PEARSON CUSTOM
COMPUTER SCIENCE

CSC106
Intermediate PC Applications With Programming
Visual Basic 2010

PEARSON

Senior Vice President, Editorial: Patrick F. Boles
Executive Marketing Manager: Nathan Wilbur
Senior Acquisitions Editor: Debbie Coniglio
Development Editor: Christina Martin
Editorial Assistant: Jeanne Martin
Operations Manager: Eric M. Kenney
Production Manager: Jennifer Berry
Art Director: Renée Sartell
Cover Designer: Kristen Kiley

Cover Art: "Blend," courtesy of Getty Images/Jason Reed; "Binary Data Flowing," courtesy of iStockphoto/Andrey Solovyev; "Beech Forest," courtesy of iStockphoto; "Small Plant," courtesy of iStockphoto/Florea Marius Catalin; "Network," courtesy of iStockphoto/Andrey Prokhorov.

Printed in the United States of America.

Please visit our website at *www.pearsonlearningsolutions.com.*

Attention Bookstores: For permission to return any unsold stock, contact us at *pe-uscustomreturns@pearson.com.*

Pearson Learning Solutions, 501 Boylston Street, Suite 900, Boston, MA 02116
A Pearson Education Company
www.pearsoned.com

ISBN 10: 1-256-23042-1
ISBN 13: 978-1-256-23042-7

Contents

Introduction to Programming and Visual Basic

TOPICS

Microsoft Visual Basic is a powerful software development system for creating applications that run on the Windows operating system. With Visual Basic, you can do the following:

- Create applications with graphical windows, dialog boxes, and menus
- Create applications that work with databases
- Create Web applications and applications that use Internet technologies
- Create applications that display graphics

Visual Basic, which is commonly referred to as VB, is a favorite tool among professional programmers. It provides tools to visually design an application's appearance, a modern programming language, and access to the latest Microsoft technologies. Powerful applications can be created with Visual Basic in a relatively short period of time.

Before plunging into learning Visual Basic, we will review the fundamentals of computer hardware and software, and then become familiar with the Visual Studio programming environment.

1 Computer Systems: Hardware and Software

CONCEPT: Computer systems consist of similar hardware devices and hardware components. This section provides an overview of computer hardware and software organization.

Hardware

The term **hardware** refers to a computer's physical components. A computer, as we generally think of it, is not an individual device, but rather a system of devices. Like the instruments in a symphony orchestra, each device plays its own part. A typical computer system consists of the following major components:

1. The central processing unit (CPU)
2. Main memory
3. Secondary storage devices
4. Input devices
5. Output devices

The organization of a computer system is shown in Figure 1.

Figure 1 The organization of a computer system

1. The CPU

When a computer is performing the tasks that a program tells it to do, we say that the computer is running or executing the program. The **central processing unit**, or **CPU**, is the part of a computer that actually runs programs. The CPU is the most important component in a computer because without it, the computer could not run software.

A **program** is a set of instructions that a computer's CPU follows to perform a task. The program's instructions are stored in the computer's memory, and the CPU's job is to fetch those instructions, one by one, and carry out the operations that they command. In memory, the instructions are stored as a series of **binary numbers**. A binary number is a sequence of 1s and 0s, such as

```
11011011
```

This number has no apparent meaning to people, but to the computer it might be an instruction to multiply two numbers or read another value from memory.

2. Main Memory

You can think of **main memory** as the computer's work area. This is where the computer stores a program while the program is running, as well as the data that the program is working with. For example, suppose you are using a word processing program to write an essay for one of your classes. While you do this, both the word processing program and the essay are stored in main memory.

Main memory is commonly known as **random-access memory**, or **RAM**. It is called this because the CPU is able to quickly access data stored at any random location in RAM. RAM is usually a volatile type of memory that is used only for temporary storage while a program is running. When the computer is turned off, the contents of RAM are erased. Inside your computer, RAM is stored in microchips.

3. Secondary Storage

The most common type of secondary storage device is the **disk drive**. A disk drive stores data by magnetically encoding it onto a circular disk. Most computers have a disk drive mounted inside their case. External disk drives, which connect to one of the computer's communication ports, are also available. External disk drives can be used to create backup copies of important data or to move data to another computer.

In addition to external disk drives, many types of devices have been created for copying data, and for moving it to other computers. For many years floppy disk drives were popular. A floppy disk drive records data onto a small floppy disk, which can be removed from the drive. The use of floppy disk drives has declined dramatically in recent years, in favor of superior devices such as USB drives. USB drives are small devices that plug into the computer's USB (universal serial bus) port, and appear to the system as a disk drive. USB drives, which use flash memory to store data, are inexpensive, reliable, and small enough to be carried in your pocket.

Optical devices such as the CD (compact disc) and the DVD (digital versatile disc) are also popular for data storage. Data is not recorded magnetically on an optical disc, but is encoded as a series of pits on the disc surface. CD and DVD drives use a laser to detect the pits and thus read the encoded data. Optical discs hold large amounts of data, and because recordable CD and DVD drives are now commonplace, they are good mediums for creating backup copies of data.

4. Input Devices

Input is any data the computer collects from the outside world. The device that collects the data and sends it to the computer is called an **input device**. Common input devices are the keyboard, mouse, scanner, and digital camera. Disk drives and CD drives can also be considered input devices because programs and data are retrieved from them and loaded into the computer's memory.

5. Output Devices

Output is any data the computer sends to the outside world. It might be a sales report, a list of names, a graphic image, or a sound. The data is sent to an **output device**, which formats and presents it. Common output devices are monitors and printers. Disk drives and CD recorders can also be considered output devices because the CPU sends data to them in order to be saved.

Software

Software refers to the programs that run on a computer. There are two general categories of software: operating systems and application software. An **operating system** or **OS** is a set of programs that manages the computer's hardware devices and controls their processes. Windows, Mac OS, and Linux are all operating systems.

Application software refers to programs that make the computer useful to the user. These programs, which are generally called applications, solve specific problems or perform general operations that satisfy the needs of the user. Word processing, spreadsheet, and database packages are all examples of application software.

 ## Checkpoint

1 List the five major hardware components of a computer system.

2 What is main memory? What is its purpose?

3 Explain why computers have both main memory and secondary storage.

4 What are the two general categories of software?

2 Programs and Programming Languages

CONCEPT: A program is a set of instructions a computer follows in order to perform a task. A programming language is a special language used to write computer programs.

What Is a Program?

Computers are designed to follow instructions. A computer program is a set of instructions that enables the computer to solve a problem or perform a task. For example, suppose we want the computer to calculate someone's gross pay—a *Wage Calculator* application. Figure 2 shows a list of things the computer should do.

Collectively, the instructions in Figure 2 are called an **algorithm**. An algorithm is a set of well-defined steps for performing a task or solving a problem. Notice these steps are sequentially ordered. Step 1 should be performed before Step 2, and so on. It is important that these instructions are performed in their proper sequence.

Figure 2 Program steps—*Wage Calculator* application

1. Display a message on the screen: *How many hours did you work?*
2. Allow the user to enter the number of hours worked.
3. Once the user enters a number, store it in memory.
4. Display a message on the screen: *How much do you get paid per hour?*
5. Allow the user to enter an hourly pay rate.
6. Once the user enters a number, store it in memory.
7. Once both the number of hours worked and the hourly pay rate are entered, multiply the two numbers and store the result in memory as the gross pay.
8. Display a message on the screen that shows the gross pay. The message must include the result of the calculation performed in Step 7.

States and Transitions

It is helpful to think of a running computer program as a combination of states and transitions. Each state is represented by a snapshot (like a picture) of the computer's memory. Using the *Wage Calculator* application example from Figure 2, the following is a memory snapshot taken when the program starts:

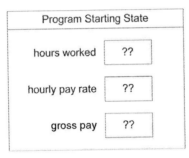

In Step 3, the number of hours worked by the user is stored in memory. Suppose the user enters the value 20. A new program state is created:

In Step 6, the hourly pay rate entered by the user is stored in memory. Suppose the user enters the value 25. The following memory snapshot shows the new program state:

In Step 7, the application calculates the amount of money earned, saving it in memory. The following memory snapshot shows the new program state:

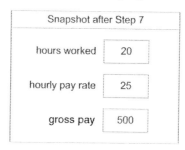

The memory snapshot produced by Step 7 represents the final program state.

Programming Languages

In order for a computer to perform instructions such as the wage calculator algorithm, the steps must be converted to a format the computer can process. As mentioned earlier, a program is stored in memory as a series of binary numbers. These numbers are known as **machine language instructions**. The CPU processes only instructions written in machine language. Our *Wage Calculator* application might look like the following at the moment when it is executed by the computer:

1010110111010100011110000110111010001111000111001101010111 *etc.*

The CPU interprets these binary or machine language numbers as commands. As you might imagine, the process of encoding an algorithm in machine language is tedious and difficult. **Programming languages**, which use words instead of numbers, were invented to ease this task. Programmers can write their applications in programming language statements, and then use special software called a **compiler** to convert the program into machine language. Names of some popular recent programming languages are shown in Table 1. This list is only a small sample—there are thousands of programming languages.

Table 1 Popular programming languages

Language	Description
Visual Basic, C#	Popular programming languages for building Windows and Web applications.
C, C++	Powerful advanced programming languages that emphasize flexibility and fast running times. C++ is also object-oriented.
Java	Flexible and powerful programming language that runs on many different computer systems. Often used to teach object-oriented programming.
Python	Simple, yet powerful programming language used for graphics and small applications.
PHP	Programming language used for creating interactive Web sites.
JavaScript	Scripting language used in Web applications that provides rich user interfaces for Web browsers.

What Is a Program Made of?

All programming languages, including Visual Basic, have certain elements in common. Let's look at the major programming language elements that you will work with when writing a program.

Keywords (Reserved Words)

Each high-level language has its own set of words that the programmer must learn in order to use the language. The words that make up a high-level programming language are known as **keywords** or **reserved words**. Each keyword has a specific meaning, and cannot be used for any other purpose.

Operators

In addition to keywords, programming languages have **operators** that perform various operations on data. For example, all programming languages have math operators that perform arithmetic. In Visual Basic, as well as most other languages, the + sign is an operator that adds two numbers. The following would add 12 and 75:

```
12 + 75
```

Variables

Programs use variables to store data in memory. A **variable** is a storage location in memory that is represented by a name. When a value is stored in a variable, it is stored in the computer's memory.

Programmers make up the names for all the variables that they use in a program. For now just remember that a variable's name is a single word that indicates what the variable is used for. For example, a program that calculates the sales tax on a purchase might use a variable named `tax` to hold that value in memory. And a program that calculates the distance from Earth to a star might use a variable named `distance` to hold that value in memory. When a program stores a value in a variable, the value is actually stored in memory at the location represented by the variable.

Syntax

In addition to keywords and operators, each language also has its own **syntax**, which is a set of rules that must be strictly followed when writing a program. The syntax rules dictate how keywords, operators, and various punctuation characters must be used in a program. When you are learning a programming language, you must learn the syntax rules for that particular language.

NOTE: Human languages also have syntax rules. Do you remember when you took your first English class, and you learned all those rules about infinitives, indirect objects, clauses, and so forth? You were learning the syntax of the English language.

Although people commonly violate the syntax rules of their native language when speaking and writing, other people usually understand what they mean. Unfortunately, program compilers do not have this ability. If even a single syntax error appears in a program, the program cannot be compiled or executed.

Statements

The individual instructions that you write in a program are called **statements**. A programming statement can consist of keywords, operators, punctuation, and other allowable programming elements, arranged in the proper sequence to perform an operation. The statements that are written in a program are commonly called **source code**, or simply **code**.

Procedures

A **procedure** is a set of programming statements that exist within a program for the purpose of performing a specific task. The program executes the procedure when the task needs to be performed.

Comments (Remarks)

Not everything that the programmer writes in a program is meant to be executed by the computer. Some parts of a program are **comments**, or **remarks**, that help the human reader of a program understand the purposes of the program statements. In Visual Basic, any statement that begins with an apostrophe (') is considered a comment. When the Visual Basic compiler sees a statement that begins with an apostrophe, it recognizes it as a comment and it skips over it.

You should always add descriptive comments to your code. The extra time it takes is well spent. Sometimes you (the programmer) will have to reread and understand your own code. Comments are a great way to remind you of what you were thinking when you created the program. In addition, you may have to modify or maintain code written by another programmer and you will appreciate the time spent to write comments!

Graphical User Interfaces

When a computer program is needed to perform a task, the programmer is the person who develops the algorithm, and writes the programming statements that perform the algorithm's steps. Once the program is complete, it is made available to those who need to use it. The people who use the program are known as **users**.

Although the programmer works directly with a program's statements, users are typically not concerned with the program's inner workings. Users want to make sure that they know how to operate the program when it is running, and that the program works as it should. The part of a program that users interact with is known as the **user interface**. On modern operating systems such as Windows, most of the programs that people use have a **graphical user interface**, or **GUI** (pronounced *gooey*). A graphical user interface typically consists of one or more windows that appear on the computer screen. A **window** is a rectangular area that contains other visual elements such as text, buttons that can be clicked with the mouse, boxes that accept keyboard input, and so forth. Let's look at an example. Follow the steps in Tutorial 1 to run a program that was copied to your system from the website, www.microsoft.com/express/Downloads/.

Tutorial 1:

Running the Wage Calculator application

Step 1: On your computer, navigate to the folder containing the student sample programs that you copied from the above website. If you are working in your school's computer lab, your instructor will tell you where the files are located.

Step 2: Inside the folder containing the student sample programs, go to the *Chap1* folder. Double-click the file *Wage Calculator.exe* (the *.exe* filename extension may not be visible). The program's window should display as shown in Figure 3. Leave the program running as you continue to read. We will perform operations with the program in Tutorial 2.

Figure 3 A graphical user interface

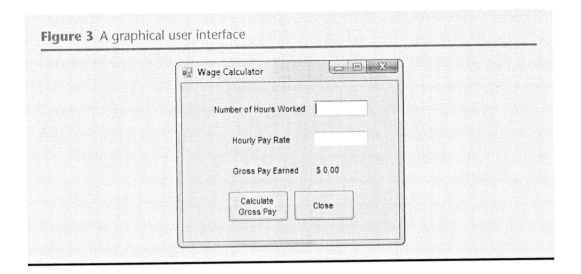

The program that you executed in Tutorial 1 calculates an employee's gross pay. Notice that inside the program's window (shown in Figure 3) there are boxes for entering the number of hours worked and the hourly pay rate. There is also a button that calculates the gross pay when it is clicked with the mouse, and a button that closes the program (stops its execution). All of these elements are part of the program's GUI, and anyone operating the program will interact with these elements.

In addition to being a programming language, Visual Basic is also a programming environment that provides tools for creating an application's graphical user interface. With Visual Basic you can design the appearance of an application's GUI, and write the code that makes the application work.

Objects and Controls

As a student studying Visual Basic, you will frequently encounter two terms: object and control. An **object** is an item in a program that contains data and has the ability to perform operations. The data that an object contains is referred to as **properties,** or **attributes.** The operations that an object can perform are called **methods.** (Recall that earlier we mentioned that a procedure is a set of programming statements that exist within a program for the purpose of performing a specific task. A method is a special type of procedure that belongs to an object.)

In the beginning of your studies you will learn how to use many different objects that are provided by Visual Basic to perform various operations in your programs.

VideoNote

Forms, Controls, and Properties

A **control** is a specific type of object that usually appears in a program's graphical user interface. For example, each of the elements that appear in the user interface in Figure 3 is a control. The window that contains the other elements is known as a **Form** control. The small boxes that accept keyboard input are known as **TextBox** controls. The areas that simply display text are known as **Label** controls. The buttons that perform operations when clicked with the mouse are known as **Button** controls. Figure 4 points out each of these controls in the user interface.

> **NOTE:** Visual Basic is an **object-oriented programming (OOP)** language. A typical VB application uses numerous objects (such as GUI controls) that work together.

Figure 4 Types of controls

Properties

A GUI control's visual appearance is determined by the control's properties. A **property** is simply a piece of data that determines some characteristic of the control. For example, many controls have a **Text property** that determines the text that is displayed by the control. If you look at Figure 4, near the top of the form you see a Label control that displays the text *Number of Hours Worked*. That Label control's Text property is set to the value *Number of Hours Worked*. Just below that Label is another Label control, and its Text property is set to the value *Hourly Pay Rate*.

Button controls also have a Text property. In Figure 4, the leftmost button's Text property is set to the value *Calculate Gross Pay*, and the rightmost button's Text property is set to the value *Close*. Forms have a Text property too, which determines the text that is displayed in the title bar at the top of the form. In Figure 4, the form's Text property is set to *Wage Calculator*. Part of the process of creating a Visual Basic application is deciding what values to store in each object's properties.

VideoNote

Event-Driven Programming

Event-Driven Programming

Programs that operate in a GUI environment must be **event-driven**. An event is an action that takes place within a program, such as the clicking of a control. All Visual Basic controls are capable of detecting various events. For example, a Button control can detect when it has been clicked and a TextBox control can detect when its contents have changed.

Names are assigned to all of the events that can be detected. For instance, when the user clicks a Button control, a Click event occurs. When the contents of a TextBox control changes, a TextChanged event occurs. If you wish for a control to respond to a specific event, you must write a set of programming statements known as an **event handler**. An event handler is a special type of procedure that executes when a specific event occurs. (Event handlers are also known as **event procedures**.) If an event occurs, and there is no event handler to respond to that event, the event is ignored.

Part of the Visual Basic programming process is designing and writing event handlers. Tutorial 2 demonstrates an event handler using the *Wage Calculator* application you executed in Tutorial 1.

Tutorial 2:
Running an application that demonstrates event handlers

Step 1: With the *Wage Calculator* application from Tutorial 1 still running, enter the value **10** in the first TextBox control. This is the number of hours worked.

Step 2: Press the [Tab] key. Notice that the cursor moves to the next TextBox control. Enter the value **15**. This is the hourly pay rate. The window should look like that shown in Figure 5.

Step 3: Click the *Calculate Gross Pay* button. Notice that in response to the mouse click, the application multiplies the values you entered in the TextBox controls and displays the result in a Label control. This action is performed by an event handler that responds to the button being clicked. The window should look like that shown in Figure 6.

Figure 5 Text boxes filled in on the *Wage Calculator* form

Figure 6 Gross pay calculated

Step 4: Next, click the *Close* button. The application responds to this event by terminating. This is because an event handler closes the application when the button is clicked.

This simple application demonstrates the essence of event-driven programming. In the next section, we examine the controls and event handlers more closely.

3 More about Controls and Programming

CONCEPT: As a Visual Basic programmer, you must design and create an application's GUI elements (forms and other controls) and the programming statements that respond to and/or perform actions (event handlers).

While creating a Visual Basic application, you will spend much of your time doing three things: creating the controls that appear in the application's user interface, setting the properties of the controls, and writing programming language statements that respond to events and perform other operations. In this section, we take a closer look at these aspects of Visual Basic programming.

Visual Basic Controls

In the previous section, you saw examples of several GUI elements, or controls. Visual Basic provides a wide assortment of controls for gathering input, displaying information, selecting values, showing graphics, and more. Table 2 lists some of the commonly used controls.

Table 2 Visual Basic controls

Control Type	Description
Button	A rectangular button-shaped object that performs an action when clicked with the mouse
CheckBox	A box that is checked or unchecked when clicked with the mouse
ComboBox	A control that is the combination of a ListBox and a TextBox
Form	A window, onto which other controls may be placed
GroupBox	A rectangular border that functions as a container for other controls
HScrollBar	A horizontal scroll bar that, when moved with the mouse, increases or decreases a value
Label	A box that displays text that cannot be changed or entered by the user
ListBox	A box containing a list of items
PictureBox	A control that displays a graphic image
RadioButton	A round button that is either selected or deselected when clicked with the mouse
TextBox	A rectangular area in which the user can enter text, or the program can display text
VScrollBar	A vertical scroll bar that, when moved with the mouse, increases or decreases a value

If you have any experience using Microsoft Windows, you are already familiar with most of the controls listed in Table 2. The materials that you downloaded from www.microsoft.com/express/Downloads/ contains a simple demonstration program in Tutorial 3 that shows you how a few of them work.

Tutorial 3:

Running an application that demonstrates various controls

Step 1: In Windows, navigate to the location where the sample program files have been copied from the above website.

Step 2: Navigate to the the *Chap1* folder.

Step 3: Double-click the file *Controls Demo.exe*. (The *.exe* extension may not be visible on your system.)

Step 4: Once the program loads and executes, the window shown in Figure 7 should appear on the screen.

Figure 7 Control demonstration screen

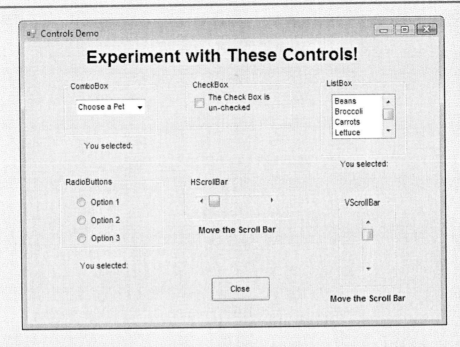

Step 5: The program presents several Visual Basic controls. Experiment with each one, noticing the following actions, which are performed by event handlers:

- When you click the small down arrow ( ) in the ComboBox control, you see a list of pets. When you select one, the name of the pet appears below the combo box.
- When you click the CheckBox control, its text changes to indicate that the check box is checked or unchecked.
- When you click an item in the ListBox control, the name of that item appears below the list box.
- When you select one of the RadioButton controls, the text below them changes to indicate which one you selected. You may only select one at a time.
- You move the horizontal scroll bar (HScrollBar) and the vertical scroll bar (VScrollBar) by doing the following:
    - Clicking either of the small arrows at each end of the bar
    - Clicking inside the bar on either side of the slider
    - Clicking on the slider and while holding down the mouse button, moving the mouse to the right or left for the horizontal scroll bar, or up or down for the vertical scroll bar.

    When you move either of the scroll bars, the text below it changes to a number. Moving the scroll bar in one direction increases the number, and moving it in the other direction decreases the number.

Step 6: Click the *Close* button to end the application.

The Name Property

The appearance of a control is determined by its properties. Some properties, however, establish nonvisual characteristics. An example is the control's **Name** property. When the programmer wishes to manipulate or access a control in a programming statement, he or she must refer to the control by its name.

When you create a control in Visual Basic, it automatically receives a default name. The first Label control created in an application receives the default name Label1. The second Label control created receives the default name Label2, and the default names continue in this fashion. The first TextBox control created in an application is automatically named TextBox1. As you can imagine, the names for each subsequent TextBox control are TextBox2, TextBox3, and so on. You can change the control's default name to something more descriptive.

Table 3 lists all the controls, by name, in the *Wage Calculator* application (Section 2), and Figure 8 shows where each is located.

Table 3 *Wage Calculator controls*

Control Name	Control Type	Description
Form1	Form	The window that holds all of the application's other controls
Label1	Label	Displays the message *Number of Hours Worked*
Label2	Label	Displays the message *Hourly Pay Rate*
Label3	Label	Displays the message *Gross Pay Earned*
txtHoursWorked	TextBox	Allows the user to enter the number of hours worked
txtPayRate	TextBox	Allows the user to enter the hourly pay rate
lblGrossPay	Label	Displays the gross pay, after the btnCalcGrossPay button has been clicked
btnCalcGrossPay	Button	When clicked, multiplies the number of hours worked by the hourly pay rate
btnClose	Button	When clicked, terminates the application

Figure 8 *Wage Calculator controls*

Control Naming Rules and Conventions

Four controls shown in Figure 8 (Form1, Label1, Label2, and Label3), still have their default names. The other five controls have programmer-defined names because those controls play an active role in the application's event handlers, and their names appear in the application's programming statements. Any control whose name appears in a programming statement should have a descriptive, programmer-defined name.

NOTE: Some programmers prefer to give all the controls in their application meaningful names, including ones whose names do not appear in programming statements.

Although you have a great deal of flexibility in naming controls, you must follow these mandatory rules:

- The first character of a control name must be a letter or an underscore character (_).
- After the first character, the remaining characters may be letters, digits, or underscore (_) characters.

It's important to remember that control names must be one word. They cannot contain spaces. Punctuation marks and other special symbols are also prohibited in control names.

In addition to these mandatory rules, there are three conventions that you should follow when naming controls:

The first three letters of the name should be a lowercase prefix indicating the control's type. In the *Wage Calculator* application, programmer-defined names use the following standard three-letter prefixes:
- `lbl` indicates a Label control.
- `txt` indicates a TextBox control.
- `btn` indicates a Button control.

There are standard prefixes for other controls as well.

2. The first letter after the prefix should be uppercase. In addition, if the name consists of multiple words, the first letter of each word should be capitalized. This makes the name more readable. For example, `txtHoursWorked` is easier to read than `txthoursworked`.

3. The part of the control name that appears after the three-letter prefix should describe the control's purpose in the application. This makes the control name very helpful to anyone reading the application's programming statements. For example, it is evident that the `btnCalcGrossPay` control is a button that calculates the gross pay.

These are not mandatory rules, but they are standard conventions that many Visual Basic programmers follow. You should use these guidelines when naming the controls in your applications as well. Table 4 describes several fictitious controls and suggests appropriate programmer-defined names for them.

Table 4 Programmer-defined control name examples

Control Description	Suggested Name
A text box in which the user enters his or her age	txtAge
A button that, when clicked, calculates the total of an order	btnCalcTotal
A label that is used to display the distance from one city to another	lblDistance
A text box in which the user enters his or her last name	txtLastName
A button that, when clicked, adds a series of numbers	btnAddNumbers

Checkpoint

5   What is an algorithm?

6   Why were computer programming languages invented?

7   What is an object? What is a control?

8   What does event-driven mean?

9   What is a property?

10 Why should the programmer change the name of a control from its default name?

11 If a control has the programmer-defined name `txtRadius`, what type of control is it?

12 What is the default name given to the first TextBox control created in an application?

13 Is `txtFirst+LastName` an acceptable control name? Why or why not?

4   The Programming Process

CONCEPT: The programming process consists of several steps, which include designing, creating, testing, and debugging activities.

Imagine building a bridge without a plan. How could it be any easier to create a complex computer program without designing its appearance and behavior? In this section, we introduce some of the most important knowledge you will gain from this text—how to begin creating a computer application. Regardless of which programming language you use in the future, good program design principles always apply.

Steps for Developing a Visual Basic Application

1. Clearly define what the application is to do.
2. Visualize the application running on the computer and design its user interface.
3. Determine the controls needed.
4. Define the values of each control's relevant properties.
5. Determine the event handlers and other code needed for each control.
6. Create a flowchart or pseudocode version of the code.
7. Check the flowchart or pseudocode for errors.
8. Start Visual Basic and create the forms and other controls identified in Step 3.
9. Use the flowcharts or pseudocode from Step 6 to write the actual code.
10. Attempt to run the application. Correct any syntax errors found and repeat this step as many times as necessary.
11. Once all syntax errors are corrected, run the program with test data for input. Correct any runtime errors. Repeat this step as many times as necessary.

These steps emphasize the importance of planning. Just as there are good ways and bad ways to paint a house, there are good ways and bad ways to write a program. A good program always begins with planning.

With the *Wage Calculator* application as our example, let's look at each of these steps in greater detail.

1. Clearly define what the application is to do.

This step requires that you identify the purpose of the application, the information to be input, the processing to take place, and the desired output. For example, the requirements for the *Wage Calculator* application are as follows:

Purpose:	To calculate the user's gross pay
Input:	Number of hours worked, hourly pay rate
Process:	Multiply number of hours worked by hourly pay rate. The result is the user's gross pay
Output:	Display a message indicating the user's gross pay

2. Visualize the application running on the computer and design its user interface.

Before you create an application on the computer, first you should create it in your mind. Step 2 is the visualization of the program. Try to imagine what the computer screen will look like while the application is running. Then, sketch the form or forms in the application. For instance, Figure 9 shows a sketch of the form presented by the *Wage Calculator* application.

Figure 9 Sketch of the *Wage Calculator* form

3. Determine the controls needed.

The next step is to determine the controls needed on each of the application's forms. You should assign names to all controls that will be accessed or manipulated in the application. Table 5 lists the controls in the *Wage Calculator* application.

Table 5 *Wage Calculator* controls

Control Type	Control Name	Description
Form	(Default)	A small form that will serve as the window onto which the other controls will be placed
Label	(Default)	Displays the message *Number of Hours Worked*
Label	(Default)	Displays the message *Hourly Pay Rate*
Label	(Default)	Displays the message *Gross Pay Earned*
TextBox	txtHoursWorked	Allows the user to enter the number of hours worked
TextBox	txtPayRate	Allows the user to enter the hourly pay rate
Label	lblGrossPay	Displays the gross pay, after the btnCalcGrossPay button has been clicked
Button	btnCalcGrossPay	When clicked, multiplies the number of hours worked by the hourly pay rate; stores the result in a variable and displays it in the lblGrossPay label
Button	btnClose	When clicked, terminates the application

4. Define the values of each control's relevant properties.

Other than Name, Text is the only control property modified in the *Wage Calculator* application. Table 6 lists the value of each control's Text property.

Table 6 *Wage Calculator* control values

Control Type	Control Name	Text Property
Form	(Default)	"Wage Calculator"
Label	(Default)	"Number of Hours Worked"
Label	(Default)	"Hourly Pay Rate"
Label	(Default)	"Gross Pay Earned"
Label	lblGrossPay	"$0.00"
TextBox	txtHoursWorked	""
TextBox	txtPayRate	""
Button	btnCalcGrossPay	"Calculate Gross Pay"
Button	btnClose	"Close"

5. Determine the event handlers and other code needed for each control.

Next, you should list the event handlers and other code that you will write. There are only two event handlers in the *Wage Calculator* application. Table 7 lists and describes them. Notice the Visual Basic names for the event handlers. btnCalcGrossPay_Click is the name of the event handler invoked when the btnCalcGrossPay button is clicked and btnClose_Click is the event handler that executes when the btnClose button is clicked.

Table 7 *Wage Calculator* event handlers

Event Handler Name	Description
btnCalcGrossPay_Click	Multiplies the number of hours worked by the hourly pay rate; these values are retrieved from the txtHoursWorked and txtPayRate TextBox controls and the result of the multiplication is stored in the lblGrossPay label's Text property
btnClose_Click	Terminates the application

6. Create a flowchart or pseudocode version of the code

A flowchart is a diagram that graphically depicts the flow of a method. It uses boxes and other symbols to represent each step. Figure 10 shows a flowchart for the btnCalcGrossPay_Click event handler.

Figure 10 Flowchart for btnCalcGrossPay_Click event handler

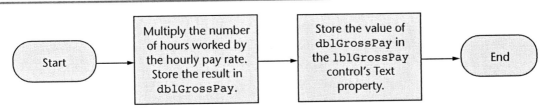

There are two types of boxes in the flowchart shown in Figure 10: ovals and rectangles. The flowchart begins with an oval labeled *Start* and ends with an oval labeled *End*. The rectangles represent a computational process or other operation. Notice that the symbols are connected with arrows that indicate the direction of the program flow.

Many programmers prefer to use pseudocode instead of flowcharts. **Pseudocode** is a cross between human language and a programming language. Although the computer can't understand pseudocode, programmers often find it helpful to plan an algorithm in a language that's almost a programming language but still very readable by humans. The following is a pseudocode version of the btnCalcGrossPay_Click event handler:

Store Number of Hours Worked × Hourly Pay Rate in the grossPay variable.
Store the value of the grossPay variable in the lblGrossPay control's Text property.

7. Check the code for errors.

In this phase the programmer reads the flowcharts and/or pseudocode from the beginning and steps through each operation, pretending that he or she is the computer. The programmer jots down the current contents of variables and properties that change and sketches what the screen looks like after each output operation. By checking each step, a programmer can locate and correct many errors.

8. Start Visual Studio and create the forms and other controls identified in Step 3.

This step is the first actual work done on the computer. Here, the programmer uses Visual Studio to create the application's user interface and arrange the controls on each form.

9. Use the flowcharts or pseudocode from Step 6 to write the actual code.

This is the second step performed on the computer. The flowcharts or pseudocode that was developed in Step 6 may be converted into code and entered into the computer using Visual Studio.

10. Attempt to run the application. Correct any syntax errors found and repeat this step as many times as necessary.

If you have entered code with syntax errors or typing mistakes, this step will uncover them. A **syntax error** is the incorrect use of a programming language element, such as a keyword, operator, or programmer-defined name. Correct your mistakes and repeat this step until the program runs.

11. Once all syntax errors are corrected, run the program with test data for input. Correct any runtime errors. Repeat this step as many times as necessary.

Runtime errors (errors found while running the program) are mistakes that do not prevent an application from executing but cause it to produce incorrect results. For example, a mistake in a mathematical formula is a common type of **runtime error**. When runtime errors are found in a program, they must be corrected and the program retested. This step must be repeated until the program reliably produces satisfactory results.

 Checkpoint

14 What four items should be identified when defining what a program is to do?

15 Describe the importance of good planning in the process of creating a Visual Basic application.

16 What does it mean to visualize a program running? What is the value of such an activity?

17 What is a flowchart?

18 What is pseudocode?

19 What is a runtime error?

20 What is the purpose of testing a program with sample data or input?

21 How much testing should you perform on a new program?

5 **Visual Studio and Visual Basic Express Edition (the Visual Basic Environment)**

CONCEPT: Visual Studio and Visual Basic Express Edition consist of tools that you use to build Visual Basic applications. The first step in using Visual Basic is learning about these tools.

NOTE: The programs in this text can be written using either Microsoft Visual Studio or Microsoft Visual Basic Express Edition. There are only minor differences between the two products. In cases where they work identically, we will refer to them as **Visual Studio**.

Before you create your first Visual Basic application, you need to know how to start Visual Studio, set up the programming environment, and understand the environment's major components. Visual Studio is an **integrated development environment (IDE)**, which means that it provides all the necessary tools for creating, testing, and debugging software. The full version of Visual Studio can be used to create applications not only with Visual Basic, but also with other languages such as Visual C++ and C#.

Visual Studio is a customizable environment. If you are working in your school's computer lab, there's a chance that someone else has customized the programming environment to suit his own preferences. If this is the case, the screens that you see may not match the ones shown in this text. For that reason it's a good idea to reset the programming environment before you create a Visual Basic application. Tutorial 4 guides you through the process.

Tutorial 4:
Starting Visual Studio and Setting Up the Environment

VideoNote

Tutorial 1-4
Walkthrough

Step 1: Find out from your instructor whether you are using Visual Studio 2010 or Visual Basic 2010 Express Edition. Then, click the *Start* button, open the *All Programs* menu, and perform one of the following:

- If you are using Visual Studio, open the *Microsoft Visual Studio 2010* program group and then execute *Visual Studio 2010.*
- If you are using Visual Basic 2010 Express Edition, open the *Microsoft Visual Studio 2010 Express* program group and then execute *Visual Basic 2010 Express.*

> **TIP:** If you are using Visual Studio rather than Visual Basic Express Edition, the first time you run the software, you will see a window entitled *Choose Default Environment Settings*. Select *Visual Basic Development Settings* from the list and click the *Start Visual Studio* button.

Step 2: Figure 11 shows the Visual Studio environment. The screen shown in the figure is known as the *Start Page*. By default, the *Start Page* is displayed when you start Visual Studio, but you may or may not see it because it can be disabled.

Figure 11 Visual Studio *Start Page*

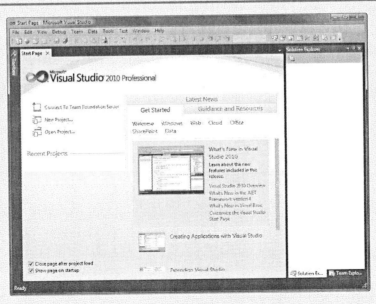

Notice the checkbox in the bottom left corner of the *Start Page* that reads *Show page on startup*. If this box is not checked, the *Start Page* will not be displayed when you start Visual Studio. If you do not see the *Start Page*, you can always display it by clicking *View* on the menu bar at the top of the screen, then clicking *Start Page*.

Step 3: This step is applicable *only* if you are using Visual Studio. If you are using Visual Basic Express Edition, skip to Step 4.

In a school computer lab, it is possible that the Visual Studio environment has been set up for a programming language other than Visual Basic. To make sure that Visual Studio looks and behaves as described in this text, you should make sure that Visual Basic is selected as the programming environment. Perform the following:

- As shown in Figure 12, click *Tools* on the menu bar and then click *Import and Export Settings . . .*
- On the screen that appears next, select *Reset all settings* and click the *Next >* button.
- On the screen that appears next, select *No, just reset settings, overwriting my current settings*, and then click the *Next >* button.
- The window shown in Figure 13 should appear next. Select *Visual Basic Development Settings* and then click the *Finish* button.
- After a moment you should see a *Reset Complete* window. Click the *Close* button and continue with the next step in the tutorial.

Figure 12 Select *Tools,* then *Import and Export Settings . . .*

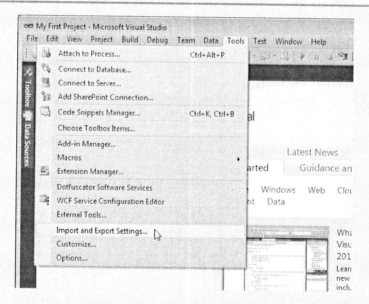

Figure 13 Select Visual Basic Development Settings

Step 4: Now you will reset Visual Studio's window layout to the default configuration. As shown in Figure 14, click *Window* on the menu bar and then click *Reset Window Layout*. Next you will see a dialog box asking *Are you sure you want to restore the default window layout for the environment?* Click *Yes*.

Figure 14 Resetting the window layout

Step 5: Visual Basic has two settings known as *Option Explicit* and *Option Strict*, which many programmers prefer to turn on because they prevent certain types of programming errors. Since you are a beginning programming student, it's a good idea that you turn these settings on, too. For now let's go through the process of turning them on. Click *Tools* on the menu bar at the top of the screen, and then click *Options*, as shown in Figure 15. This will display the *Options* window shown in Figure 16.

As shown in Figure 16, under *Projects and Solutions* (on the left side of the window), select *VB Defaults*. Then, set *Option Explicit* and *Option Strict* to *On*. After you make these settings, click *OK*.

The Visual Studio environment is now set up so you can follow the remaining tutorials in this text. If you are working in your school's computer lab, it is probably a good idea to go through these steps each time you start Visual Studio.

If you are continuing with the next tutorial, leave Visual Studio running. You can exit Visual Studio at any time by clicking *File* on the menu bar, and then clicking *Exit*.

Figure 15 Click *Tools*, and then *Options*

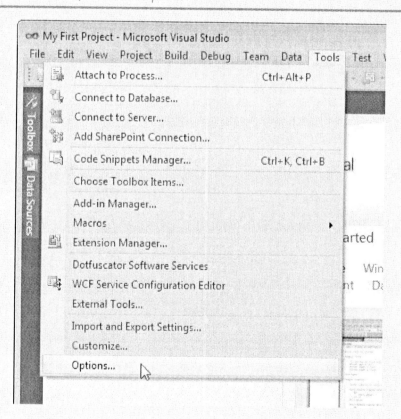

Figure 16 The *Options* window

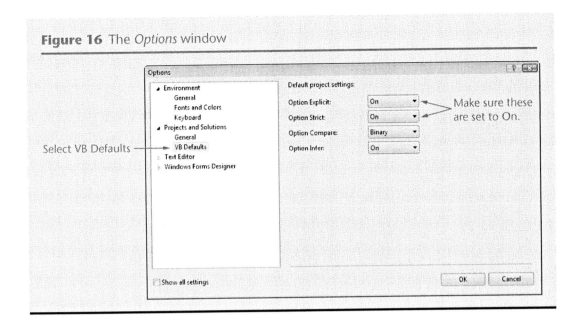

Starting a New Project

Each Visual Basic application that you create is called a **project**. When you are ready to create a new application, you start a new project. Tutorial 5 leads you through the steps of starting a new Visual Basic project.

VideoNote

Tutorial 1-5
Walkthrough

Tutorial 5:
Starting a New Visual Basic Project

Step 1: If Visual Studio is not already running, start it as you did in Tutorial 4.

Step 2: As shown in Figure 17, click *File* on the menu bar at the top of the screen, and then select *New Project*. After doing this, the *New Project* window shown in Figure 18 should be displayed.

Step 3: If you are using Visual Studio you will see *Installed Templates* at the left side of the window. Select *Visual Basic*. Then, select *Windows Forms Application*, as shown in Figure 18.

    If you are using Visual Basic Express Edition, simply select *Windows Forms Application*.

Step 4: At the bottom of the *New Project* window you see a *Name* text box. This is where you enter the name of your project. Visual Studio automatically fills this box with a default name. In Figure 18 the default name is *WindowsApplication1*. Change the project name to *My First Project*, as shown in Figure 19, and click the *OK* button.

Figure 17 Starting a new project

Figure 18 The *New Project* window

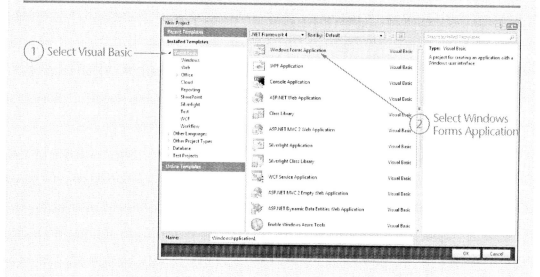

Figure 19 Changing the project name to *My First Project*

Change the project
name to *My First Project*.

NOTE: As you create a lot of Visual Basic projects, you will find that default names such as *WindowsApplication1* do not help you remember what each project does. Therefore, you should always change the name of a new project to something that describes the project's purpose.

It might take a moment for the project to be created. Once it is, the Visual Studio environment should appear similar to Figure 20. Notice that the name of the project, *My First Project*, is displayed in the title bar at the top of the Visual Studio window.

Figure 20 The Visual Studio environment with a new project open

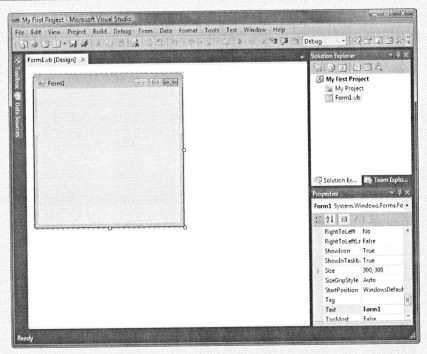

Step 5: Click *File* on the menu bar and then select *Save All*. The *Save Project* window will appear, as shown in Figure 21. The *Name* text box shows the project name that you entered when you created the project. The *Location* text box shows where a folder will be created on your system to hold the project. (The location shown on your system will be different than that shown in the figure.) If you wish to change the location, click the *Browse* button and select the desired drive and folder.

Click the *Save* button to save the project.

(Leave Visual Studio running so you can complete the next tutorial.)

Figure 21 The *Save Project* window

The Visual Studio Environment

The Visual Studio environment consists of a number of windows that you will use on a regular basis. Figure 22 shows the locations of the following windows that appear within the Visual Studio environment: the *Designer* window, the *Solution Explorer* window, and the *Properties* window. Here is a brief summary of each window's purpose:

- The *Designer* Window
  You use the *Designer* window to create an application's graphical user interface. The Designer window shows the application's form, and allows you visually design its appearance by placing the desired controls that will appear on the form when the application executes.
- The *Solution Explorer* Window
  A **solution** is a container for holding Visual Basic projects. When you create a new VB project, a new solution is automatically created to contain it. The *Solution Explorer* window allows you to navigate among the files in a Visual Basic project.
- The *Properties* Window
  When you are creating a VB application, you use the *Properties* window to examine and change a control's properties.

Figure 22 The *Designer* window, *Solution Explorer* window, and *Properties* window

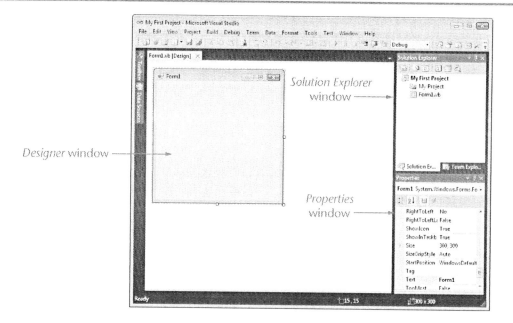

Remember that Visual Studio is a customizable environment. You can move these windows around, so they may not appear in the exact locations shown in Figure 22. You can also close the windows so they do not appear at all. If you do not see one or more of them, you can follow these steps to make them visible:

- If you do not see the *Designer* window, click *View* on the menu bar. On the *View* menu, click *Designer*. You can also press Shift+F7 on the keyboard.

- If you do not see the *Solution Explorer* window, click *View* on the menu bar. On the *View* menu, click *Solution Explorer*. (In Visual Basic Express Edition, click *View, Other Windows, Solution Explorer.*) You can also press Ctrl+Alt+L on the keyboard.
- If you do not see the *Properties* window, click *View* on the menu bar. On the *View* menu, click *Properties*. (In Visual Basic Express Edition, click *View, Other Windows, Properties.*) You can also press F4 on the keyboard.

Hidden Windows

Many windows in Visual Studio have a feature known as **Auto Hide**. When you see the pushpin icon in a window's title bar, as shown in Figure 23, you know that the window has Auto Hide capability. You click the pushpin icon to turn Auto Hide on or off for a window.

Figure 23 *Auto Hide* pushpin icon

When Auto Hide is turned on, the window is displayed only as a tab along one of the edges of the *Visual Studio* window. This feature gives you more room to view your application's forms and code. Figure 24 shows how the *Solution Explorer* and *Properties* windows appear when their Auto Hide feature is turned on. Notice the tabs that read *Solution Explorer* and *Properties* along the right edge of the screen.

The Menu Bar and the Standard Toolbar

You've already used the Visual Studio menu bar several times. This is the bar at the top of the Visual Studio window that provides menus such as *File, Edit, View, Project*, and so forth. As you learn more, you will become familiar with many of the menus.

Figure 24 The *Solution Explorer* and *Properties* windows hidden

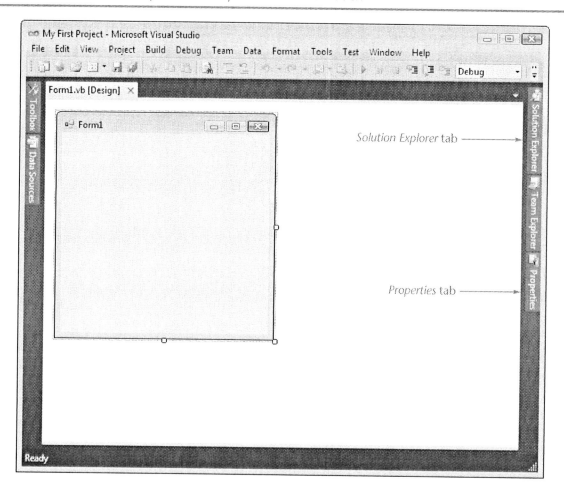

Below the menu bar is the standard toolbar. The **standard toolbar** contains buttons that execute frequently used commands. All commands that are displayed on the toolbar may also be executed from a menu, but the standard toolbar gives you quicker access to them. Figure 25 identifies the standard toolbar buttons and Table 8 gives a brief description of each.

Figure 25 Visual Studio standard toolbar buttons

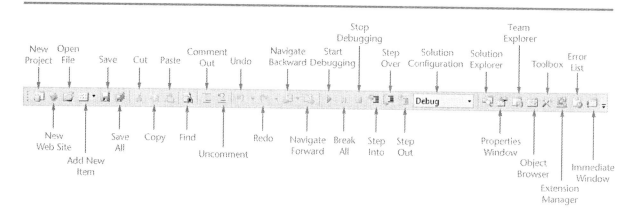

Table 8 Visual Studio toolbar buttons

Toolbar Button	Description
New Project	Starts a new project
New Web Site	Creates a new Web site (used in Web Forms applications)
Open File	Opens an existing file
Add New Item	Adds a new item such as a form to the current project
Save	Saves the file named by *filename*
Save All	Saves all of the files in the current project
Cut	Cuts the selected item to the clipboard
Copy	Copies the selected item to the clipboard
Paste	Pastes the contents of the clipboard
Find	Searches for text in your application code
Comment Out	Comments out the selected lines
Uncomment	Uncomments the selected lines
Undo	Undoes the most recent operation
Redo	Redoes the most recently undone operation
Navigate Backward	Moves to the previously active tab in the Designer window
Navigate Forward	Moves to the next active tab in the Designer window
Start Debugging	Starts debugging (running) your program
Break All	Pauses execution of your program
Stop Debugging	Stops debugging (running) your program
Step Into	Traces (steps) into the code in a procedure
Step Over	Executes the next statement without tracing into procedure calls
Step Out	Exits the current procedure while still debugging
Solution Configurations	Configures your project's executable code
Solution Explorer	Opens the *Solution Explorer* window
Properties Window	Opens the *Properties* window
Team Explorer	Opens the Team Explorer window, used in a professional development environment
Object Browser	Opens the *Object Browser* window
Toolbox	Opens the *Toolbox* window, displaying, for example, visual controls you can place on Windows forms
Extension Manager	Allows you to manage Visual Studio Extensions
Error List	Displays a list of most recent errors generated by the Visual Basic compiler
Immediate	Opens the *Immediate* window, which is used for debugging

 NOTE: Menu items and buttons cannot be used when they are grayed out.

The *Toolbox*

The *Toolbox* is a window that allows you to select the controls that you want to use in an application's user interface. When you want to place a Button, Label, TextBox, or other control on an application's form, you select it in the *Toolbox*. You will use the *Toolbox* extensively as you develop Visual Basic applications.

The *Toolbox* typically appears on the left side of the Visual Studio environment. If the *Toolbox* is in Auto Hide mode, its tab will appear as shown in Figure 26. Figure 27 shows the *Toolbox* opened, with Auto Hide turned off.

Figure 26 The *Toolbox* tab (Auto Hide turned on)

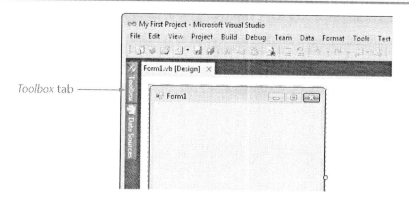

Toolbox tab

Figure 27 The *Toolbox* opened (Auto Hide turned off)

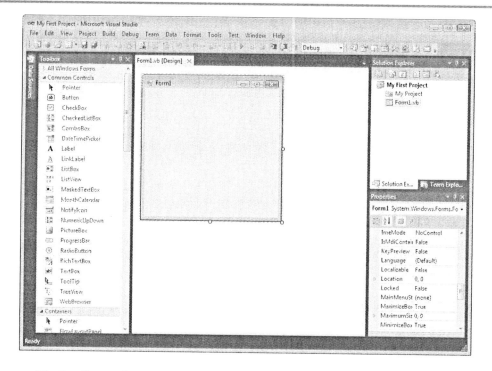

The *Toolbox* is divided into sections, and each section has a name. In Figure 27 you can see the *All Windows Forms*, *Common Controls*, and *Containers* sections. If you scroll the *Toolbox*, you will see many other sections. Each of the sections can be opened or closed. If you want to open a section of the *Toolbox*, you simply click on its name tab. To close the section, click on its name tab again. In Figure 27, the *Common Controls* section is open. You use the Common Controls section to access controls that you frequently need, such as Buttons, Labels, and TextBoxes. You can move any section to the top of the list by dragging its name with the mouse.

Using ToolTips

A **ToolTip** is a small rectangular box that pops up when you hover the mouse pointer over a button on the toolbar or in the *Toolbox* for a few seconds. The ToolTip box contains a short description of the button's purpose. Figure 28 shows the ToolTip that appears when the cursor is left sitting on the *Save All* button. Use a ToolTip whenever you cannot remember a particular button's function.

Figure 28 *Save All* ToolTip

Docked and Floating Windows

Figure 27 shows the *Toolbox*, *Solution Explorer* and *Properties* windows when they are docked, which means they are attached to one of the edges of the *Visual Studio* window. Alternatively, the windows can be **floating**. You can control whether a window is **docked** or floating as follows:

- To change a window from docked to floating, right-click its title bar and select *Float*.
- To change a window from floating to docked, right-click its title bar and select *Dock*.

Figure 29 shows Visual Studio with the *Toolbox*, *Solution Explorer* and *Properties* windows floating. When a window is floating, you can click and drag it by its title bar around the screen. You may use whichever style you prefer—docked or floating. When windows are floating, they behave as normal windows. You may move or resize them to suit your preference.

Figure 29 *Toolbox*, *Solution Explorer* and *Properties* windows floating

NOTE: A window cannot float if its Auto Hide feature is turned on.

TIP: Remember, you can always reset the window layout by clicking *Window* on the menu bar, and then selecting *Reset Window Layout*. If you accidentally close the Designer window, the *Solution Explorer* window, or the *Properties* window, you can use the *View* menu to redisplay them.

Accessing the Visual Studio Documentation

You can access the full documentation for Visual Studio by Clicking *Help* on the menu bar, and then selecting *View Help*. (Or, you can simply press Ctrl+F1.) This launches your Web browser and opens the online **Microsoft Developer Network (MSDN) library**. The MSDN library provides complete documentation for Visual Basic, as well as the other programming languages included in Visual Studio. You will also find code samples, tutorials, articles, and access to Microsoft Channel 9 Videos.

Tutorial 6:
Getting Familiar with the Visual Studio Environment

VideoNote

Tutorial 1-6
Walkthrough

This exercise will give you practice interacting with the *Solution Explorer* window, the *Properties* window, and the *Toolbox*.

Step 1: Visual Studio should still be running on your computer from the previous tutorial. If it is, continue to Step 2.

If Visual Studio is not running on your computer, repeat the steps in Tutorial 5 to start a new project. This time, however, name the project *My Second Project*. (This is necessary because you've already created a project named *My First Project*.)

Step 2: Practice turning the *Auto Hide* feature on and off for the *Solution Explorer* window, the *Properties* window, and the *Toolbox*. Recall from our previous discussion that clicking the pushpin icon in each window's title bar turns *Auto Hide* on and off. When you are finished practicing, make sure Auto Hide is turned off for each of these windows. Your screen should look like Figure 27.

Step 3: Practice floating and docking the *Solution Explorer* window, the *Properties* window, and the *Toolbox*. Recall from our previous discussion that you can make any of these windows float by right-clicking its title bar and selecting *Float*. You dock a floating window by right-clicking its title bar and selecting *Dock*.

Step 4: The *Toolbox, Solution Explorer*, and *Properties* windows each have a *Close* button (✕) in their upper right corner. Close each of these windows by clicking their *Close* button.

Step 5: Do you remember which buttons on the toolbar restore the *Solution Explorer*, *Properties* window, and *Toolbox*? If not, move your mouse cursor over any button on the toolbar, and leave it there until the ToolTip appears. Repeat this procedure on different buttons until you find the ones whose ToolTips read *Solution Explorer, Properties Window*, and *Toolbox*. (Refer to Figure 24 and Table 8 for further assistance.)

Step 6: Click the appropriate buttons on the toolbar to restore the *Solution Explorer*, the *Properties* window, and the *Toolbox*.

Step 7: Exit Visual Studio by clicking *File* on the menu bar, and then clicking *Exit*. You may see a dialog box asking you if you wish to save changes to a number of items. Click *Yes*.

Checkpoint

22 Briefly describe the purpose of the *Solution Explorer* window.

23 Briefly describe the purpose of the *Properties* window.

24 Briefly describe the purpose of the standard toolbar.

25 What is the difference between the toolbar and the *Toolbox*?

26 What is a ToolTip?

Summary

1 Computer Systems: Hardware and Software

- The major hardware components of a computer are the central processing unit (CPU), main memory, secondary storage devices, input devices, and output devices. Computer programs are stored in machine language, as a series of binary numbers.
- Main memory holds the instructions for programs that are running and data programs are working with. RAM is usually volatile, used only for temporary storage.
- The two general categories of software are operating systems and application software.

2 Programs and Programming Languages

- Although the computer can process only programs that written in machine language, programmers use languages such as Visual Basic to write programs. They then use a compiler to translate their programs to machine language.
- Keywords (reserved words), operators, variables, syntax, statements, and comments are some of the programming language elements that you will work with when writing a program.
- The part of the program that the user interacts with is called the user interface. Modern systems use graphical user interfaces.
- An object is an item in a program that contains data and has the ability to perform operations.
- A control is a type of object that usually appears in a program's graphical user interface.
- There are several types of controls available in Visual Basic. Applications in this chapter contained forms, Labels, TextBoxes, Buttons, CheckBoxes, RadioButtons, ListBoxes, ComboBoxes, and scroll bars.
- The appearance of a screen object, such as a form or other control, is determined by the object's properties.
- An event-driven program is one that responds to events or actions that take place while the program is running.

3 More about Controls and Programming

- All controls have a name. Programmers manipulate or access a control in a programming statement by referring to the control by its name. When the programmer creates a control in Visual Basic, it automatically receives a default name.
- Any control whose name appears in a programming statement should have a descriptive, programmer-defined name. Although programmers have a great deal of flexibility in naming controls, they should follow some standard guidelines.

4 The Programming Process

- This section outlines the steps for designing and creating a Visual Basic application.

5 Visual Studio and Visual Basic Express Edition (the Visual Basic Environment)

- The Visual Basic environment, which is part of Visual Studio, consists of tools used to build Visual Basic applications.
- Visual Basic can be used to create many different types of applications.

Key Terms

algorithm
application software
attributes
Auto Hide
binary number
Button
central processing unit (CPU)
CheckBox
code
ComboBox
comments
compiler
control
Designer window
disk drive
docked window
event-driven
event handler
floating window
flowchart
Form
graphical user interface (GUI)
GroupBox
hardware
HScrollBar
input
input device
integrated development
  environment (IDE)
keywords
Label
ListBox
machine language instructions
main memory
methods
Microsoft Developer Network
  (MSDN) library
Name property

object-oriented programming
  (OOP)
object
operand
operating system (OS)
operators
output
output device
PictureBox
procedure
program
programmer-defined name
programming languages
project
properties
Properties window
pseudocode
RadioButton
random-access memory (RAM)
remarks
reserved words
runtime error
secondary storage
software
source code
Solution Explorer window
standard toolbar
statement
syntax
Text property
TextBox
Toolbox window
ToolTip
user
user interface
variable
VscrollBar
window

Review Questions and Exercises

Fill-in-the-Blank

1. The job of the _____ is to fetch instructions, carry out the operations commanded by the instructions, and produce some outcome or resultant information.

2. A(n) _____ is an example of a secondary storage device.

3. The two general categories of software are _____ and _____.

4. A program is a set of _____.

5. Since computers can't be programmed in natural human language, algorithms must be written in a(n) _____ language.

6. _____ is the only language computers really process.

7. Words that have special meaning in a programming language are called _____.

8. A(n) _____ is a name that represents a storage location in memory.

9. _____ are characters or symbols that perform operations on one or more operands.

10. A(n) _____ is part of an application's code but is ignored by the compiler. It is intended for documentation purposes only.

11. The rules that must be followed when writing a program are called _____.

12. _____ is information a program gathers from the outside world.

13. _____ is information a program sends to the outside world.

14. A(n) _____ is a set of well-defined steps for performing a task or solving a problem.

15. A(n) _____ is a diagram that graphically illustrates the flow of a program.

16. _____ is a cross between human language and a programming language.

17. A(n) _____ is a piece of data that determines some characteristic of a control.

18. If you do not see the *Solution Explorer* or *Properties* windows in Visual Studio, you may use the _____ menu to bring them up.

19. You click the pushpin icon in a window's title bar to turn the _____ feature on or off.

20. You use the _____ to place Buttons, Labels, TextBoxes, and other controls on an application's forms.

21. The _____ window allows you to navigate among the files in your project.

22. The _____ window allows you to examine and change a control's properties.

23. When windows are _____, it means they are attached to one of the edges of the Visual Studio main window.

24. To dock a floating window, right-click its title bar and then select _____.

25. To reset the Visual Studio window layout, you select *Reset Window Layout* from the _____ menu.

26. All commands executed by the _____ may also be executed from a menu.

27. The _____ window shows your application's form. This is where you design your application's user interface by placing controls on the form that appears when your application executes.

28. When you want to place a Button, Label, TextBox, or other control on an application's form, you select it in the _____, and drag it onto the form in the *Designer* window.

29. You can access the full documentation for Visual Studio by Clicking _____ on the menu bar, and then selecting *View Help*.

30. A(n) _____ is a small box that is displayed when you hold the mouse cursor over a button on the toolbar or in the *Toolbox* for a few seconds.

Short Answer

1. What is the difference between main memory and secondary storage?

2. What is the difference between operating system software and application software?

3. What is an object?

4. What is a control?

5. Briefly describe what an event-driven program is.

6. From what you have read in this chapter, describe the difference between a Label control and a TextBox control. When is it appropriate to use one or the other?

7. When creating a Visual Basic application, you will spend much of your time doing what three things?

8. What is a form?

9. Summarize the mandatory rules that you must follow when naming a control.

10. What is a keyword?

11. What is the purpose of inserting comments in a program?

12. What is language syntax?

13. What is a syntax error?

14. What is a runtime error?

15. What is an operator?

16. What is a flowchart?

17. What is pseudocode?

18. What default name will Visual Basic give to the first Label control that you place on a form? What default name will Visual Basic assign to the first TextBox control that you place on a form?

19. What property determines the text that is displayed by a Label control?

20. What is *Auto Hide*? How do you turn *Auto Hide* on or off?

21. What is the *Toolbox* window in Visual Studio?

22. What is the standard toolbar in Visual Studio?

23. What is a tooltip?

24. If you do not see the *Solution Explorer* window in Visual Studio, how do you display it?

25. If you do not see the *Properties* window in Visual Studio, how do you display it?

26. Figure 30 shows the Visual Studio IDE. What are the names of the four areas that are indicated in the figure?

Figure 30 The Visual Studio IDE

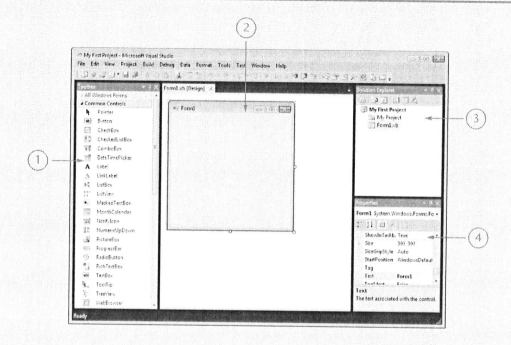

What Do You Think?

1. Are each of the following control names legal or illegal? If a name is illegal, indicate why.

   a. `txtUserName`
   b. `2001sales`
   c. `lblUser Age`
   d. `txtName/Address`
   e. `btnCalcSubtotal`

2. What type of control does each of the following prefixes usually indicate?

   a. `btn`
   b. `lbl`
   c. `txt`

3. For each of the following controls, make up a legal name that conforms to the standard control name convention described in this chapter.

   a. A TextBox control in which the user enters his or her last name
   b. A Button control that, when clicked, calculates an annual interest rate
   c. A Label control used to display the total of an order
   d. A Button control that clears all the input fields on a form

4. The following control names appear in a Visual Basic application used in a retail store. Indicate what type of control each is and guess its purpose.

   a. `txtPriceEach`
   b. `txtQuantity`
   c. `txtTaxRate`
   d. `btnCalcSale`
   e. `lblSubTotal`
   f. `lblTotal`

Programming Challenges

1. **Carpet Size**

   You have been asked to create an application for a carpet sales and installation business. The application should allow the user to enter the length and width of a room and calculate the room's area in square feet. The formula for this calculation is

   $$Area = Length \times Width$$

   In this exercise, you will gain practice using Steps 1 through 6 of the programming process described in Section 5:

   1. Clearly define what the application is to do.
   2. Visualize the application running on the computer and design its user interface.
   3. Make a list of the controls needed.
   4. Define the values of each control's properties.
   5. Make a list of methods needed for each control.
   6. Create a flowchart or pseudocode version of each method.

   Step 1: Describe the following characteristics of this application:

   > Purpose
   > Input
   > Process
   > Output

   Step 2: Draw a sketch of the application's form and place all the controls that are needed.

   Step 3: Make a list of the controls you included in your sketch. List the control type and the name of each control.

   Step 4: List the value of the Text property for each control, as needed. (Remember, some controls do not have a Text property.)

   Step 5: List each method needed. Give the name of each method and describe what each method does.

   Step 6: For each method you listed in Step 5, draw a flowchart or write pseudocode.

2. **Available Credit**

   A retail store gives each of its customers a maximum amount of credit. A customer's available credit is determined by subtracting the amount of credit used by the customer from the customer's maximum amount of credit. As you did in Programming Challenge 1, perform Steps 1 through 6 of the programming process to design an application that determines a customer's available credit.

VideoNote

Solving the
Sales Tax
Problem

3. **Sales Tax**

   Perform Steps 1 through 6 of the programming process to design an application that gets from the user the amount of a retail sale and the sales tax rate. The application should calculate the amount of the sales tax and the total of the sale.

4. **Account Balance**

   Perform Steps 1 through 6 of the programming process to design an application that gets from the user the starting balance of a savings account, the total dollar amount of the deposits made to the account, and the total dollar amount of withdrawals made from the account. The application should calculate the account balance.

Answers to Checkpoints

1 Central Processing Unit (CPU), main memory, secondary storage, input devices, and output devices

2 Main memory holds the sequences of instructions in the programs that are running and the data with which those programs are working. RAM is usually a volatile type of memory that is used only for temporary storage.

3 Program instructions and data are stored in main memory while the program is operating. Main memory is volatile and loses its content when power is removed from the computer. Secondary storage holds data for long periods of time—even when there is no power to the computer.

4 Operating systems and application software

5 A set of well-defined steps for performing a task or solving a problem

6 To ease the task of programming; programs may be written in a programming language and then converted to machine language

7 An object is an item in a program that contains data and has the ability to perform operations. A control is a specific type of object that usually appears in a program's graphical user interface.

8 An application responds to events that occur or actions that take place, such as the clicking of a mouse.

9 A property is a piece of data that determines some characteristics of a control.

10 The default name is not descriptive; it does not indicate the purpose of the control.

11 A Text Box

12 TextBox1

13 No; the + symbol is an illegal character for control names.

14 The program's purpose, information to be input, the processing to take place, and the desired output

15 Planning helps the programmer create a good design and avoid errors that may not otherwise be anticipated.

16 To imagine what the computer screen looks like when the program is running; it's the first step in creating an application's forms or windows.

17 A diagram that graphically depicts a program's flow

18 A cross between human language and a programming language

19 A mistake that does not prevent an application from executing, but causes it to produce incorrect results; a mistake in a mathematical formula is a common type of runtime error

20 To find and correct runtime errors.

21 Testing is a part of each design step. Flowcharts should be tested, code should be desk-checked, and the application should be run with test data to verify that it produces the correct output.

22 The *Solution Explorer* window shows a file-oriented view of a project. It allows quick navigation among the project files.

23 The *Properties* window shows and allows you to change most of the currently selected object's properties and their values.

24 The standard toolbar contains buttons that execute frequently used commands.

25 The toolbar contains buttons that execute frequently used menu commands. The toolbox provides buttons for placing controls.

26 A ToolTip is a small box that is displayed when you hold the mouse cursor over a button on the toolbar or in the toolbox for a few seconds. The box gives a short description of what the button does.

Creating Applications with Visual Basic

In this chapter you will develop your first application, which displays a map and written directions to the Highlander Hotel. This application uses a form with labels, a PictureBox control, and buttons. You will write your first event handlers in Visual Basic code and then you will learn to use the Label control's AutoSize, BorderStyle, and TextAlign properties. You will be introduced to clickable images, context-sensitive help, and the debugging process.

1 Focus on Problem Solving: Building the *Directions* Application

CONCEPT: In this section you create your first Visual Basic application: a window that displays a map and road directions to a hotel. In the process you learn how to place controls on a form and manipulate various properties.

The desk clerks at the historic Highlander Hotel frequently receive calls from guests requesting driving directions. Some desk clerks are not familiar with the street numbers or exits, and inadvertently give unclear or incorrect directions. The hotel manager has asked you to create an application that displays a map to the hotel. The desk clerks can refer to the application when giving directions to customers over the phone. We will use the following steps to create the application:

1. Clearly define what the application is to do.
2. Visualize the application running on the computer and design its user interface.
3. Determine the controls needed.
4. Define the values of each control's relevant properties.
5. Start Visual Basic and create the forms and other controls.

Now we will take a closer look at each of these steps.

1. Clearly define what the application is to do.

Purpose: Display a map to the Highlander Hotel
Input: None
Process: Display a form
Output: Display on the form a graphic image showing a map

2. Visualize the application running on the computer and design its user interface.

Before you create an application on the computer, first you should create it in your mind. This step is the visualization of the program. Try to imagine what the computer screen will look like while the application is running. Then draw a sketch of the form or forms in the application. Figure 1 shows a sketch of the *Directions* form presented by this application.

Figure 1 Sketch of *Directions* form

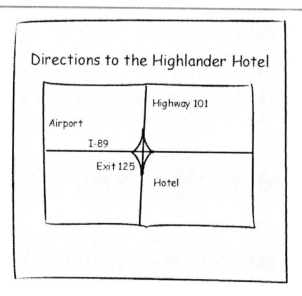

3. Determine the controls needed.

In this step you list all the needed controls. You should assign names to all the controls that will be accessed or manipulated in the application code and provide a brief description of each control. Our application needs only three controls, listed in Table 1. Because none of the controls are used in code, we will keep their default names.

Table 1 *Directions* application controls

Control Type	Control Name	Description
Form	(Default Name: *Form1*)	A small form that will serve as the window onto which the other controls will be placed
Label	(Default Name: *Label1*)	Displays the message *Directions to the Highlander Hotel*
PictureBox	(Default Name: *PictureBox1*)	Displays the graphic image showing the map to the hotel

4. Define the values of each control's relevant properties.

Each control's property settings are listed in Table 2.

Table 2 *Directions* application control properties

Property	Value
Form	
Name	*Form1*
Text	*Directions*
Label	
Name	*Label1*
Text	*Directions to the Highlander Hotel*
Font	Microsoft sans serif, bold, 16 point
PictureBox	
Name	*PictureBox1*
Image	*HotelMap.jpg*
SizeMode	*StretchImage*

Notice that in addition to the Name and Text properties, we are also setting the Font property of the Label control. We will discuss this property in detail later.

In addition to its Name property, we are setting the PictureBox control's Image and Size-Mode properties. The Image property lists the name of the file containing the graphic image. We will use *HotelMap.jpg*, which is located in the student sample programs folder named *Chap2*. The student sample programs folder can found on the website, www.microsoft.com/express/Downloads/. The **SizeMode property** is set to *StretchImage*, which allows us to resize the image. If the image is too small, we can enlarge it (stretch it). If it is too large, we can shrink it.

5. Start Visual Basic and create the forms and other controls.

Now you are ready to construct the application's form. Tutorial 1 gets you started.

Tutorial 1:
Beginning the *Directions* application

In this tutorial you begin the *Directions* application. You will create the application's form and use the *Properties* window to set the form's Text property.

Step 1: Start Visual Studio (or Visual Basic Express). Perform *one* of the following actions to create a new project:

- On the *Start Page* click the *New Project* icon
- Click *File* on the menu bar and then select *New Project...*
- Press Ctrl+N on the keyboard

The *New Project* window will appear. If you are using Visual Studio, under *Installed Templates* select *Visual Basic*. Then, in either Visual Studio or Visual Basic Express select *Windows Forms Application*.

The default project name, such as *WindowsApplication1*, appears in the *Name* text box. Replace this name with **Directions**. Click the *OK* button to close the window.

Step 2: The Visual Basic environment should be open with a blank form named *Form1* in the *Designer* window, as shown in Figure 2. Click the form to select it.

Figure 2 *Form1* displayed in the *Designer* window

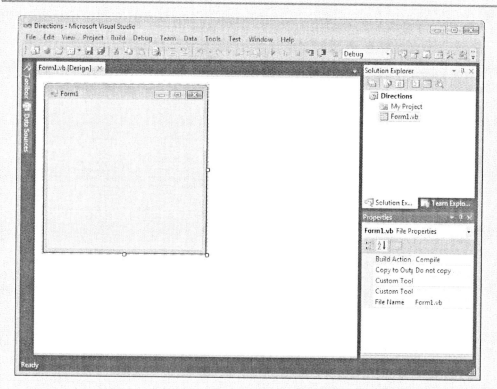

Step 3: Look at the *Properties* window. It should appear as shown in Figure 3.

Because you have selected *Form1*, the *Properties* window displays the properties for the *Form1* object. The drop-down list box at the top of the window shows the name of the selected object, *Form1*. Below that, the object's properties are displayed in two columns. The left column lists each property's name and the right column shows each property's value. The area at the bottom of the *Properties* window shows a brief description of the currently selected property.

> **TIP:** The *Properties* window has two buttons near the top that control the order of names in the window. The first ( ) sorts by category and the second ( ) sorts alphabetically. We will use the alphabetical sort in our examples.

The Text property is highlighted, which means it is currently selected. A form's Text property holds the text displayed in the form's title bar. It is initially set to the same value as the form name, so this form's Text property is set to *Form1*. Follow the instructions in Steps 4 and 5 to change the Text property to *Directions*.

Step 4: In the *Properties* window, double-click the word *Form1* inside the Text property.

Step 5: Delete the word *Form1* and type **Directions** in its place. Press the Enter key. Notice that the word *Directions* now appears in the form's title bar.

> **NOTE:** Remember, changing a form's Text property changes only the text that is displayed in the form's title bar. The form's name is still *Form1*.

Step 6: Perform *one* of the following actions to save the project:
- Click the Save All button ( ) on the standard toolbar
- Click File on the menu bar and then select Save All
- Press Ctrl+Shift+S on the keyboard

Because this is the first time you have saved the project, you will see the *Save Project* window. In that window, click the *Save* button to save the project at the specified location. Then, leave Visual Studio running for Tutorial 2, which takes you through the process of adding a Label control to the form.

Figure 3 *Properties* window showing *Form1*

Tutorial 2:

Adding a Label control to the *Directions* application

VideoNote

Tutorial 2-2
Walkthrough

Step 1: Now you are ready to add the Label control to the form. Make sure the *Common Controls* tab is open in the *Toolbox* window, as shown in Figure 4, and double-click the *Label* control icon. The label appears on the form with a dotted line around it and a small white square in its upper left corner, as shown in Figure 5. The dotted-line rectangle is called a **bounding box**—it marks the tightest rectangle that contains all parts of the control.

Figure 4 Label control tool

Figure 5 Label control on form

Step 2: Look at the *Properties* window. Because the label you just placed on the form is currently selected, the *Properties* window shows its properties (see Figure 6). The Text property is set, by default, to *Label1*. Double-click this value to select it, and replace its value by typing **Directions to the Highlander Hotel** in its place. Press the (Enter) key. When you have typed the new text into the Text property, the form appears, as shown in Figure 7. The label resizes itself to fit the contents of the Text property.

Figure 6 *Properties* window

Figure 7 Label with new text property value

Step 3: Next, you will move the label to a new location on the form. Move the mouse over the label on the form. Notice that when the mouse pointer is over the label, it becomes a four-headed arrow (⊕). Hold down the left mouse button, and drag the label to the top middle area of the form, as shown in Figure 8. From now on, we will refer to this type of operation as *dragging the control*.

Figure 8 After moving the Label control

Step 4: Save the project. Leave Visual Studio running for Tutorial 3, which takes you through the process of changing the Label control's font size and style.

Tutorial 3:
Changing the Label's font size and style

VideoNote

Tutorial 2-3
Walkthrough

In the planning phase, we indicated that the label's text should be displayed in a 16-point bold Microsoft sans serif font. These characteristics are controlled by the label's Font property. The **Font property** allows you to set the font, font style, and size of the label's text. In this tutorial you will use the Font property change the appearance of the label's text.

Step 1: With the Label selected, click the *Font* property in the *Properties* window. Notice that an ellipsis button (⬜) appears. When you click the ellipsis button, the *Font* dialog box appears, as shown in Figure 9.

Figure 9 *Font* dialog box

Step 2: *Microsoft Sans Serif* is already the selected font. Click *Bold* under *Font style*, and select *16* under *Size*. Notice that the text displayed in the *Sample* box changes to reflect your selections. Click the *OK* button.

The text displayed by the label is now in 16-point bold Microsoft sans serif. Unfortunately, not all of the label can be seen because it is too large for the form. You must enlarge the form so the entire label is visible.

Step 3: Select the form by clicking anywhere on it, except on the Label control. You will know you have selected the form when a thin dotted line with **sizing handles** appears around it. The dotted line is the form's bounding box, and the sizing handles are the small boxes, shown in Figure 10, that appear on the form's right edge, lower right corner, and bottom edge.

Step 4: Position the mouse pointer over the sizing handle that appears on the form's right edge. As shown in Figure 11, the mouse pointer becomes a two-headed arrow (⬌). Click and drag the sizing handle to widen the form. Then, select the label and move it so it appears similar to Figure 12.

Figure 10 The form selected, with sizing handles shown

Figure 11 The mouse pointer positioned over the form's right edge sizing handle

Figure 12 The form widened and the label repositioned

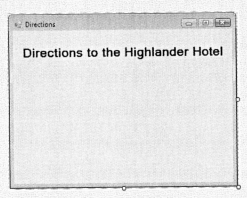

Step 5: Save the project. Leave Visual Studio running for Tutorial 4, which takes you through the process of deleting a control.

Tutorial 4:
Deleting a control

Sometimes you will find it necessary to delete a control that you have placed on a form. To delete a control, select it and press the (Delete) key on the keyboard. In this tutorial you will add another Label control to the form (one that you will not need) and then delete it.

Step 1: Double-click the *Label* icon in the *Toolbox*. Another Label control appears on the form.

Step 2: With the new Label control still selected, press the (Delete) key on the keyboard. The label is deleted from the form.

The last step in building this application is to insert the street map. In Tutorial 5 you insert a PictureBox control, which can be used to display an image.

The PictureBox Control

If you want to display a graphic image on an application's form, you use a **PictureBox control**. A PictureBox control can display images that have been saved in the bitmap, GIF, JPEG, metafile, or icon graphics formats. When a PictureBox control is placed on a form, it appears as an empty rectangle in which the image will be displayed. You can adjust the PictureBox control's size to make the image any size that you want.

The PictureBox control has several properties, but the following two properties are of particular interest:

- The **Image property** specifies the image file that is to be displayed by the control.
- The **SizeMode property** specifies how the image is to be displayed. It can be set to one of the following values:
  - **Normal**
    This is the default value. The image will be positioned in the upper-left corner of the PictureBox control. If the image is too big to fit in the PictureBox control, it will be clipped.
  - **StretchImage**
    The image will be resized both horizontally and vertically to fit in the PictureBox control. If the image is resized more in one direction than the other, it will appear stretched.
  - **AutoSize**
    The PictureBox control will be automatically resized to fit the size of the image.
  - **CenterImage**
    The image will be centered in the PictureBox control, without being resized.
  - **Zoom**
    The image will be uniformly resized to fit in the PictureBox without losing its original aspect ratio. (**Aspect ratio** is the image's width to height ratio.) This causes the image to be resized without appearing stretched.

In Tutorial 5 you will place a PictureBox control on the application's form and set the control's properties so it displays the street map image.

Tutorial 5:

Inserting a PictureBox control

VideoNote

Tutorial 2-5
Walkthrough

Step 1: Locate the *PictureBox* icon in the *Toolbox*. You will find it in the Common Controls group. (The tools are listed in alphabetical order.) When you locate the *PictureBox* tool, double-click it.

An empty PictureBox control appears on the form. Move the control to a position approximately in the center of the form, as shown in Figure 13.

Figure 13 PictureBox control placed

Step 2: Now you will specify the image that the PictureBox control will display. Locate the PictureBox control's Image property in the *Properties* window. The Image property is currently set to *(none)*, which means that no image is displayed. Click the property and notice that a browse button ([...]) appears next to the property setting. Click the browse button. The *Select Resource* window, shown in Figure 14 should appear.

Step 3: As indicated in Figure 14, in the *Select Resource* window select *Local Resource,* and then click the *Import* button. When the *Open* dialog box appears, navigate to the folder on your computer where the student sample files are located. Then, in the *Chap2* folder select the file named *HotelMap.jpg*. After you click the *OK* button, you should see the graphic shown in the *Select Resource* window, as shown in Figure 15. Click the OK button to accept the image, and you will see it displayed in the PictureBox control.

Your form should appear similar to Figure 16. As you can see from the figure, only part of the image is displayed. This is because the PictureBox control is smaller than the image, and the SizeMode property is set to its default value, *Normal.*

Figure 14 The Select Resource window

Figure 15 The HotelMap.jpg file selected

Figure 16 The HotelMap.jpg image partially displayed in the PictureBox control

Step 4: Make sure the PictureBox control is selected, and locate the SizeMode property in the Properties window. Notice that the SizeMode property is currently set to *Normal*. When you click the SizeMode property in the *Properties* window, a down arrow (▾) appears next to the property value.

Click the down arrow and a drop-down list appears, as shown in Figure 17. The list shows all of the possible values for the SizeMode property. Select *Zoom* from the list. This setting will resize the image so it fits within the bounding box of the PictureBox control, without losing the image's original aspect ratio. (In other words, the image will not appear stretched.) Figure 18 shows an example of how the form will appear.

Figure 17 A drop-down list showing the possible values of the SizeMode property

Figure 18 The image resized uniformly

Step 5: Although the image has been resized, the PictureBox shown in our example (in Figure 18) is too small. You can use the PictureBox's sizing handles to resize the PictureBox control so the image is displayed at the desired size. Resize and move the PictureBox control so the form appears similar to Figure 19.

Figure 19 The PictureBox control resized

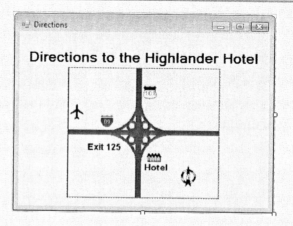

Step 6: Save the project. Leave Visual Studio running for Tutorial 6, which takes you through the process of compiling and running the application.

NOTE: You have now seen that properties are set in the *Properties* window in one of three ways:

- Typing a value for the property
- Selecting a value for the property from a drop-down list by clicking the down-arrow button (⯆)
- Establishing a value for the property with a dialog box, which appears when the *Browse* button (...) is clicked

Design Mode, Run Mode, and Break Mode

Visual Basic has three modes in which it operates as you develop and test an application. The three modes are design mode, run mode, and break mode. You have already experienced **design mode**. This is the mode in which you create an application. When you are placing controls on an application's form or writing Visual Basic code, Visual Basic is operating in design mode. (Design mode is also known as **design time**.)

When you are ready to run an application that you are developing, you can execute it without leaving the Visual Studio environment. This puts Visual Basic in **run mode** (also known as **runtime**). The application will be running on the computer, and you can interact with it as the user. There are three ways to run an application from the Visual Studio environment:

- Click the *Start Debugging* button (▶) on the toolbar
- Click *Debug* on the menu bar, then select *Start Debugging*
- Press the F5 key

When you perform one of these actions, the Visual Basic compiler will begin compiling the application. If no errors are found, the application will begin executing and Visual Basic will enter run mode. You will experience run mode in the next tutorial.

Break mode is a special mode that allows you to momentarily suspend a running application for testing and debugging purposes. It is also the mode that Visual Basic enters when a running application encounters a runtime error. (A runtime error is an error that occurs while a program is running.)

Closing a Project

To close the current project, click *File* on the menu bar, and then click *Close Project*. If you have made changes to the project since the last time you saved it, you will see a window similar to Figure 20 asking you if you want to save your changes. If you want to save your changes (in most cases you do), click *Yes*.

Figure 20 *Save changes* window

VideoNote

Tutorial 2-6
Walkthrough

Tutorial 6:
Running the application

Step 1: Now you will run the *Directions* application. It doesn't have any event handlers, so it will display only the PictureBox and Label when it runs. Perform one of the following actions to run the application:

- Click the *Start Debugging* button (▶) on the toolbar
- Click *Debug* on the menu bar, then select *Start Debugging*
- Press the F5 key

Step 2: The Visual Basic compiler will begin compiling the application. (The compiler translates the application to executable code.) After a few moments, the compiler will finish and the application will run. You should see the application's form appear on the screen, as shown in Figure 21.

Figure 21 The application running

Step 3:   Now you will stop the application (end its execution). Perform *one* of the following actions:

- Click the *Close* button () on the application window
- Click *Debug* on the Visual Studio menu bar, then select *Stop Debugging*
- Press Ctrl+Alt+Break on the keyboard

The application will stop and Visual Studio will return to Design mode.

Step 4:   If you have not recently saved the project, do so now. Then, close the project.

 TIP: Save your work often to prevent the accidental loss of changes you have made to your project.

Checkpoint

1   You want to change what is displayed in a form's title bar. Which of its properties do you change?

2   How do you insert a Label control onto a form?

3   What is the purpose of a control's sizing handles?

4   How do you delete a control?

5   What happens when you set a PictureBox control's SizeMode property to *StretchImage*?

6   What is the name of the dotted-line rectangle surrounding the Label control when looking at a form in Design mode?

7   What are the three modes in which Visual Studio operates?

How Solutions and Projects are Organized on the Disk

Now that you've created your first Visual Basic project, let's take a look at the way the project's files are organized on your computer's disk. A **solution** is a container that holds Visual Basic projects (see Figure 22). Each Visual Basic project must belong to a solution. Although it is possible for a solution to hold more than one project, each project that you will create will be saved in its own solution. So, each time you create a new project, you will also create a new solution to hold it.

Figure 22 Organization of a solution and its projects

When you save a project the first time, you see the *Save Project* window shown in Figure 23. The window shows the project name, the location on the disk where the project will be saved, and the solution name. By default the solution's name will be the same as the project's name. Notice the *Browse . . .* button that appears next to the location. You can click this button to select a different location, if you wish.

Also notice the *Create directory for solution* check box. It is a good idea to leave this box checked. It causes a directory (folder) for the solution to be created at the specified location. Inside that directory, another directory (folder) will be created for the project.

Figure 23 The *Save Project* window

Let's use Figure 23 to see an example of how the files for the *Directions* project will be organized on the disk. Notice that the location specified is:

```
C:\Users\Tony\Documents\Visual Studio 10\Projects
```

At this location, a folder named *Directions* will be created to hold the solution. If we use Windows to look inside that folder we will see that it contains the two items shown in Figure 24. Notice that one of the items is another folder named *Directions*. That is the project folder. The *Directions.sln* file is the **solution file**. It contains information needed by Visual Studio about the solution. In Windows, you can double-click the solution file and the project will be loaded into Visual Studio.

Figure 24 Contents of the *Directions* solution folder

If we look inside the project folder, also named *Directions*, we will see the contents shown in Figure 25. There are several files and other folders in the project folder, which are briefly described in Table 3. These files and folders are all created and used by Visual Studio, so you will not have to directly manipulate them. It should be mentioned, however, that in Windows you can double-click the project file (in this case *Directions.vbproj*) to load the project into Visual Studio.

Figure 25 Contents of the *Directions* project directory

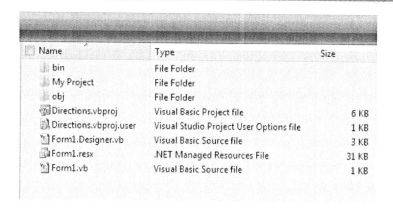

Table 3 Contents of the project folder

Item	Description
bin folder	contains the application's executable code
My Project folder	contains various application setting files
obj folder	holds temporary files that are created during the compilation process
Directions.vbproj	This is the project file. The **project file** contains information needed by Visual Studio about the *Directions* project. In Windows, you can double-click the project file and the project will be loaded into Visual Studio.
Directions.vbproj.user	This file contains information about Visual Studio's IDE settings.
Form1.Designer.vb	This file contains the Visual Basic code to generate the *Form1* form and all of the controls on it.
Form1.resx	This file contains information about various resources needed by *Form1* form.
Form1.vb	This file contains Visual Basic code that you write.

Opening an Existing Project

Once you've closed a Visual Basic project, you can open it again by performing any *one* of the following actions:

- Click *File* on the menu bar, and then select *Open Project . . .* The *Open Project* window will appear. Use the window to locate and select either the solution file (.sln) or the project file (.vbproj) for the project that you wish to open.
- Click *File* on the menu bar, and then select *Recent Projects and Solutions*. If the project is one that you have opened recently, it might be listed here. If it is, select either the solution file (.sln) or the project file (.vbproj) for the project that you wish to open.
- Use the *Start Page* to open the project. To display the *Start Page*, click *View* on the menu bar, then select *Start Page*. Then, as shown in Figure 26 either click the *Open Project* link to display the *Open Project* window, or select the name of project in the *Recent Projects* list.

Figure 26 Selecting a project from the *Recent Projects* list

Click here to display the *Open Project* window.

Or, select the project's name from this list

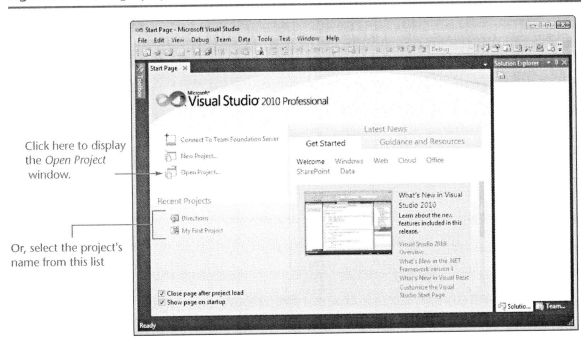

Using the *Properties* Window to Select Controls

The box that appears at the top of the *Properties* window, shown in Figure 27, shows the name of the currently selected control. This is referred to as the **object box**. In the figure, the Label1 control is currently selected in the object box. If you click inside the object box, a drop-down list will appear showing the names of all of the objects in the form. Figure 28 shows an example. You can click the name of an object in the drop-down list to select it. This has the same effect as selecting a control in the *Designer* window. The selected object's properties will be displayed in the *Properties* window.

Figure 27 Name of the currently selected control

Name of the currently selected control

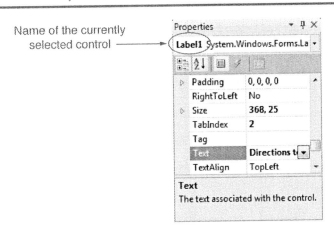

Figure 28 Drop-down list of the form's controls

Categorizing and Alphabetizing Properties

Figure 29 shows the *Categorized* and *Alphabetical* buttons, which affect the way properties are displayed in the *Properties* window. When the **Alphabetical** button is selected, the properties are displayed in alphabetical order. When the **Categorized** button is selected, related properties are displayed together in groups. Most of the time, it will be easier for you to locate a specific property if the properties are listed in alphabetical order.

Perhaps you've noticed that a few of the properties shown in the *Properties* window, including the Name property, are enclosed in parentheses. Because these properties are used so often, the Visual Basic designers enclosed them in parentheses to make them appear at the top of the alphabetical list.

In Tutorial 7 you practice using these components of the *Properties* window.

Figure 29 The Categorized and Alphabetical buttons

Categorized button

Alphabetical button

Tutorial 7:

Opening an existing project and becoming familiar with the *Properties* Window

Step 1: Start Visual Studio (or Visual Basic Express) and perform one of the actions previously discussed in this section to load the *Directions* project.

Step 2: Practice using the *Properties* window's drop-down list to select the *Label1*, *PictureBox1*, and *Form1* objects, as previously discussed in this section. Notice that as you select each object, its properties are displayed in the *Properties* window.

> **Step 3:** Select the *Label1* control and click the *Categorized* button. Scroll through the list of properties displayed in the *Properties* window. Notice there are several categories of properties. When you are finished, click the *Alphabetical* button. Scroll through the list of properties and notice that they are listed in alphabetical order.

Checkpoint

8 Describe three ways to open an existing project.

9 What are the two viewing modes for the *Properties* window? How do you select either of these modes? What is the difference between the two?

10 Open the *Directions* project. In the *Properties* window, arrange *Form1*'s properties in categorized order. Under what category does the Text property appear? Under what category does the Name property appear?

11 How can you select an object using only the *Properties* window?

Focus on Problem Solving: Responding to Events

CONCEPT: An application responds to events, such as mouse clicks and keyboard input, by executing code known as *event handlers*. In this section, you write event handlers for the *Directions* application.

VideoNote

Responding to Events

The manager of the Highlander Hotel reports that the *Directions* application has been quite helpful to the desk clerks. Some clerks, however, requested that the application be modified to display written directions as well as the map. Some also requested a more obvious way to exit the application, other than clicking the standard Windows *Close* button, located on the application's title bar.

You decide to add a button that is titled *Display Directions* to the application's form. When the user clicks the button, written directions to the hotel will appear in a Label control. You also decide to add an *Exit* button that the user can click to stop the application. Figure 30 shows the modified sketch of the form.

Figure 30 Modified *Directions* application sketch

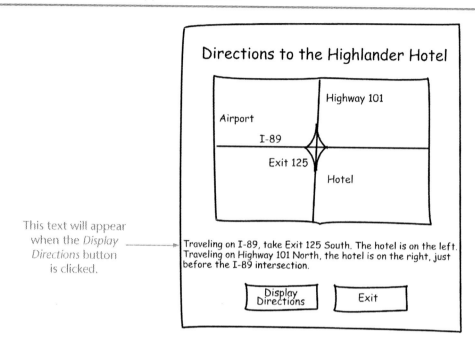

This text will appear
when the *Display
Directions* button
is clicked.

When the application runs, the Label control that displays the written directions will initially be invisible. The Label control (and most other types of controls) has a property named Visible that determines whether it can be seen. The **Visible property** is a **Boolean property**, which means that it can hold only one of two values: True or False. If a control's Visible property is set to True, the control is visible. If a control's Visible property is set to False, however, the control is invisible. When we create the new Label control, to hold the written directions, we will use the Properties window to set its Visible property to False. This will cause it to initially be invisible when the application runs. Tutorial 8 leads you through the process.

Tutorial 8:

Adding a Label control for the written directions

VideoNote

Tutorial 2-8
Walkthrough

Step 1: Start Visual Studio (or Visual Basic Express) and open the *Directions* project.

Step 2: You will place the new controls at the bottom of the form, below the image of the map. Because the form is currently too small to accommodate the new controls, you will need to enlarge it. Select the form so its sizing handles are visible. Drag the bottom edge of the form down until it looks something like the one shown in Figure 31. (Don't worry about the exact size of the form. You can adjust it again later.)

Figure 31 *Directions* project with the form enlarged

Step 3: Now you will add a new Label control to the form. Locate the Label control icon in the Toolbox and double-click it. This will create a new Label control positioned in the form's upper-left corner. Move the new Label control so it appears below the map image, at the approximate location shown in Figure 32.

Figure 32 New Label control moved below the map image

Step 4: Make sure the new Label control is still selected. In the *Properties* window, select the Text property, and then click the down-arrow button (⏷) that appears to the right of the property value. This opens an editing box as shown in Figure 33.

Figure 33 Editing box for the Label control's Text property

Step 5: Use the backspace key to delete the current contents of the editing box. Then type the following text. (Be sure to press Enter where specified.)

Traveling on I-89, take Exit 125 South. The hotel is on the left. [Enter] Traveling on Highway 101 North, the hotel is on the right, [Enter] just before the I-89 intersection.

The editing box should now appear as shown in Figure 34.

Figure 34 Editing box for the Label control's Text property

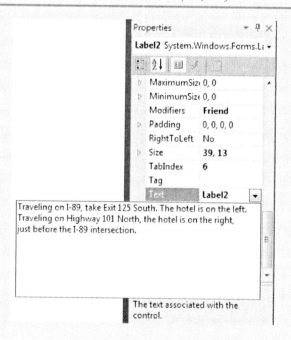

Step 6: Click the mouse anywhere outside of the editing box. This will cause the text you have typed to be saved in the Label control's Text property. The form should appear similar to Figure 35. (If necessary, move the Label control to match the approximate location shown in the figure.)

Figure 35 Label with the directions text entered

Step 7: Because we will refer to the new Label control in code, we should change the control's name to indicate its purpose. Make sure the Label control is still selected, and in the *Properties* window scroll up to the top of the property list. Near the top of the list, you will see the Name property. (Recall that the Name property is enclosed in parentheses so it appears near the top of the alphabetical listing.) Change the property's value to lblDirections, as shown in Figure 36. From this point forward we will refer to this label as the lblDirections control.

Figure 36 The Label control's name changed to lblDirections

Step 8: The last step is to change the `lblDirections` control's Visible property to False. With the control still selected, scroll down in the Properties window until you see the Visible property. Notice that the property is currently set to True. Click the down-arrow button (⯆) that appears next to the property setting. A drop-down list containing the values *True* and *False* appears, as shown in Figure 37. Select *False*.

Even though you have set the `lblDirections` control's Visible property to False, notice that it is still visible in the *Designer* window. This is because all controls are displayed in the *Designer* window, regardless of the value of their Visible property. When you run the application, however, the control will not be visible on the form.

Figure 37 Setting the Visible property

Step 9: Save the project. Leave Visual Studio running for Tutorial 9, which takes you through the process of adding a Button control and writing an event handler.

In the previous tutorial you added a Label control showing written directions to the hotel on the application's form. You named the control `lblDirections`, and you set its Visible property to False. Because its Visible property is set to False, the `lblDirections` control will not be visible on the form when the application runs. The next step is to add a Button control that, when clicked, causes the `lblDirections` control to appear at runtime. To make that happen, you will write an event handler that changes the `lblDirections` control's Visible property to True when the button is clicked. Tutorial 9 takes you through the process.

Tutorial 9:
Adding the *Display Directions* Button and its Click event handler

VideoNote

Tutorial 2-9
Walkthrough

Step 1: With the *Directions* project loaded into Visual Studio (or Visual Basic Express), click on the application's form in the *Designer* window to select it. Next, locate the Button control icon in the *Toolbox* and double-click it. This will create a new Button control positioned in the form's upper-left corner. Move the Button control so it appears at the approximate location shown in Figure 38.

Figure 38 New Button control added to the form

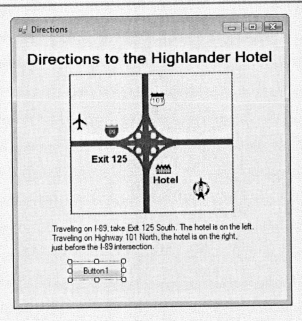

Step 2: With the button still selected, use the *Properties* window to change the button's Text property to *Display Directions*. This changes the text that is displayed on the face of the button.

Step 3: The button isn't quite large enough to accommodate this text, so use its sizing handles to increase its height, as shown in Figure 39.

Figure 39 Button control resized

Step 4: With the button still selected, scroll up in the *Properties* window and find the Name property. Notice that the button's name is currently set to `Button1`. Change the button's name to `btnDisplayDirections`.

Let's take a moment to think about why we changed the button's name. We did so because we will see the button's name appear in code later, and the default name, `Button1`, does not describe the control's purpose. The name `btnDisplayDirections` does describe the control: it is a button that displays directions.

Step 5: Now you are ready to write the Click event handler for the `btnDisplayDirections` button. (A button's Click event handler executes when the user clicks the button.) In the *Designer* window, double-click the `btnDisplayDirections` button. This causes the *Code* window to open as shown in Figure 40.

The **Code** window is a text-editing window in which you write code. Notice that some code already appears in the window. Let's briefly discuss this code. First, notice that the first and last lines of code read:

```
Public Class Form1
```

```
End Class
```

These statements are the beginning and the end of a **class declaration** for the Form1 form. For now, you just need to know that all of the code for the Form1 form (and all controls on the Form1 form) must appear inside this class declaration.

Next, notice that inside the class declaration, the following two lines of code appear:

We've left out the code that appears here.

```
Private Sub btnDisplayDirections_Click(…) Handles btnDisplayDirections.Click

End Sub
```

This is a **code template** for the `btnDisplayDirections` button's Click event handler. The template, which has been conveniently written for you, consists of the first and last lines of the event handler's code. Your job is to fill in the code that goes between these two lines. Any code that you write between these two lines will be executed when the `btnDisplayDirections` button is clicked.

NOTE: The first line of the event handler template is a very long line of code. Unless you have a large monitor, you might have to scroll the *Code* window to the right to see all of it. Because this line of code is so long, we have left out the part that appears inside the parentheses. We will frequently do this to simplify the appearance of the code in the text.

Figure 40 The Code window opened with an event handler template

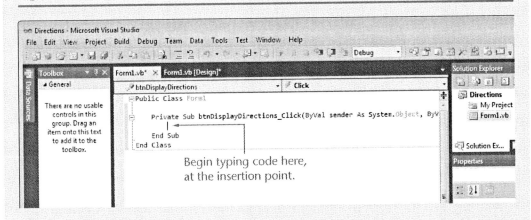

Begin typing code here,
at the insertion point.

Step 6: Figure 40 shows the flashing cursor, known as the insertion point, appearing between the first and last lines of the event handler code template. If the insertion point is not located at the position shown in the figure, use the arrow keys on the keyboard to move it to this location. Then, type the following statement exactly as it appears here:

```
lblDirections.Visible = True
```

We will discuss this statement in greater detail after the tutorial, but here is a brief explanation: when this statement executes, it will set the lblDirections control's Visible property to True. As a result, the lblDirections control will become visible on the form.

After you have typed this statement, the *Code* window should appear as shown in Figure 41.

Figure 41 The statement written in the event handler

```
Public Class Form1

    Private Sub btnDisplayDirections_Click(ByVal sender As Syster
        lblDirections.Visible = True
    End Sub
End Class
```

Did you notice that as soon as you started typing the statement, a list box popped up on the screen? This is known as the **IntelliSense** list box. The contents of the list box changes as you type. Figure 42 shows the IntelliSense list box after you have typed the characters lbl.

IntelliSense is a feature of Visual Studio that helps you write code faster. As you type code, you will see these IntelliSense boxes popping up regularly. Later in this chapter we have included a section that explains more about IntelliSense. Until you've had time to read that section, just ignore the IntelliSense boxes.

Creating Applications with Visual Basic

Figure 42 IntelliSense list box displayed

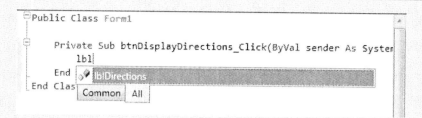

Step 7: This is a good time to save the project. Click the *Save All* button.

Step 8: Although you're not finished with the application, you can test the event handler that you just wrote. Click the *Start Debugging* button (▶) on the toolbar to run the application. After a moment the application will begin running and you will see the form displayed as shown in Figure 43. Notice that the written directions do not appear on the form.

Figure 43 The *Directions* application running

Step 9: Click the *Display Directions* button. The written directions appear on the form as shown in Figure 44.

Take a moment to review the following points about the application, and make sure you understand why it works the way that it does:

- When we created the lblDirections control, we set its Visible property to False in the *Properties* window. So, when the application starts, the control is not visible.
- When the btnDisplayDirections Button control is clicked, the event handler that you wrote sets the lblDirections control's Visible property to True, making it visible on the form.

Figure 44 The written directions displayed

Step 10: Click the form's standard close button (![close button]) to stop the application. You will continue modifying the project in the next tutorial.

Before we finish developing the *Directions* application, let's discuss the concepts we covered in Tutorial 9 in greater depth.

Creating the Click Event Handler for `btnDisplayDirections`

When a Button control appears on a form in the *Designer* window, you can double-click the Button control to edit the code for its Click event handler. You saw this happen in Step 5 of Tutorial 9. In that step, you double-clicked the `btnDisplayDirections` button. The *Code* window then opened, showing a code template for that button's Click event handler. Let's take a closer look at the code template, which is shown in Figure 45.

The first line starts with the keywords `Private Sub`. Following that is the name of the event handler, which in this case is `btnDisplayDirections_Click`. Following the name is some code that is enclosed in a set of parentheses. (As previously mentioned, we have left the contents of the parentheses out, here in the text, to simplify the figure.) After the parentheses are the words `Handles btnDisplayDirections.Click`. This tells us that the code handles the Click event when it happens to the `btnDisplayDirections` control.

The last line of the code template reads `End Sub`. These are keywords that mark the end of the event handler. Any code that you write between the first and last lines of the code template are executed, in the order in which they appear, when the event handler is invoked.

Figure 45 Event handler code template

Name of the event handler

```
Private Sub btnDisplayDirections_Click(…) Handles btnDisplayDirections.Click

End Sub
```

The event that executes
this event handler

Indentation

You probably noticed in Tutorial 9 that Visual Studio automatically indented the code that you wrote inside the event handler. Indenting the statements inside a procedure is a common programming practice that makes code much easier for human eyes to read. Although indenting the statements inside a procedure is not required (the code will still execute, even if it is not indented), it visually sets the statements apart. As a result, you can tell at a glance which statements are inside the procedure. This is helpful, especially when a program has a lot of procedures.

Changing a Control's Visible Property in Code

In design mode, setting the value of a control's property is simple. You do so using the *Properties* window. Quite often, however, you will want a control's property to change while the application is running. The *Directions* project gives us a good example. While that application is running, the value of the lblDirections control's Visible property changes to True when the user clicks the *Display Directions* button. Recall from Tutorial 9 (Step 6) that you wrote code in the btnDisplayDirections_Click event handler to make that happen. Anytime you want a control's property to change during the application's runtime, you have to write code that performs the change.

Let's look again at the statement you wrote in the btnDisplayDirections_Click event handler in Tutorial 9:

```
lblDirections.Visible = True
```

This is called an **assignment statement**. The equal sign (=) is known as the **assignment operator**. It assigns the value that appears on its right side to the item that appears on its left side. In this example, the item on the left side of the assignment operator is the expression lblDirections.Visible. This simply means the lblDirections control's Visible property. The value on the right side of the assignment operator is the value True. When this statement executes, the value True is assigned to the lblDirections control's Visible property. As a result of this assignment statement, the lblDirections control becomes visible on the application form.

NOTE: In an assignment statement, the name of the item receiving the value must be on the left side of the = operator. The following statement, for example, is wrong:

```
True = lblDirections.Visible ← ERROR!
```

NOTE: The standard notation for referring to a control's property in code is *ControlName.PropertyName*. The period that appears between the control name and the property name is called a dot.

Switching Between the *Code* Window and the *Designer* Window

Before continuing with the next tutorial, we should discuss how to switch between the *Code* window and the *Designer* window. When developing a VB application you will often find yourself switching between these two windows.

When a form is created in a VB project, the code for that form is stored in a file with the same name as the form, followed by the .vb extension. For example, the form in the *Directions* project is named Form1, so its code will be stored in a file named Form1.vb. If you still have Visual Studio running from the previous tutorial, you should see the tabs shown in Figure 46 at the top of the *Code* window. One of the tabs reads *Form1.vb*, and another one reads *Form1.vb* [*Design*]. (The tabs on your screen might not be in this order.) In the figure, the tab that reads *Form1.vb* is highlighted, indicating that the *Code* window is currently opened. To switch to the *Designer* window, click the tab that reads *Form1.vb* [*Design*]. Then, to switch back to the *Code* window, click the tab that reads *Form1.vb*.

Figure 46 *Code* window and *Designer* window Tabs

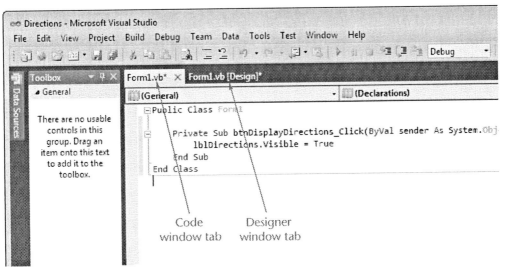

You can also use the *Solution Explorer* to switch between the *Code* window and the *Designer* window. First, make sure the form's code file is selected in the *Solution Explorer*. For example, in Figure 47 the Form1.vb file is selected. At the top of the *Solution Explorer* are two buttons that switch between the *Code* window and the *Designer* window: the *View Code* button ( ) and the *View Designer* button ( ).

Figure 47 *View Code* and *View Designer* buttons

You can also perform any of the following actions to switch between the *Code* and *Designer* windows:

- Click *View* on the menu bar and then select either *Code* or *Designer*
- Press F7 on the keyboard to switch to the *Code* window, or Shift F7 to switch to the *Designer* window

Tutorial 10:
Adding the *Exit* Button and its Click Event Handler

VideoNote

Tutorial 2-10
Walkthrough

In this tutorial you will add the final control to the *Directions* application: an *Exit* button that causes the application to end when the user clicks it.

Step 1: When you finished the previous tutorial, the *Directions* project was loaded into Visual Studio (or Visual Basic Express), and the *Code* window was opened. Use one of the techniques previously discussed to switch to the *Designer* window.

Step 2: Select the form in the *Designer* window. Next, locate the Button control icon in the *Toolbox* and double-click it. This will create a new Button control positioned in the form's upper-left corner. Move the Button control so it appears at the approximate location shown in Figure 48.

Figure 48 New Button control added to the form

Step 3: With the new button still selected, use the *Properties* window to change the button's Text property to *Exit*. This changes the text displayed on the face of the button.

Step 4: Use the button's sizing handles to make it the same height as the *Display Directions* button, as shown in Figure 49.

Figure 49 Button control resized

Step 5: With the button still selected, scroll up in the *Properties* window and find the Name property. Change the button's name to `btnExit`.

Step 6: Now you are ready to write the Click event handler for the `btnExit` button. In the *Designer* window, double-click the `btnExit` button. This causes the *Code* window to open as shown in Figure 50. Notice that a code template has been created for the `btnExit_Click` event handler.

Figure 50 The *Code* window opened with a new event handler code template

Step 7: At the current insertion point, between the first and last lines of the `btnExit_Click` event handler code template, type the following statement exactly as it is shown:

```
Me.Close()
```

When this statement executes, it will cause the form to close and the application to end. (We will discuss this statement in greater detail after the tutorial.) After you have typed this statement, the *Code* window should appear as shown in Figure 51.

Figure 51 The completed btnExit_Click event handler

```
Form1.vb* ✕  Form1.vb [Design]*

(General)                                        ▼  (Declarations)                    ▼

Public Class Form1

    Private Sub btnDisplayDirections_Click(ByVal sender As System.Object, ByV
        lblDirections.Visible = True
    End Sub

    Private Sub btnExit_Click(ByVal sender As System.Object, ByVal e As Syste
        Me.Close()
    End Sub
End Class
```

Step 8: Click the *Save All* button to save the project.

Step 9: Let's test the event handler that you just wrote. Click the *Start Debugging* button (▶) on the toolbar to run the application. After a moment the application will begin running and you will see the form displayed as shown in Figure 52.

Figure 52 The *Directions* application running

Step 10: Click the *Exit* button. The application should close.

Ending an Application with `Me.Close()`

You saw in the previous tutorial that when the statement `Me.Close()` executes, the application's form closes and the application ends. This statement is an example of a **method call**. Objects have methods, which are operations that an object can perform. If you want to execute one of an object's methods, you have to call that method.

An application's form (which is an object) has a method named `Close`. When a form's `Close` method is called, it causes the form to close. If an application has only one form, as the *Directions* application does, closing the form also ends the application's execution.

In the statement `Me.Close()`, the keyword `Me`, which appears to the left of the period, is shorthand for referring to the current form. On the right side of the period, the word `Close` is the name of the method we are calling. Next is a set of parentheses, which always appear after the name of the method in a method call.

Comments

Comments, which are also called *remarks*, are short notes that you can write in an application's code to explain what the code does. You should get into the habit of writing comments in your application code. The comments will almost certainly save you time in the future when you have to modify or debug the program. Even large and complex applications can be made easy to read and understand if they are properly commented.

In Visual Basic a comment starts with an apostrophe ('). Anything appearing after the apostrophe, to the end of the line, is ignored by the Visual Basic compiler. Here is an example of how we might use a comment to document a line of code:

```
' Make the directions visible.
lblDirections.Visible = True
```

The comment *Make the directions visible* explains in ordinary language what the next line of code does. In this example the comment uses an entire line, but it doesn't have to. A comment can be inserted at the end of a programming statement, like this:

```
lblDirections.Visible = True ' Make the directions visible.
```

In Tutorial 11 you will add comments to the code that you wrote in the *Directions* project.

Tutorial 11:
Adding comments to the *Directions* project code

Step 1: With the *Directions* project loaded into Visual Studio (or Visual Basic Express), use one of the techniques discussed earlier in this chapter to open the *Code* window.

Step 2: As shown in Figure 53, inside the `btnDisplayDirections_Click` event handler, insert the comment `' Make the directions visible.`

Figure 53 Comment inserted into the `btnDisplayDirections_Click` event handler

Step 3: As shown in Figure 54, inside the `btnExit_Click` event handler, insert the comment `' Close the form`.

Figure 54 Comment inserted into the `btnDisplayDirections_Click` event handler

Step 4: Save the project.

NOTE: From this point forward we will write comments as we write code. It's best to comment code as you write it because the code's purpose is fresh in your mind.

Checkpoint

12 How do you decide if you will keep a control's default name or assign it a new name?

13 What is a Boolean property?

14 Suppose an application has a button named `btnShowName`. The button has an event handler that executes when the user clicks it. What would the event handler be named?

15 Assume the following line appears in a button's Click event handler. What does the line cause the application to do?

    `lblGreeting.Visible = True`

16 What is the purpose of a comment (or remark)?

17 Suppose an application has a Label control named `lblSecretAnswer`. Write an assignment statement that causes the control to be hidden. (*Hint*: Use the Visible property.)

18 What is the purpose of the `Me.Close()` statement?

Changing Text Colors

You have already learned that the font style and size of text on a control can be easily changed through the *Properties* window. You can also change the text background and foreground color with the **BackColor** and **ForeColor** properties. Tutorial 12 walks you through the process.

Tutorial 12:
Changing the text colors

Step 1: With the *Directions* project loaded, open the *Designer* window.

Step 2: Select the *Label1* control. This is the Label control whose Text property reads *Directions to the Highlander Hotel*.

Step 3: In the *Properties* window, look for the BackColor property. This is the property that establishes the background color for the label text. Click the property value. A down-arrow button (⏷) appears.

Step 4: Click the down-arrow button (⏷). A drop-down list of colors appears, as shown in Figure 55.

The drop-down list has three tabs: *Custom*, *Web*, and *System*. The *System* tab lists colors defined in the current Windows configuration. The *Web* tab lists colors displayed with consistency in Web browsers. The *Custom* tab displays a color palette, as shown in Figure 56.

Select a color from one of the tabs. Notice that the label text background changes to the color you selected.

Step 5: Now look for the **ForeColor property** in the *Properties* window. When you click it, a down-arrow button (⏷) appears.

Step 6: Click the down-arrow button (⏷) and notice the same drop-down list as you saw in Step 4. Once again, select a color from one of the tabs. Notice that the label's text foreground color changes to the color you selected.

Figure 55 BackColor drop-down list

Figure 56 Custom color palette

Step 7:   Start the application to test the new colors. After you close the application, save your project.

Setting the FormBorderStyle Property and Locking Controls

The FormBorderStyle Property

Sometimes you want to prevent the user from resizing, minimizing, or maximizing a form, or from closing a form using its *Close* button (▣). You can control all of these actions by selecting an appropriate value for the form's **FormBorderStyle property**. Table 4 shows a list of the possible values for the FormBorderStyle property.

Table 4 Values for FormBorderStyle

Value	Description
Fixed3D	Displays a 3D border. The form's size is fixed and displayed with *Minimize*, *Maximize*, and *Close* buttons on its title bar. Although the form may be maximized and minimized, it may not be resized by its edges or corners.
FixedDialog	This type of border shows *Minimize*, *Maximize*, and *Close* buttons on its title bar. Although the form may be maximized and minimized, it may not be resized by its edges or corners.
FixedSingle	The form's size is fixed and uses a border that is a single line. The form is displayed with *Minimize*, *Maximize*, and *Close* buttons on its title bar. Although the form may be maximized and minimized, it may not be resized by its edges or corners.
FixedToolWindow	Intended for use with floating toolbars. Only shows the title bar with a *Close* button. May not be resized.
None	The form is displayed with no border at all. Subsequently, there is no title bar, and no *Minimize*, *Maximize*, and *Close* buttons. The form may not be resized.
Sizable	This is the default value. The form is displayed with *Minimize*, *Maximize*, and *Close* buttons on its title bar. The form may be resized, but the controls on the form do not change position.
SizableToolWindow	Like *FixedToolWindow*, but resizable.

Locking Controls

Once you have placed all the controls in their proper positions on a form, it is usually a good idea to lock them. When you lock the controls on a form, they cannot be accidentally moved at design time. They must be unlocked before they can be moved.

To lock all the controls on a form, place the cursor over an empty spot on the form and right-click. A small menu pops up. One of the selections on the menu is *Lock Controls*.

In Tutorial 13 we modify the value of the form's FormBorderStyle property so the user cannot minimize, maximize, or resize the window. We will also lock the controls on the form.

Tutorial 13:
Setting the FormBorderStyle property and locking the controls in the *Directions* application

Step 1: Open the *Directions* project in Visual Studio (or Visual Basic Express). Select the form and find the FormBorderStyle property in the *Properties* window.

Step 2: Click the FormBorderStyle property. A down-arrow button (▾) appears. Click the down-arrow button (▾) to see a list of values.

Step 3: Click *FixedSingle*.

Step 4: Start the application and test the new border style. Notice that you can move the window, but you cannot resize it by its edges or its corners.

Step 5: Click the *Exit* button to end the application.

Step 6: Now you will lock the controls. Place the cursor over an empty spot on the form and right-click. A small menu pops up.

Step 7: Click the *Lock Controls* command.

Step 8: Select any control on the form and try to move it. Because the controls are locked, you cannot move them.

Step 9: Save the project.

When you are ready to move the controls, just right-click over an empty spot on the form and select the *Lock Controls* command again. This toggles (reverses) the locked state of the controls.

 WARNING: Be careful. Locked controls can still be deleted.

 TIP: *A single control may be locked by setting its Locked property to True. It may be unlocked by setting its Locked property to False.*

Printing Your Code

To print a project's code, open the *Code* window, click *File* on the menu bar, and then click the *Print* command on the *File* menu.

Using IntelliSense

IntelliSense is a feature of Visual Studio that provides automatic code completion as you write programming statements. As you have worked through the tutorials in this chapter, you have probably noticed the IntelliSense list boxes that pop up as you write programming statements. For example, suppose you have the *Directions* project loaded, and you are about to type the following statement in the *Code* window:

```
lblDirections.Visible = True
```

As soon as you type the letter `"l"` an IntelliSense list box pops up, as shown in Figure 57. The IntelliSense system is anticipating what you are about to type. The list box shown in Figure 57 shows all the names starting with the letter `"l"` that might be a candidate for the statement you are typing. As you continue to type letters, the contents of the list box narrows. For example, after you have `"lbl"` the IntelliSense list box shows only one selection: `lblDirections`. This is shown in Figure 58. With that item selected, you can press the Tab key on the keyboard, and the `lbl` that you previously typed becomes `lblDirections`.

Figure 57 IntelliSense list box after typing the letter `"l"`

Figure 58 IntelliSense list box after typing `"lbl"`

Next, when you type a period, an IntelliSense list pops up showing every property and method belonging to the `lblDirections` object. Type `"vi"` and the choice is narrowed down to the Visible property, as shown in Figure 59. At this point, when you press the Tab key to select the Visible property, your statement automatically becomes `lblDirections.Visible`.

Figure 59 IntelliSense list box after entering "`lblDirections.vi`"

Next, if you type an = sign, another IntelliSense box appears, shown in Figure 60, showing the values False and True, which are the only possible values that can be assigned to the Visible property. Select True from the list and press the Tab key, and the statement is completed as `lblDirections.Visible = True`.

Now that you have an idea of how IntelliSense works, you are encouraged to experiment with it as you write code in future projects. With a little practice, it will become intuitive.

Figure 60 IntelliSense list box after entering "`lblDirections.Visible=`"

 Checkpoint

19 Which keyboard function key displays the *Code* window?

20 What three color categories are available when you edit a control's BackColor property?

21 What happens when you modify a Label control's BackColor property?

22 What happens when you modify a Label control's ForeColor property?

23 What property do you set in order to prevent a form from being resized when the application is running?

24 What happens when you lock the controls on a form?

25 How do you lock the controls on a form?

26 How do you unlock the controls on a form?

 3 Modifying a Control's Text Property with Code

CONCEPT: Quite often, you will need to change a control's Text property with code. This is done with an assignment statement.

While building the *Directions* application, you learned that an assignment statement assigns a value to a property while the application is running. Recall that the following statement sets the `lblDirections` control's Visible property to *True*.

```
lblDirections.Visible = True
```

87

You use the same technique to modify a control's Text property. For example, assume an application has a Label control named lblMessage. The following statement assigns the sentence *Programming is fun!* to the control's Text property.

```
lblMessage.Text = "Programming is fun!"
```

Once the statement executes, the message displayed by the lblMessage control changes to

```
Programming is fun!
```

The quotation marks in the statement are not part of the message. They simply mark the beginning and end of the set of characters assigned to the property. In programming terms, a group of characters inside a set of quotation marks is called a **string literal**.

We usually display messages on a form by setting the value of a Label control's Text property. In Tutorial 14 you open and examine an application in the student sample programs folder that demonstrates this technique.

Tutorial 14:

Examining an application that displays messages in a Label control

Step 1: Start Visual Studio and open the *KiloConverter* project from the student sample programs folder named *Chap2\KiloConverter*, from the materials you downloaded from www.microsoft.com/express/Downloads/.

Step 2: Open the *Designer* window, which displays *Form1*, as shown in Figure 61.

Step 3: Click the *Start Debugging* button (▶) to run the application.

Step 4: Once the application is running, click the *Inches* button. The form displays the number of inches equivalent to a kilometer, as shown in Figure 62.

Step 5: Experiment with the other buttons and observe the messages that are displayed when each is clicked.

Step 6: Click the *Exit* button to exit the application. Let's examine the application code. Figure 63 shows the *KiloConverter* application form with its controls labeled.

The buttons btnInches, btnFeet, btnYards, and btnMiles each change the lblMessage Text property when clicked. In the next step, you will view the *KiloConverter* event handlers.

Figure 61 *Kilometer Converter* form

Figure 62 One kilometer converted to inches

Figure 63 *KiloConverter* application controls

Step 7: Click the *View Code* button ([≡]) in the *Solution Explorer* window. The *Code* window appears, showing the following code. Examine each event handler and make sure you understand which Button control it works with, and how it changes the text that is displayed on the form.

```
Public Class Form1

    Private Sub btnExit_Click(...) Handles btnExit.Click
        ' End the application.
        Me.Close()
    End Sub

    Private Sub btnFeet_Click(...) Handles btnFeet.Click
        ' Display the conversion to feet.
        lblMessage.Text = "1 Kilometer = 3,281 feet"
    End Sub

    Private Sub btnInches_Click(...) Handles btnInches.Click
        ' Display the conversion to inches.
        lblMessage.Text = "1 Kilometer = 39,370 inches"
    End Sub

    Private Sub btnMiles_Click(...) Handles btnMiles.Click
        ' Display the conversion to miles.
        lblMessage.Text = "1 Kilometer = 0.6214 miles"
    End Sub

    Private Sub btnYards_Click(...) Handles btnYards.Click
        ' Display the conversion to yards.
        lblMessage.Text = "1 Kilometer = 1,093.6 yards"
    End Sub
End Class
```

4 The AutoSize, BorderStyle, and TextAlign Properties

CONCEPT: The Label control's AutoSize property determines whether a label will change size automatically to accommodate the amount of text in its Text property, or remain a fixed size. The BorderStyle property allows you to set a border around a Label control. The TextAlign property determines how the text is aligned within the label.

The Label control has three additional properties, AutoSize, BorderStyle, and TextAlign, which give you greater control over the label's appearance.

The AutoSize Property

The **AutoSize property** is a Boolean property that is set to *True* by default. When a label's AutoSize property is set to *True*, the label's bounding box will automatically resize to accommodate the text in the label's Text property.

When AutoSize is set to *False*, however, you can use the label's sizing handles to change its size in the *Designer* window. When the application is running, the Label control will remain the size that it was given at design time. If the text in the label's Text property is too large to fit in the control's bounding box, the text will be only partially displayed.

The BorderStyle Property

The Label control's **BorderStyle property** may have one of three values: *None*, *FixedSingle*, and *Fixed3D*. The property is set to *None* by default, which means the label will have no border. If BorderStyle is set to *FixedSingle*, the label will be outlined with a border that is a single pixel wide. If BorderStyle is set to *Fixed3D*, the label will have a recessed 3D appearance. Figure 64 shows an example of three Label controls: one with BorderStyle set to *None*, one with BorderStyle set to *FixedSingle*, and one with BorderStyle set to *Fixed3D*.

Quite often you will want to display output, such as the results of a calculation, in a Label control with a border. You will see many example applications in this text that use this approach.

Figure 64 *FixedSingle* and *Fixed3D* BorderStyle examples

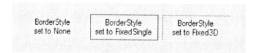

The TextAlign Property

When you set a label's AutoSize property to False and then manually resize the label, it sometimes becomes necessary to change the way the label's text is aligned. By default, a label's text is aligned with the top and left edges of the label's bounding box. For example, look at the label shown in Figure 65. When we created this label, we set the Text property to *Hello World*, we set the AutoSize property to False, and then we enlarged the size of the label as shown in the figure. Notice how the text is positioned in the label's upper-left corner.

Figure 65 Default text alignment

What if we want the text to be aligned differently within the Label? For example, what if we want the text to be centered in the label, or positioned in the lower-right corner? We can change the text's alignment in the label with the **TextAlign property**. The TextAlign property may be set to any of the following values: TopLeft, TopCenter, TopRight, MiddleLeft, MiddleCenter, MiddleRight, BottomLeft, BottomCenter, or BottomRight. Figure 66 shows nine Label controls, each with a different TextAlign value.

Figure 66 Text alignments

To change the TextAlign property, select it in the *Properties* window and then click the down-arrow button ( ) that appears next to its value. This causes a dialog box with nine buttons, as shown in the left image in Figure 67, to appear. As shown in the right image in the figure, the nine buttons represent the valid settings of the TextAlign property.

Figure 67 Setting the TextAlign property with the *Properties* window

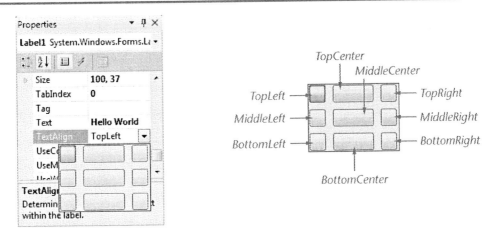

Changing a Label's TextAlign Property with Code

At design time, you set the TextAlign property's value in the *Properties* window. You can also set the property with code at runtime. You do this by using an assignment statement to assign one of the following values to the property:

```
ContentAlignment.TopLeft
ContentAlignment.TopCenter
ContentAlignment.TopRight
ContentAlignment.MiddleLeft
ContentAlignment.MiddleCenter
ContentAlignment.MiddleRight
ContentAlignment.BottomLeft
ContentAlignment.BottomCenter
ContentAlignment.BottomRight
```

For example, assume an application uses a Label control named `lblReportTitle`. The following statement aligns the control's text with the middle and center of the control's bounding box.

```
lblReportTitle.TextAlign = ContentAlignment.MiddleCenter
```

 TIP: When you write an assignment statement that stores a value in the TextAlign property, an Intellisense box appears showing all the valid values.

 Checkpoint

27 Suppose an application has a Label control named `lblTemperature`. Write a code statement that causes the label's Text property to display the message *48 degrees.*

28 What happens when a Label control's AutoSize property is set to *False*? When it is set to *True*?

29 What are the possible values for the Label control's BorderStyle property, and what result does each value produce?

30 Suppose an application has a Label control named `lblName`. Write the programming statements described by the following:
- A statement that aligns the label's text in the top right.
- A statement that aligns the label's text in the bottom left.
- A statement that aligns the label's text in the top center.

 5 Displaying Message Boxes

CONCEPT: You can use the `MessageBox.Show` method to display a message box, which is a dialog box that pops up, showing a message to the user.

Sometimes you need a convenient way to display a message to the user. In Visual Basic, you can call the `MessageBox.Show` method to pop up a message box. A **message box** is a small window, sometimes referred to as a **dialog box**, that displays a message. Figure 68 shows an example of a message box, displaying the message *Hello World!* Notice that the message box also has an *OK* button. The user must click the *OK* button to close the message box.

Figure 68 A message box

The following statement shows an example of how you would call the `MessageBox.Show` method to display the message box shown in Figure 68:

```
MessageBox.Show("Hello World!")
```

Notice that the string `"Hello World!"` appears inside the parentheses. Any string that you type inside the parentheses will be displayed in the message box when the statement executes.

Tutorial 15:
Displaying Message Boxes

In the student sample programs folder named *Chap2\French Numbers* (obtained from the materials you downloaded from the Microsoft website), you have a project named *French Numbers*. The project has been started for you, and in this tutorial you will complete it by writing the necessary event handlers.

When the project is complete, it will display the French words for the numbers 1 through 5, which are shown here:

1 un
2 deux
3 trois
4 quatre
5 cinq

The application's form has five button controls, displaying the numbers 1 through 5. The completed application will allow the user to click any of the buttons to select a number, and a message box will appear displaying the French word for the selected number. For example, if the user clicks the 2 button, a message box will appear displaying the word *deux*.

Step 1: Open the *French Numbers* project from the student sample programs folder named *Chap2\French Numbers*. Figure 69 shows the application's form, with the names of each Button control.

Figure 69 The *French Numbers* form

Step 2: Create Click event handlers for all of the button controls. When each button is clicked, it should display a message box showing the French word for the button's number, as described here:

- When the btnOne button is clicked, a message box should appear displaying *un*.
- When the btnTwo button is clicked, a message box should appear displaying *deux*.
- When the btnThree button is clicked, a message box should appear displaying *trois*.
- When the btnFour button is clicked, a message box should appear displaying *quatre*.
- When the btnFive button is clicked, a message box should appear displaying *cinq*.

In addition, write a Click event handler for the btnExit button that closes the form. When you have finished writing all of the event handlers, your code should be similar to the following. (Your event handlers might appear in a different order than those shown here, depending on the order in which you double-click each button in the *Designer* window.)

```
Public Class Form1

    Private Sub btnOne_Click(...) Handles btnOne.Click
        ' Display the French word for one.
        MessageBox.Show("un")
    End Sub

    Private Sub btnTwo_Click(...) Handles btnTwo.Click
        ' Display the French word for two.
        MessageBox.Show("deux")
    End Sub

    Private Sub btnThree_Click(...) Handles btnThree.Click
        ' Display the French word for three.
        MessageBox.Show("trois")
    End Sub

    Private Sub btnFour_Click(...) Handles btnFour.Click
        ' Display the French word for four.
        MessageBox.Show("quatre")
    End Sub

    Private Sub btnFive_Click(...) Handles btnFive.Click
        ' Display the French word for five.
        MessageBox.Show("cinq")
    End Sub

    Private Sub btnExit_Click(...) Handles btnExit.Click
        ' Close the form.
        Me.Close()
    End Sub
End Class
```

Step 3: Save the project, and then execute it. Test each button on the form to make sure it displays the correct word in a message box, as shown in Figure 70.

Figure 70 Message boxes that should be displayed by the *French Numbers* application

un	deux	trois	quatre	cinq
OK	OK	OK	OK	OK

When the user clicks 1 | When the user clicks 2 | When the user clicks 3 | When the user clicks 4 | When the user clicks 5

Checkpoint

31 What is a dialog box?

32 Write a statement that displays a message box showing the message *Welcome to our hotel!*.

33 The following statement is not written correctly. What is wrong with it?
```
MessageBoxShow("Invalid password")
```

6 Clickable Images

CONCEPT: Controls other than buttons can have Click event handlers. In this section, you learn to create PictureBox controls that respond to mouse clicks.

In this chapter, you learned that buttons can have Click event handlers. A Click event handler is executed when the user clicks the button. Other controls, such as PictureBoxes and labels, may also have Click event handlers. In Tutorial 16 you write Click event handlers for a group of PictureBox controls.

Tutorial 16:
Writing Click event handlers for PictureBox controls

Step 1: Open the *Flags* project from the student sample programs folder named *Chap2\Flags*.

Step 2: Open the *Designer* window and look at *Form1*. Figure 71 shows the form and the names of the controls on the form.

Step 3: Select the `lblMessage` control and set its TextAlign property to *MiddleCenter*, and its Font property to *Microsoft sans serif, bold, 8 points*.

Step 4: Change the form's Text property to **Flags**.

Step 5: `PictureBox1` shows the flag of the United States. Rename this control **picUSA**.

Figure 71 *Form1* of the *Flags* project

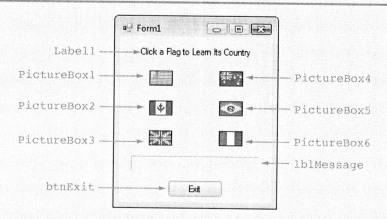

Step 6: `PictureBox2` shows the flag of Canada. Rename this control **`picCanada`**.

Step 7: `PictureBox3` shows the flag of the United Kingdom. Rename this control **`picUK`**.

Step 8: `PictureBox4` shows the flag of Australia. Rename this control **`picAustralia`**.

Step 9: `PictureBox5` shows the flag of Brazil. Rename this control **`picBrazil`**.

Step 10: `PictureBox6` shows the flag of Italy. Rename this control **`picItaly`**.

Step 11: Double-click the `picUSA` control. The *Code* window opens with a code template generated for the `picUSA_Click` event handler. Complete the event handler by writing code that assigns the string `"United States of America"` to the `lblMessge` control's Text property. The code that you should write is shown in bold here:

```
Private Sub picUSA_Click(...) Handles picUSA.Click
    ' Display United States of America.
    lblMessage.Text = "United States of America"
End Sub
```

Step 12: Repeat the process that you followed in Step 11 for each of the other PictureBox controls. The Click event handler for each PictureBox control should assign the name of its flag's country to the `lblMessage.Text` property.

Next, double-click the `btnExit` button to create a code template for the `btnExit_Click` event handler. Complete the event handler so it closes the form.

When you have completed all of these event handlers, your code should look something like the following. Note that your event handlers might not appear in the same order as the ones shown, depending on the order in which you double-clicked the controls.

```
Public Class Form1

    Private Sub picUSA_Click(...) Handles picUSA.Click
        ' Display United States of America.
        lblMessage.Text = "United States of America"
    End Sub

    Private Sub picCanada_Click(...) Handles picCanada.Click
        ' Display Canada.
        lblMessage.Text = "Canada"
    End Sub
```

```
        Private Sub picUK_Click(...) Handles picUK.Click
          ' Display United Kingdom.
          lblMessage.Text = "United Kingdom"
        End Sub
        Private Sub picAustralia_Click(...) Handles picAustralia.Click
          ' Display Australia.
          lblMessage.Text = "Australia"
        End Sub
        Private Sub picBrazil_Click(...) Handles picBrazil.Click
          ' Display Brazil.
          lblMessage.Text = "Brazil"
        End Sub
        Private Sub picItaly_Click(...) Handles picItaly.Click
          ' Display Italy.
          lblMessage.Text = "Italy"
        End Sub
        Private Sub btnExit_Click(...) Handles btnExit.Click
          ' Close the form.
          Me.Close()
        End Sub
      End Class
```

Step 13: Save the project.

Step 14: Run the application. When you click any of the flags, you should see the name of the flag's country appear in the lblMessage Label control. For example, when you click the flag of Australia, the form should appear similar to the one shown in Figure 72.

Step 15: Exit the application.

Figure 72 *Flags* application identifying flag of Australia

7 Using Visual Studio Help

The documentation for Visual Studio and Visual Basic is contained in the MSDN (Microsoft Developer Network) Library. The MSDN Library contains a wealth of information, including code samples, tutorials, and technical articles. When you install Visual Studio, you have the option of installing the MSDN Library on your computer. If you choose not to install the MSDN Library on your computer, you can still access its content on the Web.

As shown in Figure 73, you can access the MSDN Library by Clicking *Help* on the Visual Studio menu bar, and then selecting *View Help*. (Or, you can simply press Ctrl+F1.) This opens the MSDN library in your Web browser.

Figure 73 Accessing the *Visual Studio Documentation*

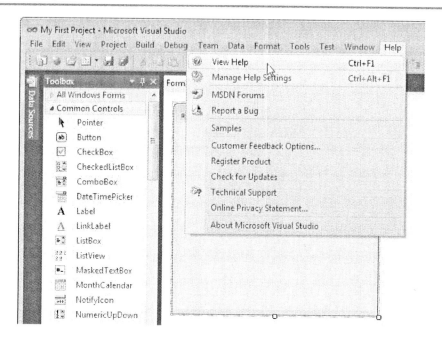

Context-Sensitive Help

The MSDN Library contains a vast amount of documentation on Visual Studio and Visual Basic. Because it contains so much information, it is often easier to find what you are looking for by using context-sensitive help. **Context-sensitive help** is help on a single topic that you are currently working on. You get context-sensitive help by selecting an item in the *Designer* window, *Code* window, *Properties* window, *Toolbox*, etc., and then pressing the F1 key. Your Web browser will launch, displaying help on the item that is selected.

For example, Figure 74 shows some code displayed in the *Code* window. Notice that the = operator has been selected (highlighted) in one of the lines of code. If we press the F1 key while the = operator is selected, we will see a help screen similar to Figure 75, displayed in a Web browser.

Notice that the left pane in the browser shows a list of topics that you can click on to get additional help. You can also use the search box that appears at the top of the left pane to search for help on specific items.

Figure 74 The = operator selected in the *Code* window

Figure 75 Help on the = operator

8 Debugging Your Application

CONCEPT: At some point, most applications contain bugs (errors) that prevent the application from operating properly. In this section, you learn fundamental debugging techniques.

Visual Basic reports errors in your project as soon as it finds them. In general, there are two types of errors: compile errors and runtime errors.

Compile errors are syntax errors, such as misspelled keywords or the incorrect use of operators or punctuation. Visual Basic checks each line of code for compile errors as soon as you enter it. When a compile error is found, it is underlined with a jagged blue line. A description of the error is also displayed in the *Error List* window. You display it by clicking *View* on the menu bar, and then selecting *Error List*.

Runtime errors are errors found while an application is running. They are not syntax errors but result if there is an attempt to perform an operation that Visual Basic cannot execute.

Tutorial 17 demonstrates how Visual Basic reports compile errors.

Tutorial 17:
Locating a compile error in Design mode

Step 1: Open the *Directions* project and open the *Code* window.

Step 2: You will modify the `btnExit_Click` procedure so it contains a syntax error. Change the spelling of the statement that reads `Me.Close()` to read `Me.Clost()`.

Step 3: Notice that the statement is now underlined with a jagged blue line as shown in Figure 76. This jagged blue underlining indicates an error.

Figure 76 Error underlined

```
Private Sub btnExit_Click(ByVal sender As System.Object,
    ' Close the form.
    Me.Clost()
End Sub
```

Step 4: Perform *one* of the following actions to open the *Error List* window:
- Click View on the menu bar, then select Error List.
- Click the Error List button ( ) on the toolbar.
- Press Ctrl+W followed by Ctrl+E on the keyboard.

Look at the *Error List* window, which should appear similar to Figure 77. It shows an error message indicating that `Clost` is not a member of `Directions.Form1`. Notice that the location of the error is also given as line 10, column 9 of the file `Form1.vb`, in the *Directions* project.

Additionally, you can double-click the error message that appears in the Error List window, and the text editing cursor in the *Code* window will be positioned at the error.

Figure 77 The *Error List* window

TIP: Sometimes you will see an error message you do not fully understand. When this happens, look at the area that shows the jagged underlining, and try to determine the problem. When you figure out what caused the error, consider how it relates to the error message.

Step 5: Correct the line of code that you changed in Step 2 so it reads `Me.Close( )`.

Checkpoint

34 What is context-sensitive help?

35 What are the two general types of errors in a Visual Basic project?

Summary

1 Focus on Problem Solving: Building the *Directions* Application

- The *Properties* window is used at design time to set control property values. The PictureBox control's SizeMode property determines how the control will place and size its image.
- Small squares (sizing handles) are used to enlarge or shrink the control. Once you place a control on a form, you can move it by clicking and dragging. To delete a control, select it and then press the [Delete] key.
- To run an application click the *Start Debugging* button on the toolbar, click the *Start Debugging* command on the *Debug* menu, or press the [F5] key. To end a running application, click the *Stop Debugging* command on the *Debug* menu or click the *Close* button on the application window.
- When you create a new project, Visual Studio automatically creates a solution with the same name as the project, and adds the project to the solution. The solution and the project are stored on the disk in a folder with the same name as the solution. The solution file ends with the *.sln* extension and the project file ends with the *.vbproj* extension.
- To open an existing project, click its name in the Recent Projects list on the *Start Page*, click *File* on the menu bar, then click *Open Project*, or click *File* on the menu bar, *Recent Projects and Solutions*, and then select the solution or project from the list.
- The *Properties* window's object box provides a drop-down list of the objects in the project. The *Alphabetical* button causes the properties to be listed alphabetically. The *Categorized* button causes related properties to be displayed in groups.

2 Focus on Problem Solving: Responding to Events

- The apostrophe (') marks the beginning of a comment in code. A comment is a note of explanation that is ignored by Visual Basic.
- The Me.Close() statement causes the current form to close. If the current form is the application's startup form, the application ends.
- To display the *Code* window, you click the *View Code* button on the *Solution Explorer* window, click *View* on the menu bar, then *Code*, or press the [F7] key on the keyboard.
- The color of a label's text is changed with the BackColor and ForeColor properties.
- Once you have placed all the controls in their proper positions on a form, it is a good idea to lock them.

3 Modifying a Control's Text Property with Code

- You may change a control's Text property with code. An assignment statement assigns a value into the property at runtime.

4 The AutoSize, BorderStyle, and TextAlign Properties

- The AutoSize property determines whether a label will change size automatically to accommodate the amount of text in its Text property, or remain a fixed size.
- The BorderStyle property allows you to set a border around a Label control.
- The TextAlign property determines how the text in a label is aligned, and may be set to any of the following values: TopLeft, TopCenter, TopRight, MiddleLeft, MiddleCenter, MiddleRight, BottomLeft, BottomCenter, or BottomRight.
- You can set the TextAlign property with code at runtime by using an assignment statement to store a valid value in the property.

5 Displaying Message Boxes

- A message box is a small window that displays a message.
- In Visual Basic you call the `MessageBox.Show` method to display a message.

6 Clickable Images

- Buttons are not the only controls that can have Click event handlers. Other controls, such as PictureBoxes and Labels, can also have Click event handlers that respond to mouse clicks.

7 Using Visual Studio Help

- You access the Visual Studio Documentation and the MSDN library by clicking *Help* on the menu bar.
- You can get context-sensitive help on a single item that is currently selected in the *Designer* window, *Code* window, *Properties* window, *Toolbox*, etc., and then pressing the F1 key.

8 Debugging Your Application

- Visual Basic checks each line of code for syntax errors as soon as you enter it. When a compile error is found, it is underlined with a jagged blue line.
- Runtime errors occur while an application is running. They are not syntax errors, but result if there is an attempt to perform an operation that Visual Basic cannot execute.

Key Terms

aspect ratio
Alphabetical button
assignment operator
assignment statement
AutoSize property
BackColor property
Boolean property
BorderStyle property
bounding box
break mode
Categorized button
class declaration
code template
Code window
compile errors
Contents button
context-sensitive help
Design mode
design time
dialog box
Font property

ForeColor property
FormBorderStyle property
Image property
Index button
IntelliSense
Method call
message box
object box
PictureBox control
project file
run mode
runtime
runtime errors
Search button
SizeMode property
sizing handles
solution
solution file
string literal
TextAlign property
Visible property

Review Questions and Exercises

Fill-in-the-Blank

1. The _____ property determines how a Label control's text is aligned.

2. A PictureBox control's _____ property lists the name of the file containing the graphic image.

3. A PictureBox control's _____ property determines how the graphic image will be positioned and scaled to fit the control's bounding box.

4. When set to _____, the TextAlign property causes text to appear in the bottom right area of a Label control.

5. The contents of a form's Text property is displayed on the form's _____ _____.

6. Anytime you select an existing control, _____ appear, which you use to resize the control.

7. A control's _____ is a transparent rectangular area that defines the control's size.

8. A Label control's _____ property establishes the font, style, and size of the label's displayed text.

9. To delete a control in the *Designer* window, select it and press the _____ _____ key.

10. The _____ control is used to display graphic images.

11. The SizeMode property of a PictureBox control is set to _____ by default.

12. When the _____ button is selected on the *Solution Explorer* window, it opens the *Code* window.

13. Clicking the _____ button in the *Properties* window causes related properties to be listed in groups.

14. Visible is a _____ property, which means it can only hold one of two values: *True* or *False*.

15. An apostrophe (') in code marks the beginning of a _____.

16. The equal sign (=) is known as the _____ operator. It copies the value on its right into the item on its left.

17. In an assignment statement, the name of the item receiving the value must be on the _____ side of the = operator.

18. Visual Basic automatically provides a code _____ , which is the first and last lines of an event handler.

19. The _____ statement causes the form to close.

20. The _____ property establishes the background color for a Label control's text.

21. The _____ property establishes the color of the type for a Label control's text.

22. The _____ property allows you to prevent the user from resizing, minimizing, or maximizing a form, or closing a form using its *Close* button.

23. When you _____ the controls on a form, they cannot be accidentally moved at design time.

24. You display text in a form's title bar by setting the value of the form's _____ property.

25. You commonly display words and sentences on a form by setting the value of a Label control's _____ property.

26. The _____ property causes the Label control to resize automatically to accommodate the amount of text in the Text property.

27. _____ errors are errors that are generated while an application is running.

True or False

Indicate whether the following statements are true or false.

1. T F: In the *Designer* window, sizing handles appear around a control that is currently selected.

2. T F: The PictureBox control has an ImageStretch property.

3. T F: The Visible property is Boolean.

4. T F: A control is hidden in the *Designer* window if its Visible property is set to *False*.

5. T F: You can delete a locked control.

6. T F: You set a control's name with its Text property.

7. T F: The TextAlign property causes a control to be aligned with other controls on the same form.

8. T F: Text is frequently the first property that the programmer changes, so it is listed in parentheses in the *Properties* window. This causes it to be displayed at the top of the alphabetized list of properties.

9. T F: Resizing handles are positioned along the edges of a control's bounding box.

10. T F: A label's text is *MiddleCenter* aligned by default.

11. T F: You can run an application in the Visual Studio environment by pressing the F5 key.

12. T F: The first line of an event handler identifies its name and the event it handles.

13. T F: You should be very cautious about, and even avoid, placing comments in your code.

14. T F: In an assignment statement, the name of the item receiving the value must be on the right side of the = operator.

15. T F: You can display the *Code* window by pressing the F7 key when the *Designer* window is visible.

16. T F: The BackColor property establishes the color of a Label control's text.

17. T F: A form's FormBorderStyle property can be used to prevent the user from resizing, minimizing, or maximizing a window, or closing the window using its *Close* button.

18. T F: When you lock the controls on a form, the user must enter a password before the application will run.

19. T F: You cannot modify a control's Text property with code.

20. T F: The *Properties* window only shows a control's properties that may be changed at design time.

21. T F: A Label control's AutoSize property is set to *True* by default.

22. T F: PictureBox controls can have a Click event handler.

Short Answer

1. Explain the difference between an object's Text property and its Name.

2. List three ways to run an application within the Visual Studio environment.

3. List three ways to display the *Code* window.

4. Why does Visual Studio indent the code between the first and last lines of an event handler?

5. How do you make a PictureBox control respond to mouse clicks?

What Do You Think?

1. Why, in the *Properties* window, do you change some properties with a drop-down list or a dialog box, while you change others by typing a value?

2. Why is it a good idea to equip a form with a button that terminates the application, if the form already has a standard Windows *Close* button in the upper right corner?

3. What is the benefit of creating PictureBox controls that respond to mouse clicks?

Find the Error

1. Open the *Error1* project from the student sample programs folder named *Chap2* *Error1*, downloaded from www.microsoft.com/express/Downloads/. Run the application. When Visual Basic reports an error, find and fix the error.

2. Open the *Error2* project from the student sample programs folder named *Chap2* *Error2*. Run the application. When Visual Basic reports an error, find and fix the error.

Programming Challenges

1. **Welcome Screen Modification**

   For this exercise, you will modify an application that displays a welcome screen for the First Gaddis Bank. After starting Visual Studio, open the *First Gaddis* project from the student sample programs folder named *Chap2\First Gaddis*. Figure 78 shows the application's form.

Figure 78 *First Gaddis welcome screen, Form1*

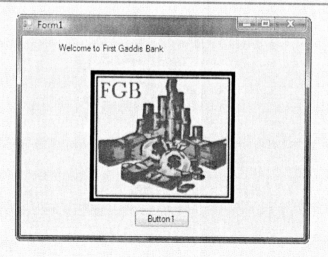

Make the following modifications to the application:

a. Change the form's title bar text to read *First Gaddis Bank*.
b. Change the label's Font property to *Microsoft sans serif, bold, 14.25 point*.
c. Change the label's text alignment to middle center.
d. Change the button's name to `btnExit`.
e. Change the button's text to read *Exit*.
f. Change the label's background color to a shade of light blue, or another color of your choice.
g. Change the form's background color to the same color you chose for the label.
h. Write a Click event handler for the button that closes the application window.

VideoNote

The Name and Address Problem

2. **Name and Address**

Create an application that displays your name and address when a button is clicked. The application's form should appear as shown in Figure 79 when it first runs. Once the *Show Info* button is clicked, the form should appear similar to the one shown in Figure 80.

Figure 79 Intitial *Name* and *Address* form

Figure 80 *Name and address* form after *Show Info* button is clicked

Here are the detailed property specifications:

a. The button that displays the name and address should be named `btnShowInfo`. Its text should read *Show Info*.
b. The button that closes the application should be named `btnExit`. Its text should read *Exit*.
c. The form should have three Label controls. The first will hold your name, the second will hold your street address, and the third will hold your city, state, and ZIP code. The labels should be named `lblName`, `lblStreet`, and `lblCityStateZip`, respectively. The labels' Font property should be set to *Times New Roman, bold, 12 point*. The labels' TextAlign property should be set to *MiddleCenter*.
d. The form's title bar should read *Name and Address*.

3. **Math Tutor Application**

You are to create a *Math Tutor* application. The application should display a simple math problem in a Label control. The form should have a button that displays the answer to the math problem in a second label, when clicked. It should also have a button that closes the application. Figure 81 shows an example of the application's form before the button is clicked to display the answer. Figure 82 shows the form

Figure 81 Initial *Math Tutor* application

Figure 82 *Math Tutor* application after *Show Answers* button is clicked

after the *Show Answer* button is clicked. Here are the detailed property specifications:

a. The button that displays the answer should be named `btnShowAnswer`. Its Text property should read *Show Answer*.

b. The button that closes the application should be named `btnExit`. Its Text property should read *Exit*.

c. The label that displays the answer to the math problem should be named `lblAnswer`.

d. The form's title bar should read *Math Tutor*.

Design Your Own Forms

4. **State Abbreviations**

The following table shows lists of six states and their official abbreviations.

State	Abbreviation
Virginia	VA
North Carolina	NC
South Carolina	SC
Georgia	GA
Alabama	AL
Florida	FL

Create an application that allows the user to select a state, and then displays that state's official abbreviation. The form should have six buttons, one for each state. When the user clicks a button, the application displays the state's abbreviation in a Label control.

5. **Latin Translator**

Look at the following list of Latin words and their meanings.

Latin	English
sinister	left
dexter	right
medium	center

Create an application that translates the Latin words to English. The form should have three buttons, one for each Latin word. When the user clicks a button, the application should display the English translation in a Label control. When the user clicks the *sinister* button, the translation should appear with middle left alignment. When the user clicks the *dexter* button, the translation should appear with middle right alignment. When the user clicks the *medium* button, the translation should appear with middle center alignment.

6. **Clickable Images**

In the *Chap2* folder, in the student sample programs, you will find the image files shown in Figure 83. Create an application that displays these images in PictureBox controls. The application should perform the following actions:

- When the user clicks the 1 image, the application should display the word *One* in a message box.
- When the user clicks the 2 image, the application should display the word *Two* in a message box.
- When the user clicks the 3 image, the application should display the word *Three* in a message box.
- When the user clicks the 4 image, the application should display the word *Four* in a message box.
- When the user clicks the 5 image, the application should display the word *Five* in a message box.

Figure 83 Image files

One.bmp   Two.bmp   Three.bmp   Four.bmp   Five.bmp

7. **Joke and Punch line**

A joke typically has two parts: a setup and a punch line. For example, this might be the setup for a joke:

How many programmers does it take to change a light bulb?

And this is the punch line:

None. That's a hardware problem.

Think of your favorite joke and identify its setup and punch line. Then, create an application that has a Label and two buttons on a form. One of the buttons should read "Setup" and the other button should read "Punch line." When the *Setup* button is clicked, display the joke's setup in the Label. When the *Punch line* button is clicked, display the joke's punch line in the Label.

Answers to Checkpoints

1 The Text property.

2 With the form selected, double-click the Label control tool in the toolbox.

3 To resize the control's bounding box.

4 Select it and press the [Delete] key.

5 The image will be resized both horizontally and vertically to fit in the PictureBox control. If the image is resized more in one direction than the other, it will appear stretched.

6 Bounding box

7 Design mode, run mode, and break mode.

8 • Click *File* on the menu bar, and then select *Open Project...* The *Open Project* window will appear. Use the window to locate and select either the solution file (.sln) or the project file (.vbproj) for the project that you wish to open.
   • Click *File* on the menu bar, and then select *Recent Projects and Solutions.* If the project is one that you have opened recently, it might be listed here. If it is, select either the solution file (.sln) or the project file (.vbproj) for the project that you wish to open.
   • Use the *Start Page* to open the project. To display the *Start Page*, click *View* on the menu bar, then select *Start Page*. Then, either click the *Open Project* link to display the *Open Project* window, or select the name of project in the *Recent Projects* list.

9 Alphabetical and categorized. Select alphabetical mode by clicking the *Alphabetical* button. Select categorized mode by clicking the *Categorized* button. When the *Alphabetical* button is clicked, the properties are displayed alphabetically. When the *Categorized* button is clicked, related properties are listed in groups.

10 Text is listed under the *Appearance* category. Name is listed under the *Design* category.

11 Select it from the list of objects displayed in the object box drop-down list.

12 If a control will be accessed in code or will have code associated with it (such as an event handler), assign it a name. Otherwise, keep the control's default name.

13 A property that may only have one of two values: *True* or *False*

14 btnShowName_Click()

15 It assigns True to the lblGreeting control's Visible property. As a result, the lblGreeting control will be visible on the application's form at runtime.

16 A comment, or remark, is a note of explanation that documents something in a program.

17 lblSecretAnswer.Visible = False

18 It closes the current form.

19 The [F7] key

20 Custom, Web, and System

21 The background color of the Label's text changes.

22 The color of the Label's text changes.

23 FormBorderStyle

24 You cannot move them until they are unlocked.

25 Right-click over an empty spot on the form and select *Lock Controls* from the pop-up menu.

26 The same way that you locked the controls: Right-click over an empty spot on the form, and select *Lock Controls* from the pop-up menu.

27 `lblTemperature.Text = "48 degrees"`

28 When AutoSize is set to *False*, you can set the bounding box of a Label control to be larger than the text it holds. When a label's AutoSize property is set to *True*, the label's bounding box automatically resizes to the length of the text in the label's Text property.

29 The BorderStyle property can hold one of the following values: *None*, *FixedSingle*, and *Fixed 3D*. When set to *None*, the label has no border. (This is the default value.) When set to *FixedSingle*, the label is outlined with a border that is a single pixel wide. When set to *Fixed3D*, the label has a recessed 3-dimensional appearance.

30 `lblName.TextAlign = ContentAlignment.TopRight`
   `lblName.TextAlign = ContentAlignment.BottomLeft`
   `lblName.TextAlign = ContentAlignment.TopCenter`

31 A dialog box is a small window that is typically used to display a message to the user. A message box is an example of a dialog box.

32 `MessageBox.Show("Welcome to our hotel!")`

33 The statement is missing the dot that should appear between `MessageBox` and `Show`. The statement should read `MessageBox.Show("Invalid password")`.

34 A help screen that is displayed for the currently selected item when the F1 key is pressed

35 Compile errors and runtime errors

Variables and Calculations

TOPICS

This chapter covers the use of text boxes to gather input from users. It also discusses the use of variables, named constants, type conversion functions, and mathematical calculations. You will be introduced to the GroupBox control as a way to organize controls on an application's form. The *Format* menu commands, which allow you to align, size, and center controls are also discussed. You will learn about the form's Load event, which happens when a form is loaded into memory, and debugging techniques for locating logic errors.

1 Gathering Text Input

CONCEPT: In this section, we use the TextBox control to gather input the user has typed on the keyboard. We also alter a form's tab order and assign keyboard access keys to controls.

The programs you have written and examined so far perform operations without requiring information from the user. In reality, most programs ask the user to enter values. For example, a program that calculates payroll for a small business might ask the user to enter the name of the employee, the hours worked, and the hourly pay rate. The program then uses this information to print the employee's paycheck.

From Chapter 3 of *Starting Out with Visual Basic® 2010*, Fifth Edition, Tony Gaddis, Kip Irvine.

A **text box** is a rectangular area on a form that accepts keyboard input. As the user types, the characters are stored in the text box. In Visual Basic, you create a text box with a **TextBox control**. Tutorial 1 examines an application that uses a TextBox control.

Tutorial 1:
Using a TextBox control

Step 1: Open the *Greetings* project from the student sample programs folder named *Chap3\Greetings*. The student sample programs folder is located at www.microsoft.com/express/Downloads.

Step 2: Click the *Start* button (▶) to run the application. The application's form appears, as shown in Figure 1. The TextBox control is the white rectangular area beneath the label that reads *Enter Your Name*.

Notice that the TextBox control shows a blinking text cursor, indicating it is ready to receive keyboard input.

Figure 1 *Greetings* project initial form

Figure 2 *Greetings* project completed form

Step 3: Type your name. As you enter characters on the keyboard, they appear in the TextBox control.

Step 4: Click the *Show Greeting* button. The message *Hello* followed by the name you entered appears in a label below the TextBox control. The form now appears similar to the one shown in Figure 2.

Step 5: Click inside the TextBox control and use the [Delete] and/or [Backspace] key to erase the name you entered. Enter another name, and then click the *Show Greeting* button. Notice that the greeting message changes accordingly.

Step 6: Click the *Exit* button to exit the application. You have returned to Design mode.

Step 7: Look at the application's form in the *Designer* window. Figure 3 shows the form with its controls.

Notice that the name of the TextBox control starts with txt, which we use as the prefix for TextBox controls. Like the Label control, the TextBox control has a Text property. However, the Label control's Text property is only for displaying information—the user cannot directly alter its contents. The TextBox control's

Text property is for input purposes. The user can alter it by typing characters into the TextBox control. Whatever the user types into the TextBox control is stored, as a string, in its Text property.

Figure 3 *Greetings* project form with controls labeled

Using the Text Property in Code

You access a TextBox control's Text property in code the same way you access other properties. For example, assume an application has a Label control named `lblInfo` and a TextBox control named `txtInput`. The following statement assigns the contents of the TextBox control's Text property into the Label control's Text property.

```
lblInfo.Text = txtInput.Text
```

The following statement shows another example. It displays the contents of the `txtInput` control's Text property in a message box:

```
MessageBox.Show(txtInput.Text)
```

Clearing a Text Box

Recall that an object contains methods, which are actions the object performs. If you want to execute an object's method, you write a statement that calls the method. The general format of such a statement is

```
Object.Method
```

Object is the name of the object and *Method* is the name of the method that is being called.

A `TextBox` control is an object, and has a variety of methods that perform operations on the text box or its contents. One of these methods is `Clear`, which clears the contents of the text box's Text property. The general format of the `Clear` method is

```
TextBoxName.Clear()
```

TextBoxName is the name of the TextBox control. Here is an example:

```
txtInput.Clear()
```

When this statement executes, the Text property of `txtInput` is cleared and the text box appears empty on the screen.

You can also clear a text box by assigning the predefined constant `String.Empty` to its Text property. Here is an example:

```
txtInput.Text = String.Empty
```

Once this statement executes, the Text property of `txtInput` is cleared and the text box appears empty on the screen.

String Concatenation

Returning to the *Greetings* application, let's look at the code for the `btnShowGreeting` control's Click event handler:

```
Private Sub btnShowGreeting_Click(...) Handles btnShowGreeting.Click
    ' Display a customized greeting to the user
    ' in the lblGreeting control.
    lblGreeting.Text = "Hello " & txtUserName.Text
End Sub
```

The assignment statement in this procedure introduces a new operator: the ampersand (`&`). When the ampersand is used in this way, it performs **string concatenation**. This means that one string is appended to another.

The `&` operator creates a string that is a combination of the string on its left and the string on its right. Specifically, it appends the string on its right to the string on its left. For example, assume an application uses a Label control named `lblMessage`. The following statement assigns the string "Good morning Charlie" to the control's Text property:

```
lblMessage.Text = "Good morning " & "Charlie"
```

In our *Greetings* application, if the user types *Becky* into the `txtUserName` control, the control's Text property is set to *Becky*. So the statement

```
lblGreeting.Text = "Hello " & txtUserName.Text
```

assigns the string `"Hello Becky"` to `lblGreeting`'s Text property.

Look again at the assignment statement. Notice there is a space in the string literal after the word *Hello*. This prevents the two strings being concatenated from running together.

In a few moments, it will be your turn to create an application using TextBox controls and string concatenation. Tutorial 2 leads you through the process.

Aligning Controls in Design Mode

Visual Studio provides a convenient way to align controls on forms. When you drag a control to a position on a form that aligns with another control, guide lines automatically appear. In Figure 4, for example, a TextBox has been placed below an existing TextBox. The blue guide lines tell us the two controls are aligned vertically. If either control is dragged sideways, the guide lines disappear.

In Figure 5, two TextBox controls are aligned horizontally, indicated by lavender guide lines. In Figure 6, guide lines appear for simultaneous vertical and horizontal alignment. All in all, this feature of Visual Studio takes the guesswork out of aligning controls, saving you a lot of time. Tutorial 2 shows you how to build the *Date String* application.

Figure 4 Vertical guide lines align two TextBox controls

Blue guide line

Figure 5 Horizontal guide lines align two TextBox controls

Lavender guide line

Figure 6 Horizontal and vertical guide lines can be used together

Tutorial 2:
Building the *Date String* application

VideoNote

Tutorial 3-2
Walkthrough

In this tutorial you will create an application that lets the user enter the following information about today's date:

- The day of the week
- The name of the month
- The numeric day of the month
- The year

When the user enters the information and clicks a button, the application displays a date string such as Friday, December 3, 2010.

Step 1: Start Visual Studio and start a new Windows Forms Application named *Date String*.

Step 2: Create the form shown in Figure 7, using the following instructions:

- You insert TextBox controls by double-clicking the TextBox icon in the Tool-Box. When a TextBox control is created, it will be given a default name. As with other controls, you can change a TextBox control's name by modifying its Name property.

- Give each control the name indicated in the figure. The labels that display *Enter the day of the week*, *Enter the month*, *Enter the day of the month*, and *Enter the year* will not be referred to in code, so they may keep their default names.
- Set the lblDateString label's AutoSize property to False, its BorderStyle property to *Fixed3D*, and its TextAlign property to *MiddleCenter*. Resize the label as shown in Figure 7, and delete the contents of the label's Text property.
- Set the form's Text property to *Date String*.

Figure 7 *Date String* form

Step 3: Next, you will write code for the btnShowDate button's Click event handler. Double-click the button to create the code template, and then enter the lines shown in bold:

```
Private Sub btnShowDate_Click(...) Handles btnShowDate.Click
    ' Concatenate the input and build the date string.
    lblDateString.Text = txtDayOfWeek.Text & ", " &
        txtMonth.Text & " " &
        txtDayOfMonth.Text & ", " &
        txtYear.Text
End Sub
```

This example introduces a new programming technique: breaking up a long statement into multiple lines. Quite often, you will find yourself writing statements that are too long to fit entirely inside the *Code* window. Your code will be hard to read if you have to scroll the *Code* window to the right to view long statements. In addition, if you or your instructor chooses to print your code, the statements that are too long to fit on one line of the page will wrap around to the next line and make your code look unorganized. For these reasons, it is usually best to break a long statement into multiple lines.

When typing most statements, you can simply press the Enter key when you reach an appropriate point to continue the statement on the next line. Remember, however, that you cannot break up a keyword, quoted string, or a name (such as a variable name or a control name).

Step 4: Switch back to the *Designer* window and double-click the `btnClear` button to create a code template for its Click event handler. Then enter the following bold code to complete the event handler:

```
Private Sub btnClear_Click(...) Handles btnClear.Click
    ' Clear the Text Boxes and lblDateString.
    txtDayOfWeek.Clear()
    txtMonth.Clear()
    txtDayOfMonth.Clear()
    txtYear.Clear()
    lblDateString.Text = String.Empty
End Sub
```

Let's review this code. The `btnClear` button allows the user to start over with a form that is empty of previous values. The `btnClear_Click` event handler clears the contents of all the TextBox controls and the `lblDateString` label. To accomplish this, the procedure calls each TextBox control's `Clear` method, and then assigns the special value `String.Empty` to `lblDateString`'s Text property. (The value `String.Empty` represents an empty string. Assigning `String.Empty` to a label's Text property clears the value displayed by the label.)

Step 5: Switch back to the *Designer* window and double-click the `btnExit` button to create a code template for its Click event handler. Then enter the following bold code to complete the event handler:

```
Private Sub btnExit_Click(...) Handles btnExit.Click
    ' Close the form.
    Me.Close()
End Sub
```

Step 6: Save the project.

Step 7: Click the *Start* button (▶) to run the application. With the application running, enter the requested information into the TextBox controls and click the *Show Date* button. Your form should appear similar to the one shown in Figure 8.

Figure 8 Running the *Date String* application

Step 8: Click the *Clear* button to test it, and then enter new values into the TextBox controls. Click the *Show Date* button.

Step 9: Click the *Exit* button to exit the application.

The Focus Method

When an application is running and a form is displayed, one of the form's controls always has the **focus**. The control having the focus is the one that receives the user's keyboard input. For example, when a TextBox control has the focus, it receives the characters that the user enters on the keyboard. When a button has the focus, pressing the (Enter) key executes the button's Click event handler.

You can tell which control has the focus by looking at the form at runtime. When a TextBox control has the focus, a blinking text cursor appears inside it, or the text inside the TextBox control appears highlighted. When a button, radio button, or check box has the focus, a thin dotted line appears around the control.

NOTE: Only controls capable of receiving some sort of input, such as text boxes and buttons, may have the focus.

Often, you want to make sure a particular control has the focus. Consider the *Date String* application, for example. When the *Clear* button is clicked, the focus should return to the txtDayOfWeek TextBox control. This would make it unnecessary for the user to click the TextBox control in order to start entering another set of information.

In code, you move the focus to a control by calling the **Focus** method. The method's general syntax is:

```
ControlName.Focus()
```

where *ControlName* is the name of the control. For instance, you move the focus to the txtDayOfWeek TextBox control with the statement txtDayOfWeek.Focus(). After the statement executes, the txtDayOfWeek control will have the focus. In Tutorial 3, you add this statement to the *Clear* button's Click event handler so txtDayOfWeek has the focus after the TextBox controls and the lblDateString label are cleared.

Tutorial 3:
Using the Focus method

Step 1: Open the *Date String* project that you created in Tutorial 2.

Step 2: Open the *Code* window and add the statements shown in bold to the btnClear_Click event handler.

```
Private Sub btnClear_Click(...) Handles btnClear.Click
    ' Clear the Text Boxes and lblDateString
    txtDayOfWeek.Clear()
    txtMonth.Clear()
    txtDayOfMonth.Clear()
    txtYear.Clear()
    lblDateString.Text = String.Empty

    ' Give the focus to txtDayOfWeek.
    txtDayOfWeek.Focus()
End Sub
```

Step 3: Run the application. Enter some information into the TextBox controls, and then click the *Clear* button. The focus should return to the txtDayOfWeek TextBox control.

Step 4: Save the project.

Controlling a Form's Tab Order with the TabIndex Property

In Windows applications, pressing the ⟨Tab⟩ key changes the focus from one control to another. The order in which controls receive the focus is called the **tab order**. When you place controls on a form in Visual Basic, the tab order will be the same sequence in which you created the controls. In many cases this is the tab order you want, but sometimes you rearrange controls on a form, delete controls, and add new ones. These modifications often lead to a disorganized tab order, which can confuse and irritate the users of your application. Users want to tab smoothly from one control to the next, in a logical sequence.

You can modify the tab order by changing a control's TabIndex property. The **TabIndex property** contains a numeric value, which indicates the control's position in the tab order. When you create a control, Visual Basic automatically assigns a value to its TabIndex property. The first control you create on a form will have a TabIndex of 0, the second will have a TabIndex of 1, and so on. The control with a TabIndex of 0 will be the first control in the tab order. The next control in the tab order will be the one with a TabIndex of 1. The tab order continues in this sequence.

You may change the tab order of a form's controls by selecting them, one-by-one, and changing their TabIndex property in the *Properties* window. An easier method, however, is to click *View* on the menu bar, and then click *Tab Order*. This causes the form to be displayed in **tab order selection mode**. In this mode, each control's existing TabIndex value is displayed on the form. Then you establish a new tab order by clicking the controls in the order you want. When you are finished, exit tab order selection mode by pressing the ⟨Esc⟩ key. Tutorial 4 shows you how to change the tab order.

Tutorial 4:
Changing the tab order

In this tutorial, you rearrange the controls in the *Date String* application, and then change the tab order to accommodate the controls' new positions.

Step 1: Open the *Date String* project that you created in Tutorials 2 and 3.

Step 2: Open the application's form in the *Designer* window. Rearrange the controls to match Figure 9. (You might want to enlarge the form temporarily so you have

Figure 9 *Date String* form

room to move some of the controls around. Don't forget to move the labels that correspond to the TextBox controls.)

Step 3:   Run the application and notice which control has the focus. Press the [Tab] key several times and observe the tab order.

Step 4:   Stop the application and return to Design mode.

Step 5:   Click *View* on the menu bar, and then click *Tab Order*. The form should switch to tab order selection mode, as shown in Figure 10. The numbers displayed in the upper left corner of each control are the existing TabIndex values.

 NOTE: Your existing TabIndex values may be different from those shown in Figure 10.

Figure 10 Form in tab order selection mode

Step 6:   Click the following controls in the order they are listed here: txtMonth, txtDayOfMonth, txtDayOfWeek, txtYear, btnShowDate, btnClear, btnExit.

Step 7:   The controls you clicked should now have the following TabIndex values displayed:

```
txtMonth:        0
txtDayOfMonth:   1
txtDayOfWeek:    2
txtYear:         3
btnShowDate:     4
btnClear:        5
btnExit:         6
```

 NOTE: The Label controls cannot receive the focus, so do not be concerned with the TabIndex values displayed for them.

Step 8:   Press the [Esc] key to exit tab order selection mode.

Step 9: Don't forget to change the `btnClear_Click` event handler so `txtMonth` gets the focus when the form is cleared. The code for the procedure is as follows, with the modified lines in bold:

```
Private Sub btnClear_Click(...) Handles btnClear.Click
    ' Clear the Text Boxes and lblDateString
    txtDayOfWeek.Clear()
    txtMonth.Clear()
    txtDayOfMonth.Clear()
    txtYear.Clear()
    lblDateString.Text = String.Empty

    ' Give the focus to txtMonth.
    txtMonth.Focus()
End Sub
```

Step 10: Run the application and test the new tab order.

Step 11: End the application and save the project.

Here are a few last notes about the TabIndex property:

- If you do not want a control to receive the focus when the user presses the [Tab] key, set its **TabStop property** to *False*.
- An error will occur if you assign a negative value to the TabIndex property in code.
- A control whose Visible property is set to *False* or whose Enabled property is set to *False* cannot receive the focus.
- GroupBox and Label controls have a TabIndex property, but they are skipped in the tab order.

Assigning Keyboard Access Keys to Buttons

An **access key**, also known as a **mnemonic**, is a key pressed in combination with the [Alt] key to access a control such as a button quickly. When you assign an access key to a button, the user can trigger a Click event either by clicking the button with the mouse or by using the access key. Users who are quick with the keyboard prefer to use access keys instead of the mouse.

You assign an access key to a button through its Text property. For example, assume an application has a button whose Text property is set to *Exit*. You wish to assign the access key [Alt]+[X] to the button, so the user may trigger the button's Click event by pressing [Alt]+[X] on the keyboard. To make the assignment, place an ampersand (&) before the letter *x* in the button's Text property: `E&xit`. Figure 11 shows how the Text property appears in the *Property* window.

Although the ampersand is part of the button's Text property, it is not displayed on the button. With the ampersand in front of the letter *x*, the letter will appear underlined as shown in Figure 12. This indicates that the button may be clicked by pressing [Alt]+[X] on the keyboard. (On many systems the underlining will not appear until the user presses the Alt key.)

Figure 11 Text property E&xit

Figure 12 Button with E&xit text

 NOTE: Access keys do not distinguish between uppercase and lowercase characters. There is no difference between [Alt]+X and [Alt]+x.

Suppose we had stored the value &Exit in the button's Text property. The ampersand is in front of the letter E, so [Alt]+[E] becomes the access key. The button will appear as shown in Figure 13.

Assigning the Same Access Key to Multiple Buttons

Be careful not to assign the same access key to two or more buttons on the same form. If two or more buttons share the same access key, a Click event is triggered for the first button created when the user presses the access key.

Displaying the & Character on a Button

If you want to display an ampersand character on a button use two ampersands (&&) in the Text property. Using two ampersands causes a single ampersand to display and does not define an access key. For example, if a button has the Text property Save && Exit the button will appear as shown in Figure 14.

Figure 13 Button with &Exit text

Exit

Figure 14 Button with text Save && Exit

Save & Exit

Accept Buttons and Cancel Buttons

An **accept button** is a button on a form that is automatically clicked when the user presses the [Enter] key. A **cancel button** is a button on a form that is automatically clicked when the user presses the [Esc] key. Forms have two properties, AcceptButton and CancelButton, which allow you to designate an accept button and a cancel button. When you select these properties in the *Properties* window, a down-arrow button ([▾]) appears, which allows you to display a drop-down list. The list contains the names of all the buttons on the form. You select the button that you want to designate as the accept button or cancel button.

Any button that is frequently clicked should probably be selected as the accept button. This will allow keyboard users to access the button quickly and easily. *Exit* or *Cancel* buttons are likely candidates to become cancel buttons. In Tutorial 5, you set access keys, accept, and cancel buttons.

Tutorial 5:
Setting access keys, accept, and cancel buttons

In this tutorial, you assign access keys to the buttons in the *Date String* application, and set accept and cancel buttons.

Step 1: Open the *Date String* project that you have worked on in Tutorials 2 through 4.

Step 2: Open the application's form in the *Designer* window.

Step 3: Select the *Show Date* button (btnShowDate) and change its text to read *Show &Date*. This assigns [Alt]+[D] as the button's access key.

Step 4: Select the *Clear* button (btnClear) and change its text to read *Clea&r*. This assigns [Alt]+[R] as the button's access key.

Step 5: Select the *Exit* button (btnExit) and change its text to read *E&xit*. This assigns [Alt]+[X] as the button's access key.

Step 6: Select the form, and then select the AcceptButton property in the *Properties* window. Click the down-arrow button ([▾]) to display the drop-down list of buttons. Select btnShowDate from the list.

Step 7: With the form still selected, select the CancelButton property in the *Properties* window. Click the down-arrow button ([▾]) to display the drop-down list of buttons. Select btnExit from the list.

Step 8: Run the application and test the buttons' new settings. Notice that when you press the [Enter] key, the *Show Date String* button's Click event hander is executed; when you press the [Esc] key, the application exits.

> **NOTE:** When the application executes, the access keys you assigned to the buttons might not be displayed as underlined characters until you press the [Alt] key.

Step 9: Save the project.

Checkpoint

1 What TextBox control property holds text entered by the user?

2 Assume an application has a label named `lblMessage` and a TextBox control named `txtInput`. Write the statement that takes text the user entered into the TextBox control and assigns it to the label's Text property.

3 If the following statement is executed, what will the `lblGreeting` control display?

```
lblGreeting.Text = "Hello " & "Jonathon, " & "how are you?"
```

4 What is string concatenation?

5 What is meant when it is said that a control has the focus?

6 Write a statement that gives the focus to the `txtLastName` control.

7 What is meant by tab order?

8 How does the TabIndex property affect the tab order?

9 How does Visual Basic normally assign the tab order?

10 What happens when a control's TabStop property is set to *False*?

11 Assume a button's Text property is set to the text *Show &Map*. What effect does the & character have?

12 What is an accept button? What is a cancel button? How do you establish these buttons on a form?

2 Variables and Data Types

CONCEPT: Variables hold data that may be manipulated, used to manipulate other data, or remembered for later use.

VideoNote

Introduction to Variables

A **variable** is a storage location in computer memory that holds data while a program is running. It is called a variable because the data it holds can be changed by statements in the program.

In this chapter, you have seen programs that store data in properties belonging to Visual Basic controls. While properties hold values that are associated with a specific control, variables are used for general purpose data storage in memory. Generally speaking, you can do a number of things with variables:

- Copy and store values entered by the user so the values can be manipulated
- Perform arithmetic on numeric values
- Test values to determine that they meet some criterion
- Temporarily hold and manipulate the value of a control property
- Remember data for later use in a program

Think of a variable as a name that represents a location in the computer's random-access memory (RAM). When a value is stored in a variable, it is actually stored in RAM. You use the assignment operator (=) to store a value in a variable, just as you do with a control property. For example, suppose a program uses a variable named `intLength`. The following statement stores the value 112 in that variable:

```
intLength = 112
```

When this statement executes, the value 112 is stored in the memory location the name `intLength` represents. As another example, assume the following statement appears in a program that uses a variable named `strGreeting` and a TextBox control named `txtName`:

```
strGreeting = "Good morning " & txtName.Text
```

Suppose the user has already entered *Holly* into the `txtName` TextBox control. When the statement executes, the variable `strGreeting` is assigned the string `"Good morning Holly"`.

Declaring Variables

A **variable declaration** is a statement that creates a variable in memory when a program executes. The declaration indicates the name you wish to give the variable and the type of data the variable will hold. Here is the general form of a variable declaration:

```
Dim VariableName As DataType
```

Here is an example of a variable declaration:

```
Dim intLength As Integer
```

Let's look at each part of this statement, and its purpose:

- The `Dim` keyword tells Visual Basic that a variable is being declared.
- `intLength` is the name of the variable.
- `As Integer` indicates the variable's data type. We know it will be used to hold integer numbers.

You can declare multiple variables with one `Dim` statement, as shown in the following statement. It declares three variables, all holding integers:

```
Dim intLength, intWidth, intHeight As Integer
```

NOTE: The keyword `Dim` stands for "dimension." This is a term for declaring a variable that goes back to some of the earliest programming languages.

Variable Names

It is your responsibility as the programmer to make up the names of the variables that you use in a program. You must follow these rules when naming a variable in Visual Basic:

- The first character must be a letter or an underscore character. (We do not recommend that you start a variable name with an underscore, but if you do, the name must also contain at least one letter or numeric digit.)
- After the first character, you may use letters, numeric digits, and underscore characters. (You cannot use spaces, periods, or other punctuation characters in a variable name.)
- Variable names cannot be longer than 1023 characters.
- Variable names cannot be Visual Basic keywords. Keywords have reserved meanings in Visual Basic, and their use as variable names would confuse the compiler.

Type Prefixes

In this text we normally begin variable names with a three- or four-letter prefix that indicates the variable's data type. For example, the variable name `intLength` begins with the three-letter prefix `int`, which indicates that it is an Integer variable. Earlier we used the name `strGreeting` as an example variable name. That name begins with the prefix `str`, indicating that it is a String variable.

The practice of beginning a variable name with a prefix is not required, but it is intended to make code more understandable. For example, when you are reading your own, or someone else's, code, and you see a variable name such as `intUnitsSold`, you immediately know that it is an Integer variable because of the `int` prefix.

The convention of using type prefixes in variable names has historically been popular among Visual Basic programmers, but not all programmers follow this practice. Your instructor may or may not require you to use them. Regardless of whether you use them or not, be consistent in the approach that you adopt.

Table 1 shows the prefixes that we use in this text, the Visual Basic data types that they are used with, and examples of each used in variable names. (We will discuss the commonly used data types in greater detail momentarily.)

Table 1 Recommended prefixes for variable names

Variable Type	Prefix	Examples
Boolean	bln	blnContinue, blnHasRows
Byte	byt	bytInput, bytCharVal
Char	chr	chrSelection, chrMiddleInitial
Date, DateTime	dat or dtm	datWhenPublished, dtmBirthDate
Decimal	dec	decWeeklySalary, decGrossPay
Double	dbl	dblAirVelocity, dblPlanetMass
Integer	int	intCount, intDaysInPayPeriod
Long	lng	lngElapsedSeconds
Object	obj	objStudent, objPayroll
Short	shrt	shrtCount
Single	sng	sngTaxRate, sngGradeAverage
String	str	strLastName, strAddress

Use Descriptive Variable Names

In addition to following the Visual Basic rules, you should always choose names for your variables that give an indication of what they are used for. For example, a String variable that holds a customer's name might be named `strCustomerName`, and an Integer variable that holds a car's speed might be named `intSpeed`. You may be tempted to give variables names like `x` and `b2`, but names like these give no clue as to what the variable's purpose is.

Because a variable's name should reflect the variable's purpose, programmers often find themselves creating names that are made of multiple words. For example, consider the following variable names:

```
inthoursworked
strcustomername
inthotdogssoldtoday
```

Unfortunately, these names are not easily read by the human eye because the words aren't separated. Because we can't have spaces in variable names, we need to find another way to separate the words in a multiword variable name, and make it more readable to the human eye.

One way to do this is to use the camel case naming convention. **Camel case** names are written in the following manner:

- The variable name starts with lowercase letters.
- The first character of the second and subsequent words is written in uppercase.

For example, the following variable names are written in camel case:

```
intHoursWorked
strCustomerName
intHotDogsSoldToday
```

This style of naming is called camel case because the uppercase characters that appear in a name may suggest a camel's humps. The camel case convention is widely used, not only in Visual Basic, but in other languages as well. We will use the camel case convention for variable names in this text.

Assigning Values to Variables

A value is put into a variable with an assignment statement. For example, the following statement assigns the value 20 to the variable `intUnitsSold`:

```
intUnitsSold = 20
```

The = operator is called the assignment operator. A variable name must always appear on the left side of the assignment operator. For example, the following would be incorrect:

```
20 = intUnitsSold
```

On the right side of the operator, you can put a literal, another variable, or a mathematical expression that matches the variable's type. In the following, the contents of the variable on the right side of the = sign is assigned to the variable on the left side:

```
intUnitsSold = intUnitsOnHand
```

Suppose `intUnitsOnHand` already equals 20. Then Figure 15 shows how the value 20 is copied into the memory location represented by `intUnitsSold`.

The assignment operator changes only the left operand. The right operand (or expression) does not change value. Sometimes your program will contain a series of statements that pass a value from one variable to the next. When the following statements execute, all three variables will contain the same value, 50:

```
Dim intA, intB, intC As Integer
intA = 50
intB = intA
intC = intB
```

Figure 15 Assigning `intUnitsOnHand` to `intUnitsSold`

A variable can hold only one value at a time. If you assign a new value to the variable, the new value replaces the variable's previous contents. There is no way to "undo" this operation. For example:

```
Dim intA, intB As Integer
intA = 50
intA = 99
```

After the second assignment statement, intA equals 99. The value 50 no longer exists in memory.

Integer Data Types

Integers are whole numbers such as –5, 26, 12345, and 0. Visual Basic has four data types, listed in Table 2, for holding integers. (For your convenience the table also shows the type prefix that we will use for variables of each of these data types.) Unsigned integers can hold only positive values (zero is considered positive). Signed integers can hold both positive and negative values.

Table 2 Integer data types

Type	Naming Prefix	Description
Byte	byt	Holds an unsigned integer value in the range 0 to 255
Short	shrt	Holds a signed integer in the range –32,768 to +32,767
Integer	int	Holds a signed integer in the range –2,147,483,648 to +2,147,483,647
Long	lng	Holds a signed integer in the range –9,223,372,036,854,775,808 to +9,223,372,036,854,775,807

The following code example shows variables of the different integer types being declared and assigned values:

```
Dim bytInches As Byte
Dim shrtFeet as Short
Dim intMiles As Integer
Dim lngNationalDebt As Long

bytInches = 26
shrtFeet = 32767
intMiles = 2100432877
lngNationalDebt = 4000000000001
```

Each type has a different storage size and range of possible values it can hold. Most of the time, you will use the Integer data type for integer-type values. Its name is easy to remember, and Integer values are efficiently processed by the computer.

Integer Literals

When you write an integer literal in your program code, Visual Basic assumes the literal is type Integer if the value fits within the allowed range for the Integer data type. A value larger than that will be assumed to be type Long. On rare occasions you may want to override the literal's default type. You do this by appending one of the following special characters to the end of the number:

I   Integer literal
L   Long integer literal
S   Short integer literal

In the following code example, an integer literal uses the L character to identify it as type Long:

```
Dim lngCounter As Long
lngCounter = 10000L
```

In the following, an integer literal uses the S character to identify it as type Short:

```
Dim shrtFeet as Short
shrtFeet = 1234S
```

 TIP: You cannot embed commas in numeric literals. The following, for example, causes an error: intMiles = 32,767

Floating-Point Data Types

Values that have fractional parts and use a decimal point must be stored in one of Visual Basic's floating-point data types. Table 3 lists the floating-point data types, showing their naming prefixes and descriptions.

Table 3 Floating-point data types

Type	Naming Prefix	Description
Single	sng	Holds a signed single precision real number with 7 significant digits, in the range of approximately plus or minus 1.0×10^{38}
Double	dbl	Holds a signed double precision real number with 15 significant digits, in the range of approximately plus or minus 1.0×10^{308}
Decimal	dec	Decimal real number, 29 significant digits. Its range (with no decimal places) is +/–79,228,162,514,264,337,593,543,950,335

Significant Digits

The significant digits measurement for each floating-point data type is important for certain kinds of calculations. Suppose you were simulating a chemical reaction and needed to calculate the number of calories produced. You might produce a number such as 1.234567824724. If you used a variable of type Single, only the first seven digits would be kept in computer memory, and the remaining digits would be lost. The last digit would be rounded upward, producing 1.234568. This loss of precision happens because the computer uses a limited amount of storage for floating-point numbers. If you did the same chemical reaction calculation using a variable of type Double, the entire result would be safely held in the number, with no loss of precision.

The Decimal data type is used in financial calculations when you need a great deal of precision. This data type helps prevent rounding errors from creeping into repeated calculations.

The following code demonstrates each floating-point data type:

```
Dim sngTemperature As Single
Dim dblWindSpeed As Double
Dim decBankBalance As Decimal

sngTemperature = 98.6
dblWindSpeed = 35.373659262
decBankBalance = 1234567890.1234567890123456789D
```

Notice that the last line requires a D suffix on the number to identify it as a Decimal literal. Otherwise, Visual Basic would assume that the number was type Double.

Floating-Point Literals

Floating-point literals can be written in either fixed-point or scientific notation. The number 47281.97, for example, would be written in scientific notation as 4.728197×10^4. Visual Basic requires the letter E just before the exponent in scientific notation. So, our sample number would be written in Visual Basic like this:

```
4.728197E+4
```

The + sign after the E is optional. Here is an example of a value having a negative exponent:

```
4.623476E-2
```

Scientific notation is particularly useful for very large numbers. Instead of writing a value such as 12340000000000000000000000000000.0, for example, it is easier to write 1.234E+31.

Boolean Data Type

A Boolean type variable can hold only one of two possible values: *True* or *False*. The values True and False are built-in Visual Basic keywords. The word Boolean is named after George Boole, a famous mathematician of the nineteenth century. (His Boolean algebra is the basis for all modern computer arithmetic.)

We use Boolean variables to hold information that is either true or false. The standard naming prefix for Boolean variables is `bln`. Here is an example:

```
Dim blnIsRegistered As Boolean
blnIsRegistered = True
```

Char Data Type

Variables of the Char data type can hold a single Unicode character. Unicode characters are the set of values that can represent a large number of international characters in different languages. To assign a character literal to a Char variable, enclose the character in double quotations marks, followed by a lowercase "c". The standard naming prefix for Char variables is `chr`. The following is an example:

```
Dim chrLetter As Char
chrLetter = "A"c
```

String Data Type

A variable of type String can hold between zero and about 2 billion characters. The characters are stored in sequence. A string literal, as you have seen earlier, is always enclosed in quotation marks. In the following code, a string variable is assigned various string literals:

```
Dim strName As String
strName = "Jose Gonzalez"
```

The standard naming prefix for String variables is `str`.

An empty string literal can be coded as `""` or by the special identifier named `String.Empty`:

```
strName = ""
strName = String.Empty
```

Date Data Type

A variable of the Date data type can hold date and time information. Date variables are assigned a prefix of `dat` or `dtm`. You can assign a date literal to a Date variable, as shown here:

```
Dim dtmBirth As Date
dtmBirth = #5/1/2010#
```

Notice that the Date literal is enclosed in # symbols. A variety of date and time formats is permitted. All of the following Date literals are valid:

```
#12/10/2010#
#8:45:00 PM#
#10/20/2010 6:30:00 AM#
```

A Date literal can contain a date, a time, or both. When specifying a time, if you omit AM or PM, the hours value is assumed to be based on a 24-hour clock. If you supply a date without the time, the time portion of the variable defaults to 12:00 AM.

In Tutorial 6, you will assign text to a variable.

Tutorial 6:

Assigning text to a variable

In this tutorial, you will modify a program that assigns the contents of text boxes to a string variable.

Step 1: Open the *Variable Demo* project from the student sample programs folder named *Chap3\Variable Demo*. This folder would have been downloaded with the other materials from www.microsoft.com/express/Downloads/.

Step 2: View the *Form1* form in the *Designer* window, as shown in Figure 16.

Step 3: Double-click the *Show Name* button, which opens the *Code* window and creates a template for the button's Click event handler. Type the following lines, shown in bold:

```
Private Sub btnShowName_Click(...) Handles btnShowName.Click
    ' Declare a string variable to hold the full name.
    Dim strFullName As String

    ' Combine the first and last names and assign the
    ' result to strFullName.
    strFullName = txtFirstName.Text & " " & txtLastName.Text

    ' Display the full name in the lblFullName label.
    lblFullName.Text = strFullName
End Sub
```

Figure 16 *Variable Demo* application, *Form1*

Step 4: In the *Designer* window, double-click the *Clear* button and insert the following lines in the *Code* window (shown in bold):

```
Private Sub btnClear_Click(...) Handles btnClear.Click
  ' Clear TextBox controls and the Label.
  txtFirstName.Clear()
  txtLastName.Clear()
  lblFullName.Text = String.Empty

  ' Set focus to txtfirstName.
  txtFirstName.Focus()
End Sub
```

Step 5: In the *Designer* window, double-click the *Exit* button and insert the following lines in the *Code* window (shown in bold):

```
Private Sub btnExit_Click(...) Handles btnExit.Click
  ' Close the form.
  Me.Close()
End Sub
```

Step 6: Save the project.

Step 7: Run the program, type in a name, and click the *Show Name* button. The output should look similar to that shown in Figure 17.

Figure 17 *Variable Demo* application, running

TIP: Code outlining is a Visual Studio tool that lets you expand and collapse sections of code. As your programs get longer, it is sometimes helpful to collapse procedures you have already written. Then you can concentrate on new sections of code. For example, Figure 18 shows the btnShowName_Click procedure from the *Variable Demo* application. Notice that a minus sign (–) appears next to its heading.

If we click the minus sign, it collapses the event handler into a single line showing its name (Figure 19). You can modify outlining options by right-clicking in the *Code* window and selecting *Outlining*.

Figure 18 Expanded btnShowName_Click handler

Click here to collapse the event handler.

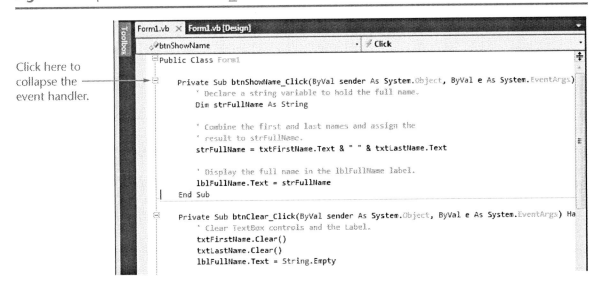

Figure 19 Collapsed btnShowName_Click handler

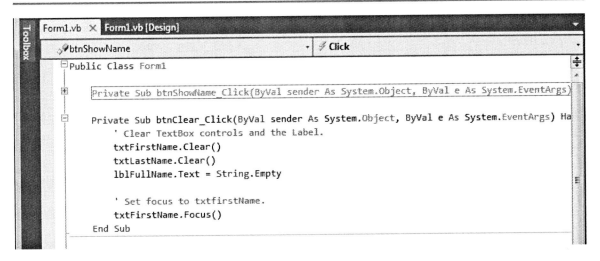

Variable Declarations and the IntelliSense Feature

When you are entering a variable declaration, Visual Studio's IntelliSense feature helps you fill in the data type. Suppose you begin to type a variable declaration such as the following:

```
Dim decPayRate As
```

If you press the (Spacebar) at this point, a list box appears with all the possible data types in alphabetical order. When the list box appears, type the first few letters of the data type name, and the box will highlight the data type that matches what you have typed. For example, after you type *dec* the Decimal data type will be highlighted. Press the (Tab) key to select the highlighted data type.

TIP: You can use the arrow keys or the mouse with the list box's scroll bar to scroll through the list. Once you see the desired data type, double-click it with the mouse.

Default Values and Initialization

When a variable is first created it is assigned a default value. Variables with a numeric data type (such as Byte, Decimal, Double, Integer, Long, and Single) are assigned the value 0. Boolean variables are initially assigned the value False, and Date variables are assigned the value 12:00:00 AM, January 1 of year 1. String variables are automatically assigned a special value called `Nothing`.

You may also specify a starting value in the `Dim` statement. This is called **initialization**. Here is an example:

```
Dim intUnitsSold As Integer = 12
```

This statement declares `intUnitsSold` as an Integer and assigns it the starting value 12. Here are other examples:

```
Dim strLastName As String = "Johnson"
Dim blnIsFinished As Boolean = True
Dim decGrossPay As Decimal = 2500
Dim chrMiddleInitial As Char = "E"c
```

Forgetting to initialize variables can lead to program errors. Unless you are certain a variable will be assigned a value before being used in an operation, always initialize it. This principle is particularly true with string variables. Performing an operation on an uninitialized string variable often results in a runtime error, causing the program to halt execution because the value `Nothing` is invalid for many operations. To prevent such errors, always initialize string variables or make sure they are assigned a value before being used in other operations. A good practice is to initialize string variables with an empty string, as shown in the following statement:

```
Dim strName As String = String.Empty
```

Local Variables

In the examples we have looked at so far, the variables are declared inside event handlers. When a variable is declared inside of a procedure, such as an event handler, it is referred to as a **local variable**. A local variable belongs to the procedure in which it is declared, and only statements inside that procedure can access the variable. (The term local is meant to indicate that the variable can be used only locally, within the procedure in which it is declared.)

An error will occur if a statement in one procedure attempts to access a local variable that belongs to another procedure. For example, assume that an application has the following two event handlers:

```
Private Sub Button1_Click(...) Handles Button1.Click
    ' Declare an Integer variable named intValue.
    Dim intValue As Integer

    ' Assign a value to the variable.
    intValue = 25
End Sub

Private Sub Button2_Click(...) Handles Button2.Click
    ' Attempt to assign a value to the intValue variable.
    ' This will cause an error!
    intValue = 0
End Sub
```

The `intValue` variable that is declared inside the `Button1_Click` event handler is a local variable that belongs that procedure. However, the assignment statement inside the `Button2_Click` event handler attempts to store a value in `intValue` variable. This will cause an error because the `intValue` variable is local to the `Button1_Click` procedure, and statements outside that procedure cannot access it. If we try to compile this code, we still get the following error message: *Name '`intValue`' is not declared.*

What if we declared `intValue` again in the `Button2_Click` event handler? Then the program would compile with no errors, but we would have created two different variables having the same name. Each variable is separate from the other:

```
Private Sub Button1_Click(...) Handles Button1.Click
    ' Declare an Integer variable named intValue.
    Dim intValue As Integer

    ' Assign a value to the variable.
    intValue = 25
End Sub

Private Sub Button2_Click(...) Handles Button2.Click
    ' Declare an Integer variable named intValue.
    Dim intValue As Integer

    ' Attempt to assign a value to the intValue variable.
    intValue = 0
End Sub
```

In this case, the `Button1_Click` event handler has a local variable named `intValue`, and the `Button2_Click` event handler has its own local variable named `intValue`. Variables in different procedures can have the same name because they are isolated from each other.

Scope

The term **scope** means the part of a program in which a variable may be accessed. Every variable has a scope, and a variable is visible only to statements in its scope. A local variable's scope begins at the `Dim` statement that declares the variable, and ends at the end of the procedure in which the variable is declared. The variable cannot be accessed by statements outside this region. That means that a local variable cannot be accessed by statements outside the procedure, or by statements that are inside the procedure but before the `Dim` statement that declares the variable.

For example, look at the following event handler code. This procedure attempts to assign a value to a variable before the variable is declared:

```
Private Sub Button1_Click(...) Handles Button1.Click
    strName = "Jane" 'ERROR!
    Dim strName As String
End Sub
```

If we try to compile this code, we will get the error message *Local variable '`strName`' cannot be referred to before it is declared.*

Duplicate Variable Names

Earlier you saw that two variables with the same name can be declared in different procedures. That is because the scope of the two variables is separate. You cannot, however, declare two variables with the same name in the same scope. For example, look at the following event handler:

```
Private Sub Button1_Click(...) Handles Button1.Click
    ' Declare an Integer variable named intValue.
    Dim intValue As Integer = 0
```

```
    ' Declare another Integer variable named intValue.
    ' ERROR!
    Dim intValue As Integer = 25
End Sub
```

This procedure declares two local variables named intValue. The second Dim statement will cause an error because a variable named intValue has already been declared. If we try to compile this code we will get the error message *Local variable 'intValue' is already declared in the current block.*

Checkpoint

13 What is a variable?

14 Show an example of a variable declaration.

15 Which of the following variable names are written with the convention used in this text?
   a. decintrestrate
   b. InterestRateDecimal
   c. decInterestRate

16 Indicate whether each of the following is a legal variable name. If it is not, explain why.
   a. count
   b. rate*Pay
   c. deposit.amount
   d. down_payment

17 What default value is assigned to each of the following variables?
   a. Integer
   b. Double
   c. Boolean
   d. Byte
   e. Date

18 Write a Date literal for the following date and time: 5:35:00 PM on February 20, 2010.

19 *Bonus question*: Find out which famous Microsoft programmer was launched into space in early 2007. Was this programmer connected in any way to Visual Basic?

3 Performing Calculations

CONCEPT: Visual Basic has powerful arithmetic operators that perform calculations with numeric variables and literals.

VideoNote

Problem
Solving with
Variables

There are two basic types of operators in Visual Basic: unary and binary. These reflect the number of operands an operator requires. A **unary operator** requires only a single operand. The negation operator, for example, causes a number to be negative:

    -5

It can be applied to a variable. The following line negates the value in intCount:

    -intCount

A **binary operator** works with two operands. The addition operator (+) is binary because it uses two operands. The following mathematical expression adds the values of two numbers:

```
5 + 10
```

The following adds the values of two variables:

```
intA + intB
```

Table 4 lists the binary arithmetic operators in Visual Basic. Addition, subtraction, multiplication, division, and exponentiation can be performed on both integer and floating-point data types. Only two operations (integer division and modulus) must be performed on integer types.

Table 4 Arithmetic operators in Visual Basic

Operator	Operation
+	Addition
−	Subtraction
*	Multiplication
/	Floating-point division
\	Integer division
MOD	Modulus (remainder from integer division)
^	Exponentiation ($x\text{^}y = x^y$)

Addition

The addition operator (+) adds two values, producing a sum. The values can be literals or variables. The following are examples of valid addition expressions:

```
intA + 10
```

```
20 + intB
```

The question is, what happens to the result? Ordinarily, it is assigned to a variable, using the assignment operator. In the following statement, intC is assigned the sum of the values from intA and intB:

```
intC = intA + intB
```

This operation happens in two steps. First, the addition takes place. Second, the sum is assigned to the variable on the left side of the = sign.

The following example adds the contents of two Double variables that hold rainfall measurements for the months of March and April:

```
dblCombined = dblMarchRain + dblAprilRain
```

Subtraction

The subtraction operator (−) subtracts the right-hand operand from the left-hand operand. In the following, the variable intC will contain the difference between intA and intB:

```
intC = intA - intB
```

Alternatively, the difference might be assigned back to the variable intA:

```
intA = intA - intB
```

The following statement uses Decimal variables. It subtracts an employee's tax amount from his or her gross pay, producing the employee's net pay:

```
decNetPay = decGrossPay - decTax
```

Addition and Subtraction in Applications

How can addition and subtraction statements be useful in an application? Suppose a college registration program needs to add the credits completed by a student during two semesters (Fall and Spring). First, the variables would be declared:

```
Dim intFallCredits, intSpringCredits, intTotalCredits As Integer
```

Then the application would assign values to `intSpringCredits` and `intFallCredits`, perhaps by asking for their input from the user. Finally, the program would calculate the total credits for the year:

```
intTotalCredits = intFallCredits + intSpringCredits
```

Multiplication

The multiplication operator (*) multiplies the right-hand operand by the left-hand operand. In the following statement, the variable `intC` is assigned the product of multiplying `intA` and `intB`:

```
intC = intA * intB
```

The following statement uses Decimal variables to multiply an item's price by the sales tax rate, producing a sales tax amount:

```
decTaxAmount = decItemPrice * decTaxRate
```

Floating-Point Division

The floating-point division operator (/) divides one floating-point value by another. The result, called the quotient, is also a floating-point number. For example, the following statement divides the total points earned by a basketball team by the number of players, producing the average points per player:

```
dblAverage = dblTotalPoints / dblNumPlayers
```

NOTE: If you divide a number by zero you get the special value `Infinity`.

Integer Division

The integer division operator (\) divides one integer by another, producing an integer result. For example, suppose we know the number of minutes it will take to finish a job, and we want to calculate the number of hours that are contained in that many minutes. The following statement uses integer division to divide the `intMinutes` variable by 60, giving the number of hours as a result:

```
intHours = intMinutes \ 60
```

Integer division does not save any fractional part of the quotient. The following statement, for example, produces the integer 3:

```
intQuotient = 10 \ 3
```

Modulus

The modulus operator (MOD) performs integer division and returns only the remainder. The following statement assigns 2 to the variable named `intRemainder`:

```
intRemainder = 17 MOD 3
```

Note that 17 divided by 3 equals 5, with a remainder of 2. Suppose a job is completed in 174 minutes, and we want to express this value in both hours and minutes. First, we can use integer division to calculate the hours (2):

```
intTotalMinutes = 174
intHours = intTotalMinutes \ 60
```

Next, we use the MOD operator to calculate the remaining minutes (54):

```
intMinutes = intTotalMinutes Mod 60
```

Now we know that the job was completed in 2 hours, 54 minutes.

Exponentiation

Exponentiation calculates a variable x taken to the power of y when written in the form $x \char`\^ y$. The value it returns is of type Double. For example, the following statement assigns 25.0 to dblResult:

```
dblResult = 5.0 ^ 2.0
```

You can use integers as operands, but the result will still be a Double:

```
dblResult = intX ^ intY
```

Negative and fractional exponents are permitted.

Getting the Current Date and Time

Your computer system has an internal clock that calculates the current date and time. Visual Basic provides the functions listed in Table 5, which allow you to retrieve the current date, time, or both from your computer. We will discuss functions in greater detail later, but for now, you can think of functions as commands recognized by Visual Basic that return useful information.

Table 5 Date and time functions

Function	Description
Now	Returns the current date and time from the system
TimeOfDay	Returns the current time from the system, without the date
Today	Returns the current date from the system, without the time

The following code demonstrates how to use the Now function:

```
Dim dtmSystemDate As Date
dtmSystemDate = Now
```

After the code executes, dtmSystemDate will contain the current date and time, as reported by the system. The TimeOfDay function retrieves only the current time from the system, demonstrated by the following statement.

```
dtmSystemTime = TimeOfDay
```

After the statement executes, dtmSystemTime will contain the current time, but not the current date. Instead, it will contain the date January 1 of year 1. The Today function retrieves only the current date from the system, demonstrated by the following statement:

```
dtmSystemDate = Today
```

After the statement executes, dtmSystemDate will contain the current date, but will not contain the current time. Instead, it will contain the time 00:00:00.

TIP: Later in this chapter you will see how to use the `ToString` method to display only the date value or time value inside a Date variable.

Combined Assignment Operators

Quite often, programs have assignment statements in the following form:

```
intNumber = intNumber + 1
```

On the right-hand side of the assignment operator, 1 is added to `intNumber`. The result is then assigned to `intNumber`, replacing the value that was previously stored there. Similarly, the following statement subtracts 5 from `intNumber`.

```
intNumber = intNumber - 5
```

Table 6 shows examples of similar statements. Assume that the variable x is set to 6 prior to each statement's execution.

Table 6 Assignment statements (Assume x = 6 prior to each statement's execution)

Statement	Operation Performed	Value of x after the Statement Executes
x = x + 4	Adds 4 to x	10
x = x - 3	Subtracts 3 from x	3
x = x * 10	Multiplies x by 10	60
x = x / 2	Divides x by 2	3

Assignment operations are common in programming. For convenience, Visual Basic offers a special set of operators designed specifically for these jobs. Table 7 shows the **combined assignment operators**, or **compound operators**.

Table 7 Combined assignment operators

Operator	Example Usage	Equivalent To
+=	x += 2	x = x + 2
-=	x -= 5	x = x - 5
*=	x *= 10	x = x * 10
/=	x /= y	x = x / y
\=	x \= y	x = x \ y
&=	strName &= lastName	strName = strName & lastName

Operator Precedence

It is possible to build **mathematical expressions** with several operators. The following statement assigns the sum of 17, x, 21, and y to the variable `intAnswer`.

```
intAnswer = 17 + x + 21 + y
```

Some expressions are not that straightforward, however. Consider the following statement:

```
dblOutcome = 12 + 6 / 3
```

What value will be stored in dblOutcome? If the addition takes place before the division, then dblOutcome will be assigned 6. If the division takes place first, dblOutcome will be assigned 14. The correct answer is 14 because the division operator has higher **precedence** than the addition operator.

Mathematical expressions are evaluated from left to right. When two operators share an operand, the operator with the highest precedence executes first. Multiplication and division have higher precedence than addition and subtraction, so 12 + 6 / 3 works like this:

- 6 is divided by 3, yielding a result of 2.
- 12 is added to 2, yielding a result of 14.

It can be diagrammed as shown in Figure 20.

Figure 20 dblOutcome = 12 + 6 / 3

```
dblOutcome = 12   +   6  /   3
                          └──┬──┘
                             ▼
dblOutcome = 12   +       2
                  └──────┬──────┘
                         ▼
dblOutcome =          14
```

The precedence of the arithmetic operators, from highest to lowest, is as follows:

1. Exponentiation (the ^ operator)
2. Multiplication and division (the * and / operators)
3. Integer division (the \ operator)
4. Modulus (the MOD operator)
5. Addition and subtraction (the + and − operators)

The multiplication and division operators have the same precedence. This is also true of the addition and subtraction operators. When two operators with the same precedence share an operand, the operator on the left executes before the operator on the right.

Table 8 shows some example mathematical expressions with their values.

Table 8 Mathematical expressions and their values

Expression	Value
5 + 2 * 4	13
2^3 * 4 + 3	35
10 / 2 − 3	2
8 + 12 * 2 − 4	28
6 − 3 * 2 + 7 − 1	6

Grouping with Parentheses

Parts of a mathematical expression may be grouped with parentheses to force some operations to be performed before others. In the following statement, the sum of x, y, and z is divided by 3. The result is assigned to dblAverage.

```
dblAverage = (x + y + z) / 3
```

Without the parentheses, however, *z* would be divided by 3, and the result added to the sum of *x* and *y*. Table 9 shows more expressions and their values.

Table 9 Additional mathematical expressions and their values

Expression	Value
(5 + 2) * 4	28
10 / (5 - 3)	5
8 + 12 * (6 - 2)	56
(6 - 3) * (2 + 7) / 3	9

More about Mathematical Operations: Converting Mathematical Expressions to Programming Statements

In algebra, the mathematical expression $2xy$ describes the value 2 times *x* times *y*. Visual Basic, however, requires an operator for any mathematical operation. Table 10 shows some mathematical expressions that perform multiplication and the equivalent Visual Basic expressions.

Table 10 Visual Basic equivalents of mathematical expressions

Mathematical Expression	Operation	Visual Basic Equivalent
$6B$	6 times *B*	6 * B
$(3)(12)$	3 times 12	3 * 12
$4xy$	4 times *x* times *y*	4 * x * y

 Checkpoint

20 What value will be stored in dblResult after each of the following statements executes?
   a. dblResult = 6 + 3 * 5
   b. dblResult = 12 / 2 - 4
   c. dblResult = 2 + 7 * 3 - 6
   d. dblResult = (2 + 4) * 3
   e. dblResult = 10 \ 3
   f. dblResult = 6 ^ 2

21 What value will be stored in intResult after each statement executes?
   a. intResult = 10 MOD 3
   b. intResult = 47 MOD 15

22 Write a statement that assigns the current time of day to the variable dtmThisTime.

23 Write a statement that assigns the current date and time to a variable named dtmCurrent.

24 How is integer division different from floating-point division?

25 What will be the final value of `dblResult` in the following sequence?

```
Dim dblResult As Double = 3.5
dblResult += 1.2
```

26 What will be the final value of `dblResult` in the following sequence?

```
Dim dblResult As Double = 3.5
dblResult *= 2.0
```

Mixing Different Data Types

Implicit Type Conversion

When you assign a value of one data type to a variable of another data type, Visual Basic attempts to convert the value being assigned to the data type of the receiving variable. This is known as an **implicit type conversion**. Suppose we want to assign the integer 5 to a variable of type Single named `sngNumber`:

```
Dim sngNumber As Single = 5
```

When the statement executes, the integer 5 is automatically converted into a single-precision real number, which is then stored in `sngNumber`. This conversion is a **widening conversion** because no data is lost.

Narrowing Conversions

If you assign a real number to an integer variable, Visual Basic attempts to perform a **narrowing conversion**. Often, some data is lost. For example, the following statement assigns 12.2 to an integer variable:

```
Dim intCount As Integer = 12.2    'intCount = 12
```

Assuming for the moment that Visual Basic is configured to accept this type of conversion, the 12.2 is rounded downward to 12. Similarly, the next statement rounds upward to the nearest integer when the fractional part of the number is .5 or greater:

```
Dim intCount As Integer = 12.5    'intCount = 13
```

Another narrowing conversion occurs when assigning a Double value to a variable of type Single. Both hold floating-point values, but Double permits more significant digits:

```
Dim dblOne As Double = 1.2342376
Dim sngTwo As Single = dblOne     'sngTwo = 1.234238
```

The value stored in `sngTwo` is rounded up to 1.234238 because variables of type Single can only hold seven significant digits.

Option Strict

Visual Basic has a configuration option named *Option Strict* that determines whether certain implicit data type conversions are legal. If you set *Option Strict* to *On*, only widening conversions are permitted (such as Integer to Single). Figure 21 shows how implicit conversion between numeric types must be in a left-to-right direction in the diagram. A Decimal value can be assigned to a variable of type Single, an Integer can be assigned to a variable of type Double, and so on. If, on the other hand, *Option Strict* is set to *Off*, all types of numeric conversions are permitted, with possible loss of data.

Figure 21 Conversions permitted with *Option Strict On*

Implicit Numeric Conversions

Byte	Integer	Long	Decimal	Single	Double

To set *Option Strict* for a single project, right-click the project name in the *Solution Explorer* window, select *Properties*, and then select the *Compile* tab, as shown in Figure 22. From the *Option Strict* drop-down list, you can select *On* or *Off*.

We recommend setting *Option Strict* to *On*, so Visual Basic can catch errors that result when you accidentally assign a value of the wrong type to a variable. When set to *On*, *Option Strict* forces you to use a conversion function, making your intentions clear. This approach helps to avoid runtime errors.

Figure 22 *Project Properties* page

Type Conversion Runtime Errors

The following statement does not compile with *Option Strict* set to *On*:

```
Dim intCount As Integer = "abc123"
```

But if *Option Strict* has been set to *Off*, a program containing this statement will compile without errors. Then, when the program executes, it will stop when it reaches this statement because the string "abc123" contains characters that prevent the string from being converted to a number. The program will generate a runtime error message. Recall that runtime errors are errors that occur while the application is running. The type of error in this case is also known as a **type conversion error** or **type mismatch error**.

Runtime errors are harder to catch than syntax errors because they occur while a program is running. Particularly in programs where the user has a number of choices (mouse clicks, keyboard input, menus, and so on), it is very difficult for a programmer to predict when runtime errors might occur. Nevertheless, there are certain conversion functions shown in the next section that reduce the chance of this type of mishap.

> **TIP:** Can the best-trained programmers avoid runtime errors? To discover the answer to that question, spend some time using commercial Web sites and notice all the little things that go wrong. Software reliability is particularly hard to guarantee when users have lots of choices.

Literals

Literals (also known as constants) have specific types in Visual Basic. Table 11 lists the more common types. Many literals use a suffix character (C, D, @, R, I, L, F, S, !) to identify their type.

Table 11 Representing literals (constants) in Visual Basic

Type	Description	Example
Boolean	Keywords *True* and *False*	`True`
Byte	Sequence of decimal digits between 0 and 255	`200`
Char	Single letter enclosed in double quotes followed by the lowercase letter *C*	`"A"c`
Date	Date and/or time representation enclosed in # symbols	`#1/20/05 3:15 PM#`
Decimal	Optional leading sign, sequence of decimal digits, optional decimal point and trailing digits, followed by the letter *D* or @	`+32.0D` `64@`
Double	Optional leading sign, sequence of digits with a decimal point and trailing digits, followed by optional letter *R*	`3.5` `3.5R`
Integer	Optional leading sign, sequence of decimal digits, followed by optional letter *I*	`-3054I` `+26I`
Long	Optional leading sign, sequence of decimal digits, followed by the letter *L*	`40000000L`
Short	Optional leading sign, sequence of decimal digits, followed by the letter *S*	`12345S`
Single	Optional leading sign, sequence of digits with a decimal point and trailing digits, followed by the letter *F* or !	`26.4F` `26.4!`
String	Sequence of characters surrounded by double quotes	`"ABC"` `"234"`

It's important to know literal types because you often assign literal values to variables. If the receiving variable in an assignment statement has a different type from the literal, an implied conversion takes place. If *Option Strict* is *On*, some conversions are automatic and others generate errors. You need to understand why.

Most of the time, you will be inclined to use no suffix with numeric literals. As long as the receiving variable's data type is compatible with the literal's data type, you have no problem:

```
Dim lngCount As Long = 25          'Integer assigned to Long
Dim dblSalary As Double = 2500.0   'Double assigned to Double
```

In the following example, however, we're trying to assign a Double to a Decimal, which is not permitted when *Option Strict* is *On*:

```
Dim decPayRate As Decimal = 35.5          'Double to Decimal (?)
```

If you know how to create numeric literals, all you have to do is append a *D* to the number. The following is valid:

```
Dim decPayRate As Decimal = 35.5D
```

Named Constants

You have seen several programs and examples where numbers and strings are expressed as literal values. For example, the following statement contains the literal numeric value 0.129:

```
dblPayment = dblPrincipal * 0.129
```

Suppose this statement appears in a banking program that calculates loan information.

In such a program, two potential problems arise. First, it is not clearly evident to anyone other than the original programmer what the number 0.129 is. It appears to be an interest rate, but in some situations there are other fees associated with loan payments. How can you determine the purpose of this statement without painstakingly checking the rest of the program?

The second problem occurs if this number is used in other calculations throughout the program and must be changed periodically. Assuming the number is an interest rate, if the rate changes from 12.9% to 13.2% the programmer will have to search through the source code for every occurrence of the number.

Both of these problems can be addressed by using named constants. A **named constant** is like a variable whose content is read-only, and cannot be changed by a programming statement while the program is running. The following is the general form of a named constant declaration:

```
Const ConstantName As DataType = Value
```

Here is an example of a named constant declaration:

```
Const dblINTEREST_RATE As Double = 0.129
```

It looks like a regular variable declaration except for the following differences:

- The word Const is used instead of Dim.
- An initialization value is required.
- By convention, all letters after the prefix are capitals.
- Words in the name are separated by the underscore character.

The keyword Const indicates that you are declaring a named constant instead of a variable. The value given after the = sign is the value of the constant throughout the program's execution.

A value must be assigned when a named constant is declared or an error will result. An error will also result if any statements in the program attempt to change the contents of a named constant.

One advantage of using named constants is that they help make programs self-documenting. The statement

```
dblPayment = dblPrincipal * 0.129
```

can be changed to read

```
dblPayment = dblPrincipal * dblINTEREST_RATE
```

A new programmer can read the second statement and know what is happening. It is evident that dblPrincipal is being multiplied by the interest rate.

Another advantage to using named constants is that consistent changes can easily be made to the program. Let's say the interest rate appears in a dozen different statements throughout the program. When the rate changes, the value assigned to the named constant in its declaration is the only value that needs to be modified. If the rate increases to 13.2% the declaration is changed to the following:

```
Const dblINTEREST_RATE as Double = 0.132
```

Every statement that uses dblINTEREST_RATE will use the new value.

It is also useful to declare named constants for common values that are difficult to remember. For example, any program that calculates the area of a circle must use the value *pi*, which is 3.14159. This value could easily be declared as a named constant, as shown in the following statement:

```
Const dblPI as Double = 3.14159
```

Explicit Type Conversions

Let's assume for the current discussion that *Option Strict* is set to *On*. If you try to perform anything other than a widening conversion, your code will not compile. Visual Basic has a set of conversion functions to solve this problem.

What Is a Function?

A **function** is a special type of procedure. When you call a function, you typically send data to the function as input. The function performs an operation using that data, and then it sends a value back as output. Figure 23 illustrates this idea.

Figure 23 A function receives input and produces a single output

Input(s) ⟶ Function ⟶ Output

When we send a piece of data as input to a function, we typically say that we are passing the data as an **argument**. When a function sends a value back as output, we typically say that the function is **returning a value**.

For example, one of the Visual Basic conversion functions is named cInt. (You can think of this as standing for "Convert to Integer.") If you have a non-integer value that you need to convert to an integer, you can call the cInt function, passing the value as an argument. The cInt function will return that value, converted to an integer. Here is a code sample that shows how the cInt function works:

```
' Declare two variables.
Dim dblRealNumber as Double = 3.2
Dim intWholeNumber As Integer = 0

' Assign the Double value to the Integer variable.
intWholeNumber = CInt(dblRealNumber)
```

The last statement assigns the value of the Double variable, dblRealNumber, to the Integer variable, intWholeNumber. Let's take a closer look. On the right side of the = operator is the expression CInt(dblRealNumber). This expression calls the CInt function, passing the value of dblRealNumber, which is 3.2, as an argument.

The CInt function converts the value 3.2 to an integer by dropping the .2. (Dropping the fractional part of a number is called **truncation**.) The value 3 is then returned from the function. The assignment operator then assigns the value 3 to the intWholeNumber variable, as shown in Figure 24.

Figure 24 Using the CInt function

The value 3 is returned from the CInt function and
assigned to the intWholeNumber variable.

Visual Basic Conversion Functions

Table 12 lists the Visual Basic conversion functions that we will use most often. The input to each conversion function is an expression, which is another name for a constant, a variable, or a mathematical expression (such as 2.0 + 4.2). The following situations require a conversion function:

- When assigning a wider numeric type to a narrower numeric type. In Figure 21, the arrow pointing from left to right indicates automatic conversions. Any conversion in the opposite direction requires a call to a conversion function. Examples are Long to Integer, Decimal to Long, Double to Single, and Double to Decimal.
- When converting between Boolean, Date, Object, String, and numeric types. These all represent different categories, so they require conversion functions.

Table 12 Commonly used type conversion functions

Function	Description
CDate(*expr*)	Converts a String expression containing a valid date, such as "10/14/2010 1:30:00 PM", to a Date. Input can also be a Date literal, such as #10/14/2010 1:30:00 PM#.
CDbl(*expr*)	Converts an expression to a Double. If the input expression is a String, a leading currency symbol ($) is permitted, as are commas. The decimal point is optional.
CDec(*expr*)	Converts an expression to a Decimal. If the input expression is a String, a leading currency symbol ($) is permitted, as are commas. The decimal point is optional.
CInt(*expr*)	Converts an expression to an Integer. If the input expression is a String, a leading currency symbol ($) is permitted, as are commas. The decimal point is optional, as are digits after the decimal point.
CStr(*expr*)	Converts an expression to a String. Input can be a mathematical expression, Boolean value, a date, or any numeric data type.

VideoNote

Converting
TextBox Input

Converting TextBox Input

The conversion functions listed in Table 12 are commonly used to convert values that the user has entered into TextBox controls. Anything entered by the user into a TextBox is stored as a string in the control's Text property. If the user has entered a numeric value into a TextBox, and you want to use that value in a calculation, you will have to convert it from a string to an appropriate numeric data type.

For example, suppose a payroll application uses a TextBox named `txtHoursWorked` to get the number of hours worked, and a TextBox named `txtPayRate` to get the hourly pay rate. If the application needs to use the values held in these controls in a calculation, the values must be converted to a numeric type. The following statement shows how we might get the value that has been entered into `txtHoursWorked`, convert that value to an Integer, and assign it to a variable named `intHoursWorked`:

```
intHoursWorked = CInt(txtHoursWorked.Text)
```

And, the following statement shows how we might get the value that has been entered into `txtPayRate`, convert that value to a Double, and assign it to a variable named `dblPayRate`:

```
dblPayRate = CDbl(txtPayRate.Text)
```

After these conversions have taken place, the `intHoursWorked` and `dblPayRate` variables can be used in calculations.

The value of a TextBox control's Text property can be converted to other values as well. For example, a TextBox can be used to get a date from the user, and then the control's Text property can be converted to the Date data type. For example, assume that an application has a TextBox named `txtBirthday`, and the user has entered a date such as *11/15/2010*. The following statement declares a Date variable named `datBirthday` and initialized it with the value in the TextBox:

```
Dim datBirthday As Date = CDate(txtBirthDay.Text)
```

Here's an example that declares a Decimal variable named `decAccountBalance`, and initializes it with the value entered into the `txtAccountBalance` TextBox:

```
Dim decAccountBalance As Decimal = CDec(txtAccountBalance.Text)
```

Converting Floating-Point Numbers to Integers

The `CInt` function is required when assigning any floating-point type to an integer. Here is an example showing a Double being converted to an integer:

```
Dim dblAmount As Double = 3.4
Dim intAmount As Integer = CInt(dblAmount)
```

Here is an example showing a Single being converted to an integer:

```
Dim sngAmount As Single = 1.2
Dim intAmount As Integer = CInt(sngAmount)
```

And, here is an example showing a Decimal being converted to an integer:

```
Dim decAmount As Decimal = 9.1
Dim intAmount As Integer = CInt(decAmount)
```

Converting Doubles and Singles to Decimals

As previously mentioned, when *Option Strict* is set to *On*, a Double value cannot be assigned directly to a Decimal variable. A Single value cannot be assigned directly to a Decimal, either. You can, however, use the `CDec` function to explicitly convert a Double or a

Single to a Decimal. The following shows an example with a Double being converted to a Decimal:

```
Dim dblAmount As Double = 123.45
Dim decAmount As Decimal = CDec(dblAmount)
```

And, the following shows an example with a Single being converted to a Decimal:

```
Dim sngAmount As Single = 4.5
Dim decAmount As Decimal = CDec(sngAmount)
```

If You Want to Know More: CInt and Rounding

The CInt function converts an expression to an Integer. If the input value contains digits after the decimal point, a special type of rounding occurs, called *banker's rounding*. Here's how it works:

- If the digit after the decimal point is less than 5, the digits after the decimal point are removed from the number. We say the number is *truncated*.
- If the digit after the decimal point is a 5, the number is rounded toward the nearest even integer.
- If the digit after the decimal point is greater than 5 and the number is positive, it is rounded to the next highest integer.
- If the digit after the decimal point is greater than 5 and the number is negative, it is rounded to the next smallest integer.

Invalid Conversions

What happens if you call a conversion function, passing a value that cannot be converted? Here's an example:

```
Dim dblSalary As Double
dblSalary = CDbl("xyz")
```

The program stops with a runtime error, displaying the dialog box shown in Figure 25. The specific type of error, also known as an **exception**, is called an *InvalidCastException*. The text inside the list box consists of hyperlinks, which take you to specific *Visual Studio Help* pages. Later in this chapter, you will learn how to catch errors like this so the program won't stop.

Figure 25 Error displayed when trying to perform an invalid conversion from String to Double

152

Tutorial 7:

Examining a *Simple Calculator* application

This tutorial examines an application that functions as a simple calculator. The application has two TextBox controls, into which you enter numbers. There are buttons for addition, subtraction, multiplication, division, exponentiation, integer division, and modulus. When you click one of these buttons, the application performs a math operation using the two numbers entered into the TextBox controls and displays the result in a label.

Step 1: Open the *Simple Calculator* project from this chapter sample programs folder named *Simple Calculator*.

Step 2: Click the *Start* button to run the application. The application's form appears, as shown in Figure 26.

Figure 26 *Simple Calculator* form

Step 3: Enter **10** into the *Number 1* TextBox control. (In the program source code, this TextBox control is named `txtNumber1`.)

Step 4: Enter **3** into the *Number 2* TextBox control. (In the program source code, this TextBox control is named `txtNumber2`.)

Step 5: Click the + button. Notice that next to the word *Operation* a large plus sign appears on the form. This indicates that an addition operation has taken place. (The plus sign is displayed in a label named `lblOperation`.) The result of 10 + 3 displays in the *Result* label, which is named `lblResult`. The form appears as shown in Figure 27.

Step 6: Click the – button. Notice that the `lblOperation` label changes to a minus sign and the result of 10 minus 3 displays in the `lblResult` label.

Step 7: Click the *, ^, /, \, and *MOD* buttons. Each performs a math operation using 10 and 3 as its operands and displays the result in the `lblResult` label.

Step 8: If you wish to experiment with other numbers, click the *Clear* button and continue.

Step 9: When you are finished, click the *Exit* button.

Figure 27 Result of 10 + 3

Step 10: Open *Form1* in the *Designer* window, if it is not already open. Double-click the + button on the application form. This opens the *Code* window, with the text cursor positioned in the `btnPlus_Click` event handler. The code is as follows:

```
Private Sub btnPlus_Click(...) Handles btnPlus.Click
    ' This event handler performs addition.
    ' Declare a variable to hold the result.
    Dim dblResult As Double

    ' Indicate "+" as the operation.
    lblOperation.Text = "+"

    ' Add the two numbers and store the result in dblResult.
    dblResult = CDbl(txtNumber1.Text) + CDbl(txtNumber2.Text)

    ' Display the result.
    lblResult.Text = CStr(dblResult)
End Sub
```

Step 11: Examine the other event handlers in this application. Most of the arithmetic operator button handlers are similar, except those for the Integer division and Modulus operators. In the Integer division operator handler, for example, the result variable is an integer, and the `CInt` function converts the contents of the TextBox controls:

```
Private Sub btnIntegerDivide_Click(...) Handles btnIntegerDivide.Click
    ' This event handler performs integer division.
    ' Declare a variable to hold the result.
    Dim intResult As Integer

    ' Indicate "\" as the operation.
    lblOperation.Text = "\"

    ' Integer-divide Number 1 by Number 2 and
    ' store the result in dblResult.
    intResult = CInt(txtNumber1.Text) \ CInt(txtNumber2.Text)

    ' Display the result.
    lblResult.Text = CStr(intResult)
End Sub
```

If You Want to Know More: Full Set of VB Conversion Functions

Table 12, shown earlier, lists the Visual Basic conversion functions that you will use most frequently. For your reference, Table 13 contains a more complete list of Visual Basic conversion functions, including some that you will use only occasionally.

Table 13 Visual Basic type conversion functions

Function	Description
CBool(*expr*)	Converts an expression to a Boolean value. The expression must be a number, a string that represents a number, or the strings `"True"` or `"False"`. Otherwise a runtime error is generated. If the expression is nonzero, the function returns *True*. Otherwise it returns *False*. For example, CBool(10) and CBool("7") return *True*, while CBool(0) and CBool("0") return *False*. If the argument is the string `"True"`, the function returns *True*, and if the expression is the string `"False"`, the function returns *False*.
CByte(*expr*)	Converts an expression to a Byte, which can hold the values 0 through 255. If the argument is a fractional number, it is rounded. If the expression cannot be converted to a value in the range of 0–255, a runtime error is generated.
CChar(*expr*)	Converts a string expression to a Char. If the string contains more than one character, only the first character is returned. For example, CChar("xyz") returns the character *x*.
CDate(*expr*)	Converts an expression to a Date. String expressions must be valid Date literals. For example, CDate("#10/14/2010 1:30:00 PM#") returns a Date with the value *1:30 PM, October 14th, 2010*. If the expression cannot be converted to a Date value, a runtime error is generated.
CDbl(*expr*)	Converts a numeric or string expression to a Double. If the expression converts to a value outside the range of a Double, or is not a numeric value, a runtime error is generated.
CDec(*expr*)	Converts a numeric or string expression to a Decimal. The CDec function can convert strings starting with a $ character, such as $1,200.00. Commas are also permitted. If the expression converts to a value outside the range of a Decimal, or is not a numeric value, a runtime error is generated.
CInt(*expr*)	Converts a numeric or string expression to an Integer. If the expression converts to a value outside the range of an Integer, or is not a numeric value, a runtime error is generated. Rounds to nearest integer.
CLng(*expr*)	Converts a numeric or string expression to a Long (long integer). If the expression converts to a value outside the range of a Long, or is not a numeric value, a runtime error is generated.
CObj(*expr*)	Converts an expression to an Object.
CShort(*expr*)	Converts a numeric or string expression to a Short (short integer). If the expression converts to a value outside the range of a Short, or is not a numeric value, a runtime error is generated.
CSng(*expr*)	Converts a numeric or string expression to a Single. If the expression converts to a value outside the range of a Single, or is not a numeric value, a runtime error is generated. The input expression may conatain commas, as in "1,234."
CStr(*expr*)	Converts a numeric, Boolean, Date, or string expression to a String. Input can be an arithmetic expression, a Boolean value, a date, or any numeric data type.

Checkpoint

27 After the statement `dblResult = 10 \ 3` executes, what value will be stored in `dblResult`?

28 After each of the following statements executes, what value will be stored in `dblResult`?

    a. `dblResult = 6 + 3 * 5`
    b. `dblResult = 12 / 2 - 4`
    c. `dblResult = 2 + 7 * 3 - 6`
    d. `dblResult = (2 + 4) * 3`

29 What value will be stored in `dblResult` after the following statement executes?

    `dblResult = CInt("28.5")`

30 Will the following statement execute or cause a runtime error?

    `dblResult = CDbl("186,478.39")`

31 What is a named constant?

32 Assuming that `intNumber` is an integer variable, what value will each of the following statements assign to it?

    a. `intNumber = 27`
    b. `intNumber = CInt(12.8)`
    c. `intNumber = CInt(12.0)`
    d. `intNumber = (2 + 4) * 3`

33 Which function converts the string "860.2" to value of type Double?

34 How would the following strings be converted by the `CDec` function?

    a. `48.5000`
    b. `$34.95`
    c. `2,300`
    d. `Twelve`

5 Formatting Numbers and Dates

Users of computer programs generally like to see numbers and dates displayed in an attractive, easy to read format. Numbers greater than 999, for instance, should usually be displayed with commas and decimal points. The value 123456.78 would normally be displayed as "123,456.78".

 TIP: Number formatting is dependent on the locale that is used by the computer's Microsoft Windows operating system. *Localization* refers to the technique of adapting your formats for various regions and countries of the world. For example, in North America a currency value is formatted as 123,456.78. In many European countries, the same value is formatted as 123.456,78. We will display only North American formats, but you can find help on using other types of formats by looking for the topic named *localization* in Visual Studio help.

ToString Method

All numeric and date data types in Visual Basic contain the `ToString` method. This method converts the contents of a variable to a string. The following code segment shows an example of the method's use.

```
Dim intNumber As Integer = 123
lblNumber.Text = intNumber.ToString()
```

In the second statement the number variable's ToString method is called. The method returns the string "123", which is assigned to the Text property of lblNumber.

By passing a formatting string to the ToString method, you can indicate what type of format you want to use when the number or date is formatted. The following statements create a string containing the number 1234.5 in Currency format:

```
Dim dblSample As Double
Dim strResult As String
dblSample = 1234.5
strResult = dblSample.ToString("c")
```

When the last statement executes, the value assigned to strResult is "$1,234.50". Notice that an extra zero was added at the end because currency values usually have two digits to the right of the decimal point. The value "c" is called a format string. Table 14 shows the format strings used for all types of floating-point numbers (Double, Single, and Decimal), assuming the user is running Windows in a North American locale. The format strings are not case sensitive, so you can code them as uppercase or lowercase letters. If you call ToString using an integer type (Byte, Integer, or Long), the value is formatted as if it were type Double.

Table 14 Standard numeric format strings

Format String	Description
N or n	Number format
F or f	Fixed-point scientific format
E or e	Exponential scientific format
C or c	Currency format
P or p	Percent format

Number Format

Number format (n or N) displays numeric values with thousands separators and a decimal point. By default, two digits display to the right of the decimal point. Negative values are displayed with a leading minus (−) sign. Example:

```
-2,345.67
```

Fixed-Point Format

Fixed-point format (f or F) displays numeric values with no thousands separator and a decimal point. By default, two digits display to the right of the decimal point. Negative values are displayed with a leading minus (−) sign. Example:

```
-2345.67
```

Exponential Format

Exponential format (e or E) displays numeric values in scientific notation. The number is normalized with a single digit to the left of the decimal point. The exponent is marked by the letter e, and the exponent has a leading + or − sign. By default, six digits display to the right of the decimal point, and a leading minus sign is used if the number is negative. Example:

```
-2.345670e+003
```

Currency Format

Currency format (c or C) displays a leading currency symbol (such as $), digits, thousands separators, and a decimal point. By default, two digits display to the right of the decimal point. Negative values are surrounded by parentheses. Example:

```
($2,345.67)
```

Percent Format

Percent format (p or P) causes the number to be multiplied by 100 and displayed with a trailing space and % sign. By default, two digits display to the right of the decimal point. Negative values are displayed with a leading minus (−) sign. The following example uses −.2345:

```
-23.45 %
```

Specifying the Precision

Each numeric format string can optionally be followed by an integer that indicates how many digits to display after the decimal point. For example, the format n3 displays three digits after the decimal point. Table 15 shows a variety of numeric formatting examples, based on the North American locale.

Table 15 Numeric formatting examples (North American locale)

Number Value	Format String	ToString( ) Value
12.3	n3	12.300
12.348	n2	12.35
1234567.1	n	1,234,567.10
123456.0	f2	123456.00
123456.0	e3	1.235e+005
.234	p	23.40%
−1234567.8	c	($1,234,567.80)

Rounding

Rounding can occur when the number of digits you have specified after the decimal point in the format string is smaller than the precision of the numeric value. Suppose, for example, that the value 1.235 were displayed with a format string of n2. Then the displayed value would be 1.24. If the next digit after the last displayed digit is 5 or higher, the last displayed digit is rounded *away from zero*. Table 16 shows examples of rounding using a format string of n2.

Table 16 Rounding examples, using the n2 display format string

Number Value	Formatted As
1.234	1.23
1.235	1.24
1.238	1.24
−1.234	−1.23
−1.235	−1.24
−1.238	−1.24

Integer Values with Leading Zeros

Integer type variables (Byte, Integer, or Long) have a special format string, D (or d), that lets you specify the minimum width for displaying the number. Leading zeros are inserted if necessary. Table 17 shows examples.

Table 17 Formatting integers, using the D (d) format string

Integer Value	Format String	Formatted As
23	D	23
23	D4	0023
1	D2	01

Formatting Dates and Times

When you call the ToString method using a Date or DateTime variable, you can format it as a short date, short time, long date, and so on. Table 18 lists the most commonly used format strings for dates and times. The following example creates a string containing "8/10/2010", called the short date format.

```
Dim dtmSample As Date = "#8/10/2010#"
Dim strResult As String = dtmSample.ToString("d")
```

The following example gets the current date and formats it with a long date format.

```
Dim strToday As String = Today().ToString("D")
```

Date/time format strings are case sensitive.

Table 18 Common date/time formats

Format String	Description
d	Short date format, which shows the month, day, and year. An example is "8/10/2010".
D	Long date format, which contains the day of the week, month, day, and year. An example is "Tuesday, August 10, 2010".
t	Short time format, which shows the hours and minutes. An example is "3:22 PM".
T	Long time format, which contains the hours, minutes, seconds, and an AM/PM indicator. An example is "3:22:00 PM".
F	Full (long) date and time. An example is "Tuesday August 10, 2010 3:22:00 PM".

Tutorial 8 examines the *Format Demo* application.

Tutorial 8:
Examining the *Format Demo* application

Step 1: Open the *Format Demo* project from this chapter sample programs folder named *Format Demo*.

Step 2: Run the application, as shown in Figure 28. The five buttons on the left are used for formatting floating-point numeric values. The five buttons on the right are for formatting dates and times. The text in each button shows which format string is used when the `ToString` method is called.

Figure 28 *Format Demo* application

Step 3: Enter the value `67895.34926` into the TextBox control at the top of the form. Click the *Number format (n)* button. You should see the output shown in Figure 29.

Step 4: Click the *Fixed-point format (f)* button. Notice how the number next to the Formatted label changes its appearance.

Step 5: Click the remaining buttons on the left side. Change the value of the number in the TextBox control, and experiment with each of the format buttons on the left side.

Step 6: Enter the following date into the TextBox: *May 5, 2010 6:35 PM*.

Step 7: Click the *Short date (d)* button. You should see the date displayed as "*5/5/2010*".

Step 8: Click the other date and time buttons in the right-hand column. Notice all the ways the date and time can be displayed.

Step 9: Close the application window by clicking the (⊠) in the upper right corner. Open the form's code window and examine the code in each button's Click event handler.

Figure 29 Showing a Number format

Checkpoint

35 Write a statement that uses the ToString method to convert the contents of a variable named dblSalary to a Currency format.

36 For each of the following numeric formats, identify the format string used as the input parameter when calling the ToString method.
   a. Currency
   b. Exponential scientific
   c. Number
   d. Percent
   e. Fixed-point

37 How can you make the ToString method display parentheses around a number in Currency format when the number is negative?

38 In the following table, fill in the expected values returned by the ToString function when specific numeric values are used with specific format strings.

Number Value	Format String	ToString( ) Value
12.3	n4	
12.348	n1	
1234567.1	n3	
123456.0	f1	
123456.0	e3	
.234	p2	
−1234567.8	c3	

39 Show an example of formatting a Date variable in Long Time format when calling the ToString method.

40 Show an example of formatting a Date variable in Long Date format when calling the ToString method.

6 Class-Level Variables

CONCEPT: Class-level variables are accessible to all procedures in a class.

Recall that a variable's scope is the part of the program in which the variable is visible. All of the variables you have created so far have had local scope, meaning that each was declared and used inside a procedure. Local variables are not visible to statements outside the procedure in which they are declared.

It's also possible to declare a class-level variable, which is accessible to all of the procedures in a class. Recall that a form's code appears inside a class. For example, suppose a project has a form named Form1. When you open the form in the *Code* window, you see that its code is contained inside a class declaration such as this:

```
Public Class Form1

    Event handlers appear here...

End Class
```

A class-level variable is declared inside a class declaration, but not inside any procedure. Class-level variables have class scope because they are visible to all statements inside the class. For example, look at the following code. The application's form has two Button controls: btnSetValue and btnShowValue.

161

```
 1 Public Class Form1
 2  ' Declare a class-level variable.
 3  Dim intValue As Integer
 4
 5  Private Sub btnSetValue_Click(...) Handles btnSetValue.Click
 6      intValue = 99
 7  End Sub
 8
 9  Private Sub btnShowValue_Click(...) Handles btnShowValue.Click
10      MessageBox.Show(intValue.ToString())
11  End Sub
12 End Class
```

Notice that the declaration of the intValue variable in line 3 is inside the class, but is not inside of either event handler. The variable has class scope, so it is visible to both of the event handlers. When the btnSetValue_Click procedure executes, the statement in line 6 assigns 99 to the variable. When the btnShowValue_Click procedure executes, the statement in line 10 displays the variable's value in a message box. (In the *Chap3* folder of student sample programs you will find the previously shown code in a project named *Class-Level Variable Demo*.)

Most programmers agree that you should not overuse class-level variables. Although they make it easy to share values between procedures, their use can also lead to problems. Here are some of the reasons:

- While debugging, if you find that the wrong value is being stored in a class-level variable, you will have to track down each statement in the class that uses the variable to determine where the bad value is coming from. In a class with lots of code, this can be tedious and time-consuming.
- When two or more procedures modify the same class-level variable, you must ensure that one procedure cannot upset the accuracy or correctness of another procedure by modifying the variable.
- Class-level variables can make a program hard to understand. A class-level variable can be modified by any statement in the class. If you are to understand any part of the class that uses a class-level variable, you have to be aware of all the other parts of the class that access that variable.

Class-Level Constants

Although you should be careful not to overuse class-level variables, it is generally acceptable to use class-level constants. A class-level constant is a named constant declared with the Const keyword, at the class level. Because a constant's value cannot be changed during the program's execution, you do not have to worry about many of the potential hazards that are associated with the use of class-level variables.

 Checkpoint

41 What is the difference between a class-level variable and a local variable?

42 Where do you declare class-level variables?

 7 **Exception Handling**

CONCEPT: A well-engineered program should report errors and try to continue. Or, it should explain why it cannot continue, and then shut down. In this section, you learn how to recover gracefully from errors, using a technique known as exception handling.

An exception is an unexpected error that occurs while a program is running, causing the program to abruptly halt. Exceptions are typically caused by circumstances outside of the programmer's control. In Tutorial 9 you will run an application and deliberately cause an exception.

Tutorial 9:
Exception Demonstration

VideoNote

Exception
Demonstration

Step 1: Open the *Exception Demo* project from this chapter sample programs folder named *Exception Demo*. Figure 30 shows the application's form. The TextBox control's name is `txtSalary`, and the Button control's name is `btnOk`.

Figure 30 The *Exception Demo* application's form

Step 2: Open the *Code* window and look at the `btnOk` button's Click event handler. The code is shown here, with line numbers inserted for reference purposes:

```
 1 Private Sub btnOk_Click(...) Handles btnOk.Click
 2   ' Declare a variable to hold the user's salary.
 3   Dim decSalary As Decimal
 4
 5   ' Get the user's input and convert it to a Decimal.
 6   decSalary = CDec(txtSalary.Text)
 7
 8   ' Display the user's salary.
 9   MessageBox.Show("Your salary is " & decSalary.ToString("c"))
10 End Sub
```

Line 3 declares a Decimal variable named `decSalary`. Line 6 uses the `CDec` function to convert the `txtSalary` control's Text property to a Decimal, and assigns the result to the `decSalary` variable. Line 9 displays a message showing the value of `decSalary` formatted as currency.

Step 3: Run the application. Enter *4000* in the TextBox and click the *OK* button. You should see a message box with the message *Your salary is $4000.00*. Click the message box's *OK* button to dismiss it.

Step 4: Change the contents of the TextBox to *Four Thousand*, as shown in Figure 31.

Because the string *Four Thousand* cannot be converted by the `CDec` function, an exception will occur when you click the *OK* button. Go ahead and try it! Click the *OK* button. The application will halt and you will see the error window shown in Figure 32.

A lot of information is displayed in the error window. Before continuing, take note of the following:

- The window's title bar shows the message *InvalidCastException was unhandled*. All exceptions have a name, and the name of the exception that just occurred is InvalidCastException. Anytime a conversion function such as

Figure 31 *Four Thousand* entered into the TextBox

Figure 32 The resulting error window

CDec fails to convert a value, it causes an InvalidCastException to occur. This message also tells us that the exception was *unhandled*. That means that the program doesn't have any code to take care of the exception. It simply allowed it to happen, and as a result the application halted.

- Just below the window's title bar you see the error message *Conversion from string "Four Thousand" to type 'Decimal' is not valid*. This tells us exactly what happened to cause the exception.
- In the *Code* window, the statement that caused the exception is highlighted.

Step 5: Close the error window. The application is now in Break mode, which is used for debugging. We will discuss break mode in greater detail later in this chapter. For now, just exit break mode by performing *one* of the following actions:

- Click the *Stop Debugging* button ( ) on the toolbar.
- Click *Debug* on the menu bar, and then select *Stop Debugging*.
- Press Ctrl + Alt + Break on the keyboard.

When an exception occurs, programmers commonly say an *exception was thrown*. As you were following the steps in Tutorial 9, an exception known as an InvalidCastException was thrown when the CDec function attempted to convert the string "Four Thousand" to a Decimal value. When an exception is thrown, it must be handled by the program. If the exception is unhandled (as was the case in Tutorial 9), the program halts.

Failure Can Be Graceful

Exceptions are typically thrown because of events outside the programmer's control. A disk file may be unreadable, for example, because of a hardware failure. The user may enter invalid data, as happened in Tutorial 9. Or, the computer may be low on memory.

Exception handling is designed to let programs recover from errors when possible. Or, if recovery is not possible, a program should fail gracefully, letting the user know why it failed. Under no circumstances should it just halt without warning. In this section we will show how you can handle exceptions.

Visual Basic, like most modern programming languages, allows you to write code that responds to exceptions when they are thrown, and prevents the program from abruptly crashing. Such code is called an **exception handler**, and is written with a **Try-Catch** statement. There are several ways to write a Try-Catch statement, but the following is a simplified general format:

```
Try
    statement
    statement
    statement
    etc...
Catch
    statement
    statement
    statement
    etc...
End Try
```

First the key word Try appears. Next, one or more statements appear which we will refer to as the **try block**. These are statements that can potentially throw an exception. After the last statement in the try block, a **Catch** clause appears. Beginning on the next line, one or more statements appear, which we will refer to as the **catch block**.

When the a Try-Catch block executes, the statements in the try block are executed in the order that they appear. If a statement in the try block throws an exception, the program immediately jumps to the Catch clause, and executes the statements in the catch block. After the last statement in the catch block has executed, the program resumes execution with any statement that appears after the End Try clause.

Let's see how a Try-Catch statement can be used in the *Exception Demo* application. A modified version of the btnOk_Click procedure is shown here, with line numbers inserted for reference:

```
 1 Private Sub btnOk_Click(...) Handles btnOk.Click
 2   ' Declare a variable to hold the user's salary.
 3   Dim decSalary As Decimal
 4
 5   Try
 6     ' Get the user's input and convert it to a Decimal.
 7     decSalary = CDec(txtSalary.Text)
 8
 9     ' Display the user's salary.
10     MessageBox.Show("Your salary is " & decSalary.ToString("c"))
11   Catch
12     ' Display an error message.
13     MessageBox.Show("Please try again, and enter a number.")
14   End Try
15 End Sub
```

In this code, when the statement in line 7 throws an exception, the program immediately jumps to the Catch clause in line 11 and begins executing the statements in the catch block. The catch block displays a message box in line 13, and that's the end of the Try-Catch statement. Figure 33 illustrates this sequence of events.

Variables and Calculations

Figure 33 Sequence of events in the `Try-Catch` statement

```
                        Try
                            ' Get the user's input and convert it to a Decimal.
When this statement  ──────►decSalary = CDec(txtSalary.Text)
throws an exception....
                            ┌ ' Display the user's salary.
    ...these lines  ────────┤  MessageBox.Show("Your salary is " & decSalary.ToString("c"))
    are skipped...          └
                        Catch
... and the statements ────►  ' Display an error message.
in the catch block are        MessageBox.Show("Please try again, and enter a number.")
executed.               End Try
```

We encourage you to modify the `btnOk_Click` procedure in the *Exception Demo* project by adding the `Try-Catch` statement as previously shown. Then, run the application again. If you enter 4000 in the TextBox and click the OK button, you will see a message box with the message *Your salary is $4000.00*, just as you did before. If you enter something that cannot be converted to a Decimal, such as the string *Four Thousand*, you will see the message box shown in Figure 34. This message box is displayed by the statement shown previously in line 13 (in the catch block).

Figure 34 Message displayed by the catch block code

Please try again, and enter a number.

OK

Tutorial 10:

Salary Calculator project with exception handling

VideoNote

Tutorial 3-10
Walkthrough

The student sample programs folder contains a partially completed project named *Salary Calculator*. When the project is complete, it will allow the user to input a person's annual salary and number of pay periods per year. With the click of a button, the program will calculate the amount of salary the user should receive per pay period.

In this tutorial you will complete the project. First, you will implement the program without exception handling, test it, and note how runtime errors occur. Then, you will add exception handling to the program and test it again.

Step 1:   Open the *Salary Calculator* project from this chapter sample programs folder named *Salary Calculator*. Figure 35 shows the application's form with the names of the several controls.

166

Figure 35 *Salary Calculator* form

Step 2: Double-click the `btnCalculate` button to open the *Code* window. Insert the following bold code shown in the lines 2 through 14 into its Click event handler. (Don't enter the line numbers! They are shown only for reference.)

```
 1 Private Sub btnCalculate_Click(...) Handles btnCalculate.Click
 2   Dim decAnnualSalary As Decimal ' Annual salary
 3   Dim intPayPeriods As Integer   ' Number of pay periods
 4   Dim decSalary As Decimal       ' Salary per pay period
 5
 6   ' Get the annual salary and number of pay periods.
 7   decAnnualSalary = CDec(txtAnnualSalary.Text)
 8   intPayPeriods = CInt(txtPayPeriods.Text)
 9
10   ' Calculate the salary per pay period.
11   decSalary = decAnnualSalary / intPayPeriods
12
13   ' Display the salary per pay period.
14   lblSalary.Text = decSalary.ToString("c")
15 End Sub
```

Let's go over the code that you just wrote:

- Lines 2 through 4 declare the local variables used in the procedure.
- Line 7 uses the `CDec` function to convert the value of the `txtAnnualSalary` control's Text property to a Decimal , and assigns the result to the `decAnnualSalary` variable.
- Line 8 uses the `CInt` function to convert the value of the `txtPayPeriods` control's Text property to an Integer, and assigns the result to the `intPayPeriods` variable.
- Line 11 divides `decAnnualSalary` by `intPayPeriods` to calculate the salary per pay period. The result is assigned to the `decSalary` variable.
- Line 14 uses the `ToString("c")` method to convert `decSalary` to a string, formatted as currency. The resulting string is assigned to the `lblSalary` control's Text property.

Step 3: Save and run the program. Enter **75000** for the annual salary, and **26** for the pay periods per year. When you click *Calculate*, the output should be $2,884.62.

Step 4: Now you will purposely cause an exception. Erase the contents of the *Pay periods per year:* text box and click the *Calculate* button. You should see an error window appear, like the one shown in Figure 36, saying *InvalidCastException*

Figure 36 Exception reported

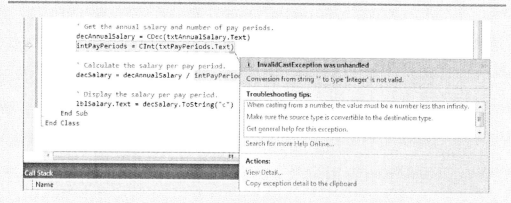

was unhandled. Notice the error message in the window reads *Conversion from string "" to type Integer is not valid*. Also notice the statement that caused the error. (Line 8 in the previously shown code.)

Close the error window and click the *Stop Debugging* button (▶) on the Visual Studio toolbar. The program should return to Design mode.

Step 5: Your next task is to add exception handling to the program to prevent the type of runtime error you just saw. You never want a program to halt like this when the user enters bad data. Revise the code in the btnCalculate_Click procedure so it looks like the following. (The new code is shown in bold. As before, don't enter the line numbers. They are shown only for reference.)

```
1 Private Sub btnCalculate_Click(...) Handles btnCalculate.Click
2     Dim decAnnualSalary As Decimal ' Annual salary
3     Dim intPayPeriods As Integer   ' Number of pay periods
4     Dim decSalary As Decimal       ' Salary per pay period
5
6     Try
7         ' Get the annual salary and number of pay periods.
8         decAnnualSalary = CDec(txtAnnualSalary.Text)
9         intPayPeriods = CInt(txtPayPeriods.Text)
10
11        ' Calculate the salary per pay period.
12        decSalary = decAnnualSalary / intPayPeriods
13
14        ' Display the salary per pay period.
15        lblSalary.Text = decSalary.ToString("c")
16     Catch
17         ' Display an error message.
18         MessageBox.Show("Error: Be sure to enter nonzero " &
19                         "numeric values.")
20     End Try
21 End Sub
```

Now, the statements that can potentially throw an exception are placed inside the try block:

- Line 8 can throw an InvalidCastException if the txtAnnualSalary control contains invalid data.
- Line 9 can throw an InvalidCastException if the txtPayPeriods control contains invalid data.

- Line 12 can also throw an exception if the `intPayPeriods` variable is set to 0. When division by zero happens, if one of the operands is a Decimal, an exception known as DivideByZeroException occurs.

If any of these exceptions occurs, the program will immediately jump to the `Catch` clause. When that happens, the statement shown in lines 18 and 19 will display an error message.

Step 6: Save and run the program. Enter *75000* for the annual salary, and leave the pay periods per year TextBox blank. When you click *Calculate*, you should see the message box shown in Figure 37. Click OK to dismiss the message box.

Figure 37 Error message box displayed

Step 7: Now let's see what happens when the program divides by zero. Leave 75000 as the annual salary and enter *0* for the pay periods per year. When you click *Calculate*, you should again see the message box shown in Figure 37. Click OK to dismiss the message box, and then close the application.

Using Nested `Try-Catch` Statements

As you saw in Tutorial 10, a procedure might contain several statements that potentially can throw an exception. If you look back at Step 5 of that tutorial, you see that lines 8, 9, and 12 each can potentially throw an exception. Regardless of which line throws an exception, the catch block displays the same error message (in lines 18 and 19). If you want to handle the exceptions separately, with a unique error message displayed for each one, you can have a set of nested `Try-Catch` statements. (When we use the term "nested," we mean that one `Try-Catch` statement appears inside another.)

The following code shows how this can be done. This is a modified version of the `btnCalculate_Click` procedure in Tutorial 10.

```
1    Private Sub btnCalculate_Click(...) Handles btnCalculate.Click
2        Dim decAnnualSalary As Decimal ' Annual salary
3        Dim intPayPeriods As Integer   ' Number of pay periods per year
4        Dim decSalary As Decimal       ' Salary per pay period
5
6        Try
7            ' Get the annual salary and number of pay periods.
8            decAnnualSalary = CDec(txtAnnualSalary.Text)
9
10           Try
11               ' Get the number of pay periods.
12               intPayPeriods = CInt(txtPayPeriods.Text)
13
```

```
14          Try
15            ' Calculate the salary per pay period.
16            decSalary = decAnnualSalary / intPayPeriods
17
18            ' Display the salary per pay period.
19            lblSalary.Text = decSalary.ToString("c")
20          Catch
21            ' Error message for division-by-zero.
22            MessageBox.Show("Pay periods cannot be zero.")
23          End Try
24
25        Catch
26          ' Error message for invalid pay periods.
27          MessageBox.Show("Pay periods must be an integer.")
28        End Try
29
30      Catch
31        ' Error message for invalid salary.
32        MessageBox.Show("Enter a numeric value for salary.")
33      End Try
34    End Sub
```

Let's take a closer look at this code:

- The first `Try` statement appears in line 6. Inside the try block, line 8 attempts to convert `txtAnnualSalary.Text` to a Decimal. If an exception is thrown, the program will jump to the `Catch` clause in line 30. When that happens, line 32 displays an error message prompting the user to enter a numeric value for the salary, and the procedure ends.
- If `txtAnnualSalary.Text` is successfully converted to a Decimal in line 8, the program continues to the nested `Try` statement in line 10. Line 12 attempts to convert `txtPayPeriods.Text` to an Integer. If an exception is thrown, the program will jump to the `Catch` clause in line 25. When that happens, line 27 displays an error message indicating that pay periods must be an integer, and the procedure ends.
- If `txtPayPeriods.Text` is successfully converted to a Decimal in line 12, the program continues to the nested `Try` statement in line 14. Then, line 16 divides `decAnnualSalary` by `intPayPeriods`. If `intPayPeriods` happens to be zero, an exception is thrown and the program jumps to the `Catch` clause in line 20. When that happens, line 22 displays an error message indicating that pay periods cannot be zero, and the procedure ends.
- If the division operation in line 16 is successful, then line 19 displays the salary in the `lblSalary` control.

(In the *Chap3* folder of student sample programs you will find the previously shown code in a project named *Nested Try*.)

If You Want to Know More: Using Multiple Catch Clauses to Handle Multiple Types of Errors

Another way to handle different types of exceptions separately, with a unique error message displayed for each one, is to have a `Catch` clause for each type of exception.

The following code shows how this can be done. This is a modified version of the `btnCalculate_Click` procedure in Tutorial 10. Notice that the `Try-Catch` statement has two `Catch` clauses: one for InvalidCastExceptions (line 17) and one for

DivideByZeroExceptions (line 21). If the code inside the try block throws an InvalidCast-Exception, the program will jump to the `Catch` clause in line 17, perform its catch block, and then exit. If the code inside the try block throws a DivideByZeroException, the program will jump to the `Catch` clause in line 21, perform its catch block, and then exit.

```
 1 Private Sub btnCalculate_Click(...) Handles btnCalculate.Click
 2   Dim decAnnualSalary As Decimal ' Annual salary
 3   Dim intPayPeriods As Integer   ' Number of pay periods
 4   Dim decSalary As Decimal       ' Salary per pay period
 5
 6   Try
 7     ' Get the annual salary and number of pay periods.
 8     decAnnualSalary = CDec(txtAnnualSalary.Text)
 9     intPayPeriods = CInt(txtPayPeriods.Text)
10
11     ' Calculate the salary per pay period.
12     decSalary = decAnnualSalary / intPayPeriods
13
14     ' Display the salary per pay period.
15     lblSalary.Text = decSalary.ToString("c")
16
17   Catch ex As InvalidCastException
18     ' An invalid value as entered.
19     MessageBox.Show("Error: Input must be numeric.")
20
21   Catch ex As DivideByZeroException
22     ' 0 was entered for pay periods.
23     MessageBox.Show("Error: Enter nonzero values.")
24   End Try
25 End Sub
```

This is a more sophisticated way of handling exceptions, but it requires you to know the names of the exception types that you want to handle ahead of time. A simple way to do this is to run the program without the `Try-Catch` statement and deliberately cause the exceptions to occur. You can then see the name of the exception in the error window that appears. (In the *Chap3* folder of student sample programs you will find the previously shown code in a project named *Multiple Exceptions*.)

If You Want to Know More: Displaying an Exception's Default Error Message

It's possible for your program to retrieve the default error message for an exception. This is the error message that you see in the error window that appears when an exception is unhandled.

When an exception occurs, an object known as an **exception object** is created in memory. The exception object has various properties that contain data about the exception. When you write a `Catch` clause, you can optionally assign a name to the exception object, as shown here:

```
Catch ex As Exception
```

This `Catch` clause specifies that the name `ex` refers to the exception object. Inside the catch block, we can use the name `ex` to access the exception object's properties. One of these is the Message property, which contains the exception's default error message. The following code shows how this can be done. This is another modified version of the `btnCalculate_Click` procedure in Tutorial 10.

```
 1 Private Sub btnCalculate_Click(...) Handles btnCalculate.Click
 2   Dim decAnnualSalary As Decimal ' Annual salary
 3   Dim intPayPeriods As Integer   ' Number of pay periods
 4   Dim decSalary As Decimal       ' Salary per pay period
 5
 6   Try
 7     ' Get the annual salary and number of pay periods.
 8     decAnnualSalary = CDec(txtAnnualSalary.Text)
 9     intPayPeriods = CInt(txtPayPeriods.Text)
10
11     ' Calculate the salary per pay period.
12     decSalary = decAnnualSalary / intPayPeriods
13
14     ' Display the salary per pay period.
15     lblSalary.Text = decSalary.ToString("c")
16
17   Catch ex As Exception
18     ' Display the default error message.
19     MessageBox.Show(ex.Message)
20   End Try
21 End Sub
```

The statement in line 19 simply passes the exception object's Message property to the `MessageBox.Show` method. This causes the default error message to be displayed in a message box. Figure 38 shows some examples.

Figure 38 Message boxes showing default exception messages

8 Group Boxes

CONCEPT: The GroupBox control is a container that is used to group other controls together.

Group Boxes

A group box is a rectangular border with an optional title that appears in the border's upper left corner. Other controls may be placed inside a group box. You can give forms a more organized look by grouping related controls together inside group boxes.

In Visual Basic, you use the **GroupBox control** to create a group box with an optional title. The title is stored in the GroupBox control's Text property. Figure 39 shows a GroupBox control. The control's Text property is set to *Personal Data*, and a group of other controls are inside the group box.

Figure 39 GroupBox containing other controls

Creating a Group Box and Adding Controls to It

To create a group box, select the *GroupBox* control from the *Containers* section of the *Toolbox* window and then draw the group box at the desired size on the form. To add another control to the group box, select the GroupBox control that you placed on the form, and then double-click the desired tool in the Toolbox to place another control inside the group box.

The controls you place inside a group box become part of a group. When you move a group box, the objects inside it move as well. When you delete a group box, the objects inside it are also deleted.

Moving an Existing Control to a Group Box

If an existing control is not inside a group box, but you want to move it to the group box, follow these steps:

1. Select the control you wish to add to the group box.
2. Cut the control to the clipboard.
3. Select the group box.
4. Paste the control.

Group Box Tab Order

The value of a control's TabIndex property is handled differently when the control is placed inside a GroupBox control. GroupBox controls have their own TabIndex property and the TabIndex value of the controls inside the group box are relative to the GroupBox control's TabIndex property. For example, Figure 40 shows a GroupBox control displayed in tab order selection mode. As you can see, the GroupBox control's TabIndex is set to 2. The TabIndex of the controls inside the group box are displayed as 2.0, 2.1, 2.2, and so on.

NOTE: The TabIndex properties of the controls inside the group box will not appear this way in the *Properties* window. They will appear as 0, 1, 2, and so on.

Figure 40 Group box TabIndex values

Assigning an Access Key to a GroupBox Control

Although GroupBox controls cannot receive the focus, you can assign a keyboard access key to them by preceding a character in their Text property with an ampersand (&). When the user enters the access key, the focus moves to the control with the lowest TabIndex value inside the group box.

Selecting and Moving Multiple Controls

It is possible to select multiple controls and work with them all at once. For example, you can select a group of controls and move them all to a different location on the form. You can also select a group of controls and change some of their properties.

Select multiple controls by using one of the following techniques:

- Position the cursor over an empty part of the form near the controls you wish to select. Click and drag a selection box around the controls. This is shown in Figure 41. When you release the mouse button, all the controls that are partially or completely enclosed in the selection box will be selected.
- Hold down the Ctrl key while clicking each control you wish to select.

After using either of these techniques, all the controls you have selected will appear with sizing handles. You may now move them, delete them, or use the *Properties* window to set many of their properties to the same value.

Figure 41 Selecting multiple controls by clicking and dragging the mouse

TIP: In a group of selected controls, it is easy to deselect a control that you have accidentally selected. Simply hold down the Ctrl key and click the control you wish to deselect.

9 The Load Event

CONCEPT: When an application's form loads into memory, an event known as the Load event takes place. You can write an event handler for the Load event, and that handler will execute just before the form is displayed.

When you run an application, the application's form is loaded into memory and an event known as the **Load event** takes place. The Load event takes place before the form is displayed on the screen. If you want to execute some code at this point, you can write the code in the form's Load event handler.

To create a Load event handler for a form, simply double-click any area of the form in the *Designer* window, where there is no other control. The *Code* window will open with a template for the form's Load event handler. The following is an example of a Load event handler that displays a message box. When the application runs, the message box will appear before the Form1 form is displayed.

```
Private Sub Form1_Load(...) Handles MyBase.Load
    MessageBox.Show("Prepare to see the form!")
End Sub
```

(In the *Chap3* folder of student sample programs you will find a project named *Load Event Demo* that demonstrates this event handler.) In the next section you will develop an application that displays the current date and time on the application's form. You will accomplish this by writing code in the form's Load event handler that retrieves the date and time from the system.

Checkpoint

43 How is a group box helpful when designing a form with a large number of controls?

44 When placing a new control inside an existing GroupBox control, what must you do before you double-click the new control in the *ToolBox*?

45 How is the clipboard useful when you want to move an existing control into a group box?

46 How does the tab order of controls inside a group box correspond to the tab order of other controls outside the group box?

47 What event happens just before a form is displayed on the screen?

10 Focus on Program Design and Problem Solving: Building the *Room Charge Calculator* Application

A guest staying at the Highlander Hotel may incur the following types of charges:

- Room charges, based on a per-night rate
- Room service charges
- Telephone charges
- Miscellaneous charges

The manager of the Highlander Hotel has asked you to create an application that calculates the guest's total charges. Figure 42 shows how the application's form should appear.

Figure 42 Sample output from the *Room Charge Calculator* application

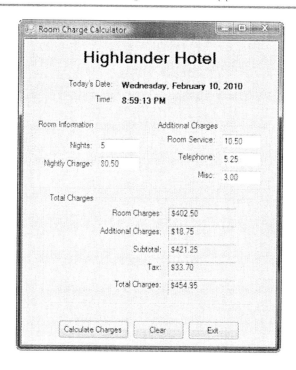

Figure 43 shows how the controls are arranged on the form with names. You can use this diagram when designing the form and assigning values to the Name property of each control. Table 20, located at the end of this section, can also be used as a reference.

Figure 43 Named controls

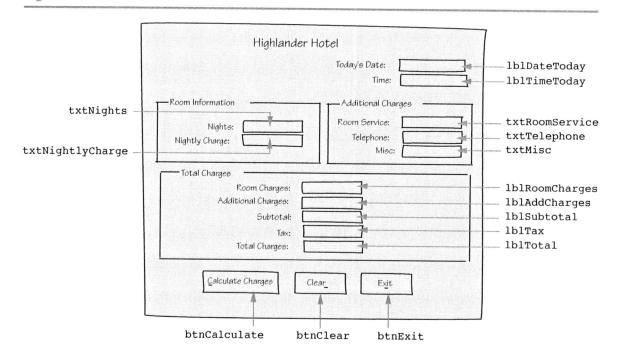

Table 19 lists and describes the event handlers needed for this application. Notice that a Load event handler is needed for the form.

Table 19 Event handlers in the *Room Charge Calculator* application

Method	Description
btnCalculate_Click	Calculates the room charges, additional charges, subtotal (room charges plus additional charges), 8% tax, and the total charges. These values are assigned to the Text properties of the appropriate labels.
btnClear_Click	Clears the TextBox controls, and the labels used to display summary charge information. This procedure also resets the values displayed in the lblDateToday and lblTimeToday labels.
btnExit_Click	Ends the application
Form1_Load	Initializes the lblDateToday and lblTimeToday labels with the current system date and time

Figure 44 shows the flowchart for the btnCalculate_Click procedure. The procedure uses the following Decimal variables:

```
decRoomCharges
decAddCharges
decSubtotal
decTax
decTotal
```

The procedure also uses a named constant, decTAX_RATE, to hold the tax rate.

Figure 44 Flowchart for btnCalculate_Click

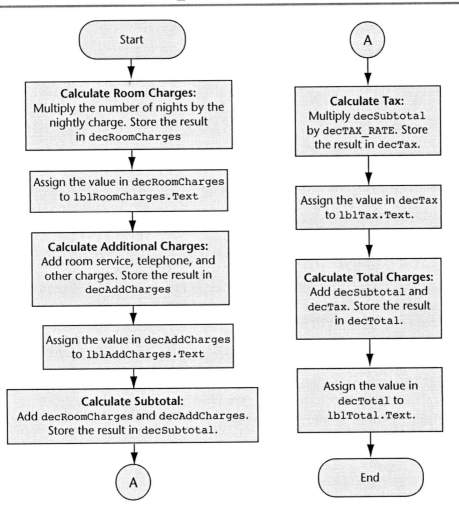

The flowchart in Figure 44 uses a new symbol: (Ⓐ)

This is called the **connector symbol** and is used when a flowchart is broken into two or more smaller flowcharts. This is necessary when a flowchart does not fit on a single page or must be divided into sections. A connector symbol, which is a small circle with a letter or number inside it, allows you to connect two flowcharts. In the flowchart shown in Figure 44, the (Ⓐ) connector indicates that the second flowchart segment begins where the first flowchart segment ends.

The flowcharts for the `btnClear_Click`, `btnExit_Click`, and `Form1_Load` procedures are shown in Figures 45, 46, and 47, respectively.

Recall that the form's `Load` procedure executes each time the form loads into memory. Tutorial 11 shows you how to create the *Room Charge Calculator* application.

Figure 45 Flowchart for `btnClear_Click`

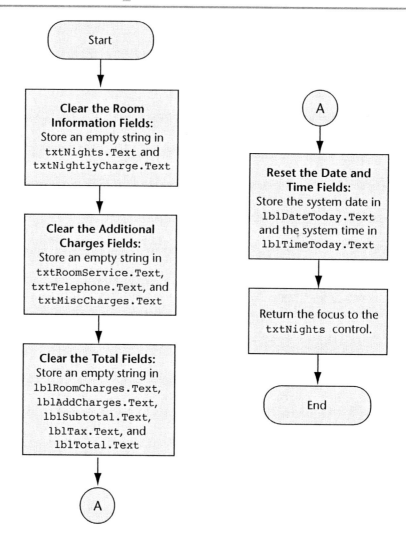

Figure 46 Flowchart for `btnExit_Click`

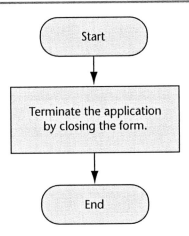

Figure 47 Flowchart for `Form1_Load` procedure

Tutorial 11:

Beginning the *Room Charge Calculator* application

Step 1: Create a new Windows Forms Application project named *Room Charge Calculator*.

Step 2: Figure 43 shows a sketch of the application's form and shows the names of the named controls. Refer to this figure as you set up the form and create the controls. Once you have completed the form, it should appear as shown in Figure 48.

Figure 48 The *Room Charge Calculator* form

TIP: Most of the controls are contained inside group boxes. Refer to Section 8 for instructions on creating controls inside a group box.

TIP: The TextBox controls are all the same size, and all the Label controls that display output are the same size. If you are creating many similar instances of a control, it is easier to create the first one, set its size and properties as needed, copy it to the clipboard, and then paste it onto the form to create another one.

Step 3: Table 20 lists the relevant property settings of all the controls on the form. Refer to this table and make the necessary property settings.

Step 4: Now you will write the application's event handlers, beginning with the form's Load event handler. Double-click any area of the form not occupied by another control. The *Code* window should open with a code template for the Form1_Load procedure. Complete the procedure by typing the following code shown in bold:

```
Private Sub Form1_Load(...) Handles MyBase.Load
    ' Get today's date from the system and display it.
    lblDateToday.Text = Now.ToString("D")

    ' Get the current time from the system and display it.
    lblTimeToday.Text = Now.ToString("T")
End Sub
```

Step 5: Double-click the *Calculate Charges* button. The *Code* window should open with a code template for the btnCalculate_Click procedure. Complete the procedure by typing the bold code shown in the following:

```
Private Sub btnCalculate_Click(...) Handles btnCalculate.Click
    ' Declare variables for the calculations.
    Dim decRoomCharges As Decimal        ' Room charges total
    Dim decAddCharges As Decimal         ' Additional charges
    Dim decSubtotal As Decimal           ' Subtotal
    Dim decTax As Decimal                ' Tax
    Dim decTotal As Decimal              ' Total of all charges
    Const decTAX_RATE As Decimal = 0.08D ' Tax rate

    Try
        ' Calculate and display the room charges.
        decRoomCharges = CDec(txtNights.Text) *
                         CDec(txtNightlyCharge.Text)
        lblRoomCharges.Text = decRoomCharges.ToString("c")

        ' Calculate and display the additional charges.
        decAddCharges = CDec(txtRoomService.Text) +
                        CDec(txtTelephone.Text) +
                        CDec(txtMisc.Text)
        lblAddCharges.Text = decAddCharges.ToString("c")

        ' Calculate and display the subtotal.
        decSubtotal = decRoomCharges + decAddCharges
        lblSubtotal.Text = decSubtotal.ToString("c")
```

```
        ' Calculate and display the tax.
        decTax = decSubtotal * decTAX_RATE
        lblTax.Text = decTax.ToString("c")

        ' Calculate and display the total charges.
        decTotal = decSubtotal + decTax
        lblTotal.Text = decTotal.ToString("c")
    Catch
        ' Error message
        MessageBox.Show("All input must be valid numeric values.")
    End Try
End Sub
```

Exception handling was used in this procedure to check for invalid input. If the user enters an invalid value in any of the text boxes, the message box shown in Figure 49 will appear, and then the user will be able to reenter the input. Imagine how much better this is than letting the program halt unexpectedly.

Figure 49 Message box displayed by the exception handler

Step 6: Open the *Design* window and double-click the *Clear* button. The *Code* window should open with a code template for the btnClear_Click procedure. Complete the procedure by typing the following code shown in bold.

```
Private Sub btnClear_Click(...) Handles btnClear.Click
    ' Clear the room info fields.
    txtNights.Clear()
    txtNightlyCharge.Clear()

    ' Clear the additional charges fields.
    txtRoomService.Clear()
    txtTelephone.Clear()
    txtMisc.Clear()

    ' Clear the decTotal fields.
    lblRoomCharges.Text = String.Empty
    lblAddCharges.Text = String.Empty
    lblSubtotal.Text = String.Empty
    lblTax.Text = String.Empty
    lblTotal.Text = String.Empty

    ' Get today's date from the operating system and display it.
    lblDateToday.Text = Now.ToString("D")

    ' Get the current time from the operating system and display it.
    lblTimeToday.Text = Now.ToString("T")

    ' Reset the focus to the first field.
    txtNights.Focus()
End Sub
```

Step 7: Open the *Design* window and double-click the *Exit* button. The *Code* window should open with a code template for the `btnExit_Click` procedure. Complete the procedure by typing the following code shown in bold.

```
Private Sub btnExit_Click(...) Handles btnExit.Click
    ' Close the form.
    Me.Close()
End Sub
```

Step 8: Save the project.

Step 9: Run the application. If there are errors, compare your code with that shown, and correct them. Once the application runs, enter test values, as shown in Figure 50 for the charges and confirm that it displays the correct output.

Figure 50 Sample output from the *Room Charge Calculator* application

Table 20 lists each control, along with any relevant property values.

Table 20 Named controls in *Room Charge Calculator* form

Control Type	Control Name	Property	Property Value
Label	(Default)	Text: Font:	Highlander Hotel MS sans serif, bold, 18 point
Label	(Default)	Text:	Today's Date:
Label	lblDateToday	Text: AutoSize: Font.Bold:	(Initially cleared) False True
Label	(Default)	Text:	Time:
Label	lblTimeToday	Text: AutoSize: Font.Bold:	(Initially cleared) False True
Group box	(Default)	Text:	Room Information
Label	(Default)	Text:	Nights:
TextBox	txtNights	Text:	(Initially cleared)
Label	(Default)	Text:	Nightly Charge:
TextBox	txtNightlyCharge	Text:	(Initially cleared)
Group box	(Default)	Text:	Additional Charges
Label	(Default)	Text:	Room Service:
TextBox	txtRoomService	Text:	(Initially cleared)
Label	(Default)	Text:	Telephone:
TextBox	txtTelephone	Text:	(Initially cleared)
Label	(Default)	Text:	Misc:
TextBox	txtMisc	Text:	(Initially cleared)
Group box	(Default)	Text:	Total Charges
Label	(Default)	Text:	Room Charges:
Label	lblRoomCharges	Text: AutoSize: BorderStyle:	(Initially cleared) False Fixed3D
Label	(Default)	Text:	Additional Charges:
Label	lblAddCharges	Text: AutoSize: BorderStyle:	(Initially cleared) False Fixed3D
Label	(Default)	Text:	Subtotal:
Label	lblSubtotal	Text: AutoSize: BorderStyle:	(Initially cleared) False Fixed3D
Label	(Default)	Text:	Tax:
Label	lblTax	Text: AutoSize: BorderStyle:	(Initially cleared) False Fixed3D

(continued)

Table 20 Named controls in *Room Charge Calculator* form (*continued*)

Control Type	Control Name	Property	Property Value
Label	(Default)	Text:	*Total Charges:*
Label	lblTotal	Text:	(Initially cleared)
		AutoSize:	*False*
		BorderStyle:	*Fixed3D*
Button	btnCalculate	Text:	*C&alculate Charges*
Button	btnClear	Text:	*Clea&r*
Button	btnExit	Text:	*E&xit*

Changing Colors with Code (Optional Topic)

The foreground and background colors of a control's text can be changed by setting the ForeColor and BackColor properties in the *Properties* window. In addition to using the *Properties* window, you can also store values in these properties with code. Visual Basic provides numerous values that represent colors, and can be assigned to the ForeColor and BackColor properties in code. The following are a few of the values:

```
Color.Black
Color.Blue
Color.Cyan
Color.Green
Color.Magenta
Color.Red
Color.White
Color.Yellow
```

For example, assume an application has a Label control named lblMessage. The following code sets the label's background color to black and foreground color to yellow:

```
lblMessage.BackColor = Color.Black
lblMessage.ForeColor = Color.Yellow
```

Visual Basic also provides values that represent default colors on your system. For example, the value SystemColors.Control represents the default control background color and SystemColors.ControlText represents the default control text color. The following statements set the lblMessage control's background and foreground to the default colors.

```
lblMessage.BackColor = SystemColors.Control
lblMessage.ForeColor = SystemColors.ControlText
```

In Tutorial 12, you will modify the *Room Charge Calculator* application so that the total charges are displayed in white characters on a blue background. This will make the total charges stand out visually from the rest of the information on the form.

Tutorial 12:

Changing a label's colors

In this tutorial, you will modify two of the *Room Charge Calculator* application's event handlers: btnCalculate_Click and btnClear_Click. In the btnCalculate_Click procedure, you will add code that changes the lblTotal control's color settings just after the total charges are displayed. In the `btnClear_Click` procedure, you will add code that reverts `lblTotal`'s colors back to their normal state.

Step 1: With the *Room Charge Calculator* project open, open the *Code* window and scroll to the `btnCalculate_Click` event handler.

Step 2: The `btnCalculate_Click` procedure is shown as follows. Add the three lines shown in bold:

```
Private Sub btnCalculate_Click(...) Handles btnCalculate.Click
    ' Declare variables for the calculations.
    Dim decRoomCharges As Decimal          ' Room charges total
    Dim decAddCharges As Decimal           ' Additional charges
    Dim decSubtotal As Decimal             ' Subtotal
    Dim decTax As Decimal                  ' Tax
    Dim decTotal As Decimal                ' Total of all charges
    Const decTAX_RATE As Decimal = 0.08D   ' Tax rate

    Try
        ' Calculate and display the room charges.
        decRoomCharges = CDec(txtNights.Text) *
                         CDec(txtNightlyCharge.Text)
        lblRoomCharges.Text = decRoomCharges.ToString("c")

        ' Calculate and display the additional charges.
        decAddCharges = CDec(txtRoomService.Text) +
                        CDec(txtTelephone.Text) +
                        CDec(txtMisc.Text)
        lblAddCharges.Text = decAddCharges.ToString("c")

        ' Calculate and display the subtotal.
        decSubtotal = decRoomCharges + decAddCharges
        lblSubtotal.Text = decSubtotal.ToString("c")

        ' Calculate and display the tax.
        decTax = decSubtotal * decTAX_RATE
        lblTax.Text = decTax.ToString("c")

        ' Calculate and display the total charges.
        decTotal = decSubtotal + decTax
        lblTotal.Text = decTotal.ToString("c")

        ' Change the colors for the total charges.
        lblTotal.BackColor = Color.Blue
        lblTotal.ForeColor = Color.White
    Catch
        ' Error message
        MessageBox.Show("All input must be valid numeric values.")
    End Try
End Sub
```

Step 3: Add the following bold lines to the end of the `btnClear_Click` procedure, just before the line at the end that calls the `Focus` method. The existing line is shown to help you find the right location:

```
' Reset the lblTotal control's colors.
lblTotal.BackColor = SystemColors.Control
lblTotal.ForeColor = SystemColors.ControlText

' Reset the focus to the first field.
txtNights.Focus()
```

Step 4:   Save the project.

Step 5:   Run and test the application. When you click the *Calculate Charges* button, the value displayed in the lblTotal label should appear in white text on a blue background. When you click the *Clear* button, the color of the lblTotal label should return to normal.

11 More about Debugging: Locating Logic Errors

CONCEPT: Visual Studio allows you to pause a program, and then execute statements one at a time. After each statement executes, you may examine variable contents and property values.

A **logic error** is a mistake that does not prevent an application from running, but causes the application to produce incorrect results. Mathematical mistakes, assigning a value to the wrong variable, or assigning the wrong value to a variable are examples of logic errors. Logic errors can be difficult to find. Fortunately, Visual Studio provides you with debugging tools that make locating logic errors easier.

Visual Studio allows you to set breakpoints in your program code. A **breakpoint** is a line you select in your source code. When the application is running and it reaches a breakpoint, the application pauses and enters Break mode. While the application is paused, you may examine variable contents and the values stored in certain control properties.

Visual Studio allows you to **single-step** through an application's code once its execution has been paused by a breakpoint. This means that the application's statements execute one at a time, under your control. After each statement executes, you can examine variable and property values. This process allows you to identify the line or lines of code causing the error. In Tutorial 13, you single-step through an application's code.

Tutorial 13:
Single-stepping through an application's code at runtime

In this tutorial, you set a breakpoint in an application's code, run it in debugging mode, and single-step through the application's code to find a logic error.

Step 1:   Open the *Average Race Times* project from the student sample programs folder named *Chap3\Average Race Times*. As a reminder, this folder can be downloaded at www.microsoft.com/express/Downloads/.

Step 2:   Run the application. The application's form appears, as shown in Figure 51.

Step 3:   This application allows you to enter the finishing times of three runners in a race, and then see their average time. Enter **25** as the time for all three runners.

Step 4:   Click the *Calculate Average* button. The application displays the incorrect value 58.3 as the average time. (The correct value should be 25.)

Figure 51 *Average Race Times* form

Step 5: Click the *Exit* button to stop the application.

Step 6: Open the *Code* window and locate the following line of code, which appears in the btnCalculate_Click event handler:

```
dblRunner1 = CDbl(txtRunner1.Text)
```

This line of code is where we want to pause the execution of the application. We must make this line a breakpoint.

Step 7: Click the mouse in the left margin of the *Code* window, next to the line of code, as shown in Figure 52.

Figure 52 Click the mouse in the left margin of the *Code* window

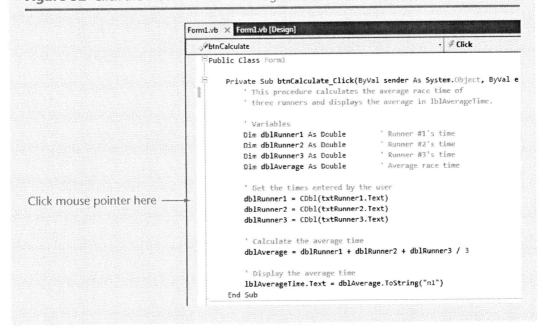

Step 8: Notice that a red dot appears next to the line in the left margin, and the line of code becomes highlighted. This is shown in Figure 53.

Figure 53 Breakpoint code highlighted

```
Form1.vb ×   Form1.vb [Design]
btnCalculate                                              ▾   Click
Public Class Form1

    Private Sub btnCalculate_Click(ByVal sender As System.Object, ByVal e
        ' This procedure calculates the average race time of
        ' three runners and displays the average in lblAverageTime.

        ' Variables
        Dim dblRunner1 As Double         ' Runner #1's time
        Dim dblRunner2 As Double         ' Runner #2's time
        Dim dblRunner3 As Double         ' Runner #3's time
        Dim dblAverage As Double         ' Average race time

        ' Get the times entered by the user
        dblRunner1 = CDbl(txtRunner1.Text)
        dblRunner2 = CDbl(txtRunner2.Text)
        dblRunner3 = CDbl(txtRunner3.Text)

        ' Calculate the average time
        dblAverage = dblRunner1 + dblRunner2 + dblRunner3 / 3

        ' Display the average time
        lblAverageTime.Text = dblAverage.ToString("n1")
    End Sub
```

The dot indicates that a breakpoint has been set on this line. Another way to set a breakpoint is to move the text cursor to the line you wish to set as a breakpoint, and then press [F9].

Step 9: Now that you have set the breakpoint, run the application. When the form appears, enter **25** as the time for each runner.

Step 10: Click the *Calculate Average* button. When program execution reaches the breakpoint, it goes into Break mode and the *Code* window reappears. The breakpoint line is shown with yellow highlighting and a small yellow arrow appears in the left margin, as shown in Figure 54.

Figure 54 Breakpoint during Break mode

```
Form1.vb ×   Form1.vb [Design]
btnCalculate                                              ▾   Click
Public Class Form1

    Private Sub btnCalculate_Click(ByVal sender As System.Object, ByVal e As Sy:
        ' This procedure calculates the average race time of
        ' three runners and displays the average in lblAverageTime.

        ' Variables
        Dim dblRunner1 As Double         ' Runner #1's time
        Dim dblRunner2 As Double         ' Runner #2's time
        Dim dblRunner3 As Double         ' Runner #3's time
        Dim dblAverage As Double         ' Average race time

        ' Get the times entered by the user
        dblRunner1 = CDbl(txtRunner1.Text)
        dblRunner2 = CDbl(txtRunner2.Text)
        dblRunner3 = CDbl(txtRunner3.Text)
```

The yellow highlighting and small arrow indicate the application's current execution point. The **execution point** is the next line of code that will execute. (The line has not yet executed.)

> **NOTE:** If the highlighting and arrow appear in a color other than yellow, the color options on your system may have been changed.

Step 11: To examine the contents of a variable or control property, hover the cursor over the variable or the property's name in the *Code* window. A small box will appear showing the variable or property's contents. For example, Figure 55 shows the result of hovering the mouse pointer over the expression `txtRunner1.Text` in the highlighted line. The box indicates that the property is currently set to 25.

Figure 55 `txtRunner1.Text` property contents revealed

```
        ' Get the times entered by the user
        dblRunner1 = CDbl(txtRunner1.Text)
        dblRunner2 = CDbl(txtRunner2.Te     txtRunner1.Text  Q ▾ "25" ⌦
        dblRunner3 = CDbl(txtRunner3.Text)

        ' Calculate the average time
        dblAverage = dblRunner1 + dblRunner2 + dblRunner3 / 3

        ' Display the average time
        lblAverageTime.Text = dblAverage.ToString("n1")
    End Sub
```

Step 12: Now hover the mouse pointer over the variable name `dblRunner1`. A box appears indicating that the variable is set to 0.0. Because the highlighted statement has not yet executed, no value has been assigned to this variable.

Step 13: You may also examine the contents of variables with the *Autos*, *Locals*, and *Watch* windows.

A description of each window follows:

- The *Autos* window (Visual Studio only) displays a list of the variables appearing in the current statement, the three statements before, and the three statements after the current statement. The current value and the data type of each variable are also displayed.
- The *Immediate* window allows you to type debugging commands using the keyboard. This window is generally used by advanced programmers.
- The *Locals* window displays a list of all the variables in the current procedure. The current value and the data type of each variable are also displayed.
- The *Watch* window allows you to add the names of variables you want to watch. This window displays only the variables you have added. Visual Studio lets you open multiple *Watch* windows, whereas Visual Basic Express offers only one *Watch* window.

You can open any of these windows by selecting *Debug* on the menu bar, then selecting *Windows,* and then selecting the window that you want to open. Use this technique to open the *Locals* window now.

The *Locals* window should appear, similar to Figure 56.

Figure 56 *Locals* window displayed

Locals		
Name	Value	Type
Me	{Average_Race_Times.Form1, Text: A...	Average_Race_Times.Form1
dblAverage	0.0	Double
dblRunner1	0.0	Double
dblRunner2	0.0	Double
dblRunner3	0.0	Double
e	{X = 16 Y = 15 Button = Left {1048576}}	System.EventArgs
sender	{Text = "Calculate &Average"}	Object

Locals Watch 2 Call Stack Immediate Window

Step 14: Now you are ready to single-step through each statement in the event handler. To do this, use the **Step Into** command. (The *Step Over* command, which is similar to *Step Into*.) You activate the *Step Into* command by one of the following methods:

- Press the F8 key.
- Select *Debug* from the menu bar, and then select *Step Into* from the *Debug* menu.

When you activate the *Step Into* command, the highlighted statement is executed. Press the F8 key now. Look at the *Watch* window and notice that the `dblRunner1` variable is now set to 25.0. Also notice that the next line of code is now highlighted.

Step 15: Press the F8 key two more times. The variables `dblRunner1`, `dblRunner2`, and `dblRunner3` should display values of 25.0 in the *Locals* window.

Step 16: The following statement, which is supposed to calculate the average of the three scores, is now highlighted:

```
dblAverage = dblRunner1 + dblRunner2 + dblRunner3 / 3
```

After this statement executes, the average of the three numbers should display next to `dblAverage`. Press F8 to execute the statement.

Step 17: Notice that the *Locals* window now reports that `dblAverage` holds the value 58.333333333333336. This is not the correct value, so there must be a problem with the math statement that just executed. Can you find it? The math statement does not calculate the correct value because the division operation takes place before any of the addition operations. You must correct the statement by inserting a set of parentheses.

From the menu, select *Debug*, and then click *Stop Debugging* to halt the application. In the *Code* window, insert a set of parentheses into the math statement so it appears as follows:

```
dblAverage = (dblRunner1 + dblRunner2 + dblRunner3) / 3
```

Step 18: Next, you will clear the breakpoint so the application will not pause again when it reaches that line of code. To clear the breakpoint, use one of the following methods:

- Click the mouse on the breakpoint dot in the left margin of the *Code* window.
- Press Ctrl+Shift+F9.
- Select *Debug* from the menu bar, and then select *Delete All Breakpoints* from the *Debug* menu.

Step 19: Run the application again. Enter **25** as each runner's time, and then click the *Calculate Average* button. This time the correct average, 25.0, is displayed.

Step 20: Click the *Exit* button to stop the application.

If You Want to Know More: Debugging Commands in the Toolbar

Visual Studio provides a toolbar for debugging commands, shown in Figure 57.

Figure 57 *Debug* toolbar commands

 Checkpoint

48 What is the difference between a syntax error and a logic error?

49 What is a breakpoint?

50 What is the purpose of single-stepping through an application?

Summary

1 Gathering Text Input

- Words and characters typed into a TextBox control are stored in the control's Text property. The standard prefix for TextBox control names is txt.
- The & operator is used to perform string concatenation.
- The control that has the focus receives the user's keyboard input or mouse clicks. The focus is moved by calling the Focus method.
- The order in which controls receive the focus when the [Tab] key is pressed at runtime is called the tab order. When you place controls on a form, the tab order will be the same sequence in which you created the controls. You can modify the tab order by changing a control's TabIndex property.
- Tab order selection mode allows you to easily view the TabIndex property values of all the controls on a form.
- If you do not want a control to receive the focus when the user presses the [Tab] key, set its TabStop property to *False*.
- You assign an access key to a button by placing an ampersand (&) in its Text property. The letter that immediately follows the ampersand becomes the access key. That letter appears underlined on the button.
- Forms have two properties named AcceptButton and CancelButton. AcceptButton refers to the control that will receive a Click event when the user presses the [Enter] key. CancelButton refers to the control that will receive a Click event when the user presses the [Esc] key.

2 Variables and Data Types

- The assignment operator (=) is used to store a value in a variable, just as with a control property. A variable's data type determines the type of information that the variable can hold.
- Rules for naming variables are enforced by the Visual Basic compiler. Naming conventions, on the other hand, are not rigid—they are based on a standard style of programming.
- When a variable is first created in memory, Visual Basic assigns it an initial value, which depends on its data type. You may also initialize a variable, which means that you specify the variable's starting value.
- Variables of the Date (DateTime) data type can hold a date and time. You may store values in a Date variable with date literals, strings, or user input.
- Each Visual Basic data type has a method named ToString that returns a string representation of the variable calling the method.

3 Performing Calculations

- A unary operator has only one operand. An example is the negation operator (minus sign).
- A binary operator has two operands. An example is the addition operator (plus sign).
- The \ symbol identifies the integer division operator.
- The * symbol identifies the multiplication operator.
- The ^ symbol identifies the exponentiation operator.
- The MOD operator returns the remainder after performing integer division.
- When two operators share an operand, the operator with the highest precedence executes first. Parts of a mathematical expression may be grouped with parentheses to force some operations to be performed before others.
- A combined assignment operator combines the assignment operator with another operator.

- The Now function retrieves the current date and time from the computer system. The TimeOfDay function retrieves the current time. The Today function retrieves the current date.
- A variable's scope determines where a variable is visible and where it can be accessed by programming statements.
- A variable declared inside a procedure is called a local variable. This type of variable is only visible from its declaring statement to the end of the same procedure. If a variable is declared inside a class, but outside of any procedure, it is called a class-level variable. If a variable is declared outside of any class or procedure, it is called a global variable.

4 Mixing Different Data Types

- Implicit type conversion occurs when you assign a value of one data type to a variable of another data type. Visual Basic attempts to convert the value being assigned to the data type of the destination variable.
- A narrowing conversion occurs when a real number is assigned to one of the integer type variables. It also occurs when a larger type is assigned to a smaller type.
- A widening conversion occurs when data of a smaller type is assigned to a variable of a larger type. An example is when assigning any type of integer to a Double.
- The *Option Strict* statement determines whether certain implicit conversions are legal. When *Option Strict* is *On*, only widening conversions are permitted. When *Option Strict* is *Off*, both narrowing and widening conversions are permitted.
- A type conversion or type mismatch error is generated when an automatic conversion is not possible.
- An explicit type conversion is performed by one of Visual Basic's conversion functions. The conversion functions discussed in this chapter are CDate (convert to date), CDbl (convert to Double), CDec (convert to Decimal), CInt (convert to Integer), and CStr (convert to String).
- The CInt function performs a special type of rounding called bankers rounding.
- Visual Basic provides several type conversion functions, such as CInt and CDbl, which convert expressions to other data types.

5 Formatting Numbers and Dates

- Ordinarily, numeric values should be formatted when they are displayed. Formatting gives your programs a more professional appearance.
- The ToString method converts the contents of a variable into a string.
- You can pass a format string as an input argument to the ToString method. The format string can be used to configure the way a number or date is displayed.
- Number format (n or N) displays numeric values with thousands separators and a decimal point.
- Fixed-point format (f or F) displays numeric values with no thousands separator and a decimal point.
- Exponential format (e or E) displays numeric values in scientific notation. The number is normalized with a single digit to the left of the decimal point.
- Currency format (c or C) displays a leading currency symbol (such as $), digits, thousands separators, and a decimal point.
- Percent format (p or P) causes the number to be multiplied by 100 and displayed with a trailing space and % sign.
- You can use the ToString method to format dates and times. Several standard formats were shown in this chapter: short date, long date, short time, long time, and full date and time.

6 Class-Level Variables

- Class-level variables are declared inside a class declaration (such as a form's class), but not inside of any procedure.
- Class-level variables are accessible to all of the procedures in a class.

7 Exception Handling

- Exception handling is a structured mechanism for handling errors in Visual Basic programs.
- Exception handling begins with the `Try` keyword, followed by one or more `Catch` blocks, followed by `End Try`.
- Some types of errors are preventable by the programmer, such as dividing by zero. Other errors may be caused by user input, which is beyond the control of the programmer.
- When a program throws an exception, it generates a runtime error. An unhandled exception causes a program to terminate and display an error message.
- You can write exception handlers that catch exceptions and find ways for the program to recover. Your exception handler can also display a message to the user.
- Exception handlers can handle multiple types of exceptions by specifically identifying different types of exceptions with different catch blocks.

8 Group Boxes

- A GroupBox control, which is used as a container for other controls, appears as a rectangular border with an optional title. You can create the GroupBox first and then create other controls inside it. Alternatively, you can drag existing controls inside the GroupBox.
- In the *Designer* window, grid lines can be used to align controls. You can select and work with multiple controls simultaneously.
- Every form causes a Load event to happen when the form loads into memory. If you need to execute code before a form is displayed, place it in the form's Load event handler.

9 Focus on Program Design and Problem Solving: Building the *Room Charge Calculator* Application

- The *Room Charge Calculator* application calculates charges for guests at an imaginary hotel. It combines many of the techniques introduced in this chapter, such as type conversion functions, formatting numbers, and formatting dates.
- Visual Basic provides numerous values that represent colors. These values may be used in code to change a control's foreground and background colors.

10 More about Debugging: Locating Logic Errors

- A logic error is a programming mistake that does not prevent an application from compiling, but causes the application to produce incorrect results.
- A runtime error occurs during a program's execution—it halts the program unexpectedly.
- A breakpoint is a line of code that causes a running application to pause execution and enter Break mode. While the application is paused, you may perform debugging operations such as examining variable contents and the values stored in control properties.
- Single-stepping is the debugging technique of executing an application's programming statements one at a time. After each statement executes, you can examine variable and property contents.

Key Terms

accept button
access key
argument
Autos window
binary operator
breakpoint
cancel button
Camel case
catch block
catch clause
code outlining
combined assignment operators
compound operators
connector symbol
exception
exception handler
exception object
execution point
focus
Focus method
function
GroupBox control
Immediate window
implicit type conversion
initialization
Load event handler
local variable
Locals window
logic error

mathematical expression
mnemonic
named constant
narrowing conversion
Option Strict
precedence
returning a value
scope (of a variable)
single-step
Step Into command
string concatenation
tab order
tab order selection mode
TabIndex property
TabStop property
text box
TextBox control
ToString method
truncation
Try block
Try-Catch statement
type conversion error
type mismatch error
variable
variable declaration
unary operator
Watch window
widening conversion

Review Questions and Exercises

Fill-in-the-Blank

1. The _____ control allows you to capture input the user has typed on the keyboard.

2. _____ is the prefix for TextBox control names.

3. _____ means that one string is appended to another.

4. The _____ character allows you to break a long statement into two or more lines of code.

5. The _____ character is actually two characters: a space followed by an underscore.

6. The control that has the _____ is the one that receives the user's keyboard input or mouse clicks.

7. The order in which controls receive the focus is called the _____.

8. You can modify the tab order by changing a control's _____ property.

9. If you do not want a control to receive the focus when the user presses the [Tab] key, set its _____ property to *False*.

10. An access key is a key that you press in combination with the _____ key to access a control such as a button quickly.

11. You define a button's access key through its _____ property.

12. A(n) _____ is a storage location in the computer's memory, used for holding information while the program is running.

13. A(n) _____ is a statement that causes Visual Basic to create a variable in memory.

14. A variable's _____ determines the type of information the variable can hold.

15. A(n) _____ variable is declared inside a procedure.

16. A(n) _____ error is generated anytime a nonnumeric value that cannot be automatically converted to a numeric value is assigned to a numeric variable or property.

17. A(n) _____ is a specialized routine that performs a specific operation, and then returns a value.

18. The _____ function converts an expression to an integer.

19. The _____ format string, when passed to the ToString method, produces a number in Currency format.

20. A(n) _____ is information that is being passed to a function.

21. When two operators share an operand, the operator with the highest _____ executes first.

22. A(n) _____ is like a variable whose content is read-only; it cannot be changed while the program is running.

23. A(n) _____ appears as a rectangular border with an optional title.

24. A form's _____ procedure executes each time a form loads into memory.

25. A(n) _____ is a line of code that causes a running application to pause execution and enter Break mode.

True or False

Indicate whether the following statements are true or false.

1. T F: The TextBox control's Text property holds the text entered by the user into the TextBox control at runtime.

2. T F: You can access a TextBox control's Text property in code.

3. T F: The string concatenation operator automatically inserts a space between the joined strings.

4. T F: You cannot break up a word with the line-continuation character.

5. T F: You can put a comment at the end of a line, after the line-continuation character.

6. T F: Only controls capable of receiving input, such as TextBox controls and buttons, may have the focus.

7. T F: You can cause a control to be skipped in the tab order by setting its `TabPosition` property to *False*.

8. T F: An error will occur if you assign a negative value to the TabIndex property in code.

9. T F: A control whose Visible property is set to *False* still receives the focus.

10. T F: GroupBox and Label controls have a TabIndex property, but they are skipped in the tab order.

11. T F: When you assign an access key to a button, the user can trigger a Click event by typing [Alt]+ the access key character.

12. T F: A local variable may be accessed by any other procedure in the same Form file.

13. T F: When a string variable is created in memory, Visual Basic assigns it the initial value 0.

14. T F: A variable's scope is the time during which the variable exists in memory.

15. T F: A variable declared inside a procedure is only visible to statements inside the same procedure.

16. T F: The `CDbl` function converts a number to a string.

17. T F: If the `CInt` function cannot convert its argument, it causes a runtime error.

18. T F: The multiplication operator has higher precedence than the addition operator.

19. T F: A named constant's value can be changed by a programming statement, while the program is running.

20. T F: The statement `lblMessage.BackColor = Color.Green` will set `lblMessage` control's background color to green.

21. T F: You can select multiple controls simultaneously with the mouse.

22. T F: You can change the same property for multiple controls simultaneously.

23. T F: To group controls in a group box, draw the controls first, then draw the group box around them.

24. T F: While single-stepping through an application's code in Break mode, the highlighted execution point is the line of code that has already executed.

Multiple Choice

1. When the user types input into a TextBox control, in which property is it stored?
   a. Input
   b. Text
   c. Value
   d. Keyboard

2. Which character is the string concatenation operator?
   a. &
   b. *
   c. %
   d. @

3. In code, you move the focus to a control with which method?

    a. `MoveFocus`
    b. `SetFocus`
    c. `ResetFocus`
    d. `Focus`

4. Which form property allows you to specify a button to be clicked when the user presses the [Enter] key?

    a. DefaultButton
    b. AcceptButton
    c. CancelButton
    d. EnterButton

5. Which form property allows you to specify a button that is to be clicked when the user presses the [Esc] key?

    a. DefaultButton
    b. AcceptButton
    c. CancelButton
    d. EnterButton

6. You can modify a control's position in the tab order by changing which property?

    a. TabIndex
    b. TabOrder
    c. TabPosition
    d. TabStop

7. You assign an access key to a button through which property?

    a. AccessKey
    b. AccessButton
    c. Mnemonic
    d. Text

8. A group box's title is stored in which property?

    a. Title
    b. Caption
    c. Text
    d. Heading

9. You declare a named constant with which keyword?

    a. `Constant`
    b. `Const`
    c. `NamedConstant`
    d. `Dim`

10. Which of the following is the part of a program in which a variable is visible and may be accessed by programming statement?

    a. segment
    b. lifetime
    c. scope
    d. module

11. If a variable named `dblTest` contains the value 1.23456, then which of the following values will be returned by the expression `dblTest.ToString("N3")`?
    a. 1.23456
    b. 1.235
    c. 1.234
    d. +1.234

12. If the following code executes, which value is assigned to `strA`?
    ```
    Dim dblTest As Double = 0.25
    Dim strA As String = dblTest.ToString("p")
    ```
    a. "0.25"
    b. "2.50"
    c. "25.00%"
    d. "0.25"

Short Answer

1. Describe the difference between the Label control's Text property and the TextBox control's Text property.

2. How do you clear the contents of a text box?

3. What is the focus when referring to a running application?

4. Write a statement that sets the focus to the `txtPassword` control.

5. How does Visual Basic automatically assign the tab order to controls?

6. How does a control's TabIndex property affect the tab order?

7. How do you assign an access key to a button?

8. How does assigning an access key to a button change the button's appearance?

9. What is the difference between the Single and Integer data types?

10. Create variable names that would be appropriate for holding each of the following information items:
    a. The number of backpacks sold this week
    b. The number of pounds of dog food in storage
    c. Today's date
    d. An item's wholesale price
    e. A customer's name
    f. The distance between two galaxies, in kilometers
    g. The number of the month (1 = January, 2 = February, and so on)

11. Why should you always make sure that a string variable is initialized or assigned a value before it is used in an operation?

12. When is a local variable destroyed?

13. How would the following strings be converted by the `CDec` function?
    a. "22.9000"
    b. "1xfc47uvy"
    c. "$19.99"
    d. "0.05%"
    e. `String.Empty`

14. Briefly describe how the `CDec` function converts a string argument to a number.

15. Complete the following table by providing the value of each mathematical expression:

Expression	Value
5 + 2 * 8	_____
20 / 5 – 2	_____
4 + 10 * 3 – 2	_____
(4 + 10) * 3 – 2	_____

16. Assuming that the variable `dblTest` contains the value 67521.584, complete the following table, showing the value returned by each function call:

Function Call	Return Value
dblTest.ToString("d2")	_____
dblTest.ToString("c2")	_____
dblTest.ToString("e1")	_____
dblTest.ToString("f2")	_____

17. Describe one way to select multiple controls in Design mode.

18. Describe three ways to set a breakpoint in an application's code.

What Do You Think?

1. Why doesn't Visual Basic automatically insert a space between strings concatenated with the & operator?

2. Why would you want to use the line-continuation character to cause a statement to span multiple lines?

3. Why are Label controls not capable of receiving the focus?

4. Why should the tab order of controls in your application be logical?

5. Why assign access keys to buttons?

6. What is the significance of showing an underlined character on a button?

7. Generally speaking, which button should be set as a form's default button?

8. Why can't you perform arithmetic operations on a string, such as `"28.9"`?

9. Suppose a number is used in calculations throughout a program and must be changed every few months. What benefit is there to using a named constant to represent the number?

10. How can you get your application to execute a group of statements each time a form is loaded into memory?

11. How can you place an existing control in a group box?

12. Visual Basic automatically reports syntax errors. Why doesn't it automatically report logic errors?

Find the Error

1. Load the *Chap3\ Error1\ Error1* project from the student sample programs folder. The `btnSum_Click` event handler has an error. Fix the error so the application correctly displays the sum of the numbers.

2. Load the *Chap3\ Error2\ Error2* project from the student sample programs folder. The application has an error. Find the error and fix it.

3. Load the *Chap3\ Error3\ Error3* project from the student sample programs folder. The `btnCalculate_Click` procedure contains an unusual error. Find the error and fix it.

Algorithm Workbench

1. Create a flowchart that shows the necessary steps for making the cookies in the following recipe:

   Ingredients:

1/2 cup butter	1/2 teaspoon vanilla
1 egg	1/2 teaspoon salt
1 cup sifted all-purpose flour	1/2 teaspoon baking soda
1/2 cup brown sugar	1/2 cup chopped nuts
1/2 cup sugar	1/2 cup semisweet chocolate chips

   Steps:
   Preheat oven to 375°.
   Cream the butter.
   Add the sugar and the brown sugar to the butter and beat until creamy.
   Beat the egg and vanilla into the mixture.
   Sift and stir the flour, salt, and baking soda into the mixture.
   Stir the nuts and chocolate chips into the mixture.
   Shape the mixture into 1/2-inch balls.
   Place the balls about one inch apart on a greased cookie sheet.
   Bake for 10 minutes.

2. A hot dog, still in its package, should be heated for 40 seconds in a microwave. Draw a flowchart showing the necessary steps to cook the hot dog.

3. The following pseudocode algorithm for the event handler `btnCalcArea_Click` has an error. The event handler is supposed to calculate the area of a room's floor. The area is calculated as the room's width (entered by the user into `txtWidth`), multiplied by the room's length (entered by the user into in `txtLength`). The result is displayed with the label `lblArea`. Find the error and correct the algorithm.

   a. Multiply the `intWidth` variable by the `intLength` variable and store the result in the `intArea` variable.

   b. Assign the value in `txtWidth.Text` to the `intWidth` variable.

   c. Assign the value in `txtLength.Text` to the `intLength` variable.

   d. Assign the value in the `intArea` variable to `lblArea.Text`.

4. The following steps should be followed in the event handler `btnCalcAvailCredit_Click`, which calculates a customer's available credit. Construct a flowchart that shows these steps.

   a. Assign the value in the TextBox control `txtMaxCredit` to the variable `decMaxCredit`.

   b. Assign the value in the `TextBox` control `txtUsedCredit` to the variable `decUsedCredit`.

   c. Subtract the value in `decUsedCredit` from `decMaxCredit`. Assign the result to `decAvailableCredit`

   d. Assign the value in `decAvailableCredit` to the label `lblAvailableCredit`.

5. Convert the flowchart you constructed in Exercise 4 into Visual Basic code.

6. Design a flowchart or pseudocode for the event handler `btnCalcSale_Click`, which calculates the total of a retail sale. Assume the program uses `txtRetailPrice`, a TextBox control that holds the retail price of the item being purchased, and `decTAX_RATE`, a constant that holds the sales tax rate. The event handler uses the items above to calculate the sales tax for the purchase and the total of the sale. Display the total of the sale in a label named `lblTotal`.

7. Convert the flowchart or pseudocode you constructed in Exercise 6 into Visual Basic code.

Programming Challenges

VideoNote

The Miles
per Gallon
Calculator
Problem

1. **Miles per Gallon Calculator**

   Create an application that calculates a car's gas mileage. The formula for calculating the miles that a car can travel per gallon of gas is:

   $$MPG = \frac{miles}{gallons}$$

   In the formula *MPG* is miles-per-gallon, *miles* is the number of miles that can be driven on a full tank of gas, and *gallons* is the number of gallons that the tank holds.

   The application's form should have TextBox controls that let the user enter the number of gallons of gas the tank holds, and the number of miles the car can be driven on a full tank. When the *Calculate MPG* button is clicked, the application should display the number of miles that the car can be driven per gallon of gas. The form should also have a *Clear* button that clears the input and results, and an *Exit* button that ends the application. The application's form should appear as shown in Figure 58.

Figure 58 *Miles per Gallon Calculator*

Use the following set of test data to determine if the application is calculating properly:

Gallons	Miles	Miles per Gallon
10	375	37.50
12	289	24.08
15	190	12.67

2. **Stadium Seating**

   There are three seating categories at an athletic stadium. For a baseball game, Class A seats cost $15 each, Class B seats cost $12 each, and Class C seats cost $9 each. Create an application that allows the user to enter the number of tickets sold for each class. The application should be able to display the amount of income generated from each class of ticket sales and the total revenue generated. The application's form should resemble the one shown in Figure 59.

Figure 59 *Stadium Seating* form

Use the following test data to determine if the application is calculating properly:

Ticket Sales	Revenue
Class A: 320	Class A: $4,800.00
Class B: 570	Class B: $6,840.00
Class C: 890	Class C: $8,010.00
	Total Revenue: $19,650.00
Class A: 500	Class A: $7,500.00
Class B: 750	Class B: $9,000.00
Class C: 1,200	Class C: $10,800.00
	Total Revenue: $27,300.00
Class A: 100	Class A: $1,500.00
Class B: 300	Class B: $3,600.00
Class C: 500	Class C: $4,500.00
	Total Revenue: $9,600.00

3. **Test Score Average**

Create an application that allows the user to enter five test scores. It should be able to calculate and display the average score. The application's form should resemble the one shown in Figure 60. Notice that the labels next to each TextBox control have been assigned an access key. Use a label to assign an access key indirectly to a TextBox control.

Figure 60 *Test Score Average* form

Use the following test data to determine if the application is calculating properly:

Test Scores   **Averages**

Test Score 1: 85   Average: 86.60
Test Score 2: 90
Test Score 3: 78
Test Score 4: 88
Test Score 5: 92

Test Score 1: 90   Average: 70.00
Test Score 2: 80
Test Score 3: 70
Test Score 4: 60
Test Score 5: 50

Test Score 1: 100   Average: 82.2
Test Score 2: 92
Test Score 3: 56
Test Score 4: 89
Test Score 5: 74

4. **Theater Revenue**

A movie theater only keeps a percentage of the revenue earned from ticket sales. The remainder goes to the movie company. Create an application that calculates and displays the following figures for one night's box office business at a theater:

a. *Gross revenue for adult tickets sold.* This is the amount of money taken in for all adult tickets sold.
b. *Net revenue for adult tickets sold.* This is the amount of money from adult ticket sales left over after the payment to the movie company has been deducted.
c. *Gross revenue for child tickets sold.* This is the amount of money taken in for all child tickets sold.
d. *Net revenue for child tickets sold.* This is the amount of money from child ticket sales left over after the payment to the movie company has been deducted.
e. *Total gross revenue.* This is the sum of gross revenue for adult and child tickets sold.
f. *Total net revenue.* This is the sum of net revenue for adult and child tickets sold.

The application's form should resemble the one shown in Figure 61.

Figure 61 *Theater Revenue* form

Assume the theater keeps 20% of its box office receipts. Use a named constant in your code to represent this percentage. Use the following test data to determine if the application is calculating properly:

Ticket Sales		Revenue	
Price per Adult Ticket:	$6.00	Gross Adult Ticket Sales:	$720.00
Adult Tickets Sold:	120	Gross Child Ticket Sales:	$288.00
Price per Child Ticket:	$4.00	Total Gross Revenue:	$1,008.00
Ticket Sales (*continued*)		Revenue (*continued*)	
Child Tickets Sold:	72	Net Adult Ticket Sales:	$144.00
		Net Child Ticket Sales:	$57.60
		Total Net Revenue:	$201.60

Design Your Own Forms

5. **How Many Widgets?**

   The Yukon Widget Company manufactures widgets that weigh 9.2 pounds each. Create an application that calculates how many widgets are stacked on a pallet, based on the total weight of the pallet. The user should be able to enter how much the pallet weighs alone and how much it weighs with the widgets stacked on it. The user should click a button to calculate and display the number of widgets stacked on the pallet. Use the following test data to determine if the application is calculating properly:

Pallet	Pallet and Widgets	Number of Widgets
100	5,620	600
75	1,915	200
200	9,400	1,000

6. **Celsius to Fahrenheit**

   Create an application that converts Celsius to Fahrenheit. The formula is $F = 1.8 * C + 32$ where F is the Fahrenheit temperature and C is the Celsius temperature. Use the following test data to determine if the application is calculating properly:

Celsius	Fahrenheit
100	212
0	32
56	132.8

7. **Currency**

   Create an application that converts U.S. dollar amounts to pounds, euros, and yen. The following conversion factors are not accurate, but you can use them in your application:

   1 dollar = 0.68 pound
   1 dollar = 0.83 euro
   1 dollar = 108.36 yen

   In your code, declare named constants to represent the conversion factors for the different types of currency. For example, you might declare the conversion factor for yen as follows:

   ```
   Const dblYEN_FACTOR As Double = 108.36
   ```

Use the named constants in the mathematical conversion statements. Use the following test data to determine whether the application is calculating properly:

Dollars	Conversion Values	
$100.00	Pounds:	68
	Euros:	83
	Yen:	10,836
$ 25.00	Pounds:	17
	Euros:	20.75
	Yen:	2,709
$ 1.00	Pounds:	0.68
	Euros:	0.83
	Yen:	108.36

8. **Monthly Sales Tax**

A retail company must file a monthly sales tax report listing the total sales for the month, and the amount of state and county sales tax collected. The state sales tax rate is 4% and the county sales tax rate is 2%. Create an application that allows the user to enter the total sales for the month. From this figure, the application should calculate and display the following:

a. The amount of county sales tax
b. The amount of state sales tax
c. The total sales tax (county plus state)

In the application's code, represent the county tax rate (0.02) and the state tax rate (0.04) as named constants. Use the named constants in the mathematical statements. Use the following test data to determine whether the application is calculating properly:

Total Sales	Tax Amounts	
9,500	County sales tax:	$190.00
	State sales tax:	$380.00
	Total sales tax:	$570.00
5,000	County sales tax:	$100.00
	State sales tax:	$200.00
	Total sales tax:	$300.00
15,000	County sales tax:	$300.00
	State sales tax:	$600.00
	Total sales tax:	$900.00

9. **Property Tax**

A county collects property taxes on the assessment value of property, which is 60% of the property's actual value. If an acre of land is valued at $10,000, its assessment value is $6,000. The property tax is then $0.64 for each $100 of the assessment value. The tax for the acre assessed at $6,000 will be $38.40. Create an application that displays the assessment value and property tax when a user enters the actual value of a property. Use the following test data to determine if the application is calculating properly:

Actual Property Value	Assessment and Tax	
100,000	Assessment value:	$ 60,000.00
	Property tax:	384.00
75,000	Assessment value:	45,000.00
	Property tax:	288.00
250,000	Assessment value:	150,000.00
	Property tax:	960.00

10. **Pizza Pi**

    Joe's Pizza Palace needs an application to calculate the number of slices a pizza of any size can be divided into. The application should do the following:

    a. Allow the user to enter the diameter of the pizza, in inches.
    b. Calculate the number of slices that can be cut from a pizza that size.
    c. Display a message that indicates the number of slices.

    To calculate the number of slices that can be cut from the pizza, you must know the following facts:

    a. Each slice should have an area of 14.125 inches.
    b. To calculate the number of slices, divide the area of the pizza by 14.125.

    The area of the pizza is calculated with the following formula:

    $$Area = \pi r^2$$

    NOTE: π is the Greek letter pi. 3.14159 can be used as its value. The variable r is the radius of the pizza. Divide the diameter by 2 to get the radius.

    Use the following test data to determine if the application is calculating properly:

Diameter of Pizza	Number of Slices
22 inches	27
15 inches	13
12 inches	8

11. **Distance Traveled**

    Assuming there are no accidents or delays, the distance that a car travels down the interstate can be calculated with the following formula:

    $$Distance = Speed \times Time$$

    Create a VB application that allows the user to enter a car's speed in miles-per-hour. When a button is clicked, the application should display the following:

    - The distance the car will travel in 5 hours
    - The distance the car will travel in 8 hours
    - The distance the car will travel in 12 hours

12. **Tip, Tax, and Total**

    Create a VB application that lets the user enter the food charge for a meal at a restaurant. When a button is clicked, it should calculate and display the amount of a 15 percent tip, 7 percent sales tax, and the total of all three amounts.

13. **Body Mass Index**

    Create a VB application that lets the user enter his or her weight (in pounds) and height (in inches). The application should calculate the user's body mass index (BMI). The BMI is often used to determine whether a person with a sedentary lifestyle is overweight or underweight for their height. A person's BMI is calculated with the following formula:

    $$BMI = weight \times 703 / height^2$$

14. **How Much Insurance?**

    Many financial experts advise that property owners should insure their homes or buildings for at least 80 percent of the amount it would cost to replace the structure. Create a VB application that lets the user enter the replacement cost of a building and then displays the minimum amount of insurance he or she should buy for the property.

15. **How Many Calories?**

    A bag of cookies holds 40 cookies. The calorie information on the bag claims that there are 10 "servings" in the bag and that a serving equals 300 calories. Create a VB application that lets the user enter the number of cookies they actually ate and then reports the number of total calories consumed.

16. **Automobile Costs**

    Create a VB application that lets the user enter the monthly costs for the following expenses incurred from operating his or her automobile: loan payment, insurance, gas, oil, tires, and maintenance. The program should then display the total monthly cost of these expenses and the total annual cost of these expenses.

Answers to Checkpoints

1 Text

2 `lblMessage.Text = txtInput.Text`

3 Hello Jonathon, how are you?

4 Appending one string to another.

5 The control is accepting keyboard and/or mouse input from the user.

6 `txtLastName.Focus()`

7 The order in which controls receive the focus when the user presses the Tab key.

8 The TabIndex property, which contains a numeric value, determines the position of a control in the tab order. The control that has the lowest TabIndex value (usually 0) on a form is the first in the tab order. The control with the next highest TabIndex (usually 1) will be the next in the tab order. This sequence continues.

9 In the order that controls are created

10 That control is skipped in the tab order.

11 The & character has two effects: It assigns an access key to the button (in this case, the access key is Alt+M because the & is in front of the M) and it causes the M to appear underlined on the button.

12 An accept button is a form's button that is clicked when the user presses the Enter key. A cancel button is a form's button that is clicked when the user presses the Esc key. You select accept and cancel buttons with the form's AcceptButton and CancelButton properties.

13 A variable is a storage location in the computer's memory; used for holding data while the program is running.

14 `Dim intCount As Integer`

15 `decInterestRate` is written with the convention used in this text.

16 a. `count`   Legal
   b. `rate*Pay`   Illegal; cannot use the * character
   c. `deposit.amount`   Illegal; cannot use a period
   d. `down_payment`   Legal

17 a. 0   d. 0
   b. 0.0   e. 12:00:00 AM, January 1 of year 1
   c. False

18 `#2/20/2010 5:35:00 PM#`

19 Charles Simonyi. He introduced the use of prefixes in variable names, called Hungarian Notation, a popular naming convention often used in Visual Basic and many other programming languages.

20 a. 21   d. 18
    b. 2   e. 3.0
    c. 17   f. 36

21 a. 1
    b. 2

22 `dtmThisTime = TimeOfDay`

23 `dtmCurrent = Now`

24 Integer division throws away any fractional part of the quotient. The result of integer division is always an integer.

25 `dblResult` will be set to `4.7`

26 `dblResult` will be set to `7.0`

27 `dblResult` will be set to `3.0`

28 a. 21
    b. 2
    c. 17
    d. 18

29 `dblResult` will be set to `28`

30 `dblResult` will be set to `186478.39`

31 A named constant is like a variable whose content is read-only, and cannot be changed by a programming statement while the program is running.

32 a. 27
    b. 13
    c. 12
    d. 18

33 `CDbl` function

34 a. 48   (rounds to nearest even integer)
    b. 35   (rounds up)
    c. 2300
    d. ** cannot be converted **

35 `dblSalary.ToString("c")`

36 a. `"c"`   d. `"p"`
    b. `"e"`   e. `"f"`
    c. `"n"`

37 `ToString("c")`

38

Number Value	Format String	ToString Value
12.3	n4	12.3000
12.348	n1	12.3
1234567.1	n3	1,234,567.100
123456.0	f1	123456.0
123456.0	e3	1.235E+005
.234	p2	23.40%
−1234567.8	c3	($1,234,567.800)

39 `datStart.ToString("T")`

40 `datBirth.ToString("D")`

41 Local variables are not visible to statements outside the procedure in which they are declared. Class-level variables are visible to all of the procedures in a class.

42 Class-level variables are declared at the class-level (inside the class, but not in any procedure).

43 You can make a form appear more organized by grouping related controls inside group boxes.

44 Select the GroupBox with the mouse.

45 Copy the control to the clipboard, select the GroupBox with the mouse, and then paste the control from the clipboard into the GroupBox.

46 The TabIndex value of the controls inside the GroupBox are relative to the GroupBox control's TabIndex property.

47 `Form_Load`

48 A compile error (or syntax error), will prevent an application from starting. Examples are misspelled keywords and incorrect use of operators or punctuation. Compiler errors are often reported as soon as you type them. A logic error is a programming mistake that does not prevent an application from starting, but causes the application to produce incorrect results. Examples are incorrect math statements and copying the wrong value to a variable.

49 A breakpoint is a line of code that causes a running application to pause execution and enter break mode. While the application is paused, you may perform debugging operations, such as examining variable contents and the values stored in control properties.

50 Single-stepping is a useful debugging technique for locating logic errors. In single-stepping, you execute an application's code one line at a time. After each line executes, you can examine variable and property contents. This process allows you to identify the line or lines of code causing the error.

Making Decisions

TOPICS

In this chapter, you will learn how programs use If...Then, If...Then...Else, and If...Then...ElseIf statements to make decisions. You will learn how to compare values using relational operators and build complex comparisons using logical operators. You will be introduced to the Select Case statement, radio buttons (which allow the user to select one choice from many possible choices), and check boxes (which allow the user to make on/off or yes/no types of selections). You will learn more about message boxes, which display messages to the user, and the process of input validation.

1 The Decision Structure

CONCEPT: The decision structure allows a program's logic to have more than one path of execution.

So far, you are probably familiar with statements that execute sequentially. This means that statements are executed one after the other, in the order in which they appear.

You might think of sequentially executed statements as the steps you take as you walk down a road. To complete the journey, you must start at the beginning and take each step, one after the other, until you reach your destination. This is illustrated in Figure 1.

Figure 1 Sequence instruction

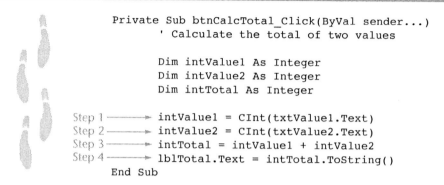

```
                Private Sub btnCalcTotal_Click(ByVal sender...)
                  ' Calculate the total of two values

                  Dim intValue1 As Integer
                  Dim intValue2 As Integer
                  Dim intTotal As Integer

Step 1 ────────► intValue1 = CInt(txtValue1.Text)
Step 2 ────────► intValue2 = CInt(txtValue2.Text)
Step 3 ────────► intTotal = intValue1 + intValue2
Step 4 ────────► lblTotal.Text = intTotal.ToString()
                End Sub
```

This type of code is called a **sequence structure** because the statements are executed in sequence, without branching in another direction. Programs often need more than one path of execution because many algorithms require a program to execute some statements only under certain circumstances. This can be accomplished with a **decision structure**.

Decision Structures in Flowcharts and Pseudocode

In a decision structure's simplest form, an expression is tested for a true or false value. If the expression is true, an action is performed. If the expression is false, the action is not performed. Figure 2 shows a flowchart segment for a decision structure. The diamond symbol represents a yes/no question, or a true/false expression. If the answer to the question is *yes* (or if the expression is true), the program follows one path. If the answer to the question is *no* (or the expression is false), the program follows another path.

In the flowchart, the action *Wear a coat* is performed only when it is cold outside. If it is not cold outside, the action is skipped. The action is **conditionally executed** because it is performed only when a certain condition (*cold outside*) exists. Figure 3 shows a more elaborate flowchart, where three actions are taken, only when it is cold outside.

Decision structures can also be expressed as pseudocode. For example, the decision structure shown in Figure 2 can be expressed as

> *If it is cold outside Then*
> > *Wear a coat.*
> *End If*

The *End If* statement marks the end of the decision structure in pseudocode. The statements appearing between *If...Then* and *End If* are executed only when it is cold outside. The decision structure shown in Figure 3, which conditionally executes three actions, can be expressed as

> *If it is cold outside Then*
> > *Wear a coat.*
> > *Wear a hat.*
> > *Wear gloves.*
> *End If*

Figure 2 Simple decision structure flowchart

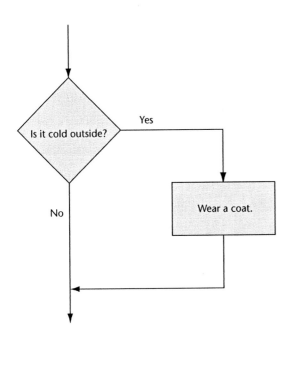

Figure 3 Three-action decision structure flowchart

VideoNote

The If...
Then
Statement

2 The If...Then Statement

CONCEPT: The If...Then statement causes other statements to execute only when an expression is true.

One way to code a decision structure in Visual Basic is with the If...Then statement. Here is the general form of the If...Then statement.

```
If expression Then
    statement
    (more statements may follow)
End If
```

The If...Then statement is really very simple: if the *expression* is true, the statement or statements that appear between the If...Then and the End If are executed. Otherwise, the statements are skipped.

Boolean Expressions and Relational Operators

The expression that is tested in an If...Then statement can be either True or False. Such an expression is known as a **Boolean expression**. Special operators known as relational operators are commonly used in Boolean expressions. A **relational operator** determines

213

whether a specific relationship exists between two values. For example, the greater-than operator (>) determines whether one value is greater than another value. The equal to operator (=) determines two values are the same. Table 1 lists the Visual Basic relational operators.

Table 1 Visual Basic relational operators

Relational Operator	Meaning
>	Greater than
<	Less than
=	Equal to
<>	Not equal to
>=	Greater than or equal to
<=	Less than or equal to

All relational operators are binary, which means they use two operands. Here is an example of an expression using the greater than operator:

```
length > width
```

This expression determines whether the value of length is greater than the value of width. If length is greater than width, the value of the expression is true. Otherwise, the value of the expression is false. Because the expression can be only true or false, it is a Boolean expression. The following expression uses the less than operator (<) to determine whether length is less than width:

```
length < width
```

Table 2 shows examples of several relational expressions that compare the variables x and y.

Table 2 Boolean expressions using relational operators

Relational Expression	Meaning
$x > y$	Is x greater than y?
$x < y$	Is x less than y?
$x >= y$	Is x greater than or equal to y?
$x <= y$	Is x less than or equal to y?
$x = y$	Is x equal to y?
$x <> y$	Is x not equal to y?

The = operator, when used in a relational expression, determines whether the operand on its left is equal to the operand on its right. If both operands have the same value, the expression is true. Assuming that a is 4, the expression $a = 4$ is true and the expression $a = 2$ is false.

There are two operators that can test more than one relationship at the same time. The >= operator determines whether the operand on its left is greater than or equal to the operand on the right. Assuming that a is 4, b is 6, and c is 4, the expressions $b >= a$ and $a >= c$ are true, and $a >= 5$ is false. When using this operator, the > symbol must precede the = symbol, with no space between them.

The <= operator determines whether the left operand is less than or equal to the right operand. Once again, assuming that *a* is 4, *b* is 6, and *c* is 4, both *a* <= *c* and *b* <= 10 are true, but *b* <= *a* is false. When using this operator, the < symbol must precede the = symbol, with no space between them.

The <> operator is the *not equal* operator. It determines whether the operand on its left is not equal to the operand on its right, which is the opposite of the = operator. As before, assuming *a* is 4, *b* is 6, and *c* is 4, both *a* <> *b* and *b* <> *c* are true because a is not equal to *b* and *b* is not equal to *c*. However, *a* <> *c* is false because *a* is equal to *c*. Values compared by a relational expression need not be exactly the same type. Suppose we compare a variable of type Single to an integer constant, as in the following:

```
sngTemperature > 40
```

In this example, the integer 40 is temporarily converted to a Single so the comparison can take place. You do not have to worry about doing this conversion. It is carried out automatically by the Visual Basic compiler. Similarly, we might want to compare a Double to a Single, as in the following:

```
dblTemperature < sngBoilingPoint
```

The value of `sngBoilingPoint` is automatically converted to type Double so the values can be compared.

Putting It All Together

Let's look at an example of an `If...Then` statement:

```
If decSales > 50000 Then
   MessageBox.Show("You've earned a bonus!")
End If
```

This statement uses the > operator to determine whether `decSales` is greater than 50000. If expression `decSales > 50000` is true, the message *You've earned a bonus!* is displayed in a message box.

The following example conditionally executes multiple statements.

```
If decSales > 50000 Then
   MessageBox.Show("You've earned a bonus!")
   decCommissionRate = 0.12
   intDaysOff = intDaysOff + 1
End If
```

Here are some specific rules to remember about the `If...Then` statement:

- The words `If` and `Then` must appear on the same line.
- Nothing other than a comment can appear after the `Then` keyword, on the same line.
- The `End If` statement must be on a line by itself. Only a comment may follow it on the same line.

Tutorial 1 examines an application that uses the `If...Then` statement.

Tutorial 1:

Examining an application that uses the If...Then statement

Step 1: Open the *Test Score Average 1* project from the student sample programs folder named *Chap4\Test Score Average 1*. The student sample programs folder can be downloaded from www.microsoft.com/express/Downloads/.

Step 2: Run the application. The form appears, as shown in Figure 4.

Step 3: Enter the following test scores in the three text boxes: **80, 90, 75**.

Step 4: Click the *Calculate Average* button. The average test score is displayed.

Step 5: Click the *Clear* button, and then enter the following test scores in the three text boxes: **100, 97, 99**.

Step 6: Click the *Calculate Average* button. This time, in addition to the average test score being displayed, the message *Congratulations! Great Job!* also appears. The form appears, as shown in Figure 5.

Figure 4 *Test Score Average* form

Figure 5 Average and message displayed

Step 7: Click the *Exit* button to terminate the application.

Step 8: Open the *Code* window and find the btnCalculate_Click event handler. The code is as follows:

```
Private Sub btnCalculate_Click(...) Handles btnCalculate.Click
    ' Variables to hold scores and the average score
    Dim dblScore1 As Double
    Dim dblScore2 As Double
    Dim dblScore3 As Double
    Dim dblAverage As Double

    ' Constant for a high score.
    Const dblHIGH_SCORE As Double = 95.0

    Try
        ' Copy the TextBox scores into the variables.
        dblScore1 = CDbl(txtScore1.Text)
        dblScore2 = CDbl(txtScore2.Text)
        dblScore3 = CDbl(txtScore3.Text)
```

```
            ' Calculate the average score.
            dblAverage = (dblScore1 + dblScore2 + dblScore3) / 3.0

            ' Display the average, rounded to 2 decimal places.
            lblAverage.Text = dblAverage.ToString("n2")

            ' If the score is high, compliment the student.
            If dblAverage > dblHIGH_SCORE Then
                lblMessage.Text = "Congratulations! Great Job!"
            End If
        Catch
            ' Display an error message.
            MessageBox.Show("Scores must be numeric.")
        End Try
    End Sub
```

Notice that at the end of the try block, the following `If...Then` statement appears:

```
If dblAverage > 95 Then
    lblMessage.Text = "Congratulations! Great Job!"
End If
```

This statement determines whether the average is greater than 95, and if so, displays *Congratulations! Great Job!* in the `lblMessage` label.

Programming Style and the `If...Then` Statement

When you type an `If...Then` statement, Visual Studio automatically indents the conditionally executed statements. This is not a syntax requirement, but a programming style convention. For example, compare the following statements:

```
If decSales > 50000 Then
    MessageBox.Show("You've earned a bonus!")
    decCommissionRate = 0.12
    intDaysOff = intDaysOff + 1
End If

If decSales > 50000 Then
MessageBox.Show("You've earned a bonus!")
decCommissionRate = 0.12
intDaysOff = intDaysOff + 1
End If
```

Both `If...Then` statements produce the same result. The first example, however, is more readable to the human eye than the second because the conditionally executed statements are indented.

NOTE: If the automatic indenting feature has been turned off, you can turn it on by clicking *Tools* on the menu bar, then clicking *Options*. In the *Options* window, perform the following:

- Click the *Show all settings* check box. Then, click *Text Editor* in the left pane, then click *Basic*, then click *Tabs*. Make sure *Smart* is selected in the dialog box under *Indenting*.
- In the left pane, click *VB Specific*. Make sure *Automatic Insertion of end constructs* and *Pretty listing (reformatting) of code* are both checked.

Using Relational Operators with Math Operators

It is possible to use a relational operator and math operators in the same expression. Here is an example:

```
If intX + intY > 20 Then
   lblMessage.Text = "It is true!"
End If
```

When a relational operator appears in the same expression as one or more math operators, the math operators always execute first. In this statement, the + operator adds intX and intY. The result is compared to 20 using the > operator. Here is another example:

```
If intX + intY > intA - intB Then
   lblMessage.Text = "It is true!"
End If
```

In this statement, the result of intX + intY is compared, using the > operator, to the result of intA − intB.

Most programmers prefer to use parentheses to clarify the order of operations. Relying on operator precedence rules is risky because the rules are hard to remember. Here is a preferred way to write the foregoing If...Then statement:

```
If (intX + intY) > (intA − intB) Then
   lblMessage.Text = "It is true!"
End If
```

Using Function Calls with Relational Operators

It is possible to compare the return value of a function call with another value, using a relational operator. Here is an example:

```
If CInt(txtInput.Text) < 100 Then
   lblMessage.Text = "It is true!"
End If
```

This If...Then statement calls the CInt function to get the integer value of txtInput.Text. The function's return value is compared to 100 by the < operator. If the result of CInt(txtInput.Text) is less than 100, the assignment statement is executed.

Using Boolean Variables as Flags

A **flag** is a Boolean variable that signals when some condition exists in the program. When the flag is set to *False*, it indicates the condition does not yet exist. When the flag is set to *True*, it means the condition does exist. Look at the following code, which uses a Boolean variable named blnQuotaMet.

```
If blnQuotaMet Then
   lblMessage.Text = "You have met your sales quota"
End If
```

The preceding statement assigns the string "You have met your sales quota" to lblMessage.Text if the Boolean variable equals *True*. If blnQuotaMet is *False*, the assignment statement is not executed. It is not necessary to use the = operator to compare the variable to *True*. The statement is equivalent to the following:

```
If blnQuotaMet = True Then
   lblMessage.Text = "You have met your sales quota"
End If
```

Checkpoint

1 Assuming *x* is 5, *y* is 6, and *z* is 8, indicate whether each of the following relational expressions equals *True* or *False*:

a. $x = 5$	T	F		e. $z <> 4$	T	F
b. $7 <= (x + 2)$	T	F		f. $x >= 6$	T	F
c. $z < 4$	T	F		g. $x <= (y * 2)$	T	F
d. $(2 + x) <> y$	T	F				

2 In the following `If...Then` statement, assume that `blnIsInvalid` is a Boolean variable. Exactly what condition is being tested?

```
If blnIsInvalid Then
    ' Do something
End If
```

3 Do both of the following `If...Then` statements perform the same operation?

```
If decSales > 10000 Then
    decCommissionRate = 0.15
End If
If decSales > 10000 Then
decCommissionRate = 0.15
End If
```

4 Of the two `If...Then` statements shown in Checkpoint 3, which is preferred, and why?

3 The `If...Then...Else` Statement

CONCEPT: The `If...Then...Else` statement executes one group of statements if the Boolean expression is true and another group of statements if the Boolean expression is false.

The `If...Then...Else` statement is an expansion of the `If...Then` statement. Here is its format:

```
If condition Then
    statement
    (more statements may follow)
Else
    statement
    (more statements may follow)
End If
```

As in an `If...Then` statement, a Boolean expression is evaluated. If the expression is true, a statement or group of statements is executed. If the expression is false, a separate group of statements is executed, as in the following.

```
If dblTemperature < 40 Then
    lblMessage.Text = "A little cold, isn't it?"
Else
    lblMessage.Text = "Nice weather we're having!"
End If
```

The `Else` clause specifies a statement or group of statements to be executed when the Boolean expression is false. In the preceding example, if the expression `dblTemperature < 40` is false, the statement appearing after the `Else` clause is executed.

VideoNote

The `If...Then...Else` Statement

The If...Then...Else statement follows only one of the two paths. If you think of the statements in a computer program as steps taken down a road, consider the If...Then...Else statement as a fork in the road. Instead of being a momentary detour, like an If...Then statement, the If...Then...Else statement causes the program execution to follow one of two exclusive paths. Figure 6 shows a flowchart for this type of decision structure.

Figure 6 Flowchart for If...Then...Else statement

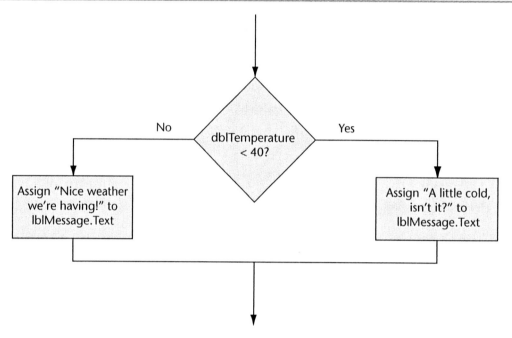

The logic shown in the flowchart in Figure 6 can also be expressed in pseudocode:

If temperature < 40 Then
  Display the message "A little cold, isn't it?"
Else
  Display the message "Nice weather we're having!"
End If

In Tutorial 2 you complete an application that uses the If...Then...Else statement.

Tutorial 2:

Completing an application that uses the
If...Then...Else statement

VideoNote

Tutorial 4-2
Walkthrough

Step 1: Open the *Test Score Average 2* project from the student sample programs folder named *Chap4\Test Score Average 2*. (This is a modification of the *Test Score Average 1* application from Tutorial 1.)

Step 2: Double-click the *Calculate Average* button. The *Code* window will open and show the btnCalculate_Click event handler, which is shown as follows. Complete the event handler by writing the code shown in bold:

```
Private Sub btnCalculate_Click(...) Handles btnCalculate.Click
    ' Variables to hold scores and the average score
    Dim dblScore1 As Double
    Dim dblScore2 As Double
    Dim dblScore3 As Double
    Dim dblAverage As Double
```

```
' Constant for a high score.
Const dblHIGH_SCORE As Double = 95.0

Try
   ' Copy the TextBox scores into the variables.
   dblScore1 = CDbl(txtScore1.Text)
   dblScore2 = CDbl(txtScore2.Text)
   dblScore3 = CDbl(txtScore3.Text)

   ' Calculate the average score.
   dblAverage = (dblScore1 + dblScore2 + dblScore3) / 3.0

   ' Display the average, rounded to 2 decimal places.
   lblAverage.Text = dblAverage.ToString("n2")

   ' If the score is high, give the student praise.
   ' Otherwise, give some encouragement.
   If dblAverage > dblHIGH_SCORE Then
      lblMessage.Text = "Congratulations! Great Job!"
   Else
      lblMessage.Text = "Keep trying!"
   End If
Catch
   ' Display an error message.
   MessageBox.Show("Scores must be numeric.")
End Try
End Sub
```

Now the application will display one of two possible messages. If the user's average score is greater than 95, the message *Congratulations! Great Job!* will appear. Otherwise, the message *Keep trying!* will appear.

Step 3: Save the project.

Step 4: Run the application and input the following test scores in the three text boxes: **80, 90, 75.**

Step 5: Click the *Calculate Average* button. As shown in Figure 7, the average test score is displayed, and the message *Keep trying!* appears.

Figure 7 *Test Score Average* form with message displayed

Step 6: Click the *Clear* button, and then enter the following test scores in the three text boxes: **100, 97, 99.**

Step 7: Click the *Calculate Average* button. This time, the message *Congratulations! Great job!* appears.

Step 8: Click the *Exit* button to terminate the application.

Checkpoint

5 Look at each of the following code segments. What value will the `If...Then...Else` statements store in the variable `intY`?

a.
```
intX = 0
If intX < 1 Then
  intY = 99
Else
  intY = 0
End If
```

b.
```
intX = 100
If intX <= 1 Then
  intY = 99
Else
  intY = 0
End If
```

c.
```
intX = 0
If intX <> 1 Then
  intY = 99
Else
  intY = 0
End If
```

4 The `If...Then...ElseIf` Statement

CONCEPT: The `If...Then...ElseIf` statement is like a chain of `If...Then...Else` statements. They perform their tests, one after the other, until one of them is found to be true.

We make certain mental decisions by using sets of different but related rules. For example, we might decide which type of coat or jacket to wear by consulting the following rules:

- If it is very cold, wear a heavy coat
- Else, if it is chilly, wear a light jacket
- Else, if it is windy, wear a windbreaker
- Else, if it is hot, wear no jacket

The purpose of these rules is to decide on one type of outer garment to wear. If it is cold, the first rule dictates that a heavy coat must be worn. All the other rules are then ignored. If the first rule does not apply (if it isn't cold) the second rule is consulted. If that rule does not apply, the third rule is consulted, and so on.

TIP: When logic rules are not expressed correctly by a program, the result is called a **logic error**. The Visual Studio Debugger can help you to identify logic errors by letting you walk through the program code, one line at a time.

The way these rules are connected is very important. If they were consulted individually, we might go out of the house wearing the wrong jacket or, possibly, more than one jacket. For instance, if it is windy, the third rule says to wear a windbreaker. What if it is both windy and very cold? Will we wear a windbreaker? A heavy coat? Both? Because of the order in which the rules are consulted, the first rule will determine that a heavy coat is needed. The remaining rules will not be consulted, and we will go outside wearing the most appropriate garment.

This type of decision making is also common in programming. In Visual Basic, it is accomplished with the `If...Then...ElseIf` statement. Here is its general format:

```
If condition Then
   statement
   (more statements may follow)
ElseIf condition Then
   statement
   (more statements may follow)
(put as many ElseIf statements as necessary)
Else
   statement
   (more statements may follow)
End If
```

This construction is like a chain of `If...Then...Else` statements. The `Else` part of one statement is linked to the `If` part of another. The chain of `If...Then...Else` statements becomes one long statement. In Tutorial 3, you complete an application that uses the `If...Then...ElseIf` statement.

Tutorial 3:
Completing an application that uses the `If...Then...ElseIf` statement

VideoNote

Tutorial 4-3
Walkthrough

In this tutorial, you will begin with the program from Tutorial 2 and add controls and program code that display the student's letter grade (*A*, *B*, *C*, *D*, *F*).

Step 1:   Open the *Test Score Average 2* project you modified in Tutorial 2.

Step 2:   Drag the form's border downward about one-half inch, and drag the `lblMessage` control and the three button controls downward on the form to make space for a new row of controls.

Step 3:   Drag the lower border of the group box downward about one-half inch to make room for a label that will display the student's letter grade.

Step 4:   Inside the group box add the new Label controls shown in Figure 8. When you add the label on the left, set its Text property to *Grade:*. When you add the label on the right, set its Name property to `lblGrade`, its AutoSize property to *False*, and set its BorderStyle property to *Fixed3D*.

Figure 8 Adding the *Grade* label inside the group box

Step 5: Double-click the *Calculate Average* button. The *Code* window will open and show the `btnCalculate_Click` event handler, which is shown as follows. Complete the event handler by writing the code shown in bold:

```
Private Sub btnCalculate_Click(...) Handles btnCalculate.Click
    ' Variables to hold scores and the average score
    Dim dblScore1 As Double
    Dim dblScore2 As Double
    Dim dblScore3 As Double
    Dim dblAverage As Double

    ' Constant for a high score.
    Const dblHIGH_SCORE As Double = 95.0

    Try
        ' Copy the TextBox scores into the variables.
        dblScore1 = CDbl(txtScore1.Text)
        dblScore2 = CDbl(txtScore2.Text)
        dblScore3 = CDbl(txtScore3.Text)

        ' Calculate the average score.
        dblAverage = (dblScore1 + dblScore2 + dblScore3) / 3.0

        ' Display the average, rounded to 2 decimal places.
        lblAverage.Text = dblAverage.ToString("n2")

        ' Display the letter grade.
        If dblAverage < 60 Then
            lblGrade.Text = "F"
        ElseIf dblAverage < 70 Then
            lblGrade.Text = "D"
        ElseIf dblAverage < 80 Then
            lblGrade.Text = "C"
        ElseIf dblAverage < 90 Then
            lblGrade.Text = "B"
        ElseIf dblAverage <= 100 Then
            lblGrade.Text = "A"
        End If

        ' If the score is high, give the student praise.
        ' Otherwise, give some encouragement.
        If dblAverage > dblHIGH_SCORE Then
            lblMessage.Text = "Congratulations! Great Job!"
        Else
            lblMessage.Text = "Keep trying!"
        End If
    Catch
        ' Display an error message.
        MessageBox.Show("Scores must be numeric.")
    End Try
End Sub
```

The `If...Then...ElseIf` statement that you wrote has a number of notable characteristics. Let's analyze how it works. First, the Boolean expression `dblAverage < 60` is tested:

```
If dblAverage < 60 Then
    lblGrade.Text = "F"
```

If dblAverage is less than 60, *F* is assigned to lblGrade.Text, and the rest of the ElseIf statements are ignored. If dblAverage is not less than 60, the next ElseIf statement executes:

```
If dblAverage < 60 Then
    lblGrade.Text = "F"
ElseIf dblAverage < 70 Then
    lblGrade.Text = "D"
```

The first If...Then statement filtered out all grades less than 60, so when this ElseIf statement executes, dblAverage must be 60 or greater. If dblAverage is less than 70, *D* is assigned to lblGrade.Text and the remaining ElseIf statements are ignored. The chain of events continues until one of the expressions is true, or the End If statement is encountered. Figure 9 uses a flowchart to describe the logic.

Figure 9 Flowchart for determining the student's letter grade

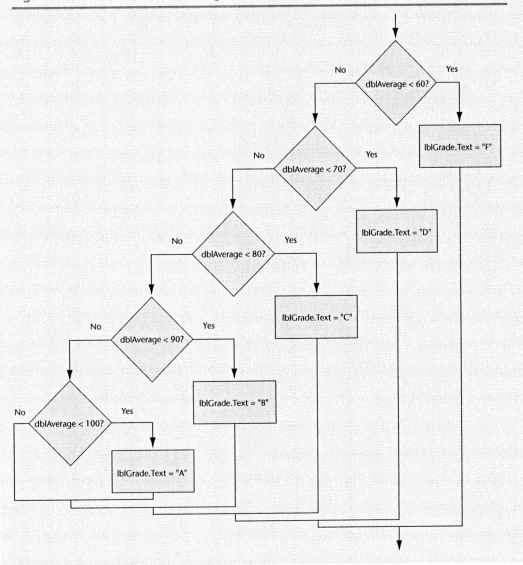

Step 6: Scroll down to the btnClear_Click event handler and add the statement shown here in bold:

```
Private Sub btnClear_Click(...) Handles btnClear.Click
    ' Clear the Text Boxes and Labels.
    txtScore1.Clear()
    txtScore2.Clear()
    txtScore3.Clear()
    lblAverage.Text = String.Empty
    lblMessage.Text = String.Empty
    lblGrade.Text = String.Empty

    ' Reset the focus.
    txtScore1.Focus()
End Sub
```

This statement will clear the contents of the lblGrade label when the user clicks the *Clear* button.

Step 7: Save the project, run the application, and input the following test scores in the text boxes: **80, 90, 75**.

Step 8: Click the *Calculate Average* button. The average test score and letter grade are displayed, along with the message *Keep trying!* (see Figure 10).

Step 9: Click the *Exit* button to terminate the application.

Figure 10 Student grade displayed

Using a Trailing Else

There is one minor problem with the test averaging applications shown so far: What if the user enters a test score greater than 100? The If...Then...ElseIf statement in the *Test Score Average 2* project handles all scores through 100, but none greater. Figure 11 shows the form when the user enters values greater than 100.

Figure 11 *Test Score Average 2 application showing values greater than 100*

The program does not give a letter grade because there is no code to handle a score greater than 100. Assuming that any grade over 100 is invalid, we can fix the program by placing an `Else` at the end of the `If...Then...ElseIf` statement, as follows:

```
' Display the letter grade.
If dblAverage < 60 Then
    lblGrade.Text = "F"
ElseIf dblAverage < 70 Then
    lblGrade.Text = "D"
ElseIf dblAverage < 80 Then
    lblGrade.Text = "C"
ElseIf dblAverage < 90 Then
    lblGrade.Text = "B"
ElseIf dblAverage <= 100 Then
    lblGrade.Text = "A"
Else
    lblGrade.Text = "Invalid Score"
End If
```

The trailing `Else` catches any value that falls through the cracks. It provides a default response when the `If...Then` or none of the `ElseIf` statements finds a true condition.

 TIP: When writing an `If...Then...ElseIf` statement, code the structure of the statement first, identifying all the conditions to be tested. For example, the code in our example might initially be written as follows:

```
If dblAverage < 60 Then
ElseIf dblAverage < 70 Then
ElseIf dblAverage < 80 Then
ElseIf dblAverage < 90 Then
ElseIf dblAverage <= 100 Then
Else
End If
```

This creates the framework of the statement. Next, insert the conditionally executed statements, as shown in bold in the following code:

```
If dblAverage < 60 Then
    lblGrade.Text = "F"
```

```
ElseIf dblAverage < 70 Then
   lblGrade.Text = "D"
ElseIf dblAverage < 80 Then
   lblGrade.Text = "C"
ElseIf dblAverage < 90 Then
   lblGrade.Text = "B"
ElseIf dblAverage <= 100 Then
   lblGrade.Text = "A"
Else
   lblGrade.Text = "Invalid Score"
End If
```

A good design approach is to decide which conditions must be tested first, and then decide what actions must be taken for each condition.

 Checkpoint

6 The following If...Then...ElseIf statement has several Boolean expressions that test the variable intX. Assuming intX equals 20, how many times will the following statement compare intX before it finds a Boolean expression that is true?

```
If intX < 10 Then
   intY = 0
ElseIf intX < 20 Then
   intY = 1
ElseIf intX < 30 Then
   intY = 2
ElseIf intX < 40 Then
   intY = 3
Else
   intY = -1
End If
```

7 In the following If...Then...ElseIf statement, if the variable intX equals 5, how many times will the code assign a value to intY?

```
If intX < 10 Then
   intY = 0
ElseIf intX < 20 Then
   intY = 1
ElseIf intX < 30 Then
   intY = 2
ElseIf intX < 40 Then
   intY = 3
End If
```

Look carefully at the following set of If...Then statements. If the variable intX equals 5, how many times will the code assign a value to intY?

```
If intX < 10 Then
   intY = 0
End If
If intX < 20 Then
   intY = 1
End If
If intX < 30 Then
   intY = 2
End If
If intX < 40 Then
   intY = 3
End If
```

5 Nested If Statements

CONCEPT: A nested **If** statement is an **If** statement in the conditionally executed code of another **If** statement. (In this section, we use the term **If** statement to refer to an **If ... Then, If...Then...Else,** or **If...Then...ElseIf** statement.)

A nested **If** statement is an If statement that appears inside another If statement. In Tutorial 4, you will examine an application that uses nested If statements. The application determines whether a bank customer qualifies for a special loan. The customer must meet one of the following qualifications:

- Earn $30,000 per year or more and have worked in his or her current job for more than two years.
- Have worked at his or her current job for more than five years.

VideoNote

Tutorial 4-4
Walkthrough

Tutorial 4:
Completing an application with a nested If statement

Step 1: Open the *Loan Qualifier* project from the student sample programs folder named *Chap4\Loan Qualifier*.

Step 2: Open *Form1* in the *Design* window. It should appear as shown in Figure 12.

Figure 12 *Loan Qualifier* application

Step 3: Double-click the *Check Qualifications* button. The *Code* window will open and show the code template for the btnCheckQual_Click event handler. Complete the event handler by writing the code shown here in bold:

```
Private Sub btnCheckQual_Click(...) Handles btnCheckQual.Click
    ' Variables to hold input data.
    Dim dblSalary As Double
    Dim intYearsOnJob As Integer

    Try
        ' Get the user's input.
        dblSalary = CDbl(txtSalary.Text)
        intYearsOnJob = CInt(txtYearsOnJob.Text)

        ' Determine whether the applicant qualifies
        ' for the special loan.
        If dblSalary > 30000 Then
            If intYearsOnJob > 2 Then
                lblMessage.Text = "The applicant qualifies."
```

229

```
            Else
               lblMessage.Text = "The applicant does not qualify."
            End If
         Else
            If intYearsOnJob > 5 Then
               lblMessage.Text = "The applicant qualifies."
            Else
               lblMessage.Text = "The applicant does not qualify."
            End If
         End If

      Catch ex As Exception
         ' Display an error message.
         MessageBox.Show("Enter numeric data please.")
      End Try
   End Sub
```

Step 4: Save and run the application. Enter **45000** for salary and **3** for years at current job. Click the *Check Qualifications* button. The message *The applicant qualifies* should appear on the form.

Step 5: Enter **15000** for salary and **3** for years at current job. Click the *Check Qualifications* button. The message *The applicant does not qualify* appears on the form.

Step 6: Experiment with other values. When you are finished, click the *Exit* button to terminate the application.

Examining the Nested If Statement in More Depth

In the *Loan Qualifier* project, the outermost If statement tests the following expression:

```
If dblSalary > 30000 Then
```

If this expression is true, the nested If statement shown in bold is executed:

```
If dblSalary > 30000 Then
   If intYearsOnJob > 2 Then
      lblMessage.Text = "The applicant qualifies."
   Else
      lblMessage.Text = "The applicant does not qualify."
   End If
Else
   If intYearsOnJob > 5 Then
      lblMessage.Text = "The applicant qualifies."
   Else
      lblMessage.Text = "The applicant does not qualify."
   End If
End If
```

However, if the expression dblSalary > 30000 is not true, the Else part of the outermost If statement causes its nested If statement, shown in bold, to execute:

```
If dblSalary > 30000 Then
   If intYearsOnJob > 2 Then
      lblMessage.Text = "The applicant qualifies."
   Else
      lblMessage.Text = "The applicant does not qualify."
   End If
```

```
Else
    If intYearsOnJob > 5 Then
        lblMessage.Text = "The applicant qualifies."
    Else
        lblMessage.Text = "The applicant does not qualify."
    End If
End If
```

Figure 13 shows a flowchart for these nested If statements.

Figure 13 Flowchart of nested If statements

6   Logical Operators

CONCEPT: Logical operators combine two or more Boolean expressions into a single expression.

Logical operators can combine multiple Boolean expressions into a compound expression. Each individual Boolean expression might be very simple. But then, you can combine them using logical operators (also called Boolean operators) to make complex decisions. Table 3 lists Visual Basic's logical operators.

Table 3 Visual Basic logical operators

Operator	Effect
And	Combines two expressions into one. Both expressions must be true for the overall expression to be true.
Or	Combines two expressions into one. One or both expressions must be true for the overall expression to be true. It is only necessary for one to be true, and it does not matter which.
Xor	Combines two expressions into one. One expression (not both) must be true for the overall expression to be true. If both expressions are true, or both expressions are false, the overall expression is false.
Not	Reverses the logical value of an expression: makes a true expression false and a false expression true.

The And Operator

The **And operator** combines two expressions into one. Both expressions must be true for the overall expression to be true. The following If statement uses the And operator:

```
If intTemperature < 20 And intMinutes > 12 Then
    lblMessage.Text = "The temperature is in the danger zone."
End If
```

In this statement, the two relational expressions are combined into a single expression. The assignment statement is executed only if intTemperature is less than 20 and intMinutes is greater than 12. If either relational expression is false, the entire expression is false and the assignment statement is not executed.

Table 4 shows a truth table for the And operator. The truth table lists all the possible combinations of values that two expressions may have, followed by the resulting value returned by the And operator connecting the two conditions. As the table shows, both Expression 1 and Expression 2 must be true for the And operator to return value of *True*.

Table 4 Truth table for the And operator

Expression 1	Expression 2	Expression 1 **And** Expression 2
True	False	False
False	True	False
False	False	False
True	True	True

> **TIP:** You must provide complete expressions on each side of the And operator. For example, the following is not correct because the code on the right side of the And operator is not a complete expression:
>
> ```
> intTemperature > 0 And < 100
> ```
>
> The expression must be rewritten as follows:
>
> ```
> intTemperature > 0 And intTemperature < 100
> ```

Short-Circuit Evaluation with AndAlso

When the And operator appears in a compound Boolean expression, Visual Basic evaluates both expressions on the left and right side of the And operator. Consider the following example in which the first expression compares dblX to zero and the second expression calls a Boolean function named CheckValue:

```
If dblX > 0 And CheckValue(dblX) Then
    lblResult.Text = "Expression is True"
Else
    lblResult.Text = "Expression is False"
End If
```

When this code executes, the expression dblX > 0 will be tested, and then the CheckValue function is called. In some situations, however, it shouldn't be necessary to call the CheckValue function to determine the value of the compound Boolean expression. If the expression dblX > 0 is false, then we know that the compound expression is false, so the function call can be skipped. Such behavior is called **short-circuit evaluation**. In Visual

Basic you use the **AndAlso** operator to achieve short-circuit evaluation. In the following example, assuming that `dblX` is less than or equal to zero, `CheckValue` is not called and *Expression is False* is displayed:

```
If dblX > 0 AndAlso CheckValue(dblX) Then
    lblResult.Text = "Expression is True"
Else
    lblResult.Text = "Expression is False"
End If
```

See the *ShortCircuit* application in the student sample programs folder named *Chap4\ShortCircuit* for an example of the `AndAlso` operator.

The Or Operator

The **Or operator** combines two expressions into one. One or both expressions must be true for the overall expression to be true. It is only necessary for one to be true, and it does not matter which. The following `If` statement uses the `Or` operator:

```
If intTemperature < 20 Or intTemperature > 100 Then
    lblMessage.Text = "The temperature is in the danger zone."
End If
```

The assignment statement will be executed if `intTemperature` is less than 20 or `intTemperature` is greater than 100. If either relational test is true, the entire expression is true and the assignment statement is executed.

Table 5 is a truth table for the `Or` operator.

Table 5 Truth table for the Or operator

Expression 1	Expression 2	Expression 1 **or** Expression 2
True	False	True
False	True	True
False	False	False
True	True	True

All it takes for an `Or` expression to be true is for one of the subexpressions to be true. It doesn't matter if the other subexpression is true or false.

> **TIP:** You must provide complete Boolean expressions on both sides of the `Or` operator. For example, the following is not correct because the code on the right side of the `Or` operator is not a complete Boolean expression:
>
> ```
> intTemperature < 0 Or > 100
> ```
>
> The expression must be rewritten as follows:
>
> ```
> intTemperature < 0 Or intTemperature > 100
> ```

Short Circuit-Evaluation with OrElse

When the `Or` operator appears in a compound Boolean expression, Visual Basic evaluates both expressions on the left and right side of the `Or` operator. Consider the following example, in which the first expression compares dblX to zero; the second calls a Boolean function named CheckValue:

```
If dblX = 0 Or CheckValue(dblX) Then
    lblResult.Text = "Expression is True"
End If
```

When this code executes, the expression dblX = 0 will be tested, and then the CheckValue function is called. In some situations, however, it shouldn't be necessary to call the CheckValue function to determine the value of the compound expression. If the expression dblX = 0 is true, then we know that the compound expression is true, so the function call can be skipped. As previously mentioned, this type of evaluation is known as short-circuit evaluation, and it can be performed with the **OrElse** operator.

In the following example, if dblX equals zero, the CheckValue function is not called:

```
If dblX = 0 OrElse CheckValue(dblX) Then
    lblResult.Text = "Expression is True"
End If
```

See the *ShortCircuit* application in the student sample programs folder named *Chap4/ShortCircuit* for an example of the OrElse operator.

The Xor Operator

Xor stands for *exclusive or*. The **Xor operator** takes two expressions as operands and creates an expression that is true when one, but not both, of the subexpressions is true. The following If statement uses the Xor operator:

```
If decTotal > 1000 Xor decAverage > 120 Then
    lblMessage.Text = "You may try again."
End If
```

The assignment statement will be executed if decTotal is greater than 1000 or decAverage is greater than 120, but not both. If both relational tests are true, or neither is true, the entire expression is false. Table 6 shows a truth table for the Xor operator.

Table 6 Truth table for the Xor operator

Expression 1	Expression 2	Expression 1 **Xor** Expression 2
True	False	True
False	True	True
False	False	False
True	True	False

TIP: You must provide complete Boolean expressions on both sides of the Xor operator. For example, the following is not correct because the code on the right side of the Xor operator is not a complete Boolean expression:

```
value < 0 Xor > 100
```

The expression must be rewritten as follows:

```
value < 0 Xor value > 100
```

The Not Operator

The **Not** operator takes a Boolean expression and reverses its logical value. In other words, if the expression is true, the Not operator returns *False*, and if the expression is false, it returns *True*. The following If statement uses the Not operator:

```
If Not intTemperature > 100 Then
    lblMessage.Text = "You are below the maximum temperature."
End If
```

First, the expression intTemperature > 100 is tested to be true or false. Then the Not operator is applied to that value. If the expression intTemperature > 100 is true, the Not operator returns *False*. If it is false, the Not operator returns *True*. This example is equivalent to asking *Is intTemperature not greater than 100?* Table 7 shows a truth table for the Not operator.

Table 7 Truth table for the Not operator

Expression	**Not** Expression
True	False
False	True

Checking Numeric Ranges with Logical Operators

When your program is determining whether a number is inside a numeric range, it's best to use the And operator. For example, the following If statement checks the value in intX to determine whether it is in the range of 20 through 40:

```
If intX >= 20 And intX <= 40 Then
    lblMessage.Text = "The value is in the acceptable range."
End If
```

The expression in the If statement is true only when intX is greater than or equal to 20 *and* less than or equal to 40. The value in intX must be within the range of 20 through 40 for this expression to be true.

When your program is determining whether a number is outside a range, it's best to use the Or operator. The following statement determines whether intX is outside the range of 20 through 40:

```
If intX < 20 Or intX > 40 Then
    lblMessage.Text = "The value is outside the acceptable range."
End If
```

It is important not to get these logical operators confused. For example, the following expression cannot be true because no value exists that is both less than 20 and greater than 40.

```
If intX < 20 And intX > 40 Then
    lblMessage.Text = "The value is outside the acceptable range."
End If
```

If You Want to Know More about Using Not, And, Or, and Xor Together

It is possible to write an expression containing more than one logical operator. For example, examine the following If statement:

```
If intX < 0 And intY > 100 Or intZ = 50 Then
    ' Perform some statement.
End If
```

Logical operators have an order of precedence. The Not operator has the highest precedence, followed by the And operator, followed by the Or operator, followed by the Xor operator. So, in the example statement, the following expression is evaluated first:

```
intX < 0 And intY > 100
```

The result of this expression is then applied to the Or operator to carry out the rest of the condition. For example, if the first expression (using And) is true, the remainder of the condition will be tested as follows:

```
True Or intZ = 50
```

If the first expression (using And) is false, however, the remainder of the condition will be tested as follows:

```
False Or intZ = 50
```

Always use parentheses in logical expressions to clarify the order of evaluation. The following If statement confirms that the And operator executes before the Or operator:

```
If (intX < 0 And intY > 100) Or intZ = 50 Then
    ' Perform some statement.
End If
```

You can use parentheses to force one expression to be tested before others. For example, look at the following If statement:

```
If intX < 0 And (intY > 100 Or intZ = 50) Then
    ' Perform some statement.
End If
```

In the statement, the expression (intY > 100 Or intZ = 50) is tested first.

If You Want to Know More about Using Math Operators with Relational and Logical Operators

It is possible to write expressions containing math, relational, and logical operators. For example, look at the following code segment:

```
intA = 5
intB = 7
intX = 100
intY = 30
If (intX > (intA * 10)) And (intY < (intB + 20)) Then
    ' Perform some statement.
End If
```

In statements containing complex conditions, math operators execute first. After the math operators, relational operators execute. Logical operators execute last. Let's use this order to step through the evaluation of the condition shown in our sample If statement. First, the math operators execute, causing the statement to become

```
If (intX > 50) And (intY < 27) Then
```

Next, the relational operators execute, causing the statement to become

```
If True And False Then
```

Since True And False equals *False*, the condition is false.

Checkpoint

8 The following truth table shows various combinations of the values *True* and *False* connected by a logical operator. Complete the table by indicating whether the result of each combination is *True* or *False*.

Logical Expression	Result
True And False	_____
True And True	_____
False And True	_____
False And False	_____
True Or False	_____
True Or True	_____
False Or True	_____
False Or False	_____
True Xor False	_____
True Xor True	_____
Not True	_____
Not False	_____

7 Comparing, Testing, and Working with Strings

CONCEPT: Visual Basic provides various methods in the **string** class that make it easy to work with strings. This section shows you how to use relational operators to compare strings, and discusses several functions and string methods that perform tests and manipulations on strings.

In the preceding examples, you saw how numbers can be compared using the relational operators. You can also use relational operators to compare strings. For example, look at the following code segment, in which strName1 and strName2 are string variables.

```
strName1 = "Mary"
strName2 = "Mark"
If strName1 = strName2 Then
   lblMessage.Text = "The names are the same"
Else
   lblMessage.Text = "The names are NOT the same"
End If
```

The = operator tests strName1 and strName2 to determine whether they are equal. Since the strings "Mary" and "Mark" are not equal, the Else part of the If statement will cause the message *The names are NOT the same* to be assigned to lblMessage.Text.

You can compare string variables with string literals as well. The following code sample uses the <> operator to determine if strMonth is not equal to *October*:

```
If strMonth <> "October" Then
   ' statement
End If
```

You can also use the >, <, >=, and <= operators to compare strings. Before we look at these operators, though, we must understand how characters are stored in memory.

Computers do not actually store characters, such as *A*, *B*, *C*, and so on, in memory. Instead, they store numeric codes that represent the characters. Visual Basic uses **Unicode**, which is a numbering system that represents all letters of the alphabet (lowercase and uppercase), the printable digits 0 through 9, punctuation symbols, and special characters. Each character is stored in memory as its corresponding Unicode number. When the computer is instructed to print the value on the screen, it displays the character that corresponds to the numeric code.

NOTE: Unicode is an international encoding system that is extensive enough to represent all the characters of most of the world's alphabets.

In Unicode, letters are arranged alphabetically. Because *A* comes before *B*, the numeric code for the letter *A* is less than the code for the letter *B*. In the following `If` statement, the relational expression `"A" < "B"` is true.

```
If "A" < "B" Then
   ' Do something
End If
```

TIP: When comparing strings, make sure they are consistent in their use of uppercase and lowercase letters. Avoid comparing `"jones"` to `"Adams"` or `"BAKER"`, for example. The ordering of strings is affected by the choice of uppercase and lowercase letters.

When you use relational operators to compare strings, the strings are compared character-by-character. For example, look at the following code segment:

```
strName1 = "Mary"
strName2 = "Mark"
If strName1 > strName2 Then
   lblMessage.Text = "Mary is greater than Mark"
Else
   lblMessage.Text = "Mary is not greater than Mark"
End If
```

The > operator compares each character in the strings `"Mary"` and `"Mark"`, beginning with the first, or leftmost characters, as shown in Figure 14.

Figure 14 String comparison

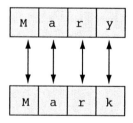

Here is how the comparison takes place:

1. The *M* in *Mary* is compared with the *M* in *Mark*. Since these are the same, the next characters are compared.
2. The *a* in *Mary* is compared with the *a* in *Mark*. Since these are the same, the next characters are compared.

3. The *r* in *Mary* is compared with the *r* in *Mark*. Since these are the same, the next characters are compared.

4. The *y* in *Mary* is compared with the *k* in *Mark*. Since these are not the same, the two strings are not equal. The character *y* is greater than *k*, so it is determined that *Mary* is greater than *Mark*.

NOTE: If one of the strings in a relational comparison is shorter in length than the other, Visual Basic treats the shorter character as if it were padded with blank spaces. For example, suppose the strings `"High"` and `"Hi"` were compared. The string `"Hi"` would be treated as if it were four characters in length, with the last two characters being spaces. Because the space character has a lower value than the alphabetic characters in Unicode, `"Hi"` would be less than `"High"`.

Testing for No Input

You can determine whether the user has entered a value into a text box by comparing the TextBox control's Text property to the predefined constant `String.Empty` as shown here:

```
If txtInput.Text = String.Empty Then
   lblMessage.Text = "Please enter a value"
Else
   ' The txtInput control contains input, so
   ' perform an operation with it here.
End If
```

The predefined constant `String.Empty` represents an **empty string**, which is a string that contains no characters.

The `If` statement copies the string *Please enter a value* to lblMessage if the txtInput control contains no input. The statements following the Else clause are executed only if txtInput contains a value. You can use this technique to determine whether the user has provided input for a required field before performing operations on that field.

NOTE: The technique we used in the preceding `If` statement does not detect a string that contains only spaces. A space is a character, just as the letter *A* is a character. If the user types only spaces into a text box, you will have to trim away the spaces to determine if any other characters were typed. Later in this section, we will discuss functions for trimming spaces from strings.

The `ToUpper` and `ToLower` Methods

The `ToUpper` and `ToLower` methods are both members of the `String` class, so they may be called with any string variable or expression. The **`ToLower` method** returns the lowercase equivalent of a string. Here is the method's general format:

```
StringExpression.ToUpper()
```

StringExpression can be any string variable or string expression. In the following example, strLittleWord and strBigWord are string variables:

```
strLittleWord = "Hello"
strBigWord = strLittleWord.ToUpper()
```

After the statement executes, `strBigWord` will contain `"HELLO"` in uppercase letters. Notice that the original string, `"Hello"` had one uppercase letter—the initial *H*. The `ToUpper` method converts only lowercase characters. Characters that are already uppercase and characters that are not alphabet letters are not converted.

> **TIP:** The `ToUpper` method does not modify the value of the string, but returns the string's uppercase equivalent. For example, after the statements in the previous example execute, `strLittleWord` still contains the original string `"Hello"`.

The **ToLower method** works just like the `ToUpper` method, except it returns a lowercase version of a string. Here is the method's general format:

```
StringExpression.ToLower()
```

In the following example, `strBigTown` and `strLittleTown` are string variables:

```
strBigTown = "NEW YORK"
strLittleTown = strBigTown.ToLower()
```

After the statements execute, the variable `strLittleTown` contains the string `"new york"`. The `ToLower` method converts only uppercase characters. Characters that are already lowercase, and characters that are not alphabet letters, are not converted.

> **TIP:** Like `ToUpper`, the `ToLower` method does not modify the original string.

You may also use the `ToUpper` and `ToLower` methods with a control's Text property. In the following example `strLastName` is a string variable:

```
strLastName = txtLastName.Text.ToUpper()
```

The `ToUpper` and `ToLower` methods are helpful in performing string comparisons. String comparisons in Visual Basic are *case sensitive*, meaning that uppercase letters are not considered the same as their lowercase counterparts. In other words, *A* is not the same as *a*. This can lead to problems when you construct `If` statements that compare strings. Tutorial 5 leads you through such an example.

Tutorial 5:
Examining an application that performs
string comparisons

Step 1: Open the *Secret Word* project from the student sample programs folder named *Chap4\ Secret Word*. Recall that the student sample programs folder can be downloaded from www.microsoft.com/express/Downloads/.

Step 2: Run the application. The form shown in Figure 15 appears.

This application asks you to enter the secret word, which might be similar to a password in some programs. The secret word is *PROSPERO*.

Step 3: Enter **prospero** in all lowercase letters, and click the *Ok* button. You will see the message *Wrong! That is NOT the secret word!*

Figure 15 *Secret Word* form

Step 4: Enter **Prospero** with an uppercase *P*, followed by all lowercase letters. Click the *Ok* button. Once again, you see the message *Wrong! That is NOT the secret word!*

Step 5: Enter **PROSPERO** in all uppercase letters and click the *Ok* button. This time you see the message *Congratulations! That is the secret word!*

Step 6: Click the *Exit* button to close the application.

Step 7: Open the *Code* window and look at the btnOk_Click event handler. The code is as follows:

```
Private Sub btnOk_Click(...) Handles btnOk.Click
    ' Compare the input entered with the secret word.
    If txtInput.Text = "PROSPERO" Then
        lblMessage.Text = "Congratulations! That " &
                          "is the secret word!"
    Else
        lblMessage.Text = "Wrong! That is NOT the secret word!"
    End If
End Sub
```

The If...Then...Else statement compares the string entered by the user to *PROSPERO* in all uppercase letters. But what if the programmer intended to accept the word without regard to case? What if *prospero* in all lowercase letters is valid as well? One solution would be to modify the If statement to test for all the other possible values. However, to test for all the possible combination of lowercase and uppercase letters would require a large amount of code.

A better approach is to convert the text entered by the user to all uppercase letters, and then compare the converted text to *PROSPERO*. When the user enters the word *prospero* in any combination of uppercase or lowercase characters, this test will return *True*. Modify the code by adding a call to the ToUpper method, as shown bold in the following code.

```
If txtInput.Text.ToUpper() = "PROSPERO" Then
    lblMessage.Text = "Congratulations! That " &
                      "is the secret word!"
Else
    lblMessage.Text = "Wrong! That is NOT the secret word!"
End If
```

Step 8: Run the application. When the form appears, Enter **prospero** in all lowercase letters and click the *Ok* button. This time you see the message *Congratulations! That is the secret word!* You can experiment with various combinations of uppercase and lowercase letters. As long as you type the word *prospero* the application will recognize it as the secret word.

Step 9: Close the project.

The ToLower method can also be used in Tutorial 5 to accomplish the same result, as shown in bold in the following code. Just make sure you compare the return value of the ToLower method to an all lowercase string.

```
If txtInput.Text.ToLower() = "prospero" Then
    lblMessage.Text = "Congratulations! That " &
                      "is the secret word!"
Else
    lblMessage.Text = "Wrong! That is NOT the secret word!"
End If
```

The IsNumeric Function

The **IsNumeric** function accepts a string as its argument and returns *True* if the string contains a number. The function returns *False* if the string's contents cannot be recognized as a number. Here is the function's general use:

```
IsNumeric(StringExpression)
```

Here is an example:

```
Dim strNumber As String
strNumber = "576"
If IsNumeric(strNumber) Then
    lblMessage.Text = "It is a number"
Else
    lblMessage.Text = "It is NOT a number"
End If
```

In this statement, the expression IsNumeric(strNumber) returns *True* because the contents of strNumber can be recognized as a number. In the following code segment, however, the expression returns *False*:

```
strNumber = "123abc"
If IsNumeric(strNumber) Then
    lblMessage.Text = "It is a number"
Else
    lblMessage.Text = "It is NOT a number"
End If
```

When you want the user to enter numeric data, the IsNumeric function is useful for checking user input and confirming that it is valid.

Determining the Length of a String

The **Length** property, a member of the string class, returns the number of characters in a string. Here is an example:

```
Dim strName As String = "Herman"
Dim intNumChars As Integer
intNumChars = strName.Length
```

The code stores 6 in intNumChars because the length of the string "Herman" is 6.

You can also determine the length of a control's Text property, as shown in the following code:

```
If txtInput.Text.Length > 20 Then
    lblMessage.Text = "Please enter no more than 20 characters."
End If
```

There are many situations in which Length is useful. One example is when you must display or print a string and have only a limited amount of space.

> **WARNING:** If you attempt to get the length of an uninitialized string variable, an exception (runtime error) occurs. You can prevent this error by initializing string variables with an empty string, as shown in the following statement:
>
> ```
> Dim str As String = String.Empty
> ```

Optional Topic: Trimming Spaces from Strings

Sometimes it is necessary to trim leading and/or trailing spaces from a string before performing other operations on the string, such as a comparison. A **leading space** is a space that appears at the beginning, or left side, of a string. For instance, the following string has three leading spaces:

```
"   Hello"
```

A **trailing space** is a space that appears at the end, or right side, of a string, after the non-space characters. The following string has three trailing spaces:

```
"Hello   "
```

The String class has three methods for removing spaces: TrimStart, TrimEnd, and Trim. Here is the general format of each method:

```
StringExpression.TrimStart()
StringExpression.TrimEnd()
StringExpression.Trim()
```

The **TrimStart** method returns a copy of the string expression with all leading spaces removed. The **TrimEnd** method returns a copy of the string expression with all trailing spaces removed. The **Trim method** returns a copy of the string expression with all leading and trailing spaces removed. The following is an example:

```
strGreeting = "   Hello   "
lblMessage1.Text = strGreeting.TrimStart()
lblMessage2.Text = strGreeting.TrimEnd()
lblMessage3.Text = strGreeting.Trim()
```

In this code, the first statement assigns the string "   Hello   " (with three leading spaces and three trailing spaces) to the named variable, strGreeting. In the second statement, the TrimStart method is called. Its return value, "Hello   ", is assigned to lblMessage1.Text. In the third statement, the TrimEnd method is called. Its return value, "   Hello", is assigned to lblMessage2.Text. In the fourth statement, the Trim method is called. Its return value, "Hello", is assigned to lblMessage3.Text.

These methods do not modify the string variable, but return a modified copy of the variable. To actually modify the string variable you must use a statement such as the following:

```
strGreeting = strGreeting.Trim()
```

After this statement executes, the strGreeting variable no longer contains leading or trailing spaces.

Like the Length property, these methods may also be used with a control's Text property. The following is an example:

```
Dim strName As String
strName = txtName.Text.Trim()
```

The `Substring` Method

The **Substring** method returns a substring, or a string within a string. There are two formats:

```
StringExpression.Substring(Start)
StringExpression.Substring(Start, Length)
```

The positions of the characters in *StringExpression* are numbered, with the first character at position 0. In the first format shown for the method, an integer argument, *Start*, indicates the starting position of the string to be extracted from *StringExpression*. The method returns a string containing all characters from the *Start* position to the end of *StringExpression*. For example, look at the following code:

```
Dim strLastName As String
Dim strFullName As String = "George Washington"
strLastName = strFullName.Substring(7)
```

After this code executes, the variable `strLastName` will contain the string `"Washington"` because `"Washington"` begins at position 7 in `strFullName`, and continues to the end of the string.

In the second format shown for `Substring`, a second integer argument, *Length*, indicates the number of characters to extract, including the starting character. For example, look at the following code:

```
Dim strFirstName As String
Dim strFullName As String = "George Washington"
strFirstName = strFullName.Substring(0, 6)
```

In this code, the `Substring` method returns the six characters that begin at position 0 in `strFullName`. After the code executes, the variable `strFirstName` contains the string `"George"`.

Optional Topic: The `IndexOf` Method

The **IndexOf** method searches for a character or a string within a string. The method has three general formats:

```
StringExpression.IndexOf(SearchString)
StringExpression.IndexOf(SearchString, Start)
StringExpression.IndexOf(SearchString, Start, Count)
```

In the first format, *SearchString* is the string or character to search for within *StringExpression*. The method returns the character position, or index, of the first occurrence of *SearchString* if it is found within *StringExpression*. If *SearchString* is not found, the method returns −1. For example, look at the following code:

```
Dim strName As String = "Angelina Adams"
Dim intPosition As Integer
intPosition = strName.IndexOf("e")
```

After this code executes, the variable position equals 3 because the character *e* is found at character position 3.

NOTE: With the `IndexOf` method, the first character position is 0.

In the second format shown for `IndexOf`, a second argument, *Start*, is an integer that specifies a starting position within *StringExpression* for the search to begin. The following is an example:

```
Dim strName As String = "Angelina Adams"
Dim intPosition As Integer
intPosition = strName.IndexOf("A", 1)
```

After the code executes, the variable `intPosition` equals 9. The `IndexOf` method begins its search at character position 1 (the second character), so the first *A* is skipped.

NOTE: The version of the `IndexOf` method used here performs a case sensitive search. When searching for *A* it does not return the position of *a*.

In the third format shown for `IndexOf`, a third argument, *Count*, is an integer specifying the number of characters within *StringExpression* to search. Here is an example:

```
Dim strName As String = "Angelina Adams"
Dim intPosition As Integer
intPosition = strName.IndexOf("A", 1, 7)
```

After the code executes, the variable position equals –1. The `IndexOf` method searches only 7 characters, beginning at character 1. Because *A* is not found in the characters searched, the method returns –1.

WARNING: An exception (runtime error) will occur if the starting position argument passed to `IndexOf` is negative or specifies a nonexistent position. Get the length of the string before calling `IndexOf`, to ensure the index is in a valid range.

The following code shows how to use the `IndexOf` method to determine if a search string exists within a string:

```
Dim strName As String = "Angelina Adams"
If strName.IndexOf("Adams") = -1 Then
    lblMessage.Text = "Adams is not found"
End If
```

Tutorial 6 completes a string searching application.

Tutorial 6:
Completing a string searching application

In this tutorial, you will write code that implements a string searching program. You will have an opportunity to try the `IsNumeric`, `Trim`, and `IndexOf` methods. The user interface is already created, so you can concentrate on the program code that makes it work. Here are its basic features:

- A string is shown at the top of the form, as shown in Figure 16, containing various character patterns (*abc*, *ABC*, 00123, and so on). It uses a blue font, which appears gray on the printed page.
- The user inputs a string into the text box, indicating which substring they want to find.
- The user clicks the *Go* button, as shown in Figure 17.

- The program displays the position in which the substring was found. You can verify the accuracy of the result by inspecting the numbers in the scale line below the string shown in blue.
- The user can change the starting index position of the search from 0 to another value. In Figure 18, the user has selected index position 4 to begin searching. The next matching occurrence of *ABC* is found at index 20.
- If the user enters a nonnumeric index, an error message box pops up, as shown in Figure 19.

Figure 16 *String Finder* application, when started

Figure 17 User enters substring they want to find, clicks *Go* button

Figure 18 Searching for *ABC* starting at index position 4

Figure 19 User has entered a nonnumeric index

Step 1: Open the *String Finder* project from the student sample programs folder named *Chap4\String Finder*. This folder can be downloaded from www.microsoft.com/express/Downloads/.

Step 2: Open *Form1* in the *Designer* window. Click each control and view its name in the *Properties* window. When you begin writing code, you will want to know the control names.

Step 3: Double-click the *Go* button. The *Code* window will open and show the code template for the btnGo_Click event handler. Complete the event handler by writing the code shown here in bold:

```
Private Sub btnGo_Click(...) Handles btnGo.Click
    ' Variable declarations
    Dim intStartIndex As Integer ' Starting index of the search
    Dim intFoundIndex As Integer ' Index of the found substring

    ' Determine whether the starting index is numeric.
    If IsNumeric(txtStartIndex.Text) Then

        ' Determine whether a string to search for was entered.
        If txtToFind.Text.Length > 0 Then
```

```
               ' Get the starting index for the search.
               intStartIndex = CInt(txtStartIndex.Text)

               ' Search for the substring.
               intFoundIndex = lblString.Text.IndexOf(txtToFind.Text,
                                                     intStartIndex)

               ' Indicate whether the search string was found.
               If intFoundIndex = -1 Then
                   lblResults.Text = "The string was not found."
               Else
                   lblResults.Text = "The string was found at index " &
                                    intFoundIndex
               End If

           Else
               ' Display an error message for an empty search string.
               MessageBox.Show("Enter a string to search for.")
           End If
       Else
           ' Display an error message for a non-numeric index.
           MessageBox.Show("The index must be a number.")
       End If
   End Sub
```

Step 4: Save and run the program. Search for the substring *ABC* starting at index 0. The program should find the string at position 3.

Step 5: Search for *ABC* starting at index 4. The program should find the string at position 20.

Checkpoint

9 Are each of the following relational expressions *True* or *False*?

a. "ABC" > "XYZ"   _____

b. "AAA" = "AA"   _____

c. "ABC123" < "abc123"   _____

10 Match the description in the right column with the method or function in the left column.

_____ IsNumeric	a. Returns the uppercase equivalent of a string.
_____ ToLower	b. Returns the number of characters in a string.
_____ ToUpper	c. Returns a copy of a string without trailing spaces.
_____ Length	d. Returns a copy of a string without leading or trailing spaces.
_____ TrimStart	e. Searches for the first occurrence of a character or string within a string.
_____ Substring	f. Accepts a string as its argument and returns *True* if the string contains a number.
_____ IndexOf	g. Returns the lowercase equivalent of a string.
_____ TrimEnd	h. Extracts a string from within a string.
_____ Trim	i. Returns a copy of a string without leading spaces.

8 More about Message Boxes

CONCEPT: Sometimes you need a convenient way to display a message to the user. This section discusses the `MessageBox.Show` method, which allows you to display a message in a dialog box.

A message box is a pop-up window that displays a message to the user. You may have had a brief introduction to the `MessageBox.Show` method, which displays a message box. In this section we will discuss the `MessageBox.Show` method in greater detail and you will learn more about its capabilities. We will discuss the following general formats of the method call:

```
MessageBox.Show(Message)
MessageBox.Show(Message, Caption)
MessageBox.Show(Message, Caption, Buttons)
MessageBox.Show(Message, Caption, Buttons, Icon)
MessageBox.Show(Message, Caption, Buttons, Icon, DefaultButton)
```

When `MessageBox.Show` executes, a message box (a Windows dialog box) pops up. For example, the following statement causes the message box shown in Figure 20 to appear:

```
MessageBox.Show("Operation complete.")
```

In the second format, *Caption* is a string to be displayed in the message box's title bar. The following statement causes the message box shown in Figure 21 to appear:

```
MessageBox.Show("Operation complete.", "Status")
```

Figure 20 Message box

Figure 21 Message box with caption

In both formats, the message box has only an *OK* button. In the third format, *Buttons* is a value that specifies which buttons to display in the message box. Table 8 lists the available values for *Buttons* and describes each.

Table 8 Message box button values

Value	Description
`MessageBoxButtons.AbortRetryIgnore`	Displays *Abort*, *Retry*, and *Ignore* buttons
`MessageBoxButtons.OK`	Displays only an *OK* button
`MessageBoxButtons.OKCancel`	Displays *OK* and *Cancel* buttons
`MessageBoxButtons.RetryCancel`	Displays *Retry* and *Cancel* buttons
`MessageBoxButtons.YesNo`	Displays *Yes* and *No* buttons
`MessageBoxButtons.YesNoCancel`	Displays *Yes*, *No*, and *Cancel* buttons

For example, the following statement causes the message box shown in Figure 22 to appear:

```
MessageBox.Show("Do you wish to continue?", "Please Confirm",
            MessageBoxButtons.YesNo)
```

Figure 22 Message box with caption and *Yes* and *No* buttons

In some versions of `MessageBox.Show`, `Icon` is a value that specifies an icon to display in the message box. The available values for `Icon` are `MessageBoxIcon.Asterisk`, `MessageBoxIcon.Error`, `MessageBoxIcon.Exclamation`, `MessageBoxIcon.Hand`, `MessageBoxIcon.Information`, `MessageBoxIcon.Question`, `MessageBoxIcon.Stop`, and `MessageBoxIcon.Warning`. Figure 23 shows the icons matching each value. Note that some values display the same icon as others.

For example, the following statement causes the message box shown in Figure 24 to appear:

```
MessageBox.Show("Do you wish to continue?", "Please Confirm",
            MessageBoxButtons.YesNo, MessageBoxIcon.Question)
```

Figure 24 Message box with caption, *Yes* and *No* buttons, and *Question* icon

Figure 23 Message box icons

MessageBoxIcon.Asterisk
MessageBoxIcon.Information

MessageBoxIcon.Error
MessageBoxIcon.Hand
MessageBoxIcon.Stop

MessageBoxIcon.Exclamation
MessageBoxIcon.Warning

MessageBoxIcon.Question

In one version of `MessageBox.Show`, the `DefaultButton` argument specifies which button to select as the default button. The default button is the button clicked when the user presses the [Enter] key. Table 9 lists the available values for this argument.

Table 9 *DefaultButton* values

Value	Description
`MessageBoxDefaultButton.Button1`	Selects the leftmost button on the message box as the default button
`MessageBoxDefaultButton.Button2`	Selects the second button from the left edge of the message box as the default button
`MessageBoxDefaultButton.Button3`	Selects the third button from the left edge of the message box as the default button

For example, the following statement displays a message box and selects `Button2` (the *No* button) as the default button:

```
MessageBox.Show("Do you wish to continue?", "Please Confirm",
          MessageBoxButtons.YesNo, MessageBoxIcon.Question,
          MessageBoxDefaultButton.Button2)
```

Determining Which Button the User Clicked

When the user clicks any button on a message box, the message box is dismissed. In code, the `MessageBox.Show` method returns an integer that indicates which button the user clicked. You can compare this value with the values listed in Table 10 to determine which button was clicked.

Table 10 `MessageBox.Show` return values

Value	Meaning
`Windows.Forms.DialogResult.Abort`	The user clicked the *Abort* button
`Windows.Forms.DialogResult.Cancel`	The user clicked the *Cancel* button
`Windows.Forms.DialogResult.Ignore`	The user clicked the *Ignore* button
`Windows.Forms.DialogResult.No`	The user clicked the *No* button
`Windows.Forms.DialogResult.OK`	The user clicked the *OK* button
`Windows.Forms.DialogResult.Retry`	The user clicked the *Retry* button
`Windows.Forms.DialogResult.Yes`	The user clicked the *Yes* button

The following code shows how an `If` statement can take actions based on which message box button the user clicked:

```
Dim intResult As Integer
intResult = MessageBox.Show("Do you wish to continue?",
          "Please Confirm", MessageBoxButtons.YesNo)

If intResult = Windows.Forms.DialogResult.Yes Then
   ' Perform an action here
ElseIf intResult = Windows.Forms.DialogResult.No Then
   ' Perform another action here
End If
```

Using `ControlChars.CrLf` to Display Multiple Lines

If you want to display multiple lines of information in a message box, use the constant **`ControlChars.CrLf`** (CrLf stands for *carriage return line feed*). Concatenate it with the string you wish to display, where you wish to begin a new line (as shown in this example):

```
MessageBox.Show("This is line 1" & ControlChars.CrLf &
          "This is line 2")
```

This statement causes the message box in Figure 25 to appear. When Visual Basic displays the string `"This is line 1" & ControlChars.CrLf & "This is line 2"`, it interprets `ControlChars.CrLf` as a command to begin a new line of output.

Figure 25 Message box displaying two lines

 TIP: In code, you can use `ControlChars.CrLf` to create multiple lines in label text too.

 ## Checkpoint

11 Match each of the message boxes in Figure 26 with the statement it displays.

Figure 26 Message boxes

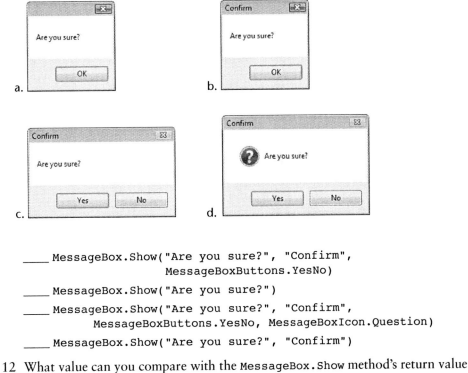

```
____ MessageBox.Show("Are you sure?", "Confirm",
                     MessageBoxButtons.YesNo)

____ MessageBox.Show("Are you sure?")

____ MessageBox.Show("Are you sure?", "Confirm",
          MessageBoxButtons.YesNo, MessageBoxIcon.Question)

____ MessageBox.Show("Are you sure?", "Confirm")
```

12 What value can you compare with the `MessageBox.Show` method's return value to determine if the user has clicked the *Abort* button?

13 The following statement displays *William Joseph Smith* in a message box. How would you modify the statement so that *William*, *Joseph*, and *Smith* appear on three separate lines?

```
MessageBox.Show("William Joseph Smith")
```

9 The Select Case Statement

CONCEPT: In a **Select Case** statement, one of several possible actions is taken, depending on the value of an expression.

The If...Then...ElseIf statement allows your program to branch into one of several possible paths. It performs a series of tests and branches when one of these tests is true. The **Select Case** statement, which is a similar mechanism, tests the value of an expression only once, and then uses that value to determine which set of statements to branch to. Following is the general format of the Select Case statement. The items inside the brackets are optional.

```
Select Case TestExpression
  [Case ExpressionList
    [one or more statements]]
  [Case ExpressionList
    [one or more statements]]
  ' Case statements may be repeated
  ' as many times as necessary.
  [Case Else
    [one or more statements]]
End Select
```

The first line starts with Select Case and is followed by a test expression. The test expression may be any numeric or string expression that you wish to test.

Starting on the next line is a sequence of one or more Case statements. Each Case statement follows this general form:

```
Case ExpressionList
  one or more statements
```

After the word Case is an expression list, so-called because it may hold one or more expressions. Beginning on the next line, one or more statements appear. These statements are executed if the value of the test expression matches any of the expressions in the Case statement's expression list.

A Case Else comes after all the Case statements. This branch is selected if none of the Case expression lists match the test expression. The entire Select Case construct is terminated with an End Select statement.

 WARNING: The Case Else section is optional. If you leave it out, however, your program will have nowhere to branch to if the test expression doesn't match any of the expressions in the Case expression lists.

Here is an example of the Select Case statement:

```
Select Case CInt(txtInput.Text)
  Case 1
    MessageBox.Show("Day 1 is Monday.")
  Case 2
    MessageBox.Show("Day 2 is Tuesday.")
  Case 3
    MessageBox.Show("Day 3 is Wednesday.")
```

```
    Case 4
       MessageBox.Show("Day 4 is Thursday.")
    Case 5
       MessageBox.Show("Day 5 is Friday.")
    Case 6
       MessageBox.Show("Day 6 is Saturday.")
    Case 7
       MessageBox.Show("Day 7 is Sunday.")
    Case Else
       MessageBox.Show("That value is invalid.")
  End Select
```

Let's look at this example more closely. The test expression is `CInt(txtInput.Text)`. The `Case` statements `Case 1`, `Case 2`, `Case 3`, `Case 4`, `Case 5`, `Case 6`, and `Case 7` mark where the program is to branch to if the test expression is equal to the values 1, 2, 3, 4, 5, 6, or 7. The `Case Else` section is branched to if the test expression is not equal to any of these values.

Suppose the user has entered 3 into the `txtInput` text box, so the expression `CInt(txtInput.Text)` is equal to 3. Visual Basic compares this value with the first `Case` statement's expression list:

```
   Select Case CInt(txtInput.Text)
➡ Case 1
       MessageBox.Show("Day 1 is Monday.")
```

The only value in the expression list is 1, and this is not equal to 3, so Visual Basic goes to the next `Case`:

```
   Select Case CInt(txtInput.Text)
     Case 1
       MessageBox.Show("Day 1 is Monday.")
➡ Case 2
       MessageBox.Show("Day 2 is Tuesday.")
```

Once again, the value in the expression list does not equal 3, so Visual Basic goes to the next `Case`:

```
   Select Case CInt(txtInput.Text)
     Case 1
       MessageBox.Show("Day 1 is Monday.")
     Case 2
       MessageBox.Show("Day 2 is Tuesday.")
➡ Case 3
       MessageBox.Show("Day 3 is Wednesday.")
```

This time, the value in the `Case`'s expression list matches the value of the test expression, so the `MessageBox.Show` statement on the next line executes. (If there had been multiple statements appearing between the `Case 3` and `Case 4` statements, all would have executed.) After the `MessageBox.Show` statement executes, the program jumps to the statement immediately following the `End Select` statement.

The Select Case Structure in Flowcharts and Pseudocode

The flowchart segment in Figure 27 shows the general form of a `Case` structure. The diamond represents the test expression, which is compared to a series of values. The path of execution follows the value matching the test expression. If none of the values matches a test expression, the default path is followed (`Case Else`).

Figure 27 General form of a Case structure

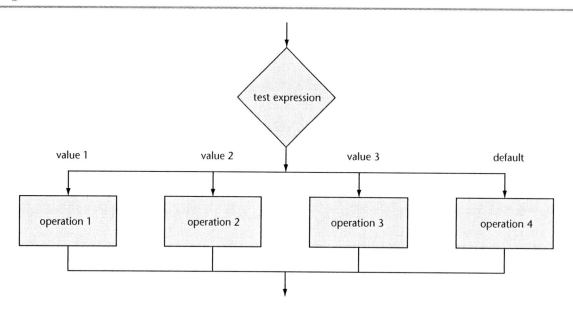

As with the `If` statement, the pseudocode for the `Select Case` statement looks very similar to the actual programming statements. The following is an example:

> *Select Case Input*
>   *Case 1*
>   *Display Message "Day 1 is Monday."*
>   *Case 2*
>   *Display Message "Day 2 is Tuesday."*
>   *Case 3*
>   *Display Message "Day 3 is Wednesday."*
>   *Case 4*
>   *Display Message "Day 4 is Thursday."*
>   *Case 5*
>   *Display Message "Day 5 is Friday."*
>   *Case 6*
>   *Display Message "Day 6 is Saturday."*
>   *Case 7*
>   *Display Message "Day 7 is Sunday."*
>   *Case Else*
>   *Display Message "That value is invalid."*
> *End Select*

More about the Expression List

The `Case` statement's expression list can contain multiple expressions, separated by commas. For example, the first `Case` statement in the following code compares `intNumber` to 1, 3, 5, 7, and 9, and the second `Case` statement compares it to 2, 4, 6, 8, and 10. In the following code, assume that `strStatus` is a string variable:

```
Select Case intNumber
   Case 1, 3, 5, 7, 9
      strStatus = "Odd"
   Case 2, 4, 6, 8, 10
      strStatus = "Even"
   Case Else
      strStatus = "Out of Range"
End Select
```

The `Case` statement can also test string values. In the following code, assume that strAnimal is a string variable:

```
Select Case strAnimal
  Case "Dogs", "Cats"
    MessageBox.Show("House Pets")
  Case "Cows", "Pigs", "Goats"
    MessageBox.Show("Farm Animals")
  Case "Lions", "Tigers", "Bears"
    MessageBox.Show("Oh My!")
End Select
```

You can use relational operators in the `Case` statement, as shown by the following example. The `Is` keyword represents the test expression in the relational comparison.

```
Select Case dblTemperature
  Case Is <= 75
    blnTooCold = True
  Case Is >= 100
    blnTooHot = True
  Case Else
    blnJustRight = True
End Select
```

Finally, you can determine whether the test expression falls within a range of values. This requires the `To` keyword, as shown in the following code.

```
Select Case intScore
  Case Is >= 90
    strGrade = "A"
  Case 80 To 89
    strGrade = "B"
  Case 70 To 79
    strGrade = "C"
  Case 60 To 69
    strGrade = "D"
  Case 0 To 59
    strGrade = "F"
  Case Else
    MessageBox.Show("Invalid Score")
End Select
```

The numbers used on each side of the `To` keyword are included in the range. So, the statement `Case 80 To 89` matches the values 80, 89, or any number in between.

TIP: The `To` keyword works properly only when the smaller number appears on its left and the larger number appears on its right. You can write an expression such as `10 To 0`, but it will not function properly at runtime.

Tutorial 7 examines a sales commission calculator application.

Tutorial 7:

Examining *Crazy Al's Sales Commission Calculator* application

Crazy Al's Computer Emporium is a retail seller of personal computers. The sales staff at Crazy Al's works strictly on commission. At the end of the month, each salesperson's commission is calculated according to Table 11.

For example, a salesperson with $16,000 in monthly sales earns a 12% commission ($1,920.00). A salesperson with $20,000 in monthly sales earns a 14% commission ($2,800.00).

Table 11 Sales commission rates

Sales This Month	Commission Rate
Less than $10,000	5%
$10,000 – $14,999	10%
$15,000 – $17,999	12%
$18,000 – $21,999	14%
$22,000 or more	16%

Because the staff is paid once per month, Crazy Al's allows each employee to take up to $1,500 per month in advance pay. When sales commissions are calculated, the amount of each employee's advance pay is subtracted from the commission. If any salesperson's commission is less than the amount of the advance, he or she must reimburse Crazy Al's for the difference.

Here are two examples:

- Beverly's monthly sales were $21,400, so her commission is $2,996. She took $1,500 in advance pay. At the end of the month she gets a check for $1,496.
- John's monthly sales were $12,600, so his commission is $1,260. He took $1,500 in advance pay. At the end of the month he must pay back $240 to Crazy Al's.

In this tutorial, you examine the *Crazy Al's Commission Calculator* application used to determine a salesperson's commission.

Step 1: Open the *Crazy Al* project from the student sample programs folder named *Chap4\Crazy Al*.

Step 2: Run the application. The form shown in Figure 28 appears.

Step 3: Enter **16000** as the amount of sales for this month (first text box).

Figure 28 *Crazy Al's Commission Calculator* form

Step 4: Enter **1000** as the amount of advance pay taken (second text box). Click the *Calculate* button. You should see the commission rate, commission, and net pay information, as shown in Figure 29.

Step 5: Click the *Clear* button to reset the contents of the input and display fields.

Figure 29 Calculations filled in

Experiment with other values for sales and advance pay.

Step 6: When you are finished, click the *Exit* button to end the application.

Step 7: Open the *Code* window and look at the btnCalculate_Click event handler. The code is as follows:

```
Private Sub btnCalculate_Click(...) Handles btnCalculate.Click
    ' Variable declarations
    Dim decSalesAmount As Decimal          ' Monthly sales amount
    Dim decAdvancePayAmount As Decimal     ' Advance pay taken
    Dim decCommissionRate As Decimal       ' Commission rate
    Dim decCommissionAmount As Decimal     ' Commission
    Dim decNetPay As Decimal               ' Net pay

    Try
        ' Get the amount of sales.
        decSalesAmount = CDec(txtSalesAmount.Text)

        ' Get the amount of advance pay.
        decAdvancePayAmount = CDec(txtAdvancePayAmount.Text)

        ' Determine the commission rate.
        Select Case decSalesAmount
            Case Is < 10000
                decCommissionRate = 0.05D

            Case 10000 To 14999
                decCommissionRate = 0.1D

            Case 15000 To 17999
                decCommissionRate = 0.12D

            Case 18000 To 21999
                decCommissionRate = 0.14D

            Case Is >= 22000
                decCommissionRate = 0.15D
        End Select
```

```
    ' Calculate the commission and net pay amounts.
    decCommissionAmount = decSalesAmount * decCommissionRate
    decNetPay = decCommissionAmount - decAdvancePayAmount

    ' Display the rate, commission, and net pay.
    lblCommissionRate.Text = decCommissionRate.ToString("p")
    lblCommissionAmount.Text = decCommissionAmount.ToString("c")
    lblNetPay.Text = decNetPay.ToString("c")

Catch
    ' Display an error message.
    MessageBox.Show("Input must be numeric.")
    End Try
End Sub
```

As you can see, the Select Case construct has a Case statement for each level of sales in the commission table.

Checkpoint

14 Convert the following If...Then...ElseIf statement into a Select Case statement.

```
If intQuantity >= 0 And intQuantity <= 9 Then
    decDiscount = 0.1
ElseIf intQuantity >= 10 And intQuantity <= 19 Then
    decDiscount = 0.2
ElseIf intQuantity >= 20 And intQuantity <= 29 Then
    decDiscount = 0.3
ElseIf intQuantity >= 30 Then
    decDiscount = 0.4
Else
    MessageBox.Show("Invalid Data")
End If
```

10 Introduction to Input Validation

CONCEPT: Input validation is the process of inspecting input values and determining whether they are valid.

The accuracy of a program's output is only as good as the accuracy of its input. Therefore, it is important that your applications perform input validation on the values entered by the user. **Input validation** is the process of inspecting input values and determining whether they are valid. In this section we will discuss ways of using decision structures to prevent data conversion exceptions, and determine whether numeric values entered by the user fall within an acceptable range.

Preventing Data Conversion Exceptions

An exception will occur if you try to convert the contents of a TextBox to a number, but the TextBox contains nonnumeric data. We introduced the Try-Catch statement, and you saw how to use it to handle those exceptions when they occur. Now that you know how to use the If...Then statement, you have more validation techniques at your disposal.

For example, suppose there is a way to determine whether a TextBox contains a value that can be successfully converted to a specific data type *before* you try to convert it to that data type. If that is possible, you can prevent data conversion exceptions from occurring in the first place. In Visual Basic, you can use a family of methods known as the **TryParse methods** to make this determination.

In computer science, the term **parse** typically means to analyze a string of characters for some purpose. The purpose of the TryParse methods is to parse a string, and try to convert the string's contents to a value of a specific data type. A TryParse method returns a Boolean value (True or False) to let you know if the conversion was successful. Table 12 describes several of the TryParse methods.

Table 12 TryParse methods

Method	Description
Integer.TryParse	Accepts two arguments: a string (argument 1) and an Integer variable (argument 2). The method attempts to convert the string (argument 1) to an Integer. If successful, the converted value is assigned to the Integer variable (argument 2) and the method returns True. If the conversion is not successful, the method returns False.
Double.TryParse	Accepts two arguments: a string (argument 1) and Double variable (argument 2). The method attempts to convert the string (argument 1) to a Double. If successful, the converted value is assigned to the Double variable (argument 2) and the method returns True. If the conversion is not successful, the method returns False.
Decimal.TryParse	Accepts two arguments: a string (argument 1) and a Decimal variable (argument 2). The method attempts to convert the string (argument 1) to a Decimal. If successful, the converted value is assigned to the Decimal variable (argument 2) and the method returns True. If the conversion is not successful, the method returns False.
Single.TryParse	Accepts two arguments: a string (argument 1) and a Single variable (argument 2). The method attempts to convert the string (argument 1) to a Single. If successful, the converted value is assigned to the Single variable (argument 2) and the method returns True. If the conversion is not successful, the method returns False.
Date.TryParse	Accepts two arguments: a string (argument 1) and a Date variable (argument 2). The method attempts to convert the string (argument 1) to a Date value. If successful, the converted value is assigned to the Date variable (argument 2) and the method returns True. If the conversion is not successful, the method returns False.

Because these methods return either True or False, they are commonly called as the Boolean expression in an If...Then statement. The following code snippet shows an example using the Integer.TryParse method. The lines are numbered for reference purposes. As you read the code, assume txtInput is the name of a TextBox control.

```
1 Dim intNumber As Integer
2
3 If Integer.TryParse(txtInput.Text, intNumber) Then
4    MessageBox.Show("Success!")
5 Else
6    MessageBox.Show("Error: Conversion failed.")
7 End If
```

The purpose of this code snippet is to convert the value of txtInput's Text property to an Integer and assign that value to the intNumber variable, which is declared in line 1. In line 3, the If...Then statement calls the Integer.TryParse method, passing txtInput.Text as argument 1 and intNumber as argument 2. Here's what happens:

- If txtInput.Text is successfully converted to an Integer, the resulting value is assigned to the intNumber variable, and the method returns True. That causes the statement in line 4 to execute.
- If txtInput.Text cannot be converted to an Integer, the method returns False. That causes the statement in line 6 (after the Else clause) to execute.

In Tutorial 8 you will look at a simple application that uses the Integer.TryParse and Decimal.TryParse methods to validate data entered by the user.

Tutorial 8:

Examining an application that uses TryParse for input validation

VideoNote

Validating Input with TryParse

Step 1: Open the *Gross Pay* project from the student sample programs folder named *Chap4\Gross Pay*. The student sample programs folder can be downloaded from www.microsoft.com/express/Downloads/. Figure 30 shows the application's form. This is a simple program that allows you to enter the number of hours worked and your hourly pay rate. When you click the *Calculate Gross Pay* button, your gross pay is calculated and displayed.

Step 2: Run the application. Enter an invalid value such as *xyz9* for the hours worked, and then click the *Calculate Gross Pay* button. Notice that a message box appears with the message *Enter a valid integer for hours worked*. Click the *OK* button to dismiss the message box.

Figure 30 The *Gross Pay* application's form

Step 3: Enter *40* for the hours worked (a valid number), and then enter an invalid value such as *abc44* for the hourly pay rate. Click the *Calculate Gross Pay* button. Notice that a message box appears, this time showing the message *Enter a valid value for hourly pay rate*. Click the *OK* button to dismiss the message box.

Step 4: With *40* still entered for the hours worked, change the hourly pay rate to *50*. Click the *Calculate Gross Pay* button. This time $2,000.00 is displayed as the gross pay.

Step 5: Click the *Exit* button to exit the application.

Step 6:   Switch to the *Code* window and locate the `btnCalculate_Click` event handler. The code is shown here, with line numbers inserted for reference:

```
1 Private Sub btnCalculate_Click(...) Handles btnCalculate.Click
2   ' Declare variables
3   Dim intHours As Integer        ' Hours worked
4   Dim decPayRate As Decimal      ' Hourly pay rate
5   Dim decGrossPay As Decimal     ' Gross pay
6
7   ' Get the hours worked.
8   If Integer.TryParse(txtHours.Text, intHours) Then
9
10     ' Get the hourly pay rate.
11     If Decimal.TryParse(txtPayRate.Text, decPayRate) Then
12       ' Calculate the gross pay.
13       decGrossPay = intHours * decPayRate
14
15       ' Display the gross pay.
16       lblGrossPay.Text = decGrossPay.ToString("c")
17     Else
18       ' Display pay rate error message.
19       MessageBox.Show("Enter a valid value for hourly pay rate.")
20     End If
21
22   Else
23     ' Display hours worked error message.
24     MessageBox.Show("Enter a valid integer for hours worked.")
25   End If
26 End Sub
```

Let's take a closer look at the code:

- Lines 3 through 5 declare the variables `intHours` (to hold hours worked), `decPayRate` (to hold the hourly pay rate), and `decGrossPay` (to hold the gross pay).
- The `If...Then` statement that begins in line 8 calls `Integer.TryParse` to convert `txtHours.Text` to an Integer and assign the result to `intHours`. If the conversion fails, the program jumps to the `Else` clause in line 22, and the message *Enter a valid integer for hours worked* is displayed in line 24. If the conversion is successful, however, the program continues with the `If...Then` statement in line 11.
- The `If...Then` statement that begins in line 11 calls `Decimal.TryParse` to convert `txtPayRate.Text` to a Decimal and assign the result to `decPayRate`. If the conversion fails, the program jumps to the `Else` clause in line 17, and the message *Enter a valid value for hourly pay rate* is displayed in line 19. If the conversion is successful, however, the program continues with the calculation in line 13.
- Line 13 multiplies `intHours` by `decPayRate` and assigns the result to `decGrossPay`.
- Line 16 displays the value of `decGrossPay`, formatted as currency.

Checking Numeric Ranges

In addition to checking for valid conversions, you sometimes need to check numeric input values to make sure they fall within a range. For example, suppose you are running the *Gross Pay* application from Tutorial 8, and instead of entering 40 as the number of hours, you accidentally enter 400. The program doesn't know that you made a mistake, so it uses the bad data that you entered to calculate the gross pay.

This error could be avoided by having an `If...Then` statement that tests the number of hours to make sure it is a reasonable value. For example, there are 168 hours in a week, so the maximum number of hours that a person can work in a week is 168. The following `If...Then` statement determines whether the variable `intHours` is in the range of 0 through 168:

```
If intHours >= 0 And intHours <= 168 Then
    decGrosspay = intHours * decPayRate
Else
    MessageBox.Show("Invalid number of hours.")
End If
```

In this code, we used the `And` logical operator to create the following Boolean expression:

```
intHours >= 0 And intHours <= 168
```

This expression is true only if the value of `intHours` is within the range of 0 through 168.

It's also possible to enter an invalid value for the hourly pay rate. Suppose the company's maximum hourly pay rate is 45. Only values in the range of 0 through 45 are valid, so we could add another `If...Then` statement (shown here in bold) that validates the value of the `decPayRate` variable:

```
If intHours >= 0 And intHours <= 168 Then
    If decPayRate >= 0 And decPayRate <= 45.0 Then
      decGrosspay = intHours * decPayRate
    Else
      MessageBox.Show("Invalid pay rate.")
    End If
Else
    MessageBox.Show("Invalid number of hours.")
End If
```

In the previous examples we determined whether a value was within a range. Sometimes you want to know if a value is outside of a range. In that case it is better to use the `Or` operator to create a Boolean expression. For example, suppose you've written an application that is a car driving simulator, and the `intSpeed` variable holds the car's current speed. In the simulation, the minimum speed limit is 35 and the maximum speed limit is 60. To determine whether `intSpeed` is outside this range, we could use the following logic:

```
If intSpeed < 35 Or intSpeed > 60 Then
    MessageBox.Show("Speed violation!")
End If
```

It's important not to get the logic of the logical operators confused when testing for a range of values. For example, the Boolean expression in the following `If...Then` statement would never test true:

```
' This is an error!
If intSpeed < 35 And intSpeed > 60 Then
    MessageBox.Show("Speed violation!")
End If
```

Obviously, `intSpeed` cannot be less than 35 and at the same time be greater than 60.

11 Focus on GUI Design: Radio Buttons and Check Boxes

CONCEPT: Radio buttons appear in groups of two or more, allowing the user to select one of several options. A check box allows the user to select an item by checking a box, or deselect the item by unchecking the box.

Radio Buttons

Radio buttons are useful when you want the user to select one choice from several possible choices. Figure 31 shows a group of radio buttons.

A radio button may be selected or deselected. Each radio button has a small circle that appears filled in when the radio button is selected, and appears empty when the radio button is deselected.

Visual Basic provides the **RadioButton control**, which allows you to create radio buttons. Radio buttons are normally grouped in one of the following ways:

- All radio buttons inside a group box are members of the same group.
- All radio buttons on a form not inside a group box are members of the same group.

Figure 32 shows two forms. The form on the left has three radio buttons that belong to the same group. The form on the right has two groups of radio buttons.

At runtime, only one radio button in a group may be selected at a time, which makes them mutually exclusive. Clicking on a radio button selects it, and automatically deselects any other radio button in the same group.

Figure 31 Radio buttons

Figure 32 Forms with radio buttons

 NOTE: The name *radio button* refers to the old car radios that had push buttons for selecting stations. Only one button could be pushed in at a time. When you pushed a button, it automatically popped out the currently selected button.

Radio Button Properties

Radio buttons have a Text property, which holds the text that is displayed next to the radio button's circle. For example, the radio buttons in the leftmost form in Figure 32 have their Text properties set to *Coffee*, *Tea*, and *Soft Drink*.

Radio buttons have a Boolean property named Checked. The **Checked property** is set to *True* when the radio button is selected and *False* when the radio button is deselected. Their default value is *False*.

Working with Radio Buttons in Code

The prefix that we use for radio button control names is rad. You determine if a radio button is selected by testing its Checked property. The following code shows an example. Assume that radChoice1, radChoice2, and radChoice3 are radio buttons in the same group:

```
If radChoice1.Checked = True Then
   MessageBox.Show("You selected Choice 1")
ElseIf radChoice2.Checked = True Then
   MessageBox.Show("You selected Choice 2")
ElseIf radChoice3.Checked = True Then
   MessageBox.Show("You selected Choice 3")
End If
```

Radio Buttons have a **CheckedChanged** event that is triggered when the user selects or delelects a radio button. If you double-click a radio button in the *Designer* window, a code template for the CheckedChange event handler is created in the *Code* window.

Assigning a TabIndex Value and an Access Key to a Radio Button

Radio button controls have a position in the form's tab order, which may be changed with the TabIndex property. As with other controls, you can assign an access key to a radio button by placing an ampersand (&) in the Text property, just before the character you wish to serve as the access key. The character will appear underlined on the form. At runtime, when the user presses the Alt+*access key* combination, the focus shifts to the radio button, and the radio button is selected.

Selecting a Radio Button in Code

You can use code to select a radio button, using an assignment statement to set the desired radio button's Checked property to *True*, for example:

```
radChoice1.Checked = True
```

TIP: If you set a radio button's Checked property to *True* in Design mode (with the *Properties* window), it becomes the default radio button for that group. It is selected when the application starts up and it remains selected until the user or application code selects another radio button.

Check Boxes

A *check box* appears as a small box, labeled with a caption. An example is shown in Figure 33.

Figure 33 Check box

Visual Basic provides the **CheckBox control**, which allows you to create check boxes. Like radio buttons, check boxes may be selected or deselected at runtime. When a check box is selected, a small check mark appears inside the box. Unlike radio buttons, check boxes are not mutually exclusive. You may have one or more check boxes on a form or in a group box, and any number of them can be selected at any given time.

The prefix that we use for a CheckBox control's name is chk. Like radio buttons, check boxes have a Checked property. When a check box is selected, or checked, its Checked property is set to *True*. When a check box is deselected, or unchecked, its Checked property is set to *False*. Here is a summary of other characteristics of the check box:

- A check box's caption is stored in the Text property.
- A check box's place in the tab order may be modified with the TabIndex property. When a check box has the focus, a thin dotted line appears around its text. You can check or uncheck it by pressing the [Spacebar].
- You may assign an access key to a check box by placing an ampersand (&) in the Text property, just before the character that you wish to serve as the access key.
- You can use code to select or deselect a check box. Simply use an assignment statement to set the desired check box's Checked property, for example:

```
chkChoice4.Checked = True
```

- You may set a check box's Checked property at design time.
- Like radio buttons, check boxes have a CheckedChanged event that is triggered whenever the user changes the state of the check box. If you have written a CheckedChanged event handler for the check box, it will execute whenever the user checks or unchecks the check box.

In Tutorial 9, you complete the code for an application that demonstrates radio buttons and check boxes.

Tutorial 9:
Completing an application with radio buttons and check boxes

Step 1: Open the *Radio Button Check Box Demo* project from the student sample programs folder named *Chap4\Radio Button Check Box Demo*.

Step 2: Open *Form1* in *Design* mode, as shown in Figure 34.

Figure 34 *Radio Button Check Box Demo* form

Step 3: Double-click the *OK* button and insert the following bold code into the btnOk_Click event handler:

```
Private Sub btnOk_Click(...) Handles btnOk.Click
    ' Determine which radio button is selected.
    If radChoice1.Checked = True Then
        MessageBox.Show("You selected Choice 1.")
    ElseIf radChoice2.Checked = True Then
        MessageBox.Show("You selected Choice 2.")
    ElseIf radChoice3.Checked = True Then
        MessageBox.Show("You selected Choice 3.")
    End If

    ' Determine which check boxes are checked.
    If chkChoice4.Checked = True Then
        MessageBox.Show("You selected Choice 4.")
    End If

    If chkChoice5.Checked = True Then
        MessageBox.Show("You selected Choice 5.")
    End If

    If chkChoice6.Checked = True Then
        MessageBox.Show("You selected Choice 6.")
    End If
End Sub
```

Step 4: Save the project and run the application.

Step 5: Click *Choice 3*, *Choice 4*, and *Choice 6*. When you click the *OK* button you should see three message boxes, one after the other, indicating your selections. Experiment by clicking different radio buttons and check boxes. Note the results you see after clicking the *OK* button.

Checkpoint

15 In code, how do you determine whether a radio button has been selected?

16 If several radio buttons are placed on a form, not inside group boxes, how many of them may be selected at any given time?

17 In code, how do you determine whether a check box has been selected?

18 If several check boxes appear on a form, how many of them may be selected at any given time?

19 How can the user check or uncheck a check box that has the focus by using the keyboard?

12 Focus on Program Design and Problem Solving: Building the *Health Club Membership Fee Calculator* Application

CONCEPT: In this section you build the *Health Club Membership Fee Calculator* application. It will use features discussed in this chapter, including decision structures, radio buttons, and check boxes.

The Bay City Health and Fitness Club charges the following monthly membership rates:

Standard adult membership: $40/month
Child (age 12 and under): $20/month
Student: $25/month
Senior citizen (age 65 and over): $30/month

The club also offers the following optional services, which increase the base monthly fee:

Yoga lessons: add $10 to the monthly fee
Karate lessons: add $30 to the monthly fee
Personal trainer: add $50 to the monthly fee

The manager of the club has asked you to create a *Health Club Membership Fee Calculator* application. It should allow the user to select a membership rate, select optional services, and enter the number of months of the membership. It should calculate the member's monthly and total charges for the specified number of months. The application should also validate the number of months entered by the user. An error message should be displayed if the user enters a number less than 1 or greater than 24. (Membership fees tend to increase every two years, so there is a club policy that no membership package can be purchased for more than 24 months at a time.)

Figure 35 shows a sketch of the application's form. The figure also shows the name of each control with a programmer-defined name.

Figure 35 Sketch of the *Health Club Membership Fee Calculator* form

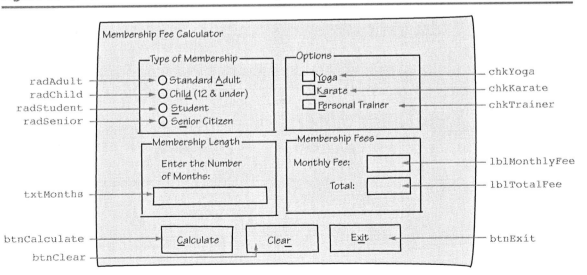

Table 13 lists each control, along with any relevant property settings.

Table 13 *Health Club Membership Fee Calculator* controls

Control Type	Control Name	Property	Property Value
Form	(Default)	Text:	*Membership Fee Calculator*
Group box	(Default)	Text:	*Type of Membership*
Radio button	radAdult	Text:	*Standard &Adult*
		Checked:	*True*
Radio button	radChild	Text:	*Chil&d (12 && under)*
Radio button	radStudent	Text:	*&Student*
Radio button	radSenior	Text:	*S&enior Citizen*
Group box	(Default)	Text:	*Options*
Check box	chkYoga	Text:	*&Yoga*
Check box	chkKarate	Text:	*&Karate*
Check box	chkTrainer	Text:	*&Personal Trainer*
Group box	(Default)	Text:	*Membership Length*
Label	(Default)	Text:	*Enter the Number of Months:*
Text box	txtMonths	Text:	
Group box	(Default)	Text:	*Membership Fees*
Label	(Default)	Text:	*Monthly Fee:*
Label	(Default)	Text:	*Total:*
Label	lblMonthlyFee	BorderStyle:	*Fixed3D*
		Text:	Initially cleared
		AutoSize:	*False*
Label	lblTotalFee	BorderStyle:	*Fixed3D*
		Text:	Initially cleared
		AutoSize:	*False*
Button	btnCalculate	Text:	*&Calculate*
Button	btnClear	Text:	*Clea&r*
Button	btnExit	Text:	*E&xit*

Table 14 lists and describes the event handlers needed for this application.

Table 14 *Health Club Membership Fee Calculator* event handlers

Event Handler	Description
btnCalculate_Click	First, this procedure validates the number of months entered by the user. Then, if the input is valid, it calculates the monthly fees and the total fee for the time period. Charges for optional services are included. If the input is not valid, it displays an error message.
btnClear_Click	Clears the text box, output labels, and check boxes, and resets the radio buttons so that radAdult is selected.
btnExit_Click	Ends the application.

Figure 36 shows a flowchart for the `btnCalculate_Click` event handler.

The number of months entered by the user is tested to determine whether it is valid. If the value is less than 1 or greater than 24, an error message is displayed. If the number of months is valid, the fees are calculated.

The first two processes in the calculation are (1) calculate the base monthly fee, and (2) calculate and add the cost of optional services. Each of these processes can be expanded into more detailed flowcharts. Figure 37 shows a more detailed view of the *calculate the base monthly fee* process.

Figure 36 Flowchart for `btnCalculate_Click`

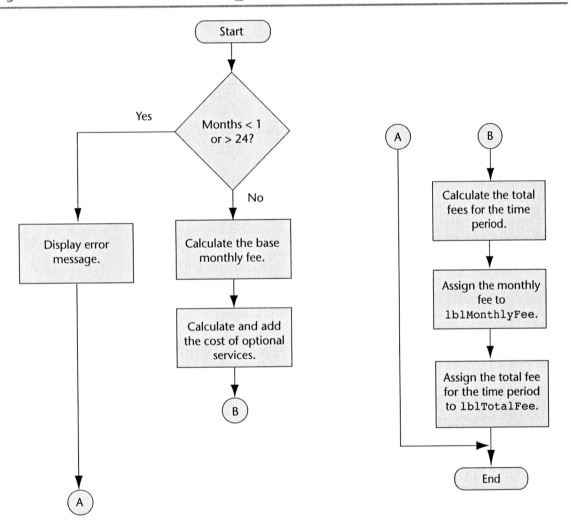

Figure 37 Flowchart of *calculate the base monthly fee* process

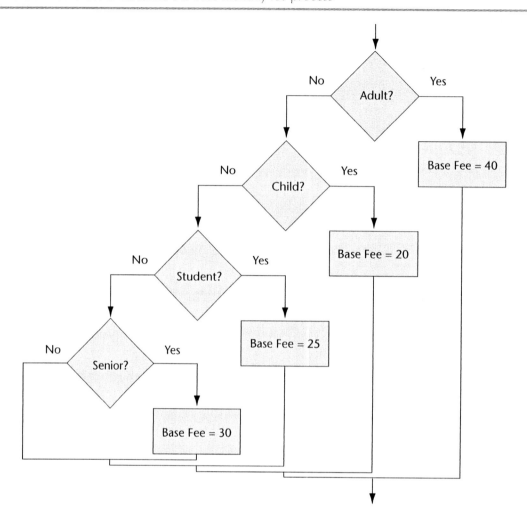

The logic in the flowchart can be expressed by the following pseudocode:

> *If Member is an Adult Then*
> *Monthly Base Fee = 40*
> *ElseIf Member is a Child Then*
> *Montlby Base Fee = 20*
> *ElseIf Member is a Student Then*
> *Monthly Base Fee = 25*
> *ElseIf Member is a Senior Citizen Then*
> *Monthly Base Fee = 30*
> *End If*

Figure 38 shows a more detailed view of the *calculate and add the cost of optional services* process.

Figure 38 Flowchart of *calculate and add the cost of optional services* process

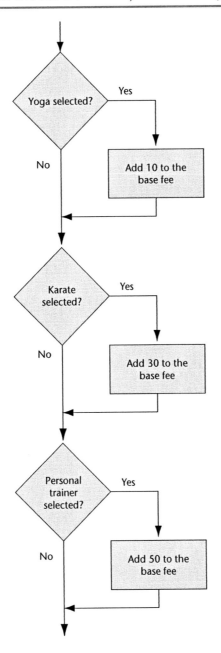

The logic in the flowchart can be expressed with the following pseudocode:

If Yoga is selected Then
  Add 10 to the monthly base fee
End If
If Karate is selected Then
  Add 30 to the monthly base fee
End If
If Personal Trainer is selected Then
  Add 50 to the monthly base fee
End If

Tutorial 10 builds the *Health Club Membership Fee Calculator* application.

Tutorial 10:

Building the *Health Club Membership Fee Calculator* application

Step 1: Create a new Windows application project named *Health Club Membership Fee Calculator*.

Step 2: Set up the form as shown in Figure 39. Create the group boxes, radio buttons, and check boxes. Refer to the sketch in Figure 35 for the control names and Table 13 for the relevant property settings of each control.

Figure 39 *Membership Fee Calculator* form

Step 3: In the *Designer* window, double-click the *Calculate* button to create the code template for the btnCalculate_Click event handler. Type the code shown here in bold. (Don't type the line numbers. We have inserted them for reference only.)

```
1 Private Sub btnCalculate_Click(...) Handles btnCalculate.Click
2     ' Declare local variables.
3     Dim decBaseFee As Decimal   ' Base Monthly Fee
4     Dim decTotalFee As Decimal  ' Total Membership Fee
5     Dim intMonths As Integer    ' Number of months
6
7     ' Constants for base fees
8     Const decADULT_FEE As Decimal = 40D
9     Const decCHILD_FEE As Decimal = 20D
10    Const decSTUDENT_FEE As Decimal = 25D
11    Const decSENIOR_FEE As Decimal = 30D
12
13    ' Constants for additional fees
14    Const decYOGA_FEE As Decimal = 10D
15    Const decKARATE_FEE As Decimal = 30D
16    Const decTRAINER_FEE As Decimal = 50D
17
18    ' Get the number of months.
19    If Integer.TryParse(txtMonths.Text, intMonths) Then
20        ' Validate the number of months.
21        If intMonths >= 1 And intMonths <= 24 Then
22            ' Determine the base monthly fee.
23            If radAdult.Checked = True Then
24                decBaseFee = decADULT_FEE
```

```
25          ElseIf radChild.Checked = True Then
26            decBaseFee = decCHILD_FEE
27          ElseIf radStudent.Checked = True Then
28            decBaseFee = decSTUDENT_FEE
29          ElseIf radSenior.Checked = True Then
30            decBaseFee = decSENIOR_FEE
31          End If
32
33          ' Look for additional services.
34          If chkYoga.Checked = True Then
35            decBaseFee += decYOGA_FEE
36          End If
37
38          If chkKarate.Checked = True Then
39            decBaseFee += decKARATE_FEE
40          End If
41
42          If chkTrainer.Checked = True Then
43            decBaseFee += decTRAINER_FEE
44          End If
45
46          ' Calculate the total fee.
47          decTotalFee = decBaseFee * intMonths
48
49          ' Display the fees.
50          lblMonthlyFee.Text = decBaseFee.ToString("c")
51          lblTotalFee.Text = decTotalFee.ToString("c")
52        Else
53          ' Error: Months is outside the range 1-24.
54          MessageBox.Show("Months must be in the range 1 - 24.")
55        End If
56      Else
57        ' Error: value entered for months is not an integer.
58        MessageBox.Show("Months must be an integer.")
59      End If
60 End Sub
```

Let's take a moment to go over this code. Lines 3 through 5 declare the following variables:

- The decBaseFee variable will hold the member's base monthly fee ($440 for an adult, $20 for a child, $25 for a student, or $30 for a senior citizen).
- The decTotalFee variable will hold the member's total monthly fee.
- The intMonths variable will hold the number of months of membership.

Lines 8 through 11 declare the following constants:

- decADULT_FEE specifies the monthly base fee for an adult membership.
- decCHILD_FEE specifies the monthly base fee for a child membership.
- decSTUDENT_FEE specifies the monthly base fee for a student membership.
- decSENIOR_FEE specifies the monthly base fee for a senior citizen membership.

Lines 14 through 16 declare the following constants:

- decYOGA_FEE specifies the additional monthly fee for yoga lessons.
- decKARATE_FEE specifies the additional monthly base fee for karate lessons.
- decTRAINER_FEE specifies the additional monthly base fee for a personal trainer.

The `If...Then` statement in line 19 calls `Integer.TryParse` to convert the value `txtMonths.Text` to an Integer, and assign the result to the `intMonths` variable. If the conversion fails, the program will branch to the `Else` clause in line 56, and the statement in line 58 displays an error message. If the conversion succeeds, the program continues to the `If...Then` statement in line 21.

Recall that the number of months must be in the range of 1 through 24. The `If...Then` statement in line 21 determines whether the value of `intMonths` falls within this range. If it does not, the program will branch to the `Else` clause in line 52, and the statement in line 54 displays an error message. If the conversion succeeds, the program continues to the `If...Then...ElseIf` statement that begins in line 23.

The user selects a radio button on the application's form to specify the type of membership. The `If...Then...ElseIf` statement that begins in line 23 determines which of the radio buttons is selected, and assigns the correct value to the `decBaseFee` variable.

Next, a series of three `If...Then` statements appears in lines 34 through 44. These statements determine whether any of the check boxes for additional services (yoga lessons, karate lessons, or a personal trainer) have been selected. If any have been selected, the `decBaseFee` variable is increased by the necessary amount.

Next, line 47 calculates the total fee by multiplying the monthly fee by the number of months. The result is assigned to the `decTotalFee` variable. Line 50 displays the monthly fee, and line 51 displays the total fee.

Step 4: Go back to the *Designer* window, and double-click the *Clear* button to create the code template for the `btnClear_Click` event handler. Type the code shown here in bold.

```
Private Sub btnClear_Click(...) Handles btnClear.Click
    ' Reset the Adult radio button.
    radAdult.Checked = True

    ' Clear the check boxes.
    chkYoga.Checked = False
    chkKarate.Checked = False
    chkTrainer.Checked = False

    ' Clear the number of months.
    txtMonths.Clear()

    ' Clear the fee labels.
    lblMonthlyFee.Text = String.Empty
    lblTotalFee.Text = String.Empty

    ' Give txtMonths the focus.
    txtMonths.Focus()
End Sub
```

Step 5: Go back to the *Designer* window, and double-click the *Exit* button to create the code template for the `btnExit_Click` event handler. Type the code shown here in bold.

```
Private Sub btnExit_Click(...) Handles btnExit.Click
    ' Close the form.
    Me.Close()
End Sub
```

Step 6: Save the project, and then run it. (If you mistyped something, and as a result have any syntax errors, correct them.)

Step 7: With the application running, enter the following test data and confirm that it displays the correct output.

Type of Membership	Monthly Fee	Total
Standard adult with yoga, karate, and personal trainer for 6 months	$130.00	$780.00
Child with karate for 3 months	$50.00	$150.00
Student with yoga for 12 months	$35.00	$420.00
Senior citizen with karate and personal trainer for 8 months	$110.00	$880.00

Step 8: End the application.

Summary

1 The Decision Structure

- Programs often need more than one path of execution. Many algorithms require a program to execute some statements only under certain circumstances. The decision structure accomplishes this.

2 The `If...Then` Statement

- The `If...Then` statement can cause other statements to execute under certain conditions.
- Boolean expressions, such as those created using relational operators, can be evaluated only as *True* or *False*.
- Math operators and function calls can be used with relational operators.

3 The `If...Then...Else` Statement

- The `If...Then...Else` statement executes one group of statements if a condition is true and another group of statements if the condition is false.

4 The `If...Then...ElseIf` Statement

- The `If...Then...ElseIf` statement is like a chain of `If...Then...Else` statements that perform their tests, one after the other, until one of them is found to be true.

5 Nested `If` Statements

- A nested `If` statement is an `If` statement in the conditionally executed code of another `If` statement.

6 Logical Operators

- Logical operators connect two or more relational expressions into one (using `And`, `Or`, `AndAlso`, `OrElse`, or `Xor`), or reverse the logic of an expression (using `Not`).
- When determining whether a number is inside a numeric range, it's best to use the `And` operator.
- When determining whether a number is outside a range, it's best to use the `Or` operator.

7 Comparing, Testing, and Working with Strings

- Relational operators can be used to compare strings.
- An empty string is represented by the constant `String.Empty`, or by two quotation marks, with no space between them.
- The `IsNumeric` function accepts a string as its argument and returns *True* if the string contains a number. The function returns *False* if the string's contents cannot be recognized as a number.
- The `Substring` method extracts a specified number of characters from within a specified position in a string.
- The `IndexOf` method is used to search for a character or a string within a string.

8 More about Message Boxes

- Message boxes are displayed with the `MessageBox.Show` method. The types of buttons and an icon to display in the message box can be specified.
- The return value of the `MessageBox.Show` method can be tested to determine which button the user clicked to dismiss the message box.

- The value `ControlChars.CrLf` can be concatenated with a string to produce multiple line displays.

9 The `Select Case` Statement

- The `Select Case` statement tests the value of an expression only once, and then uses that value to determine which set of statements to branch to.

10 Introduction to Input Validation

- The accuracy of a program's output depends on the accuracy of its input. It is important that applications perform input validation on the values entered by the user.

11 Focus on GUI Design: Radio Buttons and Check Boxes

- Radio buttons appear in groups and allow the user to select one of several possible options. Radio buttons placed inside a group box are treated as one group, separate and distinct from any other groups of radio buttons. Only one radio button in a group can be selected at any time.
- Clicking on a radio button selects it and automatically deselects any other radio button selected in the same group.
- Check boxes allow the user to select or deselect items. Check boxes are not mutually exclusive. There may be one or more check boxes on a form, and any number of them can be selected at any given time.

12 Focus on Program Design and Problem Solving: Building the *Health Club Membership Fee Calculator* Application

- This section outlines the process of building the *Health Club Membership Fee Calculator* application using the features discussed in the chapter.

Key Terms

And operator
AndAlso operator
Boolean expression
CheckBox control
CheckedChanged event
Checked property
conditionally executed (statement)
ControlChars.CrLf
decision structure
empty string
flag
If...Then
If...Then...Else
If...Then...ElseIf
IndexOf method
input validation
IsNumeric function
leading space
Length property
logic error

logical operators
nested If statement
Not operator
Or operator
OrElse operator
parse
RadioButton control
relational operator
Select Case statement
sequence structure
short-circuit evaluation
Substring method
ToLower method
ToUpper method
trailing space
Trim method
TrimEnd method
TrimStart method
Unicode
Xor operator

Review Questions and Exercises

Fill-in-the-Blank

1. A _____ structure allows a program to execute some statements only under certain circumstances.

2. A(n) _____ operator determines if a specific relationship exists between two values.

3. Boolean expressions can only be evaluated as _____ or _____.

4. A(n) _____ is a Boolean variable that signals when some condition exists in the program.

5. The _____ statement will execute one group of statements if the condition is true, and another group of statements if the condition is false.

6. The _____ statement is like a chain of If...Then...Else statements. They perform their tests, one after the other, until one of them is found to be true.

7. A _____ If statement is an If statement that appears inside another If statement.

8. _____ operators connect two or more relational expressions into one or reverse the logic of an expression.

9. The _____ method returns the uppercase equivalent of a string.

10. The _____ returns a lowercase version of a string.

11. The _____ function accepts a string as its argument and returns *True* if the string contains a number, or *False* if the string's contents cannot be recognized as a number.

12. The _____ method returns the number of characters in a string.

13. The _____ method returns a copy of a string without leading spaces.

14. The _____ method returns a copy of a string without trailing spaces.

15. The _____ method returns a copy of the string without leading or trailing spaces.

16. The _____ method extracts a specified number of characters from within a specified position in a string.

17. The value _____ can be concatenated with a string to produce multiple line displays.

18. A(n) _____ statement tests the value of an expression only once, and then uses that value to determine which set of statements to branch to.

19. _____ is the process of inspecting input values and determining whether they are valid.

20. _____ controls usually appear in groups and allow the user to select one of several possible options.

21. _____ controls may appear alone or in groups and allow the user to make yes/no, or on/off selections.

True or False

Indicate whether the following statements are true or false.

1. T F: It is not possible to write a Boolean expression that contains more than one logical operator.

2. T F: It is not possible to write Boolean expressions that contain math, relational, and logical operators.

3. T F: You may use the relational operators to compare strings.

4. T F: Clicking on a radio button selects it, and leaves any other selected radio button in the same group selected as well.

5. T F: Radio buttons that are placed inside a group box are treated as one group, separate and distinct from any other groups of radio buttons.

6. T F: When a group of radio buttons appears on a form (outside of a group box), any number of them can be selected at any time.

7. T F: You may have one or more check boxes on a form, and any number of them can be selected at any given time.

8. T F: The `If...Then` statement is an example of a sequence structure.

9. T F: An `If...Then` statement will not execute unless the conditionally executed statements are indented.

10. T F: The `Substring` method returns a lowercase copy of a string.

Multiple Choice

1. Relational operators allow you to _____ numbers.
   a. Add
   b. Multiply
   c. Compare
   d. Average

2. This statement can cause other program statements to execute only under certain conditions.
   a. `MessageBox.Show`
   b. `Decide`
   c. `If`
   d. `Execute`

3. This is a Boolean variable that signals when a condition exists.
   a. Relational operator
   b. Flag
   c. Arithmetic operator
   d. Float

4. This statement is like a chain of `If` statements. They perform their tests, one after the other, until one of them is found to be true.
   a. `If...Then`
   b. `If...Then...ElseIf`
   c. `Chain...If`
   d. `Relational`

5. When placed at the end of an If...Then...ElseIf statement, this provides default action when none of the ElseIf statements have true expressions.

   a. Trailing If
   b. Trailing Select
   c. Trailing Otherwise
   d. Trailing Else

6. When an If statement is placed inside another If statement, it is known as this type of statement.

   a. A nested If
   b. A complex If
   c. A compound If
   d. An invalid If

7. This operator connects two Boolean expressions into one. One or both expressions must be true for the overall expression to be true. It is only necessary for one to be true, and it does not matter which.

   a. And
   b. Or
   c. Xor
   d. Not

8. This operator connects two Boolean expressions into one. Both expressions must be true for the overall expression to be true.

   a. And
   b. Or
   c. Xor
   d. Not

9. This operator reverses the logical value of an Boolean expression. It makes a true expression false and a true expression true.

   a. And
   b. Or
   c. Xor
   d. Not

10. This operator connects two Boolean expressions into one. One, and only one, of the expressions must be true for the overall expression to be true. If both expressions are true, or if both expressions are false, the overall expression is false.

    a. And
    b. Or
    c. Xor
    d. Not

11. When determining whether a number is inside a numeric range, it's best to use this logical operator.

    a. And
    b. Or
    c. Xor
    d. Not

12. When determining whether a number is outside a range, it's best to use this logical operator.

    a. And
    b. Or
    c. Xor
    d. Not

13. In code you should test this property of a radio button or a check box to determine whether it is selected.

    a. Selected
    b. Checked
    c. On
    d. Toggle

14. This method attempts to convert a value to an Integer.

    a. `NumericConvert`
    b. `IntegerConvert`
    c. `Integer.TryParse`
    d. `Integer.TryConvert`

15. `strName` is a string variable. This expression returns the length of the string stored in `strName`.

    a. `Length(strName)`
    b. `strName.Length`
    c. `strName.StringSize`
    d. `CharCount(strName)`

16. Use this method to display a message box and determine which button the user clicked to dismiss the message box.

    a. `MessageBox.Show`
    b. `MessageBox.Button`
    c. `Message.Box`
    d. `MessageBox.UserClicked`

Short Answer

1. Describe the difference between the `If...Then...ElseIf` statement and a series of `If...Then` statements.

2. In an `If...Then...ElseIf` statement, what is the purpose of a trailing `Else`?

3. What is a flag and how does it work?

4. Briefly describe how the `And` operator works.

5. Briefly describe how the `Or` operator works.

6. How is the `Xor` operator different from the `Or` operator?

7. How is the `AndAlso` operator different from the `And` operator?

8. How is the `OrElse` operator different from the `Or` operator?

What Do You Think?

1. Why are the relational operators called relational?

2. When writing an `If...Then` statement to determine whether a number is inside a range, would you use the `And` operator, or the `Or` operator in the Boolean expression?

3. Why does Visual Studio automatically indent the conditionally executed statements in a decision structure?

4. Explain why you cannot convert the following If...Then...ElseIf statement into a Select Case statement.

    ```
    If dblTemperature = 100 Then
        intX = 0
    ElseIf intPopulation > 1000 Then
        intX = 1
    ElseIf dblRate < .1 Then
        intX = -1
    End If
    ```

Find the Error

1. What is syntactically incorrect in each of the following statements?

    a. ```
        If intX > 100
            MessageBox.Show("Invalid Data")
        End If
        ```
    b.  ```
        Dim str As String = "Hello"
        Dim intLength As Integer
        intLength = Length(str)
        ```
    c. ```
        If intZ < 10 Then
            MessageBox.Show("Invalid Data")
        ```
    d.  ```
        Dim str As String = "123"
        If str.IsNumeric Then
            MessageBox.Show("It is a number.")
        End If
        ```
    e. ```
        Select Case intX
            Case < 0
                MessageBox.Show("Value too low.")
            Case > 100
                MessageBox.Show("Value too high.")
            Case Else
                MessageBox.Show("Value just right.")
        End Select
        ```

### Algorithm Workbench

1.  Read the following instructions for cooking a pizza, and then design a flowchart with a decision structure that shows the necessary steps to cook the pizza with either thin and crispy or thick and chewy crust.

    a.  For thin and crispy crust, do not preheat the oven. Bake pizza at 450 degrees for 15 minutes.
    b.  For thick and chewy crust, preheat the oven to 400 degrees. Bake pizza for 20 minutes.

2.  Write an If...Then statement that assigns 0 to intX when intY is equal to 20.

3.  Write an If...Then statement that multiplies decPayRate by 1.5 when intHours is greater than 40.

4.  Write an If...Then statement that assigns 0.2 to decCommissionRate when decSales is greater than or equal to $10,000.00.

5.  Write an If...Then statement that sets the variable intFees to 50 when the Boolean variable blnIsMax equals *True*.

6.  Write an If...Then...Else statement that assigns 1 to intX when intY is equal to 100. Otherwise it should assign 0 to intX.
        ```

7. The string variable `strPeople` contains a list of names, such as *Bill Jim Susan Randy Wilma* and so on. Write code that searches people for *Gene*. If *Gene* is found in `strPeople`, display a message box indicating that *Gene* was found.

8. Write an `If...Then` statement that prints the message *The number is valid* if the variable `sngSpeed` is within the range 0 through 200.

9. Write an `If...Then` statement that prints the message *The number is not valid* if the variable `sngSpeed` is outside the range 0 through 200.

10. Convert the following `If...Then...ElseIf` statement into a `Select Case` statement.

```
If intSelection = 1 Then
    MessageBox.Show("Pi times radius squared")
ElseIf intSelection = 2 Then
    MessageBox.Show("Length times width")
ElseIf intSelection = 3 Then
    MessageBox.Show("Pi times radius squared times height")
ElseIf intSelection = 4 Then
    MessageBox.Show("Well okay then, good bye!")
Else
    MessageBox.Show("Not good with numbers, eh?")
End If
```

Programming Challenges

1. **Larger and Smaller**

   Create an application that allows the user to enter two integers on a form similar to the one shown in Figure 40. The application should determine which value is larger than the other, or it should determine that the values are equal. Before comparing the numbers, use the `TryParse` method to verify that both inputs are valid integers. If an error is found, display an appropriate message to the user. Use a Label control to display all messages. The *Exit* button should close the window.

Figure 40 *Larger and Smaller* form

VideoNote

The Roman
Numeral
Converter
Problem

2. **Roman Numeral Converter**

   Create an application that allows the user to enter an integer between 1 and 10 into a text box on a form similar to the one shown in Figure 41. Use a `Select Case` statement to identify which Roman numeral is the correct translation of the integer. Display the Roman numeral in a Label control. If the user enters an invalid value, display an appropriate error message and do not attempt the conversion. Include an *Exit* button that closes the window.

Figure 41 *Roman Numeral Converter* form

The following table lists the Roman numerals for the numbers 1 through 10.

Number	Roman Numeral
1	I
2	II
3	III
4	IV
5	V
6	VI
7	VII
8	VIII
9	IX
10	X

Input validation: Do not accept a number less than 1 or greater than 10. If the user enters a number outside this range, display an error message.

3. **Fat Percentage Calculator**

Create an application that allows the user to enter the number of calories and fat grams in a food. The application should display the percentage of the calories that come from fat. If the calories from fat are less than 30% of the total calories of the food, it should also display a message indicating the food is low in fat. (Display the message in a label or a message box.) The application's form should appear similar to the one shown in Figure 42.

One gram of fat has 9 Calories, so:
Calories from fat = fat grams * 9

The percentage of calories from fat can be calculated as:
Percentage of calories from fat = Calories from fat / total calories

Figure 42 *Fat Gram Calculator* form

Input validation: Make sure the number of calories and fat grams are numeric, and are not less than 0. Also, the number of calories from fat cannot be greater than the total number of calories. If that happens, display an error message indicating that either the calories or fat grams were incorrectly entered.

Use the following test data to determine if the application is calculating properly:

Calories and Fat	Percentage Fat
200 calories, 8 fat grams	Percentage of calories from fat: 36%
150 calories 2 fat grams	Percentage of calories from fat: 12% (a low-fat food)
500 calories, 30 fat grams	Percentage of calories from fat: 54%

4. **Running the Race**

Create an application that allows the user to enter the names of three runners and the time it took each of them to finish a race. The application should display who came in first, second, and third place. For simplicity, you can assume that the two runners will never have exactly the same finishing times. The application's form should appear similar to the one shown in Figure 43. The *Clear* button should clear all text boxes and calculated labels. The *Exit* button should close the form. Include the following input error checking: No runner name can be blank, and finishing times must be both numeric and positive.

Use the following test data to determine if the application is calculating properly:

Names and Times	Results	
John, 87 seconds	First place:	Carol
Carol, 74 seconds	Second place:	John
Shelly, 94 seconds	Third place:	Shelly

Figure 43 *Race Results* form

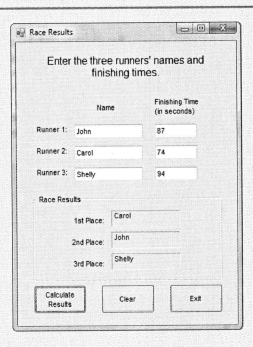

5. **Software Sales**

A software company sells three packages, Package A, Package B, and Package C, which retail for $99, $199, and $299, respectively. Quantity discounts are given according to the following table:

Quantity	Discount
10 through 19	20%
20 through 49	30%
50 through 99	40%
100 or more	50%

Create an application that allows the user to enter the number of units sold for each software package. The application's form should resemble Figure 44.

Figure 44 *Software Sales* form

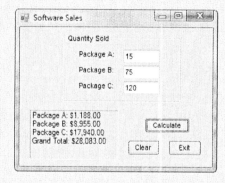

The application should calculate and display the order amounts and the grand total in a Label control. The *Clear* button must clear all text boxes and calculated labels. The *Exit* button must close the window.

Input validation: Make sure the number of units for each package is numeric, and is not negative.

Use the following test data to determine if the application is calculating properly:

Units Sold		Amount of Order	
Package A:	15 units	Package A:	$1,188.00
Package B:	75 units	Package B:	$8,955.00
Package C:	120 units	Package C:	$17,940.00
		Grand Total:	$28,083.00

Design Your Own Forms

6. **Bank Charges**

A bank charges $10 per month, plus the following check fees for a commercial checking account:

$0.10 each for less than 20 checks
$0.08 each for 20 through 39 checks
$0.06 each for 40 through 59 checks
$0.04 each for 60 or more checks

Create an application that allows the user to enter the number of checks written. The application should compute and display the bank's service fees for the month. All checks for the month are assigned the same charge, based on the total number of checks written during the month.

Input validation: Do not accept a negative value for the number of checks written. Ensure that all values are numeric. The *Clear* button must clear the text box and the label that displays the monthly service charge.

Use the following test data to determine if the application is calculating properly:

Number of Checks	Total Fees
15	$ 11.50
25	$ 12.00
45	$ 12.70
75	$ 13.00

7. **Shipping Charges**

The Fast Freight Shipping Company charges the rates listed in the following table.

Weight of the Package (in kilograms)	Shipping Rate per Mile
2 kg or less	$0.01
Over 2 kg, but not more than 6 kg	$0.015
Over 6 kg, but not more than 10 kg	$0.02
Over 10 kg, but not more than 20 kg	$0.025

Create an application that allows the user to enter the weight of the package and the distance it is to be shipped, and then displays the charges.

Input validation: Do not accept values of 0 or less for the weight of the package. Do not accept weights of more than 20 kg (this is the maximum weight the company will ship). Do not accept distances of less than 10 miles or more than 3000 miles. These are the company's minimum and maximum shipping distances. Suggestion: use the `OrElse` operator to combine the two range conditions that check for package weights that are too small or too large. Use exception handling to check for nonnumeric data.

Use the following test data to determine if the application is calculating properly:

Weight and Distance	Shipping Cost
1.5 Kg, 100 miles	$ 1.00
5 Kg, 200 miles	$ 3.00
8 Kg, 750 miles	$ 15.00
15 Kg, 2000 miles	$ 50.00

8. **Speed of Sound**

The following table shows the approximate speed of sound in air, water, and steel.

Medium	Speed
Air	1,100 feet per second
Water	4,900 feet per second
Steel	16,400 feet per second

Create an application that displays a set of radio buttons allowing the user to select air, water, or steel. Provide a text box to let the user enter the distance a sound wave will travel in the selected medium. Then, when the user clicks a button, the program should display the amount of time it will take. Format the output to two decimal places.

Input validation: Do not accept distances less than 0. Always check for nonnumeric data.

Use the following test data to determine if the application is calculating properly:

Medium and Distance	Speed of Sound
Air, 10,000 feet	9.09 seconds
Water, 10,000 feet	2.04 seconds
Steel, 10,000 feet	0.61 seconds

9. **Freezing and Boiling Points**

   The following table lists, in degrees Fahrenheit, the freezing and boiling points of several substances. Create an application that allows the user to enter a temperature. The program should then display a list of the substances that freeze at that temperature, followed by a list of substances that will boil at the same temperature.

Substance	Freezing Point	Boiling Point
Ethyl alcohol	−173°	172°
Mercury	−38°	676°
Oxygen	−362°	−306°
Water	32°	212°

   Use the following test data and sample outputs to determine if the application is calculating properly:

Temperature	Results
−20°	Water will freeze and oxygen will boil.
−50°	Mercury and water will freeze and oxygen will boil.
−200°	Ethyl alcohol, mercury, and water will freeze and oxygen will boil.
−400°	Ethyl alcohol, mercury, oxygen, and water will freeze.

10. **Long-Distance Calls**

    A long-distance provider charges the following rates for telephone calls:

Rate Category	Rate per Minute
Daytime (6:00 a.m. through 5:59 P.M.)	$0.07
Evening (6:00 p.m. through 11:59 P.M.)	$0.12
Off-Peak (12:00 a.m. through 5:59 A.M.)	$0.05

    Create an application that allows the user to select a rate category (from a set of radio buttons) and enter the number of minutes of the call, then displays the charges. Include a *Clear* button that clears the input and calculated values, and an *Exit* button that closes the window. Error checking: the minutes input by the user must be numeric, and it must be greater than zero.

    Use the following test data to determine if the application is calculating properly:

Rate Category and Minutes	Charge
Daytime, 20 minutes	$ 1.40
Evening, 20 minutes	$ 2.40
Off-peak, 20 minutes	$ 1.00

11. **Internet Service Provider, Part 1**

    An Internet service provider offers three subscription packages to its customers, plus a discount for nonprofit organizations:

    a. Package A: 10 hours of access for $9.95 per month. Additional hours are $2.00 per hour.

    b. Package B: 20 hours of access for $14.95 per month. Additional hours are $1.00 per hour.

    c. Package C: Unlimited access for $19.95 per month.

    d. Nonprofit Organizations: The service provider gives all nonprofit organizations a 20% discount on all packages.

    The user should select the package the customer has purchased (from a set of radio buttons) and enter the number of hours used. A check box captioned *Nonprofit Organization* should also appear on the form. The application should calculate and display the total amount due. If the user selects the *Nonprofit Organization* check box, a 20% discount should be deducted from the final charges. Implementation note: all rates, limits, and discounts must be declared using symbolic constants (using the const keyword).

Input validation: The number of hours used in a month cannot exceed 744. The value must be numeric.

Use the following data to determine if the application is calculating properly:

Package and Hours	The Monthly Charge
Package A, 5 hours, nonprofit	$ 7.96
Package A, 25 hours	$39.95
Package B, 10 hours, nonprofit	$11.96
Package B, 25 hours	$19.95
Package C, 18 hours, nonprofit	$15.96
Package C, 25 hours	$19.95

12. **Internet Service Provider, Part 2 (Advanced)**

Make a copy of your solution program from Programming Challenge 11. Then, using the copied program, modify it so the form has a check box captioned *Display Potential Savings*. When this check box is selected, the application should also display the amount of money that Package A customers would save if they purchased Package B or C, or the amount that Package B customers would save if they purchased Package C. If there would be no savings, the message should indicate that.

Use the following test data to determine if the application is calculating properly:

Package and Hours	Total Monthly Savings
Package A, 5 hours, nonprofit	$7.96, no savings with Packages B or C
Package A, 25 hours	$39.95, save $20.00 with Package B, and save $20.00 with Package C
Package B, 10 hours, nonprofit	$11.96, no savings with Package C
Package B, 25 hours	$19.95, no savings with Package C

13. **Mass and Weight**

Scientists measure an object's mass in kilograms and its weight in newtons. If you know the amount of mass of an object, you can calculate its weight, in newtons, with the following formula:

$$Weight = mass \times 9.8$$

Create a VB application that lets the user enter an object's mass and calculates its weight. If the object weighs more than 1000 newtons, display a message indicating that it is too heavy. If the object weighs less than 10 newtons, display a message indicating that it is too light.

14. **Book Club Points**

Serendipity Booksellers has a book club that awards points to its customers based on the number of books purchased each month. The points are awarded as follows:

- If a customer purchases 0 books, he or she earns 0 points.
- If a customer purchases 1 book, he or she earns 5 points.
- If a customer purchases 2 books, he or she earns 15 points.
- If a customer purchases 3 books, he or she earns 30 points.
- If a customer purchases 4 or more books, he or she earns 60 points.
  Create a VB application that lets the user enter the number of books that he or she has purchased this month and displays the number of points awarded.

15. **Body Mass Index Program Enhancement**

The BMI (body mass index) is often used to determine whether a person with a sedentary lifestyle is overweight or underweight for their height. A person's BMI is calculated with the following formula:

$$BMI = weight \times 703 / height^2$$

In the formula, weight is measured in pounds and height is measured in inches. Enhance the program so it displays a message indicating whether the person has optimal weight, is underweight, or is overweight. A sedentary person's weight is considered to be optimal if his or her BMI is between 18.5 and 25. If the BMI is less than 18.5, the person is considered to be underweight. If the BMI value is greater than 25, the person is considered to be overweight.

16. **Magic Dates**

The date June 10, 1960, is special because when we write it in the following format, the month times the day equals the year.

6/10/60

Create a VB application that lets the user enter a month (in numeric form), a day, and a two-digit year. The program should then determine whether the month times the day is equal to the year. If so, it should display a message saying the date is magic. Otherwise it should display a message saying the date is not magic.

17. **Time Calculator**

Create a VB application that lets the user enter a number of seconds and works as follows:

- There are 60 seconds in a minute. If the number of seconds entered by the user is greater than or equal to 60, the program should display the number of minutes in that many seconds.
- There are 3,600 seconds in an hour. If the number of seconds entered by the user is greater than or equal to 3,600, the program should display the number of hours in that many seconds.
- There are 86,400 seconds in a day. If the number of seconds entered by the user is greater than or equal to 86,400, the program should display the number of days in that many seconds.

Answers to Checkpoints

1. a. T e. T
   b. T f. F
   c. F g. T
   d. T

2. If the Boolean variable `blnIsInvalid` equals `True`.

3. Yes, they both perform the same operation. Only the indentation is different.

4. The following statement is preferred because the conditionally executed statement is indented. The indention makes the statement easier to read.
   ```
   If decSales > 10000 Then
     decCommissionRate = 0.15
   End If
   ```

5. a. 99
   b. 0
   c. 99

6. Three times

7. One time by the `If...Then...ElseIf` statement and four times by the set of `If...Then` statements

8. | Logical Expression | Result |
   |---|---|
   | `True And False` | `False` |

True And True	True
False And True	False
False And False	False
True Or False	True
True Or True	True
False Or True	True
False Or False	False
True Xor False	True
True Xor True	False
Not True	False
Not False	True

9 a. *False*
   b. *False*
   c. *True*

10 f, g, a, b, i, h, e, c, d

11 c, a, d, b

12 `DialogResult.Abort`

13 `MessageBox.Show("William" & ControlChars.CrLf &`
    `    "Joseph" & ControlChars.CrLf & "Smith")`

14
```
Select Case intQuantity
  Case 0 To 9
    decDiscount = 0.1
  Case 10 To 19
    decDiscount = 0.2
  Case 20 To 29
    decDiscount = 0.3
  Case Is >= 30
    decDiscount = 0.4
  Case Else
    MessageBox.Show("Invalid Data")
End Select
```

15 By examining its Checked property. If the property equals `True`, the radio button is selected. If the property equals `False`, the radio button is not selected.

16 Only one

17 By examining its Checked property. If the property equals `True`, the check box is selected. If the property equals `False`, the check box is not selected.

18 Any or all of them

19 By pressing the spacebar

Lists and Loops

TOPICS

This chapter begins by showing you how to use input boxes, which provide a quick and simple way to ask the user to enter data. List boxes and combo boxes are also introduced. Next, you learn to write loops, which cause blocks, or sequences of programming statements to repeat. You will also learn how to generate random numbers and use them for various purposes in a program. Finally, we cover the ToolTip control, which allows you to display pop-up messages when the user moves the mouse over controls.

1   Input Boxes

CONCEPT: Input boxes provide a simple way to gather input without placing a text box on a form.

An **input box** is a quick and simple way to ask the user to enter data. Figure 1 shows an example. In the figure, an input box displays a message to the user and provides a text box for the user to enter input. The input box also has *OK* and *Cancel* buttons.

From Chapter 5 of *Starting Out with Visual Basic® 2010*, Fifth Edition, Tony Gaddis, Kip Irvine.

You can display input boxes with the `InputBox` function. When the function is called, an input box such as the one shown in Figure 1 appears on the screen. Here is the general format:

```
InputBox(Prompt [, Title] [, Default] [, Xpos] [, Ypos])
```

Figure 1 Input box that requests the user's name

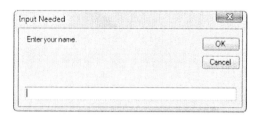

The brackets in the general format are shown around the *Title*, *Default*, *Xpos*, and *Ypos* arguments to indicate that they are optional. The first argument, *Prompt*, is a string that is displayed to the user in the input box. Normally, the string asks the user to enter a value. The optional arguments, *Title*, *Default*, *Xpos*, and *Ypos* are described as follows.

- *Title* is a string that appears in the input box's title bar. If you do not provide a value for *Title*, the name of the project appears.
- *Default* is a string to be initially displayed in the input box's text box. If you do not provide a value for *Default*, the input box's text box is left empty.
- *Xpos* and *Ypos* specify the input box's location on the screen. *Xpos* is an integer that specifies the distance of the input box's leftmost edge from the left edge of the screen. *Ypos* is an integer that specifies the distance of the topmost edge of the input box from the top of the screen. *Xpos* and *Ypos* are measured in pixels. If *Xpos* is omitted, Visual Basic centers the input box horizontally on the screen. If *Ypos* is omitted, the input box is placed near the top of the screen.

If the user clicks the input box's *OK* button or presses the Enter key, the function returns the string value from the input box's text box. If the user clicks the *Cancel* button, the function returns an empty string. To retrieve the value returned by the `InputBox` function, use the assignment operator to assign it to a variable. For example, the following statement displays the input box shown in Figure 2. Assume that `strUserInput` is a string variable that has already been declared.

```
strUserInput = InputBox("Enter your age.", "Input Needed")
```

Figure 2 Input box that requests the user's age

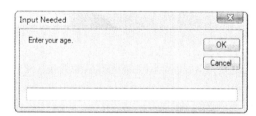

After this statement executes, the value the user entered in the input box is stored as a string in `strUserInput`. As another example, the following statement displays the input box shown in Figure 3.

```
strUserInput = InputBox("Enter the distance.", "Provide a Value",
                        "150")
```

Figure 3 Input box with default user input

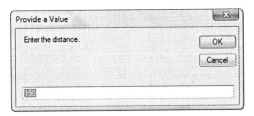

If the user clicks the *OK* button without entering a value in the text box, the input box function returns `"150"`.

NOTE: In most applications, the `InputBox` function should not be used as the primary method of input because it draws the user's attention away from the application's form. It also complicates data validation, because the box closes before validation can take place. Despite these drawbacks, it is a convenient tool for developing and testing applications.

 Checkpoint

Carefully examine the input box in Figure 4 and complete Checkpoint items 1 and 2.

Figure 4 Input box that requests a number from the user

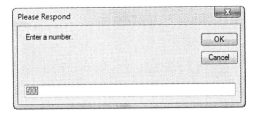

1 Write a statement that displays the input box at the default location on the screen.

2 Write a statement that displays the input box with its leftmost edge at 100 pixels from the left edge of the screen, and its topmost edge 300 pixels from the top edge of the screen.

2 List Boxes

CONCEPT: List boxes display a list of items and allow the user to select an item from the list.

The ListBox Control

A **ListBox control** displays a list of items and also allows the user to select one or more items from the list. (Informally, we refer to this control as a *list box.*) Figure 5 shows a form with two list boxes. At runtime, the user may select one of the items, causing the item to appear selected.

Figure 5 List box examples

One of the list boxes in Figure 5 does not have a scroll bar, but the other one does. A scroll bar appears when the list box contains more items than can be displayed in the space provided. In the figure, the top list box has four items (Poodle, Great Dane, German Shepherd, and Terrier), and all items are displayed. The bottom list box shows four items (Siamese, Persian, Bobtail, and Burmese), but because it has a scroll bar, we know there are more items in the list box than those four.

Creating a ListBox Control

You create a ListBox control using either of the following methods:

- Double-click the ListBox icon in the *Toolbox* window to cause a ListBox control to appear on the form. Move the control to the desired location and resize it, if necessary.
- Click the ListBox icon in the *Toolbox* window and use the mouse to draw the ListBox control on the form with the desired location and size.

In Design mode, a ListBox control appears as a rectangle. The size of the rectangle determines the size of the list box. The prefix that we will use in a ListBox control's name is `lst`, where the first character is a lowercase letter L. Let's discuss some of the list box's important properties and methods.

The Items Property

The entries in a list box are stored in a property named Items. You can store values in the **Items property** (also known as the Items collection) at design time or at runtime. To store values in the Items property at design time, follow these steps:

1. Make sure the ListBox control is selected in the *Designer* window.
2. In the *Properties* window, the setting for the Items property is displayed as *(Collection)*. When you select the Items property, an ellipsis button (...) appears.
3. Click the ellipsis button. The *String Collection Editor* dialog box appears, as shown in Figure 6.
4. Type the values that are to appear in the list box into the *String Collection Editor* dialog box. Type each value on a separate line by pressing the Enter key after each entry.
5. When you have entered all the values, click the *OK* button.

Figure 6 The *String Collection Editor* dialog box

 NOTE: Once you acquire the necessary skills, you will be able to fill the Items collection of list boxes from external data sources (such as databases).

The Items.Count Property

You can use the **Items.Count property** to determine the number of items stored in the list box. When there are no items in the Items property, the Items.Count property equals 0. For example, assume an application has a list box named lstEmployees. The following If...Then statement displays a message box when there are no items in the list box:

```
If lstEmployees.Items.Count = 0 Then
   MessageBox.Show("There are no items in the list!")
End If
```

The following statement assigns the number of items in the list box to the variable intNumEmployees:

```
intNumEmployees = lstEmployees.Items.Count
```

Item Indexing

The Items property is a collection of objects, in which each has an *index*, or number. The first object in the collection has index 0, the next has index 1, and so on. The last index value is $n - 1$, where n is the number of items in the collection. When you access the Items property in code, you must supply an index, using an expression such as the following:

```
lstEmployees.Items(0)
```

If you want to retrieve an item from a list box's Items property and assign it to a variable, you have to explicitly convert that item to the same data type as the variable. For example, suppose we want to get the first item that is stored in the lstEmployees list box and assign it to strName, which is a string variable. We would need to call the item's ToString method as shown here:

```
strName = lstEmployees.Items(0).ToString()
```

This statement gets the item that is stored at lstEmployees.Items(0), calls that item's ToString method, and assigns the resulting string to the strName variable.

Let's look at another example. Suppose an application has a list box named lstRoomNumbers that contains a list of room numbers. The following statement shows how you would assign the first item in the list box to the Integer variable intRoomNumber:

```
intRoomNumber = CInt(lstRoomNumbers.Items(0))
```

This statement gets the item that is stored at lstRoomNumbers.Items(0), converts it to an Integer with the CInt function, and assigns the resulting value to the intRoomNumber variable.

Handling Exceptions Caused by Indexes

When you use an index with the Item property, an exception is thrown if the index is out of range. Because indexes start at zero, the highest index number you can use is always one less than the collection size. You can use an exception handler to trap such an error. In the following code, assume that the variable intIndex contains a value that we want to use as an index. If the value in intIndex is out of range, the exception is handled. We display the Message property (Figure 7) of the exception object to give the user an idea of what went wrong.

```
Try
   strInput = lstMonths.Items(intIndex).ToString()
Catch ex As Exception
   MessageBox.Show(ex.Message)
End Try
```

Figure 7 Exception thrown by out of range index

Many programmers prefer to handle indexing errors using an If statement. The following code is an example in which we compare the index (in a variable named intIndex) to the Count property of the Items collection:

```
If intIndex >= 0 And intIndex < lstMonths.Items.Count Then
   strInput = lstMonths.Items(intIndex).ToString()
Else
   MessageBox.Show("Index is out of range: " & intIndex)
End If
```

The SelectedIndex Property

When the user selects an item in a list box, the item's index is stored in the **SelectedIndex** property. If no item is selected, `SelectedIndex` is set to –1. You can use the SelectedIndex property to retrieve the selected item from the Items property. For example, assume an application has a list box named `lstLocations`. The following code segment uses an `If ...Then` statement to determine whether the user has selected an item in the list box. If so, it copies the item from the Items property to the string variable `strLocation`.

```
If lstLocations.SelectedIndex <> -1 Then
   strLocation = lstLocations.Items(lstLocations.SelectedIndex).
        ToString()
End If
```

TIP: To prevent a runtime error, always test the SelectedIndex property to make sure it is not set to –1 before using it with the Items property to retrieve an item.

You can also use the SelectedIndex property to deselect an item by setting it to –1. For example, the following statement deselects any selected item in `lstLocations`:

```
lstLocations.SelectedIndex = -1
```

The SelectedItem Property

Whereas the SelectedIndex property contains the index of the currently selected item, the SelectedItem property contains the item itself. For example, suppose the list box `lstFruit` contains *Apples*, *Pears*, and *Bananas*. If the user has selected *Pears*, the following statement copies the string *Pears* to the variable `strSelectedFruit`:

```
strSelectedFruit = lstFruit.SelectedItem.ToString()
```

The Sorted Property

You can use the list box's **Sorted** property to cause the items in the Items property to be displayed alphabetically. This Boolean property is set to *False* by default, causing the items to be displayed in the order they were inserted into the list. When set to *True*, the items are sorted alphabetically.

The `Items.Add` Method

To store values in the Items property with code at runtime, use the **`Items.Add`** method. Here is the general format:

```
ListBox.Items.Add(Item)
```

`ListBox` is the name of the list box control. `Item` is the value to be added to the Items property. For example, suppose an application has a list box named `lstStudents`. The following statement adds the string "`Sharon`" to the end of the list box.

```
lstStudents.Items.Add("Sharon")
```

You can add virtually any type of values to list box, including objects. For example, the following statements add Integer, Decimal, and Date objects to list boxes.

```
Dim intNum As Integer = 5
Dim decGrossPay As Decimal = 1200D
Dim datStartDate As Date = #12/18/2010#
lstNumbers.Items.Add(intNum)
lstWages.Items.Add(decGrossPay)
lstDates.Items.Add(datStartDate)
```

When you add an object other than a string to a list box, the text displayed in the list box is the string returned by the object's ToString method.

The Items.Insert Method

To insert an item at a specific position, you must use the Items.Insert method. Here is the general format of the Items.Insert method:

```
ListBox.Items.Insert(Index, Item)
```

ListBox is the name of the list box control. *Index* is an integer argument that specifies the position where *Item* is to be placed in the Items property. *Item* is the item to add to the list.

For example, suppose the list box lstStudents contains the following items, in the order they appear: *Bill*, *Joe*, *Geri*, and *Sharon*. Since *Bill* is the first item, its index is 0. The index for *Joe* is 1, for *Geri* is 2, and for *Sharon* is 3. Now, suppose the following statement executes.

```
lstStudents.Items.Insert(2, "Jean")
```

This statement inserts *Jean* at index 2. The string that was previously at index 2 (*Geri*) is moved to index 3, and the string previously at index 3 (*Sharon*) is moved to index 4. The items in the Items property are now *Bill*, *Joe*, *Jean*, *Geri*, and *Sharon*.

The Items.Remove and Items.RemoveAt Methods

The Items.Remove and Items.RemoveAt methods both remove one item from a list box's Items property. Here is the general format of both methods:

```
ListBox.Items.Remove(Item)
ListBox.Items.RemoveAt(Index)
```

ListBox is the name of the list box control. With the Items.Remove method, *Item* is the item you wish to remove. For example, the following statement removes the string *Industrial Widget* from the lstInventory list box.

```
lstInventory.Items.Remove("Industrial Widget")
```

If you specify an item that is not in the list box, nothing is removed.

The Items.RemoveAt method removes the item at a specific index. For example, the following statement removes the item at index 4 from the lstInventory list box:

```
lstInventory.Items.RemoveAt(4)
```

 WARNING: If you specify an invalid index with the Items.RemoveAt method, an exception will occur.

The Items.Clear Method

The Items.Clear method erases all the items in the Items property. Here is the method's general format:

```
ListBox.Items.Clear()
```

For example, assume an application has a list box named lstCars. The following statement erases all items in the list.

```
lstCars.Items.Clear()
```

In Tutorial 1, you create an application with two list boxes.

Tutorial 1:
Creating list boxes

Step 1: Create a new Windows Forms Application project named *List Boxes*. Change the form's Text property to *List Box Demo*.

Step 2: On the form, create a list box as shown in Figure 8. Notice that the default name of the list box is `ListBox1`. Also notice that the name of the list box is displayed in the list box at design time. It will not appear there at runtime.

Step 3: Change the name of the list box to `lstMonths`.

Step 4: With the list box selected, click the Items property in the *Properties* window. Then click the ellipsis button (`...`) that appears.

Step 5: The *String Collection Editor* dialog box will appear. Type the following names of the months, with one name per line: `January, February, March, April, May, June, July, August, September, October, November,` and `December`. When you are finished, the dialog box should appear as shown in Figure 9. Click the *OK* button to close the dialog box.

Figure 8 A list box

Figure 9 *String Collection Editor* with months filled in

Step 6: Create another list box and make it the same size as the first one. Change its name to `lstYears`. Enter the following items in its Items property: **2008, 2009, 2010, 2011,** and **2012**.

Step 7: Create two buttons on the form. Name the first `btnOk`, and change its Text property to *OK*. Name the second `btnReset` and change its Text property to *Reset*. The form should look similar to Figure 10.

Figure 10 The form with two list boxes and two buttons

Step 8: Double-click the btnOk button to generate a Click event handler code template. Complete the event handler by writing the following bold code shown in lines 2 through 15.

```
1 Private Sub btnOk_Click(...) Handles btnOk.Click
2   Dim strInput As String ' Holds selected month and year
3
4   If lstMonths.SelectedIndex  = -1 Then
5     ' No month is selected
6     MessageBox.Show("Select a month.")
7   ElseIf lstYears.SelectedIndex = -1 Then
8     ' No year is selected
9     MessageBox.Show("Select a year.")
10  Else
11    ' Get the selected month and year
12    strInput = lstMonths.SelectedItem.ToString() &
13      " " & lstYears.SelectedItem.ToString()
14    MessageBox.Show("You selected " & strInput)
15  End If
16 End Sub
```

Let's take a closer look at the code. The If statement in line 4 determines whether lstMonths.SelectedIndex is equal to −1, which would mean that the user has not selected anything from the lstMonths list box. If that is true, line 6 displays a message box telling the user to select a month.

If the user has selected an item from lstMonths, the ElseIf clause in line 7 determines whether lstYears.SelectedIndex is equal to −1, which would mean that the user has not selected anything from the lstYears list box. If that is true, line 9 displays a message box telling the user to select a year.

If the user has selected items in both lstMonths and lstYears, the program jumps to the Else clause in line 10. The statement that appears in lines 11 and 12 creates a string containing the selected month, followed by a space, followed by the selected year. For example, if the user selected *April* in lstMonths and *2011* in lstYears, the string "April 2011" would be created and assigned to the strInput variable. Then line 14 displays the string in a message box.

Step 9: Double-click the btnReset button to add a Click event handler code template. Write the following code shown in bold:

```
Private Sub btnReset_Click(...) Handles btnReset.Click
    ' Reset the list boxes.
    lstMonths.SelectedIndex = -1
    lstYears.SelectedIndex = -1
End Sub
```

When this button is clicked, the SelectedIndex property of both list boxes is set to –1. This deselects any selected items.

Step 10: Run the application. Without selecting any item in either list box, click the *OK* button. A message box appears instructing you to *Select a month*.

Step 11: Select *March* in lstMonths, but do not select an item from lstYears. Click the *OK* button. This time a message box appears instructing you to *Select a year*.

Step 12: With *March* still selected in lstMonths, select *2012* in lstYears. Click the *OK* button. Now a message box appears with the message *You selected March 2012*. Click the message box's *OK* button to dismiss it.

Step 13: Click the *Reset* button. The items you previously selected in lstMonths and lstYears are deselected.

Step 14: Close the application and save it.

More about the Items Collection

You've learned that a list box's Items property is a special type of container known as a *collection*. Collections are commonly used to store groups of objects, and as you learn more about Visual Basic, you will see that collections are used in many places. What you have learned about a list box's Items collection applies to other collections as well. Table 1 lists several important methods and properties that collections have.

Table 1 Several methods and properties of collections

Method or Property	Description
Add (*item As Object*)	Method: adds *item* to the collection, returning its index position.
Clear ( )	Method: removes all items in the collection. No return value.
Contains (*value As Object*)	Method: returns *True* if *value* is found at least once in the collection.
Count	Property: returns the number of items in the collection. Read-only, so you can read it but not change it.
IndexOf (*value As Object*)	Method: returns the Integer index position of the first occurrence of *value* in the collection. If *value* is not found, the return value is –1.
Insert (*index As Integer, item As Object*)	Method: insert *item* in the collection at position *index*. No return value.
Item (*index As Integer*)	Property: returns the object located at position *index*.
Remove (*value As Object*)	Method: removes *value* from the collection. No return value.
RemoveAt (*index As Integer*)	Method: removes the item at the specified *index*. No return value.

You have already seen examples of the Add, Clear, Insert, Remove, and RemoveAt methods. Let's look at examples of the remaining methods and properties shown in the table. Assume that lstMonths is the same list box that you created in Tutorial 1. The following If...Then statement determines whether the lstMonths list box's Items property contains "March". If so, it displays the message "March is found in the list." Otherwise, it displays "March is NOT found in the list."

```
If lstMonths.Items.Contains("March") Then
   MessageBox.Show("March is found in the list.")
Else
   MessageBox.Show("March is NOT found in the list.")
End If
```

In the following statement, intIndex is assigned the value 2 because *March* is located at index 2 in the collection.

```
intIndex = lstMonths.Items.IndexOf("March")
```

In the following statement, strMonth is assigned the string "April" because it is at index position 3 in the collection.

```
Dim strMonth As String = lstMonths.Items.Item(3).ToString()
```

 ## Checkpoint

3 What is the index of the first item stored in a list box's Items property?

4 Which list box property holds the number of items stored in the Items property?

5 If a list box has 12 items stored in it, what is the index of the twelfth item?

6 Which list box property holds the item that has been selected from the list?

7 Which list box property holds the index of the item that has been selected from the list?

8 Assume lstNames is a list box with 15 items and strSelectedName is a string variable. Write a statement that assigns the second item in lstNames to strSelectedName.

 3 # Introduction to Loops: The Do While Loop

CONCEPT: A loop is a repeating structure that contains a block of program statements.

Decision structures direct the flow of a program along two or more paths. A **repetition structure**, or **loop** causes one or more statements to repeat. Visual Basic has three types of loops: the Do While loop, the Do Until loop, and the For...Next loop. The difference among them is how they control the repetition.

VideoNote

The
Do While
Loop

The Do While Loop

The Do While loop has two important parts: (1) a Boolean expression that is tested for a *True* or *False* value, and (2) a statement or group of statements that is repeated as long as the Boolean expression is true. Figure 11 shows a flowchart of a Do While loop.

Figure 11 Flowchart of a Do While loop

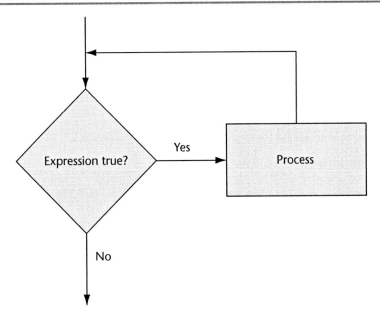

Notice the use of the diamond symbol for testing a Boolean expression. If the expression is true, the structure performs a process. Then it tests the Boolean expression again; if the expression is still true, the process is repeated. This continues as long as the Boolean expression is true when it is tested.

Here is the general format of the **Do While** loop in code:

```
Do While BooleanExpression
   statement
   (more statements may follow)
Loop
```

The statement that reads Do While is the beginning of the loop, and the statement that reads Loop is the end of the loop. The statements that appear between these two lines are known as the *body of the loop*. When the loop runs, the *BooleanExpression* is tested. If it is true, then the statements in the body of the loop are executed. Then the loop starts over and the *BooleanExpression* is tested again. If it is still true, the statements in the body of the loop are executed. This cycle repeats until the *BooleanExpression* is false.

Because the statements in the body of the loop are executed only under the condition that the Boolean expression is true, they are called **conditionally executed statements**. The Do While loop works like an If statement that executes over and over. As long as the Boolean expression is true, the conditionally executed statements will repeat. Each repetition of the loop is called an **iteration**. In Tutorial 2, you complete an application that demonstrates the Do While loop.

Tutorial 2:
Completing an application that uses the Do While loop

VideoNote

Tutorial 5-2
Walkthrough

Step 1: Open the *Do While Demo* project from the student sample programs folder named *Chap5\Do While Demo*. The student sample programs folder can be downloaded from www.microsoft.com/express/Downloads/.

Step 2: In the *Designer* window for *Form1*, double-click the *Run Demo* button to display the *Code* window.

Step 3: Complete the btnRunDemo_Click event handler by writing the following bold code shown in lines 2 through 7.

```
1 Private Sub btnRunDemo_Click(...) Handles btnRunDemo.Click
2    Dim intCount As Integer = 0
3
4    Do While intCount < 10
5       lstOutput.Items.Add("Hello")
6       intCount += 1
7    Loop
8 End Sub
```

Let's take a closer look at the code. Line 2 declares an Integer variable named intCount, and initializes it with the value 0. Line 4 is the beginning of a Do While loop that will execute as long as intCount is less than 10.

The first statement in the body of the loop appears in line 5. It adds the word *Hello* to the lstOutput list box. Then, line 6 uses the += combined assignment operator to add 1 to intCount.

The key word Loop appears in line 7. This marks the end of the Do While loop, and causes the loop to start over at line 4. Each time the loop starts over, the expression intCount < 10 is tested. If the expression is true, the statements in the body of the loop (lines 5 and 6) are executed. If the expression is false, the loop stops and the program resumes with the statement that immediately follows the Loop statement in line 7. (In this code, the event handler ends immediately after the loop.)

Step 4: Save and run the application. Click the *Run Demo* button. The output should appear as shown in Figure 12.

Figure 12 Output from the *Do While Demo* application

Infinite Loops

In all but rare cases, loops must contain within themselves a way to terminate. This means that something inside the Do While loop must eventually make the test expression false. The loop in the *Do While Demo* application stops when the variable intCount is no longer less than 10.

If a loop does not have a way of stopping, it is called an **infinite loop**. Infinite loops keep repeating until the program is interrupted. Here is an example:

```
intCount = 0
Do While intCount < 10
   lstOutput.Items.Add("Hello")
Loop
```

This loop will execute forever because it does not contain a statement that changes intCount. Each time the test expression is evaluated, intCount will still be equal to 0.

Programming Style and Loops

When you type the code for a loop, Visual Studio automatically indents the statements in the body of the loop. This is not a syntax requirement, but a programming style convention. For example, compare the following loops:

```
Do While intCount < 10
   lstOutput.Items.Add("Hello")
   intCount += 1
Loop

Do While intCount < 10
lstOutput.Items.Add("Hello")
intCount += 1
Loop
```

These two loops do the same thing, but the second one does not use proper indentation. In the first loop, you can quickly see which statements are repeated by the loop because they are indented.

NOTE: If the automatic indenting feature has been turned off, you can turn it on by clicking *Tools* on the menu bar, then clicking *Options*. In the *Options* window, perform the following:

- Click the *Show all settings* check box. Then, click *Text Editor* in the left pane, then click *Basic*, then click *Tabs*. Make sure *Smart* is selected in the dialog box under *Indenting*.
- In the left pane, click *VB Specific*. Make sure *Automatic Insertion of end constructs* and *Pretty listing (reformatting) of code* are both checked.

Counters

A **counter** is a variable that is regularly incremented or decremented each time a loop iterates. To increment a variable means to add 1 to its value. To decrement a variable means to subtract 1 from its value.

The following statements increment the variable intX:

```
intX = intX + 1
intX += 1
```

The following statements decrement the variable intX.

```
intX = intX − 1
intX -= 1
```

Often, a program must control or keep track of the number of iterations a loop performs. For example, the loop in the *Do While Demo* application adds *Hello* to the list box 10 times. Let's look at part of the code again.

```
Do While intCount < 10
    lstOutput.Items.Add("Hello")
    intCount += 1
Loop
```

In the code, the variable `intCount`, which starts at 0, is incremented each time through the loop. When `intCount` reaches 10, the loop stops. As a counter variable, it is regularly incremented in each iteration of the loop. In essence, `intCount` keeps track of the number of iterations the loop has performed.

TIP: `intCount` must be properly initialized. If it is initialized to 1 instead of 0, the loop will iterate only nine times.

Pretest and Posttest `Do While` Loops

The `Do While` loop can be written as a pretest loop or a posttest loop. The difference between these two types of loop is as follows:

- In a **pretest loop**, the Boolean expression is tested first. If the expression is true, the loop then executes the statements in the body of the loop. This process repeats until the Boolean expression is false.
- In a **posttest loop**, the statements in the body of the loop are executed first, and then the Boolean expression is tested. If the Boolean expression is true, the loop repeats. If the Boolean expression is false, the loop stops.

The examples that you have seen so far have all been pretest loops. An important characteristic of a pretest loop is that it will never execute if its Boolean expression is false to start with. For example, look at the following code:

```
Dim intCount As Integer = 100
Do While intCount < 10
    MessageBox.Show("Hello World!")
    intCount += 1
Loop
```

In this code the variable `intCount` is initialized with the value 100. When the `Do While` loop begins to execute, it tests the expression `intCount < 10`. Because this expression is false to start with, the loop immediately ends. The statements in the body of the loop never execute.

The `Do While` loop can also be written as a posttest loop, using the following general format:

```
Do
    Statement
    (More statements may follow)
Loop While BooleanExpression
```

Notice that in this general format, the `While BooleanExpression` clause appears at the end, after the `Loop` keyword. A loop written this way is a posttest `Do While` loop, and it tests its Boolean expression after each loop iteration. The flowchart in Figure 13 shows the logic of a posttest `Do While` loop.

Figure 13 Logic of the posttest Do While loop

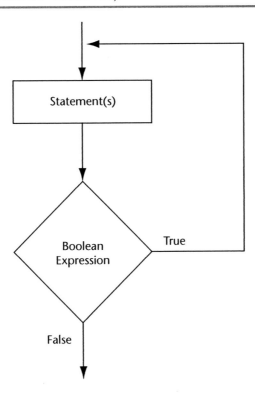

A posttest loop will always perform at least one iteration, even if its Boolean expression is false to start with. For example, look at the following code:

```
Dim intCount As Integer = 100
Do
    MessageBox.Show("Hello World!")
    intCount += 1
Loop While intCount < 10
```

In this code the variable intCount is initialized with the value 100. Then the loop begins to execute. Because this is a posttest loop, it first executes the statements in the body of the loop, and then tests the expression intCount < 10. The expression is false, so the loop stops after the first iteration.

In Tutorial 3, you will modify the *Do While Demo* application to use a posttest loop.

Tutorial 3:
Modifying the *Do While Demo* application to use a posttest loop

VideoNote

Tutorial 5-3
Walkthrough

Step 1: Open the *Do While Demo* project from the student sample programs folder named *Chap5\Do While Demo*.

Step 2: Open the *Code* window. When you wrote the btnRunDemo_Click event handler in Tutorial 2, you used a pretest Do While loop. In this step you will modify the loop so it is a posttest loop. Change the code to appear as follows. The modified lines of code are shown in bold.

```
Private Sub btnRunDemo_Click(...) Handles btnRunDemo.Click
    Dim intCount As Integer = 0

    Do
        lstOutput.Items.Add("Hello")
        intCount += 1
    Loop While intCount < 10
End Sub
```

Step 3: Run the application and click the *Run Demo* button. The loop should display *Hello* 10 times in the list box.

Step 4: Click the *Exit* button to end the application. Go back to the code for the `btnRunDemo_Click` event handler and change the less-than operator to a greater-than operator in the loop's Boolean expression. After doing this, the loop should appear as:

```
Do
    lstOutput.Items.Add("Hello")
    intCount += 1
Loop While intCount > 10
```

Although the expression `intCount > 10` is false to begin with, the statements in the body of the loop should execute once because this is a posttest loop.

Step 5: Run the application and click the *Run Demo* button. The loop should display *Hello* one time in the list box.

Step 6: Click the *Exit* button to end the application.

Keeping a Running Total

Many programming tasks require you to calculate the total of a series of numbers. For example, suppose you are writing a program that calculates a business's total sales for a week. The program would read the sales for each day as input and calculate the total of those numbers.

Programs that calculate the total of a series of numbers typically use two elements:

- A loop that reads each number in the series.
- A variable that accumulates the total of the numbers as they are read.

The variable that is used to accumulate the total of the numbers is called an **accumulator**. It is often said that the loop keeps a **running total** because it accumulates the total as it reads each number in the series. Figure 14 shows the general logic of a loop that calculates a running total.

When the loop finishes, the accumulator will contain the total of the numbers that were read by the loop. Notice that the first step in the flowchart is to set the accumulator variable to 0. This is a critical step. Each time the loop reads a number, it adds it to the accumulator. If the accumulator starts with any value other than 0, it will not contain the correct total when the loop finishes.

Let's look at an example. The application in Tutorial 4 calculates a company's total sales for five days by taking daily sales figures as input and keeping a running total of them as they are gathered.

Figure 14 Logic for calculating a running total

Tutorial 4:
Using a loop to keep a running total

In this tutorial, you will use an input box and a loop to enter five separate sales amount values. The values will be added to a total, which will be displayed.

Step 1: Open the *Running Total* project from the student sample programs folder named *Chap5\Running Total*.

Step 2: Open *Form1* in Design mode and double-click the *Enter Sales* button.

Step 3: Complete the btnEnterSales_Click event handler by writing the following bold code shown in lines 2 through 28.

```
 1 Private Sub btnEnterSales_Click(...) Handles btnEnterSales.Click
 2    Const intNUM_DAYS As Integer = 5 ' The number of days
 3    Dim intCount As Integer = 1      ' Loop counter
 4    Dim decSales As Decimal = 0      ' To hold daily sales
 5    Dim decTotal As Decimal = 0      ' To hold the total sales
 6    Dim strInput As String           ' To hold string input
 7
 8    ' Get the sales for each day.
 9    Do While intCount <= intNUM_DAYS
10       ' Get a daily sales amount from the user.
11       strInput = InputBox("Enter the sales for day " &
12                        intCount.ToString())
13
14       ' Convert the input to a Decimal.
```

```
15      If Decimal.TryParse(strInput, decSales) Then
16        ' Add the daily sales to the total sales.
17        decTotal += decSales
18
19        ' Add 1 to the loop counter.
20        intCount += 1
21      Else
22        ' Display an error message for invalid input.
23        MessageBox.Show("Enter a numeric value.")
24      End If
25    Loop
26
27    ' Display the total sales.
28    lblTotal.Text = decTotal.ToString("c")
29 End Sub
```

Let's take a closer look at the code. Here is a summary of the constant and variable declarations:

- Line 2 declares a constant named intNUM_DAYS, set to the value 5. This is the number of days of sales data we want to get from the user.
- Line 3 declares a variable named intCount that will be used as a loop counter. Notice that the variable is initialized with the value 1.
- Line 4 declares a variable named decSales that will be used to hold daily sales amounts.
- Line 5 declares a variable named decTotal that will hold the total sales. This is the accumulator variable. Notice that decTotal is initialized with the value 0. It is important that decTotal starts with the value 0 so the sum of all the sales amounts will be correct.
- Line 6 declares a variable named strInput that will hold the user's input, which is returned from the InputBox function.

The Do While loop that begins in line 9 executes as long as intCount is less than or equal to intNUM_DAYS. The statement in lines 11 and 12 displays an input box prompting the user to enter the sales for a specified day. (The first time the loop iterates, it will prompt the user to *Enter the sales for day 1*, the second time it will prompt *Enter the sales for day 2*, and so on.) The user's input is assigned, as a string, to the strInput variable.

Because the user's input is returned as a string, we need to convert it to a Decimal so we can perform math with it. That means that an exception will be thrown if the user has entered nonnumeric input. To prevent an exception, the If...Then statement in line 15 calls the Decimal.TryParse method to convert strInput to a Decimal, and store the result in the decSales variable. This method returns True if the conversion is successful, or False if the value cannot be converted to a Decimal. If the method returns False, the program will jump to the Else clause in line 21, display the error message in line 23, and then the loop starts over. If the user's input is successfully converted to a Decimal, however, decSales is added to the decTotal variable in line 17, and 1 is added to intCount in line 20. The loop then starts over.

After the loop finishes, line 28 displays the total sales in the lblTotal label.

Step 4: Save and run the program. Click the *Enter Sales* button. The input box shown in Figure 15 asks the user to enter the sales for day 1. Enter 1000, and click the OK button. (If you prefer, you may press the (Enter) key.)

Figure 15 Input box

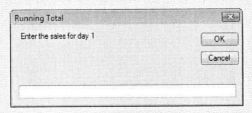

Step 5: The application will present input boxes asking for the sales for days 2, 3, 4, and 5. Enter the following amounts:

Day 2: **2000**
Day 3: **3000**
Day 4: **4000**
Day 5: **5000**

Step 6: After you enter the sales amount for all five days, the application should display the total sales as shown in Figure 16.

Step 7: End the program. You're finished.

Figure 16 Total sales displayed

Letting the User Control the Loop

Sometimes the user must decide how many times a loop should iterate. In Tutorial 5, you examine a modification of the *Running Total* application. This version of the program asks the user how many days he or she has sales figures for. The application then uses that value to control the number of times the Do While loop repeats.

Tutorial 5:
Examining an application that uses a user-controlled loop

Step 1: Open the *User Controlled* project, from the student sample programs folder named *Chap5\User Controlled*.

Step 2: Run the application. When the form appears, click the *Enter Sales* button. The input box shown in Figure 17 appears.

Step 3: The input box asks you to enter the number of days you have sales figures for. Enter 3 and click the *OK* button (or press (Enter)).

Figure 17 Input box

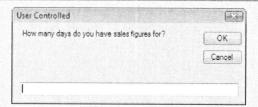

Step 4: Because you entered 3 for the number of days, the application presents three input boxes asking for the sales for days 1, 2, and 3. Enter the following values when asked:

Day 1: **1000**
Day 2: **2000**
Day 3: **3000**

Step 5: After you enter the sales figure for day 3, the application's form displays $6,000.00 as the total sales.

Step 6: Click the *Exit* button to terminate the application.

Step 7: Open the *Code* window and look at the `btnEnterSales_Click` event handler. Notice that this version of the code does not declare the constant `intNUM_DAYS`, as was used in Tutorial 4. This event handler has a new variable named `intNumDays`, declared as follows:

```
Dim intNumDays As Integer ' To hold the number of days
```

The following code that gets the number of days from the user, converts that input to an integer, and assigns the result to `intNumDays`:

```
' Get the number of days from the user.
strInput = InputBox("How many days do you have sales figures for?")

' Convert the user's input to an integer.
intNumDays = CInt(strInput)
```

After this code executes, `intNumDays` will hold the number of days specified by the user. Then, notice the first line of the `Do While` loop:

```
Do While intCount <= intNumDays
```

The loop repeats while `intCount` is less than or equal to `intNumDays`, the value specified by the user. As a result, the number of loop iterations will be equal to the number of days specified by the user.

 Checkpoint

9 How many times will the following code segment display the message box?

```
Dim intCount As Integer = 0
Do While intCount < 10
    MessageBox.Show("I love Visual Basic!")
Loop
```

10 How many times will the following code segment display the message box?

```
Dim intCount As Integer = 0
Do While intCount < 10
    MessageBox.Show("I love Visual Basic!")
    intCount += 1
Loop
```

11 How many times will the following code segment display the message box?

```
Dim intCount As Integer = 100
Do
    MessageBox.Show("I love Visual Basic!")
    intCount += 1
Loop While intCount < 10
```

12 In the following code segment, which variable is the counter and which is the accumulator?

```
Dim intA As Integer
Dim intX As Integer
Dim intY As Integer
Dim intZ As Integer
Dim strInput As String
intX = 0
intY = 0
strInput = InputBox("How many numbers do you wish to enter?")
intZ = CInt(strInput)
Do While intX < intZ
    strInput = InputBox("Enter a number.")
    intA = CInt(strInput)
    intY += intA
    intX += 1
Loop
MessageBox.Show("The sum of those numbers is " & intY.ToString())
```

13 The following loop adds the numbers 1 through 5 to the lstOutput list box. Modify the loop so that instead of starting at 1 and counting to 5, it starts at 5 and counts backward to 1.

```
Dim intCount As Integer = 1
Do While intCount <= 5
    lstOutput.Items.Add(intCount)
    intCount += 1
Loop
```

14 Write a Do While loop that uses an input box to ask the user to enter a number. The loop should keep a running total of the numbers entered and stop when the total is greater than 300.

15 If you want a Do While loop always to iterate at least once, which form should you use, pretest or posttest?

4 The Do Until and For...Next Loops

CONCEPT: The Do Until loop iterates until its test expression is true. The For...Next loop uses a counter variable and iterates a specific number of times.

The Do Until Loop

The Do While loop iterates as long as a Boolean expression is true. Sometimes, however, it is more convenient to write a loop that iterates *until* an expression is true—that is, a loop that iterates as long as an expression is false, and then stops when the expression becomes true.

For example, consider a machine in an automobile factory that paints cars as they move down the assembly line. When there are no more cars to paint, the machine stops. If you were programming such a machine, you might want to design a loop that causes the machine to paint cars until there are no more cars on the assembly line.

A loop that iterates until a condition is true is known as a **Do Until** loop. The Do Until loop can be written as either a pretest or a posttest loop. Here is the general format of a pretest Do Until loop:

```
Do Until BooleanExpression
    Statement
    (More statements may follow)
Loop
```

Here is the general format of a posttest Do Until loop:

```
Do
    Statement
    (More statements may follow)
Loop Until BooleanExpression
```

In Tutorial 6, you examine an application that uses the Do Until loop. The application asks the user to enter test scores, and then displays the average of the scores.

Tutorial 6:

Examining an application that uses the Do Until loop

Step 1: Open the *Test Scores* project from the student sample programs folder named *Chap5\Test Scores*. Recall that this folder can be downloaded with other materials from www.microsoft.com/express/Downloads/.

Step 2: Run the application. The form appears, as shown in Figure 18.

Step 3: Click the *Get Scores* button. The input box shown in Figure 19 appears.

Figure 18 *Test Score Average* form

Figure 19 Input box

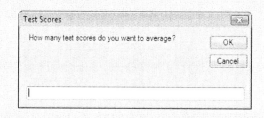

Step 4: Enter **5** for the number of test scores and click the *OK* button (or press [Enter]).

Step 5: Because you entered 5 for the number of test scores, the application presents five input boxes asking for scores 1, 2, 3, 4, and 5. Enter the following values when asked.

Test Score 1: **98**   Test Score 3: **100**   Test Score 5: **92**
Test Score 2: **87**   Test Score 4: **74**

Step 6: After you enter the fifth test score, the test score average 90.2 is displayed on the application form. Click the *Exit* button to end the application.

Step 7: Open the *Code* window. The application's code is shown, with line numbers for reference, at the end of the tutorial. Let's look at the `btnGetScores_Click` event handler in greater detail:

- Local variables are declared in lines 6 through 11. Notice that the `dblTotal` variable (line 8) is initialized to 0. This variable is used as an accumulator. Also notice that the `intCount` variable (line 11) is initialized to 1. This variable is used as a loop counter.
- Line 14 displays the input box prompting the user for the number of test scores. The input is assigned to `strInput`.
- The `If...Then` statement in line 17 uses the `Integer.TryParse` method to convert `strInput` to an Integer, and store the result in `intNumScores`. If the conversion is successful, the `Integer.TryParse` method returns `True` and the program continues to line 20. If the conversion fails (because of invalid input), the `Integer.TryParse` method returns `False`, and the program jumps to the `Else` clause in line 45. If this happens, line 47 displays an error message, and the event handler ends.
- The `Do Until` loop that begins in line 20 iterates until `intCount` is greater than `intNumScores`. Inside the loop, lines 22 and 23 prompt the user for a test score, storing the user's input in `strInput`. The `If...Then` statement in line 26 uses the `Double.TryParse` method to convert `strInput` to a Double, and store the result in `dblTestScore`. If the conversion is successful, the `Double.TryParse` method returns `True` and the program continues to line 29. If the conversion fails (because of invalid input), the `Double.TryParse` method returns `False`, and the program jumps to the `Else` clause in line 33. If this happens, line 35 displays an error message, and the event handler ends.
- Line 29 uses the `+=` operator to add `dblTestScore` to the accumulator variable `dblTotal`.
- Line 32 uses the `+=` operator to add 1 to the counter variable `intCount`.
- After the loop has finished, the `If...Then` statement in line 40 determines whether `intNumScores` is greater than 0. If so, line 41 calculates the average test score, and line 42 displays the average in the `lblAverage` label.

```
1  Public Class Form1
2
3    Private Sub btnGetScores_Click(...) Handles btnGetScores.Click
4      ' This procedure gets the test scores, then calculates and
5      ' displays the average.
6      Dim intNumScores As Integer   ' The number of test scores
7      Dim dblTestScore As Double    ' To hold a test score
8      Dim dblTotal As Double = 0    ' Accumulator, initialized to 0
9      Dim dblAverage As Double      ' The average of the test scores
10     Dim strInput As String        ' To hold user input
11     Dim intCount As Integer = 1   ' Counter variable, initialized to 1
12
13     ' Prompt the user for the number of test scores.
14     strInput = InputBox("How many test scores do you want to average?")
15
16     ' Convert the input to an integer.
17     If Integer.TryParse(strInput, intNumScores) Then
18
19       ' Get the test scores.
20       Do Until intCount > intNumScores
```

```
21          ' Prompt the user for a score.
22          strInput = InputBox("Enter test score " &
23                              intCount.ToString())
24
25          ' Convert the input to a Double.
26          If Double.TryParse(strInput, dblTestScore) Then
27
28             ' Add the score to the accumulator.
29             dblTotal += dblTestScore
30
31             ' Add 1 to the counter.
32             intCount += 1
33          Else
34             ' Invalid test score.
35             MessageBox.Show("Enter a numeric test score.")
36          End If
37       Loop
38
39       ' Calculate and display the average.
40       If intNumScores > 0 Then
41          dblAverage = dblTotal / intNumScores
42          lblAverage.Text = dblAverage.ToString()
43       End If
44
45    Else
46       ' Invalid number of test scores.
47       MessageBox.Show("Enter an integer value for number of test scores.")
48    End If
49 End Sub
50
51 Private Sub btnExit_Click(...) Handles btnExit.Click
52    ' Close the form.
53    Me.Close()
54 End Sub
55 End Class
```

The For...Next Loop

VideoNote

The
For...
Next Loop

The For...Next loop is ideal for situations that require a counter because it initializes, tests, and increments a counter variable. Here is the format of the **For...Next** loop:

```
For CounterVariable = StartValue To EndValue [Step Increment]
   statement
   (more statements may follow)
Next [CounterVariable]
```

As usual, the brackets are not part of the syntax, but indicate the optional parts. Let's look closer at the syntax.

- *CounterVariable* is the variable to be used as a counter. It must be a numeric variable.
- *StartValue* is the value the counter variable will be initially set to. This value must be numeric.
- *EndValue* is the value the counter variable is tested against just prior to each iteration of the loop. This value must be numeric.
- The Step *Increment* part of the statement is optional. If it is present, *Increment* (which must be a numeric expression) is the amount added to the counter variable at the end of each iteration. If the Step *Increment* part of the statement is omitted, the counter variable is incremented by 1 at the end of each iteration.

- The `Next` [*CounterVariable*] statement marks the end of the loop and causes the counter variable to be incremented. Notice that the name of the counter variable is optional.

Here is an example of the `For...Next` loop:

```
For intCount = 1 To 10
   MessageBox.Show("Hello")
Next
```

This loop executes the `MessageBox.Show("Hello")` statement 10 times. The following steps take place when the loop executes.

1. `intCount` is set to 1 (the start value).
2. `intCount` is compared to 10 (the end value). If `intCount` is less than or equal to 10, continue to Step 3. Otherwise the loop is exited.
3. The `MessageBox.Show("Hello")` statement in the body of the loop is executed.
4. `intCount` is incremented by 1.
5. Go back to Step 2 and repeat this sequence.

The flowchart shown in Figure 20 shows loop's actions.

 WARNING: It is incorrect to place a statement in the body of the `For...Next` loop that changes the counter variable's value. For example, the following loop increments `intX` twice for each iteration.

```
' Warning!
For intCount = 1 To 10
   MessageBox.Show("Hello")
   intCount += 1
Next
```

Figure 20 Flowchart of `For...Next` loop

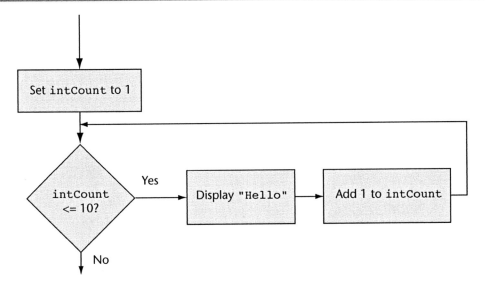

In Tutorial 7, you examine an application that demonstrates the `For...Next` loop.

 NOTE: Because the `For...Next` loop performs its test prior to each iteration, it is a pretest loop. Unlike the `Do While` and `Do Until` loops, this is the only form the `For...Next` loop may be written in.

Tutorial 7:

Examining an application that uses the For...Next loop

Step 1: Open the *For Next Demo 1* project from the student sample programs folder named *Chap5\For Next Demo 1.*

Step 2: Run the application. The form appears as shown in Figure 21.

Step 3: Click the *Run Demo* button. The form now appears as shown in Figure 22.

Figure 21 *For...Next Demo 1* form

Figure 22 Results of For...Next loop

Step 4: Click the *Exit* button to terminate the application.

Step 5: Open the *Code* window and find the `btnRunDemo_Click` event handler. The code is as follows:

```
Private Sub btnRunDemo_Click(...) Handles btnRunDemo.Click
    Dim intCount As Integer      ' Loop counter
    Dim intSquare As Integer     ' To hold squares
    Dim strTemp As String        ' To hold output

    For intCount = 1 To 10
      ' Calculate the square of intCount.
      intSquare = CInt(intCount ^ 2)

      ' Create a string to display.
      strTemp = "The square of " & intCount.ToString() &
        " is " & intSquare.ToString()

      ' Add the string to the list box.
      lstOutput.Items.Add(strTemp)
    Next
  End Sub
```

Figure 23 illustrates the order of the steps taken by the For...Next loop in this program.

Figure 23 Steps in `For...Next` loop

Step 1: Initialize `intCount` to 1.

Step 2: Compare `intCount` to 10. If `intCount` is greater than 10, terminate the loop. Otherwise, go to Step 3.

```
For intCount = 1 To 10
       ' Calculate the square of intCount.
       intSquare = CInt(intCount ^ 2)

       ' Create a string to display.
       strTemp = "The square of " & intCount.ToString() &
           " is " & intSquare.ToString()

       ' Add the string to the list box.
       lstOutput.Items.Add(strTemp)
Next
```

Step 3: Execute the body of the loop.

Step 4: Increment `intCount` by 1. Go back to Step 2.

In Tutorial 8, you complete a partially written application. The application will use a graphic image and a `For...Next` loop to perform a simple animation.

Tutorial 8:

Completing an application that uses the `For...Next` loop

Step 1: Open the *For Next Demo 2* project from the student sample programs folder named *Chap5\For Next Demo 2*.

Step 2: Open the application's form, as shown in Figure 24.

Figure 24 *For Next Demo 2* form

The propeller cap graphic is displayed by a PictureBox control. The PictureBox control has a Left property that specifies the distance from the left edge of the form to the left edge of the PictureBox control. (The distance is measured in pixels.) In this tutorial, you will write a `For...Next` loop that makes the image move across the form by increasing the value of the PictureBox control's Left property.

NOTE: The PictureBox control's Left property does not appear in the Properties window. You access the Left property in code.

Step 3: Double-click the *Go!* button, and then complete the btnGo_Click event handler by writing the following bold code.

```
Private Sub btnGo_Click(...) Handles btnGo.Click
    Dim intCount As Integer ' Loop counter

    ' Move the image across the form.
    For intCount = 16 To 328
       picPropellerCap.Left = intCount
    Next
End Sub
```

Look at the first line of the For...Next loop:

```
For intCount = 16 To 328
```

The start value for intCount is 16, and its end value is 328. Inside the loop, the following statement stores the value of intCount in the PictureBox control's Left property:

```
picPropellerCap.Left = intCount
```

As the loop iterates, the value in the Left property grows larger, which causes the PictureBox control to move across the form.

Step 4: Run the application. Each time you click the *Go!* button, the propeller cap image should move from the form's left edge to its right edge.

Step 5: Click the *Exit* button to end the application. If you wish, open the *Code* window and experiment with different start and end values for the For...Next loop.

Specifying a Step Value

The **step value** is the value added to the counter variable at the end of each iteration of the For...Next loop. By default, the step value is 1. You can specify a different step value with the Step keyword. For example, look at the following code:

```
For intCount = 0 To 100 Step 10
    MessageBox.Show(intCount.ToString())
Next
```

In this loop, the starting value of intCount is 0 and the ending value of intCount is 100. The step value is 10, which means that 10 is added to intCount at the end of each iteration. During the first iteration intCount is 0, during the second iteration intCount is 10, during the third iteration intCount is 20, and so on.

You may also specify a negative step value if you want to decrement the counter variable. For example, look at the following loop:

```
For intCount = 10 To 1 Step -1
    MessageBox.Show(intCount.ToString())
Next
```

In this loop the starting value of intCount is 10 and the ending value of intCount is 1. The step value is –1, which means that 1 is subtracted from intCount at the end of each iteration. During the first iteration intCount is 10, during the second iteration intCount is 9, and so on.

Summing a Series of Numbers with the `For...Next` Loop

The `For...Next` loop can be used to calculate the sum of a series of numbers, as shown in the following code:

```
Dim intCount As Integer          ' Loop counter
Dim intTotal As Integer = 0      ' Accumulator

' Add the numbers 1 through 100.
For intCount = 1 To 100
    intTotal += intCount
Next

' Display the sum of the numbers.
MessageBox.Show("The sum of 1 through 100 is " & intTotal.ToString())
```

This code uses the variable `intTotal` as an accumulator, and calculates the sum of the numbers from 1 through 100. The counter variable, `intCount`, has a starting value of 1 and an ending value of 100. During each iteration, the value of `intCount` is added to `intTotal`.

You may also let the user specify how many numbers to sum, as well as the value of each number. For example, look at the following code:

```
 1 Dim intCount As Integer          ' Loop counter
 2 Dim intMaxCount As Integer       ' To hold the maximum count
 3 Dim dblTotal As Double = 0.0     ' Accumulator
 4 Dim strInput As String           ' To hold user input
 5 Dim dblNum As Double             ' To hold a number
 6
 7 ' Get the number of numbers to sum.
 8 strInput = InputBox("How many numbers to you want to sum?")
 9 intMaxCount = CInt(strInput)
10
11 ' Add the user-specified numbers.
12 For intCount = 1 To intMaxCount
13     ' Get a number.
14     strInput = InputBox("Enter a number.")
15     dblNum = CDbl(strInput)
16
17     ' Add the number to the accumulator.
18     dblTotal += dblNum
19 Next
20
21 ' Display the sum of the numbers.
22 MessageBox.Show("The sum of those numbers is " &
23                 dblTotal.ToString())
```

For simplicity, we have left out exception handlers, or other code to validate the user input. Line 8 prompts the user for the number of numbers to sum, and line 9 stores the user's input in the `intMaxCount` variable. In line 12, which is the beginning of the For...Next loop, the `intCount` variable has a starting value of 1, and an ending value of `intMaxCount`. As a result, the number of iterations will be the value stored in `intMaxCount`.

In line 14, an input box is used to prompt the user for a number. In line 15, the value entered by the user is stored in the `dblNum` variable. Line 18 adds `dblNum` to the `dblTotal` variable, which is the accumulator.

Optional Topic: Breaking Out of a Loop

In rare circumstances, you might find it necessary to stop a loop before it goes through all of its iterations. Visual Basic provides the `Exit Do` statement, that allows you to prematurely break out of a Do While loop, and the Exit For statement, that allows you to prematurely break out of a For...Next loop. The way they work is simple:

- When a Do While loop is executing, if it encounters an Exit Do statement, the loop immediately ends.
- When a For...Next loop is executing, if it encounters an Exit For statement, the loop immediately ends.

You should do your best to avoid using these statements, however. They bypass the normal logic that terminates the loop, and make the code more difficult to understand and debug.

Deciding Which Loop to Use

Although most repetitive algorithms can be written with any of the three types of loops, each works best in different situations.

The Do While Loop

Use the Do While loop when you wish the loop to repeat as long as the test expression is true. You can write the Do While loop as a pretest or posttest loop. Pretest Do While loops are ideal when you do not want the code in the loop to execute if the test expression is false from the beginning. Posttest loops are ideal when you always want the code in the loop to execute at least once.

The Do Until Loop

Use the Do Until loop when you wish the loop to repeat until the test expression is true. You can write the Do Until loop as a pretest or posttest loop. Pretest Do Until loops are ideal when you do not want the code in the loop to execute if the test expression is true from the beginning. Posttest loops are ideal when you always want the code in the loop to execute at least once.

The For...Next Loop

The For...Next loop is a pretest loop that first initializes a counter variable to a starting value. It automatically increments the counter variable at the end of each iteration. The loop repeats as long as the counter variable is not greater than an end value. The For...Next loop is primarily used when the number of required iterations is known.

 Checkpoint

16 How many times will the code inside the following loop execute? What will be displayed in the message box?

```
intX = 0
Do Until intX = 10
    intX += 2
Loop
MessageBox.Show(intX.ToString())
```

17 Write a For...Next loop that adds every fifth number, starting at zero, through 100, to the list box lstOutput.

18 Write a For...Next loop that repeats seven times, each time displaying an input box that asks the user to enter a number. The loop should also calculate and display the sum of the numbers entered.

19 Which type of loop is best to use when you know exactly how many times the loop should repeat?

20 Which type of loop is best to use when you want the loop to repeat as long as a condition exists?

21 Which type of loop is best to use when you want the loop to repeat until a condition exists?

Nested Loops

CONCEPT: A loop that is contained inside another loop is called a nested loop.

A **nested loop** is a loop inside another loop. A clock is a good example of something that works like a nested loop. The second hand, minute hand, and hour hand all spin around the face of the clock. The hour hand, however, makes only one revolution for every 60 of the minute hand's revolutions. And it takes 60 revolutions of the second hand for the minute hand to make one revolution. This means that for every complete revolution of the hour hand, the second hand revolves 3,600 times.

The following is a code segment with a `For...Next` loop that partially simulates a digital clock. It displays the seconds from 0 through 59 in a label named `lblSeconds`.

```
For intSeconds = 0 To 59
    lblSeconds.Text = intSeconds.ToString()
Next
```

We can add a minutes variable and another label, and nest the loop inside another loop that cycles through 60 minutes:

```
For intMinutes = 0 To 59
    lblMinutes.Text = intMinutes.ToString()
    For intSeconds = 0 To 59
        lblSeconds.Text = intSeconds.ToString()
    Next
Next
```

To make the simulated clock complete, another variable, label, and loop can be added to count the hours:

```
For intHours = 0 To 23
    lblHours.Text = intHours.ToString()
    For intMinutes = 0 To 59
        lblMinutes.Text = intMinutes.ToString()
        For intSeconds = 0 To 59
            lblSeconds.Text = intSeconds.ToString()
        Next
    Next
Next
```

The innermost loop will iterate 60 times for each iteration of the middle loop. The middle loop will iterate 60 times for each iteration of the outermost loop. When the outermost loop has iterated 24 times, the middle loop will have iterated 1,440 times and the innermost loop will have iterated 86,400 times.

The simulated clock example brings up a few points about nested loops:

- An inner loop goes through all of its iterations for each iteration of an outer loop.
- Inner loops complete their iterations before outer loops do.
- To get the total number of iterations of a nested loop, multiply the number of iterations of all the loops.

Checkpoint

22 What values will the following code segment add to the lstNumbers list box?

```
For intX = 1 To 3
    lstNumbers.Items.Add(intX)
    For intY = 1 To 2
        lstNumbers.Items.Add(intY)
    Next
Next
```

23 How many times will the value in intY be displayed in the following code segment?

```
For intX = 1 To 20
    For intY = 1 To 30
        MessageBox.Show(intY.ToString())
    Next
Next
```

6 | Multicolumn List Boxes, Checked List Boxes, and Combo Boxes

CONCEPT: A multicolumn list box displays items in columns with a horizontal scroll bar, if necessary. A checked list box displays a check box next to each item in the list. A combo box performs many of the same functions as a list box, and it can also let the user enter text.

Multicolumn List Boxes

The ListBox control has a Multicolumn property that can be set to *True* or *False*. By default, it is set to *False*. If you set Multicolumn to *True*, it causes the list box to display its list in columns. You set the size of the columns, in pixels, with the ColumnWidth property. For example, suppose a form has a list box named lstNumbers, as shown in Figure 25.

The list box's Multicolumn property is set to *True*, and its ColumnWidth property is set to *30*. The following code adds the numbers 0 through 100 to a list box:

```
For intNumber = 0 To 100
    lstNumbers.Items.Add(intNumber)
Next
```

After the code executes, the list box appears as shown in Figure 26.

Notice that a horizontal scroll bar automatically appears in the list box. The user may scroll through the list and select a number.

Checked List Boxes

The CheckedListBox control is a variation of the ListBox control. It supports all ListBox properties and methods discussed in Section 2. Each item in a CheckedListBox control, however, is displayed with a check box next to it. Figure 27 shows an example.

An item in a checked list box may be selected and/or checked. Only one item in a checked list box may be selected at a given time, but multiple items may be checked.

Figure 25 List box

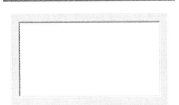

Figure 26 List box with multicolumn display

Figure 27 Checked list box

This is how the CheckOnClick property determines whether items become checked:

- When set to *False*, the user clicks an item once to select it, and then clicks it again to check it (or uncheck it, if it is already checked).
- When set to *True*, the user clicks an item only once to both select it and check it (or uncheck it, if it is already checked).

The CheckOnClick property is set to *False* by default. Because this setting makes working with the control a bit complicated, you may prefer setting it to *True* for most applications.

You can access the selected item in a checked list box exactly as you do with a regular list box: through the SelectedIndex and SelectedItem properties. These properties only indicate which item is selected, however, and do not report which items are checked. You access the checked items through the GetItemChecked method, which has the following general format:

```
CheckedListBox.GetItemChecked(Index)
```

CheckedListBox is the name of the CheckedListBox control. *Index* is the index of an item in the list. If the item is checked, the method returns *True*. Otherwise, it returns *False*. For example, assume an application has a checked list box name clbCities. (clb is the prefix for checked list boxes.) The following code counts the number of checked items:

```
Dim intIndex As Integer            ' List box index
Dim intCheckedCities As Integer = 0  ' To count the checked cities

' Step through the items in the list box, counting
' the number of checked items.
For intIndex = 0 To clbCities.Items.Count - 1
    If clbCities.GetItemChecked(intIndex) = True Then
        intCheckedCities += 1
    End If
Next

' Display the number of checked cities.
MessageBox.Show("You checked " & intCheckedCities.ToString() &
                " cities.")
```

As another example, assume an application uses the controls shown in Figure 28. The checked list box on the left is clbCities and the list box on the right is lstChecked. The *OK* button, btnOk, uses the following Click event handler:

```
Private Sub btnOk_Click(...) Handles btnOk.Click
    Dim intIndex As Integer ' List box index

    For intIndex = 0 To clbCities.Items.Count - 1
        If clbCities.GetItemChecked(intIndex) = True Then
            lstChecked.Items.Add(clbCities.Items(intIndex))
        End If
    Next
End Sub
```

The `btnOk_Click` event handler adds the items checked in the `clbCities` control to the `lstChecked` control. Figure 29 shows how the controls appear after the user has checked three cities and clicked the *OK* button.

Figure 28 Checked list box
and a list box

Figure 29 Cities checked

Combo Boxes

Combo boxes and list boxes are similar in the following ways:

- They both display a list of items to the user.
- They both have Items, Items.Count, SelectedIndex, SelectedItem, and Sorted properties.
- They both have `Items.Add`, `Items.Clear`, `Items.Remove`, and `Items.RemoveAt` methods.
- All of these properties and methods work the same with combo boxes and list boxes.

Additionally, a combo box has a rectangular area that works like a text box. The user may either select an item from the combo box's list or type text into the combo box's text input area.

Like a text box, the combo box has a Text property. If the user types text into the combo box, the text is stored in the Text property. Also, when the user selects an item from the combo box's list, the item is copied to the Text property.

The prefix that we use for combo box names is `cbo`.

Combo Box Styles

There are three different styles of combo boxes: the drop-down combo box, the simple combo box, and the drop-down list combo box. You can select a combo box's style with its DropDownStyle property. Let's look at the differences of each style.

The Drop-Down Combo Box

This is the default setting for the combo box DropDownStyle property. At runtime, a drop-down combo box appears like the one shown in Figure 30.

This style of combo box behaves like either a text box or a list box. The user may either type text into the box (like a text box) or click the down arrow (⏷). If the user clicks the down arrow, a list of items drops down, as shown in Figure 31.

Now the user may select an item from the list. When the user selects an item, it appears in the text input area at the top of the box, and is copied to the combo box's Text property.

NOTE: When typing text into the combo box, the user may enter a string that does not appear in the drop-down list.

Figure 30 A drop-down combo box

Figure 31 A list drops down when the user clicks the down arrow

 TIP: When the combo box has the focus, the user may also press [Alt] + [↓] to drop the list down. This is also true for the drop-down list combo box.

The Simple Combo Box

With the simple style of combo box, the list of items does not drop down but is always displayed. Figure 32 shows an example.

As with the drop-down combo box, this style allows the user to type text directly into the combo box or select from the list. When typing, the user is not restricted to the items that appear in the list. When an item is selected from the list, it is copied to the text input area and to the combo box's Text property.

Drop-Down List Combo Box

With drop-down list combo box style, the user may not type text directly into the combo box. An item must be selected from the list. Figure 33 shows a drop-down list combo box.

When the user clicks the down arrow, a list of items appears, as shown in Figure 34.

Figure 33 The drop-down list combo box

Figure 32 The simple combo box

Figure 34 A list drops down when the user clicks the down arrow

When the user selects an item from the list, it is copied to the text area at the top of the combo box and to the Text property. Because the user can only select items from the list, it is not possible to enter text that does not appear in the list.

Getting the User's Input from a Combo Box

As with the list box, you can determine which item has been selected from a combo box's list by retrieving the value in the SelectedIndex or SelectedItem properties. If the user has typed text into the combo box's text area, however, you cannot use the SelectedIndex or SelectedItem properties to get the text. The best way to get the user's input is with the Text property, which contains either the user's text input or the item selected from the list.

> **NOTE:** The drop-down list combo box's Text property is read-only. You cannot change its value with code.

List Boxes versus Combo Boxes

The following guidelines help you decide when to use a list box and when to use a combo box.

- Use a drop-down or simple combo box when you want to provide the user a list of items to select from but do not want to limit the user's input to the items on the list.
- Use a list box or a drop-down list combo box when you want to limit the user's selection to a list of items. The drop-down list combo box generally takes less space than a list box (because the list doesn't appear until the user clicks the down arrow), so use it when you want to conserve space on the form.

In Tutorial 9, you create three styles of combo boxes.

Tutorial 9:
Creating combo boxes

In this tutorial, you will create each of the three styles of combo boxes.

Step 1: Create a new Windows Forms Application project named *Combo Box Demo*.

Step 2: Set up the form like the one shown in Figure 35. Create three combo boxes: cboCountries (drop-down combo box), cboPlays (simple combo box), and cboArtists (drop-down list combo box).

Step 3: Enter the following items into the Items property of the cboCountries combo box: **England, Ireland, Scotland**, and **Wales**. Set the combo box's Sorted property to *True*.

Step 4: Enter the following items into the Items property of the cboPlays combo box: **Hamlet, Much Ado about Nothing, Romeo and Juliet, A Comedy of Errors**, and **The Merchant of Venice**. Set the combo box's Sorted property to *True*.

Step 5: Enter the following items into the Items property of the cboArtists combo box: **Michelangelo, Raphael**, and **da Vinci**.

Figure 35 *Combo Box Demo* form

Step 6: The btnShow_Click event handler should perform the following tasks:

- Copy the selected item or typed text from the cboCountries combo box to the lblCountry.Text property.
- Copy the selected item or typed text from the cboPlays combo box to the lblPlay.Text property.
- Copy the selected item from the cboArtists combo box to the lblArtist. Text property.

Enter the following code shown in bold for the btnShow_Click event handler:

```
Private Sub btnShow_Click(...) Handles btnShow.Click
    ' Display the combo box selections.
    lblCountry.Text = cboCountries.Text
    lblPlay.Text = cboPlays.Text
    lblArtist.Text = cboArtists.Text
End Sub
```

Step 7: The btnReset_Click event handler should deselect any items that are selected in the combo boxes. As with list boxes, this is accomplished by setting the SelectedIndex property to –1. The procedure should also set the Text property of lblCountry, lblPlay, and lblArtist to String.Empty. Enter the following code, shown in bold, for the btnReset_Click event handler.

```
Private Sub btnReset_Click(...) Handles btnReset.Click
    ' Reset the combo boxes.
    cboCountries.SelectedIndex = -1
    cboCountries.Text = String.Empty
    cboPlays.SelectedIndex = -1
    cboPlays.Text = String.Empty
    cboArtists.SelectedIndex = -1
    ' Note: cboArtists.Text is read-only.

    ' Reset the labels.
    lblCountry.Text = String.Empty
    lblPlay.Text = String.Empty
    lblArtist.Text = String.Empty
End Sub
```

NOTE: If the user types characters into a combo box's text input area, those characters are not cleared by setting the SelectedIndex property to –1. You must set the Text property to `String.Empty` to accomplish that.

Step 8: The `btnExit_Click` event handler should end the application. Write the code for that event handler.

Step 9: Save the project and run the application. Experiment with the combo boxes by trying a combination of text input and item selection. For example, select an item from the `cboCountries` list and type text into the `cboPlays`' text input area. Click the `btnShow` button to see what you have entered.

Step 10: End the application when you are finished experimenting with it.

Checkpoint

24 What is the index of the first item stored in a list box or combo box's Items property?

25 Which list box or combo box property holds the number of items stored in the Items property?

26 Which list box or combo box property holds the index of the item selected from the list?

27 What is the difference between a drop-down and drop-down list combo box?

28 What is the best method of getting the user's input from a combo box?

29 Suppose you want to place a list box on a form, but it would take up too much space. What other control might you use?

7 Random Numbers

CONCEPT: Visual Basic provides tools to generate random numbers and initialize the sequence of random numbers with a random seed value.

Computer applications such as games and simulations often create what appear to be random events. A program simulating a traffic intersection, for example, might generate random numbers of simulated vehicles. Based on information provided during the simulation, planners can estimate the average amount of time drivers spend waiting at the stoplight. Similarly, random numbers can simulate the movements of stock prices, using various rules about how stock prices change.

Unfortunately, computers aren't capable of generating truly random numbers (unless you have an old, malfunctioning computer—then it might fail from time to time, generating truly random results.) Instead, computers use carefully crafted formulas that are based on years of research to generate pseudo-random numbers. **Pseudo-random** numbers only seem to be random. For most applications that require random numbers, however, pseudo-random numbers work just as well.

To generate random numbers in Visual Basic, you have to create a special type of object known as a `Random` object in memory. `Random` objects have methods and properties that make generating random numbers fairly easy. Here is an example of a statement that creates a `Random` object:

```
Dim rand As New Random
```

This statement declares a variable named `rand`. The expression `New Random` creates a `Random` object in memory. After this statement executes, the `rand` variable will refer to the `Random` object. As a result, you will be able to use the `rand` variable to call the object's methods for generating random numbers. (There is nothing special about the variable name `rand` used in this example. You can use any legal variable name.)

The `Next` Method

Once you have created a `Random` object, you can call its `Next` method to get a random integer number. The following code shows an example:

```
' Declare an Integer variable.
Dim intNum As Integer

' Create a Random object.
Dim rand As New Random

' Get a random integer and assign it to intNum.
intNum = rand.Next()
```

After this code executes, the `intNum` variable will contain a random number. If you call the `Next` method with no arguments, as shown in this example, the returned integer is somewhere between 0 and 2,147,483,647. Alternatively, you can pass an argument that specifies an upper limit to the generated number's range. In the following statement, the value assigned to `intNum` is somewhere between 0 and 99:

```
intNum = rand.Next(100)
```

The random integer's range does not have to begin at zero. You can add or subtract a value to shift the numeric range upward or downward. In the following statement, we call the `Next` method to get a random number in the range of 0 through 9, and then we add 1 to it. So, the number assigned to `intNum` will be somewhere in the range of 1 through 10:

```
intNum = rand.Next(10) + 1
```

The following statement shows another example. It assigns a random integer to `intNum` between −50 and +49:

```
intNum = rand.Next(100) - 50
```

The `NextDouble` Method

You can call a `Random` object's `NextDouble` method to get a random floating-point number between 0.0 and 1.0 (not including 1.0). The following code shows an example:

```
' Declare a Double variable.
Dim dblNum As Double

' Create a Random object.
Dim rand As New Random

' Get a random number and assign it to dblNum.
dblNum = rand.NextDouble()
```

After this code executes, the `dblNum` variable will contain a random floating-point number in the range of 0.0 up to (but not including) 1.0. If you want the random number to fall within a larger range, multiply it by a scaling factor. The following statement assigns a random number between 0.0 and 500.0 to `dblNum`:

```
dblNum = rand.NextDouble() * 500.0
```

The following statement generates a random number between 100.0 and 600.0:

```
dblNum = (rand.NextDouble() * 500.0) + 100.0
```

In Tutorial 10 you will create a VB application that uses random numbers to simulate a coin toss.

Tutorial 10:
Creating the Coin Toss Application

In this tutorial you will create an application that simulates the tossing of a coin. Each time the user tosses the coin, the application will use a Random object to get a random integer in the range of 0 through 1. If the random number is 0, it means the tails side of the coin is up, and if the random number is 1, it means the heads side is up. The application will display an image of a coin showing either the heads side or the tails side, depending on the value of the random number.

Step 1: Create a new Windows Forms application named *Coin Toss*.

Step 2: Set up the form with two PictureBox controls and two buttons, like the one shown in Figure 36. In the student sample programs, in the *Chap5* folder, you will find two image files named Heads.bmp and Tails.bmp. Set the picHeads control's Image property to the Heads.bmp file, and set the picTails control's Image property to the Tails.bmp file. Remember that the student sample programs folder can be downloaded from www.microsoft.com/express/Downloads/.

Step 3: Set the Visible property to False for both the picHeads control and the picTails control. (You will still see the images on the form in the *Designer* window, but they will be invisible when the application runs.)

Figure 36 The *Coin Toss* form

Step 4: Double-click the btnToss button to create a code template for its Click event handler. Complete the event handler by writing the following bold code shown in lines 2 through 20.

```
1 Private Sub btnToss_Click(...) Handles btnToss.Click
2   Dim intSideUp As Integer ' To indicate which side is up
3   Dim rand As New Random    ' Random number generator
4
```

```
 5   ' Get a random number in the range of 0 through 1.
 6   ' 0 means tails up, and 1 means heads up.
 7   intSideUp = rand.Next(2)
 8
 9   ' Display the side that is up.
10   If intSideUp = 0 Then
11       ' 0 means tails is up, so display the tails
12       ' image and hide the heads image.
13       picTails.Visible = True
14       picHeads.Visible = False
15   Else
16       ' 1 means heads is up, so display the heads
17       ' image and hide the tails image.
18       picHeads.Visible = True
19       picTails.Visible = False
20   End If
21 End Sub
```

Let's take a closer look at the code. Line 2 declares an Integer variable named intSideUp. This variable will hold a random number that indicates which side of the coin is up. Line 3 creates a Random object, using the name rand to refer to that object.

Line 7 calls the rand object's Next method, passing 2 as an argument. This means that the method will return a value in the range of 0 through 1. The random number is assigned to the intSideUp variable.

The If statement in line 10 determines whether intSideUp is equal to 0. If so, it means that the tails side of the coin is up, so line 12 makes the picTails control visible and line 13 makes the picHeads control invisible.

If the intSideUp variable is not equal to 0, then the heads side of the coin is up. In that case, the Else clause in line 15 takes over. Line 18 makes the picHeads control visible and line 19 makes the picTails control invisible.

Step 5: Write an event handler for the btnExit button. The button should close the form when it is clicked.

Step 6: Save the application, and then run it. Initially you will not see the coin on the form. When you click the *Toss the Coin* button, however, one of the two images (heads up or tails up) will be displayed, as shown in Figure 37. Click the button several times to simulate several coin tosses. When you are finished, exit the application.

Figure 37 The *Coin Toss* form with heads up and tails up

Random Number Seeds

The formula used to generate random numbers has to be initialized with a value known as a seed value. The **seed value** is used in the calculation that returns the next random number in the series. When a `Random` object is created in memory, it retrieves the system time from the computer's internal clock, and uses that as the seed value. The system time is an integer that represents the current date and time, down to a hundredth of a second.

If a `Random` object uses the same seed each time it is created, it will always generate the same series of random numbers. Because the system time changes every hundredth of a second, it is the preferred value to use as the seed in most cases. However, you can specify a different integer value as the seed, if you desire, when you create a `Random` object. Here is an example:

```
Dim rand As New Random(1000)
```

In this example, the `Random` object that is created uses 1000 as the seed value. Each time a `Random` object is created with this statement, it will generate the same series of random numbers. That may be desirable when running specific tests and validations, but decidedly boring if the program is a computer game or simulation.

Checkpoint

30 What does a `Random` object's `Next` method return?

31 What does a `Random` object's `NextDouble` method return?

32 Write code that creates a `Random` object and then assigns a random integer in the range of 1 through 100 to the variable `intRandomNumber`.

32 Write code that creates a `Random` object and then assigns a random integer in the range of 100 through 400 to the variable `intRandomNumber`.

34 What does a `Random` object use as its seed value if you do not specify one?

35 What happens if the same seed value is used each time a `Random` object is created?

8 Simplifying Code with the `With...End With` Statement

CONCEPT: The `With...End With` statement allows you to simplify a series of consecutive statements that perform operations using the same object.

Sometimes you must write several consecutive statements that perform operations on the same control or other object. The following code shows an example of several operations being performed with a text box named `txtName`:

```
txtName.Clear()
txtName.ForeColor = Color.Blue
txtName.BackColor = Color.Yellow
txtName.BorderStyle = BorderStyle.Fixed3D
```

In Visual Basic you can simplify this code using the **`With...End With`** statement, as shown here:

```
With txtName
  .Clear()
  .ForeColor = Color.Blue
```

```
      .BackColor = Color.Yellow
      .BorderStyle = BorderStyle.Fixed3D
   End With
```

Notice that the With...End With statement we refer to the txtName control only once, in the first line. That eliminates the need to repeatedly type txtName at the beginning of each line that appears inside the statement.

9 ToolTips

CONCEPT: ToolTips are a standard and convenient way of providing help to the users of an application. The ToolTip control allows you to assign pop-up hints to the other controls on a form.

A **ToolTip** is a small box displayed when the user holds the mouse cursor over a control. The box shows a short description of what the control does. Most Windows applications use ToolTips as a way of providing immediate and concise help to the user.

The **ToolTip control** allows you to create ToolTips for other controls on a form. Place a ToolTip control in your application just as you place other controls: double-click the ToolTip icon in the Toolbox. When you do so, a ToolTip control appears in an area at the bottom of the *Designer* window, as shown in Figure 38.

Figure 38 ToolTip control

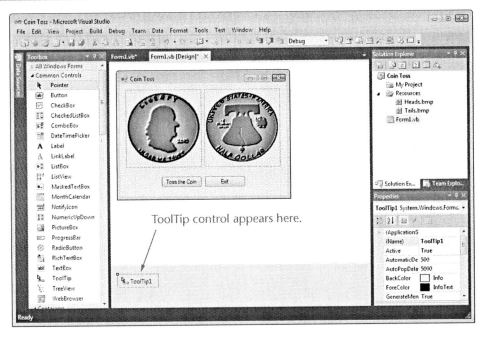

Because the ToolTip control is invisible at runtime, it does not appear on the form at design time. Instead, it appears in an area known as the component tray. The **component tray** is a resizable region at the bottom of the *Design* window that holds invisible controls.

When you add a ToolTip control to a form, a new property is added to all the other controls. The new property is named *ToolTip* on *ToolTipControl*, where *ToolTipControl* is the name of the ToolTip control. For example, suppose you add a ToolTip control to a form and keep the default name *ToolTip1*. The new property that is added to the other controls will be named *ToolTip on ToolTip1*. This new property holds the string that is displayed as the control's ToolTip.

ToolTip Properties

You can select the ToolTip control in the component tray and then examine its properties in the *Properties* window. The InitialDelay property determines the amount of time, in milliseconds, that elapses between the user pointing the mouse at a control and the ToolTip's appearance. The default setting is 500. (One millisecond is 1/1000th of a second, so 500 milliseconds is half of a second.)

The AutoPopDelay property is also a measure of time in milliseconds. It determines how long a ToolTip remains on the screen once it is displayed. The default setting is 5000. The ReshowDelay property holds the number of milliseconds that will elapse between the displaying of different ToolTips as the user moves the mouse from control to control. The default setting is 100.

You can set these properties individually, or set them all at once with the AutomaticDelay property. When you store a value in the AutomaticDelay property, InitialDelay is set to the same value, AutoPopDelay is set to 10 times the value, and ReshowDelay is set to one-fifth the value. In Tutorial 11, you add ToolTips to an application.

Tutorial 11:
Adding ToolTips to an application

Step 1: Load the *Coin Toss* project that you completed in Tutorial 10 and open the form in the *Designer* window.

Step 2: Scroll down in the Toolbox until you find the ToolTip icon ( ). Double-click the icon to add a ToolTip control to the component tray. Notice that the default name of the ToolTip control is *ToolTip1*.

Step 3: When you add the ToolTip1 control, Visual Basic automatically adds a new property named *ToolTip on ToolTip1* to all other controls on the form. In the *Designer* window select the btnToss Button control, and then locate the ToolTip on ToolTip1 property in the *Properties* window.

Step 4: Set the btnToss Button control's ToolTip on ToolTip1 property to *Click to toss the coin.*

Step 5: In the *Designer* window select the btnExit Button control, and then set its ToolTip on ToolTip1 property to *Click to exit.*

Step 6: Save the project and the run it. The image on the left in Figure 39 shows the tooltip that should appear when you hold the mouse cursor over the btnToss button, and the image on the right shows shows the tooltip that should appear when you hold the mouse cursor over the btnExit button.

Figure 39 Tooltips displayed

10 Focus on Program Design and Problem Solving: Building the *Vehicle Loan Calculator* Application

CONCEPT: In this section, you build the *Vehicle Loan Calculator* application. The application uses a loop, input validation, and ToolTips. This section also covers some of the Visual Basic intrinsic financial functions.

Visual Basic has several built-in functions for performing financial calculations. You will build a program named *Vehicle Loan Calculator*. It uses the following functions: Pmt, IPmt, and PPmt. Let's look at each function in detail before continuing with the case study.

The Pmt Function

The Pmt function returns the periodic payment amount for a loan. It assumes the loan has a fixed interest rate. Here is the general form of the **Pmt** function call:

```
Pmt(PeriodicInterestRate, NumberOfPeriods, —LoanAmount)
```

Descriptions of each argument follow:

1. *PeriodicInterestRate*: You usually know a loan's annual interest rate; this function, however, needs to know the loan's periodic interest rate. A loan is divided into periods, and you make a payment each period. The periodic interest rate is the rate of interest per period of the loan. For example, if you make monthly payments on a loan, the period is each month. If the annual interest rate is 9%, then the periodic interest rate is .09 divided by 12, which is .0075.
2. *NumberOfPeriods*: For a loan that requires monthly payments, this is the total number of months of the loan. For example, a three-year loan is given for 36 months.
3. *LoanAmount*: This is the amount being borrowed, which must be negative.

NOTE: The Pmt function can also be used to calculate payments on a savings plan. When using it for that purpose, specify the desired value of the savings as a positive number.

Here is an example of the function call:

```
dblPayment = Pmt(dblAnnInt / 12, 24, -5000)
```

In this statement, dblAnnInt contains the annual interest rate, 24 is the number of months of the loan, and the amount of the loan is $5,000. After the statement executes, dblPayment holds the fixed monthly payment amount.

The IPmt Function

The IPmt function returns the interest payment for a specific period on a loan. It assumes the loan has a fixed interest rate, with fixed monthly payments. Here is the general format of the **IPmt** function call:

```
IPmt(PeriodicInterestRate, Period, NumberOfPeriods, —LoanAmount)
```

Descriptions of each argument follow:

1. *PeriodicInterestRate*: As with the Pmt function, this function must know the periodic interest rate. (See the description of argument 1 for the Pmt function.)

2. *Period*: This argument specifies the period for which you wish to calculate the payment. The argument must be at least 1, and no more than the total number of periods of the loan.
3. *NumberofPeriods*: The total number of periods of the loan. (See the description of argument 2 for the Pmt function.)
4. *LoanAmount*: As with the Pmt function, the loan amount must be expressed as a negative number.

Here is an example of the function call:

```
dblInterest = IPmt(dblAnnInt / 12, 6, 24, -5000)
```

In this statement, dblAnnInt contains the annual interest rate, 6 is the number of the month for which you wish to calculate the payment, 24 is the number of months of the loan, and the amount of the loan is $5,000. After the statement executes, dblInterest holds the amount of interest paid in month 6 of the loan.

The PPmt Function

The PPmt function returns the principal payment for a specific period on a loan. It assumes the loan has a fixed interest rate, with fixed monthly payments. Here is the general format of the **PPmt function** call:

```
PPmt(PeriodicInterestRate, Period, NumberOfPeriods, —LoanAmount)
```

Descriptions of each argument follow:

1. *PeriodicInterestRate*: As with the Pmt function, this function must know the periodic interest rate. (See the description of argument 1 for the Pmt function.)
2. *Period*: This argument specifies the period for which you wish to calculate the payment. The argument must be at least 1, and no more than the total number of periods of the loan.
3. *NumberOfPeriods*: The total number of periods of the loan. (See the description of argument 2 for the Pmt function.)
4. *LoanAmount*: As with the Pmt function, the loan amount must be expressed as a negative number.

Here is an example of the function call:

```
dblPrincipal = PPmt(dblAnnInt / 12, 6, 24, -5000)
```

In this statement, dblAnnInt contains the annual interest rate, 6 is the number of the month for which you wish to calculate the payment, 24 is the number of months of the loan, and the amount of the loan is $5,000. After the statement executes, dblPrincipal holds the amount of principal paid in month 6 of the loan.

The Case Study

The Central Mountain Credit Union finances new and used vehicles for its members. A credit union branch manager asks you to write an application named Vehicle Loan Calculator that displays the following information for a loan:

- The monthly payment amount
- The amount of the monthly payment applied toward interest
- The amount of the monthly payment applied toward principal

The credit union currently charges 8.9% annual interest for new vehicle loans and 9.5% annual interest on used vehicle loans.

Figure 40 shows a sketch of the *Vehicle Loan Calculator* application's form.

Figure 40 Sketch of the *Vehicle Loan Calculator* form

Table 2 lists each control, along with any relevant property settings.

Table 2 *Vehicle Loan Calculator* controls

Control Type	Control Name	Property	Property Value
Form	(Default)	Text:	*Loan Calculator*
ToolTip	(Default)		(Retain default property settings)
GroupBox	(Default)	Text: TabIndex:	*Vehicle && Loan Information* 0
Label	(Default)	Text:	*Cost of Vehicle:*
Text box	txtCost	ToolTip on ToolTip1:	*Enter the cost of the vehicle here.*
Label	(Default)	Text:	*Amount of Down Payment:*
Text box	txtDownPayment	ToolTip on ToolTip1:	*Enter the amount of the down payment here.*
Label	(Default)	Text:	*Number of Months:*

(continued)

341

Table 2 *Vehicle Loan Calculator controls (continued)*

Control Type	Control Name	Property	Property Value
Text box	txtMonths	ToolTip on ToolTip1:	*Enter the number of months of the loan here.*
GroupBox	(Default)	Text:	*New or Used Vehicle?*
RadioButton	radNew	Text: ToolTip on ToolTip1: Checked	*&New* *Click here if the vehicle is new.* True
RadioButton	radUsed	Text: ToolTip on ToolTip1: Checked	*&Used* *Click here if the vehicle is used.* False
GroupBox	(Default)	Text:	*Interest and Principal Payments*
Label	(Default)	Text:	*Annual Interest Rate:*
Label	lblAnnualRate	BorderStyle: AutoSize: ToolTip on ToolTip1:	*Fixed3D* *False* *Annual interest rate*
ListBox	lstOutput		
Button	btnCalculate	Text: ToolTip on ToolTip1:	*&Calculate* *Click here to calculate the payment data.*
Button	btnClear	Text: ToolTip on ToolTip1:	*C&lear* *Click here to clear the form.*
Button	btnExit	Text: ToolTip on ToolTip1:	*E&xit* *Click here to exit.*

Table 3 lists and describes the event handlers needed in this application.

Table 3 *Vehicle Loan Calculator event handlers*

Method	Description
btnCalculate_Click	Calculates and displays a table in the list box showing interest and principal payments for the loan
btnClear_Click	Resets the interest rate, clears the text boxes, and clears the list box
btnExit_Click	Ends the application
radNew_CheckedChanged	Updates the annual interest rate if the user selects a new vehicle loan
radUsed_CheckedChanged	Updates the annual interest rate if the user selects a used vehicle loan

The following pseudocode shows the general logic for the btnCalculate_Click event handler. Note that the pseudocode does not indicate input validation, and the actual arguments that need to be passed to the Pmt, IPmt, and PPmt functions are not shown.

> *Get VehicleCost from the form*
> *Get DownPayment from the form*
> *Get Months from the form*
>
> *Loan = VehicleCost – DownPayment*
> *MonthlyPayment = Pmt()*

```
For Count = 0 To Months
    Interest = IPmt()
    Principal = PPmt()
    Display Month, Payment, Interest, and Principal in list box
Next
```

These event handlers change the annual interest rate when the user clicks the radNew and radUsed radio buttons. Pseudocode for the radNew_CheckedChanged event handler is as follows:

```
If radNew is selected Then
    Annual Interest Rate = 0.089
    Display Annual Interest Rate in lblAnnInt
End If
```

Pseudocode for the radUsed_CheckedChanged event handler is as follows:

```
If radUsed is selected Then
    Annual Interest Rate = 0.095
    Display Annual Interest Rate in lblAnnInt
End If
```

In Tutorial 12 you build the *Vehicle Loan Calculator* application.

Tutorial 12:

Building the *Vehicle Loan Calculator* application

Step 1: Create a new Windows Forms Application project named *Loan Calculator*.

Step 2: Set up the form as shown in Figure 41. Refer to Figure 40 for the names of the programmer-defined control names, and Table 1 for the important property settings.

Figure 41 *Loan Calculator* form

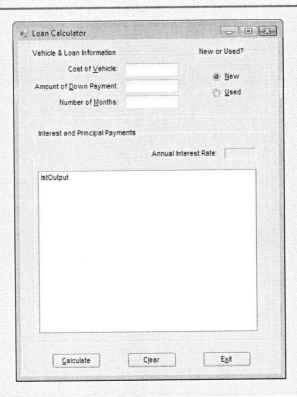

Step 3: Once you have placed all the controls on the form and set their properties, you can write the application's code. Open the *Code* window and write the comments and class-level variable declarations shown as follows in bold. This code should not appear inside of any event handler.

```
Public Class Form1
    ' Class-level constants
    Const dblMONTHS_YEAR As Double = 12 ' Months per year
    Const dblNEW_RATE As Double = 0.089 ' Interest rate, new cars
    Const dblUSED_RATE As Double = 0.095 ' Interest rate, used cars

    ' Class-level variable to hold the annual interest rate
    Dim dblAnnualRate As Double = dblNEW_RATE
End Class
```

The variable, dblAnnualRate, which holds the annual interest rate, is declared as a class-level variable because it will be accessed by multiple procedures. It is initialized with dblNEW_RATE because a new vehicle loan will be selected by default.

Step 4: Create the code template for the btnCalculate_Click event handler. Complete the event handler by writing the following bold code.

```
Private Sub btnCalculate_Click(...) Handles btnCalculate.Click
    Dim dblVehicleCost As Double       ' Vehicle cost
    Dim dblDownPayment As Double       ' Down payment
    Dim intMonths As Integer           ' Number of months for the loan
    Dim dblLoan As Double              ' Amount of the loan
    Dim dblMonthlyPayment As Double    ' Monthly payment
    Dim dblInterest As Double          ' Interest paid for the period
    Dim dblPrincipal As Double         ' Principal paid for the period
    Dim intCount As Integer            ' Counter for the loop
    Dim strOut As String               ' Used to hold a line of output

    ' Get the vehicle cost.
    If Double.TryParse(txtCost.Text, dblVehicleCost) Then

        ' Get the down payment.
        If Double.TryParse(txtDownPayment.Text, dblDownPayment) Then

            ' Get the number of months.
            If Integer.TryParse(txtMonths.Text, intMonths) Then

                ' Calculate the amount of the loan.
                dblLoan = dblVehicleCost - dblDownPayment

                ' Calculate the monthly payment
                dblMonthlyPayment = Pmt(dblAnnualRate / dblMONTHS_YEAR,
                                    intMonths, -dblLoan)

                ' Clear the list box.
                lstOutput.Items.Clear()

                For intCount = 1 To intMonths
                    ' Calculate the interest for this period.
                    dblInterest = IPmt(dblAnnualRate / dblMONTHS_YEAR,
                                    intCount, intMonths, -dblLoan)
```

```
                    ' Calculate the principal for this period.
                    dblPrincipal = PPmt(dblAnnualRate / dblMONTHS_YEAR,
                                        intCount, intMonths, -dblLoan)

                    ' Start building the output string with the month.
                    strOut = "Month: " & intCount.ToString()

                    ' Add the payment amount to the output string
                    strOut &= " Payment: " & dblMonthlyPayment.ToString("c")

                    ' Add the interest amount to the output string.
                    strOut &= " Interest: " & dblInterest.ToString("c")

                    ' Add the principal for the period.
                    strOut &= " Principal: " & dblPrincipal.ToString("c")

                    ' Add the output string to the list box
                    lstOutput.Items.Add(strOut)
                Next

            Else
                ' Error message for invalid months.
                MessageBox.Show("Ener an integer for months.")
            End If
        Else
            ' Error message for invalid down payment.
            MessageBox.Show("Ener a numeric value for down payment.")
        End If
    Else
        ' Error message for invalid vehicle cost.
        MessageBox.Show("Ener a numeric value for vehicle cost.")
    End If
End Sub
```

Step 5: Create the code template for the `btnClear_Click` event handler. Complete the event handler by writing the following bold code.

```
Private Sub btnClear_Click(...) Handles btnClear.Click
    ' Reset the interest rate, clear the text boxes
    ' and clear the list box. Set default interest
    ' rate for new car loans.

    radNew.Checked = True
    dblAnnualRate = dblNEW_RATE
    lblAnnualRate.Text = dblNEW_RATE.ToString("p")
    txtCost.Clear()
    txtDownPayment.Clear()
    txtMonths.Clear()
    lstOutput.Items.Clear()

    ' Reset the focus to txtCost.
    txtCost.Focus()
End Sub
```

Step 6: Create the code template for the `btnExit_Click` event handler. Complete the event handler by writing the following bold code.

```
Private Sub btnExit_Click(...) Handles btnExit.Click
    ' Close the form.
    Me.Close()
End Sub
```

Step 7: Create the code template for the `radNew_CheckedChanged` event handler. (You can easily create the code template by opening the *Designer* window and double-clicking the radNew control.) Complete the event handler by writing the following bold code.

```
Private Sub radNew_CheckedChanged(...) Handles radNew.CheckedChanged
    ' If the New radio button is checked, then
    ' the user has selected a new car loan.
    If radNew.Checked = True Then
        dblAnnualRate     = dblNEW_RATE
        lblAnnualRate.Text = dblNEW_RATE.ToString("p")
    End If
End Sub
```

Step 8: Create the code template for the `radUsed_CheckedChanged` event handler. (You can easily create the code template by opening the *Designer* window and double-clicking the radUsed control.) Complete the event handler by writing the following bold code.

```
Private Sub radUsed_CheckedChanged(...) Handles radUsed.CheckedChanged
    ' If the Used radio button is checked, then
    ' the user has selected a used car loan.
    If radUsed.Checked = True Then
        dblAnnualRate = dblUSED_RATE
        lblAnnualRate.Text = dblUSED_RATE.ToString("p")
    End If
End Sub
```

Step 9: Attempt to run the application. If there are errors, compare your code and property settings with those listed to locate them.

Step 10: Save the project.

Summary

1 Input Boxes

- Input boxes provide a simple way to gather input from the user.

2 List Boxes

- A list box control displays a list of items and allows the user to select one or more items from the list.

3 Introduction to Loops: The Do While Loop

- A repetition structure, or loop, causes one or more statements to repeat. Each repetition of a loop is called an iteration.
- The Do While loop has an expression that is tested for *True* or *False* value and a statement or group of statements that is repeated as long as an expression is true.

4 The Do Until and For...Next Loops

- The Do Until loop repeats until its test expression is true.
- The For...Next loop initializes, tests, and increments a counter variable.
- The Do While and Do Until loops may be written as either pretest or posttest loops. The For...Next loop is a pretest loop.
- The Exit Do and Exit For statements, when placed inside the body of a loop, stop the execution of the loop and cause the program to jump to the statement immediately following the loop.

5 Nested Loops

- A loop located inside another loop is called a nested loop. It is used when a task performs a repetitive operation and each iteration of that operation is itself a repetitive operation.

6 Multicolumn List Boxes, Checked List Boxes, and Combo Boxes

- A multicolumn list box displays items in columns with a horizontal scroll bar, if necessary.
- A checked list box displays a check box next to each item in the list.
- There are three different styles of combo box: the drop-down combo box, the simple combo box, and the drop-down list combo box. You select a combo box's style with its DropDownStyle property.

7 Random Numbers

- A Random object has methods that generate random sequences of numbers.
- A Random object's Next method returns the next random integer in a series.
- A Random object's NextDouble method returns a random value between 0.0 and 1.0.

8 Simplifying Code with the With...End With Statement

- The With...End With statement allows you to simplify a series of consecutive statements that perform operations using the same object.

9 ToolTips

- The ToolTip control allows you to create ToolTips (pop-up hints) for other controls on the same form.
- The ToolTip control is invisible at runtime; it appears in the component tray at design time.

10 Focus on Program Design and Problem Solving: Building the *Vehicle Loan Calculator* Application

- This section outlines the process of building the *Vehicle Loan Calculator* application using a loop.
- The Pmt function returns the periodic payment amount for a loan. The IPmt function returns the required interest payment for a specific period on a loan. The PPmt function returns the principal payment for a specific period on a loan.

Key Terms

accumulator	loop
combo box	nested loop
conditionally executed statements	Next method
counter	NextDouble method
Do Until loop	posttest loop
Do While loop	Pmt function
Exit Do statement	PPmt function
Exit For statement	pretest loop
For...Next loop	pseudo-random (numbers)
infinite loop	Random object
input box	repetition structure
IPmt function	running total
Items property	Seed value
Items.Add method	SelectedIndex property
Items.Count property	SelectedItem property
Items.Insert method	Sorted property
Items.Remove method	step value
Items.RemoveAt method	tooltip
iteration	ToolTip control
ListBox control	With...End With statement

Review Questions and Exercises

Fill-in-the-Blank

1. A(n) _____ provides a simple way to gather input without placing a text box on a form.

2. A(n) _____ displays a list of items and allows the user to select an item from the list.

3. A(n)_____ causes one or more statements to repeat.

4. If a loop does not have a way of stopping, it is called a(n) _____ loop.

5. A(n)_____ is a variable that is regularly incremented or decremented each time a loop iterates.

6. A(n)_____ loop evaluates its test expression after each iteration.

7. Each repetition of the loop is called a(n) _____.

8. The _____ statement, when placed inside the body of a Do While loop, stops the execution of the loop and causes the program to jump to the statement immediately following the loop.

9. A loop that is inside another loop is called a _____ loop.

10. A (n) _____ object has methods that can generate a sequence of random numbers.

11. The _____ method generates a random integer.

12. The _____ method generates a random floating-point value.

13. The _____ function returns the periodic payment amount for a loan.

14. The _____ function returns the principal payment for a specific period on a loan.

15. The _____ function returns the required interest payment for a specific period on a loan.

Multiple Choice

1. You display input boxes with this function.
   a. InBox
   b. Input
   c. InputBox
   d. GetInput

2. An input box returns the value entered by the user as this.
   a. String
   b. Integer
   c. Single
   d. Boolean

3. Visual Basic automatically adds this to a list box when it contains more items than can be displayed.
   a. Larger list box
   b. Scroll bar
   c. Second form
   d. Message box

4. A list box or combo box's index numbering starts at this value.
   a. 0
   b. 1
   c. −1
   d. any value you specify

5. This property holds the index of the selected item in a list box.
   a. Index
   b. SelectedItem
   c. SelectedIndex
   d. Items.SelectedIndex

6. This method erases one item from a list box.

   a. `Erase`
   b. `Items.Remove`
   c. `Items.RemoveItem`
   d. `Clear`

7. The `Do While` statement marks the beginning of a `Do While` loop, and the `Loop` statement marks the end. The statements between these are known as one of the following.

   a. Processes of the loop
   b. Functions of the loop
   c. Substance of the loop
   d. Body of the loop

8. This type of loop evaluates its test expression before each iteration.

   a. Out-test
   b. Pretest
   c. Posttest
   d. In-test

9. One of the following is a sum of numbers that accumulates with each iteration of a loop.

   a. Counter
   b. Running total
   c. Summation function
   d. Iteration count

10. This type of loop is ideal for situations that require a counter because it is specifically designed to initialize, test, and increment a counter variable.

    a. `Do While`
    b. `Do Until`
    c. `For...Next`
    d. `Posttest Do Until`

11. You do this to get the total number of iterations of a nested loop.

    a. Add the number of iterations of all the loops
    b. Multiply the number of iterations of all the loops
    c. Average the number of iterations of all the loops
    d. Get the number of iterations of the outermost loop

12. When this ListBox control's property is set to *True*, it causes the ListBox control to display its list in multiple columns.

    a. Columns
    b. Multicolumn
    c. ColumnList
    d. TableDisplay

13. This control has a rectangular area that functions like a text box.

    a. List box
    b. Drop-down list box
    c. Combo box
    d. Input label

14. This is the prefix that we use for combo box names.

    a. `cbo`
    b. `com`
    c. `cbx`
    d. `cob`

15. With this style of combo box, the list of items does not drop down, but is always displayed.
    a. Drop-down combo box
    b. Simple combo box
    c. Drop-down list combo box
    d. Simple drop-down combo list box

16. This combo box property will contain the user's text input or the item selected from the list.
    a. Input
    b. Caption
    c. List
    d. Text

17. Which of the following statements creates a `Random` object and initializes the sequence of random numbers with the seed value 25?
    a. `InitRandom(25)`
    b. `Rnd(25)`
    c. `Dim rand As New Seed(25)`
    d. `Dim rand As New Random(25)`

True or False

Indicate whether the following statements are true or false.

1. T F: If you do not provide a value for an input box's title, an error will occur.

2. T F: If the user clicks an input box's *Cancel* button, the function returns the number −1.

3. T F: The `Items.RemoveAt` method always removes the last item in a list box (the item with the highest index value).

4. T F: Infinite loops keep repeating until the program is interrupted.

5. T F: A loop's conditionally executed statements should be indented.

6. T F: A pretest loop always performs at least one iteration, even if the test expression is false from the start.

7. T F: The `Do While` loop may be written as either a pretest or posttest loop.

8. T F: In a `For...Next` loop, the *Counter Variable* must be numeric.

9. T F: The *Step Increment* part of the `For...Next` statement is optional.

10. T F: The `For...Next` loop is a posttest loop.

11. T F: In a nested loop, the inner loop goes through all of its iterations for each iteration of an outer loop.

12. T F: To create a checked list box, you draw a regular list box and set its Checked property to *True*.

13. T F: A drop-down list combo box allows the user to either select an item from a list or type text into a text input area.

14. T F: If a `Random` object is initialized with the same seed value each time it is created, it will produce the same series of random numbers each time.

Short Answer

1. What buttons automatically appear on an input box?

2. Where is an input box positioned if you leave out the xpos and ypos arguments?

3. Write a statement that adds *Spinach* to the list box lstVeggies at index 2.

4. Write a statement that removes the item at index 12 of the combo box cboCourses.

5. Describe the two important parts of a Do While loop.

6. In general terms, describe how a Do While loop works.

7. Why should you indent the statements in the body of a loop?

8. Describe the difference between pretest loops and posttest loops.

9. Why are the statements in the body of a loop called conditionally executed statements?

10. What is the difference between the Do While loop and the Do Until loop?

11. Which loop should you use in situations where you wish the loop to repeat as long as the test expression is true?

12. Which type of loop should you use in situations where you wish the loop to repeat until the test expression is true?

13. Which type of loop should you use when you know the number of required iterations?

14. What feature do combo boxes have that list boxes do not have?

15. With one style of combo box the user may not type text directly into the combo box, but must select an item from the list. Which style is it?

16. With one style of combo box the Text property is read-only. Which style?

17. What value does a Random object use as its seed if you do not specify a seed value?

What Do You Think?

1. Why is it critical that counter variables are properly initialized?

2. Why should you be careful not to place a statement in the body of a For...Next loop that changes the value of the loop's counter variable?

3. You need to write a loop that iterates until the user enters a specific value into an input box. Which type of loop should you choose? Why?

4. You need to write a loop that will repeat 224 times. Which type of loop will you choose? Why?

5. You need to write a loop that iterates as long as a variable has a specific value stored in it. Which type of loop will you choose? Why?

6. Why is a computer's system time a good source of random seed values?

7. You use the statement lstNames.Items.RemoveAt(6) to remove an item from a list box. Does the statement remove the sixth or seventh item in the list? Why?

8. What kind of control(s) do you use when you want to provide the user a list of items to select from, but do not want to limit the user's input to the items on the list?

9. What kind of control(s) do you use when you want to limit the user's selection to a list of items?

Find the Error

Identify the syntactically incorrect statements in the following:

1. Loop
```
    intX = intX + 1
Do While intX < 100
```

2. Do
```
    lstOutput.Items.Add("Hello")
    intX = intX + 1
While intCount < 10
```

3. Loop Until intX = 99
```
    intX = intX + 1
Do
```

4. For intX = 1
```
    lstOutput.Items.Add(intX)
Next
```

Algorithm Workbench

1. An event handler named `btnShow_Click` must add the numbers 1 through 20 to a list box named `lstNumbers`. Design a flowchart for this event handler.

2. Write the code that you would insert into the code template for the event handler described in Question 1.

3. Write a `Do While` loop that uses an input box to get a number from the user. The number should be multiplied by 10 and the result stored in the variable product. The loop should iterate as long as product contains a value less than 100.

4. Write a `Do While` loop that uses input boxes to get two numbers from the user. The numbers should be added and the sum displayed message box. An input box should ask the user whether he or she wishes to perform the operation again. If so, the loop should repeat; otherwise it should terminate.

5. Write a `For...Next` loop that adds the following set of numbers to the list box `lstNumbers`.

   0, 10, 20, 30, 40, 50 . . . 1000

6. Write a loop that uses an input box to get a number from the user. The loop should iterate 10 times and keep a running total of the numbers entered.

7. Convert the following pretest `Do While` loop to a posttest `Do While` loop:

```
intX = 1
Do While intX > 0
  strInput = InputBox("Enter a number")
  intX = CInt(strInput)
Loop
```

8. Convert the following `Do While` loop to a `Do Until` loop:

```
strInput = String.Empty
Do While strInput.ToUpper <> "Y"
  strInput = InputBox("Are you sure you want to quit?")
Loop
```

9. Convert the following `Do While` loop to a `For...Next` loop:

```
intCount = 0
Do While intCount < 50
  lstOutput.Items.Add(intCount)
  intCount += 1
Loop
```

10. Convert the following `For...Next` loop to a `Do While` loop:

```
For intX = 50 To 0 Step -1
  lstOutput.Items.Add(intX)
Next
```

11. Rewrite the following statements so they appear inside a `With` block:

```
txtName.Text = "(unknown)"
txtName.Font.Size = 10
txtName.BackColor = Color.Red
```

Programming Challenges

VideoNote

The Sum of Numbers Problems

1. **Sum of Numbers**

   Create an application that displays a form similar to the one shown in Figure 42. When the *Enter Numbers* button is clicked, the application should display the input box shown in Figure 43.

   The input box asks the user to enter a positive integer value. Notice that the default input value is 10. When the *OK* button is clicked, the application should display a message box with the sum of all the integers from 1 through the value entered by the user, as shown in Figure 44.

Figure 42 *Sum of Numbers* form

Figure 43 *Sum of Numbers* input box

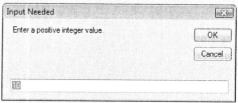

Figure 44 *Sum of Numbers* message box

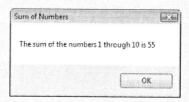

If the user enters a negative value, the application should display an error message. Use the following test data to determine if the application is calculating properly:

Value	Sum
5	15
10	55
20	210
100	5050

2. **Distance Calculator**

   If you know a vehicle's speed and the amount of time it has traveled, you can calculate the distance it has traveled as follows:

   $$Distance = Speed * Time$$

For example, if a train travels 40 miles per hour for 3 hours, the distance traveled is 120 miles. Create an application with a form similar to the one shown in Figure 45.

When the user clicks the *Calculate* button, the application should display an input box asking the user for the speed of the vehicle in miles-per-hour, followed by another input box asking for the amount of time, in hours, that the vehicle has traveled. Then it should use a loop to display in a list box the distance the vehicle has traveled for each hour of that time period. Figure 46 shows an example of what the application's form should look like.

Figure 45 *Distance Calculator*

Figure 46 *Distance Calculator* completed

Use the following test data to determine if the application is calculating properly.

Vehicle Speed: 60
Hours Traveled: 7

Hour	Distance Traveled
1	60
2	120
3	180
4	240
5	300
6	360
7	420

3. **Workshop Selector**

Table 4 shows a training company's workshops, the number of days of each, and their registration fees.

Table 4 Workshops and registration fees

Workshop	Number of Days	Registration Fee
Handling Stress	3	$595
Time Management	3	$695
Supervision Skills	3	$995
Negotiation	5	$1,295
How to Interview	1	$395

The training company conducts its workshops in the six locations shown in Table 5. The table also shows the lodging fees per day at each location.

Table 5 Training locations and lodging fees

Location	Lodging Fees per Day
Austin	$95
Chicago	$125
Dallas	$110
Orlando	$100
Phoenix	$92
Raleigh	$90

When a customer registers for a workshop, he or she must pay the registration fee plus the lodging fees for the selected location. For example, here are the charges to attend the Supervision Skills workshop in Orlando:

Registration: $995
Lodging: $100 × 3 days = $300
Total: $1,295

Design an application with a form that resembles the one shown in Figure 47.

Figure 47 *Workshop Selector* form

The application should allow the user to select a workshop from one list box and a location from another list box. When the user clicks the *Add Workshop* button, the application should add the total cost of the selected workshop at the selected location in the third list box. When the user clicks the *Calculate Total* button, the total cost of all the selected workshops should be calculated and displayed in the label. The *Reset* button should deselect the workshop and location from the first two list boxes, clear the third list box, and clear the total cost label.

4. **Hotel Occupancy**

The ElGrande Hotel has eight floors and 30 rooms on each floor. Create an application that calculates the occupancy rate for each floor, and the overall occupancy rate for the hotel. The occupancy rate is the percentage of rooms occupied, and may be calculated by dividing the number of rooms occupied by the number of rooms. For example, if 18 rooms on the first floor are occupied, the occupancy rate is as follows:

$$18 / 30 = .6 \text{ or } 60\%$$

The application's form should appear similar to the one shown in Figure 48.

Figure 48 *Hotel Occupancy* form

When the user clicks the *Complete Report* button, a loop should execute and iterate eight times. Each time the loop iterates, it should display an input box for one of the hotel's floors. The input box should ask the user to enter the number of rooms occupied on that floor. As the user enters a value for each floor, the loop should calculate the occupancy rate for that floor, and display the information for that floor in the list box. When the number of occupied rooms has been entered for all the floors, the application should display the total number of rooms occupied and the overall occupancy rate for the hotel. (The hotel has a total of 240 rooms.)

Figure 49 shows an example of the form after occupancy information has been provided for all the floors.

The *Clear* button should clear all the appropriate controls on the form. The *Exit* button should end the application. Use the values shown in Figure 49 to confirm that your application is performing the correct calculations.

Figure 49 Completed *Hotel Occupancy* form

5. **Rainfall Statistics**

Create an application that allows the user to enter each month's amount of rainfall (in inches) and calculates the total and average rainfall for a year. Figure 50 shows the application's form.

Once the user has entered the amount of rainfall for each month, he or she may click the *Calculate* button to display the total and average rainfall. The *Clear* button should clear all the text boxes and labels on the form. The *Exit* button should end the application.

Figure 50 *Rainfall Statistics* form

Rainfall Statistics		
Rainfall Data		
January	July	
Februar	August	
March	September	
April	October	
May	November	
June	December	
	Total Rainfall	
	Average Rainfall	
Calculate	Clear	Exit

6. **Bar Chart**

Create an application that prompts the user to enter today's sales for five stores. The program should then display a simple bar graph comparing each store's sales. Create each bar in the bar graph by displaying a row of asterisks (*) in a list box. Each asterisk in a bar represents $100 in sales.

Figure 51 shows the form with the bar chart displayed. The sales data entered was $1000 for store #1, $1200 for store #2, $1800 for store #3, $800 for store #4, and $1900 for store #5.

Figure 51 *Bar Chart* form

358

7. **Grade Report**

Create an application that allows a teacher to enter three test scores each for three students. The application should calculate each student's average test score and assign a letter grade based on the following grading scale:

Average Test Score	Letter Grade
90 or greater	A
80 through 89	B
70 through 79	C
60 through 69	D
Below 60	F

The application should prompt the user for each student's name and three test scores. Figure 52 shows an example of how the application's form might appear after all the data has been entered.

Figure 52 *Grade Report* form

Design Your Own Forms

8. **Celsius to Fahrenheit Table**

Recall that the formula for converting Celcius temperatures to Fahrenheit is

$$F = 1.8 * C + 32$$

In the formula, F is the Fahrenheit temperature and C is the Celsius temperature.

For this exercise, create an application that displays a table of the Celsius temperatures 0 through 20 and their Fahrenheit equivalents. The application should use a loop to display the temperatures in a list box.

9. **Population**

Create an application that will predict the approximate size of a population of organisms. The user should select or enter the starting number of organisms in a combo box, enter the average daily population increase (as a percentage) in a text box, and select or enter the number of days the organisms will be left to multiply in another combo box. For example, assume the user enters the following values:

Starting number of organisms: 2
Average daily increase: 30%
Number of days to multiply: 10

The application should display the following table of data.

Day	Approximate Population
1	2
2	2.6
3	3.38
4	4.394
5	5.7122
6	7.42586
7	9.653619
8	12.5497
9	16.31462
10	21.209

Be sure to add appropriate ToolTips for each control on the form.

10. **Pennies for Pay**

Susan is hired for a job, and her employer agrees to pay her every day. Her employer also agrees that Susan's salary is one penny the first day, two pennies the second day, four pennies the third day, and continuing to double each day. Create an application that allows the user to select or enter into a combo box the number of days that Susan will work, and calculates the total amount of pay she will receive over that period of time.

11. **Payroll**

Create an application that displays payroll information. The application should allow the user to enter the following data for four employees:

- Number of hours worked
- Hourly pay rate
- Percentage to be withheld for state income tax
- Percentage to be withheld for federal income tax
- Percentage to be withheld for FICA

The application should calculate and display the following data for each employee in a list box:

- Gross pay (the number of hours worked multiplied by the hourly pay rate)
- State income tax withholdings (gross pay multiplied by state income tax percentage)
- Federal income tax withholdings (gross pay multiplied by federal income tax percentage)
- FICA withholdings (gross pay multiplied by FICA percentage)
- Net pay (the gross pay minus state income tax, federal income tax, and FICA)

When the calculations are performed, be sure to check for the following error:

- If any employee's state income tax plus federal tax plus FICA is greater than the employee's gross pay, display an error message stating that the withholdings are too great.

Be sure to add appropriate ToolTips for each control on the form.

12. **Ocean Levels**

Assuming the ocean's level is currently rising at about 1.5 millimeters per year, create an application that displays the number of millimeters that the ocean will have risen each year for the next 10 years.

13. **Calories Burned**

Running on a particular treadmill you burn 3.9 calories per minute. Create an application that uses a loop to display the number of calories burned after 10, 15, 20, 25, and 30 minutes.

14. **Budget Analysis**

Create an application that lets the user enter the amount that he or she has budgeted for a month. A loop should then use input boxes to prompt the user for his or her expenses for the month, and keep a running total. When the loop finishes, the program should display the amount that the user is over or under budget.

15. **Speed Conversion Chart**

Your friend Amanda, who lives in the United States, just bought an antique European sports car. The car's speedometer works in kilometers per hour. The formula for converting kilometers per hour to miles per hour is:

$$MPH = KPH * 0.6214$$

In the formula, MPH is the speed in miles per hour and KPH is the speed in kilometers per hour. Amanda is afraid she will get a speeding ticket, and has asked you to write a program that displays a list of speeds in kilometers per hour with their values converted to miles per hour. The list should display the speeds from 60 kilometers per hour through 130 kilometers per hour, in increments of 5 kilometers per hour. (In other words, it should display 60 kph, 65 kph, 70 kph, and so forth, up through 130 kph.)

16. **Dice Simulator**

Create an application that simulates rolling a pair of dice. When the user clicks a button, the application should generate two random numbers, each in the range of 1 through 6, to represent the value of the dice. Use PictureBox controls to display the dice. (In the student sample programs, in the *Chap5* folder, you will find six images named Die1.bmp, Die2.bmp, Die3.bmp, Die4.bmp, Die5.bmp, and Die6.bmp, that you can use in the PictureBoxes.)

17. **Addition Tutor**

Create an application generates two random integers, each in the range of 100 through 500. The numbers should be displayed as an addition problem on the application's form, such as

$$247 + 129 = ?$$

The form should have a text box for the user to enter the problem's answer. When a button is clicked, the application should do the following:

- Check the user's input and display a message indicating whether it is the correct answer.
- Generate two new random numbers and display them in a new problem on the form.

18. **Random Number Guessing Game**

Create an application that generates a random number in the range of 1 through 100, and asks the user to guess what the number is. If the user's guess is higher than the random number, the program should display "Too high, try again." If the user's guess is lower than the random number, the program should display "Too low, try again." The program should use a loop that repeats until the user correctly guesses the random number.

19. **Random Number Guessing Game Enhancement**

Enhance the program that you wrote for Programming Challenge 18 so it keeps a count of the number of guesses that the user makes. When the user correctly guesses the random number, the program should display the number of guesses.

Answers to Checkpoints

1. ```
   strInput = InputBox("Enter a number", "Please Respond", "500")
   ```

2. ```
   strInput = InputBox("Enter a number", "Please Respond",
                       "500" 100, 300)
   ```

3. 0

4. `Items.Count`

5. 11

6. SelectedItem

7. SelectedIndex

8. `strSelectedName = lstNames.Items(1).ToString()`

9. The loop is an infinite loop because it does not change the value of `intCount`.

10. Ten times

11. One time

12. `intX` is the counter and `intY` is the accumulator.

13. ```
    Dim intCount As Integer = 5

    Do While intCount >= 1
      lstOutput.Items.Add(intCount)
      intCount -= 1
    Loop
    ```

14. ```
    Dim intTotal As Integer = 0
    Dim intNumber As Integer

    Do While intTotal <= 300
      intNumber = CInt(InputBox("Enter a number"))
      intTotal += intNumber
    Loop
    ```

15. Posttest

16. The loop will execute five times. The message box will display 10.

17. ```
    Dim intCount As Integer

    For intCount = 0 To 100 Step 5
      lstOutput.Items.Add(intCount)
    Next
    ```

18. ```
    Dim intCount As Integer
    Dim intTotal As Integer
    Dim intNum As Integer

    intTotal = 0
    For intCount = 0 To 7
      intNum = CInt(InputBox("Enter a number"))
      intTotal += intNum
    Next
    MessageBox.Show("The total is " & intTotal.ToString())
    ```

19. The `For` loop

20. The `Do While` loop

21. The `Do Until` loop

22 1, 1, 2, 2, 1, 2, 3, 1, 2

23 600 times

24 0

25 Items.Count

26 SelectedIndex

27 A drop-down combo box allows the user to type text into its text area. A drop-down list combo box does not allow the user to type text. The user can only select an item from the list.

28 By retrieving the value in the Text property

29 A drop-down list combo box

30 It returns a random integer value somewhere between 0 and 2,147,483,647.

31 It returns a random floating-point number between 0.0 and 1.0 (not including 1.0).

32 `Dim rand as New Random`

   `intRandomNumber = rand.Next(101)`

33 `Dim rand as New Random`

   `intRandomNumber = rand.Next(301) + 100`

34 When a `Random` object is created in memory, it retrieves the system time from the computer's internal clock, and uses that as the seed value.

35 If a `Random` object uses the same seed each time it is created, it will always generate the same series of random numbers.

Procedures and Functions

A **procedure** is a collection of statements that performs a task. Event handlers, for example, are procedures. A **function** is a collection of statements that performs a task and then returns a value to the part of the program that executed it. You have already used many of Visual Basic's built-in functions such as CInt and IsNumeric.

This chapter discusses how to write general purpose procedures and functions. These procedures do not respond to events, but execute when they are called by statements. You will learn how to create, call, and pass arguments to these procedures as well as various techniques for debugging applications that use them.

In common object-oriented terminology, the term **method** is used to mean both procedures and functions.

1 Procedures

CONCEPT: You can write your own general purpose procedures that perform specific tasks. General purpose procedures are not triggered by events, but are called from statements in other procedures.

A procedure is a collection of statements that performs a task. An event handler or event procedure is a type of procedure that is executed when an event, such as a mouse click, occurs while the program is running. This section discusses general purpose procedures that are not triggered by events, but executed by statements in other procedures.

By writing your own procedures, you can **modularize** an application's code, that is, break it into small, manageable procedures. Imagine a book with a thousand pages that was not divided into chapters or sections. Finding a single topic in the book would be very difficult. Real-world applications can easily have thousands of lines of code, and unless they are modularized, they can be very difficult to modify and maintain.

Procedures can reduce the amount of duplicated code in a program. If a specific task is performed in several places, a procedure for performing that task can be written once and executed anytime it is needed.

Tutorial 1 walks you through an example application that uses a procedure.

Tutorial 1:
Examining an application with a procedure

Step 1: Open the *Procedure Demo* project from the student sample programs folder named *Chap6\Procedure Demo*. The student sample programs folder can be downloaded from www.microsoft.com/express/Downloads/. The application's form is shown in Figure 1. The form has a list box named lstOutput and two buttons: btnGo and btnExit.

Figure 1 *Procedure Demo* form

Step 2: Open the *Code* window and find the procedure named `DisplayMessage`, which is shown here:

```
Sub DisplayMessage()
  ' This is a procedure that displays a message.
  lstOutput.Items.Add("")
  lstOutput.Items.Add("Hello from the DisplayMessage procedure.")
  lstOutput.Items.Add("")
End Sub
```

The declaration of a procedure begins with a `Sub` statement and ends with an `End Sub` statement. The code that appears between these two statements is the body of the procedure. When the `DisplayMessage` procedure executes, it displays a blank line in the list box, followed by the string `"Hello from the DisplayMessage procedure."`, followed by another blank line.

Figure 2 shows the parts of the Sub statement.

Figure 2 First line of `DisplayMessage` procedure

The first line of the procedure begins with the word `Sub`, followed by the name of the procedure, followed by a set of parentheses. In this procedure, the parentheses are empty. Later, you will see procedures having items inside the parentheses.

> **NOTE:** An event handler is associated with a control, so its name is commonly prefixed with the control's name. For example, the `btnGo` button's Click event handler is named `btnGo_Click`. Since a general purpose procedure is not associated with a control, we do not usually prefix its name with any control name.

Step 3: General purpose procedures are not executed by an event. Instead, they must be called. Look at the following code for the `btnGo_Click` event handler. The statement in line 7 calls the `DisplayMessage` procedure.

```
1 Private Sub btnGo_Click(...) Handles btnGo.Click
2   ' Display some text in the list box.
3   lstOutput.Items.Add("Hello from the btnGo_Click procedure.")
4   lstOutput.Items.Add("Now I am calling the DisplayMessage procedure.")
5
6   ' Call the DisplayMessage procedure.
7   DisplayMessage()
8
9   ' Display some more text in the list box.
10   lstOutput.Items.Add("Now I am back in the btnGo_Click procedure.")
11 End Sub
```

This type of statement, known as a **procedure call**, causes the procedure to execute. A procedure call is simply the name of the procedure that is to be executed. Parentheses follow the name of the procedure. You can also use the **Call** keyword, as shown here:

```
Call DisplayMessage()
```

The Call keyword is optional, and is not used in this text.

When a procedure call executes, the application branches to the procedure and executes its body. When the procedure has finished, control returns to the procedure call and resumes executing at the next statement. Figure 3 illustrates how this application branches from the btnGo_Click procedure to the DisplayMessage procedure call, and returns to the btnGo_Click procedure.

Figure 3 Procedure call

```
Private Sub btnGo_Click(...) Handles btnGo.Click
    ' Display some text in the list box.
    lstOutput.Items.Add("Hello from the btnGo_Click procedure.")
    lstOutput.Items.Add("Now I am calling the DisplayMessage procedure.")

    ' Call the DisplayMessage procedure.
    DisplayMessage()

    ' Display some more text in the list box.
    lstOutput.Items.Add("Now I am back in the btnGo_Click procedure.")
End Sub


Sub DisplayMessage()
    ' This procedure displays a message in the list box.
    lstOutput.Items.Add("")
    lstOutput.Items.Add("Hello from the DisplayMessage procedure.")
    lstOutput.Items.Add("")
End Sub
```

Procedure is called

Branch back

Step 4: Run the application. Click the *Go* button. The form should appear as shown in Figure 4.

Figure 4 Results of *Procedure Demo*

As you can see, the statements in the `btnGo_Click` event handler executed up to the `DisplayMessage` procedure call. At that point, the application branched to the `DisplayMessage` procedure and executed all of its statements. When the `DisplayMessage` procedure finished, the application returned to the `btnGo_Click` event handler and resumed executing at the line following the `DisplayMessage` call.

Step 5: Click the *Exit* button to end the application.

Declaring a Procedure

The general format of a **procedure declaration** is as follows:

```
[AccessSpecifier] Sub ProcedureName ([ParameterList])
   [Statements]
End Sub
```

The items shown in brackets are optional. *AccessSpecifier* specifies the accessibility of the procedure. This is an important issue because some applications have more than one form. When you use the `Private` access specifier, the procedure may be accessed only by other procedures declared in the same class or form. When a procedure begins with `Public`, it may also be accessed by procedures declared in other forms. If you leave out the access specifier, it defaults to `Public`.

Following the keyword **Sub** is the name of the procedure. You should always give the procedure a name that reflects its purpose. You should also adopt a consistent style of using uppercase and lowercase letters. For procedure names, we use **Pascal casing**, which capitalizes the first character and the first character of each subsequent word in the procedure name. All other characters are lowercase. Using different styles of capitalization for variables and procedures lets the reader of your code know what type of entity a name belongs to.

Inside the parentheses is an optional *ParameterList*. A **parameter** is a special variable that receives a value being passed into a procedure. Later in this chapter, you will see procedures that use parameters to accept data passed into them.

The last line of a procedure declaration is the `End Sub` statement. Between the `Sub` statement and the `End Sub` statement, you write the statements that execute each time the procedure is called.

Tutorial 2 guides you through the process of writing procedures. In the tutorial, you will complete an application that uses two procedures, in addition to its event handlers.

Tutorial 2:
Creating and Calling Procedures

VideoNote

Tutorial 6-2
Walkthrough

The *Chap6* folder in the student sample programs contains a partially created project named *Lights*. In this tutorial you will complete the project so it simulates a light being turned off or on. The project's form is shown in Figure 5.

Figure 5 The *Lights* project's form

The form has the following controls:

- A PictureBox control named `picLightOn`, showing the image of a light bulb turned on. Initially, this PictureBox's Visible property is set to True.
- A PictureBox control name `picLightOff`, showing the image of a light bulb turned off. Initially, this PictureBox's Visible property is set to False.
- A Label control named `lblLightState` that will display either "ON" or "OFF". Initially, this control's Text property is set to "ON".
- A Button control named `btnSwitchLight` that turns the light off or on.
- A Button control named `btnExit` that closes the form.

When the user clicks the *Switch Light* button, the state of the light will be reversed. In other words, if the light is currently on, it will be turned off. If the light is currently off, it will be turned on.

When the light is turned on, the following actions will take place:

- The `picLightOn` control's Visible property is set to True
- The `picLightOff` control's Visible property is set to False.
- The `lblLightState` label's Text property is assigned the string "ON".

When the light is turned off, the following actions will take place:

- The `picLightOff` control's Visible property is set to True
- The `picLightOn` control's Visible property is set to False.
- The `lblLightState` label's Text property is assigned the string "OFF".

Step 1: Open the *Lights* project from the *Chap6* folder in the sample student programs.

Step 2: Open the *Code* window and type the following two procedures, shown in lines 3 through 23. (Don't type the line numbers. They are shown here for reference only.)

```
1 Public Class Form1
2
3   Sub TurnLightOn()
4     ' Display the "Light On" image.
5     picLightOn.Visible = True
6
```

```
 7          ' Hide the "Light Off" image.
 8          picLightOff.Visible = False
 9
10          ' Change the label text.
11          lblLightState.Text = "ON"
12      End Sub
13
14      Sub TurnLightOff()
15          ' Display the "Light Off" image.
16          picLightOff.Visible = True
17
18          ' Hide the "Light On" image.
19          picLightOn.Visible = False
20
21          ' Change the label text.
22          lblLightState.Text = "OFF"
23      End Sub
24 End Class
```

Before continuing, let's take a closer look at the code. Line 3 is the beginning of a procedure named TurnLightOn. The purpose of this procedure is to simulate the light turning on. When this procedure executes, line 5 makes the picLightOn control visible, line 8 hides the picLightOff control, and line 11 sets the lblLightState control's Text property to "ON".

Line 14 is the beginning of a procedure named TurnLightOff. The purpose of this procedure is to simulate the light turning off. When this procedure executes, line 16 makes the picLightOff control visible, line 19 hides the picLightOn control, and line 22 sets the lblLightState control's Text property to "OFF".

Step 3: Open the *Designer* window and double-click the btnSwitchLight button to create a code template for its Click event handler. Complete the event handler by writing the bold code, shown here in lines 2 through 7. (Don't type the line numbers. They are shown here for reference only.)

```
1 Private Sub btnSwitchLight_Click(...) Handles btnSwitchLight.Click
2   ' Reverse the state of the light.
3   If picLightOn.Visible = True Then
4     TurnLightOff()
5   Else
6     TurnLightOn()
7   End If
8 End Sub
```

Let's review this code. The If...Then statement in line 3 determines whether the picLightOn control is visible. If it is, it means the light is turned on, so the statement in line 4 calls the TurnLightOff procedure to turn the light off. Otherwise, the Else clause in line 5 takes over, and the TurnLightOn procedure is called on line 6 to turn the light on.

Step 4: Open the *Designer* window and double-click the btnExit button to create a code template for its Click event handler. Complete the event handler as shown here:

```
Private Sub btnExit_Click(...) Handles btnExit.Click
  ' Close the form.
  Me.Close()
End Sub
```

Step 5: Save the project, and then run the application. The form should initially appear as shown on the left in Figure 6. When you click the *Switch Light* button, the form should appear as shown on the right in the figure. Each time you click the *Switch Light* button, the state of the light should reverse.

Figure 6 Light on and off

Step 6: When you are finished, exit the application.

If You Want to Know More: Static Local Variables

If a procedure is called more than once in a program, the values stored in the procedure's local variables do not remain between procedure calls. This is because the local variables are created in memory when the procedure starts, and destroyed when the procedure terminates. For example, look at the following procedure:

```
Sub ShowLocal()
   Dim intLocalNum As Integer
   MessageBox.Show(intLocalNum.ToString())
   intLocalNum = 99
End Sub
```

When this procedure is called, `intLocalNum` is created in memory and automatically initialized to 0, so the message box displays 0. Although the last statement in the `ShowLocal` procedure stores 99 in `intLocalNum`, the variable is destroyed when the procedure terminates. The next time this procedure is called, `intLocalNum` is recreated and initialized to 0 again. So, each time the procedure executes, it will display 0 in the message box.

Sometimes you want a procedure to remember the value stored in a local variable between procedure calls. This can be accomplished by making the variable static. **Static local variables** are not destroyed when a procedure terminates. They exist for the lifetime of the application, although their scope is only the procedure in which they are declared.

To declare a static local variable, replace `Dim` with `Static`. Here is the general format of a **Static** variable declaration.

```
Static VariableName As DataType
```

For example, look at the following procedure:

```
Sub ShowStatic()
   Static intStaticNum As Integer
   MessageBox.Show(intStaticNum.ToString())
   intStaticNum += 1
End Sub
```

Notice that `intStaticNum` is declared `Static`. When the procedure is called, `intStaticNum` is automatically initialized to 0 and its value is displayed in the message box. The last statement adds 1 to `intStaticNum`. Because the variable is static, it retains its value between procedure calls. The second time the procedure is called, `intStaticNum` equals 1. Likewise, the third time the procedure is called, `intStaticNum` equals 2, and so on.

NOTE: Static variables should only be used in those rare cases when a procedure must retain the value of a local variable between calls to the procedure. Also, you cannot declare a class-level variable using `Static`. Only variables declared inside a procedure may be static.

Checkpoint

1 Figure 7 shows an application's form.

The list box is named `lstOutput`. The buttons are named `btnGo` and `btnExit`. The application's procedures are as follows:

```
Private Sub btnGo_Click(...) Handles btnGo.Click
   Dim intNumber As Integer
   Dim strInput As String

   strInput = InputBox("Enter a number")
   intNumber = CInt(strInput)

   If intNumber < 10 Then
     Message1()
     Message2()
   Else
     Message2()
     Message1()
   End If
End Sub

Private Sub btnExit_Click(...) Handles btnExit.Click
   'Close the form.
   Me.Close()
End Sub

Sub Message1()
   lstOutput.Items.Add("Able was I")
End Sub

Sub Message2()
   lstOutput.Items.Add("I saw Elba")
End Sub
```

Suppose you run this application and click the btnGo button. What will the application display in the list box if you enter 10 in the input box? What if you enter 5?

Figure 7 *Checkpoint 1 application form*

2 What is the difference between a regular local variable and a static local variable?

2 Passing Arguments to Procedures

CONCEPT: When calling a procedure, you can pass it values known as arguments.

VideoNote

Passing Arguments to Procedures

Values passed to procedures are called **arguments.** You are already familiar with how to use arguments. In the following statement, the CInt function is called and an argument, txtInput.Text, is passed to it:

```
intValue = CInt(txtInput.Text)
```

There are two ways to pass an argument to a procedure: by value or by reference. Passing an argument **by value** means that only a copy of the argument is passed to the procedure. Because the procedure has only a copy, it cannot make changes to the original argument. When an argument is passed **by reference,** however, the procedure has access to the original argument and can make changes to it.

In order for a procedure to accept an argument, it must be equipped with a parameter. A parameter is a special variable that receives an argument being passed into a procedure. Here is an example procedure that uses a parameter:

```
Sub DisplayValue(ByVal intNumber As Integer)
  ' This procedure displays a value in a message box.
  MessageBox.Show(intNumber.ToString())
End Sub
```

Notice the statement inside the parentheses in the first line of the procedure (repeated below).

```
ByVal intNumber As Integer
```

This statement declares the variable intNumber as an integer parameter. The **ByVal** keyword indicates that arguments passed into the variable are passed by value. This parameter variable enables the DisplayValue procedure to accept an integer argument.

TIP: The declaration of a parameter looks like a regular variable declaration, except the word `ByVal` is used instead of `Dim`.

Here is an example of how you would call the procedure and pass an argument to it:

```
DisplayValue(5)
```

The argument, 5, is listed inside the parentheses. This value is passed into the procedure's parameter variable, `intNumber`. This is illustrated in Figure 8.

Figure 8 Passing 5 to `DisplayValue`

```
DisplayValue(5)              The value 5
                          is copied into the
                          parameter variable
                             intNumber.

Sub DisplayValue(ByVal intNumber As Integer)
    ' This procedure displays a value in a message box.
    MessageBox.Show(intNumber.ToString())
End Sub
```

You may also pass variables and the values of expressions as arguments. For example, the following statements call the `DisplayValue` procedure, passing various arguments:

```
DisplayValue(intX)
DisplayValue(intX * 4)
DisplayValue(CInt(txtInput.Text))
```

The first statement passes the value in the variable `intX` as the argument. The second statement passes the value of the expression `intX * 4` as the argument. The third statement passes the value returned from `CInt(txtInput.Text)` as the argument. Tutorial 3 guides you through an application that demonstrates argument passing.

 Tutorial 3:

Examining an application that demonstrates passing an argument to a procedure

Step 1: Open the *Argument Demo* project from the student sample programs folder named *Chap6\Argument Demo*. The application's form is shown in Figure 9. The application's form has four buttons: `btnDemo1`, `btnDemo2`, `btnDemo3`, and `btnExit`.

Figure 9 *Argument Demo* form

Step 2: In addition to the event handlers for each of the form's buttons, the application uses the `DisplayValue` procedure described earlier. Open the *Code* window and locate the `btnDemo1_Click` event handler. The code is as follows:

```
Private Sub btnDemo1_Click(...) Handles btnDemo1.Click
    'This event handler calls the DisplayValue procedure,
    'passing 5 as an argument.
    DisplayValue(5)
End Sub
```

This event handler calls `DisplayValue` with 5 as the argument.

Step 3: Locate the `btnDemo2_Click` event handler. The code is as follows:

```
Private Sub btnDemo2_Click(...) Handles btnDemo2.Click
    ' Call the DisplayValue procedure several times,
    ' passing different arguments each time.
    DisplayValue(5)
    DisplayValue(10)
    DisplayValue(2)
    DisplayValue(16)

    ' The value of an expression is passed to the
    ' DisplayValue procedure.
    DisplayValue(3 + 5)
End Sub
```

This event handler calls the `DisplayValue` procedure five times. Each procedure call is given a different argument. Notice the last procedure call:

```
DisplayValue(3 + 5)
```

This statement passes the value of an expression as the argument. When this statement executes, the value 8 is passed to `DisplayValue`.

Step 4: Locate the `btnDemo3_Click` event handler. The code is as follows:

```
Private Sub btnDemo3_Click(...) Handles btnDemo3.Click
    ' Use a loop to call the DisplayValue procedure
    ' passing a variable as the argument.
    Dim intCount As Integer

    For intCount = 1 To 10
        DisplayValue(intCount)
    Next
End Sub
```

This event handler has a local variable named `intCount`. It uses a `For...Next` loop to call the `DisplayValue` procedure ten times, each time passing the `intCount` variable as the argument.

Step 5: Run the application and click the *Demo 1* button. A message box appears displaying the value 5.

Step 6: Click the *Demo 2* button. Five successive message boxes are displayed, showing the values 5, 10, 2, 16, and 8.

Step 7: Click the *Demo 3* button. Ten successive message boxes are displayed, showing the values 1 through 10.

Step 8: Click the *Exit* button to end the application.

Passing Multiple Arguments

Often, it is useful to pass more than one argument to a procedure. For example, the following is a procedure that accepts two arguments:

```
Sub ShowSum(ByVal intNum1 As Integer, ByVal intNum2 As Integer)
    Dim intSum As Integer ' Local variable to hold a sum

    ' Get the sum of the two arguments.
    intSum = intNum1 + intNum2

    ' Display the sum.
    MessageBox.Show("The sum is " & intSum.ToString())
End Sub
```

Assuming that `intValue1` and `intValue2` are Integer variables, the following is an example call to the `ShowSum` procedure:

```
ShowSum(intValue1, intValue2)
```

When a procedure with multiple parameters is called, the arguments are assigned to the parameters in left-to-right order, as shown in Figure 10.

Figure 10 Multiple arguments passed to multiple parameters

The following procedure call causes 5 to be assigned to the `intNum1` parameter and 10 to be assigned to `intNum2`:

```
ShowSum(5, 10)
```

However, the following procedure call causes 10 to be assigned to the `intNum1` parameter and 5 to be assigned to `intNum2`:

```
ShowSum(10, 5)
```

More about Passing Arguments by Reference

You have learned that when the `ByVal` keyword is used in the declaration of a parameter variable, an argument is passed by value to the parameter. This means that a copy of the argument is passed to the parameter variable. If the parameter's value is changed inside the procedure, it has no effect on the original argument.

When an argument is passed by reference, however, the procedure has access to the original argument. Any changes made to the parameter variable are actually performed on the original argument. Use the **ByRef** keyword in the declaration of a parameter variable to cause arguments to be passed by reference to the parameter. Here is an example:

```
Sub GetName(ByRef strName as String)
    ' Get the user's name
    strName = InputBox("Enter your name.")
End Sub
```

This procedure uses ByRef to declare the strName parameter. Any argument assigned to the parameter is passed by reference, and any changes made to strName are actually made to the argument passed into it. For example, assume the following code calls the procedure and displays the user name:

```
' Declare a string variable
Dim strUserName As String

' Get the user's name
GetName(strUserName)

' Display the user's name
MessageBox.Show("Your name is" & strUserName)
```

This code calls the GetName procedure and passes the string variable strUserName, by reference, into the strName parameter. The GetName procedure displays an input box instructing the user to enter his or her name. The user's input is stored in the strName variable. Because strUserName was passed by reference, the value stored in strName is actually stored in strUserName. When the message box is displayed, it shows the name entered by the user.

Tutorial 4 further demonstrates how passing an argument by reference differs from passing it by value.

Tutorial 4:
Working with ByVal and ByRef

In this tutorial, you examine a procedure that accepts a ByVal argument. Then you change ByVal to ByRef, to see how the procedure behaves differently.

Step 1: Open the *ByVal ByRef Demo* project from the student sample programs folder named *Chap6\ByVal ByRef Demo*. Remember, the student sample programs folder can be downloaded from www.microsoft.com/express/ Downloads/. The application's form is shown in Figure 11. The form has a list box named lstOutput and two buttons named btnGo and btnExit.

Figure 11 *ByVal ByRef Demo* form

Step 2: Open the *Code* window and look at the btnGo_Click event handler.

```
Private Sub btnGo_Click(...) Handles btnGo.Click
    Dim intNumber As Integer = 100

    lstOutput.Items.Add("Inside btnGo_Click the value of " &
                        "intNumber is " &
                        intNumber.ToString())

    lstOutput.Items.Add("Now I am calling ChangeArg.")

    ChangeArg(intNumber)
    lstOutput.Items.Add("Now back in btnGo_Click, " &
                        "the value of intNumber is " &
                        intNumber.ToString())
End Sub
```

The variable intNumber is initialized to 100. This procedure calls the ChangeArg procedure and passes intNumber as the argument.

Step 3: Now look at the ChangeArg procedure. The code is as follows:

```
Sub ChangeArg(ByVal intArg As Integer)
    ' Display the value of intArg.
    lstOutput.Items.Add(" ")
    lstOutput.Items.Add("Inside the ChangeArg procedure, " &
                        "intArg is " & intArg.ToString())
    lstOutput.Items.Add("I will change the value of intArg.")

    ' Assign 0 to intArg.
    intArg = 0

    ' Display the value of intArg.
    lstOutput.Items.Add("intArg is now " & intArg.ToString())
    lstOutput.Items.Add(" ")
End Sub
```

Notice that the parameter variable, intArg, is declared ByVal.

Step 4: Run the application and click the *Go!* button. The form should appear as shown in Figure 12. Although the ChangeArg procedure sets intArg to 0, the value of intNumber did not change. This is because the ByVal keyword was used in the declaration of intArg. (intArg was passed by value).

Figure 12 Results with argument passed by value

Step 5: Click the *Exit* button to end the application.

Step 6: Open the *Code* window. Change ByVal in the ChangeArg procedure to ByRef. The first line of the procedure should now look like this:

```
Sub ChangeArg(ByRef intArg As Integer)
```

Step 7:   Run the application again and click the *Go!* button. The form should appear as shown in Figure 13. This time, when `ChangeArg` sets `intArg` to 0, it changes the value of `intNumber` to 0. This is because the `ByRef` keyword was used in the declaration of `intArg`.

Figure 13 Results with argument passed by reference

Step 8:   Click the *Exit* button to end the application.

 NOTE: You have learned how to pass variables as arguments to procedures. You can also pass constants and expressions as arguments to procedures. Although you can pass both variable and nonvariable arguments by reference, only variable arguments can be changed by the procedure receiving the arguments. If you pass a nonvariable argument by reference to a procedure, the procedure cannot change the argument.

 Checkpoint

3 On paper, write the code for a procedure named `TimesTen`. The procedure must have an Integer parameter variable named `intValue`. The procedure must multiply the parameter by 10 and display the result in a message box.

4 Write a statement that calls the `TimesTen` procedure you wrote in Checkpoint 3. Pass the number 25 as the argument.

5 On paper, write the code for a procedure named `PrintTotal`. The procedure must have the following parameters:

```
intNum1 As Integer
intNum2 As Integer
intNum3 As Integer
```

The procedure must calculate the total of the three numbers and display the result in a message box.

6 Write a statement that calls the `PrintTotal` procedure you wrote in Checkpoint 5. Pass the variables `intUnits`, `intWeight`, and `intCount` as the arguments. The three arguments will be assigned to the `intNum1`, `intNum2`, and `intNum3` parameters.

7 Suppose you want to write a procedure that accepts an argument, and uses the argument in a mathematical operation. You want to make sure that the original argument is not altered. Should you declare the parameter `ByRef` or `ByVal`?

3 Functions

CONCEPT: A function returns a value to the part of the program that called the function.

VideoNote

Functions

This section shows you how to write functions. Like a procedure, a function is a set of statements that perform a task when the function is called. In addition, a function returns a value that can be used in an expression.

You called built-in Visual Basic functions many times. For instance, you used the CInt function to convert strings to integers. You also used the ToString function, which converts numbers to strings. Now you will learn to write your own functions that return values in the same way as built-in functions.

Declaring a Function

The general format of a function declaration is as follows:

```
[AccessSpecifier] Function FunctionName ([ParameterList]) As DataType
    [Statements]
End Function
```

A function declaration is similar to a procedure declaration. *AccessSpecifier* is optional, and specifies the accessibility of the function. As with procedures, you may use the keywords Private, Public, Protected, Friend, and Protected Friend as access specifiers. If you do not include an access specifier, it defaults to Public. Next is the keyword Function, followed by the name of the function. Inside the parentheses is an optional list of parameters. Following the parentheses is As *DataType*, where *DataType* is any data type. The data type listed in this part of the declaration is the data type of the value returned by the function.

The last line of a function declaration is the End Function statement. Between the Function statement and the End Function statements, are statements that execute when the function is called. Here is an example of a completed function:

```
1 Function Sum(ByVal dblNum1 As Double, ByVal dblNum2 As Double) As Double
2     Dim dblResult As Double
3
4     ' Add the two arguments.
5     dblResult = dblNum1 + dblNum2
6
7     ' Return the result.
8     Return dblResult
9 End Function
```

This code shows a function named Sum that accepts two arguments, adds them, and returns their sum. (Everything you have learned about passing arguments to procedures applies to functions as well.) The Sum function has two parameter variables, dblNum1 and dblNum2, both of the Double data type. Notice that the words As Double appear after the parentheses. This indicates that the value returned by the function will be of the Double data type.

Inside the function, the statement shown in line 2 declares a local variable named dblResult. The statement shown in line 5 adds the parameter variables dblNum1 and dblNum2, and assigns the result to dblResult. The Return statement in line 8 causes the function to end execution and return a value to the part of the program that called the function. The general format of the Return statement, when used to return a value from a function, is as follows:

```
Return Expression
```

Expression is the value to be returned. It can be any expression having value, such as a variable, a constant, or a mathematical expression. In this case, the Sum function returns the value in the dblResult variable. However, we could have eliminated the dblResult variable, and returned the expression dblNum1 + dblNum2, as shown in the following code:

```
Function Sum(ByVal dblNum1 As Double, ByVal dblNum2 As Double) As Double
    Return dblNum1 + dblNum2
End Function
```

The data type of the Return statement's expression should be the same as the function's return type, or convertible to the function's return type. For example, if the Sum function returns a Double, the value of the Return statement's expression must be Double, or a type that automatically converts to Double. If the return value cannot be converted to the function's return data type, a runtime error occurs.

Calling a Function

Assuming that dblTotal, dblValue1, and dblValue2 are variables of type Double, here is an example of how you might call the Sum function:

```
dblTotal = Sum(dblValue1, dblValue2)
```

This statement passes the variables dblValue1 and dblValue2 as arguments. It assigns the value returned by the Sum function to the variable dblTotal. So, if dblValue1 is 20.0 and dblValue2 is 40.0, the statement assigns 60.0 to dblTotal.

Figure 14 illustrates how the arguments are passed to the function and how a value is returned from the function.

Figure 14 Arguments passed and a value returned

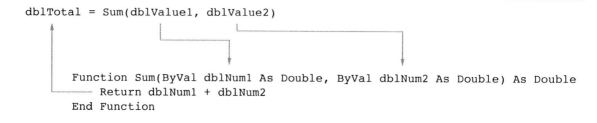

```
dblTotal = Sum(dblValue1, dblValue2)



    Function Sum(ByVal dblNum1 As Double, ByVal dblNum2 As Double) As Double
        Return dblNum1 + dblNum2
    End Function
```

In Tutorial 5, you will create a simple application that uses a function to calculate the sale price of a retail item.

Tutorial 5:
Creating and Calling a Function

VideoNote

Tutorial 6-5
Walkthrough

In this tutorial you will create an application that calculates the sale price of a retail item. The application will allow the user to enter the item's regular retail price and the discount percentage. It will then calculate the sale price using the following formula:

$$Sale\ Price = Retail\ Price - (Retail\ Price \times Discount\ Percentage)$$

For example, if an item's retail price is $100 and the discount percentage is 25 percent (.25), then the sale price is $75.

In the application's code you will write a function named `SalePrice` that accepts the item's retail price and the discount percentage as arguments. The function will then return the sale price as a Decimal.

Step 1: Start a new Windows Forms Application project named *Sale Price Calculator*. Set up the application's form as shown in Figure 15.

Figure 15 *Sale Price Calculator* form

Step 2: Open the *Code* window and write the `SalePrice` function, as shown here in the bold code, in lines 3 through 12. (Don't type the line numbers. They are shown here for reference.)

```
1 Private Class Form1
2
3     Function SalePrice(ByVal decRetail As Decimal,
4                  ByVal decPercentage As Decimal) As Decimal
5         Dim decSalePrice As Decimal ' To hold the sale price
6
7         ' Calculate the sale price.
8         decSalePrice = decRetail - (decRetail * decPercentage)
9
10        ' Return the sale price.
11        Return decSalePrice
12    End Function
13 End Class
```

Let's take a closer look at the function's code. Notice that the function has two parameter variables: `decRetail` and `decPercentage`. When we call this function we will pass an item's retail price and the discount percentage as arguments. In line 5 we declare a local variable named `decSalePrice` that will be used to hold the sale price. Line 8 calculates the item's sale price, and assigns that value to the `decSalePrice` variable. Then, line 11 returns the value of the `decSalePrice` variable.

Step 3: Open the *Designer* window and double-click the `btnCalc` button. Complete the Click event handler with the bold code shown here in lines 2 through 26. (Don't type the line numbers. They are shown here for reference.)

```
1 Private Sub btnCalc_Click(...) Handles btnCalc.Click
2     Dim decRetail As Decimal      ' To hold the retail price
3     Dim decPercentage As Decimal ' To hold the discount percentage
4     Dim decSalePrice As Decimal   ' To hold the sale price
5
```

```
 6        ' Get the retail price.
 7        If Decimal.TryParse(txtRetailPrice.Text, decRetail) Then
 8
 9            ' Get the discount percentage.
10            If Decimal.TryParse(txtDiscountPct.Text, decPercentage) Then
11
12                ' Get the sale price.
13                decSalePrice = SalePrice(decRetail, decPercentage)
14
15                ' Display the sale price.
16                lblSalePrice.Text = decSalePrice.ToString("c")
17
18            Else
19                ' Error message for invalid discount percentage.
20                MessageBox.Show("Enter a numeric discount percentage.")
21            End If
22
23        Else
24            ' Error message for invalid retail price.
25            MessageBox.Show("Enter a numeric retail price.")
26        End If
27 End Sub
```

Let's take a closer look at the code. Lines 2, 3, and 4 declare local variables to hold the item's retail price (decRetail), the discount percentage (decPercentage), and the sale price (decSalePrice).

The If...Then statement in line 7 uses the Decimal.TryParse method to convert txtRetailPrice.Text to a Decimal, and stores the result in decRetail. If the conversion is successful, the Decimal.TryParse method returns True and the program continues to line 10. If the conversion fails (because of invalid input in the txtRetailPrice control), the Decimal.TryParse method returns False, and the program jumps to the Else clause in line 23. If this happens, line 25 displays an error message, and the event handler ends.

The If...Then statement in line 10 uses the Decimal.TryParse method to convert txtDiscountPct.Text to a Decimal, and stores the result in decPercentage. If the conversion is successful, the Decimal.TryParse method returns True and the program continues to line 13. If the conversion fails (because of invalid input in the txtDiscountPct control), the Decimal.TryParse method returns False, and the program jumps to the Else clause in line 18. If this happens, line 20 displays an error message, and the event handler ends.

Line 13 calls the SalePrice function, passing decRetail and decPercentage as arguments. The function uses these values to calculate a sale price, which is returned and assigned to decSalePrice. Line 16 displays the sale price in the lblSalePrice label.

Step 4: Open the *Designer* window and double-click the btnExit button to create a code template for its Click event handler. Complete the event handler as shown here:

```
Private Sub btnExit_Click(...) Handles btnExit.Click
    ' Close the form.
    Me.Close()
End Sub
```

Step 5: Save the project, and then run the application. Enter 100 for the retail price and .25 for the discount percentage. When you click the *Calculate Sale Price* button, the application should display $75.00 as the sale price, as shown in Figure 16.

Figure 16 Sale price calculated

Step 6: When you are finished, exit the application.

If You Want to Know More about Functions: Returning Nonnumeric Values

When writing functions, you are not limited to returning numeric values. You can return nonnumeric values, such as strings and Boolean values. For example, here is the code for a function that returns a String:

```
Function FullName(ByVal strFirst As String,
                  ByVal strLast As String) As String
    ' Local variable to hold the full name
    Dim strName As String

    ' Append the last name to the first name and
    ' assign the result to strName.
    strName = strFirst & " " & strLast

    ' Return the full name.
    Return strName
End Function
```

Here is an example of a call to this function:

```
strCustomer = FullName("John", "Martin")
```

After this call, the string variable `strCustomer` will hold `"John Martin"`.

Here is an example of a function that returns a Boolean value:

```
Function IsValid(intNum As Integer) As Boolean
    Dim blnStatus As Boolean

    If intNum >= 0 And intNum <= 100 Then
      blnStatus = True
    Else
      blnStatus = False
    End If

    Return blnStatus
End Function
```

This function returns *True* if its argument is within the range 0 to 100. Otherwise, it returns *False*. The following code segment has an If...Then statement with an example call to the function:

```
intValue = 20
If IsValid(intValue) Then
    MessageBox.Show("The value is within range.")
Else
    MessageBox.Show("The value is out of range.")
End If
```

When this code executes, it displays *The value is within range.* in a message box. Here is another example:

```
intValue = 200
If IsValid(intValue) Then
    MessageBox.Show("The value is within range.")
Else
    MessageBox.Show("The value is out of range.")
End If
```

When this code executes, it displays *The value is out of range.* in a message box.

Checkpoint

8   Look at the following function declaration and answer the questions below.
```
Function Distance(ByVal sngRate As Single,
                  ByVal sngTime As Single) As Single
```
   a.   What is the name of the function?
   b.   When you call this function, how many arguments do you pass to it?
   c.   What are the names of the parameter variables and what are their data types?
   d.   This function returns a value of what data type?

9   Write the first line of a function named Days. The function should return an integer value. It should have three integer parameters: intYears, intMonths, and intWeeks. All arguments should be passed by value.

10 Write an example function call statement for the function described in Checkpoint 9.

11 Write the first line of a function named LightYears. The function should return a value of the Single data type. It should have one parameter variable, lngMiles, of the Long data type. The parameter should be declared so that the argument is passed by value.

12 Write an example function call statement for the function described in Checkpoint 11.

13 Write the entire code for a function named TimesTwo. The function should accept an integer argument and return the value of that argument multiplied by two.

4 More about Debugging: Stepping Into, Over, and Out of Procedures and Functions

CONCEPT: Visual Basic debugging commands allow you to single-step through applications with procedure and function calls. The *Step Into* command allows you to single-step through a called procedure or function. The *Step Over* command allows you to execute a procedure or function call without single-stepping through its lines. The *Step Out* command allows you to execute all remaining lines of a procedure or function you are debugging without stepping through them.

You should be familiar with how to set a breakpoint in your application's code and to single-step through the code's execution. Let's find out how to step into or step over a procedure or function and step out of a procedure or function.

When an application is in Break mode, the **Step Into** command causes the currently highlighted line (the execution point) to execute. If that line contains a call to a procedure or a function, the next highlighted line is the first line in that procedure or function. In other words, the *Step Into* command allows you to single-step through a procedure or function when it is called. Activate the *Step Into* command using one of the following methods:

- Press the F8 key
- Select *Debug* from the menu bar, and then select *Step Into* from the *Debug* menu
- Click the *Step Into* button (🖫) on the *Debug Toolbar*, if the toolbar is visible

Like the *Step Into* command, the **Step Over** command causes the currently highlighted line to execute. If the line contains a procedure or function call, however, the procedure or function is executed without stepping through its statements. Activate the *Step Over* command using one of the following methods:

- Press Shift+F8
- Select *Debug* from the menu bar, and then select *Step Over* from the *Debug* menu
- Click the *Step Over* button (🖫) on the *Debug Toolbar*, if the toolbar is visible

Use the **Step Out** command when single-stepping through a procedure or function, if you want the remainder of the procedure or function to complete execution without single-stepping. After the procedure or function has completed, the line following the procedure or function call is highlighted, and you may resume single-stepping. Activate the *Step Out* command using one of the following methods:

- Press Ctrl+Shift+F8
- Select *Debug* from the menu bar, and then select *Step Out* from the *Debug* menu
- Click the *Step Out* button (🖫) on the *Debug Toolbar* , if the toolbar is visible

In Tutorials 6, 7, and 8 you practice using each of these commands.

Tutorial 6:
Practicing the *Step Into command*

In this tutorial, you use the *Sale Price Calculator* project to practice single-stepping through procedures and functions.

Step 1: Open the *Sale Price Calculator* project from Tutorial 5.

Step 2: Open the *Code* window and set a breakpoint at the line in the btnCalc_Click event handler shown in Figure 17.

Figure 17 Location of breakpoint

```
Form1.vb  ×  Form1.vb [Design]
Form1                                                      ▾  (Declarations)
Public Class Form1

    Private Sub btnCalc_Click(ByVal sender As System.Object, ByVal e As System.E
        Dim decRetail As Decimal          ' To hold the retail price
        Dim decPercentage As Decimal      ' To hold the discount percentage
        Dim decSalePrice As Decimal       ' To hold the sale price

        ' Get the retail price.
        If Decimal.TryParse(txtRetailPrice.Text, decRetail) Then

            ' Get the discount percentage.
            If Decimal.TryParse(txtDiscountPct.Text, decPercentage) Then

                ' Get the sale price.
                decSalePrice = SalePrice(decRetail, decPercentage)

                ' Display the sale price.
                lblSalePrice.Text = decSalePrice.ToString("c")

            Else
                ' Error message for invalid discount percentage
                MessageBox.Show("Enter a numeric discount percentage.")
            End If

        Else
            ' Error message for invalid retail price.
            MessageBox.Show("Enter a numeric retail price.")
        End If
    End Sub
End Class
```

TIP: Set a breakpoint by clicking the mouse while the pointer is positioned in the left margin, next to the line of code. You can also move the text cursor to the line you wish to set as a breakpoint, and then press [F9]

Step 3: Run the application in Debug mode, and enter 100 for the retail price and .25 for the discount percentage.

Step 4: Click the *Calculate Sale Price* button. The application enters Break mode with the breakpoint line highlighted.

Step 5: Notice that the highlighted line contains a call to the SalePrice function. Press [F8] to execute the *Step Into* command.

Step 6: Because you pressed [F8], the first line of the SalePrice function is highlighted next. You will now single-step through the statements inside the SalePrice function. Continue pressing the [F8] key to single-step though the SalePrice function. When the End Function line is highlighted, press [F8] once more to return to the line that called the function.

Step 7: Press [F5] or click *Debug* on the menu bar and then click *Continue* to exit Break mode and resume normal execution. (Leave the project open in Visual Studio. You will use it in the next tutorial.)

Tutorial 7:
Practicing the *Step Over* command

Step 1: Make sure the *Sale Price Calculator* project is still open in Visual Studio from the previous tutorial. The breakpoint should still be set as shown in Figure 18.

Figure 18 Location of breakpoint

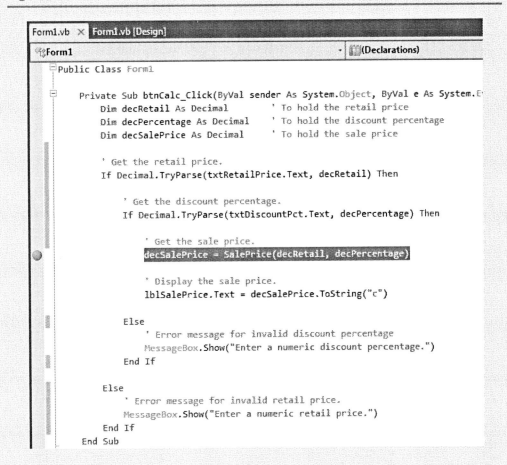

```vb
Public Class Form1

    Private Sub btnCalc_Click(ByVal sender As System.Object, ByVal e As System.E
        Dim decRetail As Decimal          ' To hold the retail price
        Dim decPercentage As Decimal      ' To hold the discount percentage
        Dim decSalePrice As Decimal       ' To hold the sale price

        ' Get the retail price.
        If Decimal.TryParse(txtRetailPrice.Text, decRetail) Then

            ' Get the discount percentage.
            If Decimal.TryParse(txtDiscountPct.Text, decPercentage) Then

                ' Get the sale price.
                decSalePrice = SalePrice(decRetail, decPercentage)

                ' Display the sale price.
                lblSalePrice.Text = decSalePrice.ToString("c")

            Else
                ' Error message for invalid discount percentage
                MessageBox.Show("Enter a numeric discount percentage.")
            End If

        Else
            ' Error message for invalid retail price.
            MessageBox.Show("Enter a numeric retail price.")
        End If
    End Sub
End Sub
```

Step 2: Run the application in Debug mode and enter **100** for the retail price and **.25** for the discount percentage.

Step 3: Click the *Calculate Sale Price* button. The application enters Break mode with the breakpoint line highlighted.

Step 4: Notice that the highlighted line contains a call to the `SalePrice` function. Press Shift + F8 to execute the *Step Over* command. This executes the function call without stepping through it. The next line is now highlighted.

Step 5: Press F5 or click *Debug* on the menu bar and then click *Continue* to exit Break mode and resume normal execution. (Leave the project open in Visual Studio. You will use it in the next tutorial.)

Tutorial 8:

Practicing the *Step Out* command

Step 1: Make sure the *Sale Price Calculator* project is still open in Visual Studio from the previous tutorial. The breakpoint should still be set as shown in Figure 19.

Figure 19 Location of breakpoint

```vb
Form1.vb ×  Form1.vb [Design]
Form1                                                    ▼   (Declarations)
Public Class Form1

    Private Sub btnCalc_Click(ByVal sender As System.Object, ByVal e As System.E
        Dim decRetail As Decimal          ' To hold the retail price
        Dim decPercentage As Decimal      ' To hold the discount percentage
        Dim decSalePrice As Decimal       ' To hold the sale price

        ' Get the retail price.
        If Decimal.TryParse(txtRetailPrice.Text, decRetail) Then

            ' Get the discount percentage.
            If Decimal.TryParse(txtDiscountPct.Text, decPercentage) Then

                ' Get the sale price.
                decSalePrice = SalePrice(decRetail, decPercentage)

                ' Display the sale price.
                lblSalePrice.Text = decSalePrice.ToString("c")

            Else
                ' Error message for invalid discount percentage
                MessageBox.Show("Enter a numeric discount percentage.")
            End If

        Else
            ' Error message for invalid retail price.
            MessageBox.Show("Enter a numeric retail price.")
        End If
    End Sub
End Sub
```

Step 2: Run the application in Debug mode and enter 100 for the retail price and .25 for the discount percentage.

Step 3: Click the *Calculate Sale Price* button. The application enters Break mode with the breakpoint line highlighted.

Step 4: Notice that the highlighted line contains a call to the `SalePrice` function. Press `F8` to execute the *Step Into* command.

Step 4: Because you pressed `F8`, the first line of the `SalePrice` function is highlighted next. Press the `F8` key once again to advance to the next line in the function.

Step 5: Instead of continuing to step through the function, you will now step out of the function. Press `Ctrl`+`Shift`+`F8` to execute the *Step Out* command. Single-stepping is suspended while the remaining statements in the `SalePrice` function execute. You are returned to the `btnCalc_Click` event handler, at the line containing the function call.

Step 6: Press `F5` or click *Debug* on the menu bar and then click *Continue* to exit Break mode and resume normal execution.

TIP: When the current execution point does not contain a procedure or function call, the *Step Into* and *Step Over* commands perform identically.

 Checkpoint

14 Suppose you are debugging an application in Break mode, and are single-stepping through a function that has been called. If you want to execute the remaining lines of the function and return to the line that called the function, what command do you use? What key(s) do you press to execute this command?

15 Suppose you are debugging an application in Break mode and the current execution point contains a procedure call. If you want to single-step through the procedure that is being called, what command do you use? What key(s) do you press to execute this command?

16 Suppose you are debugging an application in Break mode, and the current execution point contains a function call. If you want to execute the line, but not single-step through the function, what command do you use? What key(s) do you press to execute this command?

5 Focus on Program Design and Problem Solving: Building the *Bagel and Coffee Price Calculator* Application

CONCEPT: In this section you build the *Bagel and Coffee Price* Calculator application. It uses procedures and functions to calculate the total of a customer order.

Brandi's Bagel House has a bagel and coffee delivery service for the businesses in her neighborhood. Customers may call in and order white and whole wheat bagels with a variety of toppings. Additionally, customers may order three different types of coffee. Here is a complete price list:

Bagels:
White bagel $1.25
Whole wheat bagel $1.50

Toppings:
Cream cheese $0.50
Butter $0.25
Blueberry jam $0.75
Raspberry jam $0.75
Peach jelly $0.75

Coffee:
Regular coffee $1.25
Cappuccino $2.00
Café au lait $1.75

(*Note:* Delivery for coffee alone is not offered.)

Brandi, the owner, has asked you to write an application that her staff can use to record an order as it is called in. The application should display the total of the order, including 6% sales tax. Figure 20 shows a sketch of the application's form and identifies all the controls with programmer-defined names.

Figure 20 Sketch of *Brandi's Bagel House* form

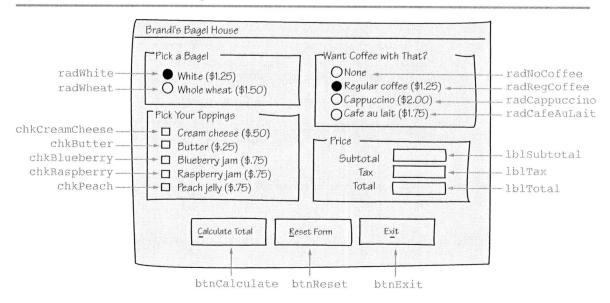

Table 1 lists each control, along with any relevant property settings.

Table 1 *Bagel and Coffee Calculator* controls

Control Type	Control Name	Property	Property Value
Form	(Default)	Text:	*Brandi's Bagel House*
ToolTip	(Default)		(Retain all default property settings.)
GroupBox	(Default)	Text:	*Pick a Bagel*
RadioButton	radWhite	Text:	*White ($1.25)*
		Checked:	*True*
		ToolTip on ToolTip1:	*Click here to choose a white bagel.*
RadioButton	radWheat	Text:	*Whole Wheat ($1.50)*
		ToolTip on ToolTip1:	*Click here to choose a whole wheat bagel.*
GroupBox	(Default)	Text:	*Pick Your Toppings*
CheckBox	chkCreamCheese	Text:	*Cream Cheese ($.50)*
		ToolTip on ToolTip1:	*Click here to choose cream cheese.*
CheckBox	chkButter	Text:	*Butter ($.25)*
		ToolTip on ToolTip1:	*Click here to choose butter.*
CheckBox	chkBlueberry	Text:	*Blueberry Jam ($.75)*
		ToolTip on ToolTip1:	*Click here to choose blueberry jam.*
CheckBox	chkRaspberry	Text:	*Raspberry Jam ($.75)*
		ToolTip on ToolTip1:	*Click here to choose raspberry jam.*

(continued)

Table 1 *Bagel and Coffee Calculator* controls (*continued*)

Control Type	Control Name	Property	Property Value
CheckBox	chkPeach	Text: ToolTip on ToolTip1:	*Peach Jelly ($.75)* *Click here to choose peach jelly.*
GroupBox	(Default)	Text:	*Want coffee with that?*
RadioButton	radNoCoffee	Text: ToolTip on ToolTip1:	None *Click here to choose no coffee.*
RadioButton	radRegCoffee	Text: Checked: ToolTip on ToolTip1:	*Regular Coffee ($1.25)* *True* *Click here to choose regular coffee.*
RadioButton	radCappuccino	Text: ToolTip on ToolTip1:	*Cappuccino ($2.00)* *Click here to choose cappuccino.*
RadioButton	radCafeAuLait	Text: ToolTip on ToolTip1:	*Cafe au lait ($1.75)* *Click here to choose cafe au lait.*
GroupBox	(Default)	Text:	*Price*
Label	(Default)	Text:	*Subtotal*
Label	lblSubtotal	Text: AutoSize: BorderStyle:	 *False* *Fixed3D*
Label	(Default)	Text:	*Tax*
Label	lblTax	Text: AutoSize: BorderStyle:	 *False* *Fixed3D*
Label	(Default)	Text:	*Total*
Label	lblTotal	Text: AutoSize: BorderStyle:	 *False* *Fixed3D*
Button	btnCalculate	Text: ToolTip on ToolTip1:	*&Calculate Total* *Click here to calculate the total of the order.*
Button	btnReset	Text: ToolTip on ToolTip1:	*&Reset Form* *Click here to clear the form and start over.*
Button	btnExit	Text: ToolTip on ToolTip1:	*E&xit* *Click here to exit.*

Table 2 lists and describes the methods (event handlers procedures, and functions) used in this application.

Table 2 Methods for *Bagel and Coffee Calculator*

Method	Type of Method	Description
btnCalculate_Click	Event handler	Calculates and displays the total of an order. Calls the following functions: BagelCost, CoffeeCost, ToppingCost, and CalcTax.
btnExit_Click	Event handler	Ends the application.

(*continued*)

393

Table 2 Methods for *Bagel and Coffee Calculator (continued)*

Method	Type of Method	Description
btnReset_Click	Event handler	Resets the controls on the form to their initial values. Calls the following procedures: ResetBagels, ResetToppings, ResetCoffee, ResetPrice.
BagelCost	Function	Returns the price of the selected bagel.
ToppingCost	Function	Returns the total price of the selected toppings.
CoffeeCost	Function	Returns the price of the selected coffee.
CalcTax	Function	Accepts the amount of a sale as an argument. Returns the amount of sales tax on that amount. The tax rate is stored in a class-level constant, decTAX_RATE.
ResetBagels	Procedure	Resets the bagel type radio buttons to their initial value.
ResetToppings	Procedure	Resets the topping check boxes to unchecked.
ResetCoffee	Procedure	Resets the coffee radio buttons to their initial values.
ResetPrice	Procedure	Sets the Text property of the lblSubtotal, lblTax, and lblTotal labels to String.Empty.

Figure 21 shows a flowchart for the btnCalculate_Click event handler. This procedure calculates the total of an order and displays its price. Notice that very little math is actually performed in this procedure, however. It calls the BagelCost, ToppingCost, CoffeeCost, and CalcTax functions to get the values it needs.

Notice that a new flowchart symbol, which represents a call to a procedure or function, is introduced.

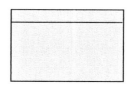

Pseudocode for the btnCalculate_Click procedure is as follows:

subtotal = BagelCost() + ToppingCost() + CoffeeCost()
tax = CalcTax(subtotal)
total = subtotal + tax

lblSubtotal.Text = subtotal
lblTax.Text = tax
lblTotal.Text = total

Figure 22 shows a flowchart for the btnReset_Click event handler. The purpose of this procedure is to reset all the radio buttons, check boxes, and labels on the form to their initial values. This operation has been broken into the following procedures: ResetBagels, ResetToppings, ResetCoffee, ResetPrice. When btnReset_Click executes, it simply calls these procedures.

Figure 21 Flowchart for `btnCalculate_Click` event handler

Figure 22 Flowchart for `btnReset_Click` event handler

Pseudocode for the `btnReset_Click` procedure is as follows:

ResetBagels()
ResetToppings()
ResetCoffee()
ResetPrice()

Figure 23 shows a flowchart for the `BagelCost` function. This function determines whether the user has selected white or whole wheat, and returns the price of that selection.

Pseudocode for the `BagelCost` function is as follows:

If White Is Selected Then
  cost of bagel = 1.25
Else
  cost of bagel = 1.5
End If
Return cost of bagel

Figure 23 Flowchart for `BagelCost` function

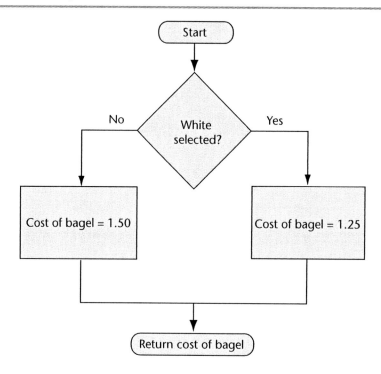

Figure 24 shows a flowchart for the `ToppingCost` function. This function examines the topping check boxes to determine which toppings the user has selected. The total topping price is returned.

Pseudocode for the `ToppingCost` function is as follows:

cost of topping = 0.0
If Cream Cheese Is Selected Then
  cost of topping += 0.5
End If
If Butter Is Selected Then
  cost of topping += 0.25
End If
If Blueberry Is Selected Then
  cost of topping += 0.75
End If
If Raspberry Is Selected Then
  cost of topping += 0.75
End If
If Peach Is Selected Then
  cost of topping += 0.75
End If
Return cost of topping

Figure 24 Flowchart for `ToppingCost` function

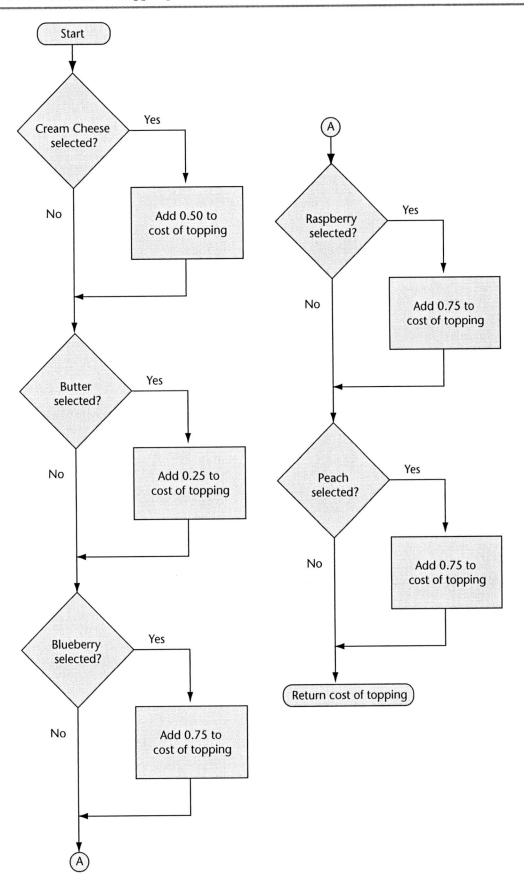

Figure 25 shows a flowchart for the CoffeeCost function. This function examines the coffee radio buttons to determine which coffee (if any) the user has selected. The price is returned.

Figure 25 Flowchart for CoffeeCost function

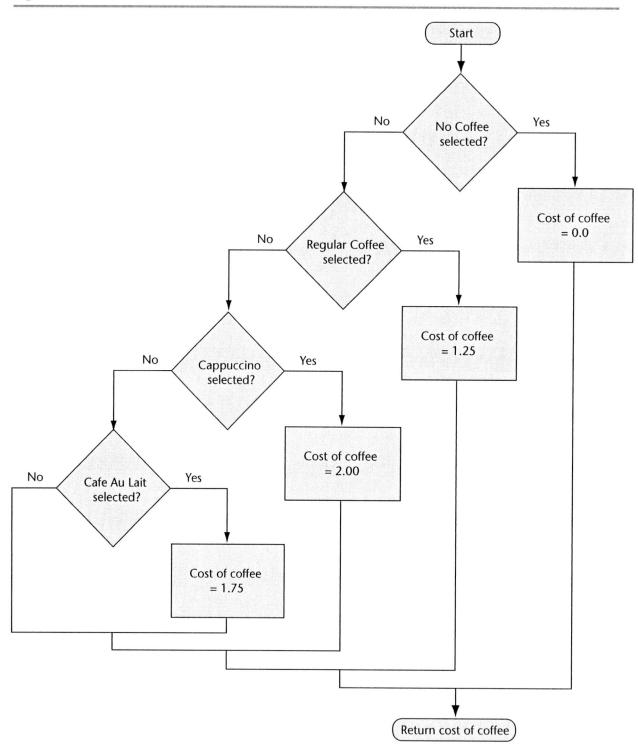

Pseudocode for the `CoffeeCost` function is as follows:

> *If No Coffee Is Selected Then*
>   *cost of coffee = 0*
> *ElseIf Regular Coffee Is Selected Then*
>   *cost of coffee = 1.25*
> *ElseIf Cappuccino Is Selected Then*
>   *cost of coffee = 2*
> *ElseIf Café Au Lait Is Selected Then*
>   *cost of coffee = 1.75*
> *End If*
> *Return cost of coffee*

Figure 26 shows a flowchart for the `CalcTax` function. Note that `CalcTax` accepts an argument, which is passed into the `amount` parameter variable. (The tax rate will be stored in a class-level constant.) The amount of sales tax is returned.

Pseudocode for the `CalcTax` function is as follows:

> *sales tax = amount * tax rate*
> *Return sales tax*

Figure 27 shows a flowchart for the `ResetBagels` procedure. This procedure resets the bagel radio buttons to their initial values.

Pseudocode for the `ResetBagels` procedure is as follows:

> *radWhite = Selected*
> *radWheat = Deselected*

Figure 26 Flowchart for `CalcTax` function

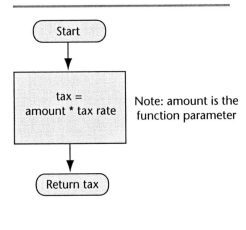

Figure 27 Flowchart for `ResetBagels` procedure

Figure 28 shows a flowchart for the `ResetToppings` procedure. This procedure unchecks all the topping check boxes.

Pseudocode for the ResetToppings procedure is as follows:

chkCreamCheese = Unchecked
chkButter = Unchecked
chkBlueberry = Unchecked
chkRaspberry = Unchecked
chkPeach = Unchecked

Figure 29 shows a flowchart for the ResetCoffee procedure. This procedure resets the coffee radio buttons to their initial values.

Pseudocode for the ResetCoffee procedure is as follows:

radNoCoffee = Deselected
radRegCoffee = Selected
radCappuccino = Deselected
radCafeAuLait = Deselected

Figure 28 Flowchart for ResetToppings procedure

Figure 29 Flowchart for ResetCoffee procedure

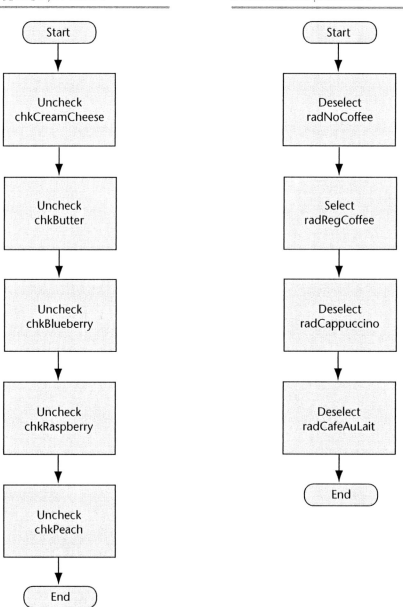

Figure 30 shows a flowchart for the `ResetPrice` procedure. This procedure copies an empty string to `lblSubtotal`, `lblTax`, and `lblTotal`.

Pseudocode for the `ResetPrice` procedure is as follows:

lblSubtotal.Text = String.Empty
lblTax.Text = String.Empty
lblTotal.Text = String.Empty

Figure 30 Flowchart for `ResetPrice` procedure

In Tutorial 9, you build the *Bagel House* application.

Tutorial 9:
Building the *Bagel House* application

Step 1: Create a new Windows Forms Application project named *Bagel House*.

Step 2: Set up the form as shown in Figure 31. Refer to Figure 20 and Table 1 for specific details about the controls and their properties.

Step 3: Once you have placed all the controls on the form and set their properties, you can begin writing the code. Start by opening the *Code* window and writing the class-level declarations shown in bold:

```
Public Class Form1

    ' Class-level declarations
    Const decTAX_RATE As Decimal = 0.06D      ' Tax rate
```

```
Const decWHITE_BAGEL As Decimal = 1.25D    ' Cost of a white bagel
Const decWHEAT_BAGEL As Decimal = 1.5D     ' Cost of a whole wheat bagel
Const decCREAM_CHEESE As Decimal = 0.5D    ' Cost of cream cheese topping
Const decBUTTER As Decimal = 0.25D         ' Cost of butter topping
Const decBLUEBERRY As Decimal = 0.75D      ' Cost of blueberry topping
Const decRASPBERRY As Decimal = 0.75D      ' Cost of raspberry topping
Const decPEACH As Decimal = 0.75D          ' Cost of peach topping
Const decREG_COFFEE As Decimal = 1.25D     ' Cost of regular coffee
Const decCAPPUCCINO As Decimal = 2D        ' Cost of cappuccino
Const decDAFE_AU_LAIT As Decimal = 1.75D   ' Cost of Cafe au lait

End Class
```

Figure 31 *Brandi's Bagel House* form

Step 4: Now write the btnCalculate_Click, btnReset_Click, and btnExit_Click event handlers, as follows:

```
Private Sub btnCalculate_Click(...) Handles btnCalculate.Click
    ' This procedure calculates the total of an order.
    Dim decSubtotal As Decimal    ' Holds the order subtotal
    Dim decTax As Decimal         ' Holds the sales tax
    Dim decTotal As Decimal       ' Holds the order total

    decSubtotal = BagelCost() + ToppingCost() + CoffeeCost()
    decTax = CalcTax(decSubtotal)
    decTotal = decSubtotal + decTax

    lblSubtotal.Text = decSubtotal.ToString("c")
    lblTax.Text = decTax.ToString("c")
    lblTotal.Text = decTotal.ToString("c")
End Sub
```

```
Private Sub btnReset_Click(...) Handles btnReset.Click
  ' This procedure resets the controls to default values.
  ResetBagels()
  ResetToppings()
  ResetCoffee()
  ResetPrice()
End Sub

Private Sub btnExit_Click(...) Handles btnExit.Click
  ' Close the form.
  Me.Close()
End Sub
```

Step 5: Write the code for the following functions and procedures:

```
Function BagelCost() As Decimal
  ' This function returns the cost of the selected bagel.
  Dim decBagel As Decimal

  If radWhite.Checked = True Then
    decBagel = decWHITE_BAGEL
  Else
    decBagel = decWHEAT_BAGEL
  End If

  Return decBagel
End Function

Function ToppingCost() As Decimal
  ' This function returns the cost of the toppings.
  Dim decCostOfTopping As Decimal = 0D

  If chkCreamCheese.Checked = True Then
    decCostOfTopping += decCREAM_CHEESE
  End If

  If chkButter.Checked = True Then
    decCostOfTopping += decBUTTER
  End If

  If chkBlueberry.Checked = True Then
    decCostOfTopping += decBLUEBERRY
  End If

  If chkRaspberry.Checked = True Then
    decCostOfTopping += decRASPBERRY
  End If

  If chkPeach.Checked = True Then
    decCostOfTopping += decPEACH
  End If

  Return decCostOfTopping
End Function

Function CoffeeCost() As Decimal
  ' This function returns the cost of the selected coffee.
  Dim decCoffee As Decimal
```

```
      If radNoCoffee.Checked Then
        decCoffee = 0D
      ElseIf radRegCoffee.Checked = True Then
        decCoffee = decREG_COFFEE
      ElseIf radCappuccino.Checked = True Then
        decCoffee = decCAPPUCCINO
      ElseIf radCafeAuLait.Checked = True Then
        decCoffee = decDAFE_AU_LAIT
      End If

      Return decCoffee
  End Function

  Function CalcTax(ByVal decAmount As Decimal) As Decimal
      ' This function receives the sale amount and
      ' returns the amount of sales tax.
      Return decAmount * decTAX_RATE
  End Function

  Sub ResetBagels()
      ' This procedure resets the bagel selection.
      radWhite.Checked = True
  End Sub

  Sub ResetToppings()
      ' This procedure resets the topping selection.
      chkCreamCheese.Checked = False
      chkButter.Checked = False
      chkBlueberry.Checked = False
      chkRaspberry.Checked = False
      chkPeach.Checked = False
  End Sub

  Sub ResetCoffee()
      ' This procedure resets the coffee selection.
      radRegCoffee.Checked = True
  End Sub

  Sub ResetPrice()
      ' This procedure resets the price.
      lblSubtotal.Text = String.Empty
      lblTax.Text = String.Empty
      lblTotal.Text = String.Empty
  End Sub
```

Step 6: Save and run the program. If there are errors, use debugging techniques you have learned to find and correct them.

Step 7: When you're sure the application is running correctly, save it one last time.

Summary

1 Procedures

- The declaration for a procedure begins with a Sub statement and ends with an End Sub statement. The code that appears between these two statements is the body of the procedure.
- When a procedure call executes, the application branches to that procedure and executes its statements. When the procedure has finished, the application branches back to the procedure call and resumes executing at the next statement.
- Static local variables are not destroyed when a procedure returns. They exist for the lifetime of the application, although their scope is limited to the procedure in which they are declared.
- To declare a static local variable, substitute the word Static for Dim.

2 Passing Arguments to Procedures

- A parameter is a special variable that receives an argument value passed into a procedure or function. If a procedure or function has a parameter, you must supply an argument when calling the procedure or function.
- When a procedure or function with multiple parameters is called, arguments are assigned to the parameters in left-to-right order.
- There are two ways to pass an argument to a procedure: by value or reference. Passing an argument by value means that only a copy of the argument is passed to the procedure. Because the procedure has only a copy, it cannot make changes to the original argument. When an argument is passed by reference, however, the procedure has access to the original argument and can make changes to it.

3 Functions

- A function returns a value to the part of the program that called it. Similar to a procedure, it is a set of statements that perform a task when the function is called.
- A value is returned from a function by the Return statement.

4 More about Debugging: Stepping Into, Over, and Out of Procedures and Functions

- Visual Basic debugging commands (*Step Into*, *Step Over*, and *Step Out*) allow you to step through application code and through called procedures and function.

5 Focus on Program Design and Problem Solving: Building the *Bagel and Coffee Price Calculator* Application

- This section outlines the process of building the *Bagel and Coffee Price Calculator* application, with a focus on program design and problem solving.

Key Terms

arguments
by reference (pass argument)
by value (pass argument)
ByRef
ByVal
Call keyword
event handler
event procedure
function
method
modularize

parameter
Pascal casing
procedure
procedure call
procedure declaration
Static
static local variables
Step Out command
Step Over command
Sub keyword

Review Questions and Exercises

Fill-in-the-Blank

1. A(n) _____ is a named block of code that performs a specific task and does not return a value.

2. A(n) _____ statement causes a procedure to be executed.

3. A(n) _____ is a named block of statements that executes and returns a value.

4. You return a value from a function with the _____ statement.

5. _____ local variables are not destroyed when a procedure returns.

6. Values passed to a procedure or function are called _____.

7. A(n) _____ is a special variable that receives an argument passed to a procedure or function.

8. When an argument is passed by _____ a copy of the argument is assigned to the parameter variable.

9. When an argument is passed by _____ the procedure has access to the original argument.

10. The _____ debugging command allows you to single-step through a called procedure or function.

Multiple Choice

1. Which of the following terms means to divide an application's code into small, manageable procedures?
    a. Break
    b. Modularize
    c. Parameterize
    d. Bind

2. Which type of statement causes a procedure to execute?
    a. Procedure declaration
    b. Access specifier
    c. Procedure call
    d. Step Into

3. What happens when a procedure finishes executing?

    a. The application branches back to the procedure call, and resumes executing at the next line

    b. The application terminates

    c. The application waits for the user to trigger the next event

    d. The application enters Break mode

4. In what way is a function different from a procedure?

    a. A procedure returns a value and a function does not

    b. A function returns a value and a procedure does not

    c. A function must be executed in response to an event

    d. There is no difference

5. What type of local variable retains its value between calls to the procedure or function in which it is declared?

    a. `Private`

    b. `Persistent`

    c. `Permanent`

    d. `Static`

6. What is an argument?

    a. A variable that a parameter is passed into

    b. A value passed to a procedure or function when it is called

    c. A local variable that retains its value between procedure calls

    d. A reason not to create a procedure or function

7. What keyword is used in a parameter declaration to specify that the argument is passed by value?

    a. `ByVal`

    b. `Val`

    c. `Value`

    d. `AsValue`

8. When an argument is passed to a procedure this way, the procedure has access to the original argument and may make changes to it.

    a. By value

    b. By address

    c. By reference

    d. By default

9. Which of the following is a debugging command that causes a procedure or function to execute without single-stepping through the procedure's or function's code?

    a. *Step Into*

    b. *Step Through*

    c. *Jump Over*

    d. *Step Over*

10. Which of the following is a debugging command that is used when you are stepping through a procedure's code and you wish to execute the remaining statements in the procedure without single-stepping through them?

    a. *Jump Out*

    b. *Step Through*

    c. *Step Out*

    d. *Step Over*

True or False

Indicate whether the following statements are true or false.

1. T F: A general purpose procedure is associated with a specific control.

2. T F: You must use the `Call` keyword to execute a procedure.

3. T F: The declaration of a parameter variable looks like a regular variable declaration, except `ByVal` or `ByRef` is used instead of `Dim`.

4. T F: You can pass more than one argument to a procedure or function.

5. T F: If you write a procedure or function with a parameter variable, you do not have to supply an argument when calling the procedure.

6. T F: If you are debugging an application in Break mode and you want to single-step through a procedure that will be called in the highlighted statement, you use the *Step Over* command.

Short Answer

1. Why do nonstatic local variables lose their values between calls to the procedure or function in which they are declared?

2. What is the difference between an argument and a parameter variable?

3. Where do you declare parameter variables?

4. If you are writing a procedure that accepts an argument and you want to make sure that the procedure cannot change the value of the argument, what do you do?

5. When a procedure or function accepts multiple arguments, does it matter what order the arguments are passed in?

6. How do you return a value from a function?

What Do You Think?

1. What advantage is there to dividing an application's code into several small procedures?

2. How would a static local variable be useful?

3. Give an example in which passing an argument by reference would be useful.

4. Suppose you want to write a procedure to perform an operation. How do you decide if the procedure should be a procedure or a function?

5. When debugging an application, why would you not want to single-step through every procedure or function?

Find the Error

Locate the errors in the following code examples:

1.
```
Sub DisplayValue(Dim intNumber As Integer)
    ' This displays a value.
    MessageBox.Show(intNumber.ToString())
End Sub
```

2. The following is a procedure:
```
Sub Greeting(ByVal strName As String)
    ' This procedure displays a greeting.
    MessageBox.Show("Hello " & strName)
End Sub
```

And the following is a call to the procedure:
```
Greeting()
```

3. The following is a function:
```
Function Product(ByVal intNum1 As Integer, ByVal intNum2
                    As Integer) As Integer
    Dim intResult As Integer
    intResult = intNum1 * intNum2
End Function
```

4. The following is a function:
```
Sub Sum(ByVal intNum1 As Single, ByVal intNum2 As Single)
        As Single
    Dim intResult As Single
    intResult = intNum1 + intNum2
    Return intResult
End Sub
```

Algorithm Workbench

1. The following statement calls a function named Half that returns a Decimal, which is half of the argument. Write the function.
```
intResult = Half(intNumber)
```

2. An application contains the following function:
```
Function Square(ByVal intValue As Integer) As Integer
    Return intValue ^ 2
End Function
```
Write a statement that passes the value 4 to this function and assigns its return value to a variable named intResult.

3. Write a procedure named TimesTen that accepts a single Integer argument. When the procedure is called, it should display the product of its argument multiplied by 10 in a message box.

4. An application contains the following procedure:
```
Sub Display(ByVal intArg1 As Integer, ByVal strArg2 As String,
            ByVal sngArg3 As Single)
    MessageBox.Show("Here are the values: " &
                    intArg1.ToString() & " " &
                    strArg2 & " " & sngArg3.ToString())
End Sub
```
Write a statement that calls the procedure and passes it the following variables:
```
Dim strName As String
Dim intAge As Integer
Dim sngIncome As Single
```

Programming Challenges

1. **Retail Price Calculator**

   Write an application that accepts from the user the wholesale cost of an item and its markup percentage. (For example, if an item's wholesale cost is $5 and its retail price is $10, then the markup is 100%.)

   The program should contain a function named CalculateRetail that receives the wholesale cost and markup percentage as arguments, and returns the retail price of the item. The application's form should look something like the one shown in Figure 32.

Figure 32 *Retail Price Calculator* form

Figure 33 *Hospital Charges* form

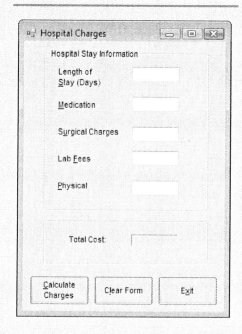

When the user clicks the *Get Retail* button, the program should do the following:

- Verify that the values entered by the user for the wholesale cost and the markup percent are numeric and not negative
- Call the `CalculateRetail` function
- Display the retail cost as returned from the function

2. **Hospital Charges**

   Create an application that calculates the total cost of a hospital stay. The application should accept the following input:

   - The number of days spent in the hospital
   - The amount of medication charges
   - The amount of surgical charges
   - The amount of lab fees
   - The amount of physical rehabilitation charges

   The hospital charges $350 per day. The application's form should resemble the one shown in Figure 33.

   Create the following functions:

`CalcStayCharges`	Calculates and returns the base charges for the hospital stay. This is computed as $350 times the number of days in the hospital.
`CalcMiscCharges`	Calculates and returns the total of the medication, surgical, lab, and physical rehabilitation charges.
`CalcTotalCharges`	Calculates and returns the total charges.

   Input Validation: Do not accept a negative value for length of stay, medication charges, surgical charges, lab fees, or physical rehabilitation charges.

3. **Order Status**

The Middletown Wire Company sells spools of copper wiring for $100 each. The normal delivery charge is $10 per spool. Rush delivery costs $15 per spool. Create an application that displays the status of an order. The status should include the following:

- The number of spools ready to ship
- The number of spools on back order
- The shipping and handling charges
- The total amount due

The application's form should resemble the one shown in Figure 34.

Figure 34 *Order Status* form

The user should enter the number of spools ordered into the text box, and check the *Rush Delivery* check box if rush delivery is desired. When the *Calculate Total* button is clicked, an input box should appear asking the user to enter the number of spools currently in stock. If the user has ordered more spools than are in stock, a portion of the order is back-ordered. For example, if the user orders 200 spools and there are only 150 spools in stock, then 150 spools are ready to ship and 50 spools are back-ordered.

The application should have the following functions, called from the *Calculate Total* button's Click event handler:

GetInStock	Displays an input box asking the user to enter the number of spools in stock. The function should return the value entered by the user.
ReadyToShip	Accepts the following arguments: the number of spools in stock and the number of spools ordered. The function returns the number of spools ready to ship.
BackOrdered	Accepts the following arguments: the number of spools in stock and the number of spools ordered. The function returns the number of spools on back order. If no spools are on back order, it returns 0.

411

ShippingCharges   Accepts the following arguments: the number of spools ready to ship and the per-spool shipping charges. The function returns the total shipping and handling charges.

The application should have the following procedures, called from the *Clear Form* button's Click event handler:

ResetSpools   Clears the text box and the check box.

ResetDelivery   Clears the labels that display the delivery information.

Input Validation: Do not accept orders for less than one spool.

4. **Joe's Automotive**

Joe's Automotive performs the following routine maintenance services:

- Oil change—$26.00
- Lube job—$18.00
- Radiator flush—$30.00
- Transmission flush—$80.00
- Inspection—$15.00
- Muffler replacement—$100.00
- Tire rotation—$20.00

Joe also performs other nonroutine services and charges for parts and labor ($20 per hour). Create an application that displays the total for a customer's visit to Joe's. The form should resemble the one shown in Figure 35. *Note:* Visual Studio lets you use an apostrophe in a project's name, but the apostrophe will prevent you from being able to run the project after it has been created.

Figure 35 *Joe's Automotive* form

The application should have the following functions:

OilLubeCharges   Returns the total charges for an oil change and/or a lube job, if any.

FlushCharges   Returns the total charges for a radiator flush and/or a transmission flush, if any.

`MiscCharges`	Returns the total charges for an inspection, muffler replacement, and/or a tire rotation, if any.
`OtherCharges`	Returns the total charges for other services (parts and labor), if any.
`TaxCharges`	Returns the amount of sales tax, if any. Sales tax is 6%, and is only charged on parts. If the customer purchased services only, no sales tax is charged.
`TotalCharges`	Returns the total charges.

The application should have the following procedures, called when the user clicks the *Clear* button:

`ClearOilLube`	Clears the check boxes for oil change and lube job.
`ClearFlushes`	Clears the check boxes for radiator flush and transmission flush.
`ClearMisc`	Clears the check boxes for inspection, muffler replacement, and tire rotation.
`ClearOther`	Clears the text boxes for parts and labor.
`ClearFees`	Clears the labels that display the labels in the section marked *Summary*.

Input validation: Do not accept negative amounts for parts and labor charges.

Design Your Own Forms

5. **Password Verifier**

   You will develop a software package that requires users to enter their passwords. Your software requires users' passwords to meet the following criteria:

   - The password should be at least six characters long
   - The password should contain at least one numeric digit and at least one alphabetic character

   Create an application that asks the user to enter a password. The application should use a function named `IsValid` to verify that the password meets the criteria. It should display a message indicating whether the password is valid or invalid.

   The `IsValid` function should accept a string as its argument and return a Boolean value. The string argument is the password to be checked. If the password is valid, the function should return *True*. Otherwise, it should return *False*.

6. **Travel Expenses**

   Create an application that calculates and displays the total travel expenses for a business trip. The user must provide the following information:

   - Number of days on the trip
   - Amount of airfare, if any
   - Amount of car rental fees, if any
   - Number of miles driven, if a private vehicle was used
   - Amount of parking fees, if any
   - Amount of taxi charges, if any
   - Conference or seminar registration fees, if any
   - Lodging charges, per night

The company reimburses travel expenses according to the following policy:

- $37 per day for meals
- Parking fees, up to $10.00 per day
- Taxi charges up to $20.00 per day
- Lodging charges up to $95.00 per day
- If a private vehicle is used, $0.27 per mile driven

The application should calculate and display the following:

- Total expenses incurred by the business person
- The total allowable expenses for the trip
- The excess that must be paid by the business person, if any
- The amount saved by the business person if the expenses were under the total allowed

The application should have the following functions:

CalcMeals	Calculates and returns the amount reimbursed for meals.
CalcMileage	Calculates and returns the amount reimbursed for mileage driven in a private vehicle.
CalcParkingFees	Calculates and returns the amount reimbursed for parking fees.
CalcTaxiFees	Calculates and returns the amount reimbursed for taxi charges.
CalcLodging	Calculates and returns the amount reimbursed for lodging.
CalcTotalReimbursement	Calculates and returns the total amount reimbursed.
CalcUnallowed	Calculates and returns the total amount of expenses that are not allowable, if any. These are parking fees that exceed $10.00 per day, taxi charges that exceed $20.00 per day, and lodging charges that exceed $95.00 per day.
CalcSaved	Calculates and returns the total amount of expenses under the allowable amount, if any. For example, the allowable amount for lodging is $95.00 per day. If a business person stayed in a hotel for $85.00 per day for five days, the savings would $50.00.

Input validation: Do not accept negative numbers for any dollar amount or for miles driven in a private vehicle. Do not accept numbers less than 1 for the number of days.

7. **Paint Job Estimator**

A painting company has determined that for every 115 square feet of wall space, one gallon of paint and eight hours of labor are required. The company charges $18.00 per hour for labor. Create an application that allows the user to enter the number of rooms to be painted and the price of the paint per gallon. The application should use input boxes to ask the user for the square feet of wall space in each room. It should then display the following information:

- The number of gallons of paint required
- The hours of labor required
- The cost of the paint
- The labor charges
- The total cost of the paint job

Input validation: Do not accept a value less than 1 for the number of rooms. Do not accept a value less than $10.00 for the price of paint. Do not accept a negative value for square footage of wall space.

8. **Falling Distance**

   When an object is falling because of gravity, the following formula can be used to determine the distance the object falls in a specific time period:

   $$d = \tfrac{1}{2}\,gt^2$$

   The variables in the formula are as follows: d is the distance in meters, g is 9.8, and t is the amount of time in seconds that the object has been falling.

   Create a VB application that allows the user to enter the amount of time that an object has fallen and then displays the distance that the object fell. The application should have a function named `FallingDistance`. The `FallingDistance` function should accept an object's falling time (in seconds) as an argument. The function should return the distance in meters that the object has fallen during that time interval.

9. **Kinetic Energy**

   In physics, an object that is in motion is said to have kinetic energy. The following formula can be used to determine a moving object's kinetic energy:

   $$KE = \tfrac{1}{2}\,mv^2$$

   In the formula KE is the kinetic energy, m is the object's mass in kilograms, and v is the object's velocity in meters per second.

   Create a VB application that allows the user to enter an object's mass and velocity and then displays the object's kinetic energy. The application should have a function named `KineticEnergy` that accepts an object's mass (in kilograms) and velocity (in meters per second) as arguments. The function should return the amount of kinetic energy that the object has.

10. **Prime Numbers**

    A prime number is a number that can be evenly divided by only itself and 1. For example, the number 5 is prime because it can be evenly divided by only 1 and 5. The number 6, however, is not prime because it can be evenly divided by 1, 2, 3, and 6.

    Write a Boolean function named `IsPrime` which takes an integer as an argument and returns *true* if the argument is a prime number or *false* otherwise. Use the function in an application that lets the user enter a number and then displays a message indicating whether the number is prime.

TIP: Recall that the MOD operator divides one number by another and returns the remainder of the division. In an expression such as `intNum1 MOD intNum2`, the MOD operator will return 0 if `intNum1` is evenly divisible by `intNum2`.

11. **Prime Number List**

    This exercise assumes you have already written the `IsPrime` function in Programming Challenge 10. Create another application that uses this function to display all of the prime numbers from 1 through 100 in a list box. The program should have a loop that calls the `IsPrime` function.

Answers to Checkpoints

1 If you enter 10, the following will be displayed:

   I saw Elba
   Able was I

   If you enter 5, the following will be displayed:

   Able was I
   I saw Elba

2 Static local variables retain their value between procedure calls. Regular local variables do not.

3
```
Sub TimesTen(ByVal intValue As Integer)
   Dim intResult As Integer
   intResult = intValue * 10
   MessageBox.Show(intResult.ToString())
End Sub
```

4
```
TimesTen(25)
```

5
```
Sub PrintTotal(ByVal intNum1 As Integer, ByVal intNum2 As Integer,
               ByVal intNum3 As Integer)
   Dim intTotal As Integer
   intTotal = intNum1 + intNum2 + intNum3
   MessageBox.Show(intTotal.ToString())
End Sub
```

6
```
PrintTotal(intUnits, intWeight, intCount)
```

7 ByVal

8 a. Distance
   b. Two
   c. sngRate and sngTime; they are both Singles
   d. Single

9
```
Function Days(ByVal intYears As Integer, ByVal intMonths As Integer,
              ByVal intWeeks As Integer) As Integer
```

10 `intNumDays = Days(intY, intM, intW)`

11 `Function LightYears(ByVal lngMiles As Long) As Single`

12 `sngDistance = LightYears(m)`

13
```
Function TimesTwo(intNumber As Integer) As Integer
   Return intNumber * 2
End Function
```

14 Step Out; Ctrl + Shift + F8

15 Step Into; F8

16 Step Over; Shift + F8

Arrays and More

TOPICS

This chapter discusses arrays, which are like groups of variables that allow you to store sets of data. A single-dimensional array is useful for storing and working with a single set of data, while a multidimensional array can be used to store and work with multiple sets of data. This chapter presents many array programming techniques, such as summing and averaging the elements in an array, summing all columns in a two-dimensional array, searching an array for a specific value, and using parallel arrays. The Enabled, Anchor, and Dock properties, and Timer controls, are also covered.

1 Arrays

CONCEPT: An array is like a group of variables with one name. You store and work with values in an array by using a subscript.

Sometimes it is necessary for an application to store multiple values of the same type. Often it is better to create an array than several individual variables. An **array** is a like group of variables that have a single name. All of the values stored within an array are called **elements**, and all are of the same data type. You access the individual elements in an array through a subscript. A **subscript**, also known as an **index**, is a number that identifies a specific element within an array.

Subscript numbering begins at 0, so the subscript of the first element in an array is 0 and the subscript of the last element in an array is one less than the total number of elements. For example, consider an array of seven integers. The subscript of the first element in the array is 0 and the subscript of the last element in the array is 6.

Declaring an Array

You declare an array much like you declare a regular variable. Here is the general format of an array declaration:

```
Dim ArrayName (UpperSubscript) As DataType
```

Let's take a closer look at the syntax.

- *ArrayName* is the name of the array.
- *UpperSubscript* is the value of the array's highest subscript. This must be a positive integer, a positive Integer named constant, or an Integer variable containing a positive number.
- *DataType* is a Visual Basic data type.

Let's look at some examples.

```
Dim intHours(6) As Integer
```

This statement declares `intHours` as an array of integers. The number inside the parentheses, 6, indicates that the array's highest subscript is 6. Figure 1 shows that this array consists of seven elements with the subscripts 0 through 6. The figure shows that numeric array elements are initialized to the value 0.

Figure 1 `intHours` array

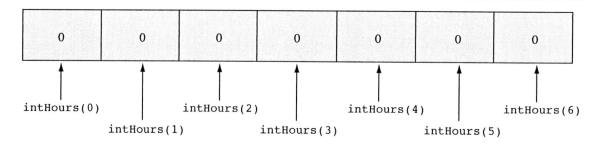

$$intHours(0) \quad intHours(2) \quad intHours(4) \quad intHours(6)$$
$$intHours(1) \quad intHours(3) \quad intHours(5)$$

NOTE: Like regular string variables, the uninitialized elements of a string array are set to the special value `Nothing`. Before doing any work with the elements of a string array, you must store values in them, even if the values are empty strings. Later you will see how to initialize arrays at the same time they are declared.

The following is another example of an array declaration:

```
Dim decPay(4) As Decimal
```

This statement declares `decPay` as an array of five Decimal values, as shown in Figure 2, with subscripts 0 through 4. The following example uses the contents of an Integer variable to specify the array size:

```
Dim intSize As Integer = 4
Dim decPay(intSize) As Decimal
```

Figure 2 decPay array

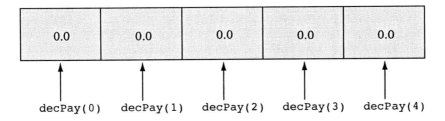

decPay(0) decPay(1) decPay(2) decPay(3) decPay(4)

Implicit Array Sizing and Initialization

You can implicitly size an array by omitting the upper subscript in the declaration and providing an initialization list. An array initialization list is a set of numbers enclosed in a set of braces, with the numbers separated by commas. The following is an example of an array declaration that uses an initialization list:

```
Dim intNumbers() As Integer = { 2, 4, 6, 8, 10, 12 }
```

This statement declares intNumbers as an array of integers. The numbers 2, 4, 6, 8, 10, and 12 are stored in the array. The value 2 will be stored in element zero, 4 will be stored in element one, and so on. Notice that no upper subscript is provided inside the parentheses. The array is large enough to hold the values in the initialization list. In this example, the array has six elements, as shown in Figure 3.

Figure 3 intNumbers array

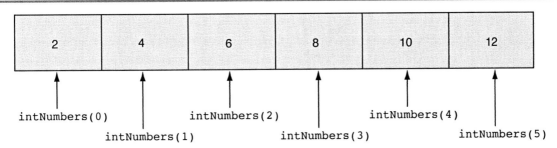

intNumbers(0) intNumbers(2) intNumbers(4)
intNumbers(1) intNumbers(3) intNumbers(5)

The following code declares an implicitly sized array of strings.

```
Dim strFriends() As String = { "Joe", "Geri", "Bill", "Rose" }
```

You can initialize an array with empty strings, as shown here.

```
Dim strFriends() As String = { "", "", "", "" }
```

It is a good idea to initialize a string array, particularly if there is a chance that your program will access its elements before any data has been stored there. Performing an operation on a string array element results in a runtime error if no data has been stored in the element.

NOTE: You cannot provide both an initialization list and an upper subscript in an array declaration.

Using Named Constants as Subscripts in Array Declarations

To make programs easier to maintain and debug, programmers often use a named constant as the upper subscript in an array declaration, as shown in the following code:

```
Const intMAX_SUBSCRIPT As Integer = 100
Dim intArray(intMAX_SUBSCRIPT) As Integer
```

Quite often, when you write code that processes an array, you have to refer to the value of the array's upper subscript. You will see examples of this later in the chapter. When you declare a named constant to represent an array's upper subscript, you can use that constant any time that you need to refer to the array's last subscript in code. Then, if you ever need to modify the program so the array is a different size, you need only to change the value of the named constant.

Working with Array Elements

You can store a value in an array element with an assignment statement. On the left of the = operator, use the name of the array with the subscript of the element you wish to assign. For example, suppose `intNumbers` is an array of integers with subscripts 0 through 5. The following statements store values in each element of the array:

```
intNumbers(0) = 100
intNumbers(1) = 200
intNumbers(2) = 300
intNumbers(3) = 400
intNumbers(4) = 500
intNumbers(5) = 600
```

TIP: The expression `intNumbers (0)` is pronounced *intNumbers sub zero*.

Figure 4 shows the values assigned to the elements of the array after these statements execute.

Figure 4 `intNumbers` array with assigned values

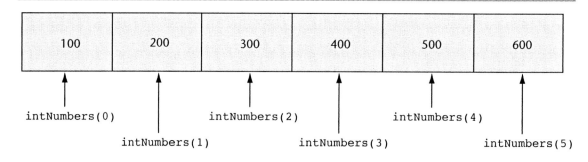

Accessing Array Elements with a Loop

VideoNote

Accessing
Array Elements
with a Loop

You can assign an integer to a variable and then use the variable as a subscript. This makes it possible to use a loop to cycle through an entire array, performing the same operation on each element. This can be helpful if you want to process the elements in a large array because writing individual statements would require a lot of typing.

For example, the following code declares `intSeries` as an array of 10 integers. The array's subscripts are 0 through 9. The `For...Next` loop stores the value 100 in each of its elements, beginning at subscript 0:

```
Const intMAX_SUBSCRIPT As Integer = 9
Dim intSeries(intMAX_SUBSCRIPT) As Integer
Dim intCount As Integer

For intCount = 0 To intMAX_SUBSCRIPT
   intSeries(intCount) = 100
Next
```

The variable `intCount`, used as the loop counter, takes on the values 0 through 9 as the loop repeats. The first time through the loop, `intCount` equals 0, so the statement `intSeries(intCount) = 100` assigns 100 to `intSeries(0)`. The second time the loop executes, the statement stores 100 in `intSeries(1)`, and so on. Figure 5 illustrates how the loop is set up so the counter variable begins with the first array subscript and ends with the last array subscript.

Figure 5 A `For...Next` loop using a counter variable to step through an array

The following example uses a `Do While` loop to perform the same operation:

```
Const intMAX_SUBSCRIPT As Integer = 9
Dim intSeries(intMAX_SUBSCRIPT) As Integer
Dim intCount As Integer = 0

Do While intCount <= intMAX_SUBSCRIPT
   intSeries(intCount) = 100
   intCount += 1
Loop
```

We mentioned earlier that it is a good idea to initialize a string array if there is a chance that the program will access its elements before data has been stored there. It might be cumbersome, however, to provide a separate initializer for each array element. Instead, you can use a loop to initialize the array's elements. For example, the following code stores an empty string in each element of `strNames`, a 1000-element array of strings:

```
Const intMAX_SUBSCRIPT As Integer = 999
Dim strNames(intMAX_SUBSCRIPT) As String
Dim intCount As Integer

For intCount = 0 To intMAX_SUBSCRIPT
   strNames(intCount) = String.Empty
Next
```

Array Bounds Checking

The Visual Basic runtime system performs **array bounds checking**, meaning that it does not allow a statement to use a subscript outside the range of valid subscripts for an array. For example, in the following declaration, the array named intValues has a subscript range of 0 through 10:

```
Const intMAX_SUBSCRIPT As Integer = 10
Dim intValues(intMAX_SUBSCRIPT) As Integer
```

If a statement uses a subscript that is less than 0 or greater than 10 with this array, the program will throw an exception.

The compiler does not display an error message at design time when you write a statement that uses an invalid subscript. For example, the loop in the following code uses out-of-range subscripts:

```
Const intMAX_SUBSCRIPT As Integer = 10
Dim intValues(intMAX_SUBSCRIPT) As Integer
Dim intIndex As Integer

For intIndex = 0 To 20
  intValues(intIndex) = 99
Next
```

At runtime, this loop executes until intIndex equals 11. At that point, when the assignment statement tries to use intIndex as a subscript, an exception is thrown, as shown in Figure 6.

Figure 6 Exception window reporting index outside the bounds of the array

Tutorial 1:

Using an array to hold a list of random lottery numbers

In this tutorial you will create an application that randomly generates lottery numbers. When a button is clicked, the application will generate five 2-digit integer numbers and store them in an array. The contents of the array will then be displayed on the application's form in labels.

Step 1: Create a new Windows Forms Application project named *Lottery Numbers*.

Step 2: Set up the project's form with Label and Button controls as shown in Figure 7. Set the following properties for each of the Label controls:
- AutoSize = False
- BorderStyle = Fixed3D
- TextAlign = MiddleCenter
- Clear the Text property

Figure 7 The *Lottery Numbers* form

Step 3: Complete the code for the form's event handlers as shown in the following. (Don't type the line numbers. They are shown for reference.)

```
1 Public Class Form1
2
3     Private Sub btnGenerate_Click(...) Handles btnGenerate.Click
4         ' Create an array to hold five lottery numbers.
5         Const intMAX_SUBSCRIPT As Integer = 4        ' The maximum subscript
6         Dim intNumbers(intMAX_SUBSCRIPT) As Integer ' Array declaration
7         Dim intCount As Integer                     ' Loop counter
8
9         ' Create a Random object.
10        Dim rand As New Random
11
12        ' Fill the array with random numbers.
13        ' Each number will be in the range 0-99.
14        For intCount = 0 To intMAX_SUBSCRIPT
15            intNumbers(intCount) = rand.Next(100)
16        Next
17
18        ' Display the array elements in the labels.
19        lblFirst.Text = intNumbers(0).ToString()
20        lblSecond.Text = intNumbers(1).ToString()
21        lblThird.Text = intNumbers(2).ToString()
22        lblFourth.Text = intNumbers(3).ToString()
23        lblFifth.Text = intNumbers(4).ToString()
24    End Sub
25
26    Private Sub btnExit_Click(...) Handles btnExit.Click
27        ' Close the form.
28        Me.Close()
29    End Sub
30 End Class
```

Let's take a closer look at the code for the btnGenerate_Click event handler. Line 5 declares the constant intMAX_SUBSCRIPT, set to the value 4, and line 6 declares an Integer array named intNumbers. The constant intMAX_SUBSCRIPT is used as the upper subscript. As shown in Figure 8, the intNumbers array will have five elements, and their subscripts will be 0 through 4. Line 7 declares a variable named intCount that will be used as a loop counter.

Figure 8 The `intNumbers` array and its subscripts

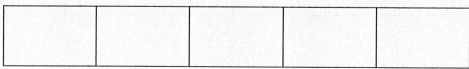

intNumbers(0) intNumbers(1) intNumbers(2) intNumbers(3) intNumbers(4)

Line 10 creates a `Random` object, using the name `rand` to refer to that object. Then, the `For...Next` loop in line 14 executes. If you study line 14 carefully you will see that the loop will iterate five times:

- During the first iteration, `intCount` will be set to 0.
- During the second iteration, `intCount` will be set to 1.
- During the third iteration, `intCount` will be set to 2.
- During the fourth iteration, `intCount` will be set to 3.
- During the fifth iteration, `intCount` will be set to 4.

The statement inside the loop in line 15 gets a random number in the range of 0 through 99 and assigns it to `intNumbers(intCount)`. As a result,

- The first random number will be assigned to `intNumbers(0)`.
- The second random number will be assigned to `intNumbers(1)`.
- The third random number will be assigned to `intNumbers(2)`.
- The fourth name random number will be assigned to `intNumbers(3)`.
- The fifth random number will be assigned to `intNumbers(4)`.

The statements in lines 19 through 23 display the values of the array elements by assigning their values to the Label controls. Notice that we call each array element's `ToString` method to convert its value to a string, as shown in line 19:

```
lblFirst.Text = intNumbers(0).ToString()
```

The value stored in `intNumbers(0)` is an integer, so the expression `intNumbers(0).ToString()` converts that value to a string. The resulting string is then assigned to the `lblFirst` control's Text property. This technique is used to convert the remaining array elements to strings and assign their values to the other Label controls in lines 20 through 23.

Step 4: Save the project, and run the application. Click the *Generate Numbers* button. You should see random numbers displayed in each of the Label controls, similar to Figure 9.

Figure 9 Array elements displayed in the Label controls

Using Array Elements to Store Input

Array elements can be used to hold data entered by the user. For example, the following code gets numbers from the user and stores them in the `intSeries` array:

```
Const intMAX_SUBSCRIPT As Integer = 9
Dim intSeries(intMAX_SUBSCRIPT) As Integer
Dim intCount As Integer

For intCount = 0 To intMAX_SUBSCRIPT
  intSeries(intCount) = CInt(InputBox("Enter a number."))
Next
```

In Tutorial 2 you will create an application that uses input boxes to read a sequence of strings as input, and stores those strings in an array.

Tutorial 2:
Using an array to hold a list of names entered by the user

VideoNote

Tutorial 8-2
Walkthrough

In this tutorial you will create an application that uses an array to hold five strings. The application will have a button that allows you to enter the names of five friends. It will store those names in the array, and then display the contents of the array in a list box.

Step 1: Create a new Windows Forms Application project named *Friend List*.

Step 2: Set up the project's form with a ListBox and two Button controls as shown in Figure 10.

Figure 10 The *Friend List* project's form

Step 3: Complete the code for the form's event handlers as shown in the following. (Don't type the line numbers. They are shown for reference.)

```
 1 Public Class Form1
 2
 3     Private Sub btnEnterNames_Click(...) Handles btnEnterNames.Click
 4         Const intMAX_SUBSCRIPT As Integer = 4     ' The max subscript
 5         Dim strNames(intMAX_SUBSCRIPT) As String ' Array to hold names
 6         Dim intCount As Integer                   ' Loop counter
 7
 8         ' Tell the user what we are about to do.
 9         MessageBox.Show("I'm going to ask you to enter the names " &
10                         "of five friends.")
11
```

```
12          ' Get the names and store them in the array.
13          For intCount = 0 To intMAX_SUBSCRIPT
14              strNames(intCount) = InputBox("Enter a friend's name.")
15          Next
16
17          ' Clear the list box of its current contents.
18          lstFriends.Items.Clear()
19
20          ' Display the contents of the array in the list box.
21          For intCount = 0 To intMAX_SUBSCRIPT
22              lstFriends.Items.Add(strNames(intCount))
23          Next
24      End Sub
25
26      Private Sub btnExit_Click(...) Handles btnExit.Click
27          ' Close the form.
28          Me.Close()
29      End Sub
30  End Class
```

Let's take a closer look at the code for the btnEnterNames_Click event handler. Line 4 declares the constant intMAX_SUBSCRIPT, set to the value 4, and line 5 declares a String array named strNames. The constant intMAX_SUBSCRIPT is used as the upper subscript. As shown in Figure 11, the strNames array will have five elements, and their subscripts will be 0 through 4. Line 6 declares a variable named intCount that will be used as a loop counter.

Figure 11 The strNames array and its subscripts

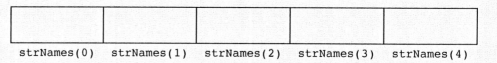

| strNames(0) | strNames(1) | strNames(2) | strNames(3) | strNames(4) |

Lines 9 and 10 display a message box preparing the user to enter five names. Then, the For...Next loop in line 13 executes five times:

- During the first iteration, intCount will be set to 0.
- During the second iteration, intCount will be set to 1.
- During the third iteration, intCount will be set to 2.
- During the fourth iteration, intCount will be set to 3.
- During the fifth iteration, intCount will be set to 4.

The statement inside the loop, in line 14, does the following: (1) It displays an input box prompting the user to enter a friend's name, and (2) it assigns the value entered by the user to strNames(intCount). As a result,

- The first name the user enters will be assigned to strNames(0).
- The second name the user enters will be assigned to strNames(1).
- The third name the user enters will be assigned to strNames(2).
- The fourth name the user enters will be assigned to strNames(3).
- The fifth name the user enters will be assigned to strNames(4).

Line 18 clears the contents of the `lstFriends` list box. Then, another `For...Next` loop executes in line 21. Just like the previous `For...Next` loop, this loop uses the `intCount` variable to step through the elements of the `strNames` array. When this loop executes, the statement in line 22 adds an array element to the `lstFriends` list box. After the loop has finished, each name that is stored in the `strNames` array will be displayed in the list box.

Step 4: Save the project, and run the application. Click the *Enter Names* button, and then enter five names in the resulting input boxes. After you enter the last one, you should see the names displayed in the list box, similar to Figure 12.

Figure 12 Names displayed in the list box

Getting the Length of an Array

Arrays have a Length property that holds the number of elements in the array. For example, assume the following declaration:

```
Dim strNames() As String = { "Joe", "Geri", "Rose" }
```

The `strNames` array has a total of 3 elements, with an upper subscript of 2. The array's Length property returns the value 3. The following is an example of code that uses the Length property:

```
For intCount = 0 to strNames.Length - 1
    MessageBox.Show(strNames(intCount))
Next
```

The code uses the expression `strNames.Length - 1` as the loop's upper limit, because the value in the Length property is 1 greater than the array's upper subscript. As you will learn later, it's possible to change an array's size while an application is running. You can use the Length property to get the current value of an array's size.

Processing Array Contents

You can use array elements just like regular variables in operations. For example, assuming `intHours` is an array of Integers, the following statement multiplies `intHours(3)` by the variable `decPayRate` and stores the result in `decGrossPay`:

```
decGrossPay = intHours(3) * decPayRate
```

Assuming `intTallies` is an array of Integers, the following statement adds 1 to `intTallies(0)`:

```
intTallies(0) += 1
```

And, assuming `decPay` is an array of Decimals, the following statement displays `decPay(5)` in a message box:

```
MessageBox.Show(decPay(5).ToString())
```

In Tutorial 3 you will complete an application that performs calculations using array elements.

Tutorial 3:

Completing an application that uses array elements in a calculation

VideoNote

Tutorial 8-3
Walkthrough

JJ's House of Pizza has six employees, each paid $12 per hour. In this tutorial, you complete an application that stores the number of hours worked by each employee in an array. The application uses the values in the array to calculate each employee's gross pay.

Step 1: Open the *Simple Payroll* project located in the student sample programs folder named *Chap8\Simple Payroll*. The student sample programs folder can be downloaded from www.microsoft.com/express/Downloads/. Figure 13 shows the project's form, which has already been created for you.

Figure 13 *Simple Payroll* form

Step 2: Complete the code for the Button control event handlers as shown in the following. (Don't type the line numbers. They are shown for reference.)

```
1 Public Class Form1
2
3     Private Sub btnCalcPay_Click(...) Handles btnCalcPay.Click
4         ' Constants
5         Const decHOURLY_PAY_RATE As Decimal = 12D
6         Const intMAX_SUBSCRIPT As Integer = 5
7
```

```
 8              ' Array and other variables
 9              Dim dblHoursArray(intMAX_SUBSCRIPT) As Double
10              Dim intCount As Integer = 0    ' Loop counter
11              Dim decEmpPay As Decimal       ' To hold gross pay
12
13              ' Prepare the user to enter each employee's hours.
14              MessageBox.Show("I'm going to ask you for each " &
15                              "employee's hours worked.")
16
17              ' Get the hours worked by the employees.
18              Do While intCount < dblHoursArray.Length
19                  Try
20                      dblHoursArray(intCount) =
21                          CDbl(InputBox("Employee number " &
22                                        (intCount + 1).ToString()))
23                      intCount += 1
24                  Catch
25                      ' Display an error message for invalid hours.
26                      MessageBox.Show("Enter a valid number of " &
27                                      "hours for that employee.")
28                  End Try
29              Loop
30
31              ' Clear the list box.
32              lstOutput.Items.Clear()
33
34              ' Calculate and display each employee's gross pay.
35              For intCount = 0 To dblHoursArray.Length - 1
36                  decEmpPay = CDec(dblHoursArray(intCount) *
37                      decHOURLY_PAY_RATE)
38
39                  lstOutput.Items.Add("Employee " &
40                                      (intCount + 1).ToString() &
41                                      " earned " &
42                                      decEmpPay.ToString("c"))
43              Next
44      End Sub
45
46      Private Sub btnExit_Click(...) Handles btnExit.Click
47          ' Close the form.
48          Me.Close()
49      End Sub
50 End Class
```

Let's take a closer look at the `btnCalcPay_Click` event handler. Here is a summary of the declarations that appear in lines 5 through 11:

- Line 5 declares the constant `decHOURLY_PAY_RATE` for the employee hourly pay rate.
- Line 6 declares the constant `intMAX_SUBSCRIPT` for the array's upper subscript.
- Line 9 declares `dblHoursArray`, an array of Doubles, to hold all of the employees' hours worked.
- Line 10 declares `intCount`, which will be used as a loop counter (initialized to 0), and to step through the `dblHoursArray` array.
- Line 11 declares `decEmpPay`, a Decimal to hold an employee's gross pay.

Lines 14 and 15 display a message box, letting the user know that we are about to ask for each employee's hours worked. The `Do While` loop that begins in line 18 uses the `intCount` variable to step through the `dblHoursArray` array. Recall that `intCount` was initialized with 0. The loop executes as long as `intCount` is less than `dblHoursArray.length`.

Inside the loop a `Try-Catch` statement is used to catch any exceptions that might occur if the user enters a non-numeric value. The statement that appears in lines 20 through 22 performs the following actions:

- It displays an input box prompting the user with an employee number.
- It uses the `CDbl` function to convert the user's input to a Double.
- It assigns the resulting value to the array element `dblHoursArray(intCount)`.

If the user enters an invalid value, the program will branch to the `Catch` clause in line 24, display an error message in lines 26 and 27, and then the loop starts over. If the user enters a valid value, however, line 23 adds 1 to the `intCount` variable. The loop then starts over.

Once the user has entered values for all of the array elements, line 32 clears the list box, and then the `For...Next` loop in line 35 begins. This loop also uses the `intCount` variable to step through each array element. Lines 36 and 37 use an array element to calculate an employee's gross pay, and lines 39 through 42 add a string to the list box reporting the employee's gross pay.

Step 3: Save the project, and run the application. Click the *Calculate Payroll* button. A series of input boxes should appear, asking you to enter the number of hours worked for employees 1 through 6. Enter the following values in order:

Employee 1:	**10**
Employee 2:	**40**
Employee 3:	**20**
Employee 4:	**15**
Employee 5:	**10**
Employee 6:	**30**

After you enter the hours for employee 6, the form should appear, as shown in Figure 14.

Step 4: Click the *Exit* button to end the program.

Figure 14 *Simple Payroll* application, after entering hours for all employees

Accessing Array Elements with a For Each Loop

Visual Basic provides a special loop known as the For Each loop. The For Each loop can simplify array processing when your task is simply to step through an array, retrieving the value of each element. The loop can read the array elements, but it cannot modify their values. The For Each loop is written in the following general form:

```
For Each var As type In array
    statements
Next
```

In the general form, *var* is the name of a variable that will be created just for use with the loop, *type* is the data type of the array, and *array* is the name of an array. The loop will iterate once for every element in the array. Each time the loop iterates, it copies an array element to the *var* variable. For example, the first time the loop iterates, the *var* variable will contain the value of *array*(0), the second time the loop iterates, the *var* variable will contain the value of *array*(1), and so forth. This continues until the loop has stepped through all of the elements in the array.

For example, suppose we have the following array declaration:

```
Dim intArray() As Integer = {10, 20, 30, 40, 50, 60}
```

The following For Each loop displays all of the array values in a ListBox control named lstShow:

```
For Each intVal As Integer In intArray
    lstShow.Items.Add(intVal)
Next
```

Optional Topic: Using the For Each Loop with a ListBox

A For Each loop can also be used to process the items in a collection. Suppose we would like to search for a city name in the Items collection of a ListBox control named lstCities. We will assume that the user has entered a city name into a TextBox control named txtCity. Figure 15 shows an example of the program at runtime. Here are the statements that execute the search:

```
For Each strCity As String In lstCities.Items
  If strCity = txtCity.Text Then
    lblResult.Text = "The city was found!"
  End If
Next
```

Figure 15 Searching for a city name in a ListBox control

Checkpoint

1 Write declaration statements for the following arrays:

a. intEmpNums, an array of 100 integers
b. decPayRate, an array of 24 Decimal variables
c. intMiles, an array of integers initialized to the values 10, 20, 30, 40, and 50
d. strNames, an array of strings with an upper subscript of 12
e. strDivisions, an array of strings initialized to the values "North", "South", "East", and "West".

2 Identify the error in the following declaration:

```
Dim intNumberSet(4) As Integer = { 25, 37, 45, 60 }
```

3 Look at the following array declarations and indicate the number of elements in each array:

a. Dim dblNums(100) As Double
b. Dim intValues() As Integer = { 99, 99, 99 }
c. Dim intArray(0) As Integer

4 What is array bounds checking?

5 Assume that a procedure has the following array declaration:

```
Const intMAX_SUBSCRIPT As Integer = 25
Dim intPoints(intMAX_SUBSCRIPT) As Integer
```

Write a For...Next loop that displays each of the array's elements in message boxes.

6 Rewrite your answer to Checkpoint 5, using a For Each loop.

7 What values are displayed in the message boxes by the following code? (Use a calculator if necessary.)

```
Const dblRATE As Double = 0.1
Const intMAX_SUBSCRIPT As Integer = 3
Dim intBalance(intMAX_SUBSCRIPT) As Integer
Dim intCount As Integer
Dim dblResult As Double

intBalance(0) = 100
intBalance(1) = 250
intBalance(2) = 325
intBalance(3) = 500

For intCount = 0 To intMAX_SUBSCRIPT
  dblResult = intBalance(intCount) * dblRATE
  MessageBox.Show(dblResult.ToString())
Next
```

 2 More about Array Processing

CONCEPT: There are many uses for arrays, and many programming techniques can be applied to them. You can total values and search for data. Related information may be stored in multiple parallel arrays. In addition, arrays can be resized at runtime.

How to Total the Values in a Numeric Array

To total the values in a numeric array, use a loop with an accumulator variable. The loop adds the value in each array element to the accumulator. For example, assume the following array declaration exists in an application, and values have been stored in the array:

```
Const intMAX_SUBSCRIPT As Integer = 24
Dim intUnits(intMAX_SUBSCRIPT) As Integer
```

The following code adds each array element to the intTotal variable:

```
Dim intTotal As Integer = 0
Dim intCount As Integer

For intCount = 0 To (intUnits.Length — 1)
   intTotal += intUnits(intCount)
Next
```

NOTE: The first statement in the previous example sets intTotal to 0. Recall that an accumulator variable must be set to 0 before it is used to keep a running total or the sum will not be correct. Although Visual Basic automatically initializes numeric variables to 0, this statement emphasizes that intTotal must equal 0 before the loop starts.

The previous example demonstrated how to use a For...Next loop to total all of the values in a numeric array. You can also use a For Each loop, as shown in the following code. Assume intUnits is an Integer array.

```
Dim intTotal As Integer = 0

For Each intVal As Integer In intUnits
    intTotal += intVal
Next
```

After the loop finishes, intTotal will contain the total of all the elements in intUnits.

Calculating the Average Value in a Numeric Array

The first step in calculating the average value in an array is to sum the values. The second step is to divide the sum by the number of elements in the array. Assume the following declaration exists in an application, and values have been stored in the array:

```
Const intMAX_SUBSCRIPT As Integer = 24
Dim intUnits(intMAX_SUBSCRIPT) As Integer
```

The following loop calculates the average value in the intUnits array. The average is stored in the dblAverage variable.

```
Dim intTotal As Integer = 0
Dim dblAverage As Double
Dim intCount As Integer

For intCount = 0 To (intUnits.Length - 1)
   intTotal += intUnits(intCount)
Next

' Use floating-point division to compute the average.
dblAverage = intTotal / intUnits.Length
```

The statement that calculates the average (`dblAverage`) must be placed after the end of the loop. It should execute only once.

Finding the Highest and Lowest Values in an Integer Array

Earlier in this chapter, when explaining For Each loops, we showed you how to find the largest value in an array. Let's look at a similar example that uses a For Next loop and accesses each array element using a subscript. Assume that the following array declaration exists in an application, and that values have been stored in the array:

```
Dim intUnits() As Integer = {1, 2, 3, 4, 5}
Dim intCount As Integer      ' Loop counter
Dim intHighest As Integer    ' To hold the highest value

' Get the first element.
intHighest = intNumbers(0)

' Search for the highest value.
For intCount = 1 To (intNumbers.Length - 1)
    If intNumbers(intCount) > intHighest Then
        intHighest = intNumbers(intCount)
    End If
Next
```

The code begins by assigning the value in the first array element to the variable `intHighest`. Next, the loop compares all remaining array elements, beginning at subscript 1, to `intHighest`. Each time it finds a value in the array greater than `intHighest`, the value is copied into `intHighest`. When the loop finishes, `intHighest` equals the largest value in the array.

Lowest Value

The following code, which finds the lowest value in the array, is very similar to the code for finding the highest value. When the loop finishes, `intLowest` equals the smallest value in the array.

```
Dim intUnits() As Integer = {1, 2, 3, 4, 5}
Dim intCount As Integer      ' Loop counter
Dim intLowest As Integer     ' To hold the lowest value

' Get the first element.
intLowest = intNumbers(0)

' Search for the lowest value.
For intCount = 1 To (intNumbers.Length - 1)
    If intNumbers(intCount) < intLowest Then
        intLowest = intNumbers(intCount)
    End If
Next
```

Copying One Array's Contents to Another

Assume that an application has the following statements:

```
Const intMAX_SUBSCRIPT As Integer = 2
Dim intOldValues(intMAX_SUBSCRIPT) As Integer
Dim intNewValues(intMAX_SUBSCRIPT) As Integer
intOldValues(0) = 10
```

```
intOldValues(1) = 100
intOldValues(2) = 200
```

Suppose we want to copy the contents of the intOldValues array to the intNewValues array. We might be tempted to use a single assignment statement, such as the following:

```
intNewValues = intOldValues
```

Although this statement compiles, it does not copy the intOldValues array to the intNewValues array. Instead it causes the names intNewValues and intOldValues to reference the same array in memory.

Arrays in Visual Basic are object variables. Recall that an object variable is a variable that holds a reference to an object. When you use the assignment operator to assign one array to another, the two array variables end up referencing to the same array. For example, after the statement intNewValues = intOldValues executes, the intNewValues variable refers to the same array as the intOldValues variable. This situation is illustrated in Figure 16.

Figure 16 State of the arrays before and after the assignment statement

The danger of assigning intNewValues to intOldValues is that we are no longer working with two arrays, but one. If we were to change the value of any element in the intNewValues array, we would automatically be changing the same element of the intOldValues array. This action would probably be accidental, resulting in a program bug.

Rather than using a single assignment statement to copy an array, we would have to use a loop to copy the individual elements from intOldValues to intNewValues, as shown in the following code:

```
For intCount = 0 To (intOldValues.Length-1)
    intNewValues(intCount) = intOldValues(intCount)
Next
```

This loop copies intOldValue's elements to the intNewValues array. When finished, two separate arrays exist.

Parallel Arrays

Sometimes it is useful to store related data in two or more related arrays, also known as parallel arrays. For example, assume an application has the following array declarations:

```
Const intMAX_SUBSCRIPT As Integer = 4
Dim strNames(intMAX_SUBSCRIPT) As String
Dim strAddresses(intMAX_SUBSCRIPT) As String
```

The strNames array stores the names of five people, and the strAddresses array stores the addresses of the same five people. The information for one person is stored in the same relative location in each array. For instance, the first person's name is stored at strNames(0), and the same person's address is stored at strAddresses(0), as shown in Figure 17.

Figure 17 strNames and strAddresses parallel arrays

To access the information, use the same subscript with both arrays. For example, the following loop displays each person's name and address in a list box named lstPeople:

```
For intCount = 0 To intMAX_SUBSCRIPT
    lstPeople.Items.Add("Name: " & strNames(intCount) &
                        " Address: " & strAddresses(intCount))
Next
```

The arrays strNames and strAddresses are examples of parallel arrays. **Parallel arrays** are two or more arrays that hold related data. The related elements in each array are accessed with a common subscript. Parallel arrays are especially useful when the related data are of unlike types. For example, an application could store the names and ages of five people in the following arrays:

```
Const intMAX_SUBSCRIPT As Integer = 4
Dim strNames(intMAX_SUBSCRIPT) As String
Dim intAges(intMAX_SUBSCRIPT) As Integer
```

Tutorial 4 examines an application that uses parallel arrays: one to hold the names of the months, and one to hold the number of days in each month.

Tutorial 4:
Using parallel arrays

In this tutorial you will create an application that displays the number of days in each month. The application will use two parallel arrays: a String array that is initialized with the names of the months, and an Integer array that is initialized with the number of days in each month. When a button is clicked, the application will display its output in a list box.

Step 1: Create a new Windows Forms Application project named *Months and Days*.

Step 2: Set up the project's form with a ListBox and two Button controls as shown in Figure 18.

Figure 18 The *Months and Days* project's form

Step 3: Complete the code for the form's event handlers as shown in the following. (Don't type the line numbers. They are shown for reference.)

```
 1 Public Class Form1
 2
 3     Private Sub btnDisplay_Click(...) Handles btnDisplay.Click
 4         Dim intCount As Integer     ' Loop counter
 5
 6         ' Array with the names of the months
 7         Dim strMonths() As String = {"January", "February", "March",
 8                                      "April", "May", "June", "July",
 9                                      "August", "September", "October",
10                                      "November", "December"}
11
12         ' Array with the days of each month
13         Dim intDays() As Integer = {31, 28, 31,
14                                     30, 31, 30,
15                                     31, 31, 30,
16                                     31, 30, 31}
```

```
17
18            ' Display a list of the months and days.
19            For intCount = 0 To strMonths.Length - 1
20                lstOutput.Items.Add(strMonths(intCount) & " has " &
21                                    intDays(intCount).ToString() &
22                                    " days.")
23            Next
24        End Sub
25
26        Private Sub btnExit_Click(...) Handles btnExit.Click
27            ' Close the form.
28            Me.Close()
29        End Sub
30 End Class
```

Let's take a closer look at the code for the `btnDisplay_Click` event handler. Line 4 declares the `intCount` variable that we will use as a loop counter. Lines 7 through 10 declare a String array named `strMonths`. The `strMonths` array is initialized with the names of the months, so it has twelve elements. Lines 13 through 16 declare an Integer array named `intDays`. The `intDays` array is initialized with the number of days in each month, so it also has twelve elements.

The `strMonths` and `intDays` arrays have the parallel relationship shown in Figure 19. In this relationship, `strMonths(n)` contains the name of a month, and `intDays(n)` contains the number of days in that same month.

Figure 19 Parallel arrays

The `For...Next` loop that begins in line 19 uses the `intCount` variable to step through the parallel arrays, displaying a line of output in the `lstOutput` list box. In the first iteration the string "January has 31 days." will be added to the list box. In the second iteration the string "February has 28 days." will be added to the list box. This continues for each element in the arrays.

Step 4: Save the project, and run the application. Click the *Display the Months and Days* button. You should see the output shown in Figure 20.

Figure 20 Output displayed in the list box

Step 5: Click the *Exit* button to end the application.

Parallel Relationships between Arrays, List Boxes, and Combo Boxes

Items stored in a list box or a combo box have a built-in index. The index of the first item is 0, the index of the second item is 1, and so on. Because this indexing scheme corresponds with the way array subscripts are used, it is easy to create parallel relationships between list boxes, combo boxes, and arrays.

For example, assume that an application has a list box named `lstPeople`. The following statements store three names in the list box:

```
lstPeople.Items.Add("Jean James")
lstPeople.Items.Add("Kevin Smith")
lstPeople.Items.Add("Joe Harrison")
```

When these statements execute, `"Jean James"` is stored at index 0, `"Kevin Smith"` is stored at index 1, and `"Joe Harrison"` is stored at index 2. Also assume the application has an array of strings named `strPhoneNumbers`. This array holds the phone numbers of the three people whose names are stored in the list box. The following statements store phone numbers in the array:

```
strPhoneNumbers(0) = "555-2987"
strPhoneNumbers(1) = "555-5656"
strPhoneNumbers(2) = "555-8897"
```

The phone number stored at element 0 (`"555-2987"`) belongs to the person whose name is stored at index 0 in the list box (`"Jean James"`). Likewise, the phone number stored at element 1 belongs to the person whose name is stored at index 1 in the list box, and so on. When the user selects a name from the list box, the following statement displays the person's phone number:

```
MessageBox.Show(strPhoneNumbers(lstPeople.SelectedIndex))
```

The SelectedIndex property holds the index of the selected item in the list box. This statement uses the index as a subscript in the `strPhoneNumbers` array.

439

It is possible however, for the SelectedIndex property to hold a value outside the bounds of the parallel array. When no item is selected, the SelectedIndex property holds −1. The following code provides error checking:

```
With lstPeople
  If .SelectedIndex > -1 And
     .SelectedIndex < strPhoneNumbers.Length Then
     MessageBox.Show(strPhoneNumbers(.SelectedIndex))
  Else
     MessageBox.Show("That is not a valid selection.")
  End If
End With
```

Searching Arrays

Applications not only store and process information stored in arrays, but also often search arrays for specific items. The most basic method of searching an array is the **sequential search**. It uses a loop to examine the elements in an array, one after the other, starting with the first. It compares each element with the value being searched for, and stops when the value is found or the end of the array is reached. If the value being searched for is not in the array, the algorithm unsuccessfully searches to the end of the array.

The pseudocode for a sequential search is as follows:

found = False
subscript = 0
Do While found is False and subscript < array's length
  If array(subscript) = searchValue Then
    found = True
    position = subscript
  End If
  subscript += 1
End While

In the pseudocode, *found* is a Boolean variable, *position* and *subscript* are integers, *array* is an array of any type, and *searchValue* is the value being searched for. When the search is complete, if the *found* variable equals *False*, the search value was not found. If *found* equals *True*, position contains the subscript of the array element containing the search value.

For example, suppose an application stores test scores in an array named *scores*. The following pseudocode searches the array for an element containing 100:

' Search for a 100 in the array.
found = False
count = 0
Do While Not found And count < scores.Length
  If scores(count) = 100 Then
    found = True
    position = count
  End If
  count += 1
Loop

' Was 100 found in the array?
If found Then
  Display "Congratulations! You made a 100 on test " & (position + 1)

Else
    Display "You didn't score a 100, but keep trying!"
End If

Sorting an Array

Programmers often want to sort, or arrange the elements of an array in **ascending order**, which means its values are arranged from lowest to highest. The lowest value is stored in the first element, and the highest value is stored in the last element. To sort an array in ascending order, use the `Array.Sort` method. The general format is as follows:

```
Array.Sort(ArrayName)
```

ArrayName is the name of the array you wish to sort. For example, assume that the following declaration exists in an application:

```
Dim intNumbers() As Integer = {7, 12, 1, 6, 3}
```

The following statement will sort the array in ascending order:

```
Array.Sort(intNumbers)
```

After the statement executes, the array values are in the following order: 1, 3, 6, 7, 12.

When you pass an array of strings to the `Array.Sort` method, the array is sorted in ascending order according to the Unicode encoding scheme. Generally, the sort occurs in alphabetic order. But to be more specific about the order, numeric digits are first, upper-case letters are second, and lowercase letters are last. For example, assume the following declaration:

```
Dim strNames() As String = {"dan", "Kim", "Adam", "Bill"}
```

The following statement sorts the array in ascending order:

```
Array.Sort(strNames)
```

After the statement executes, the values in the array appear in this order: `"Adam"`, `"Bill"`, `"Kim"`, `"dan"`.

Dynamically Sizing Arrays

You can change the number of elements in an array at runtime, using the `ReDim` statement. The general format of the `ReDim` statement is as follows:

```
ReDim [Preserve] Arrayname (UpperSubscript)
```

The word `Preserve` is optional. If it is used, any existing values in the array are preserved. If `Preserve` is not used, existing values in the array are destroyed. *Arrayname* is the name of the array being resized. *UpperSubscript* is the new upper subscript and must be a positive whole number. If you resize an array and make it smaller than it was, elements at the end of the array are lost.

For example, the following statement resizes `strNames` so that 25 is the upper subscript:

```
ReDim Preserve strNames(25)
```

After this statement executes, `strNames` has 26 elements. Because the `Preserve` keyword is used, any values originally stored in `strNames` will still be there.

When you do not know at design time the number of elements you will need in an array, you can declare an array without a size, and use the `ReDim` statement later to give it a size. For example, suppose you want to write a test-averaging application that averages any number of tests. You can initially declare the array with no size, as follows:

```
Dim dblScores() As Double
```

441

Currently, dblScores equals Nothing, but is capable of referencing an array of Double values. Later, when the application has determined the number of test scores, a ReDim statement will give the array a size. The following code shows an example of such an operation:

```
intNumScores = CInt(InputBox("Enter the number of test scores."))
If intNumScores > 0 Then
    ReDim dblScores (intNumScores - 1)
Else
    MessageBox.Show("You must enter 1 or greater.")
End If
```

This code asks the user to enter the number of test scores. If the user enters a value greater than 0, the ReDim statement sizes the array with intNumScores − 1 as the upper subscript. (Because the subscripts begin at 0, the upper subscript is intNumScores − 1.)

Checkpoint

8 Suppose intValues is an array of 100 integers. Write a For...Next loop that totals all the values stored in the array.

9 Suppose intPoints is an array of integers, but you do not know the size of the array. Write code that calculates the average of the values in the array.

10 Suppose strSerialNumbers is an array of strings. Write a single statement that sorts the array in ascending order.

11 What is displayed by the message boxes in the following code segment? (You may need to use a calculator.)

```
Const intMAX_SUBSCRIPT As Integer = 4
Dim intTimes(intMAX_SUBSCRIPT) As Integer
Dim intSpeeds(intMAX_SUBSCRIPT) As Integer
Dim intDists(intMAX_SUBSCRIPT) As Integer
Dim intCount As Integer

intSpeeds(0) = 18
intSpeeds(1) = 4
intSpeeds(2) = 27
intSpeeds(3) = 52
intSpeeds(4) = 100

For intCount = 0 To 4
  intTimes(intCount) = intCount
Next

For intCount = 0 To 4
  intDists(intCount) = intTimes(intCount) * intSpeeds(intCount)
Next

For intCount = 0 To 4
  MessageBox.Show(intTimes(intCount).ToString() & " " &
                  intSpeeds(intCount).ToString() & " " &
                  intDists(intCount).ToString())
Next
```

12 Assume that decSales is an array of 20 Decimal values. Write a statement that resizes the array to 50 elements. If the array has existing values, they should be preserved.

13 Assume that intValidNumbers is an array of integers. Write code that searches the array for the value 247. If the value is found, display a message indicating its position in the array. If the value is not found, display a message indicating so.

3 Procedures and Functions That Work with Arrays

CONCEPT: You can pass arrays as arguments to procedures and functions. You can return an array from a function. These capabilities allow you to write procedures and functions that perform general operations with arrays.

Passing Arrays as Arguments

Quite often you will want to write procedures or functions that process the data in arrays. For example, procedures can be written to store data in an array, display an array's contents, and sum or average the values in an array. Usually such procedures accept an array as an argument.

The following procedure accepts an integer array as an argument and displays the sum of the array's elements:

```
' The DisplaySum procedure displays the sum of the elements in the
' argument array.

Sub DisplaySum(ByVal intArray() As Integer)
   Dim intTotal As Integer = 0 ' Accumulator
   Dim intCount As Integer      ' Loop counter

   For intCount = 0 To (intArray.Length - 1)
      intTotal += intArray(intCount)
   Next

   MessageBox.Show("The total is " & intTotal.ToString())
End Sub
```

The parameter variable is declared as an array with no upper subscript specified inside the parentheses. The parameter is an object variable that references an array that is passed as an argument. To call the procedure, pass the name of an array, as shown in the following code:

```
Dim intNumbers() As Integer = { 2, 4, 7, 9, 8, 12, 10 }
DisplaySum(intNumbers)
```

When this code executes, the DisplaySum procedure is called and the intNumbers array is passed as an argument. The procedure calculates and displays the sum of the elements in intNumbers.

Passing Arrays by Value and by Reference

Array parameters can be declared ByVal or ByRef. Be aware, however, that the ByVal keyword does not restrict a procedure from accessing and modifying the argument array's elements. For example, look at the following SetToZero procedure:

```
' Set all the elements of the array argument to zero.

Sub SetToZero(ByVal intArray() As Integer)
   Dim intCount As Integer ' Loop counter

   For intCount = 0 To intArray.Length - 1
      intArray(intCount) = 0
   Next
End Sub
```

This procedure accepts an integer array as its argument and sets each element of the array to 0. Suppose we call the procedure, as shown in the following code:

```
Dim intNumbers() As Integer = { 1, 2, 3, 4, 5 }
SetToZero(intNumbers)
```

After the procedure executes, the intNumbers array will contain the values 0, 0, 0, 0, and 0.

Although the ByVal keyword does not restrict a procedure from accessing and modifying the elements of an array argument, it does prevent an array argument from being assigned to another array. For example, the following procedure accepts an array as its argument, and then assigns the parameter to another array:

```
' Assign the array argument to a new array. Does this work?

Sub ResetValues(ByVal intArray() As Integer)
   Dim newArray() As Integer = { 0, 0, 0, 0, 0}
   intArray = newArray
End Sub
```

Suppose we call the procedure, as shown in the following code:

```
Dim intNumbers() As Integer = { 1, 2, 3, 4, 5 }
ResetValues(intNumbers)
```

After the procedure executes, the intNumbers array still contains the values 1, 2, 3, 4, and 5. If the parameter array had been declared with the ByRef keyword, however, the assignment would have affected the argument, and the intNumbers array would contain the values 0, 0, 0, 0, and 0 after the procedure executed.

Returning an Array from a Function

You can return an array from a function. For example, the following function prompts the user to enter four names. The names are then returned in an array.

```
' Get three names from the user and return them as an array
' of strings.

Function GetNames() As String()
   Const intMAX_SUBSCRIPT As Integer = 2
   Dim strNames(intMAX_SUBSCRIPT) As String
   Dim intCount As Integer

   For intCount = 0 To 3
      strNames(intCount) = InputBox("Enter name " &
         (intCount + 1).ToString())
   Next

   Return strNames
End Function
```

The function has a return type of String(), indicating that it returns an array of strings. The return value can be assigned to any array of strings. The following code shows the function's return value being assigned to strCustomers:

```
Dim strCustomers() As String
strCustomers = GetNames()
```

After the code executes, the strCustomers array contains the names entered by the user.

An array returned from a function must be assigned to an array of the same type. For example, if a function returns an array of integers, its return value can be assigned only to an array of integers. In Tutorial 5, you examine an application containing several functions that work with arrays.

Tutorial 5:
Examining an application that passes an array
to procedures and functions

In this tutorial, you examine the *Sales Data* application, which asks the user for sales figures for five days. It calculates and displays the total sales, average sales, highest sales amount, and lowest sales amount.

Step 1: Open the *Sales Data* project located in the student sample programs folder named *Chap8\Sales Data*. Recall that the student sample programs folder can be downloaded from www.microsoft.com/express/Downloads/.

Step 2: Before we look at the code, let's see the application in action. Run the application. Figure 21 shows the project's form. Click the *Calculate Sales Data* button.

Figure 21 *Sales Data* form

Step 3: A series of five input boxes will appear, asking you to enter the sales for days 1 through 5. Enter the following amounts for each input box:

Day 1:   **1000**
Day 2:   **2000**
Day 3:   **3000**
Day 4:   **4000**
Day 5:   **5000**

After you enter the sales amount for day 5, the application's form should appear as shown in Figure 22.

Figure 22 *Sales Data* form with sales data displayed

Step 4:   Click the *Exit* button to end the application.

Step 5:   Now we will examine the application's code. Open the *Code* window and look at the `btnCalculate_Click` event handler. The code is shown here, with line numbers for reference:

```
1 Public Class Form1
2
3     Private Sub btnCalculate_Click(...) Handles btnCalculate.Click
4         ' Create an array to hold sales amounts.
5         Const intMAX_SUBSCRIPT As Integer = 4
6         Dim decSales(intMAX_SUBSCRIPT) As Decimal
7
8         ' Other local variables
9         Dim decTotalSales As Decimal     ' To hold the total sales
10        Dim decAverageSales As Decimal ' To hold the average sales
11        Dim decHighestSales As Decimal ' To hold the highest sales
12        Dim decLowestSales As Decimal   ' To hold the lowest sales
13
14        ' Get sales amounts from the user.
15        GetSalesData(decSales)
16
17        ' Get the total sales, average sales, highest sales
18        ' amount and lowest sales amount.
19        decTotalSales = TotalArray(decSales)
20        decAverageSales = AverageArray(decSales)
21        decHighestSales = Highest(decSales)
22        decLowestSales = Lowest(decSales)
23
24        ' Display the results.
25        lblTotal.Text = decTotalSales.ToString("c")
26        lblAverage.Text = decAverageSales.ToString("c")
27        lblHighest.Text = decHighestSales.ToString("c")
28        lblLowest.Text = decLowestSales.ToString("c")
29    End Sub
30
```

Here is a summary of the declarations that appear in lines 5 through 12:

- Line 5 declares the constant `intMAX_SUBSCRIPT`, set to the value 4. This will be the upper subscript of the array that holds sales amount.

- Line 6 declares `decSales` as an array of Decimals, using `intMAX_SUB-SCRIPT` as the upper subscript. The array has five elements, one for each day of sales.
- Line 9 declares `decTotalSales` as a Decimal, to hold the total sales amount.
- Line 10 declares `decAverageSales` as a Decimal, to hold the average sales amount.
- Line 11 declares `decHighestSales` as a Decimal, to hold the highest sales amount.
- Line 12 declares `decLowestSales` as a Decimal, to hold the lowest sales amount.

Line 15 calls the `GetSalesData` procedure, passing the `decSales` array as an argument. The `GetSalesData` procedure displays the input boxes prompting the user to enter sales amounts for each day. It stores the amounts entered by the user in the array that is passed as an argument.

Line 19 calls the `TotalArray` function, passing the `decSales` array as an argument. The function returns the total of the values in the array, and that value is assigned to the `decTotalSales` variable.

Line 20 calls the `AverageArray` function, passing the `decSales` array as an argument. The function returns the average of the values in the array, and that value is assigned to the `decAverageSales` variable.

Line 21 calls the `Highest` function, passing the `decSales` array as an argument. The function returns the highest value in the array, and that value is assigned to the `decHighestSales` variable.

Line 22 calls the `Lowest` function, passing the `decSales` array as an argument. The function returns the lowest value in the array, and that value is assigned to the `decLowhestSales` variable.

The statements in lines 25 through 28 display the sales data in the Label controls on the application's form.

Just below the `btnCalculate_Click` event handler is the `GetSalesData` procedure, shown here with line numbers for reference:

```
31    ' The GetSalesData procedure accepts a Decimal array argument.
32    ' It fills the array with sales amounts entered by the user.
33
34    Sub GetSalesData(ByRef decSales() As Decimal)
35        Dim intCount As Integer = 0 ' Loop counter, set to 0
36
37        ' Fill the decSales array with values entered by the user.
38        Do While intCount < decSales.Length
39            Try
40                ' Get the sales for a day.
41                decSales(intCount) =
42                    CDec(InputBox("Enter the sales for day " &
43                                  (intCount + 1).ToString()))
44                ' Increment intCount.
45                intCount += 1
46            Catch
47                ' Display an error message for invalid input.
48                MessageBox.Show("Enter a valid numeric value.")
49            End Try
50        Loop
51    End Sub
52
```

Line 35 declares intCount, which will be used as a loop counter, and to step through the decSales array parameter. Notice that intCount is initialized to 0.

The Do While loop that begins in line 38 uses the intCount variable to step through the decSales array parameter. Recall that intCount was initialized with 0. The loop executes as long as intCount is less than decSales.length.

Inside the loop a Try-Catch statement is used to catch any exceptions that might occur if the user enters a non-numeric value. The statement that appears in lines 41 through 43 performs the following actions:

- It displays an input box prompting the user to enter the sales for a specific day.
- It uses the CDec function to convert the user's input to a Decimal.
- It assigns the resulting value to the array element decSales(intCount).

If the user enters an invalid value, the program will branch to the Catch clause in line 46, display an error message in line 48, and then the loop starts over. If the user enters a valid value, however, line 45 adds 1 to the intCount variable. The loop then starts over. When the loop is finished, the decSales array parameter will contain the sales amounts entered by the user, and the procedures ends.

Next is the TotalArray function, shown here with line numbers for reference. The function accepts a Decimal array as an argument. It uses a loop to step through the array's elements, adding their values to an accumulator variable. The total of the array's elements is then returned.

```
53    ' The TotalArray function accepts a Decimal array as an
54    ' argument and returns the total of its values.
55
56    Function TotalArray(ByVal decValues() As Decimal) As Decimal
57        Dim decTotal As Decimal = 0 ' Accumulator
58        Dim intCount As Integer      ' Loop counter
59
60        ' Calculate the total of the array's elements.
61        For intCount = 0 To (decValues.Length - 1)
62            decTotal += decValues(intCount)
63        Next
64
65        ' Return the total.
66        Return decTotal
67    End Function
68
```

Next is the AverageArray function, shown here with line numbers for reference. The function accepts a Decimal array as an argument, and returns the average of the array's values.

```
69    ' The AverageArray function accepts a Decimal array as an
70    ' argument and returns the total of its values.
71
72    Function AverageArray(ByVal decValues() As Decimal) As Decimal
73        Return TotalArray(decValues) / decValues.Length
74    End Function
75
```

Next is the Highest function, shown here with line numbers for reference. The function accepts a Decimal array as an argument, and returns the highest value found in the array.

```
76        ' The Highest function accepts a Decimal array as an
77        ' argument and returns the highest value it contains.
78
79        Function Highest(ByVal decValues() As Decimal) As Decimal
80            Dim intCount As Integer    ' Loop counter
81            Dim decHighest As Decimal ' To hold the highest value
82
83            ' Get the first value in the array.
84            decHighest = decValues(0)
85
86            ' Search for the highest value.
87            For intCount = 1 To (decValues.Length - 1)
88                If decValues(intCount) > decHighest Then
89                    decHighest = decValues(intCount)
90                End If
91            Next
92
93            ' Return the highest value.
94            Return decHighest
95        End Function
96
```

Next is the Lowest function, shown here with line numbers for reference. The function accepts a Decimal array as an argument, and returns the lowest value found in the array.

```
97        ' The Lowest function accepts a Decimal array as an
98        ' argument and returns the lowest value it contains.
99
100       Function Lowest(ByVal decValues() As Decimal) As Decimal
101           Dim intCount As Integer    ' Loop counter
102           Dim decLowest As Decimal ' To hold the lowest value
103
104           ' Get the first value in the array.
105           decLowest = decValues(0)
106
107           ' Search for the lowest value.
108           For intCount = 1 To (decValues.Length - 1)
109               If decValues(intCount) < decLowest Then
110                   decLowest = decValues(intCount)
111               End If
112           Next
113
114           ' Return the lowest value.
115           Return decLowest
116       End Function
117
```

Next is the btnExit_Click event handler, shown here with line numbers for reference:

```
118       Private Sub btnExit_Click(...) Handles btnExit.Click
119         ' Close the form.
120         Me.Close()
121       End Sub
122   End Class
```

4 Multidimensional Arrays

CONCEPT: You may create arrays with more than two dimensions to hold complex sets of data.

Two-Dimensional Arrays

The arrays presented so far have had only one subscript. An array with one subscript is called a **one-dimensional array**, and is useful for storing and working with a single set of data. Sometimes, though, it is necessary to work with multiple sets of data. For example, in a grade-averaging program, a teacher might record all of one student's test scores in an array. If the teacher has 30 students, that means there must be 30 arrays to record the scores for the entire class. Instead of declaring 30 individual arrays, it would be better to declare a two-dimensional array.

A **two-dimensional array** is like an array of arrays. It can be used to hold multiple sets of values. Think of a two-dimensional array as having rows and columns of elements, as shown in Figure 23. This figure shows an array having three rows (numbered 0, 1, and 2) and four columns (numbered 0, 1, 2, and 3). There are a total of 12 elements in the array.

Figure 23 Rows and columns

	Column 0	Column 1	Column 2	Column 3
Row 0				
Row 1				
Row 2				

To declare a two-dimensional array, two sets of upper subscripts are required, the first for the rows and the second for the columns. The general format of a two-dimensional array declaration is as follows:

```
Dim ArrayName (UpperRow,UpperColumn) As DataType
```

Let's take a closer look at the syntax.

- `ArrayName` is the name of the array.
- `UpperRow` is the value of the array's highest row subscript. This must be a positive integer.
- `UpperColumn` is the value of the array's highest column subscript. This must be a positive integer.
- `DataType` is a Visual Basic data type.

An example declaration of a two-dimensional array with three rows and four columns follows, and is shown in Figure 24. The highest row subscript is 2 and the highest column subscript is 3.

```
Dim dblScores (2, 3) As Double
```

Figure 24 Declaration of a two-dimensional array

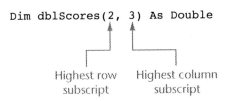

As with one-dimensional arrays, it is a good practice to use named constants to specify the upper subscripts. Here is an example:

```
Const intMAX_ROW As Integer = 2
Const intMAX_COL As Integer = 3
Dim dblScores(intMAX_ROW, intMAX_COL) As Double
```

When data in a two-dimensional array is processed, each element has two subscripts, the first for its row and the second for its column. Using the dblScores array as an example, the elements in row 0 are referenced as follows:

```
dblScores(0, 0)
dblScores(0, 1)
dblScores(0, 2)
dblScores(0, 3)
```

The elements in row 1 are referenced as follows:

```
dblScores(1, 0)
dblScores(1, 1)
dblScores(1, 2)
dblScores(1, 3)
```

The elements in row 2 are referenced as follows:

```
dblScores(2, 0)
dblScores(2, 1)
dblScores(2, 2)
dblScores(2, 3)
```

Figure 25 illustrates the array with the subscripts shown for each element.

Figure 25 Subscripts for each element of the dblScores array

	Column 0	Column 1	Column 2	Column 3
Row 0	dblScores(0, 0)	dblScores(0, 1)	dblScores(0, 2)	dblScores(0, 3)
Row 1	dblScores(1, 0)	dblScores(1, 1)	dblScores(1, 2)	dblScores(1, 3)
Row 2	dblScores(2, 0)	dblScores(2, 1)	dblScores(2, 2)	dblScores(2, 3)

To access one of the elements in a two-dimensional array, you must use two subscripts. For example, the following statement stores the number 95 in `dblScores(2, 1)`:

```
dblScores(2, 1) = 95
```

Programs often use nested loops to process two-dimensional arrays. For example, the following code prompts the user to enter a score, once for each element in the array:

```
For intRow = 0 To intMAX_ROW
    For intCol = 0 To intMAX_COL
        dblScores(intRow, intCol) = CDbl(InputBox("Enter a score."))
    Next
Next
```

And the following code displays all the elements in the `dblScores` array:

```
For intRow = 0 To intMAX_ROW
    For intCol = 0 To intMAX_COL
        lstOutput.Items.Add(dblScores(intRow, intCol).ToString())
    Next
Next
```

Implicit Sizing and Initialization of Two-Dimensional Arrays

As with a one-dimensional array, you may provide an initialization list for a two-dimensional array. Recall that when you provide an initialization list for an array, you cannot provide the upper subscript numbers. When initializing a two-dimensional array, you must provide the comma to indicate the number of dimensions. The following is an example of a two-dimensional array declaration with an initialization list:

```
Dim intNumbers(,) As Integer = { {1, 2, 3} ,
                                 {4, 5, 6} ,
                                 {7, 8, 9} }
```

Initialization values for each row are enclosed in their own set of braces. In this example, the initialization values for row 0 are `{1, 2, 3}`, the initialization values for row 1 are `{4, 5, 6}`, and the initialization values for row 2 are `{7, 8, 9}`. So, this statement declares an array with three rows and three columns.

The values are assigned to the `intNumbers` array in the following manner:

```
intNumbers(0, 0) is set to 1
intNumbers(0, 1) is set to 2
intNumbers(0, 2) is set to 3

intNumbers(1, 0) is set to 4
intNumbers(1, 1) is set to 5
intNumbers(1, 2) is set to 6

intNumbers(2, 0) is set to 7
intNumbers(2, 1) is set to 8
intNumbers(2, 2) is set to 9
```

Summing the Columns of a Two-Dimensional Array

You can use nested loops to sum the columns in a two-dimensional array. The following code sums each column of an array named `intValues`. The outer loop controls the column subscript and the inner loop controls the row subscript. The variable `intTotal` accumulates the sum of each column.

```
' Sum the columns.
For intCol = 0 To intMAX_COL
    ' Initialize the accumulator.
    intTotal = 0
    ' Sum all rows within this column.
    For intRow = 0 To intMAX_ROW
        intTotal += intValues(intRow, intCol)
    Next
    ' Display the sum of the column.
    MessageBox.Show("Sum of column " & intCol.ToString() &
                    " is " & intTotal.ToString())
Next
```

Tutorial 6:
Completing the *Seating Chart* application

In this tutorial, you will complete the *Seating Chart* application. When completed, the application will display an airplane seating chart and allow the user to select a seat number. The application will display the price of the selected seat.

Step 1: Open the *Seating Chart* project located in the student sample programs folder named *Chap8\Seating Chart*. Figure 26 shows the application's form, which has

Figure 26 The *Seating Chart* application's form

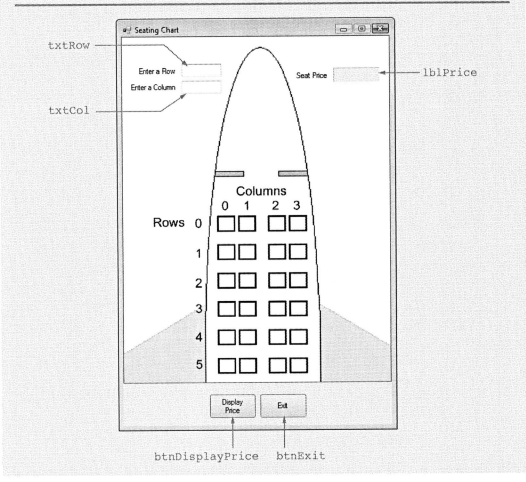

already been created for you. The seating chart image (which is displayed in a PictureBox control) shows the seats on the plane, arranged in rows and columns. When the completed application runs, the user will enter valid row and column numbers in the txtRow and txtCol text boxes, and then click the *Display Price* button. The price of the selected seat will be displayed in the lblPrice label.

The following table shows the seat prices:

	Columns			
	0	1	2	3
Row 0	$450	$450	$450	$450
Row 1	$425	$425	$425	$425
Row 2	$400	$400	$400	$400
Row 3	$375	$375	$375	$375
Row 4	$375	$375	$375	$375
Row 5	$350	$350	$350	$350

When you write the code for the application, you will create a two-dimensional array to hold these values.

Step 2: Complete the code for the form's event handlers as shown in the following. (Don't type the line numbers. They are shown for reference.)

```
1 Public Class Form1
2
3     Private Sub btnDisplayPrice_Click(...) Handles btnDisplayPrice.Click
4         ' Variables for the selected row and column
5         Dim intRow, intCol As Integer
6
7         ' Constants for the maximum row and column subscripts
8         Const intMAX_ROW As Integer = 5
9         Const intMAX_COL As Integer = 3
10
11        ' Array with seat prices
12        Dim decPrices(,) = {{450D, 450D, 450D, 450D},
13                            {425D, 425D, 425D, 425D},
14                            {400D, 400D, 400D, 400D},
15                            {375D, 375D, 375D, 375D},
16                            {375D, 375D, 375D, 375D},
17                            {350D, 350D, 350D, 350D}}
18
19        Try
20            ' Get the selected row and column numbers.
21            intRow = CInt(txtRow.Text)
22            intCol = CInt(txtCol.Text)
23
24            ' Make sure the row and col are within range.
25            If intRow >= 0 And intRow <= intMAX_ROW Then
26                If intCol >= 0 And intCol <= intMAX_COL Then
27                    ' Display the selected seat's price.
28                    lblPrice.Text = decPrices(intRow, intCol).ToString("c")
29                Else
30                    ' Error message for invalid column.
```

```
31                      MessageBox.Show("Column must be 0 through " &
32                                      intMAX_COL.ToString())
33                  End If
34              Else
35                  ' Error message for invalid row.
36                  MessageBox.Show("Row must be 0 through " &
37                                  intMAX_ROW.ToString())
38              End If
39          Catch
40              ' Error message for non-integer input.
41              MessageBox.Show("Row and column must be integers.")
42          End Try
43      End Sub
44
45      Private Sub btnExit_Click(...) Handles btnExit.Click
46          ' Close the form.
47          Me.Close()
48      End Sub
49 End Class
```

Let's take a closer look at the btnDisplayPrice_Click event handler. Line 5 declares the intRow and intCol variables. These will hold the row and column numbers that the user enters. Lines 8 and 9 declare the constants inMAX_ROW (set to 5) and intMAX_COL (set to 3). These values are the upper row and column numbers in the array that will hold the seat prices.

Lines 12 through 17 declare decPrices, a two-dimensional array of Decimals, initialized with the seat prices previously shown.

A Try-Catch statement begins in line 19, to deal with any non-numeric values entered by the user. In line 21 we get the row number entered by the user into the txtRow text box, convert it to an Integer, and store the result in the intRow variable. If an exception is thrown because of a non-numeric value, the program will jump to the Catch clause in line 39.

In line 22 we get the column number entered by the user into the txtCol text box, convert it to an Integer, and store the result in the intCol variable. If an exception is thrown because of a non-numeric value, the program will jump to the Catch clause in line 39.

Next we want to make sure the selected row and column numbers are within the correct range. The valid row numbers are 0 through 5, and the valid column numbers are 0 through 3. The If...Then statement in line 25 determines whether intRow is within the correct range. If it is not, the Else clause in line 34 displays an error message. If intRow is within the correct range, the If...Then statement in line 26 determines whether intCol is within the correct range. If it is not, the Else clause in line 29 displays an error message. Otherwise, the program continues with line 28. Line 28 uses intRow and intCol as subscripts, to retrieve the selected seat's price from the decPrices array, and then displays that value in the lblPrice label.

Step 3: Save the project, and then run the application. Experiment by entering row and column numbers for different seats, and comparing the displayed price with the table previously shown. Figure 27 shows the application's form with row 2, column 3 selected. When you are finished, click the *Exit* button to end the application.

Figure 27 Row 2, column 3 selected

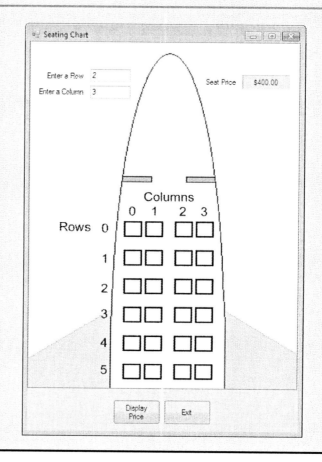

Three-Dimensional Arrays and Beyond

You can create arrays with up to 32 dimensions. The following is an example of a three-dimensional array declaration:

```
Dim decSeats(9, 11, 14) As Decimal
```

This array can be thought of as 10 sets of 12 rows, with each row containing 15 columns. This array might be used to store the prices of seats in an auditorium, in which there are 15 seats in a row, 12 rows in a section, and 10 sections in the room.

Figure 28 represents a three-dimensional array as pages of two-dimensional arrays.

Arrays with more than three dimensions are difficult to visualize but can be useful in some programming applications. For example, in a factory warehouse where cases of widgets are stacked on pallets, an array of four dimensions can store a part number for each widget. The four subscripts of each element can represent the pallet number, case number, row number, and column number of each widget. Similarly, an array with five dimensions could be used if there were multiple warehouses.

Figure 28 A three-dimensional array

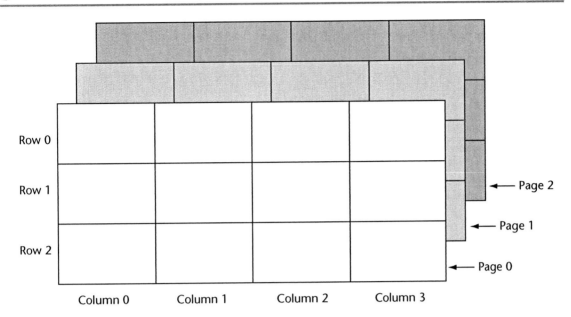

Row 0
Row 1
Row 2

Column 0 Column 1 Column 2 Column 3

Page 2
Page 1
Page 0

 Checkpoint

14 Declare a two-dimensional array of integers named intGrades. It should have 30 rows and 10 columns.

15 How many elements are in the following array?

```
Dim decSales(5, 3) As Decimal
```

16 Write a statement that assigns 56893.12 to the first column of the first row of the decSales array declared in Checkpoint 15.

17 Write a statement that displays in a message box the contents of the last column of the last row of the array decSales declared in Checkpoint 15.

18 Declare a two-dimensional Integer array named intSettings large enough to hold the following table of numbers:

```
12    24    32    21    42
14    67    87    65    90
19     1    24    12     8
```

19 How many rows and columns does the array declared in the following statement have?

```
Dim intMatrix(,) As Integer = { { 2, 4, 7, 0, 3} ,
   { 6, 5, 12, 8, 6} , { 9, 0, 14, 6, 0} ,
   { 16, 7, 9, 13, 10} }
```

20 A movie rental store keeps DVDs on 50 racks with 10 shelves each. Each shelf holds 25 DVDs. Declare a three-dimensional array of strings large enough to represent the store's storage system. Each element of the array holds a movie title.

Focus on GUI Design: The Enabled Property and the Timer Control

CONCEPT: You can disable controls by setting their Enabled property to *False*. The Timer control allows your application to execute a procedure at regular time intervals.

The Enabled Property

Most controls have a Boolean property named Enabled. When a control's **Enabled property** is set to *False*, it is considered disabled, which means it cannot receive the focus and cannot respond to events generated by the user. Additionally, many controls appear dimmed, or grayed out, when their Enabled property is set to *False*. For example, Figure 29 shows a form with three buttons that have their Enabled property set to *False*.

Figure 29 Controls with Enabled property set to *False*

By default, a control's Enabled property is set to *True*. If you change a control's Enabled property to *False* at design time, the control is initially disabled when the application runs.

You can also change the Enabled property's value with code at runtime. For example, assume an application has a radio button named `radBlue`. The following statement disables the control:

```
radBlue.Enabled = False
```

Sometimes you do not want the user to access controls. For example, consider an application that calculates the price of two different models of a new car. One model comes only in red, yellow, and black, while the other model comes only in white, green, and orange. As soon as the user selects a model, the application can disable colors not available for that model.

The Timer Control

The **Timer control** allows an application to automatically execute code at regular time intervals. It is useful when you want an application to perform an operation at certain times or after an amount of time has passed. For example, a Timer control can perform simple animation by moving a graphic image across the screen, or it can cause a form to be hidden after a certain amount of time.

Double-click the Timer icon in the toolbox to place a Timer control on a form. (The Timer control is in the *Components* section of the toolbox.) Because the Timer control is invisible at runtime, it appears in the component tray at design time. The prefix that we will use for a Timer control's name is `tmr`.

Timer Events

When you place a Timer control on a form, it responds to Tick events as the application is running. A Tick event is generated at regular time intervals. If the control has a Tick event handler, it is executed each time a Tick event occurs. Therefore, the code that you write in the Tick event handler executes at regular intervals.

To create a Tick event handler code template, double-click a Timer control that has been placed in the form's component tray.

Timer Control Properties

The Timer control has two important properties: Enabled and Interval. When the Enabled property is set to *True*, the Timer control responds to Tick events. When the Enabled property is set to *False*, the Timer control does not respond to Tick events (code in the control's Tick event handler does not execute).

The **Interval property** can be set to a value of 1 or greater. The value stored in the Interval property is the number of milliseconds that elapse between timer events. A millisecond is a thousandth of a second, so setting the Interval property to 1000 causes a timer event to occur every second.

In Tutorial 7, you examine an application that demonstrates a Timer control.

Tutorial 7:
The *Timer Demo*

Step 1: Open the *Timer Demo* project from the sample student programs folder named *Chap8\Timer Demo*. The application's form is shown in Figure 30. Notice that the Timer control appears as a stopwatch in the component tray.

Figure 30 *Timer Demo* form

Step 2: Run the application. The form shown in Figure 31 appears.

Figure 31 *Timer Demo* application running

Step 3: The number appearing under the *Seconds Counter* label is initially set to 0, but it increments every second. After a few seconds, click the *Stop Timer* button to halt the timer.

Step 4: When you click the *Stop Timer* button, the button's text changes to *Start Timer*. Click the button again to start the timer.

Step 5: After a few seconds, click the *Exit* button to end the application.

Step 6: With the *Designer* window open, select the Timer control.

Step 7: With the Timer control selected, look at the *Properties* window. The name of the control is `tmrSeconds`. Its Enabled property is initially set to *True*, and its Interval property is set to *1000*.

Step 8: Open the *Code* window and notice that a class-level variable named `intSeconds` is declared.

Step 9: Look at the `tmrSeconds_Tick` event handler. The code is as follows:

```
Private Sub tmrSeconds_Tick(...) Handles tmrSeconds.Tick
    ' Update the seconds display by one second.
    intSeconds += 1
    lblCounter.Text = intSeconds.ToString()
End Sub
```

Each time the `tmrSeconds_Tick` event handler executes, it adds 1 to `intSeconds` and then copies its value to the `lblCounter` label. Because the Timer control's Interval property is set to *1000*, this event handler executes every second (unless the Timer control's Enabled property equals *False*).

Step 10: The button that stops and starts the timer is named `btnToggleTimer`. Look at the `btnToggleTimer_Click` event handler. The code is as follows:

```
Private Sub btnToggleTimer_Click(...) Handles btnToggleTimer.Click
    ' Toggle the timer.
  If tmrSeconds.Enabled = True Then
    tmrSeconds.Enabled = False
    btnToggleTimer.Text = "&Start Timer"
  Else
    tmrSeconds.Enabled = True
    btnToggleTimer.Text = "&Stop Timer"
  End If
End Sub
```

If `tmrSeconds.Enabled` equals *True*, the code sets it to *False* and changes the button's text to *&Start Timer*. Otherwise, it sets the property to *True* and changes the button's text to *&Stop Timer*.

In Tutorial 8 you will use a Timer control to create a game application.

Tutorial 8:
Creating the *Catch Me* game

In this tutorial you will create a game application that displays a button. Every second, the button will move to a new, random location on the application's form. The user wins the game when he or she clicks the button.

There are a few button and form properties that will prove useful:

- The current form is identified by the keyword Me.
- The width and height, in pixels, of a form or other control is controlled by its Width and Height properties.
- The position of a button within a form is controlled by its Top and Left properties. Vertical pixel coordinates start at 0 at the top of a form, and grow in a downward direction, as shown in Figure 32.

Figure 32 Pixel coordinates in a Visual Basic form

The *Catch Me* game application will have a Timer control with its Interval property set to 1000. As a result, it will generate a Tick event once every second. The Timer control's Tick event handler will generate two random numbers, and assign these random numbers to the Button control's Top and Left properties. As a result, the Button control will move to a random location on the form. The Button control's Click event handler will disable the Timer control (to stop the button from moving around on the form) and display a message indicating that the user won the game.

Step 1: Create a new Windows Forms Application project named *Catch Me*. Set up the application's form as shown in Figure 33. Name the Button control btnCatchMe, and center it vertically and horizontally in the form.

Figure 33 The Catch Me application's form

Step 2: Create a Timer control and name it tmrGameTimer. Set its Enabled property to *True* and its Interval property to 1000.

Step 3: The complete code for the application is shown at the end of this tutorial, with line numbers shown for reference. Double-click the tmrGameTimer control that you created in Step 2. This opens the *Code* window and creates a code template for the tmrGameTimer_Tick event handler. Complete the event handler by entering the code shown in lines 4 through 16.

Let's take a closer look at the code:

- Line 5 creates a Random object that we will use to generate random numbers.
- Line 8 declares two variables: intNewLeft and intNewTop. These variables will hold the random numbers for the button's new location.
- Line 11 generates a random integer and assigns it to intNewLeft. Notice that the argument passed to the rand.Next method is the expression Me.Width − btnCatchMe.Width. This will make sure that the random number is not a value that will place the Button control off the right edge of the form.
- Line 12 generates a random integer and assigns it to intNewTop. The expression Me.Height − btnCatchMe.Height will make sure that the random number is not a value that will place the Button control off the bottom edge of the form.
- Line 15 assigns intNewLeft to btnCatchMe.Left.
- Line 16 assigns intNewTop to btnCatchMe.Top.

Step 4: In the *Designer* window, double-click the btnCatchMe Button control. This opens the *Code* window and creates a code template for the btnCatchMe_Click event handler. Complete the event handler by entering the code shown in lines 20 through 24.

Let's take a closer look at the code:

- Line 21 sets the Timer control's Enabled property to *False*. This stops the Timer from generating Tick events.
- Line 24 displays a message box letting the user know he or she won.

Step 5: Save the project and run the application. After you've gotten good at the game, you can make it more challenging by changing the Timer control's Interval property to a lower value. This will decrease the amount of time between button moves.

```
1 Public Class Form1
2
3   Private Sub tmrGameTimer_Tick(...) Handles tmrGameTimer.Tick
4       ' Create a Random object.
5       Dim rand As New Random
6
7       ' Variables to hold XY coordinates
8       Dim intNewLeft, intNewTop As Integer
9
10      ' Get random XY coordinates.
11      intNewLeft = rand.Next(Me.Width - btnCatchMe.Width)
12      intNewTop = rand.Next(Me.Height - btnCatchMe.Height)
13
14      ' Move the button to the new location.
15      btnCatchMe.Left = intNewLeft
16      btnCatchMe.Top = intNewTop
17   End Sub
18
19   Private Sub btnCatchMe_Click(...) Handles btnCatchMe.Click
20       ' Disable the timer.
21       tmrGameTimer.Enabled = False
22
23       ' Display a message.
24       MessageBox.Show("You win!")
25   End Sub
26 End Class
```

6 Focus on GUI Design: Anchoring and Docking Controls

CONCEPT: Controls have two properties, Anchor and Dock, which allow you to control the control's position on the form when the form is resized at runtime.

The Anchor Property

By default, when a user resizes a form at runtime, the positions of controls on the form do not change with respect to the top and left edges of the form. For example, in Figure 34, the image on the left shows the form before the user resizes it and the image on the right shows the form after the user resizes it.

Figure 34 A form before and after the user resizes it

Before resizing

After resizing

When the user resizes the form, the positions of the list box and buttons do not change. Controls have an **Anchor property**, which allows you to anchor the control to one or more edges of a form. When a control is anchored to a form's edge, the distance between the control's edge and the form's edge remains constant when the form is resized at runtime.

When you click the Anchor property in the *Properties* window, the pop-up window shown in Figure 35 appears. Notice that the top and left bars are selected, indicating that the con-

Figure 35 Anchor property selected

trol is anchored to the top and left edges of the form. This is the Anchor property's default setting. To change the Anchor property's setting, select the bars that correspond to the edges of the form you wish to anchor the control to. For example, Figure 36 shows how the Anchor property appears when the control is anchored to the bottom and right edges.

Figure 36 Anchor property set to the bottom and right edges

Figure 37 shows a form before and after it is resized. This time, the button controls are anchored to the bottom and right edges of the form and the list box is anchored to the top and left edges.

It is possible to anchor a control to opposing sides, such as the top and the bottom, or the left and the right. This approach causes the control to be resized when the form is resized. For example, look at Figure 38. The PictureBox control is anchored to all four edges of the form, and its SizeMode property is set to *StretchImage*. When the form is resized, the PictureBox control is resized.

Figure 37 Buttons anchored to the bottom and right edges of the form

Figure 38 PictureBox control anchored to all four edges of the form

The Dock Property

When a control is docked, it is positioned directly against one of the edges of a form. Additionally, the length or width of a docked control is changed to match the length or width of the form's edge. For example, the form in Figure 39 has four docked buttons. A button is docked to each of the form's edges.

Figure 39 Form with docked buttons

Buttons are automatically sized to fill up the edge to which they are docked. Use the **Dock property** to dock a control against a form's edge. In the *Properties* window, the pop-up window shown in Figure 40 appears. The figure illustrates how each button in the pop-up window affects the control. The square button in the center causes the control to fill the entire form.

Figure 40 Dock property selected

Checkpoint

21 Suppose a form has check box controls named `chkFreePizza` and `chkFreeCola`, and a radio button control named `radLifeTimeMember`. Write code that enables the check boxes if the radio button is selected.

22 If you want a Timer control to execute its Tick event handler every half second, what value do you store in its Interval property?

23 What is the purpose of the Anchor property?

24 What is the purpose of the Dock property?

7 ## Focus on Problem Solving: Building the *Demetris Leadership Center* Application

CONCEPT: In this section you build an application that uses data stored in parallel arrays.

The Demetris Leadership Center (DLC) publishes the books, videos, and CDs listed in Table 1.

Table 1 Demetris Leadership Center products

Product Title	Product Description	Product Number	Unit Price
Six Steps to Leadership	Book	914	$12.95
Six Steps to Leadership	CD	915	$14.95
The Road to Excellence	Video	916	$18.95
Seven Lessons of Quality	Book	917	$16.95
Seven Lessons of Quality	CD	918	$21.95

Suppose the vice president of sales has asked you to write a sales reporting program that does the following:

- Prompts the user for the units sold of each product
- Displays a sales report showing detailed sales data for each product and the total revenue from all products sold

The Application's Form

Figure 41 shows a sketch of the application's form with its controls labeled.

Table 2 lists each of the form's controls (excluding the menu controls) along with relevant property settings.

Figure 41 Sketch of the application's form

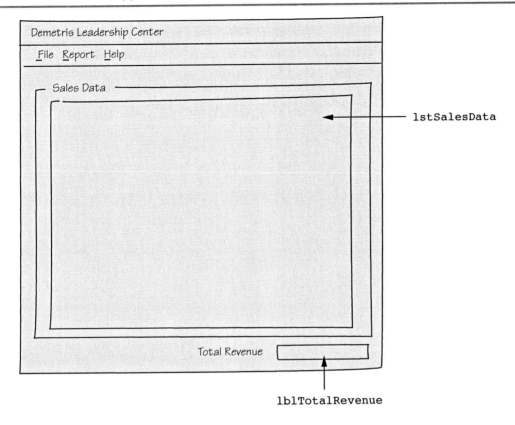

Table 2 Controls and property settings

Control Type	Control Name	Property	Property Value
Form	Form1 (default)	Text:	*Demetris Leadership Center*
GroupBox	(Default)	Text:	*Sales Data*
Label	(Default)	Text:	*Total Revenue*
Label	lblTotalRevenue	Text: AutoSize BorderStyle:	*False* *Fixed3D*
ListBox	lstSalesData	AutoSize	*False*
MenuStrip	(Default)		See Table 3 for details

Figure 42 shows a sketch of the menu system on the application's form.

Figure 42 Menu system

File	Report		Help
Exit Ctrl+Q	Enter Sales Data Display Sales Report	Ctrl+E Ctrl+D	About

Table 3 lists the menu item object names, text, and shortcut keys.

Table 3 Menu item names, text properties, and shortcut keys

Menu Item Name	Text	Shortcut Key
mnuFile	&File	
mnuFileExit	E&xit	Ctrl + Q
mnuReport	&Report	
mnuReportData	&Enter Sales Data	Ctrl + E
mnuReportDisplay	&Display Sales Report	Ctrl + D
mnuHelp	&Help	
mnuHelpAbout	&About	

Table 4 describes the form's class-level declarations.

Table 4 Class-level declarations

Name	Description
IntMAX_SUBSCRIPT	A constant, set to 8, holding the upper subscript of the class-level arrays, and the upper limit of counters used in loops that process information in the arrays
strProdNames	An array of strings; this array holds the names of the DLC products
strDesc	An array of strings; this array holds the descriptions of the DLC products
intProdNums	An array of integers; this array holds the product numbers of the DLC products
decPrices	An array of Decimal variables; this array holds the prices of the DLC products
intUnitsSold	An array of integers; this array holds the number of units sold for each of the DLC products

The five arrays are parallel arrays, meaning that the same subscript can be used to access data relating to the same item. Table 5 lists and describes the methods in the form file.

Table 5 Methods

Method	Description
InitArrays	Procedure; assigns the names, descriptions, product numbers, and unit prices of the DLC products to the class-level arrays
mnuFileExit_Click	Ends the application
mnuReportData_Click	Prompts the user for sales data
mnuReportDisplay_Click	Calculates and displays the revenue for each product and the total revenue
mnuHelpAbout_Click	Displays an *About* box
Form1_Load	Calls the InitArrays procedure

In Tutorial 9, you build the *Demetris Leadership Center Sales Reporting* application.

Tutorial 9:

Building the *Demetris Leadership Center Sales Reporting* application

Step 1: Create a new Windows Forms Application project named *Demetris Sales*.

Step 2: Set up the form as shown in Figure 43.

Figure 43 The application's main form

Refer to Table 2 for the control names and their property settings, and to Figure 41 for the locations of the controls in the control arrays. Refer to Figure 42 for the menu layout and to Table 3 for the menu item properties. Be sure to select `frmMain` as the startup object.

Step 3: The following shows the code for the application. Use this as a reference as you complete the application. (Don't type the line numbers. They are shown for reference.)

```
1 Public Class Form1
2     ' This application displays a sales report for the Demetris
3     ' Leadership Center.
4
5     ' Class-level declarations
6     Const intMAX_SUBSCRIPT As Integer = 4        ' Upper subscript
7     Dim strProdNames(intMAX_SUBSCRIPT) As String  ' Product names
8     Dim strDesc(intMAX_SUBSCRIPT) As String       ' Descriptions
9     Dim intProdNums(intMAX_SUBSCRIPT) As Integer ' Product numbers
10    Dim decPrices(intMAX_SUBSCRIPT) As Decimal    ' Unit prices
11    Dim intUnitsSold(intMAX_SUBSCRIPT) As Integer ' Units sold
12
13    Private Sub Form1_Load(...) Handles MyBase.Load
14        ' Initialize the arrays with product data.
15        InitArrays()
16    End Sub
17
```

```
18      Private Sub InitArrays()
19          ' Initialize the arrays.
20          ' First product
21          strProdNames(0) = "Six Steps to Leadership"
22          strDesc(0) = "Book"
23          intProdNums(0) = 914
24          decPrices(0) = 12.95D
25
26          ' Second product
27          strProdNames(1) = "Six Steps to Leadership"
28          strDesc(1) = "CD"
29          intProdNums(1) = 915
30          decPrices(1) = 14.95D
31
32          ' Third product
33          strProdNames(2) = "The Road to Excellence"
34          strDesc(2) = "Video"
35          intProdNums(2) = 916
36          decPrices(2) = 18.95D
37
38          ' Fourth product
39          strProdNames(3) = "Seven Lessons of Quality"
40          strDesc(3) = "Book"
41          intProdNums(3) = 917
42          decPrices(3) = 16.95D
43
44          ' Fifth product
45          strProdNames(4) = "Seven Lessons of Quality"
46          strDesc(4) = "CD"
47          intProdNums(4) = 918
48          decPrices(4) = 21.95D
49      End Sub
50
51      Private Sub mnuFileExit_Click(...) Handles mnuFileExit.Click
52          ' Close the form.
53          Me.Close()
54      End Sub
55
56      Private Sub mnuReportData_Click(...) Handles mnuReportData.Click
57          Dim intCount As Integer = 0 ' Loop counter
58
59          Do While intCount <= intMAX_SUBSCRIPT
60              Try
61                  ' Get the units sold for a product.
62                  intUnitsSold(intCount) = CInt(
63                      InputBox("Enter units sold of product number " &
64                              intProdNums(intCount)))
65
66                  ' Increment intCount.
67                  intCount += 1
68              Catch
69                  ' Error message for invalid input.
70                  MessageBox.Show("Enter a valid integer.")
71              End Try
72          Loop
73      End Sub
74
```

```
75      Private Sub mnuReportDisplay_Click(...) Handles mnuReportDisplay.Click
76            ' Calculates and displays the revenue for each
77            ' product and the total revenue.
78            Dim intCount As Integer
79            Dim decRevenue As Decimal
80            Dim decTotalRevenue As Decimal
81
82            ' Display the sales report header.
83            lstSalesData.Items.Add("SALES REPORT")
84            lstSalesData.Items.Add("-------------------")
85
86            ' Display sales data for each product.
87            For intCount = 0 To intMAX_SUBSCRIPT
88
89                ' Calculate product revenue.
90                decRevenue = intUnitsSold(intCount) * decPrices(intCount)
91
92                ' Display the product data.
93                lstSalesData.Items.Add("Product Number: " &
94                                        intProdNums(intCount))
95                lstSalesData.Items.Add("Name: " &
96                                        strProdNames(intCount))
97                lstSalesData.Items.Add("Description: " &
98                                        strDesc(intCount))
99                lstSalesData.Items.Add("Unit Price: " &
100                                        decPrices(intCount).ToString("c"))
101                lstSalesData.Items.Add("Units Sold: " &
102                                        intUnitsSold(intCount).ToString())
103                lstSalesData.Items.Add("Product Revenue: " &
104                                        decRevenue.ToString("c"))
105                lstSalesData.Items.Add("")
106
107                ' Accumulate revenue.
108                decTotalRevenue = decTotalRevenue + decRevenue
109            Next
110
111            ' Display total revenue.
112            lblTotalRevenue.Text = decTotalRevenue.ToString("c")
113      End Sub
114
115      Private Sub mnuHelpAbout_Click(...) Handles mnuHelpAbout.Click
116            ' Display an About box.
117            MessageBox.Show("Displays a sales report for DLC.", "About")
118      End Sub
119 End Class
```

Step 4:   Save the project.

Step 5:   Run the application. On the application's form, click the *Report* menu, and then click *Enter Sales Data*. You will be prompted with input boxes to enter the units sold for each of the DLC products. Enter the following units' sold values:

Product number 914: **140**
Product number 915: **85**
Product number 916: **129**
Product number 917: **67**
Product number 918: **94**

Step 6: Click the *Report* menu, and then click *Display Sales Report*. Your form should now appear similar to the one shown in Figure 44. Scroll through the sales data displayed in the list box.

Figure 44 Sales report displayed

Step 7: Exit the application.

Summary

1 Arrays

- An array is a like group of variables with a single name. The variables within an array are called elements and are of the same data type.
- Individual variables in an array are accessed through a subscript, which is a number that pinpoints a specific element within an array. Subscript numbering begins at zero. When you declare an array you can specify the upper subscript.
- You can implicitly size an array by omitting the upper subscript in the declaration statement and providing an initialization list. An array initialization list is a set of numbers enclosed in a set of braces, with the numbers separated by commas.
- Array elements are processed in the same way as regular variables, but when working with array elements, you must provide a subscript.
- You can store a subscript number in a variable and then use the variable as a subscript. You can use a loop to cycle through an entire array, performing the same operation on each element.
- Visual Basic performs array bounds checking at runtime; it does not allow a statement to use a subscript outside the range of subscripts for an array.
- The For Each statement is a special loop designed specifically to access values from arrays and array-like structures.

2 More about Array Processing

- Arrays have a Length property that holds the number of elements in the array.
- To sum the numbers stored in an array, use a loop with an accumulator variable that adds all the elements. To average the numbers stored in an array, first sum all the values, and then divide the sum by the number of elements.
- To copy the values in one array to another, use a loop to copy the individual elements.
- You can create a parallel relationship between list boxes, combo boxes, and arrays.
- The sequential search algorithm uses a loop to examine the elements in an array. It compares each element with the value being searched for, and stops when the value is found or the end of the array is encountered. If the value being searched for is not in the array, the algorithm will unsuccessfully search to the end of the array.
- The Array.Sort method sorts the elements of an array in ascending order, which means the lowest value is stored in the first element and the highest value is stored in the last element.
- You can change the number of elements in an array at runtime with the ReDim statement.

3 Procedures and Functions That Work with Arrays

- Procedures and functions may be written to accept arrays as arguments. Functions may also be written to return arrays.

4 Multidimensional Arrays

- A single-dimensional array has one subscript, and is useful for storing and working with a single set of data. Two-dimensional arrays can hold multiple sets of values. Think of a two-dimensional array as having rows and columns of elements.
- To declare a two-dimensional array, two sets of upper subscripts are required: the first one for the rows and the second one for the columns. A two-dimensional array may be implicitly sized by omitting the upper subscripts from the declaration and providing an initialization list.

- When data in a two-dimensional array is processed, each element has two subscripts: one for its row and one for its column. Nested loops can be used to sum the rows or columns of a two-dimensional numeric array.
- The For Each loop can be used to sum all the values in a numeric two-dimensional array.
- Visual Basic allows arrays of up to 32 dimensions.

5 Focus on GUI Design: The Enabled Property and the Timer Control

- When a control's Enabled property is set to *False*, it is considered disabled, which means it cannot receive the focus, cannot respond to events generated by the user, and appears dimmed or grayed out on the form.
- The Timer control is invisible at runtime. At design time it appears in the component tray. The standard prefix for a Timer control's name is tmr.
- The Timer control responds to Tick events. When a Tick event occurs, the Tick event handler is executed.
- When the Timer control's Enabled property is set to *True*, the Timer control responds to Tick events. When the Enabled property is set to *False*, the Timer control does not respond to Tick events and the code in the Tick event handler does not execute.
- The Timer control's Interval property can be set to a positive nonzero value that is the number of milliseconds to elapse between Tick events.

6 Focus on GUI Design: Anchoring and Docking Controls

- When a control is anchored to a form's edge, the distance between the control's edge and the form's edge remains constant, even when the user resizes the form.
- When a control is docked, it is positioned directly against one of the edges of a form. Additionally, the length or width of a docked control is changed to match the length or width of the form's edge.

7 Focus on Problem Solving: Building the *Demetris Leadership Center* Application

- This section outlines the process of building the *Demetris Leadership Center* application, which processes data used in parallel arrays.

Key Terms

Anchor property
array
array bounds checking
ascending order
Dock property
elements
Enabled property
For Each loop

index
Interval property
one-dimensional array
parallel arrays
sequential search
subscript
Timer control
two-dimensional array

Review Questions and Exercises

Fill-in-the-Blank

1. You access the individual variables in an array through a(n) _____, which is a number that indentifies a specific element within an array.

2. The _____ loop is a special loop designed specifically to access values from arrays and array-like structures.

3. _____ arrays are two or more arrays that hold related data. The related elements in each array are accessed with a common subscript.

4. The _____ algorithm uses a loop to examine the elements in an array sequentially, starting with the first one.

5. The _____ statement resizes an array at runtime.

6. The _____ property holds the number of elements in an array.

7. Declaring a two-dimensional array requires two sets of _____.

8. When a control's _____ property is set to *False*, it is considered disabled.

9. The _____ property causes the distance between a control's edge and the form's edge to remain constant, even when the form is resized.

10. The _____ property causes a control to be positioned directly against one of the form's edges.

11. The _____ control allows an application to automatically execute code at regularly timed intervals.

12. The Timer control's _____ property specifies the number of milliseconds between timer events.

Multiple Choice

1. Which of the following describes the storage locations within an array?
   a. Boxes
   b. Elements
   c. Subvariables
   d. Intersections

2. Which of the following identifies a specific element within an array?
   a. Element specifier
   b. Determinator
   c. Locator
   d. Subscript

3. Which of the following is the lower subscript of an array?
   a. 1
   b. { }
   c. 0
   d. -1

4. When does array bounds checking occur?
   a. Runtime
   b. Design time
   c. Break time
   d. All of the above

5. Which of the following properties determines the number of elements in an array?
   a. Size
   b. Elements
   c. Length
   d. NumberElements

6. To access related data in a set of parallel arrays, how should you access the elements in the arrays?
   a. Using the same array name
   b. Using the same subscript
   c. Using the index −1
   d. Using the `GetParallelData` function

7. Which statement resizes the `intNumbers` array to 20 elements?
   a. `ReDim intNumbers(19)`
   b. `ReDim intNumbers(20)`
   c. `Resize intNumbers() To 19`
   d. `Resize intNumbers() To 20`

8. Which statement resizes the intNumbers array and does not erase the values already stored in the array?
   a. `ReDim intNumbers(99)`
   b. `ReDim Preserve intNumbers(99)`
   c. `Preserve intNumbers(99)`
   d. `ReSize Preserve intNumbers(99)`

9. Which of the following is an apt analogy for two-dimensional array elements?
   a. Feet and inches
   b. Books and pages
   c. Lines and statements
   d. Rows and columns

10. Which statement disables the control `lblResult`?
    a. `lblResult.Disabled = True`
    b. `Disable lblResult`
    c. `lblResult.Enabled = False`
    d. `lblResult.Dimmed = True`

11. The Timer control Interval property may be set to what type of value?
    a. 0 or greater
    b. A fractional number
    c. A negative number
    d. 1 or greater

12. Which of the following properties can you use to cause a control to fill an entire form?
    a. Fill
    b. Dock
    c. Anchor
    d. Stretch

True or False

Indicate whether the following statements are true or false.

1. T F: The upper subscript of an array must be a positive whole number.

2. T F: Numeric array elements are automatically initialized to −1.

3. T F: You may not use a named constant as a subscript in an array declaration.

4. T F: Visual Basic allows you to use a variable as a subscript when processing an array with a loop.

5. T F: You get an error message at design time when you write code that attempts to access an element outside the bounds of an array.

6. T F: The value stored in an array's Length property is the same as the array's upper subscript.

7. T F: You should use a loop to copy the values of one array to another array.

8. T F: Parallel arrays are useful when working with related data of unlike types.

9. T F: The ReDim statement may be used with any array.

10. T F: The value stored in the Timer control's Interval property specifies an interval in seconds.

11. T F: It is possible to anchor a control to a form's opposing edges.

12. T F: When a control is docked to a form's edge, the width or height of the control is adjusted to match the size of the form's edge.

Short Answer

1. Write code that declares a string array with three elements, and then stores your first, middle, and last names in the array's elements.

2. What values are displayed by the following code?

```
Const intMAX_SUBSCRIPT As Integer = 4
Dim intValues(intMAX_SUBSCRIPT) As Integer
Dim intCount As Integer

For intCount = 0 To intMAX_SUBSCRIPT
    intValues(intCount) = intCount + 1
Next

For intCount = 0 To intMAX_SUBSCRIPT
    MessageBox.Show(intValues(intCount).ToString())
Next
```

3. The following code segment declares a 20-element array of integers called intFish. When completed, the code should ask how many fish were caught by fisherman 1 through 20 and store this information in the array. Complete the program.

```
Sub FishCatchArray()
    Const intMAX_SUBSCRIPT As Integer = 19
    Dim intFish(intMAX_SUBSCRIPT) As Integer

    ' You must finish this procedure. It should ask how
    ' many fish were caught by fisherman 1 - 20 and
    ' store this information in the intFish array.
End Sub
```

4. What output is generated by the following code segment? (You may need to use a calculator.)

```
Const decRATE As Decimal = 0.1D
Const intMAX_SUBSCRIPT As Integer = 4
Dim decBalance(intMAX_SUBSCRIPT) As Decimal
Dim decDue As Decimal
Dim intCount As Integer

decBalance(0) = 100
decBalance(1) = 250
decBalance(2) = 325
decBalance(3) = 500
decBalance(4) = 1100
```

```
For intCount = 0 To intMAX_SUBSCRIPT
    decDue = decBalance(intCount) * decRATE
    MessageBox.Show(decDue.ToString())
Next
```

5. Write a statement that assigns 145 to the first column of the first row of the array declared in the following statement:

```
Dim intNumberArray(9, 11) As Integer
```

6. Write a statement that assigns 18 to the last column of the last row of the array declared in Question 5.

7. Assuming that an application uses a Timer control named `tmrClock`, write a statement that stops the timer from responding to timer events.

What Do You Think?

1. The following code totals the values in two Integer arrays: `intNumberArray1` and `intNumberArray2`. Both arrays have 25 elements. Will the code print the correct sum of values for both arrays? Why or why not?

```
Dim intTotal As Integer = 0      ' Accumulator
For intCount = 0 To 24
    intTotal += intNumberArray1(intCount)
Next
MessageBox.Show("Total for intNumberArray1 is " &
                intTotal.ToString())
For intCount = 0 To 24
    intTotal += intNumberArray2(intCount)
Next
MessageBox.Show("Total for intNumberArray2 is " &
                intTotal.ToString())
```

2. How many elements are in the following array?

```
Dim dblSales (5, 3) As Double
```

3. How many elements are in the following array?

```
Dim dblValues (3, 3) As Double
```

4. Suppose an application uses a Timer control named `tmrControl`. Write a programming statement that sets the time between timer events at three seconds.

Find the Error

1. ```
Dim intReadings(-99) As Integer
```

2. ```
Dim intTable(10) As Integer ' Stores 11 values
Dim intIndex As Integer
Dim intMaxNum As Integer = 11
For intIndex = 0 To intMaxNum
    intTable(intIndex) = CInt(InputBox("Enter the next value:"))
Next
```

3. ```
Dim intValues(3) = { 2, 4, 6 }
```

4. ```
' tmrTimer is a Timer control
tmrTimer.Interval = 0
```

Algorithm Workbench

1. Assume `strNames` is a string array with 20 elements. Write a `For Each` loop that prints each element of the array.

2. Suppose you need to store information about 12 countries. Declare two arrays that may be used in parallel to store the names of the countries and their populations.

3. Write a loop that uses the arrays you declared in Question 2 to print each country's name and population.

4. The arrays `intNumberArray1` and `intNumberArray2` have 100 elements. Write code that copies the values in `intNumberArray1` to `intNumberArray2`.

5. Write the code for a sequential search that determines whether the value –1 is stored in the array named `intValues`. The code should print a message indicating whether the value was found.

6. Suppose an application stores the following data about employees:
   - Name, stored in a list box named `lstNames`
   - Employee number, stored in an array of strings named `strEmpNums`

   There is a parallel relationship between the list box and the array. Assume that the user has selected an employee's name from the list box. Write code that displays (in a message box) the employee number for the selected employee.

7. Declare a two-dimensional array of integers named `intGrades`. It should have 30 rows and 10 columns.

8. Assume that `dblValues` is a two-dimensional array of Doubles with 10 rows and 20 columns. Write a For Each statement that sums all the elements in the array and stores the sum in the variable `dblTotal`.

9. Write nested code using For...Next loops that performs the same operation requested in Question 8.

10. Suppose an application uses a two-dimensional array named `intDays`. Write code that sums each row in the array and displays the result.

    ```
    Dim intDays(29, 5) As Integer
    ```

11. Write code that sums each column in the array in Question 10.

12. Write code that uses a For Each statement to sum all of the elements in the array in Question 10.

Programming Challenges

1. **Largest/Smallest Array Values**

   Create an application that lets the user enter 10 values into an array. The application should display the largest and smallest values stored in the array. Figure 45 shows an example of the application's form after all 10 values have been entered, with the largest and smallest values displayed.

Figure 45 *Largest/Smallest Array Values* form

2. **Rainfall Statistics**

Create an application that lets the user enter the rainfall for each of 12 months into an array. The application should calculate and display the following statistics: total rainfall for the year, the average monthly rainfall, and the months with the highest and lowest amounts of rainfall. Figure 46 shows an example of the application's form after each month's rainfall amount has been entered and the statistics have been displayed.

Figure 46 *Rainfall Statistics* form

3. **Random Sentences**

Create an application that produces random sentences as output. Create five arrays of strings, one each for nouns, adjectives, verbs, prepositions, and articles. Each array should hold several words of that part of speech. For example, the strArticles array could hold the strings "the" and "a"; the strNouns array could hold "Martian", "baby", "skunk", "computer", and "mosquito"; the strPrepositions array could hold "around", "through", "under", "over", and "by"; and so on.

The application should generate sentences by randomly choosing eight words (randomly generating eight array indices) from these arrays, always constructing sentences by using the parts of speech in the following order: article, adjective, noun, verb, preposition, article, adjective, noun.

For example, a sentence might be "The shiny computer flew over a huge mosquito." In this example, "The" and "a" were randomly chosen from the articles array, "shiny" and "huge" from the adjectives array, "computer" and "mosquito" from the nouns array, "flew" from the verbs array, and "over" from the prepositions array. Be careful to produce sentences that have the proper spacing, uppercase and lowercase letters, and a period at the end.

Design your form with buttons to display the next sentence, to clear all sentences currently displayed, and to close the application. Display your sentences, one per line, in a list box. Allow enough room to display at least 10 sentences. Figure 47 shows an example of the form using a list box. The figure shows the form with three sentences generated.

Figure 47 *Random Sentences* form

4. **Driver's License Exam**

The local Registry of Motor Vehicles office has asked you to create an application that grades the written portion of the driver's license exam. The exam has 20 multiple choice questions. Here are the correct answers to the questions:

1.	B	6.	A	11.	B	16.	C
2.	D	7.	B	12.	C	17.	C
3.	A	8.	A	13.	D	18.	B
4.	A	9.	C	14.	A	19.	D
5.	C	10.	D	15.	D	20.	A

Your application should store the correct answers in an array. A form, such as the one shown in Figure 48, should allow the user to enter answers for each question.

When the user clicks the *Score Exam* button, the application should display another form showing whether each question was answered correctly or incorrectly, and whether the student passed or failed the exam. A student must correctly answer 15 of the 20 questions to pass the exam.

Input validation: Only accept the letters A, B, C, or D as answers.

Figure 48 *Driver's License Exam* form

5. **PIN Verifier**

The National Commerce Bank has hired you to create an application that verifies a customer personal identification number (PIN). A valid PIN is a seven-digit number that meets the following specifications:

Digit 1: Must be in the range of 7 through 9
Digit 2: Must be in the range of 5 through 7

Digit 3: Must be in the range of 0 through 4
Digit 4: Must be in the range of 0 through 9
Digit 5: Must be in the range of 6 through 9
Digit 6: Must be in the range of 3 through 6
Digit 7: Must be in the range of 4 through 8

Notice that each digit must fall into a range of numbers. Your application should have two arrays: `intMinimum` and `intMaximum`. The `intMinimum` array should hold the minimum values for each digit, and the `intMaximum` array should hold the maximum values for each digit.

The application should allow the user to enter seven digits on a form similar to the one shown in Figure 49. When the *Verify* button is clicked, the application should use the `intMinimum` and `intMaximum` arrays to verify that the numbers fall into acceptable ranges.

Figure 49 *PIN Verifier* form

Design Your Own Forms

6. **Employee Directory**

    Create an employee directory application that shows employee names in a list box on the main form. When the user selects a name from the list box, the application should display the employee's ID number, department name, and telephone number on a separate form.

    The application should store all employee ID numbers, department names, and telephone numbers in separate arrays. The arrays and the list box should have a parallel relationship.

7. **Grade Book**

    Suppose a teacher has five students who have taken four tests. The teacher uses the following grading scale to assign a letter grade to a student, based on the average of his or her four test scores.

Test Score	Letter Grade
90–100	A
80–89	B
70–79	C
60–69	D
0–59	F

    Create an application that uses an array of strings to hold the five student names, an array of five strings to hold each student's letter grades, and five arrays of four single precision numbers to hold each student's set of test scores.

Equip the application with a menu or a set of buttons that allows the application to perform the following:

- Display a form that allows the user to enter or change the student names and their test scores.
- Calculate and display each student's average test score and a letter grade based on the average.

Input validation: Do not accept test scores less than zero or greater than 100.

8. **Grade Book Modification**

Modify the *Grade Book* application in Programming Challenge 7 so it drops each student's lowest score when determining the test score averages and letter grades.

9. **Charge Account Validation**

Create an application that allows the user to enter a charge account number. The application should determine whether the number is valid by comparing it to the numbers in the following list:

5658845	4520125	7895122	8777541	8451277	1302850
8080152	4562555	5552012	5050552	7825877	1250255
1005231	6545231	3852085	7576651	7881200	4581002

The list of numbers should be stored in an array. A sequential search should be used to locate the number entered by the user. If the user enters a number that is in the array, the program should display a message indicating the number is valid. If the user enters a number that is not in the array, the program should display a message indicating the number is invalid.

VideoNote
The Lottery
Application

10. **Lottery Application**

Create an application that simulates a lottery. The application should have an array of five integers and should generate a random number in the range 0 through 9 for each element in the array. The array is permitted to contain duplicate values. The user should then enter five digits, which the application will compare to the numbers in the array. A form should be displayed showing how many of the digits matched. If all of the digits match, display a form proclaiming the user as a grand prize winner.

11. **Soccer Team Score Application**

Suppose a soccer team needs an application to record the number of points scored by its players during a game. Create an application that asks how many players the team has, and then asks for the names of each player. The program should declare an array of strings large enough to hold the player names, and declare an array of integers large enough to hold the number of points scored by each player. The application should have a menu system or buttons that perform the following:

- Display a form allowing the user to enter the players' names.
- Display a form that can be used during a game to record the points scored by each player.
- Display the total points scored by each player and by the team.

Input validation: Do not accept negative numbers as points.

12. **Number Analysis Program**

    Create an application that lets the user enter 10 numbers. The program should store the numbers in an array and then display the following data:
    - The lowest number in the array
    - The highest number in the array
    - The total of the numbers in the array
    - The average of the numbers in the array

13. **Phone Number Lookup**

    Create an application that has two parallel arrays: a `String` array named `strPeople` that is initialized with the names of seven of your friends and a `String` array named `strPhoneNumbers` that is initialized with your friends' phone numbers. The program should allow the user to enter a person's name (or part of a person's name). It should then search for that person in the `strPeople` array. If the person is found, it should get that person's phone number from the `strPhoneNumbers` array and display it. If the person is not found in the `strPeople` array, the program should display a message indicating this.

14. **Rock, Paper, Scissors Game**

    Create an application that lets the user play the game of "Rock, Paper, Scissors" against the computer. The program should work as follows:

    (1) When the program begins, a random number in the range of 1 through 3 is generated. If the number is 1, then the computer has chosen rock. If the number is 2, then the computer has chosen paper. If the number is 3, then the computer has chosen scissors. (Don't display the computer's choice yet.)

    (2) The user clicks a button to select his or her choice of rock, paper, or scissors.

    (3) The computer's choice is displayed.

    (4) A winner is selected according to the following rules:
    - If one player chooses rock and the other player chooses scissors, then rock wins. (Rock smashes scissors.)
    - If one player chooses scissors and the other player chooses paper, then scissors wins. (Scissors cuts paper.)
    - If one player chooses paper and the other player chooses rock, then paper wins. (Paper covers rock.)
    - If both players make the same choice, the game must be played again to determine the winner.

Answers to Checkpoints

1 a. `Dim intEmpNums(99) As Integer`
   b. `Dim decPayRate(23) As Decimal`
   c. `Dim intMiles() As Integer = { 10, 20, 30, 40, 50 }`
   d. `Dim strNames(12) As String`
   e. `Dim strDivisions() As String = {"North", "South", "East", "West"}`

2 The upper boundary (4) cannot appear inside the parentheses when an initialization list is provided.

3 a. 101
  b. 3
  c. 1

4 The runtime system throws an exception if a subscript is outside the range of subscripts for an array.

5
```
For intCount = 0 To intMAX_SUBSCRIPT
   MessageBox.Show(intPoints(intCount).ToString())
Next
```

6
```
Dim intNumber As Integer
For Each intNumber In intPoints
   MessageBox.Show(intNumber.ToString())
Next
```

7 a. 10.00
b. 25.00
c. 32.50
d. 50.00

8
```
intTotal = 0              ' Initialize accumulator.
For intCount = 0 To 99
   intTotal += intValues(intCount)
Next
```

9
```
intTotal = 0              ' Initialize accumulator.
For intCount= 0 To (points.Length - 1)
   intTotal += intPoints(intCount)
Next
dblAverage = intTotal / points.Length
```

10
```
Array.Sort(strSerialNumbers)
```

11
```
0 18 0
1 4 4
2 27 54
3 52 156
4 100 400
```

12
```
ReDim Preserve decSales(49)
```

13 (Code example)
```
blnFound = False
intCount = 0
Do While Not blnFound And intCount < intValidNumbers.Length
   If intValidNumbers (intCount) = 247 Then
     blnFound = True
     intPosition = intCount
   End If
   intCount+= 1
Loop
'Was 100 found in the array?
If blnFound Then
   MessageBox.Show("The value was found at position " &
                   intPosition.ToString())
Else
   MessageBox.Show("The value was not found.")
End If
```

14
```
Dim intGrades(29, 9) As Integer
```

15 24 elements (6 rows by 4 columns)

16
```
decSales(0, 0) = 56893.12
```

17
```
MessageBox.Show(decSales(5, 3).ToString())
```

18 ```
Dim intSettings(2, 4) As Integer
```

19 Four rows and five columns

20 ```
Dim strMovies(49, 9, 24) As String
```

21 ```
If radLifeTimeMember.Checked = True Then
   chkFreePizza.Enabled = True
   chkFreeCola.Enabled = True
End If
```

22 500   .

23 It allows you to anchor the control to one or more edges of a form. When a control is anchored to a form's edge, the distance between the control's edge and the form's edge will remain constant, even when the user resizes the form.

24 It allows you to dock a control. When a control is docked, it is positioned directly against one of the edges of a form. Additionally, the length or width of a docked control is changed to match the length or width of the form's edge.
```

Files, Printing, and Structures

TOPICS

1	Using Files	3	The PrintDocument Control
2	The OpenFileDialog, SaveFileDialog, FontDialog, and ColorDialog Controls	4	Structures

This chapter shows you how to save data to sequential text files and then read the data back into an application. You will learn how to use the OpenFileDialog, SaveFileDialog, ColorDialog, and FontDialog controls. You can use these to equip your application with standard Windows dialog boxes for opening and saving files and for selecting colors and fonts. We discuss the PrintDocument control and how to print reports from your application. Finally, you learn how to package units of data together into structures.

1 Using Files

CONCEPT: A file is a collection of data stored on a computer disk. Data can be saved in a file and later reused.

Applications you have created so far require you to re-enter data each time the program runs because the data kept in controls and variables is stored in RAM, and disappears once the program stops running. To retain data between the times it runs, an application must have a way of saving the data.

Data is saved in a **file**, on a computer disk. Once saved, the data remains after the program stops running, and can be retrieved and used at a later time. In this chapter, you write applications that create files to save data. These applications do not rely on the user to re-enter data each time the application runs.

From Chapter 9 of *Starting Out with Visual Basic*® *2010*, Fifth Edition, Tony Gaddis, Kip Irvine.

The Process of Using a File

The following steps must be taken when a file is used by an application:

1. The file must be opened. If the file does not yet exist, opening it means creating it.
2. Data is written to the file or read from the file.
3. When the application is finished using the file, the file is closed.

When a Visual Basic application is actively working with data, the data is located in memory, usually in variables and/or control properties. When data is written to a file, it is copied from the variables or control properties, as shown in Figure 1.

Figure 1 Writing data to a file

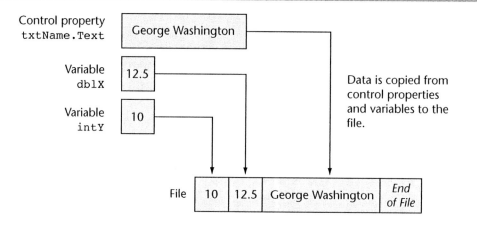

When data is read from a file, it is copied from the file into variables and/or control properties, as shown in Figure 2.

Figure 2 Reading data from a file

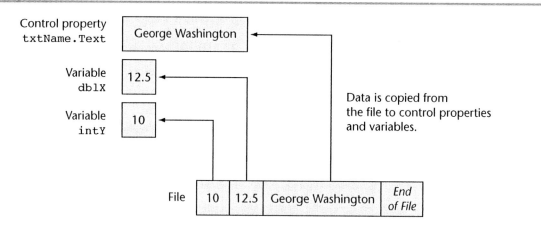

The terms input file and output file are often used. An **input file** is a file from which a program reads data. It is called an input file because the data stored in it serves as input to the program. An **output file** is a file into which a program writes data. It is called an output file because the program stores output in the file.

There are two types of files: text and binary. A **text file** contains plain text and may be opened in a text editor such as Windows Notepad. Data in **binary files** is stored as pure binary data; the content cannot usually be viewed with a text editor.

There are also two methods of accessing files: sequential-access and random-access. A **sequential-access file** is like a stream of data that must be read from its beginning to its end. To read an item stored in the middle or at the end of a sequential-access file, an application must read all the items in the file before it.

Data in a **random-access file** may be accessed in any order. An application can jump to any item in a random-access file without first reading the preceding items. The difference between sequential-access and random-access files is like the difference between a cassette tape and a CD. When listening to a CD, you don't need to listen to or fast-forward over unwanted songs. You simply jump to the track that you want to listen to.

Because most Visual Basic programmers prefer to use databases rather than random-access or binary files, we discuss only sequential-access text files in this chapter. Binary and random-access files are discussed in Appendix F, located on the Student Resources CD.

Writing to Files with `StreamWriter` Objects

VideoNote

Writing Data
to a File

There are two basic ways to open a text file so you can write data to it: You can create a new file, or you can open an existing file so data can be appended to it. The actual writing to the file is performed by a **StreamWriter** object. There are two required steps:

1. Declare a `StreamWriter` variable.
2. Call either the `File.CreateText` or `File.AppendText` method. If you want to create a new file, call `File.CreateText` and assign its return value to the `StreamWriter` variable. Or, to append to an existing text file, call `File.AppendText` and assign its return value to the `StreamWriter` variable.

Before using `StreamWriter` objects, you must insert the following `Imports` statement at the top of your form's code file. This will make the **StreamWriter** classes available to your program:

```
Imports System.IO
```

> **NOTE:** It is possible to omit the `Imports System.IO` statement, but then every reference to the `StreamWriter` class must use its fully qualified name, which is `System.IO.StreamWriter`.

Creating a Text File

First, we will show you how to create a new text file. Begin by declaring a `StreamWriter` variable, using the following general format:

```
Dim ObjectVar As StreamWriter
```

ObjectVar is the name of the object variable. You may use `Private` or `Public` in place of `Dim` if you are declaring the object variable at the class-level or module-level. Here's an example:

```
Dim phoneFile As StreamWriter
```

Next, call the **File.CreateText** method, passing it the name of a file. For example:

```
phoneFile = File.CreateText("phonelist.txt")
```

Notice how the return value from `File.CreateText` is assigned to the `StreamWriter` variable named `phoneFile`.

The filename that you pass to the `File.CreateText` method can optionally contain a complete path, such as *C:\data\vbfiles\phonelist.txt*. If you use only a filename with no path, Visual Basic assumes that the file will be created in the same location as the application's executable file, which by default is your project's *\bin\Debug* folder.

If the file cannot be created, the `File.CreateText` method will throw an exception. For example, an exception will occur if you specify a nonexistent path, or your application does not have the required permission to create a file in the specified location.

Opening an Existing File and Appending Data to It

If a text file already exists, you may want to add more data to the end of the file. This is called *appending* to the file. First, you declare a `StreamWriter` variable:

```
Dim phoneFile As StreamWriter
```

Then you call the **`File.AppendText`** method, passing it the name of an existing file. For example:

```
phoneFile = File.AppendText("phonelist.txt")
```

Any data written to the file will be written to the end of the file's existing contents.

If the file that you specify as an argument to the `File.AppendText` method does not exist, it will be created. If the file cannot be opened or created, the method will throw an exception. For example, an exception will occur if you specify a nonexistent path, or your application does not have the required permission to create a file in the specified location.

WARNING: It is possible to move an application's executable file to a location other than the project's *bin* directory. Doing so changes the default location where the files are created.

Writing Data to a File

The **`WriteLine`** method of the `StreamWriter` class writes a line of data to a file. The following is the general format of the method:

```
ObjectVar.WriteLine(Data)
```

ObjectVar is the name of a `StreamWriter` object variable. *Data* represents constants or variables whose contents will be written to the file. The `WriteLine` method writes the data to the file and then writes a newline character immediately after the data. A **newline character** is an invisible character that separates text by breaking it into another line when displayed on the screen.

NOTE: The newline character is actually stored as two characters: a carriage return (character code 13) and a linefeed character (character code 10).

To further understand how the `WriteLine` method works, let's look at an example. Assume that an application opens a file and writes three students' first names and their scores to the file with the following code:

```
Dim studentFile As StreamWriter

Try
    ' Open the file.
    studentFile = File.CreateText("StudentData.txt")

    ' Write data to the file.
    studentFile.WriteLine("Jim")
```

```
    studentFile.WriteLine(95)
    studentFile.WriteLine("Karen")
    studentFile.WriteLine(98)
    studentFile.WriteLine("Bob")
    studentFile.WriteLine(82)
  Catch
    MessageBox.Show("Error: The file cannot be created.")
  End try
```

You can visualize the data being written to the file in the following manner:

Jim<*newline*>95<*newline*>Karen<*newline*>98<*newline*>Bob<*newline*>82<*newline*>

The newline characters are represented here as <*newline*>. You do not actually see the newline characters, but when the file is opened in a text editor such as Notepad, its contents appear as shown in Figure 3. As you can see from the figure, each newline character causes the data that follows it to be displayed on a new line.

TIP: Each time the `WriteLine` method executes, it writes a separate line of text to the file.

In addition to separating the contents of a file into lines, the newline character also serves as a delimiter. A **delimiter** is an item that separates other items. When you write data to a file using `WriteLine`, newline characters are the delimiters. Later, you will see that data must be separated in order for it to be read from the file.

Figure 3 File contents displayed in Notepad

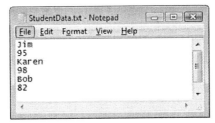

Writing a Blank Line to a File

The `WriteLine` method can write a blank line to a file by calling the method without an argument.

```
    textFile.WriteLine()
```

The `Write` Method

The `Write` method, a member of the `StreamWriter` class, writes an item of data to a file without writing a newline character. The general format is as follows:

```
    ObjectVar.Write(Data)
```

ObjectVar is the name of a `StreamWriter` object variable. *Data* represents the contents of a constant or variable that is to be written to the file. This method can be used to write data to a file without terminating the line with a newline character. For example, assume an application has a `StreamWriter` object variable named `outputFile`, as well as the following variables:

```
    Dim strName As String = "Jeffrey Smith"
    Dim intId As Integer = 47895
    Dim strPhone As String = "555-7864"
```

The contents of all three variables are written to a single line in the file:

```
outputFile.Write(strName)
outputFile.Write(" ")
outputFile.Write(intId)
outputFile.Write(" ")
outputFile.WriteLine(strPhone)
```

The first statement writes the `strName` variable to the file. The second statement writes a space character (`" "`), the third statement writes the `intId` variable, and the fourth statement writes another space. The last statement uses the `WriteLine` method to write the phone number, followed by a newline character. Here is a sample of the output:

```
Jeffrey Smith 47895 555-7864
```

Closing a File

The opposite of opening a file is closing it. The `StreamWriter` class has a method named `Close` that closes a file. The following is the method's general format:

```
ObjectVar.Close()
```

`ObjectVar` is a `StreamWriter` object variable. After the method executes, the file that was referenced by `ObjectVar` is closed. For example, `salesFile` is an object variable that references a `StreamWriter` object. The following statement closes the file associated with `salesFile`.

```
salesFile.Close()
```

To avoid losing data, your application should always close files after it is finished using them. Computers typically create one or more buffers (memory areas) when a file is opened. When an application writes data to a file, that data is first written to the **buffer**. When the buffer is filled, all data stored there is written to the file. This technique improves the system's performance because writing data to memory is faster than writing it to a disk. The **Close method** writes any unsaved information remaining in the file buffer and releases memory allocated by the `StreamWriter` object.

> **NOTE:** Once a file is closed, you must reopen it before performing any operations on it.

In Tutorial 1, you examine an application that writes data about three fictional persons to a file.

Tutorial 1:

Completing an application that writes data to a file

Step 1: Open the *File WriteLine* demo project from the student sample programs folder named *Chap9\File WriteLine Demo*. The student sample programs folder can be downloaded from www.microsoft.com/express/Downloads/. The application form is shown in Figure 4.

Step 2: Complete the code for the form's event handlers as shown in the following. (Don't type the line numbers. They are shown for reference.) Be sure to write the `Imports` statement shown in line 1.

```
1 Imports System.IO
2
3 Public Class Form1
4
```

Figure 4 *File WriteLine Demo* form

```
               btnCreateFile   btnExit

 5  Private Sub btnCreateFile_Click(...) Handles btnCreate File.Click
 6      ' Constant for the number of friends
 7      Const intNUM_FRIENDS As Integer = 3
 8
 9      ' Local variables
10      Dim strFilename As String       ' File name
11      Dim strFriend As String         ' Name of a friend
12      Dim strPhone As String          ' To hold a phone number
13      Dim intCount As Integer         ' Loop counter
14      Dim friendFile As StreamWriter  ' Object variable
15
16      ' Get the file name from the user.
17      strFilename = InputBox("Enter the filename.")
18
19      Try
20        ' Open the file.
21        friendFile = File.CreateText(strFilename)
22
23        ' Get the data and write it to the file.
24        For intCount = 1 To intNUM_FRIENDS
25          ' Get a friend's name.
26          strFriend = InputBox("Enter the name of friend " &
27                               "number " & intCount.ToString())
28
29          ' Get a friend's phone number.
30          strPhone = InputBox("Enter the that friend's " &
31                              "phone number.")
32
33          ' Write the data to the file.
34          friendFile.WriteLine(strFriend)
35          friendFile.WriteLine(strPhone)
36        Next
37
38        ' Close the file.
39        friendFile.Close()
40      Catch
41        ' Error message
42        MessageBox.Show("That file cannot be created.")
43      End Try
44  End Sub
45
46  Private Sub btnExit_Click(...) Handles btnExit.Click
47      ' Close the form.
48      Me.Close()
49  End Sub
50 End Class
```

Let's examine the `btnCreateFile_Click` event handler closer. Here is a summary of the declarations that appear in lines 7 through 14:

- Line 7: The `intNUM_FRIENDS` constant is set to 3. This is the number of friends for whom we will store data.
- Line 10: The `strFilename` variable will hold the path and filename of the file that the application will create.
- Line 11: The `strFriend` variable will hold the name of a friend.
- Line 12: The `strPhone` variable will hold a friend's phone number.
- Line 13: The `intCount` variable will be used as a loop counter.
- Line 14: The `friendFile` variable is an object variable that will be used to open the file and write data to it.

Line 17 uses an input box to prompt the user to enter a filename. The filename is assigned to the `strFilename` variable.

The `Try–Catch` statement that begins in line 19 will catch any exceptions that are thrown. Line 21 tries to create the file specified by the path and filename entered by the user. If the file cannot be created, an exception is thrown and the program jumps to the `Catch` clause in line 40. If the file is successfully created, the `For...Next` loop in line 24 begins to execute. As the loop is written, it will iterate three times, with the `intCount` variable taking on the values 1 through 3.

Inside the loop, the statement in lines 26 through 27 uses an input box to prompt the user for a friend's name. The name entered by the user is assigned to the `strFriend` variable. Then the statement in lines 30 through 31 uses an input box to prompt the user for that friend's phone number. The phone number entered by the user is assigned to the `strPhone` variable. Line 34 writes the friend's name to the file, and line 35 writes the phone number to the file. Then, the loop starts over.

When the loop is finished, line 39 closes the file.

Step 3: Save the project. Run the application and click the *Create File* button. When prompted to enter the filename, provide the path of a disk location that can be written to. For example, if you enter *C:\MyFriends.txt*, the application will create the file *MyFriends.txt* in the root directory of drive C. If you enter *C:\Temp\MyFriends.txt* the application will create the file *MyFriends.txt* in the *C:\Temp* folder. Enter a path and filename and make a note of it because you will use the same file later in this tutorial and again in Tutorial 2.

 NOTE: If you are working in a school computer lab, you may be restricted to saving files only at certain disk locations. Ask your instructor or lab manager for these locations.

Step 4: Enter the following names, ages, and addresses as you are prompted for this data. After you have entered the data for the third friend, the application returns to the main form. Click the *Exit* button.

	Name	Phone
Friend 1	Jim Weaver	555-1212
Friend 2	Mary Duncan	555-2323
Friend 3	Karen Warren	555-3434

Step 5: In Windows, locate the file that was created when you ran the application. Double-click the file's name to open it in the Notepad text editor. The contents of the file should appear as shown in Figure 5.

Figure 5 Contents of the file displayed in Notepad

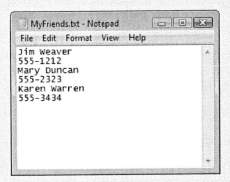

As you can see, each item is written to a separate line in the file because a new-line character separates each item.

Step 6: Close the *Notepad* window that displays the text file.

Appending a File

When we **append** a file, we write new data immediately following existing data in the file. If an existing file is opened with the `AppendText` method, data written to the file is appended to the file's existing data. If the file does not exist, it is created.

For example, assume the file *MyFriends.txt* exists and contains the following data, from Tutorial 1:

Jim Weaver
555-1212
Mary Duncan
555-2323
Karen Warren
555-3434

The following statments open the file in append mode and write additional data to the file:

```
' Declare an object variable
Dim friendFile As StreamWriter
' Open the file.
friendFile = File.AppendText("MyFriends.txt")
' Write the data.
friendFile.WriteLine("Bill Johnson")
friendFile.WriteLine("555—4545")
' Close the file.
friendFile.Close()
```

After this code executes, the *MyFriends.txt* file will contain the following data:

Jim Weaver
555-1212
Mary Duncan
555-2323
Karen Warren
555-3434
Bill Johnson
555-4545

Reading Files with StreamReader Objects

VideoNote

Reading Data
from a File

To read data from a sequential text file, use a **StreamReader** object. A StreamReader object is an instance of the **StreamReader** class, which provides methods for reading data from a file. The process of creating a StreamReader object is similar to that of creating a StreamWriter object, which we discussed in the previous section. First, you declare an object variable with a declaration statement in the following general format:

```
Dim ObjectVar As StreamReader
```

ObjectVar is the name of the object variable. As with other variables, you may use the Private or Public access specifier if you are declaring the object variable at the class level or module level.

You must create an instance of the StreamReader object and store its address in the object variable with the **File.OpenText** method. The method's general format is as follows:

```
File.OpenText(Filename)
```

Filename is a string or a string variable specifying the path and/or name of the file to open. This method opens the file specified by *Filename* and returns the address of a StreamReader object that may be used to write data to the file. If the file does not exist, or it cannot be opened for any reason, an exception will occur.

The following are examples:

```
Dim customerFile As StreamReader
customerFile = File.OpenText("customers.txt")
```

The first statement creates an object variable named customerFile. The second statement opens the file *customers.txt* and returns the address of a StreamReader object that may be used to read data from the file. The address of the StreamReader object is assigned to the customerFile variable.

As in the case of the StreamWriter class, you need to write the following Imports statement at the top of your code file:

```
Imports System.IO
```

Reading Data from a File

The **ReadLine** method in the StreamReader class reads a line of data from a file. The general format of the method is as follows:

```
ObjectVar.ReadLine()
```

ObjectVar is the name of a StreamReader object variable. The method reads a line from the file associated with *ObjectVar* and returns the data as a string. For example, assume that customerFile is a StreamReader object variable and strCustomerName is a string variable. The following statement reads a line from the file and stores it in the variable:

```
strCustomerName = customerFile.ReadLine()
```

Data is read in a forward-only direction. When the file is opened, its **read position,** the position of the next item to be read, is set to the first item in the file. As data is read, the read position advances through the file. For example, consider the file named *Quotation.txt*, as shown in Figure 6. As you can see from the figure, the file has three lines of text. Suppose a program opens the file with the following code:

```
Dim textFile As StreamReader
textFile = File.OpenText("Quotation.txt")
```

Figure 6 Text file with three lines

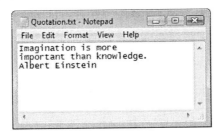

When this code opens the file, its read position is at the beginning of the first line, as illustrated in Figure 7.

Figure 7 Initial read position

Read position ————▶ Imagination is more
important than knowledge.
Albert Einstein

The following statement reads a line from the file, beginning at the current read position, and ending at the end-of-line marker:

```
strInput = textFile.ReadLine()
```

After the statement executes, the `strInput` variable contains the string `"Imagination is more"`. The invisible end-of-line marker is skipped, and the read position is placed at the beginning of the second line. Figure 8 illustrates the current read position.

Figure 8 Read position after first line is read

Imagination is more
Read position ————▶ important than knowledge.
Albert Einstein

If the `ReadLine` method is called again, the second line is read from the file and the file's read position is advanced to the third line. After all lines have been read, the read position will be at the end of the file.

Closing the File

Close an open `StreamReader` object by calling the `Close` method. The general format is as follows:

```
ObjectVar.Close()
```

In Tutorial 2, you complete an application that uses the `ReadLine` statement to read the file you created in Tutorial 1.

Tutorial 2:

Completing an application that reads a file

Step 1: Open the *File ReadLine Demo* project from the student sample programs folder named *Chap9\File ReadLine Demo*. The application's form, which has already been created for you, is shown in Figure 9.

Figure 9 *File ReadLine Demo* form

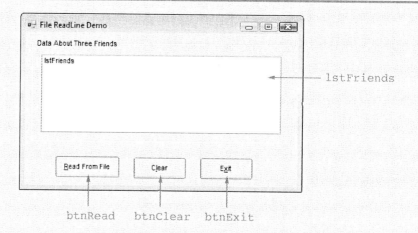

Step 2: Complete the code for the form's event handlers as shown in the following. (Don't type the line numbers. They are shown for reference.) Be sure to write the `Imports` statement shown in line 1.

```
1  Imports System.IO
2
3  Public Class Form1
4
5    Private Sub btnRead_Click(...) Handles btnRead.Click
6      ' Constant for the number of friends
7      Const intNUM_FRIENDS As Integer = 3
8
9      ' Local variables
10     Dim friendFile As StreamReader    ' Object variable
11     Dim strFilename As String         ' File name
12     Dim strFriend As String           ' Name of a friend
13     Dim strPhone As String            ' To hold a phone number
14     Dim intCount As Integer           ' Loop counter
15
16     ' Get the file name from the user.
17     strFilename = InputBox("Enter the filename.")
18
19     Try
```

```
20        ' Open the file.
21        friendFile = File.OpenText(strFilename)
22
23        ' Read the data.
24        For intCount = 1 To intNUM_FRIENDS
25            ' Read a name and phone number from the file.
26            strFriend = friendFile.ReadLine()
27            strPhone = friendFile.ReadLine()
28
29            ' Display the data in the list box.
30            lstFriends.Items.Add("Friend Number " & intCount.ToString())
31            lstFriends.Items.Add("Name: " & strFriend)
32            lstFriends.Items.Add("Phone: " & strPhone)
33            lstFriends.Items.Add("") ' Add a blank line
34        Next
35
36        ' Close the file.
37        friendFile.Close()
38      Catch
39        MessageBox.Show("That file cannot be opened.")
40      End Try
41    End Sub
42
43    Private Sub btnlear_Click(...) Handles btnlear.Click
44        ' Clear the list box.
45        lstFriends.Items.Clear()
46    End Sub
47
48    Private Sub btnExit_Click(...) Handles btnExit.Click
49        ' Close the form.
50        Me.Close()
51    End Sub
52 End Class
```

Let's examine the btnRead_Click event handler. Here is a summary of the declarations that appear in lines 7 through 14:

- Line 7: The intNUM_FRIENDS constant is set to 3. This is the number of friends for whom we will read data from the file.
- Line 10: The friendFile variable is an object variable that will be used to open the file and read data from it.
- Line 11: The strFilename variable will hold the path and filename of the file that the application will open.
- Line 12: The strFriend variable will hold the name of a friend that is read from the file.
- Line 13: The strPhone variable will hold a friend's phone number that is read from the file.
- Line 14: The intCount variable will be used as a loop counter.

Line 17 uses an input box to prompt the user to enter a filename. The filename is assigned to the strFilename variable.

The Try–Catch statement that begins in line 19 will catch any exceptions that are thrown. Line 21 tries to open the file specified by the path and filename entered by the user. If the file cannot be opened, an exception is thrown and the program jumps to the Catch clause in line 38. If the file is successfully created, the For...Next loop in line 24 begins to execute. As the loop is written, it will iterate three times, with the intCount variable taking on the values 1 through 3.

Inside the loop, the statement in line 26 reads a line of data from the file and assigns it to the `strFriend` variable, and line 27 reads the next line of data from the file and assigns it to the `strPhone` variable. Lines 30 through 33 add this friend's data to the list box, followed by a blank line. Then, the loop starts over. When the loop is finished, line 39 closes the file.

Step 3: Save the project. Run the application and click the *Read From File* button. An input box will appear asking for the filename. Enter the path and filename that you used to create the file in Step 3 of Tutorial 1. When you click the *OK* button on the input box, the data is read from the file and displayed in the list box, as shown in Figure 10. If you did not type the path and filename exactly as you did in Tutorial 1, you will see a message box indicating that the file was not found. In that case, click the *Read From File* button again, this time entering the correct path and filename.

Figure 10 Data displayed in the list box

Step 4: Click the *Exit* button to end the application.

Determining Whether a File Exists

The `File.OpenText` method throws an exception if the file it is trying to open does not exist. To prevent an exception, you can call the **File.Exists** method to determine whether a file exists before you attempt to open it. The general format of the method is as follows:

```
File.Exists(Filename)
```

Filename is the name of a file, which may include the path. The method returns *True* if the file exists or *False* if the file does not exist. The following code shows an example of how to use the method to determine if a file exists prior to trying to open the file:

```
If File.Exists(strFilename) Then
  ' Open the file.
  inputFile = File.OpenText(strFilename)
Else
  MessageBox.Show(strFilename & " does not exist.")
End If
```

Using `vbTab` to Align Display Items

The predefined `vbTab` constant moves the print position forward to the next even multiple of 8. You can use it to align columns in displayed or printed output more effectively. The following is a simple example, displayed in a list box, of a reference line followed by three lines displaying tabs and characters:

```
ListBox1.Items.Add("012345678901234567890")
ListBox1.Items.Add("X" & vbTab & "X")
ListBox1.Items.Add("XXXXXXXXXXXX" & vbTab & "X")
ListBox1.Items.Add(vbTab & vbTab & "X")
```

In the output in Figure 11, the vbTab constant in the second line moves the print position forward to column 8 before displaying the letter *X*. (Print positions are numbered starting at 0.) In lines three and four, the print position moves to column 16 before displaying the final letter *X*.

Figure 11 Demonstrating tabs in a list box

Briefly returning to the *ReadLine Demo* application from Tutorial 2, a slightly better way to display the person's information is to insert tabs between the labels and names in the list box. Here is the appropriately modified code from the loop inside the btnRead_Click event handler:

```
' Display the data in the list box.
lstFriends.Items.Add("Friend Number " & vbTab & intCount.ToString())
lstFriends.Items.Add("Name: " & vbTab & vbTab & strFriend)
lstFriends.Items.Add("Phone: " & vbTab & vbTab & strPhone)
lstFriends.Items.Add("") ' Add a blank line
```

The resulting output from this code appears in Figure 12.

Figure 12 *ReadLine Demo,* using tabs in the list box

Detecting the End of a File

The *File ReadLine Demo* application in Tutorial 2 is designed to read exactly three records. This is because we know how many records are stored in the file. In many cases, however, the amount of data in a file is unknown. When this is the case, use the **Peek method** to determine when the end of the file has been reached. The general format of the Peek method is as follows:

```
ObjectVar.Peek
```

ObjectVar is an object variable referencing a `StreamReader` object. This method looks ahead in the file, without moving the current read position, and returns the next character that will be read. If the current read position is at the end of the file (where there are no more characters to read), the method returns −1. The following example uses a `Do Until` loop that uses the `Peek` method to determine when the end of the *Scores.txt* file has been reached. The loop reads all the lines from the file and adds them to the `lstResults` list box.

```
Dim scoresFile As StreamReader
Dim strInput As String
scoresFile = File.OpenText("Scores.txt")
Do Until scoresFile.Peek = -1
   strInput = scoresFile.ReadLine()
   lstResults.Items.Add(strInput)
Loop
scoresFile.Close()
```

Tutorial 3 examines an application that detects the end of a file.

Tutorial 3:

Examining an application that detects the end of a file

VideoNote

Tutorial 9-3
Walkthrough

Step 1: Open the *File Demo* project from the student sample program folder named *Chap9\File Demo*. Recall that the folder can be downloaded from www.microsoft.com/express/Downloads/. Run the application. The form is shown in Figure 13.

Figure 13 *File Demo* form

Step 2: Click the *Create File* button. An input box appears and asks: *How many integers do you want to enter?* Enter **5** and press Enter.

Step 3: Because you indicated you want to enter five numbers, the application will prompt you five times with an input box to enter a number. Enter the following numbers: **2**, **4**, **6**, **8**, and **10**. The application writes these numbers to a file.

Step 4: After you have entered the last number, click the *Read File* button. The application reads the numbers from the file and prints them in the list box, as shown in Figure 14. Click the *Exit* button to end the application.

Figure 14 *File Demo* form with numbers displayed

Step 5: Open the *Code* window. The first part of the form's class, including the
btnCreate_Click event handler, are shown here with line numbers for reference.

```
1 Imports System.IO
2
3 Public Class Form1
4   ' Class-level constant for the filename
5   Private Const strFILENAME As String = "Numbers.txt"
6
7   Private Sub btnCreate_Click(...) Handles btnCreate.Click
8     ' Local variables
9     Dim outputFile As StreamWriter    ' Object variable
10    Dim intMaxNumbers As Integer      ' The number of values
11    Dim intCount As Integer = 0       ' Loop counter, set to 0
12    Dim intNumber As Integer          ' To hold user input
13
14    Try
15      ' Get the number of numbers from the user.
16      intMaxNumbers = CInt(InputBox("How many integers do " &
17                                    "you want to enter?"))
18
19      Try
20        ' Create the file.
21        outputFile = File.CreateText(strFILENAME)
22
23        ' Get the numbers and write then to the file.
24        Do While intCount < intMaxNumbers
25          Try
26            ' Get an integer.
27            intNumber = CInt(InputBox("Enter an integer."))
28
29            ' Write that integer to the file.
30            outputFile.WriteLine(intNumber)
31
32            ' Increment intCount.
33            intCount += 1
34          Catch
35            ' Error message for invalid integer.
36            MessageBox.Show("The last value you entered was not " &
37                            "a valid integer. Try again.")
38          End Try
```

```
39          Loop
40
41            ' Close the file.
42            outputFile.Close()
43
44      Catch
45          ' Error message for file creation error.
46          MessageBox.Show("Error creating the file " & strFILENAME)
47      End Try
48
49    Catch
50        ' Error message for invalid number of numbers.
51        MessageBox.Show("Enter a valid integer please.")
52    End Try
53  End Sub
54
```

Let's take a closer look at this code. Line 1 shows the Imports System.IO statement, and the form's class declaration begins in line 3. Line 5 declares a class-level constant named strFILENAME for the name of the file that we will be working with.

Here is a summary of the declarations that appear in lines 9 through 12:

- Line 9: The outputFile variable is an object variable that will be used to open the file and write data to it.
- Line 10: The intMaxNumbers variable will hold the number of integer values that will be written to the file.
- Line 11: The intCount variable will be used as a loop counter.
- Line 12: The intNumber variable will hold a number entered by the user, to be written to the file. Notice that we explicitly initialize intCount to 0.

Notice that a Try-Catch statement begins in line 14, and then lines 16 through 17 use an input box to prompt the user for the number of integer values that he or she wants to enter. If the user enters an invalid value, the CInt function in line 16 will throw an exception and the program will jump to the Catch clause in line 49.

If the user enters a valid integer value, the program can proceed to create the file. Notice that another Try-Catch statement begins in line 19, and then line 21 creates the file. If for any reason the file cannot be created, the File.CreateText method will throw an exception and the program will jump to the Catch clause in line 44.

If the file is successfully created, the program can proceed to get the numbers from the user and write them to the file. The Do While loop that begins in line 24 iterates as long as intCount is less than intMaxNumbers. Notice that inside the loop a Try-Catch statement begins in line 25, and then line 27 uses an input box to prompt the user for an integer. If the user enters an invalid value, the CInt function in line 27 will throw an exception and the program will jump to the Catch clause in line 34. If the user enters a valid integer, line 30 writes it to the file, and line 33 increments intCount. After the loop finishes, line 42 closes the file.

Step 6: Now scroll down and look at the btnRead_Click event handler, shown here with line numbers for reference:

```
55   Private Sub btnRead_Click(...) Handles btnRead.Click
56     ' Local variables
57     Dim inputFile As StreamReader ' Object variable
58     Dim strInput As String        ' To hold a line of input
59
60     Try
61       ' Open the file.
62       inputFile = File.OpenText(strFILENAME)
63
64       ' Clear the list box.
65       lstOutput.Items.Clear()
66
67       ' Read the file's contents.
68       Do Until inputFile.Peek = -1
69         ' Read a line from the file.
70         strInput = inputFile.ReadLine()
71
72         ' Add the line of input to the list box.
73         lstOutput.Items.Add(strInput)
74       Loop
75
76       ' Close the file.
77       inputFile.Close()
78     Catch
79       ' Error message for file open error.
80       MessageBox.Show(strFILENAME & " cannot be opened.")
81     End Try
82   End Sub
```

Let's take a closer look at this code. Here is a summary of the declarations that appear in lines 57 and 58:

- Line 57: The inputFile variable is an object variable that will be used to open the file and read data from it.
- Line 58: The strInput variable will hold a line of input that is read from the file.

Notice that a Try-Catch statement begins in line 60, and then line 62 opens the file. If the file cannot be opened, the File.OpenText method will throw an exception and the program will jump to the Catch clause in line 78. (This will happen, for example, if the user clicks the *Read File* button before the file has been created.)

If the file is successfully opened, line 65 clears the list box's contents. Then the Do Until loop in line 68 begins executing. The loop will iterate until the inputFile.Peek method returns −1, indicating that the end of the file has been reached. During each loop iteration, line 70 reads a line from the file and assigns it to the strInput variable, and line 73 adds strInput to the list box. After the loop finishes, line 77 closes the file.

Other `StreamReader` Methods

The `StreamReader` class also provides the `Read` and `ReadToEnd` methods, which we briefly discuss. The general format of the `Read` method is as follows:

```
ObjectVar.Read
```

ObjectVar is the name of a `StreamReader` object variable. The **Read method** reads only the next character from a file and returns the integer code for the character. To convert the integer code to a character, use the **Chr function**, as shown in the following code:

```
Dim textFile As StreamReader
Dim strInput As String = String.Empty
textFile = File.OpenText("names.txt")
Do While textFile.Peek <> —1
   strInput &= Chr(textFile.Read)
Loop
textFile.Close()
```

This code opens the *names.txt* file. The `Do While` loop, which repeats until it reaches the end of the file, executes the following statement:

```
strInput &= Chr(textFile.Read)
```

This statement gets the integer code for the next character in the file, converts it to a character with the `Chr` function, and concatenates that character to the string variable `strInput`. When the loop has finished, the string variable `strInput` contains the entire contents of the file *names.txt*.

The general format of the `ReadToEnd` method is as follows:

```
ObjectVar.ReadToEnd
```

ObjectVar is the name of a `StreamReader` object variable. The **ReadToEnd method** reads and returns the entire contents of a file, beginning at the current read position. The following is an example:

```
Dim textFile As StreamReader
Dim strInput As String
textFile = File.OpenText("names.txt")
strInput = textFile.ReadToEnd()
textFile.Close()
```

The statement `strInput = textFile.ReadToEnd()` reads the file's contents and stores it in the variable `strInput`.

Working with Arrays and Files

Saving the contents of an array to a file is easy. Use a loop to step through each element of the array, writing its contents to the file. For example, assume an application has the following array declaration:

```
Dim intValues() As Integer = {1, 2, 3, 4, 5, 6, 7, 8, 9, 10}
```

The following code opens a file named *Values.txt* and writes the contents of each element of the values array to the file:

```
Dim outputFile as StreamWriter
outputFile = File.CreateText("Values.txt")
For intCount = 0 To (intValues.Length — 1)
   outputFile.WriteLine(intValues(intCount))
Next
outputFile.Close()
```

Reading the contents of a file into an array is equally straightforward. The following code opens the *Values.txt* file and reads its contents into the elements of the intValues array:

```
Dim inputFile as StreamReader
inputFile = File.OpenText("Values.txt")
For intCount = 0 To (intValues.Length − 1)
    intValues(intCount) = CInt(inputFile.ReadLine())
Next
inputFile.Close()
```

NOTE: This code does not check for the end of file, so it assumes the file contains enough values to fill the array. Also, an exception will be thrown by the CInt function if the file contains a value that cannot be converted to an integer.

Checkpoint

1 What are the three steps in the process of using a file?

2 What type of object variable must you create to open a file for writing? For reading?

3 Write a statement that creates the file *Test.txt* so that you may write data to it. If the file already exists, its contents should be erased.

4 Write a statement that writes the contents of the variable intX to a line in the file you opened in Checkpoint 3.

5 Write a statement that opens the file *Test.txt* for reading.

6 Write a statement that reads a line from the file you opened in Checkpoint 5, into the variable intX.

7 How do you determine that a file already exists?

8 When reading a file, how does a program know it has reached end of the file?

2 The OpenFileDialog, SaveFileDialog, FontDialog, and ColorDialog Controls

CONCEPT: Visual Basic provides dialog controls that equip your applications with standard Windows dialog boxes for operations such as opening files, saving files, and selecting fonts and colors.

The OpenFileDialog and SaveFileDialog Controls

So far, the applications in this chapter that open a file either specify the filename as part of the code or require the user to enter the path and filename. Most Windows users, however, are accustomed to using a dialog box to browse their disk for a file to open or for a location to save a file. You can use the OpenFileDialog and SaveFileDialog controls to equip applications with standard dialog boxes used by most Windows applications.

The OpenFileDialog Control

The **OpenFileDialog control** displays a standard Windows *Open* dialog box, such as the one shown in Figure 15. The *Open* **dialog box** is useful in applications that work with files. It gives users the ability to browse for a file to open, instead of typing a long path and file-name.

Figure 15 Windows *Open* dialog box

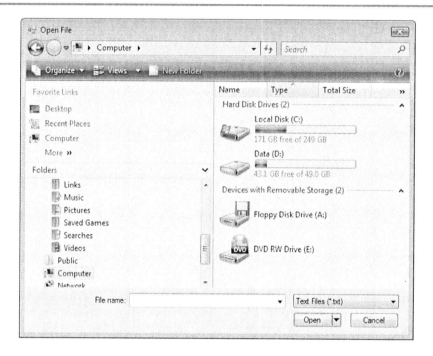

Adding the OpenFileDialog Control to Your Project

To place an OpenFileDialog control on a form, double-click the *OpenFileDialog* tool under the *Dialogs* tab in the *Toolbox* window. Because the control is invisible at runtime, it appears in the component tray at design time. We will use the prefix ofd when naming the control.

Displaying an Open Dialog Box

Display an *Open* dialog box by calling the OpenFileDialog control's ShowDialog method. The following is the method's general format:

```
ControlName.ShowDialog()
```

ControlName is the name of the OpenFileDialog control. For example, assuming ofdOpenFile is the name of an OpenFileDialog control, the following statement calls its ShowDialog method:

```
ofdOpenFile.ShowDialog()
```

ShowDialog returns one of the values Windows.Forms.DialogResult.OK or Windows.Forms.DialogResult.Cancel, indicating which button, *OK* or *Cancel*, the user clicked to close the dialog box. When the user selects a file with the *Open* dialog box, the file's path and name are stored in the control's **Filename property**.

The following code displays an *Open* dialog box and determines whether the user has selected a file. If so, the filename is displayed as follows:

```
If ofdOpenFile.ShowDialog() = Windows.Forms.DialogResult.OK Then
    MessageBox.Show(ofdOpenFile.FileName)
Else
    MessageBox.Show("You selected no file.")
End If
```

The Filter Property

The *Open* dialog box has a *Files of type* list box, which displays a filter that specifies the type of files visible in the dialog box. Filters typically use the wildcard character (*) followed by a file extension. For example, the *.txt filter specifies that only files ending in .txt (text files) are to be displayed. The *.doc filter specifies that only files ending in.doc (Microsoft Word files) are to be displayed. The *.* filter allows all files to be displayed.

The dialog box in Figure 16 shows a list box with *.txt and *.* filters.

Figure 16 *Open* dialog box with *.txt and *.* filters

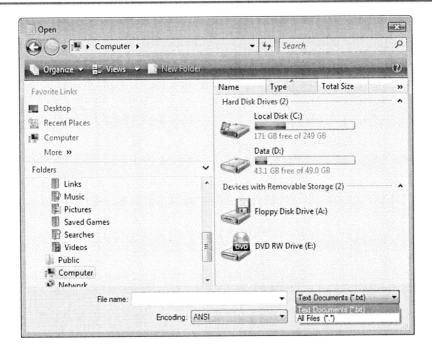

Use the **Filter property** to set the filters in the *Files of type* list box. This property can be set in the *Properties* window at design time, or by code at runtime. When storing a value in the Filter property, store a string containing a description of the filter and the filter itself. The description and the filter are separated with the pipe (|) symbol. For example, assuming an application has an OpenFileDialog control named ofdOpenFile, the following statement sets the Filter property for text files:

```
ofdOpenFile.Filter = "Text files (*.txt)|*.txt"
```

The part of the string appearing before the pipe symbol is a description of the filter, and is displayed in the *Files of type* list box. The part of the string appearing after the pipe symbol is the actual filter. In our example, the description of the filter is Text files (*.txt) and the filter is *.txt.

The pipe symbol is also used to separate multiple filters. For example, the following statement stores two filters in ofdOpenFile.Filter: *.txt and *.*:

```
ofdOpenFile.Filter = "Text files (*.txt)|*.txt|All Files (*.*)|*.*"
```

The description of the first filter is Text files (*.txt), and the filter is *.txt. The description of the second filter is All files (*.*), and the filter is *.*.

The InitialDirectory Property

By default, the *Open* dialog box displays the current directory (or folder). You can specify another directory to be initially displayed by storing its path in the **InitialDirectory** property. For example, the following code stores the path *C:\Data* in ofdOpenFile.Initial-Directory before displaying an *Open* dialog box:

```
ofdOpenFile.InitialDirectory = "C:\Data"
ofdOpenFile.ShowDialog()
```

When the *Open* dialog box is displayed, it shows the contents of the directory *C:\Data*.

The Title Property

You can change the default text displayed in the *Open* dialog box's title bar by storing a string in the control's **Title property**.

Using the *Open* Dialog Box to Open a File

The following code assumes ofdOpenFile is the name of an OpenFileDialog control. It demonstrates how to set the Filter, InitialDirectory, and Title properties, display the *Open* dialog box, retrieve the filename entered by the user, and open the file.

```
' Configure the Open dialog box and display it.
With ofdOpenFile
   .Filter = "Text files (*.txt)|*.txt|All files (*.*)|*.*"
   .InitialDirectory = "C:\Data"
   .Title = "Select a File to Open"
   If.ShowDialog() = Windows.Forms.DialogResult.OK Then
      inputFile = File.OpenText(.Filename)
   End If
End With
```

The SaveFileDialog Control

The **SaveFileDialog control** displays a standard Windows *Save As* dialog box. Figure 17 shows an example.

The *Save As* dialog box is useful in applications that work with files. It gives users the ability to browse their disks and to choose a location and name for the file.

The SaveFileDialog control has much in common with the OpenFileDialog control. Double-click the *SaveFileDialog* tool in the toolbox to place the control on a form. Because the control is invisible at runtime, it appears in the component tray at design time. We will use the prefix sfd when naming the control.

Display a *Save As* dialog box by calling the SaveFileDialog control's ShowDialog method. The following is the method's general format:

```
ControlName.ShowDialog()
```

ControlName is the name of the SaveFileDialog control. For example, assuming `sfdSaveFile` is the name of a SaveFileDialog control, the following statement calls its `ShowDialog` method:

```
sfdSaveFile.ShowDialog()
```

This method returns one of the values `Windows.Forms.DialogResult.OK` or `Windows.-Forms.DialogResult.Cancel` indicating which button, *OK* or *Cancel*, the user clicked to dismiss the dialog box.

Figure 17 Windows *Save As* dialog box

The Filename property holds the name of the file selected or entered by the user. The Filter, InitialDirectory, and Title properties work with the *Save As* dialog box the same way they do with the *Open* dialog box. The following code assumes that `sfdSaveFile` is the name of a common dialog control. It demonstrates how to set the Filter, InitialDirectory, and Title properties, display the *Save As* dialog box, retrieve the filename entered by the user, and open the file.

```
' Configure the Save As dialog box and display it.
With sfdSaveFile
    .Filter = "Text files (*.txt)|*.txt|All files (*.*)|*.*"
    .InitialDirectory = "C:\Data"
    .Title = "Save File As"
    ' If the user selected a file, open it for output.
    If.ShowDialog() = Windows.Forms.DialogResult.OK Then
        outputFile = System.IO.File.OpenText(.Filename)
    End If
End With
```

In Tutorial 4, you gain experience using the OpenFileDialog and SaveFileDialog controls by creating a simple text editor application. You will also learn about the TextBox control's MultiLine property, WordWrap property, and TextChanged event.

Tutorial 4:

Creating a simple text editor application

In this tutorial, you will create a simple text editing application that allows you to create documents, save them, and open existing documents. The application will use a Multiline TextBox control to hold the document text. It will also use the menu system shown in Figure 18.

Figure 18 Simple Text Editor menu system

Table 1 lists the required menu items, showing the contents of their Text and ShortcutKeys properties.

Table 1 Menu items and their Text and ShortcutKeys properties

Menu Item Name	Text Property	ShortcutKeys Property
mnuFile	&File	(None)
mnuFileNew	&New	Ctrl+N
mnuFileOpen	&Open...	Ctrl+O
mnuFileSave	&Save	Ctrl+S
mnuFileSaveAs	Save &As...	(None)
mnuFileExit	E&xit	Ctrl+Q
mnuHelp	&Help	(None)
mnuHelpAbout	&About	(None)

Some of the menu item Text property values end with an ellipsis (...). It is a standard Windows convention for a menu item's text to end with an ellipsis if the menu item displays a dialog box.

Step 1: Create a new Windows Forms Application project named *Simple Text Editor*.

Step 2: Set the form's Text property to *Simple Text Editor*. Create a MenuStrip control on the form and add the menu items listed in Table 1. Set their Text and ShortcutKeys properties to the values shown in the table. The form should appear similar to the one shown in Figure 19.

Figure 19 Initial *Simple Text Editor* form

Step 3: Add a TextBox control to the form named `txtDocument`. TextBox controls have a Boolean property named **MultiLine**, which is set to *False* by default. When this property is set to *True*, the height of the TextBox control can be enlarged and its text can span multiple lines. Set the MultiLine property of the `txtDocument` control to *True*. TextBox controls also have a **WordWrap property** that, when set to *True*, causes long text lines to wrap around to the following line. By default, WordWrap is set to *True*.

Step 4: Enlarge the size of the `txtDocument` control so it fills most of the form, as shown in Figure 20.

Figure 20 *Simple Text Editor* form with text box enlarged

Step 5: Set the `txtDocument` control's Anchor property to *Top, Bottom, Left, Right*. This will cause the TextBox control to resize automatically if the user resizes the form.

Step 6: Add OpenFileDialog and SaveFileDialog controls to the form. (You will find these controls under the *Dialogs* group in the Toolbox.) Name the OpenFileDialog control **ofdOpenFile**. Name the SaveFileDialog control **sfdSaveFile**.

Step 7: Set the Title property of the **ofdOpenFile** control to *Open File*. Set the Title property of the **sfdSaveFile** control to *Save File As*. Set the Filter property to *Text Files (*.txt) | *.txt* for both controls.

Step 8: Now you are ready to write the code for the application. At the end of the tutorial you will find all of the code shown in one listing. (Don't type any of the line numbers. They are shown for reference only.) First, open the *Code* window and type the **Imports** statement shown in line 1.

Step 9: Inside the form's class declaration, type the comment and the class-level declarations shown in lines 4 through 6. The **strFilename** variable will hold the filename under which the text box's contents are saved. The **blnIsChanged** variable is a flag to indicate whether the text box's contents have been changed since the last time they were saved. We need this flag so we can warn the user anytime he or she is about to clear the current document without saving it.

Step 10: Type the code for the **ClearDocument** procedure shown in lines 8 through 17. The **ClearDocument** procedure clears the **txtDocument** control's Text property, sets **strFilename** to an empty string, and sets **blnIsChanged** to *False*.

Step 11: Type the code for the **OpenDocument** procedure shown in lines 22 through 46. The **OpenDocument** procedure displays an *Open* dialog box, opens the file selected by the user, and reads its contents into the text box.

Step 12: Type the code for the **SaveDocument** procedure shown in lines 50 through 69. The **SaveDocument** procedure saves the contents of the text box to the file specified by the **strFilename** variable.

Step 13: Now you will write the code for the **txtDocument_TextChanged** event handler, shown in lines 71 through 74. This event handler will execute anytime the **txtDocument** TextBox control's Text property changes. When that happens, we want to set the **blnIsChanged** variable to *True* to indicate that the current document has changed. Here's how to write the event handler:

In the *Code* window, select *txtDocument* in the class drop-down list box (which is in the upper-left area of the *Code* window), and then select *TextChanged* in the method name drop-down list box (which is in the upper-right area of the *Code* window). This will create a code template for the event handler. Simply type the contents of lines 72 and 73 to complete the event handler.

Step 14: Next, write the Click event handlers for the menu items. The code for all of the event handlers is shown in lines 76 through 141.

Step 15: Last, you will write the code for the **Form1_FormClosing** event handler, shown in lines 143 through 157. The purpose of this event handler is to warn the user if he or she attempts to exit the application without saving the contents of the text box. Here's how to write the event handler:

In the *Code* window, select *(Form1 Events)* in the class drop-down list box (in the upper-left area of the *Code* window), and then select *FormClosing* in the method name drop-down list box (in the upper-right area of the *Code* window). This will create a code template for the event handler. Simply type the contents of lines 144 through 156 to complete the event handler.

514

Step 16: Save and run the application. If you entered all the code correctly, you should see the form shown in Figure 21. Enter some text into the text box. Experiment with each of the menu commands to see if the application operates correctly. When you are finished, exit the application.

Figure 21 *Simple Text Editor* form

```
 1 Imports System.IO
 2
 3 Public Class Form1
 4     ' Class-level variables
 5     Private strFilename As String = String.Empty ' Document filename
 6     Dim blnIsChanged As Boolean = False          ' File change flag
 7
 8     Sub ClearDocument()
 9       ' Clear the contents of the text box.
10       txtDocument.Clear()
11
12       ' Clear the document name.
13       strFilename = String.Empty
14
15       ' Set isChanged to False.
16       blnIsChanged = False
17     End Sub
18
19   ' The OpenDocument procedure opens a file and loads it
20   ' into the TextBox for editing.
21
22     Sub OpenDocument()
23       Dim inputFile As StreamReader ' Object variable
24
25       If ofdOpenFile.ShowDialog = Windows.Forms.DialogResult.OK Then
26         ' Retrieve the selected filename.
27         strFilename = ofdOpenFile.FileName
28
29         Try
30           ' Open the file.
31           inputFile = File.OpenText(strFilename)
```

```
32
33              ' Read the file's contents into the TextBox.
34              txtDocument.Text = inputFile.ReadToEnd
35
36              ' Close the file.
37              inputFile.Close()
38
39              ' Update the isChanged variable.
40              blnIsChanged = False
41          Catch
42              ' Error message for file open error.
43              MessageBox.Show("Error opening the file.")
44          End Try
45      End If
46  End Sub
47
48  ' The SaveDocument procedure saves the current document.
49
50  Sub SaveDocument()
51      Dim outputFile As StreamWriter ' Object variable
52
53      Try
54          ' Create the file.
55          outputFile = File.CreateText(strFilename)
56
57          ' Write the TextBox to the file.
58          outputFile.Write(txtDocument.Text)
59
60          ' Close the file.
61          outputFile.Close()
62
63          ' Update the isChanged variable.
64          blnIsChanged = False
65      Catch
66          ' Error message for file creation error.
67          MessageBox.Show("Error creating the file.")
68      End Try
69  End Sub
70
71  Private Sub txtDocument_TextChanged(...) Handles txtDocument.TextChanged
72      ' Indicate the text has changed.
73      blnIsChanged = True
74  End Sub
75
76  Private Sub mnuFileNew_Click(...) Handles mnuFileNew.Click
77      ' Has the current document changed?
78      If blnIsChanged = True Then
79          ' Confirm before clearing the document.
80          If MessageBox.Show("The current document is not saved. " &
81                          "Are you sure?", "Confirm",
82                          MessageBoxButtons.YesNo) =
83                  Windows.Forms.DialogResult.Yes Then
84              ClearDocument()
85          End If
86      Else
```

```
 87              ' Document has not changed, so clear it.
 88              ClearDocument()
 89            End If
 90        End Sub
 91
 92        Private Sub mnuFileOpen_Click(...) Handles mnuFileOpen.Click
 93          ' Has the current document changed?
 94          If blnIsChanged = True Then
 95            ' Confirm before clearing and replacing.
 96            If MessageBox.Show("The current document is not saved. " &
 97                            "Are you sure?", "Confirm",
 98                            MessageBoxButtons.YesNo) =
 99                        Windows.Forms.DialogResult.Yes Then
100              ClearDocument()
101              OpenDocument()
102            End If
103          Else
104            ' Document has not changed, so replace it.
105            ClearDocument()
106            OpenDocument()
107          End If
108        End Sub
109
110        Private Sub mnuFileSave_Click(...) Handles mnuFileSave.Click
111          ' Does the current document have a filename?
112          If strFilename = String.Empty Then
113            ' The document has not been saved, so
114            ' use Save As dialog box.
115            If sfdSaveFile.ShowDialog = Windows.Forms.DialogResult.OK Then
116              strFilename = sfdSaveFile.FileName
117              SaveDocument()
118            End If
119          Else
120            ' Save the document with the current filename.
121            SaveDocument()
122          End If
123        End Sub
124
125        Private Sub mnuFileSaveAs_Click(...) Handles mnuFileSaveAs.Click
126          ' Save the current document under a new filename.
127          If sfdSaveFile.ShowDialog = Windows.Forms.DialogResult.OK Then
128            strFilename = sfdSaveFile.FileName
129            SaveDocument()
130          End If
131        End Sub
132
133        Private Sub mnuExit_Click(...) Handles mnuExit.Click
134          ' Close the form.
135          Me.Close()
136        End Sub
137
138        Private Sub mnuHelpAbout_Click(...) Handles mnuHelpAbout.Click
139          ' Display an about box.
140          MessageBox.Show("Simple Text Editor version 1.0")
141        End Sub
```

```
142
143  Private Sub Form1_FormClosing(...) Handles Me.FormClosing
144     ' If the document has not been changed, confirm
145     ' before exiting.
146     If blnIsChanged = True Then
147        If MessageBox.Show("The current document is not saved. " &
148                           "Do you wish to discard your changes?",
149                           "Confirm",
150                           MessageBoxButtons.YesNo) =
151                           Windows.Forms.DialogResult.Yes Then
152           e.Cancel = False
153        Else
154           e.Cancel = True
155        End If
156     End If
157  End Sub
158 End Class
```

The ColorDialog and FontDialog Controls

The ColorDialog Control

The **ColorDialog control** displays a standard Windows *Color* dialog box. Figure 22 shows a default *Color* dialog box, on the left. When the user clicks the *Define Custom Colors* button, the dialog box expands to become the fully open *Color* dialog box shown on the right.

Double-click the *ColorDialog* icon in the *Dialogs* section of the toolbox to place the control on a form. Because the control is invisible at runtime, it appears in the component tray at design time. We will use the prefix cd when naming the control.

Figure 22 Windows *Color* dialog box

Color dialog box   Fully open *Color* dialog box

Display a *Color* dialog box by calling its `ShowDialog` method. For example, assuming `cdColor` is the name of a ColorDialog control, the following statement calls its `ShowDialog` method:

```
cdColor.ShowDialog()
```

This method returns one of the values, `Windows.Forms.DialogResult.OK` or `Windows.Forms.DialogResult.Cancel`, indicating which button, *OK* or *Cancel*, the user clicked to dismiss the dialog box. The Color property will hold a value representing the color selected by the user. This value can be used with control properties that designate color, such as ForeColor and BackColor. For example, the following code displays the *Color* dialog box and then sets the color of the text displayed by the `lblMessage` label to that selected by the user:

```
If cdColor.ShowDialog() = Windows.Forms.DialogResult.OK Then
   lblMessage.ForeColor = cdColor.Color
End If
```

By default, black is initially selected when the *Color* dialog box is displayed. If you wish to set the initially selected color, you must set the Color property to the desired color value. For example, the following code sets the initially selected color to blue:

```
cdColor.Color = Color.Blue
If cdColor.ShowDialog() = Windows.Forms.DialogResult.OK Then
   lblMessage.ForeColor = cdColor.Color
End If
```

The following code sets the initially selected color to the color of the `lblMessage` label before displaying the dialog box:

```
cdColor.Color = lblMessage.ForeColor
If cdColor.ShowDialog() = Windows.Forms.DialogResult.OK Then
   lblMessage.ForeColor = cdColor.Color
End If
```

The FontDialog Control

The **FontDialog control** displays a standard Windows *Font* dialog box. Figure 23 shows the default *Font* dialog box on the left, and a *Font* dialog box with a *Color* drop-down list on the right.

Figure 23 Windows *Font* dialog box

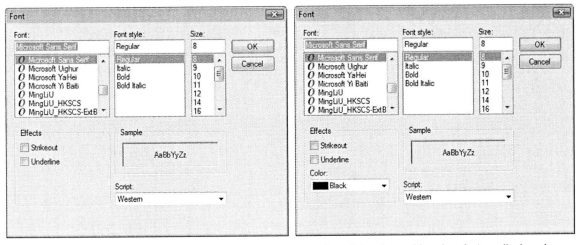

Default *Font* dialog box   *Font* dialog box with color choices displayed

Double-click the *FontDialog* icon in the *Dialogs* section of the toolbox to place the control on a form. Because the control is invisible at runtime, it appears in the component tray at design time. We will use the prefix fd when naming the control.

You display a *Font* dialog box by calling the FontDialog control's ShowDialog method. For example, assuming fdFont is the name of a FontDialog control, the following statement calls its ShowDialog method:

```
fdFont.ShowDialog()
```

By default, the *Font* dialog box does not allow the user to select a color. Color is controlled by the FontDialog control's ShowColor property, which can be set to *True* or *False*. When set to *True*, the *Font* dialog box appears with a *Color* drop-down list, shown on the right in Figure 23.

The ShowDialog method returns one of the values Windows.Forms.DialogResult.OK or Windows.Forms.DialogResult.Cancel indicating which button, *OK* or *Cancel*, the user clicked to dismiss the dialog box. The Font property will hold a value representing the font settings selected by the user. The Color property will hold a value representing the color selected by the user. For example, the following code displays the *Font* dialog box and then sets the lblMessage control's font to that selected by the user.

```
If fdFont.ShowDialog() = Windows.Forms.DialogResult.OK Then
    lblTest.Font = fdFont.Font
End If
```

The following code displays a *Font* dialog box with a drop-down list of colors. It then sets the lblMessage control's font and color to the values selected by the user.

```
fdFont.ShowColor = True
If fdFont.ShowDialog() = Windows.Forms.DialogResult.OK Then
    lblTest.Font = fdFont.Font
    lblTest.ForeColor = fdFont.Color
End If
```

 Checkpoint

9 Why is it a good idea to use the *Open* and *Save As* dialog boxes in applications that work with files?

10 What is the purpose of the following OpenFileDialog and SaveFileDialog properties?

> Filter
> InitialDirectory
> Title
> Filename

11 Suppose you want an *Open* dialog box to have the following filters: text files (*.txt), Microsoft Word files (*.doc), and all files (*.*). What string would you store in the Filter property?

12 When the user selects a color with the *Color* dialog box, where is the color value stored?

13 When the user selects font settings with the *Font* dialog box, where are the font setting values stored?

14 How do you display a *Font* dialog box with a drop-down list of colors?

15 When the user selects a color with the *Font* dialog box, where is the color value stored?

3 The PrintDocument Control

CONCEPT: The PrintDocument control allows you to send output to the printer.

The **PrintDocument control** gives your application the ability to print output on the printer. Double-click the *PrintDocument* tool in the Printing section of the *Toolbox* window to place a PrintDocument control on a form. Because the control is invisible at runtime, it appears in the component tray at design time. We will use the prefix pd when naming the control.

The `Print` Method and the `PrintPage` Event

The PrintDocument control has a **Print method** that starts the printing process. The method's general format is as follows:

```
PrintDocumentControl.Print()
```

When the `Print` method is called, it triggers a PrintPage event. You must write code in the PrintPage event handler to initiate the actual printing. To create a PrintPage event handler code template, double-click the PrintDocument control in the component tray. The following is an example:

```
Private Sub pdPrint_PrintPage(...) Handles pdPrint.PrintPage

End Sub
```

Inside the **PrintPage event handler,** you can write code that sends text to the printer using a specified font and color, at a specified location. We will use the following general format to call the e.Graphics.DrawString method:

```
e.Graphics.DrawString(String, New Font(FontName, Size,
    Style), Brushes.Black, HPos, VPos)
```

String is the string to be printed. *FontName* is a string holding the name of the font to use. *Size* is the size of the font in points. *Style* is the font style. Valid values are FontStyle.Bold, FontStyle.Italic, FontStyle.Regular, FontStyle.Strikeout, and FontStyle.Underline. *HPos* is the horizontal position of the output. This is the distance of the output, in points, from the left margin of the paper. *VPos* is the vertical position of the output. This is the distance of the output, in points, from the top margin of the paper. The Brushes.Black argument specifies that output should be printed in black.

The following PrintPage event handler prints the contents of a TextBox control, txtInput, in a regular 12 point Times New Roman font. The horizontal and vertical coordinates of the output are 10 and 10.

```
Private Sub pdPrint_PrintPage(...) Handles pdPrint.PrintPage
    e.Graphics.DrawString(txtInput.Text, New Font("Times New Roman",
                12, FontStyle.Regular), Brushes.Black, 10, 10)
End Sub
```

The following PrintPage event handler prints the string "Sales Report" in a bold 18 point Courier font. The horizontal and vertical coordinates of the output are 150 and 80.

```
Private Sub pdPrint_PrintPage(...) Handles pdPrint.PrintPage
    e.Graphics.DrawString("Sales Report", New Font("Courier",
                18, FontStyle.Bold), Brushes.Black, 150, 80)
End Sub
```

The following PrintPage event handler prints the contents of a file. Assume that `strFilename` is a class-level string variable containing the name of the file whose contents are to be printed.

```
Private Sub pdPrint_PrintPage(...) Handles pdPrint.PrintPage
    Dim inputFile As StreamReader ' Object variable
    Dim intX As Integer = 10       ' X coordinate for printing
    Dim intY As Integer = 10       ' Y coordinate for printing

    Try
       ' Open the file.
       inputFile = File.OpenText(strFilename)

       ' Read all the lines in the file.
       Do While inputFile.Peek <> -1
          ' Print a line from the file.
          e.Graphics.DrawString(inputFile.ReadLine(), New Font
             ("Courier", 10, FontStyle.Regular), Brushes.Black,
              intX, intY)

          ' Add 12 to intY.
          intY += 12
       Loop

       ' Close the file.
       inputFile.Close()
    Catch
       ' Error message for file open error.
       MessageBox.Show("Error: could not open file.")
    End Try
End Sub
```

The variables `intX` and `intY` specify the horizontal and vertical positions of each line of printed output. The statement `intY += 12` inside the loop increases the vertical distance of each line by 12 points from the top of the page. The output is printed in a 10 point font, so there are 2 points of space between each line.

In Tutorial 5, you will modify the *Simple Text Editor* application you created in Tutorial 4 by adding a *Print* command to the *File* menu.

Tutorial 5:
Adding printing capabilities to the *Simple Text Editor* application

Step 1: Open the *Simple Text Editor* project you created in Tutorial 4.

Step 2: Add a *Print* menu item and separator bar to the *File* menu, as shown in Figure 24. To add the *Print* menu item, right-click on the *Exit* MenuItem. From the pop-up menu, select *Insert*, then *MenuItem*. Set the Text property to &Print and the Name Property to `mnuFilePrint`. To add a separator bar, right-click on the *Exit* MenuItem, and select *Insert*, then *Separator*.

Step 3: Add a PrintDocument control to the form. (The PrintDocument control is in the *Printing* section of the Toolbox.) Name the control `pdPrint`.

Step 4: Double-click the `pdPrint` control to create a code template for the `pdPrint_PrintPage` event handler. Complete the event handler by entering the following code shown in bold:

```
Private Sub pdPrint_PrintPage(...) Handles pdPrint.PrintPage
    ' Print the contents of the text box.
    e.Graphics.DrawString(txtDocument.Text, New Font ("MS Sans Serif",
        12, FontStyle.Regular), Brushes.Black, 10, 10)
End Sub
```

Figure 24 Print menu item and separator bars added

Step 5: Add the following mnuFilePrint_Click event procedure.

```
Private Sub mnuFilePrint_Click(...) Handles mnuFilePrint.Click
    ' Print the current document.
    pdPrint.Print()
End Sub
```

Step 6: Save and run the application. Enter some text into the text box or load an existing file. Test the new *Print* command. The contents of the text box should be printed on the printer.

Step 7: Exit the application.

Formatted Reports with `String.Format`

Reports typically contain the following sections:

- A **report header**, printed first, contains the name of the report, the date and time the report was printed, and other general information about the data in the report.
- The **report body** contains the report's data and is often formatted in columns.
- An optional **report footer** contains the sum of one or more columns of data.

Printing Reports with Columnar Data

Report data is typically printed in column format, with each column having an appropriate heading. To properly align printed data in columns, you can use a monospaced font to ensure that all characters occupy the same amount of space, and use the `String.Format` method to format the data into columns. Let's take a closer look at each of these topics.

Monospaced Fonts

Most printers normally use proportionally spaced fonts such as MS sans serif. In a proportionally spaced font, the amount of space occupied by a character depends on the width of the character. For example, the letters *m* and *w* occupy more space than the letters *i* and *j*. Using proportionally spaced fonts, you may have trouble aligning data properly in

523

columns. To remedy the problem, you can select a monospaced font such as Courier New. All characters in a monospaced font use the same amount of space on the printed page.

Using `String.Format` to Align Data along Column Boundaries

The `String.Format` method is a versatile tool for formatting strings. In this section, we discuss how to use the method to align data along column boundaries. The method is used in the following general format:

```
String.Format(FormatString, Arg0, Arg1 [,...])
```

`FormatString` is a string containing text and/or formatting specifications. `Arg0` and `Arg1` are values to be formatted. The `[,...]` notation indicates that more arguments may follow. The method returns a string that contains the data provided by the arguments `Arg0`, `Arg1`, and so on, formatted with the specifications found in `FormatString`.

Let's look at an example of how `FormatString` can be used to format data into columns. The following code produces a string with the numbers 10, 20, and 30 aligned into columns of ten characters wide each. The resulting string is stored in the variable `strTemp`.

```
Dim strTemp As String
Dim intX, intY, intZ As Integer
intX = 10
intY = 20
intZ = 30
strTemp = String.Format("{0, 10} {1, 10} {2, 10} ", intX, intY, intZ)
```

The string `"{0, 10} {1, 10} {2, 10}"` is the format string. The variable `intX` is argument 0, the variable `intY` is argument 1, and the variable `intZ` is argument 2. This is illustrated in Figure 25.

Figure 25 Arguments of the `String.Format` method

The contents of the format string specify how the data is to be formatted. In our example, the string has three sets of numbers inside curly braces. The first set is `{0, 10}`. This specifies that argument 0 (the variable `intX`) is to be placed in a column ten spaces wide. The second set is `{1, 10}`. This specifies that argument 1 (the variable `intY`) is to be placed in a column ten spaces wide. The third set, `{2, 10}`, specifies that argument 2 (the variable `intZ`) is to be placed in a column ten spaces wide. Figure 26 labels all these parts. There are no spaces between the sets.

Figure 26 Format specifications

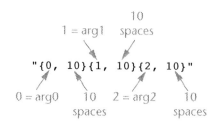

After the last statement in the previous code executes, the variable strTemp contains the string "   10   20   30". The numbers are placed in columns of ten spaces each, as illustrated in Figure 27. In our example, the numbers are right justified inside the columns. If you use a negative value for a column width in the format string, the column is left justified. For example, using the variables intX, intY, and intZ from the previous code example, the method call

```
String.Format("{0, -10} {1, -10} {2, -10} ", intX, intY, intZ)
```

produces the string "10   20   30   ".

Let's examine a code sample that prints a sales report with a header, two columns of data, and a footer. The data is printed from the following parallel arrays:

```
Dim strNames As String() = {"John Smith", "Jill McKenzie",
                            "Karen Suttles", "Jason Mabry",
                            "Susan Parsons"}
Dim decSales As Decimal() = {2500.0, 3400.0, 4200.0,
                             2200.0, 3100.0}
```

Figure 27 Column widths

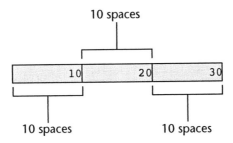

The strNames array contains five salespeople's names and the decSales array contains each salesperson's sales. The For...Next loop in the following event handler prints each line of data and uses an accumulator, decTotal, to sum the sales amounts. The contents of decTotal are printed in the footer to show the total sales.

```
Private Sub pdPrint_PrintPage(...) Handles pdPrint.PrintPage
    Dim intCount As Integer       ' Loop counter
    Dim decTotal As Decimal = 0   ' Accumulator
    Dim intVertPosition As Integer ' Vertical printing position

    ' Print the report header.
    e.Graphics.DrawString("Sales Report", New Font("Courier New", 12,
        FontStyle.Bold), Brushes.Black, 150, 10)

    e.Graphics.DrawString("Date and Time: " & Now.ToString(),
        New Font("Courier New", 12, FontStyle.Bold),
        Brushes.Black, 10, 38)

    ' Print the column headings.
    e.Graphics.DrawString(String.Format("{0, 20} {1, 20} ",
        "NAME", "SALES"), New Font("Courier New", 12,
        FontStyle.Bold), Brushes.Black, 10, 66)
```

```
      ' Print the body of the report.
      intVertPosition = 82
      For intCount = 0 To 4
          e.Graphics.DrawString(String.Format("{0, 20} {1, 20} ",
              strNames(intCount), decSales(intCount).ToString("c")),
              New Font("Courier New", 12, FontStyle.Regular),
              Brushes.Black, 10, intVertPosition)

          decTotal += decSales(intCount)
          intVertPosition += 14
      Next

      ' Print the report footer.
      e.Graphics.DrawString("Total Sales: " & decTotal.ToString("c"),
          New Font("Courier New", 12, FontStyle.Bold),
          Brushes.Black, 150, 165)
  End Sub
```

The report printed by this code appears similar to the following:

```
        Sales Report

Date and Time: 10/14/2010 11:12:34 AM

            Name          Sales
      John Smith       $2,500.00
   Jill McKenzie       $3,400.00
   Karen Suttles       $4,200.00
    Jason Mabry        $2,200.00
   Susan Parsons       $3,100.00

    Total Sales:      $15,400.00
```

 Checkpoint

16 How do you trigger a PrinterDocument control's PrintPage event?

17 Assume an application has a PrintDocument control named pdPrint. Write a statement in the control's PrintPage event handler that prints your first and last name in an 18 point bold MS sans serif font. Print your name at 100 points from the page's left margin and 20 points from the page's top margin.

18 Name the three sections most reports have.

19 What is the difference between a proportionally spaced font and a monospaced font?

20 Assume that an application has a PrintDocument control named *pdPrint*. Write a statement in the control's PrintPage event handler that prints the contents of the variables a and b in a 12 point regular Courier New font. The contents of a should be printed in a column 12 characters wide, and the contents of b should be printed in a column 8 characters wide. Print the data 10 points from the page's left margin and 50 points from the page's top margin.

21 Rewrite the answer you wrote to Checkpoint 20 so the contents of the variable a are left justified.

4   Structures

CONCEPT: Visual Basic allows you to create your own data types, into which you may group multiple data fields.

So far you have created applications that keep data in individual variables. If you need to group items, you can create arrays. Arrays, however, require elements to be of the same data type. Sometimes a relationship exists between items of different types. For example, a payroll system might use the variables shown in the following declaration statements:

```
Dim intEmpNumber As Integer    ' Employee number
Dim strFirstName As String     ' Employee's first name
Dim strLastName As String      ' Employee's last name
Dim dblHours As Double         ' Number of hours worked
Dim decPayRate As Decimal      ' Hourly pay rate
Dim decGrossPay As Decimal     ' Gross pay
```

All these variables are related because they can hold data about the same employee. The `Dim` statements, however, create separate variables and do not establish relationships.

Instead of creating separate variables that hold related data, you can group the related data. A **structure** is a data type you can create that contains one or more variables known as fields. The fields can be of different data types. Once a structure has been created, variables of the structure may be declared.

You create a structure at the class- or module-level with the **Structure** statement:

```
[AccessSpecifier] Structure StructureName
    FieldDeclarations
End Structure
```

AccessSpecifier is shown in brackets, indicating that it is optional. If you use the `Public` access specifier, the structure is accessible to statements outside the class or module. If you use the `Private` access specifier, the structure is accessible only to statements in the same class or module. *StructureName* is the name of the structure. *FieldDeclarations* is one or more declarations of fields, as regular `Dim` statements. The following is an example:

```
Structure EmpPayData
    Dim intEmpNumber As Integer
    Dim strFirstName As String
    Dim strLastName As String
    Dim dblHours As Double
    Dim decPayRate As Decimal
    Dim decGrossPay As Decimal
End Structure
```

This statement declares a structure named `EmpPayData`, having six fields.

TIP: Structure names and class names should begin with uppercase letters. This serves as a visual reminder that the structure or class name is not a variable name.

TIP: If you want a structure to be available to multiple forms in a project, place the `Structure` statement, with the `Public` access specifier, in a module.

The `Structure` statement does not create a variable—it creates a new data type by telling Visual Basic what the data type contains. You declare variables of a structure using `Dim` statements, just as you would with any other data type. For example, the following statement declares a variable called `deptHead` as an `EmpPayData` variable:

```
Dim deptHead As EmpPayData
```

The `deptHead` variable can store six values because the `EmpPayData` data type is made of six fields, as illustrated in Figure 28.

Access the fields with the dot operator. For example, the following statements assign values to all six fields of the `deptHead` variable.

```
deptHead.intEmpNumber = 1101
deptHead.strFirstName = "Joanne"
deptHead.strLastName = "Smith"
deptHead.dblHours = 40.0
deptHead.decPayRate = 25
deptHead.decGrossPay = CDec(deptHead.dblHours) *
                        deptHead.decPayRate
```

Figure 28 `deptHead` variable

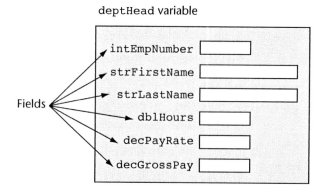

The following statement adds the `intEmpNumber` field to the `lstEmployeeList` list box:

```
lstEmployeeList.Items.Add(deptHead.intEmpNumber)
```

You can optionally use the `With` statement to simplify access to structure fields:

```
With deptHead
    .intEmpNumber = 1101
    .strFirstName = "Joanne"
    .strLastName = "Smith"
    .dblHours = 40.0
    .decPayRate = 25
    .decGrossPay = CDec(.dblHours) * .decPayRate
End With
```

Passing Structure Variables to Procedures and Functions

You may pass structure variables to procedures and functions. For example, the following procedure declares an `EmpPayData` parameter, passed by reference:

```
Sub CalcPay(ByRef employee As EmpPayData)
   ' This procedure accepts an EmpPayData variable
   ' as its argument. The employee's gross pay
   ' is calculated and stored in the grossPay
   ' field.
   With employee
      .decGrossPay =.dblHours * .decPayRate
   End With
End Sub
```

Arrays as Structure Members

Structures can contain array fields, but the arrays cannot be assigned initial sizes. An example is shown in the following statement:

```
Structure StudentRecord
   Dim strName As String
   Dim dblTestScores() As Double
End Structure
```

After declaring a structure variable, you can use the ReDim statement to establish a size for the array. Then you access the array elements with a subscript, as shown in the following example:

```
Dim student As StudentRecord
ReDim student.dblTestScores(4)
student.strName = "Mary McBride"
student.dblTestScores(0) = 89.0
student.dblTestScores(1) = 92.0
student.dblTestScores(2) = 84.0
student.dblTestScores(3) = 96.0
student.dblTestScores(4) = 91.0
```

Arrays of Structures

You may also declare an array of structures. For example, the following statement declares employees as an array of 10 EmpPayData variables:

```
Const intMAX_SUBSCRIPT As Integer = 9
Dim employees(intMAX_SUBSCRIPT) As EmpPayData
```

To access the individual elements in the array, use a subscript as shown in the following statement:

```
employees(0).intEmpNumber = 1101
```

When working with an array of structure variables in which the structure contains an array field, use the ReDim statement to establish a size for the array field of each element. For example, the StudentRecord discussed in the previous section has a field named dblTestScores, which is an array of five numbers. Suppose an application declares an array of StudentRecord variables as follows:

```
Const intMAX_SUBSCRIPT As Integer = 9
Dim students(intMAX_SUBSCRIPT) As StudentRecord
```

A loop, such as the following, can be used to set a size for each `testScores` array:

```
For intIndex = 0 To intMax_SUBSCRIPT
   ReDim students(intIndex).dblTestScores(4)
Next
```

You can use the array fields once they have been given a size. For example, the following statement stores 95 in `dblTestScores(0)` inside `students(5)`:

```
students(5).dblTestScores(0) = 95.0
```

Tutorial 6 examines an application that uses a structure.

Tutorial 6:

Examining an application with a structure

In this tutorial, you examine a modified version of the *File WriteLine Demo* project from Tutorial 1. This version of the project uses a structure to store the friend data.

Step 1: Open the *Structure File WriteLine Demo* project from the student sample programs folder named *Chap9\Structure File WriteLine Demo*. Recall that the folder can be downloaded from www.microsoft.com/express/Downloads/.

Step 2: Open the *Code* window. The following statements declare the `FriendInfo` structure:

```
Structure FriendInfo
   Dim strName As String   ' To hold a name
   Dim strPhone As String ' To hold a phone number
End Structure
```

Step 3: Look at the `btnCreateFile_Click` event handler. The procedure uses the structure variable `myFriend` to hold the names, ages, and addresses entered by the user. The `friendFile.WriteLine` statements write the contents of the structure variable's fields to the file.

```
Private Sub btnCreateFile_Click(...) Handles btnCreateFile.Click
   ' Constant for the number of friends
   Const intNUM_FRIENDS As Integer = 3

   ' Local variables
   Dim strFilename As String      ' File name
   Dim intCount As Integer        ' Loop counter
   Dim friendFile As StreamWriter  ' Object variable
   Dim myFriend As FriendInfo      ' Structure variable

   ' Get the file name from the user.
   strFilename = InputBox("Enter the filename.")

   Try
      ' Open the file.
      friendFile = File.CreateText(strFilename)

      ' Get the data and write it to the file.
      For intCount = 1 To intNUM_FRIENDS
         ' Get a friend's name.
         myFriend.strName = InputBox("Enter the name of friend " & _
                              "number " & intCount.ToString())
```

```
                ' Get a friend's phone number.
                myFriend.strPhone = InputBox("Enter the that friend's " &
                                             "phone number.")


                ' Write the data to the file.
                friendFile.WriteLine(myFriend.strName)
                friendFile.WriteLine(myFriend.strPhone)
            Next

            ' Close the file.
            friendFile.Close()
        Catch
            ' Error message
            MessageBox.Show("That file cannot be created.")
        End Try
    End Sub
```

Step 4: Run the application and, as you did in Tutorial 1, click the *Save Data to File* button. Enter a filename and data for three of your friends. The procedure saves the data.

Step 5: Exit the application.

Checkpoint

22 Write a statement that declares a structure named Movie. The structure should have fields to hold the following data about a movie.

The name of the movie
The director of the movie
The producer of the movie
The year the movie was released

23 Write a statement that declares a variable of the Movie structure that you created in Checkpoint 22.

24 Write statements that store the following data in the variable you declared in Checkpoint 23. (Do not use the With statement.)

The name of the movie: *Wheels of Fury*
The director of the movie: *Arlen McGoo*
The producer of the movie: *Vincent Van Dough*
The year the movie was released: *2010*

25 Rewrite the statements you wrote in Checkpoint 24 using the With statement.

Summary

1 Using Files

- Data is saved in a file, which is stored on a computer's disk.
- For an application to use a file, the file must be opened (which creates the file if it does not exist), data is either written to the file or read from the file, and the file is closed.
- There are two types of files: text and binary. There are two methods of accessing data in files: sequential-access and random-access.
- When a sequential file is opened, its read position is set to the first item in the file. As data is read, the read position advances through the file.
- The contents of an array are saved to a file using a loop that steps through each element of the array, writing its contents to the file.
- By specifying a namespace with the Imports statement, you can refer to names in that namespace without fully qualifying them.
- The `File.CreateText` method creates a new file or replaces an existing one. The `File.AppendText` method opens a file so more data can be appended to the end of the file. The `File.OpenText` method opens a file for reading.

2 The OpenFileDialog, SaveFileDialog, FontDialog, and ColorDialog Controls

- The OpenFileDialog control displays a standard Windows *Open* dialog box. The SaveFileDialog control displays a standard Windows *Save As* dialog box. The ColorDialog control displays a standard Windows *Color* dialog box. The FontDialog control displays a standard Windows *Font* dialog box.

3 The PrintDocument Control

- The PrintDocument control allows your application to print output. You write the code that handles the printing in the `PrintPage` event handler. You trigger a PrintPage event by calling the `Print` method. You use the `e.Graphics.DrawString` method to send output to the printer.
- Reports typically have a header, body, and footer.
- To align printed data properly in columns, you must use a monospaced font to ensure that all characters occupy the same amount of space; you use the `String.Format` method to format the data into columns.

4 Structures

- A structure is a defined data type that you create, which contains one or more variables known as fields. Fields can be of different data types. You can create a structure with the `Structure` statement. Once you have defined a structure, you may declare instances of it.

Key Terms

append	delimiter
binary files	file
buffer	`File.AppendText` method
`Chr` function	`File.CreateText` method
`Close` method	`File.Exists` method
Color dialog box	`File.OpenText` method
ColorDialog control	Filename property

Filter property
Font dialog box
FontDialog control
InitialDirectory property
input file
MultiLine property
newline character
Open dialog box
OpenFileDialog control
output file
Peek method
Print method
PrintDocument control
PrintPage event handler
random-access file
Read method
read position
ReadLine method

ReadToEnd method
report body
report footer
report header
Save As dialog box
SaveFileDialog control
sequential-access file
StreamReader class
StreamReader object
StreamWriter class
StreamWriter object
structure
Structure statement
text file
Title property
Write method
WriteLine method

Review Questions and Exercises

Fill-in-the-Blank

1. Before a file can be used, it must be _____.

2. When a file is opened, a(n) _____ is created, which is a small holding section of memory that data is first written to.

3. When it is finished using a file, an application should always _____ it.

4. To write data to a sequential file, use a(n) _____ object.

5. To read data from a sequential file, use a(n) _____ object.

6. The _____ method writes a line to a file.

7. The _____ method reads a line from a file.

8. The _____ character is a delimiter that marks the end of a line in a file.

9. The _____ control allows you to print data directly to the printer.

10. You write code that handles printing in the _____ event handler.

11. All of the characters printed with a(n) _____ font occupy the same amount of space.

12. The _____ control displays an *Open* dialog box for selecting or entering a filename.

13. The _____ control displays a *Save As* dialog box for selecting or entering a file.

14. The _____ control displays a *Color* dialog box for selecting a color.

15. The _____ control displays a *Font* dialog box for selecting a font.

16. A(n) _____ is a data type that you create, containing one or more variables, which are known as fields.

Multiple Choice

1. Which two types of files are discussed in this chapter?
   a. Real and integer
   b. Microsoft Access and Microsoft Word
   c. Text and binary
   d. Encrypted and decrypted

2. You use this type of object to write data to a file.
   a. `FileWriter`
   b. `OuputFile`
   c. `File`
   d. `StreamWriter`

3. You use this type of object to read data from a file.
   a. `FileReader`
   b. `StreamReader`
   c. `File`
   d. `Inputfile`

4. This method creates a file if it does not exist, and erases the contents of the file if it already exists.
   a. `File.OpenText`
   b. `File.AppendText`
   c. `File.CreateText`
   d. `File.OpenNew`

5. This method creates a file if it does not exist. If it already exists, data written to it will be added to the end of its existing contents.
   a. `File.OpenText`
   b. `File.AppendText`
   c. `File.CreateText`
   d. `File.OpenNew`

6. This statement writes a line of data to a file, terminating it with a newline character.
   a. `WriteLine`
   b. `SaveLine`
   c. `StoreLine`
   d. `Write`

7. This statement writes an item of data to a file, and does not terminate it with a newline character.
   a. `WriteItem`
   b. `SaveItem`
   c. `StoreItem`
   d. `Write`

8. This statement reads a line from a file.
   a. `Read`
   b. `ReadLine`
   c. `GetLine`
   d. `Input`

9. You use this method to detect when the end of a file has been reached.
   a. End
   b. Peek
   c. LastItem
   d. FileEnd

10. You use this method to determine if a file exists.
    a. System.File.Exists
    b. IO.Exists
    c. File.Exists
    d. Exists.File

11. Assuming that ofdOpen is an OpenFileDialog control, the following statement displays the dialog box.
    a. ofdOpen.Display()
    b. Show(ofdOpen)
    c. ofdOpen.OpenDialog()
    d. ofdOpen.ShowDialog()

12. This property determines the types of files displayed in an *Open* or a *Save As* dialog box.
    a. FileTypes
    b. Filter
    c. Types
    d. FileDisplay

13. This property determines the directory, or folder first displayed in an *Open* or *Save As* dialog box.
    a. InitialDirectory
    b. InitialFolder
    c. Location
    d. Path

14. When the user selects a file with an *Open* or *Save As* dialog box, the file's path and name are stored in this property.
    a. Filename
    b. PathName
    c. File
    d. Item

15. When a PrintDocument control's Print method executes, it triggers this event.
    a. StartPrint
    b. PrintPage
    c. PagePrint
    d. SendPage

16. Inside the appropriate PrintDocument event handler you use this method to actually send output to the printer.
    a. e.Graphics.DrawString
    b. e.PrintText
    c. e.Graphics.SendOutput
    d. Print

17. You can use this method to align data into columns.
    a. `Align`
    b. `Format.Align`
    c. `Format.Column`
    d. `String.Format`

18. This statement allows you to create a data type that contains one or more variables, known as fields.
    a. `UserDefined`
    b. `DataType`
    c. `Structure`
    d. `Fields`

True or False

Indicate whether the following statements are true or false.

1. T F: A file must be opened before it can be used.

2. T F: An input file is a file that a program can write data to.

3. T F: To read a record stored in the middle or at the end of a sequential-access file, an application must read all records in the file before it.

4. T F: The `File.CreateText` method creates a `StreamReader` object and returns a reference to the object.

5. T F: If you specify only a filename when opening a file, Visual Basic will assume the file's location to be the same folder from which the application is running.

6. T F: In addition to separating the contents of a file into lines, the newline character also serves as a delimiter.

7. T F: If you call the `WriteLine` method with no argument, it writes a blank line to the file.

8. T F: A file's read position is set to the end of the file when a file is first opened.

9. T F: The `Peek` method causes the read position to advance by one character.

10. T F: The Title property holds the name of the file the user selected with an *Open* or *Save As* dialog box.

11. T F: You can specify the font to use when sending output to the printer.

12. T F: You must use a proportionally spaced font when aligning data in columns.

13. T F: A structure may hold variables of different data types.

14. T F: `Structure` statements can appear inside a procedure or function.

15. T F: Structures may not contain arrays.

16. T F: You may declare an array of structure variables.

Short Answer

1. What are the three steps that must be taken when a file is used by an application?

2. What happens when you close a file with the `Close` method?

3. What is a file's read position? Where is the read position when a file is first opened for reading?

4. What is the difference between the `WriteLine` method and the `Write` method?

5. What happens when you use the `File.OpenText` method to open a file that does not exist?

6. What has happened when the `Peek` method returns –1?

7. What does the `ReadLine` method return when it reads a blank line?

8. What does the `Read` method return?

9. What is the difference between the `Print` method and the `PagePrint` event handler?

10. Where must `Structure` statements appear?

What Do You Think?

1. How do you think a file buffer increases system performance?

2. Why should you call the `Peek` method before calling the `ReadLine` method?

3. You are using the `ReadLine` method to read data from a file. After each line is read, it is added to a list box. What error can potentially occur, and how do you prevent it?

4. An application has the forms MainForm and GetDataForm, and the module `MainModule`. You want a structure to be available only to procedures in the `MainModule` module. Where do you place the `Structure` statement, and which access specifier do you use: `Public` or `Private`?

5. Suppose an application properly aligns the contents of a report into columns using the `String.Format` method. But, when the same report is printed on paper, the columns do not align as they should. What is the most likely cause of the problem?

Find the Error

What is wrong with the following code?

1.
```
Dim myFile As System.IO.StreamReader
myFile = File.CreateText("names.txt")
```

2.
```
If Not System.Exists(strFilename) Then
    MessageBox.Show(strFilename & " does not exist.")
End If
```

3.
```
Do Until myFile.Peek = ""
    strInput = myFile.ReadLine()
    lstResults.Items.Add(strInput)
Loop
```

4. (Assume that `ofdOpen` is an OpenFileDialog control.)
```
ofdOpen.Filter = "Text files (*.txt)&*.txt"
```

5. (Assume that `pdPrint` is a PrintDocument control.)
```
Private Sub pdPrint_PrintPage(...) Handles pdPrint.PrintPage
    pdPrint.Print("Hello World!", New Font("Times New Roman",
        12, FontStyle.Regular), Brushes.Black, 10, 10)
End Sub
```

6. The following Structure statement appears in a form:

```
Structure PersonInfo
   Dim strName As String
   Dim intAge As Integer
   Dim strPhone As String
End Structure
```

The following statement appears in the same form:

```
PersonInfo.strName = "Jill Smith"
```

Algorithm Workbench

1. Suppose a file named *DiskInfo.txt* already exists, and you wish to add data to the data already in the file. Write the statements necessary to open the file.

2. Suppose you wish to create a new file named *NewFile.txt* and write data to it. Write the statements necessary to open the file.

3. Assuming an application uses a list box named `lstInventory`, write code that writes the contents of the list box to the file *Inventory.txt*.

4. Assuming an application has an array of integers named `intNumbers`, write code that writes the contents of the array to the file *numbers.txt*.

5. Write a `Structure` statement that creates a structure to hold the following data about a savings account. The structure should be declared in a module and be available to all modules in the project.

```
Account number (String)
Account balance (Decimal)
Interest rate (Double)
Average monthly balance (Decimal)
```

6. Assume that `CustomerData` is a structure. The following statement declares customers as an array of ten `CustomerData` variables:

```
Dim customers(9) As CustomerData
```

Write a statement that stores `"Jones"` in the `strLastName` field of the `customers(7)`.

7. Using the variables: `strProductName`, `intProductNum`, and `decProductPrice`, write a `String.Format` statement that returns a string with `strProductName`'s value in a column of ten spaces, `intProductNum`'s value in a column of eight spaces, and `decProductPrice`'s value in a column of six spaces.

8. Assume an application uses an OpenFileDialog control named `ofdOpen`. Write statements that display an *Open* dialog box with the initial directory *C:\Becky\Images* and use the following filters: *JPEG images (*.jpg)* and *GIF images (*.gif)*.

Programming Challenges

1. **Employee Data, Part 1**

   Create an application that allows the user to enter the following employee data: First Name, Middle Name, Last Name, Employee Number, Department, Telephone Number, Telephone Extension, and E-mail Address. The valid selections for department are Accounting, Administration, Marketing, MIS, and Sales. Once the data is entered, the user should be able to save it to a file. Figure 29 shows an example of

Figure 29 *Employee Data* form for saving employee records

the application's form. The form shown in Figure 29 has a combo box for selecting the department; a *Save Record* button, which writes the record to a file; a *Clear* button, which clears the text boxes; and an *Exit* button. Write code in the `Form_Load` event handler that allows the user to enter the name of the file.

2. **Employee Data, Part 2**

   Create an application that reads the records stored in the file created by Programming Challenge 1.

   Write code in the form's Load event handler that allows the user to enter the name of the file, and opens the file. The form shown in Figure 30 has a *Next Record* button, which reads a record from the file and displays its fields; a *Clear* button, which clears the labels; and an *Exit* button. When the user clicks the *Next Record* button, the application should read the next record from the file and display it. When the end of the file is encountered, a message should be displayed.

Figure 30 *Employee Data* form for reading employee records

3. Student Test Scores

A teacher has six students and wants you to create an application that stores their grade data in a file and prints a grade report. The application should have a structure that stores the following student data: Name (a string), Test Scores (an array of five Doubles), and Average (a Double). Because the teacher has six students, the application should use an array of six structure variables.

The application should allow the user to enter data for each student, and calculate the average test score.

Figure 31 shows an example form.

Figure 31 *Student Test Scores* form

Student Test Scores

File   Report   Help

Student Data

Name   Test Scores   Average

Calculate
Averages

The user should be able to save the data to a file, read the data from the file, and print a report showing each student's test scores and average score. The form shown in Figure 31 uses a menu system. You may use buttons instead if you prefer.

Input validation: Do not accept test scores less than zero or greater than 100.

4. Video Collection

Create an application that stores data about your DVD collection in a file. The application should have a structure to hold the following fields: Video Name, Year Produced, Running Time, and Rating. The application should allow the user to save the data to a file, search the file for a video by name, and print a report listing all the video records in the file. Figure 32 shows an example form.

Figure 32 *Video Collection* form

Design Your Own Forms

VideoNote

The Random
Number File
Generator
Problem

5. **Random Number File Generator**

Create an application that generates a series of 100 random numbers in the range of 1 through 1,000. Save the series of numbers in a file.

6. **Number Analysis**

Create an application that reads the numbers from the file your application created for Programming Challenge 5. (If you have not completed that assignment, use the file named *NumberSet.txt* in the *Chap9* folder on the student disk. It contains a series of 100 real numbers.) Your application should perform the following:

- Display the total of the numbers
- Display the average of the numbers
- Display the highest number in the file
- Display the lowest number in the file

7. **Font and Color Tester**

Create an application that tests the way different fonts and color combinations appear. The application should display some text in a label, and have a menu with the items *Select Font* and *Select Color*.

The *Select Font* menu item should display a *Font* dialog box with a *Color* drop-down list. The application should change the text displayed in the label to the font and color selected in the dialog box.

The *Select Color* menu item should display a *Color* dialog box. The application should change the background color of the label to the color selected in the dialog box.

8. **Simple Text Editor Modification**

Modify the *Simple Text Editor* application that you created in this chapter by adding a *View* menu to the menu system. The *View* menu should have two items: *Font* and *Color*.

The *Font* menu item should display a *Font* dialog box with a *Color* drop-down list. The application should change the text displayed in the text box to the font and color selected in the dialog box.

The *Color* menu item should display a *Color* dialog box. The application should change the background color of the text box to the color selected in the dialog box.

9. **Image Viewer**

You can load an image into a PictureBox control at runtime by calling the `Image.FromFile` method. For example, assume that `picImage` is a PictureBox control and `filename` is a variable containing the name of a graphic file. The following statement loads the graphic file into the PictureBox control:

```
picImage.Image = Image.FromFile(filename)
```

Create an application that has a PictureBox control on a form. The PictureBox control should be configured so it fills the entire area of the form and resizes when the user resizes the form.

The application should have a *File* menu with an *Open* command. The *Open* command should display an *Open* dialog box, displaying files of the following graphic types:

- Bitmaps (**.bmp*)
- JPEG images (**.jpg*)
- GIF images (**.gif*)

When the user selects a file with the *Open* dialog box, the application should display the image in the PictureBox control.

10. **Employee Data, Part 3**

Create an application that performs the following operations with the employee file created by the application in Programming Challenge 1:

- Uses an *Open* dialog box to allow the user to select the file
- Allows the user to enter a new employee record and then saves the record to the file
- Allows the user to enter an employee number and searches for a record containing that employee number. If the record is found, the record is displayed.
- Displays all records, one after the other
- Prints an employee record

Equip your application with either a menu system or a set of buttons to perform these operations.

11. **Customer Accounts**

Create an application that uses a structure to store the following data about a customer account: Last Name, First Name, Customer Number, Address, City, State, ZIP Code, Telephone Number, Account Balance, and Date of Last Payment. The application should allow the user to save customer account records to the file, search the file for a customer by last name or customer number, and print a report listing all the customer records in the file.

Input validation: When entering a new record, make sure the user enters data for all fields. Do not accept negative numbers for the account balance.

12. **Rainfall Statistics File**

In Programming Challenge 2 of the chapter "Arrays and More," you created an application that allows the user to enter the amount of rainfall for each month and then displays rainfall statistics. Modify the application so it can save the monthly rainfall amounts entered by the user to a file and read the monthly rainfall amounts from a file.

13. **Charge Account Number File**

In Programming Challenge 9 of the chapter "Arrays and More," you created an application that allows the user to enter a charge account number. The program determines whether the account number is valid by comparing it to numbers in an array. Modify the application so it compares the number to the numbers in a file. Create the file using Notepad or another text editor.

Answers to Checkpoints

1 (1) open the file, (2) write data to the file or read data from the file, and (3) close the file

2 `StreamWriter, StreamReader`

3 `outputFile = System.IO.File.CreateText("Test.txt")`

4 `outputFile.WriteLine(intX)`

5 `inputFile = System.IO.File.OpenText("Test.txt")`

6 `intX = inputFile.ReadLine`

7 With the `System.IO.File.Exists` method

8 With the `Peek` method; when `Peek` returns -1, the end of the file has been reached

9 Most Windows users are accustomed to using a dialog box to browse their disk for a file to open, or for a location to save a file.

10 Filter: These list boxes display a filter that specifies the type of files that are visible in the dialog box. You store a string in the Filter property that specifies the filter(s) available in the list boxes.

InitialDirectory: You store the path of the directory whose contents are to be initially displayed in the dialog box.

Title: The string stored in this property is displayed in the dialog box's title bar.

Filename: The filename selected or entered by the user is stored in this property.

11
```
Text files (*.txt)|*.txt|Word files (*.doc)|*.doc|
All files(*.*)
```

12 The ColorDialog control's Color property.

13 The FontDialog control's Font property.

14 By setting the FontDialog control's ShowColor property to *True* before calling the ShowDialog method.

15 in the FontDialog control's Color property.

16 By calling the control's Print method.

17
```
e.Graphics.DrawString("Joe Smith", New Font("MS sans Serif",
      18, FontStyle.Bold), Brushes.Black, 100, 20)
```

18 Header, body, and footer.

19 The characters in a proportionally spaced font do not occupy the same amount of horizontal space. All the characters in a monospaced font use the same amount of space.

20
```
e.Graphics.DrawString(String.Format("{0,12} {1,8} ", a, b),
      New Font("Courier", 12, FontStyle.Regular),
      Brushes.Black, 10, 50)
```

21
```
e.Graphics.DrawString(String.Format("{0,-12} {1,8} ", a, b),
      New Font("Courier", 12, FontStyle.Regular),
      Brushes.Black, 10, 50)
```

22
```
Structure Movie
    strName As String
    strDirector As String
    strProducer As String
    intYear As Integer
End Structure
```

23
```
Dim film As Movie
```

24 The following statements assume the variable is named `film`:
```
film.strName = "Wheels of Fury"
film.strDirector = "Arlen McGoo"
film.strProducer = "Vincent Van Dough"
film.intYear = 2010
```

25 The following statements assume the variable is named `film`:
```
With film

    .strName = "Wheels of Fury"
    .strDirector = "Arlen McGoo"
    .strProducer = "Vincent Van Dough"
    .intYear = 2010
End With
```

Advanced User Interface Controls and Techniques

I n addition to the fundamental Visual Basic controls, there are many more controls available in Visual Basic and this chapter introduces you to several of them. It also discusses some advanced programming techniques, and user interface design guidelines. The examples shown in this chapter can be found in the Student Sample Program Files folder on the website, www.microsoft.com/express/Downloads/.

Scroll Bars

Scroll bars provide a visual way to adjust a value within a range of values. These types of controls display a slider that may be dragged along a track. Visual Basic provides a horizontal scroll bar control named **HScrollBar**, and a vertical scroll bar control named **VScrollBar**. Figure 1 shows examples of each of these controls. You can find these controls in the Toolbox, in the *All Windows Forms* group.

Here is a summary of the important properties of each of these controls:

- The Value property is an integer value that is adjusted as the user moves the control's slider. (The default value is 0.)
- The Minimum property is the lower limit of the scrollable range. (The default value is 0.)
- The Maximum property is the upper limit of the scrollable range. (The default value is 100.)
- The LargeChange property is the integer amount by which the Value property changes when the user clicks the scroll bar area that lies to either side of the slider. This is also the amount by which the Value property changes when the user presses the Page Up or Page Down keys on the keyboard while the control has the focus. (The default value is 10.)
- The SmallChange property is the integer amount by which the Value property changes when the user clicks one of the arrows that appear at either end of a scroll bar control. (The default value is 1.)

From Appendix A of *Starting Out with Visual Basic® 2010*, Fifth Edition, Tony Gaddis, Kip Irvine.

Figure 1 Horizontal and vertical scroll bars

When a horizontal scroll bar's slider is moved toward its left side, the Value property is decreased. When the slider is moved toward the scroll bar's right side, the Value property is increased. When a vertical scroll bar's slider is moved toward its top, the Value property is decreased. When the slider is moved toward the scroll bar's bottom, the Value property is increased.

When the user moves the slider on a scroll bar control, a Scroll event occurs. If you write a Scroll event handler for the control, the event handler will execute any time the slider is moved. To generate a code template for the Scroll event handler, simply double-click the scroll bar control in the *Designer* window.

Figure 2 shows the form in an example application that demonstrates the HScrollBar control. The HScrollBar control is named `hsbScrollBar` and the label that displays the value is named `lblValue`. The form's code follows. This project can be found on the Student CD. You will also find a similar project that demonstrates the VScrollBar control.

Figure 2 HScrollBar Demo application form

```
Public Class Form1

    Private Sub Form1_Load(...) Handles MyBase.Load
        ' Set the property values for the scroll bar control.
        ' These properties can also be set at Design
        ' time in the Properties window.
        hsbScrollBar.Value = 0
        hsbScrollBar.Minimum = 0
        hsbScrollBar.Maximum = 100
        hsbScrollBar.LargeChange = 10
        hsbScrollBar.SmallChange = 1
```

```
      ' Display the scroll bar's initial value
      ' in the label control.
      lblValue.Text = hsbScrollBar.Value.ToString()
   End Sub

   Private Sub hsbScrollBar_Scroll(...) Handles hsbScrollBar.Scroll
      ' Display the scroll bar value.
      lblValue.Text = hsbScrollBar.Value.ToString()
   End Sub
End Class
```

Using a TabControl to Organize a Form

A **TabControl** allows you to create a user interface that is made of multiple pages, with each page containing its own set of controls. The TabControl appears as a container on a form, with one or more tabs positioned along its top edge. Each tab represents a different page, known as a **TabPage**. When the user clicks a tab, the control displays that page. You can find the TabControl in the Toolbox, in the *Containers* group.

When you insert a new TabControl, it will contain two TabPage controls named Tab-Page1 and TabPage2. This is shown in Figure 3. Keep in mind that a TabControl is a container that contains TabPage controls. When you are working with a TabControl in the Designer window, you can select the TabControl (the container) or you can select the individual TabPage controls that it contains. When you work with a TabControl for the first time, you should practice selecting each of the controls in the group so you know at all times which one you are working with.

Figure 3 a TabControl with two TabPages

Each of the TabPage controls has its own set of properties that can be changed in the *Properties* window. For example, to change the text that is displayed on a TabPage's tab, you change that TabPage control's Text property.

As previously mentioned, a TabControl contains two TabPage controls when first inserted in a form. To add more TabPages, select the TabControl, and then select its TabPages property. (Click the ellipses button ... that appears next to the TabPages property window.) This opens the TabPage Collection Editor, shown in Figure 4. This window allows you to add new TabPages, remove existing TabPages, and edit each TabPage properties.

Figure 4 *TabPage Collection Editor* window

Figure 5 shows the *TabControl Demo* application that can be found on the Microsoft website. The application's form has a TabControl with three TabPages. Each TabPage contains a PictureBox control displaying an image. (There is no code in the application.)

Figure 5 *TabControl Demo* application

The WebBrowser Control

The **WebBrowser** control (found in the *Common Controls* group in the *Toolbox*) allows you to display a Web page on an application's form. The control has a property named Url that can be set to a Web page's URL (Uniform Resource Locator). At runtime, that Web page will be displayed in the control.

At design time, you can use the Properties window set the Url property. You simply type a valid URL such as http://www.gaddisbooks.com into the property's value box. If you want to set the Url property in code, you must create a Uri object (Uniform Resource Identifier) and assign that object to the property. Here is an example:

```
WebBrowser1.Url = New Uri("http://www.gaddisbooks.com")
```

Alternatively, you can call the control's Navigate method to display a Web page, as shown here:

```
WebBrowser1.Navigate(New Uri("http://www.gaddisbooks.com"))
```

In either of these approaches, an exception will be thrown if an invalid Web address is used.

When a Web page has finished loading, a DocumentCompleted event occurs. If you want to perform some action after a page has loaded, you can write a handler for this event. (Just double-click the WebBrowser control in the Designer window to create a code template for the DocumentCompleted event handler.)

Figure 6 shows the *WebBrowser Demo* application on the Microsoft website. The application's form has a WebBrowser control named `WebBrowser1`, a TextBox control named `txtURL`, and a Button control named `btnGo`. When the user clicks the `btnGo` button, the application sets the `WebBrowser1` control's Url property to the address that has been typed into the `txtURL` text box. The application's code follows.

```
Public Class Form1

    Private Sub btnGo_Click(...) Handles btnGo.Click
        Try
            WebBrowser1.Url = New Uri(txtURL.Text)
        Catch ex As Exception
            ' Error message for an invalid Web address.
            MessageBox.Show(ex.Message)
        End Try
    End Sub
End Class
```

Figure 6 *WebBrowser Demo* application

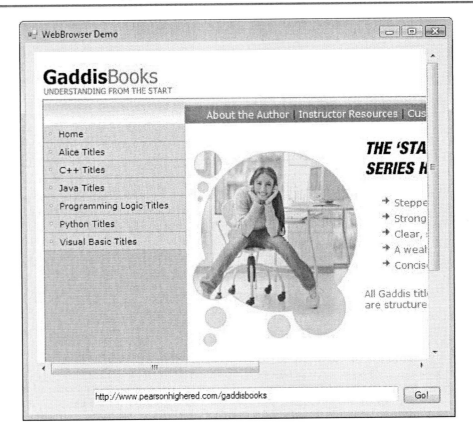

The ErrorProvider Component

The **ErrorProvider** component (found in the *Components* group in the *Toolbox*) allows you to indicate that the user has entered an invalid value by displaying a blinking error icon (◉) next to a specific control on the application's form. When the user hovers the mouse pointer over the icon, an error message is displayed as a tooltip.

When you insert an ErrorProvider component, it appears in the component tray at the bottom of the Designer window, with a default name such as ErrorProvider1. In code, when the user enters an invalid value with a specific control, you call the ErrorProvider component's SetError method. Here is the general format for calling the method:

```
ErrorProviderName.SetError(ControlName, ErrorMessage)
```

In the general format, *ErrorProviderName* is the name of the ErrorProvider component, *ControlName* is the name of the control that you want to display the error icon next to, and *ErrorMessage* is the error message to associate with the error. Here is an example:

```
ErrorProvider1.SetError(txtPayRate, "Invalid pay rate")
```

This statement uses the ErrorProvider1 component to display an error icon next to the txtPayRate control. When the user hovers the mouse pointer over the error icon, the message *Invalid pay rate* will be displayed as a tooltip.

The error icon will remain displayed next to the specified control until you call the SetError method again, passing the same control name as the first argument, and String.Empty as the second argument. Here is an example:

```
ErrorProvider1.SetError(txtPayRate, String.Empty)
```

Figure 7 shows the *ErrorProvider Demo* application on the Microsoft website. The user enters a number of hours in the txtHours TextBox, a numeric pay rate in the txtPayRate TextBox, and then clicks the btnCalc button to calculate gross pay. If a non-numeric value is entered for either the hours or the pay rate, an ErrorProvider component displays an error icon next to the control containing the invalid value. In Figure 7 the user has entered an invalid value for the pay rate. The application's code follows.

Figure 7 *ErrorProvider Demo* application

```
Public Class Form1

    Private Sub btnCalc_Click(...) Handles btnCalc.Click
        ' Variables for hours, pay rate, and gross pay
        Dim dblHours, dblPayRate, dblGrossPay As Double

        ' Clear any existing errors.
        ErrorProvider1.SetError(txtHours, String.Empty)
        ErrorProvider1.SetError(txtPayRate, String.Empty)

        ' Get values and calculate gross pay.
        Try
            ' Get the hours worked.
            dblHours = CDbl(txtHours.Text)
```

```
       Try
         ' Get the pay rate.
         dblPayRate = CDbl(txtPayRate.Text)

           ' Calculate the gross pay.
           dblGrossPay = dblHours * dblPayRate

           ' display the gross pay.
           lblGrossPay.Text = dblGrossPay.ToString("c")
         Catch ex As Exception
           ' Invalid pay rate
           ErrorProvider1.SetError(txtPayRate, "Pay rate must be numeric.")
         End Try
       Catch ex As Exception
         ' Invalid hours
         ErrorProvider1.SetError(txtHours, "Hours must be numeric.")
       End Try
    End Sub
  End Class
```

Writing Code to Select Text in a TextBox

TextBox controls have two properties, **SelectionStart** and **SelectionLength,** that you can use to make the process of correcting invalid input more convenient for the user. When the user enters an invalid value, you can display an error message and then use these properties to automatically select the invalid input for the user. Then, the user can immediately retype the input without having to use the mouse to select the TextBox.

The SelectionStart and SelectionLength properties can be used in code to automatically select the text in a text box. The SelectionStart property holds the position of the first selected character in the text box. The SelectionLength property holds the number of characters that are selected. For example, look at the following code and assume that txtName is a text box that the user has typed input into:

```
txtName.Focus()
txtName.SelectionStart = 0
txtName.SelectionLength = 5
```

The first statement gives txtName the focus. The second statement establishes that the first character in txtName (which is at position 0), is the first selected character. The next statement establishes that five characters will be selected. Together, the statements cause the first five characters in txtName to be selected.

So, how do you use similar code to select all the text in a TextBox? You use the TextBox's Length property to get the length of the text, and assign that value to the TextBox 's SelectionLength property. Here is an example:

```
txtName.Focus()
txtName.SelectionStart = 0
txtName.SelectionLength = txtName.Text.Length
```

After these statements execute, all of the contents of the txtName TextBox will be selected. When the user types a key, that keystroke will immediately erase all of the selected text.

Figure 8 shows the *Selected Text Demo* application on the Microsoft website. This is a modified version of the *ErrorProvider Demo* application previously shown. In this version, after the ErrorProvider displays an error icon, the content of the TextBox containing the invalid input is automatically selected. In the figure, the user has entered an invalid value for the hours. The application's code follows.

Figure 8 *Selected Text Demo* application

```
Public Class Form1

    Private Sub btnCalc_Click(...) Handles btnCalc.Click
        ' Variables for hours, pay rate, and gross pay
        Dim dblHours, dblPayRate, dblGrossPay As Double

        ' Clear any existing errors.
        ErrorProvider1.SetError(txtHours, String.Empty)
        ErrorProvider1.SetError(txtPayRate, String.Empty)

        ' Get values and calculate gross pay.
        Try
            ' Get the hours worked.
            dblHours = CDbl(txtHours.Text)

            Try
                ' Get the pay rate.
                dblPayRate = CDbl(txtPayRate.Text)

                ' Calculate the gross pay.
                dblGrossPay = dblHours * dblPayRate

                ' display the gross pay.
                lblGrossPay.Text = dblGrossPay.ToString("c")
            Catch ex As Exception
                ' Invalid pay rate
                ErrorProvider1.SetError(txtPayRate, "Pay rate must be numeric.")

                ' Select the invalid input.
                txtPayRate.Focus()
                txtPayRate.SelectionStart = 0
                txtPayRate.SelectionLength = txtPayRate.Text.Length
            End Try
        Catch ex As Exception
            ' Invalid hours
            ErrorProvider1.SetError(txtHours, "Hours must be numeric.")
            ' Select the invalid input.
            txtHours.Focus()
            txtHours.SelectionStart = 0
            txtHours.SelectionLength = txtHours.Text.Length
        End Try
    End Sub
End Class
```

Using Control-Level Validation

Visual Basic provides another approach to input validation that can be useful when a form contains many fields that must be validated, or when more complex validation must be applied to user input.

Most controls have a Boolean property named **CausesValidation** that is set to *True* by default. When the focus is shifting from one control to another, if the control that is receiving the focus has its CausesValidation property set to True, then a Validating event will occur for the control that is losing the focus.

Suppose an application has two text box controls: txtFirst and txtSecond. The user has just entered a value into txtFirst and pressed the Tab key, which should shift the focus from txtFirst to txtSecond. But txtSecond's CausesValidation property is set to *True*, so txtFirst's Validating event is triggered before the focus shifts. The txtFirst control has a Validating event handler, which is executed as a result of the Validating event being triggered.

The Validating event handler contains code that checks the value in txtFirst. If the value is invalid, the event handler does the following:

- It displays an error message instructing the user to reenter the data.
- It cancels the event, which prevents the focus from shifting. This lets the user correct the invalid value.

If the value is valid, however, the event handler allows the focus to shift.

The Validating event handler has a parameter named e. This parameter is a special type of object known as a CancelEventArgs object. It has a Boolean property named Cancel that, if set to True, will prevent the focus from shifting after the handler finishes executing. If the e.Cancel property is set to False, however, the focus will continue to shift after the handler finishes executing.

Figure 9 shows the *Validation Demo* application on the Microsoft website. The user enters a number of hours in the txtHours TextBox, a numeric pay rate in the txtPayRate TextBox, and then clicks the btnCalc button to calculate gross pay. The CausesValidation property of all the controls on the form is set to True. The txtHours control has a Validating event handler that executes when focus shifts away from txtHours. It makes sure the hours entered is a valid number and within the range of 0 through 40. The txtPayRate control also has a Validating event handler, that executes when focus shifts away from txtPayRate. It makes sure the pay rate is a valid number and is 0 or greater. The application's code follows.

Figure 9 *Validation Demo* application

NOTE: The form has a FormClosing event handler that sets e.Cancel to False. This is a necessary workaround in case the user tries to close the form without entering a value into the txtHours TextBox. Without this statement in the FormClosing event handler, the user will not be able to close the form without entering a valid value in txtHours.

```
Public Class Form1

    Private Sub btnCalc_Click(...) Handles btnCalc.Click
        ' Variables for hours, pay rate, and gross pay
        Dim dblHours, dblPayRate, dblGrossPay As Double

        ' Get the hours worked.
        dblHours = CDbl(txtHours.Text)

        ' Get the pay rate.
        dblPayRate = CDbl(txtPayRate.Text)

        ' Calculate the gross pay.
        dblGrossPay = dblHours * dblPayRate

        ' display the gross pay.
        lblGrossPay.Text = dblGrossPay.ToString("c")
    End Sub

    Private Sub txtHours_Validating(...) Handles txtHours.Validating
        Try
            ' Get the hours, as a Double.
            Dim dblHours As Double = CDbl(txtHours.Text)

            ' Make sure it's in the range 0 - 40.
            If dblHours >= 0.0 And dblHours <= 40.0 Then
                ' The input is okay, so do NOT cancel the event.
                e.Cancel = False
            Else
                ' The input is out of range, so display an
                ' error message.
                MessageBox.Show("Hours must be in the range 0 through 40.")
                ' Now cancel the event.
                e.Cancel = True
            End If
        Catch ex As Exception
            ' The input is not a valid number, so display
            ' an error message.
            MessageBox.Show("Hours must be a valid number.")

            ' Cancel the event.
            e.Cancel = True
        End Try
    End Sub

    Private Sub txtPayRate_Validating(...) Handles txtPayRate.Validating
        Try
            ' Get the pay rate, as a Double.
            Dim dblPayRate As Double = CDbl(txtPayRate.Text)

            ' Make sure it's 0 or greater.
            If dblPayRate >= 0.0 Then
                ' The input is okay, so do NOT cancel the event.
                e.Cancel = False
```

```
      Else
         ' The input is out of range, so display an
         ' error message.
         MessageBox.Show("Pay rate must be 0 or greater.")

         ' Now cancel the event.
         e.Cancel = True
         End If
      Catch ex As Exception
         ' The input is not a valid number, so display
         ' an error message.
         MessageBox.Show("Pay rate must be a valid number.")

         ' Cancel the event.
         e.Cancel = True
      End Try
   End Sub

   Private Sub Form1_FormClosing(...) Handles Me.FormClosing
      e.Cancel = False
   End Sub
End Class
```

The DateTimePicker and MonthCalendar Controls

The DateTimePicker and MonthCalendar controls (found in the Toolbox's *Common Controls* group) provide a much simpler and more reliable way for users to enter dates on a form than typing them into a TextBox. Both of these controls display a small scrollable calendar, showing an entire month, that the user may pick a date from. The selected date is stored, as a Date value, in the control's Value property. Initially, the Value property is set to the current date, and the current date will appear selected in the control's calendar.

When the user selects a date from either of these controls, a ValueChanged event is triggered. If you write a ValueChanged event handler for the control, the event handler will execute any time a date is selected. To generate a code template for the ValueChanged event handler, simply double-click the DateTimePicker or MonthCalendar control in the *Designer* window.

The difference between the two controls is that a DateTimePicker is a drop-down control (showing the calendar only when the user clicks an arrow) and the MonthCalendar always displays the calendar.

Figure 10 shows the *Date Demo* application on the Microsoft website. The user selects a date from the DateTimePicker control's drop-down calendar, and then the selected date is displayed in the lblDate label control. The application's code follows.

```
Public Class Form1

   Private Sub DateTimePicker1_ValueChanged(...) Handles
      DateTimePicker1.ValueChanged
      lblDate.Text = DateTimePicker1.Value.ToShortDateString
   End Sub
End Class
```

Figure 10 The *Date Demo* application

User Interface Design Guidelines

When developing an application, you should carefully plan the design of its user interface. A correctly designed user interface should be simple, self explanatory, and without distracting features. This remainder of this chapter covers several important areas of user interface design.

Adhere to Windows Standards

The users of your application are probably experienced with other Windows applications. They will expect your application to provide the features and exhibit the behavior that is common to all Windows applications. The guidelines provided here cover many of the Windows standards. Additionally, you should carefully study applications such as Microsoft Word and Microsoft Excel to observe their forms, menus, controls, and behavior.

Provide a Menu System

Avoid using too many buttons on a form. If an application provides many commands or operations for the user to choose from, place them in a menu system. Of course, an application that uses a menu system will have some menus and menu commands that are unique to that application. However, there are many menu commands that are common to most, if not all, applications. Windows applications that use a menu system normally have the following standard menus:

- **File menu commands.** *New, Open, Close, Save, Save As, Print,* and *Exit*
- **Edit menu commands.** *Copy, Cut, Paste,* and *Select All.* If an application provides searching capabilities, such as *Find* or *Replace* commands, they are typically found on the *Edit* menu.
- **Help menu commands.** *About*

Color

Use of color should be tailored to your audience. Business applications should use at most one or two colors, preferably subdued. Multimedia applications (such as Windows Media player) tend to be more colorful and use more graphics. In any event, it's a good idea to show your program to potential users and get their feedback. The color combinations that you consider attractive may not be appealing to others. The following are some general color usage guidelines for business applications:

- **Use dark text on a light background.** Combining certain colors for text and background makes the text difficult to read. Use dark colors for the text and light colors for the background. The contrast between dark and light colors makes the text easier to read.
- **Use predefined Windows colors.** Windows uses a predefined set of colors for forms, controls, text, and so on. These colors may be customized by the user. To ensure that your application conforms to a customized color scheme, you should use the predefined system colors. To find the system colors in the *Properties* window, select a color-related property such as *BackColor*. Then click the property's down-arrow button to display a pop-up list of colors. Select the *System* tab to display the system colors.
- **Avoid bright colors.** Bright colors are not recommended in business applications because they can distract the user and make the application appear cluttered and unprofessional. Additionally, users with color-defective vision can have difficulty trying to distinguish between certain colors.

Text

The use of nonstandard or multiple fonts can be distracting and makes your forms difficult to read. The following are some suggestions regarding font usage:

- **Use default fonts.** In most cases, stick with the default font for labels and text boxes. Avoid using italic and underlined styles, as they are less readable than plain fonts.
- **Use standard type sizes.** For ordinary text, Microsoft recommends 8, 9, or 11 point type. For window title bars, Microsoft recommends 10 point type.
- **Limit your exceptions to these rules.** If you insist on changing the font and/or font size, do so sparingly; do not use more than two fonts and two font sizes on a form.

Define a Logical Tab Order

Recall that a control's TabIndex property specifies the control's position in the tab order. The user expects the focus to shift logically when the Tab key is pressed. Typically, the control in the upper left corner of the form will be first in the tab order. The control that appears below it or next to it will be next. The tab order will continue in this fashion. If the focus shifts randomly around the form, a user may become confused and frustrated.

Assign Tool Tips

Recall that a tool tip is a small box that is displayed when you hold the mouse cursor over a control for a few seconds. The box gives a short description of what the button does. You can define tool tips for a form by creating a ToolTip control.

Provide Keyboard Access

Many users are proficient with the keyboard and can perform operations with it faster than with the mouse. For their convenience, you should develop your applications so they support both mouse and keyboard input. The following are some suggestions:

- **Use keyboard access keys.** Assign keyboard access keys to buttons, option buttons, check boxes, and menu items.
- **Assign a default button.** If a form uses buttons, you should always make the one that is most frequently clicked the default button. Do this by selecting that button as the form's AcceptButton. Recall that when a button is selected in a form's Accept-Button property, the button's Click event procedure is triggered when the user presses the Enter key while the form is active.
- **Assign a cancel button.** If a form has a cancel button, you should select it in the form's CancelButton property. Recall that when a button is selected in a form's CancelButton property, the button's Click event procedure is triggered when the user presses the Escape key while the form is active.

Group Controls

If a form has several controls, try to simplify the form's layout by grouping related controls inside group boxes. This visually divides the form's surface area into separate sections, making it more intuitive for the user.

Form Location

To center a form when it first appears, set its StartPosition property to *CenterScreen*.

Converting Mathematical Expressions to Programming Statements

I n mathematical expressions, it is not always necessary to use an operator for multiplication. For example, the expression $2xy$ is understood to mean "2 times x times y." Visual Basic, however, requires an operator for any mathematical operation. Table 1 shows some mathematical expressions that perform multiplication and the equivalent Visual Basic expression.

Table 1 Math expressions in Visual Basic

Mathematical Expression	Operation	Visual Basic Equivalent
$6b$	6 times b	6 * b
(3)(12)	3 times 12	3 * 12
$4xy$	4 times x times y	4 * x * y

When converting mathematical expressions to Visual Basic programming statements, you may have to insert parentheses that do not appear in the mathematical expression. For example, look at the following expression:

$$x = \frac{a + b}{c}$$

To convert this to a Visual Basic statement, $a + b$ will have to be enclosed in parentheses:

```
x = (a + b) / c
```

Table 2 shows more mathematical expressions and their Visual Basic equivalents.

From Appendix C of *Starting Out with Visual Basic*® *2010*, Fifth Edition, Tony Gaddis, Kip Irvine.

Table 2 More math expressions in Visual Basic

Mathematical Expression	Visual Basic Expression
$y = 3\dfrac{x}{2}$	`y = x / 2 * 3`
$z = 3bc + 4$	`z = 3 * b * c + 4`
$a = \dfrac{3x + 2}{4a - 1}$	`a = (3 * x + 2) / (4 * a - 1)`

ex